RUSSIA AND THE FORMER SOVIET UNION

RUSSIA AND THE FORMER SOVIET UNION

A Bibliographic Guide to English Language Publications, 1986-1991

Helen F. Sullivan
and
Robert H. Burger

Slavic and East European Library
University of Illinois at Urbana-Champaign

1994
Libraries Unlimited, Inc.
Englewood, Colorado

LIBRARIES UNLIMITED, INC.
P.O. Box 6633
Englewood, CO 80155-6633
1-800-237-6124

Library of Congress Cataloging-in-Publication Data

Sullivan, Helen F.
   Russia and the former Soviet Union : a bibliographic guide to
English language publications, 1986-1991 / Helen F. Sullivan and
Robert H. Burger.
   xii, 380 p. 17x25 cm.
   "This volume will continue, and to some extent, expand on the
bibliographies of Stephan Horak"
   Includes bibliographical references and indexes.
   ISBN 1-56308-046-X
1. Russia--Bibliography. 2. Soviet Union--Bibliography.
I. Burger, Robert H. (Robert Harold), 1947- . II. Horak, Stephan
M., 1920- Russia, the USSR, and Eastern Europe. III. Title.
Z2491.S89 1994
[DK17]
016.947--dc20   94-5233
                                            CIP

To Chuck and Ann

*Blessed and fortunate are we
who wed thee*

Contents

11 THE RUSSIAN EMPIRE PRIOR TO 1917 AND THE USSR (*continued*)

INTRODUCTION

This volume will continue and, to some extent, expand on the bibliographies of Stephan Horak. His bibliography, *Russia, the USSR and Eastern Europe*, provided students, scholars, and librarians with five-year compilations of English language materials on the area. They had the added benefit of annotations for each title, helping those unfamiliar with the field in their selection of materials.

The momentous changes in the Soviet Union and Eastern Europe have provided the impetus for the publication of even more titles than in the past. Areas of interest to scholars have expanded to include democratization, perestroika, glasnost, computers, information policy, and business. The diversity and quantity of materials make an annotated bibliography of sources more important than ever in identifying research sources.

Some of the changes in the field will be reflected in this publication. First, this will be the first of two volumes. The large number of publications made it necessary to divide the bibliography into one volume on the Soviet Union and a second on Eastern Europe. Second, subject areas previously of little or no interest to students of the area will be represented according to their increasing significance.

This is a representative selection of titles as opposed to a comprehensive listing. The titles were selected from two sources, *The American Bibliography of Slavic and East European Studies* and *Books in Print*. English language titles published from 1986 to 1991 made up the pool of selected titles. Certain categories of material were excluded: serials, occasional papers, juvenile literature, most publications under fifty pages, locally published genealogies, gallery guides, most reprints of materials published outside the chronological scope, and books not readily available to the compilers. The test for this last category of materials was the availability of the book in the Illinois interlibrary loan network (ILLINET). Some seminal publications under fifty pages were included.

As with all bibliographies attempting a representative selection rather than comprehensive coverage, some titles were not selected that technically fell within our scope. The compilers believed their first responsibility to be an inclusion of all major works on the area. The importance of the works was determined either by critical acclaim and coverage, uniqueness of subject matter or perspective, or significance of the author. There will, no doubt, be some omissions because of oversight and lack of time. We apologize for these omissions and will try to include them in the future.

We have tried to maintain an arrangement similar to Horak's volume. Titles are divided into sections by major subject area and are consecutively numbered. Each entry includes complete bibliographic information, a descriptive annotation and information, if available, on where the book was reviewed. The bibliographic description of each title includes full author, title, dates, place of publication, publisher, extent, ISBN, and series information. Volumes published as part of a series are accessible through the individual volume title. Earlier volumes in this series often included quotations from book reviews. While we have abandoned that practice, citations to book reviews are provided when available. Citations were taken from the *American Bibliography of Slavic and East European Studies*.

The annotations included here are descriptive rather than critical. They are intended to assist the student in choosing individual works on a topic of interest by describing the topic, arrangement, bias, intended audience, and special features of each book. Since both compilers contributed annotations and we each have different areas of expertise, the annotations necessarily vary in emphasis and detail. Further, some works did not readily lend themselves to such straightforward description (for example, novels). In some cases, the best descriptions of the book were found in the introduction and conclusion. Those quotations are included in the annotations with appropriate attribution. Annotations for books on Ukraine published from 1986 to 1990 are taken from Bohdan Wynar's bibliography

Ukraine: A Bibliographic Guide to English-Language Publications. They appear here in edited form by permission of the author.

Access is provided through the general subject arrangement and the author and subject indexes. While the author index is self-explanatory, a word on the compilation of the subject index might be helpful. The subject headings are based on the Library of Congress use, with some additions for more specific access. Unless otherwise indicated, all headings refer to Russia or the former Soviet Union. The numbers after each heading refer to individual citations in the main bibliography. While we tried to make the headings as specific as we deemed useful, certain headings still had an extremely large number of entries. We apologize for any difficulties this creates for the user.

Procite was used to organize all the data for this bibliography and to generate the indexes, with further modification using Microsoft Word.

As with most books, this one could not have been completed without the assistance or forbearance of many people. We wish to gratefully acknowledge the excellent editorial support of Bohdan Wynar. We are grateful for his permission to reproduce annotations from his bibliography, *Ukraine: A Bibliographic Guide to English-Language Publications.*

Jennifer Warner and Nell Burger tolerated our terrible writing to input and organize our annotations. Charles Mode made it possible for me to continue work on this bibliography in many ways, but most materially by transporting books to be annotated. Finally, all the Slavic Reference Service Staff, Julia Guachman, Jeanne Holba, and Richard Seitz have been extremely tolerant, often finding their computers unavailable to them. To all these people we owe a special debt and have greatly appreciated their help and support.

I wish to specially thank my coauthor, Robert Burger, for all his help. He has made what could have been a painfully difficult process a joy—part of his gift as a teacher.

Helen Sullivan

Part I

GENERAL AND INTERRELATED THEMES

Chapter 1
GENERAL REFERENCE WORKS

1. Kulikowski, Mark, **A Bibliography of Slavic Mythology**. Columbus, Ohio: Slavica, 1989. 137 p. ISBN: 0893572039.

Kulikowski's bibliography is divided into two parts: primary sources and secondary sources. Within each part, items are listed alphabetically by author. A brief subject index facilitates access to the entries. Each annotation includes location symbols of libraries that hold the cited work.

2. **Political and Economic Encyclopedia of the Soviet Union and Eastern Europe**, edited by Stephen White with contributions by Patrick Artesian... et al. Harlow: Longman, 1990. xii, 328 p. *Longman Current Affairs*, ISBN: 0582060362. Includes index.

This encyclopedia contains substantial articles on each of the countries of the U.S.S.R. and Eastern Europe. They focus on the economic and political development of each country, especially in the most recent period. There are other, shorter entries covering many other isolated topics including political parties and personalities, churches, political concepts, geographical units, arms control, and sports. The information is current as of March 31, 1990. The volume is arranged alphabetically with some references to other entries of relevance. It includes a detailed index for additional access.

3. Wynar, Lubomyr R., **Guide to American Ethnic Press: Slavic and East European Newspapers and Periodicals**. Kent, Ohio: Center for the Study of Ethnic Publications, Kent State University, 1986. 280 p. Includes indexes.

This is the first annotated directory of current Slavic newspapers and periodicals published in the United States. It covers 17 Slavic and East European groups, with a separate section devoted to the multi-ethnic Yugoslavian press. With 580 newspapers and periodicals covered, this guide offers almost complete bibliographic information, including library holdings, title of publication, translation of title (if the title is not in English), year the publication started, editorial address and telephone number, sponsoring organization, editor's name, language(s) used in the publication, frequency, circulation, annual subscription rate, and a brief annotation describing the nature of the publication and its special features. The Ukrainian section includes 103 publications, and in most cases the information is current. Some exceptions, e.g., *Minutes of the Seminar in Ukrainian Studies Held at Harvard University* or *Recenzija* (both items are no longer published), are probably due to the failure of the respective editors to respond to the survey. This work supplements L. Wynar and A. Wynar's more inclusive *Enclyclopedic Directory of Ethnic Newspapers and Periodicals in the United States*, 2nd ed. (Littleton, Colo., Libraries Unlimited, 1976. 248 p.) which covered 77 Ukrainian publications. Reviews: N. Sonevysky. *American Reference Books Annual* 1987, entry 884. Bohdan S. Wynar.

Chapter 2
HISTORY

4. Okey, Robin, **Eastern Europe, 1740-1985: Feudalism to Communism**. 2nd ed. Minneapolis: University of Minnesota Press, 1986. 283 p. ISBN: 08166156616. Includes index and bibliography (p. 255-271).

A general history of Eastern Europe from the eighteenth to the twentieth century. This is the second edition of this work and it contains an updated bibliography and chronology and additions to the final chapter to cover events through 1985. "From the mid-eighteenth century on, in Okey's view, Eastern Europe was a region struggling to achieve the modernity that seemed embodied in its western neighbors. His book traces the effort of East Europeans to overcome a legacy of underdevelopment and dependence, from the era of the Enlightenment through the liberal and nationalist movements of the nineteenth century down through the postwar years of the twentieth." (back cover) The book is chronologically and topically arranged covering the enlightenment, liberalism, the rise of nationalism, economics, and political development. The bibliography is arranged to coincide with topics covered in each chapter and consists of English language publications.

Chapter 3
ECONOMICS

5. Adam, Jan, **Economic Reforms in the Soviet Union and Eastern Europe Since the 1960's**. New York, N.Y.: St. Martin's Press, 1989. xvi, 264 p. ISBN: 0312020848. Includes index and bibliography (p. 243-255).

Adam's book is essentially an examination of changes in systems of management in the Soviet Union, Czechoslovakia, Hungary, and Poland. An appendix chapter by Horst Betz covers the GDR. Romania and Bulgaria are excluded. His monograph is divided into three sections with a total of eleven chapters. Part One describes the traditional Soviet system of management of the economy and uses this description as a sort of archetypical paradigm of the centrally planned economy. Part Two, consisting of five chapters, examines the common and contrasting features of reforms of the 1960s for the countries studied. Subsequent chapters in this part each cover a specific country's reform activity during that decade. Part Three is structured in a similar way with the same number and type of chapters. The focus throughout is on industrial reform; agriculture is excluded from analysis. Review: *Slavic Review* 49:4:688-90 (Winter 1990).

6. Bleaney, M. F., **Do Socialist Economies Work?: The Soviet and East European Experience**. Oxford: B. Blackwell, 1988. xii, 171 p. ISBN: 0631153063. Includes index and bibliography (p. 162-168).

Bleaney wishes to place emphasis not on the details of the planning mechanism itself, but rather on the economic behavior underlying such a system of central planning. He focuses, therefore, on the responses of enterprises to the economic environment in which they must act, the actions of planners within such a system, and the ways in which political leaders attempt to influence the process. His book's first two chapters provide a historical introduction to the formation of the Soviet economic system and economic growth, investment cycles and agriculture in the USSR and Eastern Europe since 1945. Chapters 3 and 4 discuss the planning mechanism and the various actors within this system. Chapters 5, 6, and 8 deal with planning in Poland, Hungary, and Yugoslavia. Chapter 7 provides a comparison between east and west and chapter 9 an assessment and answer posed by his title.

7. Brabant, Jozef M. van, **Integrating Eastern Europe into the Global Economy: Convertibility Through a Payments Union**. Dordrecht: Kluwer Academic, 1991. xv, 262 p. *International Studies in Economics and Econometrics*, v. 25. ISBN: 0792313526. Includes index and bibliographical references (p. 237-249).

Brabant intends this book to be "a modest contribution to the ongoing deliberations about how to ease the fairly tight constraints on the external payments of many countries of the eastern part of Europe." (p. vii) In doing so he explains several angles: (1) "the disintegration of the postwar framework for economic cooperation;" (2) "the disarray brought about by incisive economic transportation;" and (3) "various national, regional, and international interest groups at work there." (p. vii) He covers the prevailing socioeconomic situation, the collapse and dissolution of the CMEA, economic union in Eastern Europe, paths to convertibility, technical aspects of a payments union, macroeconomic surveillance and transition, downside risks of a payments union, and enlarging the European economic space.

8. ———, **The Planned Economies and International Economic Organizations**. Cambridge: Cambridge University Press, 1991. xv, 318 p. *Soviet and East European Studies*, v. 77. ISBN: 0521383501. Includes bibliographical references (p. 284-300) and index.

Van Brabant's monograph is an inquiry into the desirability and feasibility of finding a way to enable centrally planned economies around the world, Asian as well as European, to become more closely associated with the world economic, trading, monetary and financial frameworks. The book is divided into five chapters. Chapter one examines the period 1941-1947 and the wartime planning for a new economic order. Chapter two reviews the basic features of CPEs, their economic organization and management. Chapter three reviews the key features of international monetary arrangements and zeroes in on Eastern Europe in particular. Chapter four summarizes the role that CPEs have and have not played in the international trading system, especially GATT. The final, fifth chapter is concerned with making recommendations for reform and reconstitution of international economic relations. Review: *Foreign Affairs* 70:5: 188 (Winter 1991-92).

9. ———, **Remaking Eastern Europe: On the Political Economy of Transition**. Dordrecht: Kluwer Academic Publishers, 1990. xiv, 223 p. *International Studies in Economics and Econometrics*, v. 23. ISBN: 0792309553. Includes bibliographical references (p. 201-210) and index.

Van Brabant presents a detailed analysis of the state of East European economic affairs for the period 1985-1990. He maintains that recent political and economic events have created a framework within which the centrally-planned economies of Eastern Europe could be analyzed. He tries to answer the difficult question of how these countries can solicit and manage regional and international support for abandoning centrally planned economies. His study is not confined to the economics of such a transition, but to the politics of transition as well. The author, with some recognition of irony, suggests that the CMEA itself can be a vehicle for helping these countries make this difficult transition. The CMEA, after all, is a regional cooperative. Van Brabant examines realistically the past difficulties of CMEA cooperation, the various reform proposals that have been offered, the possibilities for east-west assistance, the idea of a Marshall Plan for Eastern Europe, the crucial issue of property rights and privatization, the possible remaking of the CMEA, and the relation of these economies to the global economic system.

10. **Economic Adjustment and Reform in Eastern Europe and the Soviet Union: Essays in Honor of Franklyn D. Holzman**, edited by Josef C. Brada, Ed A. Hewett, and Thomas A. Wolf. Durham, N.C.: Duke University Press, 1988. xxv, 428 p. *Duke Press Policy Studies*, no. 0020-6555. ISBN: 0822308525. Includes index and bibliography (p. 401-417).

This festschrift for Franklin D. Holzman consists of fifteen essays in five parts. The entire work deals in one way or another with economic reform in the Soviet Union and Eastern Europe and the prospect for the integration of these centrally planned economies with the larger world economy. Part one is an overview of economic stabilization, structural adjustment, and economic reform in these areas. Part two describes macroeconomic stabilization, especially in Hungary and Yugoslavia. Part three deals with structural adjustment and intra-CMEA economic relations. Part four focuses on the role of the centrally planned economies in the IMF, the World Bank, and GATT. Finally, part five gives more detailed views of economic systems and reforms, especially in Hungary, Poland, and the Soviet Union. A bibliography of the works of Franklin D. Holzman is included in the volume.

11. **Socialist Agriculture in Transition: Organizational Response to Failing Performance**, edited by Josef C. Brada and Karl-Eugen Wadekin. Boulder, CO: Westview Press, 1988. ix, 445 p. *Westview Special Studies on the Soviet Union and Eastern Europe*, ISBN: 0813373441. Includes bibliographies.

This volume contains papers presented at a conference held at Gigren, France in July 1984. Its purpose is to gain a comprehensive picture of Soviet and East European agriculture. The twenty-nine papers are arranged in nine sections. These sections are devoted to agrarian structures; problems of Soviet agriculture in Hungary, the GDR, Yugoslavia, China, and Vietnam; resource allocation; and international trade. Reviews: *Problems of Communism* 39:2:120-24 (March-April 1990). *Slavic Review* 49:1: 128-29 (Spring 1990). *Journal of Comparative Economics* 14:1:133- 37 (March 1990).

12. Cochrane, Nancy Joan, **Agriculture Statistics of Eastern Europe and the Soviet Union, 1965-1985**. Washington, DC: U.S. Dept. of Agriculture, Economic Research Service, Agriculture and Trade Analysis Division, 1989. iv, 129 p. *Statistical Bulletin*, no. 778. Includes bibliography (p. 10-11).

An update of an earlier publication, this statistical handbook adds data not in the 1983 volume. Data on Albania were excluded due to their scarcity. The introductory notes provide information of agricultural organizations in the USSR and Eastern Europe. Statistical yearbooks for each country served as the source materials along with the Council for Mutual Assistance (CMEA) Yearbook (from 1971 on). A list of suggested readings is included.

13. Collins, Susan Margaret, and Dani Rodrik, **Eastern Europe and the Soviet Union in the World Economy**. Washington, DC: Institute for International Economics, 1991. xiii, 152 p. *Policy Analyses in International Economics*, v. 32. ISBN: 0881321575. Includes bibliographical references (p. 151-152).

With the countries of Eastern Europe entering the world economy, there is an urgent need to evaluate the impact this will have. The present book, "assesses the likely effects of the emerging market economies on world trade and capital flows, and through them on such key variables as interest rates and growth in developing countries. Implications are derived for the United States, Germany, the European Community as a whole, Japan, and different sets of developing nations." (p. xi) The authors initially provide an overview and road map in an introductory chapter and then proceed to evaluate the consequences for international trade, capital flows, and macroeconomic performance. They conclude by speculating on policy implications.

14. **Power, Purpose, and Collective Choice: Economic Strategy in Socialist States**, edited by Ellen Comisso and Laura D'Andrea Tyson. Ithaca, N.Y.: Cornell University Press, 1986. 422 p. *Cornell Studies in Political Economy*.

Recognizing that the connection between political power and purpose is different from that of the OECD (Organization for Economic Cooperation and Development) states and the NICs (newly industrialized countries), the contributors to this volume proceed to describe, analyze, and evaluate economic strategy within the European members of the CMEA. Their 14 papers are arranged under four rubrics: Comparing Responses to International Disturbances, Eastern Europe as a Region, Economic Strategy inside the CMEA, and Responding to International Economic Change outside the CMEA. The essays were written based on data available through 1985, thus not privy to the tumultuous changes that would disturb this part of the world in the subsequent half decade. Concluding that economic strategy is related to state structure, but not following it, Comisso states that "even socialism turns out to be much more the governing of men than the administration of things." (p. 400).

15. Dembinski, Pawel H., **The Logic of the Planned Economy: The Seeds of the Collapse**, translated by Kevin Cook. Oxford: Clarendon Press, 1991. x, 249 p. ISBN: 0198286864. Includes index and bibliographical references (p. 235-238).

The purpose of this well-organized, clearly written work is to analyze the CPEs (centrally planned economies) from the social science point of view. Dembinski believes it is imperative to conceptualize the "otherness" of such economies by accurately defining what is meant by such terms as price, profit, and enterprise within the special environment that the CPEs inhabit. This will remove the "semantic haze" that often obscures western analyses of CPEs. The book's 8 chapters are arranged in three sections: The Essence of the System, describes how the system works; Internal Dilemmas portrays the role of planning, nature of the enterprise, and the function of money; and finally part 3, External Dilemmas, explains the problems of relations to society, the arms race, and trade with the West. Such a structure fulfills the author's two-fold objective of answering the question: were these inescapable internal contradictions that threatened the system? If the answer were yes, then at what critical level would the system collapse. Essentially the author contends that there was no way that adherence to Marxist ideology would allow the economic system to reach the levels of efficiency necessary to survive the dilemmas identified.

16. Deutsch, Robert, **The Food Revolution in the Soviet Union and Eastern Europe**. Boulder, CO: Westview Press, 1986. xxii, 256 p. *Westview Special Studies on the Soviet Union and Easter Europe, 0163-6057*, ISBN: 0813371619. Includes indexes and bibliography (p. 149-241).

Besides analyzing the economic performance of the East European socialist economies, Deutsch also examines the ways in which these different economies have attempted to meet the rise in consumer demand, especially for food. In addition to the agricultural economic aspects of the problem, the author also investigates the effect of rising food consumption on international relations. Reviews: *American Academy of Political and Social Science Annals* 491:164-65 (May 1987). *Canadian Slavonic Papers* 29:1:99-100 (March 1987). *Contemporary Sociology* 16:4:494-95 (July 1987).

17. **Economic Reforms in Eastern Europe and the Soviet Union**, edited by Hubert Gabrisch. Boulder, CO: Westview Press, 1989. vii, 214 p. *Westview Special Studies in International Economics; Yearbook, Vienna Institute for Comparative Economic Studies*, v. 1-1988. ISBN: 0813376521. Includes bibliography (p. 166-169).

Aiming to contribute to the assessment of generalized and national factors that help or hinder the economic transition from a Stalinist to a democratic order, this collection of ten essays focuses on the problems and characteristics of the reform movement that took place from 1981-1988. The book is divided into three parts: I. Basic Thinking about the Problem; II. Country Studies, which examines the Soviet Union, Bulgaria, Czechoslovakia, Hungary, and Poland; and III. Special Areas of Reform, i.e. the banking system among CMEA countries, foreign trade, and joint ventures. In the 80s the main difference from earlier periods is that the Soviet Union is supporting these reforms. The basic problem is common among these centrally planned economies: how to design a system that will protect against unemployment and at the same time to bolster the chronically underutilized production capabilities. The theme of this work centers on the problems and characteristics of this latest reform movement. Review: *Canadian Slavonic Papers* 32:4: 527 (December 1990).

18. **Planned Economies: Confronting the Challenges of the 1980s**, edited by John P. Hardt and Carl H. McMillan. Cambridge: Cambridge University Press, 1988. xiv, 191 p. ISBN: 0521344611. Includes bibliographical references and index.

These nine essays, all presented at the Third World Conference for Soviet and East European Studies, are arranged in three sections. Section one deals with new conditions of economic management (investment, self-financing, and information and computers). Section two concerns structural changes in the natural resource sector (especially energy resources), and section three tackles problems of national and international integration.

19. **Dismantling the Command Economy in Eastern Europe**. Boulder, CO: Westview Press, 1991. ix, 280 p. *Vienna Institute for Comparative Economic Studies Yearbook*, v. 3. ISBN: 0813381371. Includes bibliographical references.

The sixteen essays by various contributors are divided into three parts. In part one, the general issues section, the two essays deal with various issues in the transitions from command economies to market economies and to exchange economies. In part two, selected aspects of transition, the focus is on money and monetary policy, exchange rate policies and convertibility, east-west economic relations, energy prospects, and unemployment and social security measures. Part three, country specific transition policies, covers Bulgaria, Czechoslovakia, GDR, Hungary, Poland, Soviet Union, and Yugoslavia. Romania is not examined in part three but is covered under various topics in part two. The material presented in this yearbook offers current data and opinion as of 1991, prior to the collapse of the Soviet Union.

20. Jeffries, Ian, **A Guide to the Socialist Economies**. London: Routledge, 1990. xxii, 322 p. ISBN: 0415007461. Includes bibliographical references and index.

"The basic aim of this book is to give the reader some idea of the rich variety of economic systems to be found among socialist countries today and to highlight and explain some of the major problems facing them." (p. xiii) Since all these economies either adopted or had the Soviet system imposed on them, it starts with an analysis of the Soviet system and then proceeds to the communist economies of Eastern Europe and Asia.

21. Jonas, Paul, **Essays on the Structure and Reform of Centrally Planned Economic Systems**. Boulder, CO: Social Sciences Monographs, 1990. xx, 211 p. *East European Monographs*, no. 275. ISBN: 0880331720.

In these essays, Jonas shows with analytical tools how the Soviet revolutionaries tried to make the ideology of scientific socialism operational. The essays fall into two groups: those concentrating on the structure and growth of the Soviet economic system and those dealing with reform and integration into the world economic system, especially the European Economic Community. Specific topics include examination of the structural price mechanism, the dynamics of the Soviet development path, black market proliferation, international trade and economic integration, joint ventures, currency convertibility, and the Gerschenkron effect.

22. Lavigne, Marie, **International Political Economy and Socialism**, translated by David Lambert. Cambridge, England: Cambridge University Press, 1991. 412 p. ISBN: 0521334276, 0521336635 (pbk.). Includes bibliographical references (p. 394-409) and index.

Lavigne identifies three trading areas—technology, energy, and agriculture—upon which depends the future of Eastern Europe in world trade and finance. In nine chapters, she then explores whether trade within Comecon will expand or contract, what weight political factors will have and other questions relating to these issues. She has added a 1990 postscript in order to try to give the most recent perspective on the effects of political change in 1989. Review: *Foreign Affairs* 70:4:171 (Fall 1991).

23. **Foreign Economic Liberalization: Transformations in Socialist and Market Economies**. Boulder, CO: Westview Press, 1991. xii, 288 p. ISBN: 0813381983, 0813381991 (pbk.). Includes bibliographical references and index.

About one-half of the essays appearing in this book were originally presented at a 1989 conference, held in Budapest, on attempts at liberalization. The other half of the 22 essays have been added since that conference. The focus of the book is the liberalization of market economies and the possibilities for liberalization of socialist economies. The four divisions are tied together by the editor's introductory essay (Part I) which "contrasts economic liberalizations in market economies and in the countries of Central and Eastern Europe." (p. 5) It argues why foreign economic liberalization must be part of the transition from centrally planned to market economies, and it describes the different approaches taken by Hungary and Poland in this sphere. Part II (10 essays) describes various market economy experiences around the world. Part III (6 essays) explores Hungary's experiences and policy options. Finally, Part IV (5 essays) evaluates liberalization in Central and Eastern Europe and China. Reviews: *Orbis* 35:4:617 (Fall 1991). *Foreign Affairs* 70:4:173 (Fall 1991).

24. **Trade Unions in Communist States**, edited by Alex Pravda and Blair A. Ruble. Boston: Allen & Unwin, 1986. xiii, 281 p. ISBN: 0043311083. Includes bibliographical references and index.

The editors hope that these eleven essays fill a gap in the literature of comparative surveys of trade unions. By and large such surveys ignore communist trade unions, reasoning that they have little in common with their non-communist counterparts. While communist labor unions mobilize rather than defend labor, they also have the potential of becoming mediating organizations in communist states, albeit under party control. The first essay presents the Leninist model of the trade unions. The last chapter provides comparisons and contrasts between communist and capitalist trade unions. The intervening chapters are case studies of trade unions in the USSR, China, Poland, Hungary, the GDR, Czechoslovakia, Romania, and Yugoslavia. Review: *Canadian Slavonic Papers* 29:2-3:326-27 (June-September 1987).

25. Prybyla, Jan S., **Market and Plan Under Socialism: The Bird in the Cage**. Stanford, Calif: Hoover Institution Press, Stanford University, 1987. xv, 348 p. *Hoover Press Publication*, no. 335. ISBN: 081798352X (pbk.), 0817983511. Includes index and bibliography (p. 317-335).

Prybyla explores the influence of the classical state plan in the Soviet Union, China, Yugoslavia, and Hungary. In part one, Concepts, the typology of plan models is described as well as the theoretical foundations of the neoclassical offshoots. In part two, Cases, he examines in more detail the specifics of these plans such as the role of the collective farm, information, consideration, and motivation as key factors in these plans, and how the conceptual base in part one has been realized in China, Hungary, and Yugoslavia.

26. Williamson, John, **The Economic Opening of Eastern Europe**. Washington, DC: Institute for International Economics, 1991. x, 92 p. *Policy Studies in International Economics*, v. 31. ISBN: 0881321869. Includes bibliographical references (p. 91-92).

This book "analyzes the external aspects of the economic policies that are being adopted" by the emerging market economies in Eastern Europe. (p. ix) Sandwiched between an introduction and conclusion are three chapters. One presents the background for the reversal from planned to market economy. A second identifies the salient issues invoked including concepts of convertibility, payments union proposal, trade and exchange rate policy, and parallel currencies. A third chapter presents the positions of individual countries in their path to a market economy.

27. Winiecki, Jan, **The Distorted World of Soviet-Type Economies**. Pittsburgh, Pa.: University of Pittsburgh Press, 1988. xi, 230 p. *Russian and East European Studies*, no. 8. ISBN: 0822911493. Includes index and bibliography (p. 212-223).

By using the term Soviet type economies to describe those economic systems in Eastern Europe (GDR, Bulgaria, Poland, Czechoslovakia, Romania, Hungary, and the Soviet Union), Winiecki hopes to encompass economic systems excluded by the term centrally planned economies, notably Hungary. He maintains that Hungary still retains linkages between the political and economic systems that characterize the Soviet system generally. He attempts to point out the links between deviations from Western economic rationality at the behavioral, microeconomic level and resultant economic losses or gains forgone at the aggregate level. The book is divided into three parts. Part one deals with the dynamics of the system—economic growth and prices. Part two explores the structure of the economic system as it is influenced by the dynamics of the system, and part three examines the resulting impact of dynamics and structure on foreign trade and technology transfer. A conclusion summarizes his findings. Reviews: *Journal of Comparative Economics* 14:1:171-73 (1990). *Journal of Economic Literature* 28:1:77-78 (March 1990). *Canadian-American Slavic Studies* 24:4:499-501 (Winter 1990).

Chapter 4
GOVERNMENT AND LAW

28. **Communist Politics: A Reader**, edited by Stephen White and Daniel Nelson. London: Macmillan Education, 1986. xii, 416 p. ISBN: 0333414063. Includes index and bibliography (p. 380-410).

Reprints of what the editors consider a fair representation of some of the best work on communist politics appear in this reader. The nineteen essays are arranged in five parts. Part One (ch. 1) describes the historical origins of the Communist movement. Part Two (ch. 2-6) deals with structures of government and elections, especially in the USSR, Poland, Yugoslavia, and China. Part Three (ch. 7-10) explores various facets of the Communist Party by examining it in the USSR, Poland, Cuba, and China. Part Four (ch. 16-19) examines policy outcomes and provides comparative perspectives between East and West. Reviews: *Slavic Review* 46:3-4:615-17 (Fall-Winter 1987).

Chapter 5
INTERNATIONAL RELATIONS, FOREIGN TRADE

29. Cynkin, Thomas M., **Soviet and American Signalling in the Polish Crisis**, foreword by Robert L. Pfaltzgraff. Basingstoke: Macmillan, 1988. ix, 263 p. ISBN: 0333446925. Includes index and bibliography (p. 252-254).
Cynkin examines "the patterns of interaction that characterise superpower relations in the case of a crisis such as that which unfolded in Poland reaching its climax in early December 1981 and resulting in the imposition of martial law. Central to the analysis... is a comprehensive examination of the crisis management strategies of the USA and the USSR within the context of a variety of signals transmitted between Washington and Moscow." (p. viii) Review: *Slavic Review* 49:2:299-300 (Summer 1990).

30. Dawisha, Karen, **Eastern Europe, Gorbachev, and Reform: The Great Challenge**. 2nd ed. Cambridge: Cambridge University Press, 1990. xv, 319 p. ISBN: 0521384983, 0521386527 (pbk.). Includes bibliographical references.
The second edition of Dawisha's book updates the earlier edition by including changes to the Spring of 1990. In other aspects, the book remains essentially the same. The work is divided into two parts, with an introduction. Part one (ch. 2-4) gives a historical perspective of Soviet-East European elections over the past 45 years by examining political, economic, cultural and military factors. Part two (ch. 5-8) focuses on meeting the challenges that lie ahead. In this part she analyzes the reactions of East European leaders to the challenges facing their regimes, the short-term policy agendas in the political, economic, and social spheres, and how they all can move beyond the threat of use of force by the Soviet Union. Effects on the West and influences from the West are also taken into account. Several useful appendices are included. Topics covered include a chronology of Eastern European events from February 1945 to April 1990; Soviet and East European leadership successions 1945-1990; Eastern European Communist Parties, successors, leaders and memberships; and Eastern European elections and major contenders, 1990. Reviews: *Problems of Communism* 39:3:99-103 (May-June 1990). *Conflict* 10:3:275-77 (September 1990). *Current History* 89:551:425 (December 1990). *Canadian Slavonic Papers* 32:4:528-29 (December 1990). *Canadian-American Slavic Studies* 24:4:493-95 (Winter 1990).

31. **European Détente: Case Studies of the Politics of East-West Relations**, edited by Kenneth Dyson. London: Pinter, 1986. xi, 279 p. ISBN: 0861875575. Includes bibliographical references and index.
These eleven essays derive from an Anglo-German conference held at the University of Bradford. The overall purpose of the volume is to place European détente in its historical context and then to draw conclusions about the proper conduct of East-West relations from this analysis. In examining détente - easing the strained relations between states—Germany has been and continues to be a key element. Three of the eleven essays focus on Germany. Other topics include the Conference on Security and Cooperation in Eastern Europe and the Helsinki Final Act, the Soviet Union and European détente, national independence and Atlanticism, the dialectic of French policies, Britain and European political cooperation. Dyson concludes the volume with his three-dimensional view of East-West relations.

32. **East-West Agricultural Trade**, edited by James R. Jones. Boulder, CO.: Westview Press, 1986. xvii, 256 p. *Westview Special Studies in International Economics and Business*, ISBN: 081337135X. Includes bibliographies.

This is "the first study to focus specifically on the economies of agricultural trade issues in centrally planned economies, [and] contains recent findings of economists who have examined the decision making processes and the trends that relate to agricultural trade with the West by Eastern Europe, the Soviet Union, and China. Future prospects for agricultural trade with these countries are considered, as are the bilateral trading relations between these countries and the United States." (front piece) Reviews: *American Academy of Political and Social Science Annals* 491:164-65 (May 1987). *Soviet Union* 14:1:138-40 (1987).

33. **East-West Relations and Divided Nation Problems in the Gorbachev Era: German and Korean Perspectives**. Seoul: Institute of East and West Studies, Yonsei University, 1988. xiv, 441 p. *East and West Studies Series*, no. 4. Includes bibliographical references and index.

This collection of 22 essays is an outgrowth of the 3rd and 4th Korean-German conferences. Its focus is the understanding of factors that lead to international crises, which arise from conflicts of interests among nations. The essays are grouped in four sections. Section one (1-16) examines security issues in the global and regional context. Section II (7-11) focuses on the role of the Soviet Union in Eastern Europe and Asia and the possible change in Soviet policy under Gorbachev. Section III (12-16) analyzes east-west economic relations. Korean-Hungarian economic relations are the subject of two of these five essays. Section IV (17-22) looks at the various issues surrounding international relations in Germany and Korea and speculations regarding their future courses.

34. **The Uncertain Future: Gorbachev's Eastern Bloc**, edited by Nicholas N. Kittrie and Ivan Volgyes. New York: Paragon House Publishers, 1988. iii, 281 p. *"A PWPA Book"*, ISBN: 0943852617. Includes index and bibliography (p. 271-277).

In the light of improved relations between the superpowers, this volume was "undertaken to record and realistically review the historical as well as contemporary forces within the eastern bloc countries." (p. 7) Individual essays explore political reform, the decreasing importance of ideology, economic conditions and policy, human rights, the effect of reforms, the Warsaw Pact and changes in the military balance, and U.S. policy towards Eastern Europe.

35. Nelson, Daniel N., **Elite-Mass Relations in Communist Systems**. Basingstoke: Macmillan, 1988. x, 217 p. ISBN: 0333428218. Includes bibliography (p. 191-202).

Nelson states in his introduction, the study of communist politics " requires more attention to the 'base' of such systems rather than to their 'apex.' " (p. 1) His goal is to develop the means for gauging change in elite-mass relationships—the when, how and to what extent people will challenge the legitimacy of party rule and how, when and to what extent their leaders will respond. Nelson's focus in this type of analysis is the changing relationship between the party and the people and institutions at the local level. Seven of the eight chapters were previously published in journals in slightly altered form. He has provided an introduction and conclusion to make these essays cohere into a unified whole. Topics covered include vertical integration and political control; women in local communist politics in Poland and Romania; leadership; public opinion and public policy; Leninists and political inequalities; and workers and political alienation. Review: *Journal of Politics* 52:1:323-326 (February 1990).

36. Ploss, Sidney I., **Moscow and the Polish Crisis: An Interpretation of Soviet Policies and Intentions**. Boulder, CO: Westview Press, 1986. ix, 182 p. *Westview Special Studies on the Soviet Union and Eastern Europe*, 0163-6057. ISBN: 0813303516. Includes bibliographical references and index.

In 1980, in the midst of the Polish crisis, the West was uncertain about the Soviets' response to unrest. When martial law was declared, Secretary of State Alexander Haig maintained that it came without warning. Ploss, however, says that it was clear from analysis of the Soviet press what would happen. Using propaganda analysis, Ploss shows how the press was the best source for tracing policy decisions and leadership debates. Reviews: *Canadian Slavonic Papers* 29:2-3:354-55 (June-September 1987). *Political Science Quarterly* 102:1:178 (Spring 1987). *International Journal* 42:1:167-68 (Winter 1987-88).

37. Rachwald, Arthur R., **In Search of Poland: The Superpowers' Response to Solidarity, 1980-1989**. Stanford, CA: Hoover Institution Press, 1990. xii, 149 p. ISBN: 0817989625 (pbk.), 0817989617. Includes bibliographical references and index.

Rachwald examines the Soviet Union's resistance to Solidarity, the independent trade union movement in Poland. His "analysis of lengthy encounters between martial law authorities and Solidarity in the years following the 13 December 1981 crackdown on the union portrays Soviet failure to contain or reverse the political aspirations of the Polish people." (p. viii) He also examines Polish internal politics and its response to international affairs during this period.

38. **The Soviet Bloc and the Third World: The Political Economy of East-South Relations**, edited by Brigitte H. Schulz and William W. Hansen. Boulder, CO: Westview Press, 1989. ix, 246 p. *Westview Special Studies on the Soviet Union and Eastern Europe*, ISBN: 0813375134. Includes bibliographies and index.

These essays cover specific topics dealing with the political economy of Soviet and East European relations with the Third World. Review: *Foreign Affairs* 69:2:173 (Spring 1990).

39. **East-West Tensions in the Third World**. New York: W.W. Norton, 1986. 243 p. ISBN: 0393023109. Includes index.

These seven essays formed the background papers for the Seventieth American Assembly held in November 1985. The Final Report of the Assembly has been included as an appendix. For the most part, the authors of these papers reject the two usual methods of dealing with conflict in the Third World. The sphere of influence approach and the code of conduct approach, whereby rules for competition have been worked out, have given way to a working out of specific limitations on the kind and degree of intervention in local and regional situations. After an overview of the problem, contributors explore U.S.-Soviet rivalry in the Middle East, Latin America, Asia, and Africa. Two final essays focus economic and military competition in the Third World in general. Review: *Foreign Service Journal* 65:10:15-17 (November 1988).

40. Wallace, William V., and Roger A. Clarke, **Comecon, Trade and the West**. New York: St. Martin's Press, 1986. xi, 176 p. ISBN: 0312151047. Includes index and bibliography (p. 170-172).

The authors offer a comprehensive view of Comecon (the Soviet dominated Council for Mutual Economic Assistance) by examining the progress of Comecon and the barriers to coordination from Stalin to Brezhnev. Several subsequent chapters then cover further historical developments after Brezhnev, including the actions taken at the 27th Party Congress. Various problems facing Comecon, including the economic development of individual CMEA countries, its relations with the EEC, economic reforms, and trade are also discussed.

Chapter 6
POLITICAL THEORIES, NATIONALISM, COMMUNISM, RELIGION

41. **Soviet Nationality Policies: Ruling Ethnic Groups in the USSR**, edited by Henry R. Huttenbach. London: Mansell, 1990. xiv, 302 p. *Studies in Issues*, no. 6. ISBN: 0720120551. Includes index.

The essays in this volume cover the origins and development of Soviet nationality policy from 1917 to the present. The fifteen essays are arranged in three parts. Part one deals with determining the character of Soviet nationality policy. Part two focuses on the development of policy that strove for a Homo Sovieticus and examines the role of education, rituals, and population redistribution. Part three observes Soviet nationality policies in action and provides an analysis of them.

Chapter 7
LANGUAGE AND LITERATURE

42. **Case in Slavic**, edited by Richard D. Brecht and James S. Levine. Columbus, OH: Slavica, 1986. 467 p. ISBN: 0893571660. Includes bibliography (p. 453-467).

A selection of scholarly essays on the many facets of case in the Slavic languages. Although no Soviet work is included, the editors have sought to provide a sampling of the literature on case currently being produced. "The present volume represents a sampling of current work on Slavic case done within the Case Grammar, Government-Binding, Localist, Meaning-Text, Operational and Prague School-Jakobsonian frameworks by linguists in the U.S., Canada, Australia, Western and Eastern Europe. Together the papers here clearly demonstrate a commonality of interest that cuts across theory-specific issues."(p. 7) The volume is divided into two sections, one on metatheory and the other on various aspects of case, morphology, syntax, semantics and pragmatics.

43. **International Conference of Slavists: American Contributions to the Tenth International Congress of Slavists: Sofia, September 1988: Literature**, edited by Jane Gary Harris. Columbus, OH: Slavica, 1988. 433 p. ISBN: 0893571911. Includes bibliographies.

Like its companion volumes in other disciplines, this collection of essays in Slavic literature was written by Americans in attendance at the 10th International Congress of Slavists, held in Sofia in 1988. There is no unifying theme.

44. **The Supernatural in Slavic and Baltic Literature: Essays in Honor of Victor Terras**, edited by Amy Mandelker and Roberta Reeder. Columbus, OH: Slavica Publishers, 1988. 482 p. ISBN: 089357192X. Includes bibliographies.

While it has been recognized that one distinctive feature of Russian literature has been the close relationship between the fictional world and the empirical world of everyday life, the 26 essays presented here show "that in Russian literature of the nineteenth and early twentieth centuries there is also pervasive use of the supernatural." (p. xi) The essays are conveniently arranged under the rubrics of "Nineteenth Century Russian Literature," "Twentieth Century Russian Literature," "Baltic Literature," and Slavic and Baltic Folk-lore." A bibliography of the works of Victor Terras is also included.

45. Nobel Symposium (62nd: 1985: Stockholm, Sweden), **The Slavic Literatures and Modernism: a Nobel Symposium, August 5-8, 1985**, edited by Nils Ake Nilsson. Stockholm, Sweden: Almqvist & Wiksell International, 1986. 318 p. *Historieoch Antikvitets Academien*, v. 16. ISBN: 917402180X. Includes bibliographies.

The symposium's purpose was to bring together scholars to discuss problems that are common to most of the Slavic literatures: Russian Polish, Czech, Yugoslav and Bulgarian. The focus was on the avant-garde movements of the 1910s and 1920s.

46. Perkowski, Jan Louis, **The Darkling: A Treatise on Slavic Vampirism**. Columbus, OH: Slavica Publishers, 1989. 169 p. ISBN: 0893572004.

Perkowski was often asked at talks and lectures the questions: are there any real vampires? and was Dracula a vampire? Seeing that his audience was dissatisfied with his responses, he attempted to answer these questions more fully in this book. His approach is primarily literary and folkloristic. The nine book chapters deal with Dracula the vampire, origins of the European vampire, differences between the Slavic terms used for vampire and werewolf, daemon contamination, testimony from various Slavic folktales, the English literary vampire, and an examination of the psychological underpinnings of vampire beliefs and their mechanism of transmission. Review: *Slavic and East European Journal* 34:4:567-68 (Winter 1990).

47. Stankiewicz, Edward, **The Slavic Languages: Unity in Diversity**. New York: Mouton de Gruyter, 1986. xv, 472 p. ISBN: 0899252737. Includes bibliographies and indexes.

A collection of essays by Edward Stankiewicz on a wide range of topics relating to Slavic languages in general. Some essays focus on problems peculiar to Russian such as "The Place and Function of Stress in Russian Nominal Forms with a Zero in the Ending" and "The Accentuation of the Russian Verb." "This volume is a collection of selected papers dealing with comparative and historical problems of Slavic linguistics. Their arrangement reflects, on the one hand, the shifting interests of Slavic linguistic scholarship as it has evolved over the last three decades, and, on the other hand, the various phases and facets of my own work." (p. vii) References are included at the end of each essay. Reviews: *Canadian Slavonic Papers* 29:2-3:365-66 (June-September 1987).

48. Terry, Garth M., **East European Languages and Literatures**. Nottingham: Astra Press, 1988. xvi, 128 p. *Astra Soviet and East European Bibliographies*, no, 8. ISBN: 0946134138. Includes index.

Supplements the compiler's earlier work *East European Languages and Literatures: A Subject and Name Index to Articles in English Language Journals, 1900-1977*. These two supplements cover materials published from 1985-1990. Sources for the citations are Festschriften, conferences proceedings, collected papers, English language journals, and articles omitted from the earlier volumes. Since the volume tries to present a picture of Western scholarship, East European publications are not included. All Slavic languages are covered as well as Hungarian, Romanian, and the Baltic languages. Albania, East Germany, and Greece are excluded. The entries are arranged by subject. Abbreviations of Festschriften and journals are listed in a table at the beginning of the volume.

49. World Congress for Soviet and East European Studies (3rd: 1985: Washington, D. C.), **Aspects of Modern Russian and Czech Literature: Selected Papers of the Third World Congress for Soviet and East European Studies**, edited by Arnold McMillin. Columbus, OH: Slavica Publishers, 1989. 239 p. ISBN: 0893571946. Includes bibliographical references.

These papers reflect the broad interests of literary scholars who took part in the Third World Congress for Soviet and East European Studies. Most of the articles are on Russian literature, with three on Solzhenitsyn. Three essays are devoted to Czech literature.

Chapter 8
MILITARY AFFAIRS

50. Vale, Lawrence J., **The Limits of Civil Defence in the USA, Switzerland, Britain, and the Soviet Union: The Evolution of Policies Since 1945**. New York: St. Martin's Press, 1987. xii, 268 p. ISBN: 0312000829. Includes index and bibliography (p. 233-257).

The intellectual framework of this book is framed by four questions: "1. How have ideas about civil defense evolved? 2. Who should be responsible for implementing civil defense? 3. What sorts of rationales are put forth to justify civil defense? 4. What are the technical and political limits of civil defence?" (p. 2) After examining these theoretical considerations, Vale provides four case studies of the development of civil defense and its rationale.

51. Stourac, Richard, and Kathleen McCreery, **Theatre as a Weapon: Workers' Theatre in the Soviet Union, Germany, and Britain, 1917-1934**. London: Routledge and Kegan Paul, 1986. xvi, 336 p. *Theatre Production Studies*, ISBN: 0710097700. Includes index and bibliography (p. 324-326).

The first section of this work focuses on Workers' Theatre in Russian from 1917-1934. Such topics as the role of propaganda, Meyerhold, the cinema, Eisenstein, and the Proletkult are discussed. An appendix includes the repertoire of the Blue Blouse Movement. There is also an index of theatre groups, plays, songs, and sketches. Although the section on this type of theatre in the Soviet Union make up only one third of this volume, the authors claim to be filling a void in the existing literature. Review: *Theater Journal* 40:1:133 (March 1988).

Chapter 10
SOCIETY, SOCIAL ISSUES, SOCIOLOGY

52. **The Reemergence of Civil Society in Eastern Europe and the Soviet Union**,
    edited by Zbigniew Rau. Boulder, CO: Westview Press, 1991. xi, 181 p. ISBN:
    0813384044.

The essays appearing in this volume were originally presented at a conference at the
University of Texas at Austin on April 20-21, 1990. "The purpose of this volume is to
analyze the developments in the former Soviet bloc from the perspective of the ruled. The
key explanatory tool in this analysis is the notion of civil society; its conceptual framework
is the interaction between the civil society and the state." (p. 3) Individual essays explore
this topic in Poland, Estonia, Ukraine, and on the Crimean Tatars.

53. Shipler, David K., **Russia: Broken Idols, Solemn Dreams**. Rev. and updated ed.
    New York: Penguin Books, 1989. xvi, 462 p. ISBN: 0140122710.

In this revised edition of Shipler's best seller, the author has added an epilogue describing
his trip after Gorbachev came to power. The rest of the book remains the same. In it Shipler
"wanted to look beneath the surface, past the leadership changes, dissidents' trials, economic statistics, and diplomatic negotiations, to dimensions of attitude and culture where
the task was not so much to answer questions as to ask them, to find the right points of
curiosity and wonder, and to give them reasonable voice." (p. xiii).

54. Tanner, Marcus, **Ticket to Latvia: A Journey from Berlin to the Baltic**. 1st
    American ed. New York: Holt, 1990. 197 p. ISBN: 08050113466.

A travel account of a correspondent for the London *Independent* as he travels from Eastern
Europe to Russia. The book is arranged by city with descriptions of Berlin, Prague, Warsaw,
Cracow, Vilnius, Riga, and Leningrad. This impressionistic account dwells on the effect of
Soviet domination of the area.

Part II

SPECIFIC THEMES

Chapter 11
THE RUSSIAN EMPIRE PRIOR TO
1917 AND THE USSR

GENERAL REFERENCE WORKS

Bibliographies

55. Arans, David, **How We Lost the Civil War: Bibliography of Russian Émigré Memoirs on the Russian Revolution, 1917-1921**. Newtonville, Mass.: Oriental Research Partners, 1988. 200 p. *ORP Russian Bibliography Series*, no. 6. ISBN: 089250343. Includes index.

This bibliography of memoirs of Russian émigrés "contains only those memoirs that were published separately or were included in collections of memoirs." (p. 6) The entries are arranged by subject and within each category alphabetically. Each entry is in Cyrillic characters followed by an English translation. The entries are annotated by brief phrases describing the events described, followed by notable figures mentioned in the text. An index facilitates access to this listing.

56. Center for Research Libraries, **Soviet Serials Currently Received at the Center for Research Libraries**, edited by Sergei P. Ignashev. 4th ed. Chicago: Center for Research Libraries, 1990. vi, 305 p. Includes indexes.

This is the fourth edition of the Center for Research Libraries serial listing. It includes 1287 titles of periodicals, irregular serials, annuals, and numbered monographic series, received as of June 1, 1990. Newly added features include beginning publication dates, International Standard Book Numbers, earlier titles, series authority records, and the first issue available. The bibliography includes a subject index organized into five subject categories: science, technology, humanities, social science, and agriculture. Additional information on holdings distribution is drawn from OCLC.

57. **Economic and Political Reform in the USSR 1989: Abstracts of Soviet Social Science Periodicals**, edited by Leonid Khotin and Yakov Berger. Informatics and Prognostics, 1989. 2 v. Includes indexes.

A two volume set of abstracts from Soviet material dealing with the reforms of perestroika. Many sources were used but the main criteria for selection were: 1) articles from archival materials, 2) articles with results of sociological studies, 3) statistical and socio-demographical articles, 4) articles illustrating the debate over reforms, and 5) articles focusing on regional issues. One factor that makes this source unique is its focus on regional publications, which are often unavailable in the West. "The goals of this volume are to provide Western scholars with new information on the development of different areas of social, political and economic activity and thought in different regions and republics in the Soviet Union in order to help them create a social, political and economic 'map' of the current situation in the USSR and facilitate the cross-pollination between areas of Soviet studies." (p. vii) Numerous indexes give the reader a variety of access points including geographic and subject access.

58. **Russian Travelers to the Christian East from the Twelfth to the Twentieth Century**, edited by Theofanis G. Stavrou and Peter R. Weisensel. Columbus, Ohio: Slavica Publishers, 1986. li, 925 p. ISBN: 0893571571. Includes index.

A bibliography of traveler's accounts from 1106 to 1914. Any travel account including newspaper articles, officer's memoirs and traveler's light impressions have been selected. Material omitted are scholarly studies if there is no reference to a specific journey, political reports, works on the natural sciences and tourist guides. The word "Russian" here is meant to refer to the original language of publication or the nationality of the author. The "Christian East" includes areas associated with the origins of orthodoxy. Each entry includes the author, title, city, and date of publication and a code indicating many of the libraries that hold the volumes. Entries are arranged chronologically. Annotations are also included with each entry. Access is enhanced through the detailed index. Reviews: *Canadian Slavonic Papers* 29:2-3:294-95 (June-September 1987).

Biographies

59. Brands, H. W., **Inside the Cold War: Loy Henderson and the Rise of the American Empire, 1918-1961**. New York: Oxford University Press, 1991. xiv, 337 p. ISBN: 019406707X. Incudes bibliographical references and index.

The biography of American statesman Loy Henderson. A large part of his life was tied up with the Soviet Union. This brings an unusual perspective on Soviet development from 1918-1961, focusing on how it fit into America's empire building. Reviews: *Orbis* 35:3:465 (Summer 1991). *Foreign Affairs* 70:4:174 (Fall 1991).

60. Buloff, Joseph, **From the Old Marketplace**, translated by Joseph Singer. Cambridge, Mass.: Harvard University Press, 1991. 335 p. ISBN: 0674325036.

Buloff, actor and theater director, grew up in post-WWI Vilnius. His memoir of his childhood describes colorful inhabitants of that time and place and his own inner struggle to become someone in the midst of persecution and brutality.

61. Chavchavadze, David, **Crowns and Trenchcoats: A Russian Prince in the CIA: an Autobiography**. New York, N.Y.: Atlantic International Publications, 1990. 315 p. ISBN: 093831107. Includes index.

Chavchavadze has written an interesting autobiography of his life, focusing especially on that time spent in the CIA. He was born in 1924, a direct descendant of the Romanovs and King George XII of Georgia.

62. Chukovskaia, Lidiia Korneevna, **To the Memory of Childhood**, translated by Eliza Kellogg Klose. Evanston, IL: Northwestern University Press, 1988. 168 p. ISBN: 0810107899. Includes bibliographies.

This is a memoir of the childhood of Lidiia Chukovskaia, daughter of Russian author Kornei Chukovsky. A biographical glossary of Russian writers, artists and intellectuals is included as an aid for the reader. Reviews: *New York Times Review of Books* 37:2:12-16 (February 15, 1990). *Slavic Review* 49:1:148-49 (Spring 1990).

63. Conte, Francis, **Christian Rakovski: 1873-1941; A Political Biography**, translated from the French by A.P.M. Bradley. Boulder, CO: East European Monographs, 1989. vi, 517 p. ISBN: 0880331534. Includes bibliographical references.

Rakovski, a Bulgarian who joined the Bolshevik party, participated in the revolution, then was expelled from the party in 1927 as a member of the Trotskyite opposition, and was a victim of the show trials of the mid-1930's. Conte portrays the early years of Rakovski and then focuses most intensely on his activities from 1914 to 1930.

64. Doder, Dusko, and Louise Branson, **Gorbachev: Heretic in the Kremlin**. New York, N.Y.: Viking, 1990. x, 450 p. ISBN: 0670824720. Includes bibliographical references.

Doder and Branson, both journalists, have written a book that "penetrates both Gorbachev's character... and the character of the nation that is reeling under his reforms." (book jacket) After covering his youth and early years in the party, they spent most of their energy focusing on Gorbachev's activities in power. The book is based on interviews with hundreds of people, including several officials such as Yakovlev, Dobrinin, Aganbegin, and Abalkin.

65. Durman, Karel, **The Time of the Thunderer: Mikhail Katkov, Russian Nationalist Extremism and the Failure of the Bismarckian System, 1871-1887**. Boulder, CO: East European Monographs, 1988. ix, 609 p. *East European Monographs*, no. 237. ISBN: 0880331348. Includes index and bibliography (p. 585-598).

A biography of Mikhail Katkov, editor of the 19th century paper *Moskovskiia vedomosti*. Katkov is seen as a "pivotal personality" of the period, influencing popular opinion on public policy. The book is divided into three parts, each covering a period of Katkov's life. The author uses Katkov's life to demonstrate another point. "Russian statesmen and foreign observers alike declared newspapers, journals, and journalists the only force capable of challenging the autocratic government. Most certainly, nothing can illuminate this thesis and the whole extremist impact on tsardom's policies better than the case of Mikhail Nikiforovich Katkov." (p. 7) The biography is framed in these terms. Review: *American Historical Review* 95:3:870-871 (June 1990).

66. Furmann, Joseph T., **Rasputin: A Life**. New York: Praeger, 1990. x, 276 p. ISBN: 027593215X. Includes index and bibliography (p. 257-266).

A biography of Grigory Rasputin, the monk who wielded such tremendous influence over Tsar Nicholas II's family. The biography covers all periods of his life although the years 1850 to 1900 are somewhat sketchier due to a general lack of information in the period. A lengthy bibliography is included.

67. Glotzer, Albert, **Trotsky: Memoir and Critique**. Buffalo, NY: Prometheus Books, 1989. 343 p. ISBN: 087975544X. Includes bibliographical references.

Glotzer was born in Belorus and emigrated to Chicago at the age of five. His family had a history of political involvement. This memoir primarily covers the period from 1931, when Trotsky was exiled to Turkey, to 1940 when he was assassinated. It not only provides insight into Trotsky's later years, but is important for the history of American communism as well. Review: *Foreign Affairs* 69:3:183 (Summer 1990).

68. Gorbachev, Raisa, **I Hope**, translated by David Floyd. 1st ed. New York: Harper Collins Publishers, 1991. 207 p. ISBN: 0060168528.

Personal reminiscences of the wife of the first Soviet president. The book is organized as a sort of interview by Georgi Priakhin of Raisa Gorbachev. The volume is largely autobiographical in nature and numerous photographs are included. Review: *New York Times Review of Books* 38:21:72-81 (December 19, 1991).

69. Gromyko, Andrei Andreevich, **Memories**. London: Hutchinson, 1989. x, 365 p. ISBN: 0091738083.

In the fall of 1988 Andrei Gromyko, diplomat, ambassador, and from 1985-1988 Chairman of the Presidium of the Supreme Soviet of the USSR, retired at the age of 79. These memoirs are both a personal and political account of the fascinating era through which he lived and in which he played a pivotal part.

70. Gurevich, David, **From Lenin to Lennon**. 1st ed. San Diego: Harcourt Brace Jovanovich, 1991. 307 p. ISBN: 0151498253.
Memoirs of the life of a Russian émigré during the sixties in the Soviet Union. The author parallels the events of his life with those of the United States during the same period. *New York Times Book Review* 9 (June 2, 1991).

71. **A Biographic Directory of Soviet Regional Party Leaders**, compiled by Gavin Helf. Munich: Radio Free Europe/Radio Liberty, 1987. 2 v.
This two volume guide was drawn from material from the Radio Liberty Archive. A guide to regional Party officials has been previously unavailable. Since many of the individuals in regional positions later gain national importance, such a resource is quite useful. Entries include status, nationality, birthdate, education, family background, expertise and experience, political ties, military record, synopsis of career, and a list of speeches and publications and prominent activities. A knowledge of Russian is generally assumed, though basic information on some acronyms is provided in the preface.

72. Ignatieff, Michael, **The Russian Album**. 1st American ed. New York: Viking, 1987. 191 p. "*Elisabeth Sifton Books,*" ISBN: 0670810576. Includes index.
Using his grandmother's and grandfather's memoirs, the author recreates the history of his family from the 1880s to the end of World War II. Review: *Orbis* 32:2:330-31 (Spring 1988).

73. Jurgens, Urda, **Raisa**, translated from the German by Sylvia Clayton. London: Weidenfeld and Nicolson, 1990. 166 p. ISBN: 0297811029. Includes index.
A German biography of the popular Soviet First Lady. The author is an East German journalist who has traveled extensively with the Gorbachevs. The book covers her life as the child of a railway worker to her days in the Kremlin.

74. Kaiser, Robert G., **Why Gorbachev Happened: His Triumphs and His Failure**. New York: Simon & Schuster, 1991. 476 p. ISBN: 0671736922. Includes bibliographical references (p. 453-456) and index.
Kaiser looks at key events in the Gorbachev revolution. In straightforward language, often using the words of the participants themselves, he explains "why Gorbachev come to power, why he was the kind of man who could do what he has done, why his comrades in the Soviet Union's Communist Party let him do it, why the Soviet Empire at home and abroad crumbled as quickly as it did, and why his revolution went away." (p. 11) Reviews: *Foreign Affairs* 70:4:179-80 (Fall 1991). *New York Times Book Review* 9 (May 12, 1991). *Antioch Review* 49:4:607-09 (Fall 1991). *New York Times Review of Books* 38:18:53-59 (November 7, 1991).

75. Kanatchikov, Semen, **A Radical Worker in Tsarist Russia: The Autobiography of Semen Ivanovich Kanatchikov**, translated and edited by Reginald E. Zelnik. Stanford, CA: Stanford University Press, 1986. xxx, 472 p. ISBN: 0804713235. Includes bibliography (p. 469-472).
These memoirs are of a rather obscure Russian revolutionary peasant-craftsman. Kanatchikov begins his recollections in 1879, when he was born; his memoir breaks off abruptly in 1905 just before that year's famed revolution. The adult years recounted in his work all took place in Moscow, when he was employed there as a pattern-maker. His writings give a fascinating portrayal of city and village life at the end of the nineteenth and

early twentieth centuries. The translation is well annotated and includes an introduction and biographical post script by the editor. Review: *American Historical Review* 92:3: 711-12.

76. Khrushchev, Sergei, **Khrushchev on Khrushchev: An Inside Account of the Man and His Era**, edited and translated by William Taubman. 1st ed. Boston: Little, Brown, 1990. xiii, 423 p. ISBN: 0316491942. Includes index.

This biography of the last seven years of Khrushchev's life, from 1964 to 1971, was written by his son. Sergei Khrushchev was one of the few in whom Khrushchev ever confided. The author does occasionally refer to past events in the Soviet leader's life to illuminate his last seven years.

77. Levchenko, Stanislav, **On the Wrong Side: My Life in the KGB**. McLean, Va: Pergamon-Brassey's International Defense Publishers, 1988. xi, 244 p. ISBN: 008034478X.

The personal memoirs of former KGB agent Stanislav Levchenko. The author focuses on the lack of freedom in the USSR. He hopes to inform Americans of the conditions people lived in under the Soviet regime. He concludes the book with a "personal primer on the USSR and the KGB" in which he presents answers to the questions he has been most frequently asked. Reviews: *Problems of Communism* 39:1:101-08 (January-February 1990). *Seapower* 32:9: 49-50 (September 1989).

78. Markovna, Nina, **Nina's Journey: A Memoir of Stalin's Russia and the Second World War**. Washington, DC: Regnery Gateway, 1989. viii, 400 p. ISBN: 0895265508.

The personal memoir of one survivor of the Stalinist period. The author now lives in the U.S. Review: *National Review* 42:2:52 (February 1990).

79. McClellan, Irina Igorevna, **Of Love and Russia**. 1st ed. New York: Norton, 1989. 320 p. ISBN: 0393026809.

This is an autobiography of a Russian woman who married an American history professor. The KGB would not allow her to emigrate for eleven and one half years. Her painful separation is explicitly described. It offers another look at the cruelty imposed by the Soviet authorities as they meddled unnecessarily in private lives.

80. Medvedev, Zhores A., **Gorbachev**. 1st ed. New York: Norton, 1986. x, 272 p. ISBN: 0393023087. Includes index and bibliography (p. 247-257).

This biography of Mikhail Gorbachev was written shortly after his ascension to power in 1985. Medvedev provides sketches of his childhood and youth, his coming of age in Stavropol, his job as Kraikom secretary, his appointment as head of agriculture, standing as Andropov's ally, and an assessment of Gorbachev in power. In that part of the book dealing with Gorbachev in power, Medvedev concentrates on tracing the steps Gorbachev took in getting the country moving again, and assesses domestic and foreign policy in Gorbachev's first years. Review: *Soviet Union* 14 :1:106-7 (1987).

81. Mikoian, Anastas Ivanovich, **Memoirs of Anastas Mikoyan**, translated by Katherine T. O'Connor and Diana L. Burgin. Madison, Conn.: Sphinx Press, 1988. v. Includes index.

Memoirs of Bolshevik revolutionary Anastas Ivanovich Mikoyan. They are unusual in that they are the only memoirs covering the prerevolutionary, revolutionary, and postrevolutionary period written by a major figure in the communist party. This first volume covers the period up to 1920.

82. McNeal, Robert Hatch, **Stalin: Man and Ruler**. Houndmills, Basingstoke, Hampshire: Macmillan in association with St. Antony's College, Oxford, 1988. xvi, 389 *St. Antony's/Macmillan Series*, ISBN: 0333373510. Includes bibliography (p. 324-334).

McNeal uses official documents, personal papers and other available sources for this biography of Stalin. He also incorporates the "evidence of the Stalin cult" into this biography. Recognizing the elusiveness and deviousness of Stalin himself, he tries to separate Stalin's life from the general history of the Soviet Union, especially after 1930.

83. Nekrich, A. M., **Forsake Fear: Memoirs of an Historian**, translated by Donald Lineburgh. Boston: Unwin Hyman, 1991. vi, 293 p. ISBN: 0044456824. Includes index.

This is the first English language edition of a work that originally appeared in Russian in 1979, printed in London. It is the memoir of Russian historian Aleksandr Nekrich. It traces his career through the Soviet academic world during the late Stalinist era and through the 1960s. Mr. Nekrich's experiences give the reader a first hand account of the repression imposed on Soviet scholars. The translators hoped that the similarities between the post-Stalinist period and the Gorbachev era might also be apparent. Many of the major figures and events of the dissident movement are included here. Review: *Russian History* 18:2:252-53 (Summer 1991).

84. Petroff, Serge, **The Red Eminence: A Biography of Mikhail A. Suslov**. Clifton, New Jersey: The Kingston Press, Inc., 1988. vii, 273 p. ISBN: 0940670135. Includes bibliographical references and index.

A biography of the powerful political figure Mikhail Suslov, tracing his entire life. The author believes that Suslov was largely responsible for the general policy of anti-reform following Stalin's death. "...The post-Stalin years were years of painful transition—years during which the traditional forces of anti-reform had coalesced around one man whose fierce devotion to the slowing down of the process of change had contributed to nearly thirty years of post-Stalinist conservatism barely touched by the political and cultural thaw of the Khrushchev years." (p. 6) Reviews: *Russian Review* 49:2:231-32 (April 1990). *Slavic Review* 49:4:651-52 (Winter 1990).

85. Pomper, Philip, **Lenin, Trotsky, and Stalin: The Intelligentsia and Power**. New York: Columbia University Press, 1990. xiii, 446 p. ISBN: 0231069065. Includes bibliographical references (p. 409-431).

Pomper has set himself the task of "integrating the psychobiographies and political careers of Lenin, Trotsky, and Stalin." He examines and interprets "the formation and transformation of three personalities, first in family and school environments, then in revolutionary politics and finally, in power." (p. x).

86. Rahr, Alexander G., **A Biographic Directory of 100 Leading Soviet Officials**, compiled by Alexander G. Rahr. Munich: Radio Liberty Research, 1988. 241 p.

"The directory contains detailed information about the careers of current members of top Soviet Party and government bodies, officials of the armed forces and diplomats, as well as other officials who are believed to have a good chance of attaining top-level posts in the next few years." (p. 1) Each entry includes information such as present positions, date and place of birth, nationality, family background, higher education, a chronological listing of career posts, speeches, publications, experience and expertise, and awards.

87. Rapoport, Yakov, **The Doctors' Plot of 1953**. Cambridge, Mass.: Harvard University Press, 1991. viii, 280 p. ISBN: 0674214773. Includes index.

The autobiographical account of the author's part in the Doctors' Plot and the effect it had on his life. In a broader sense, this book gives a brief history of the Stalinist repression. The volume presents an individual's view of the prison system, antisemitism, and other aspects of the Stalin terror. Reviews: *New York Times Book Review* 25 (March 24, 1991). *Canadian Slavonic Papers* 33:2:213-14 (June 1991).

88. Ratushinskaia, Irina, **Grey Is the Color of Hope**, translated by Alyona Kojevnikov. 1st American ed. New York: Knopf, 1988. 355 p. ISBN: 0394571401.

This autobiographical work by the poet deals primarily with her imprisonment in a Soviet prison camp in Moldavia. Reviews: *World Literature Today* 64:1:146-47 (Winter 1990). *Slavic Review* 49:2:310-11 (Summer 1990). *Freedom at Issue* 114:43-44 (May-June 1990).

89. ———, **In the Beginning**. London: Hodder and Stoughton, 1990. 320 p. ISBN: 034041698X.

An autobiography of one of the better known prisoners of conscience. Ratushinskaia is a poet and her recently translated works are found under the literature section.

90. Rhinelander, Anthony L. H., **Prince Michael Vorontsov: Viceroy to the Tsar**. Montreal: McGill-Queen's University Press, 1990. viii, 279 p. ISBN: 0773507477. Includes index and bibliographical references (p. 265-274).

In 1823 Alexander I appointed Vorontsov governor-general of "new Russia" the tsar's southern Ukrainian domain. In 1844 his authority was extended to include Caucasia. In the author's words, under Vorontsov "New Russia was transformed from a relatively empty borderland into the empire's garden and bread- basket and sanitarium. Medieval, middle eastern Caucasia was propelled into the modern western world." (p. 3) Rhinelander begins his book with Vorontsov's upbringing and military training, then explores his governorship of New Russia, then Caucasia, and ends with Vorontsov's retirement and eventual death at age 72.

91. Robinson, Robert, and Jonathan Slevin, **Black on Red: A Black American's 44 Years Inside the Soviet Union**. Washington, DC: Acropolis Books, 1988. 436 p. ISBN: 0874918855. Includes index.

Robinson, a black toolmaker from Detroit, left the U.S. for the Soviet Union in 1930 and escaped, with the help of Idi Amin, in 1974. This autobiography chronicles his life in the Soviet Union during that period.

92. Schmidt-Hauer, Christian, **Gorbachev: The Path to Power**. Topsfield, Mass.: Salem House, 1986. 218 p. ISBN: 088162215X. Includes index.

This political biography of Mikhail Gorbachev traces his rise through the party ranks to his appointment as General Secretary of the Party in 1985. The author sketches the historical context in which his rise occurred as well as the political maneuvering within the party.

93. Sheehy, Gail, **The Man Who Changed the World: The Lives of Mikhail S. Gorbachev**. 1st ed. New York, NY: Harper Collins, 1990. xiv, 401 p. ISBN: 0060165472. Includes bibliographical references (p. 385-387) and index.

Passages author Sheehy has written an engaging biography of the personal life of Mikhail Gorbachev. Her work was based on interviews with relatives and associates of Gorbachev and spans the time from his youth through the crises of 1990.

94. Spence, Richard B., **Boris Savinkov: Renegade on the Left**. Boulder, CO: East European Monographs, 1991. v, 540 p. *East European Monographs*, no. 316. ISBN: 0880332131. Includes bibliographical references (p. 487-519).

The biography of Savinkov, "student radical, assassin, political émigré, military commissar, government minister, diplomat, and international conspirator" focuses on the last period of his life, from 1917 to 1925. (p. 1).

95. Taylor, Sally J., **Stalin's Apologist: Walter Duranty, the New York Times Man in Moscow**. New York: Oxford University Press, 1990. 404 p. ISBN: 0195057007. Includes index and bibliographical references (p. 391-397).

This is a biography of *New York Times* foreign correspondent Walter Duranty. "...Duranty created the leader of the Soviet Union, much as a novelist creates a set of memorable characters." (p. 5) His writing influenced much of what at least his readership thought of the Soviet Union from the time of the revolution through collectivization and the purges.

96. Tucker, Robert C., **Stalin in Power: The Revolution from Above, 1928-1941**. 1st ed. New York: Norton, 1990. xix, 707 p. ISBN: 039302881X. Includes index and bibliographical references (p. 671-683).

Tucker presents an account of the events of 1928-1941, when Stalin consolidated his power and carried out the second Russian revolution from above, that threw off the power of the kulaks through mass collectivization. Tucker intends "to show how and why this second revolution took place, how it developed in stages and with what consequences, and what parts Stalin and others played in it and why." (p. xiv) The second revolution was "a return to a state-sponsored revolution from above, aimed primarily at making Russia a mighty industrial power able to fend for itself in an unfriendly international setting and to expand its borders as opportunity allowed." (p. xiv).

97. Vassiltchikov, Marie, **Berlin Diaries, 1940-1945**. 1st American ed. New York: Knopf, 1987. xv, 324 p. ISBN: 0394556240. Includes index.

A first hand account of the life of a young Russian émigré in Germany during the war years. The author was born in Russia, but raised in the West and came to Berlin as a young woman to find work when the rest of Europe still languished in a depression economy. The diary has been published intact with few changes to the original text, thus maintaining its spontaneity. A glossary is provided to explain some of the German terms.

98. Wedziagolski, Karol, **Boris Savinkov: Portrait of a Terrorist**, translated by Margaret Patoski. Clifton, NJ: The Kingston Press, Inc., 1988. 249 p . ISBN: 0940670143. Includes index.

A biography of Boris Savinkov, revolutionary, writer, politician, and terrorist. In prerevolutionary Russia he was an assassin for the Party of the Social Revolutionaries. The biography is arranged chronologically. Included is an appendix of letters from Savinkov to Iosif Pilslovki. This is a translation of Wedziagolski's book, originally in Russian and in some ways incomplete. Review: *Russian History* 17:4:447-49 (Winter 1990).

99. Yeltsin, Boris Nikolaevich, **Against the Grain: An Autobiography**, translated by Michael Glenny. New York: Summit Books, 1990. 263 p. ISBN: 0671700553.

Yeltsin recounts the turbulent events of his and Russia's recent past. The book is structured around the events of the election campaign of 1989 with Mr. Yeltsin recounting more distant events as they are brought to mind by circumstances of the campaign.

Handbooks and Encyclopedias

100. **Research Guide to the Russian and Soviet Censuses**, edited by Ralph S. Clem. Ithaca: Cornell University Press, 1986. 323 p. *Studies in Soviet History and Society*, ISBN: 0801418380. Includes index.

A useful study of and guide to the census taken in pre-revolutionary Russia from 1917 through those of the Soviet period up to 1979. This volume is divided into two parts. The first is comprised of essays on various research problems associated with census data. Such questions as the methodology used, how census data can be used in education and literary studies are examined. The second part is an index and guide to the various censuses. It includes a list of tables, a keyword cross-index, and an index by geographical unit. Anyone working with census materials will find this work useful.

101. **Drifting Apart?: The Superpowers and Their European Allies**, edited by Christopher Coker. 1st ed. London: Brasset's Defense Publishers, 1989. xvii, 182 p. ISBN: 0080367119. Includes bibliographies and index.

Many of the essays here were generated by a conference held in 1988 by the Standing Committee on Atlantic Organization. The resulting volume is one side of the few comparative studies to NATO and the Warsaw Pact. "A diverse and renowned group of scholars, the authors explain the economic dilemmas of the superpowers in dealing with their respective European allies." (back cover) The essays are divided into six sections covering defense economics, NATO's problems in defense spending, the Warsaw Pact countries' difficulties in defense spending, an examination of the role new technologies might play, the changes within the alliances and a look to the possible futures for the alliances. No common theme runs through the essays. However, all authors agreed that an economic crisis is facing both alliances; that its main cause is defense spending; that changes in the military will be necessary with the superpower allies shouldering more of the burden and that new technologies may ease financial difficulties but create political problems.

102. **Soviet Government Officials, 1922-41: A Handlist**, edited by R. W. Davies. Birmingham: Centre for Russian and East European Studies, 1989. xi, 410 p. ISBN: 0704410575.

"This handbook provides information on the senior Soviet government officials in the central legislative and executive bodies of the USSR, in the Peoples Commissariats at the USSR level and in the commissars and committees attached to these agencies." (p.i) It covers the period 1922 to June 22, 1941. These are the three listings: institutional listing, chronological listing, and alphabetical listing.

103. Grimstead, Patricia Kennedy, **A Handbook for Archival Research in the USSR**. New York: International Research and Exchanges Board, 1989. xxxiv, 430 p. Includes bibliographical references.

Grimstead's extremely useful handbook is what every researcher needs to navigate the intricacies of the Russian archival system. The author describes the State Archival Administration and the State Archival Fund, explains how archival materials are arranged and described, offers suggestions regarding archival access, and delineates the steps in preparing to carry out archival research. She also offers an annotated listing of general aids for archival research, instructions on how to obtain microfilm, and hints for general deportment in conducting research. An updated version for 1993 with recent name changes is now available from IREX.

104. Laird, Roy D., and Betty A. Laird, **A Soviet Lexicon: Important Concepts, Terms, and Phrases**. Lexington, MA: Lexington Books, 1988. 201 p. ISBN: 066916738X.

"This book is designed to provide a basic understanding of the words, concepts and phrases essential to interpreting the Soviet system, its politics and economics, its problems, successes, failures, and goals." (p. 1) The authors provide an introductory chapter explaining the arrangement and scope of the lexicon and a brief introductory sketch of the Soviet system followed by the lexicon. A list of full and candidate members of the Politburo from 1917-1987, the Soviet constitution, and the Rules of the Communist Party of the Soviet Union are included in appendices.

105. Lazic, Branko M., **Biographical Dictionary of the Comintern**, in collaboration with Milorad M. Drachkovitch. New, rev., and expanded ed. Stanford, Calif.: Hoover Institution Press, 1986. lv, 532 p. ISBN: 0817984011.

This expanded edition now includes 753 biographies and 435 pseudonyms. Two-hundred twenty nine biographies from the original edition have been corrected or additional information supplied to them. Individuals were included if they were part of the Comintern's overall directorate, people who spoke at Comintern Congresses from 1919 to 1935 or were delegates to the enlarged plenary meetings of the Executive Committee from 1922 to 1933, members of the Comintern "apparatus" (secret emissaries, etc.), leaders of the international organizations, and graduates of the four principle Comintern schools. Reviews: *Historical Review* 16:1: 29-30 (Fall 1987). *Orbis* 31:1:155-56 (Spring 1987).

106. Richardson, Paul E., and David F. Kelley, **Moscow Business Survival Guide**. 2nd ed. Waitsfield, Vt.: Russian Information Service, 1991. 187 p. Includes index.

This is the second edition of the survival guide with several revisions. "The goods and services section has been expanded and reverified. A city map has been added, as has a telephone directory. New laws, acts, devaluation and price increases are covered in detail." (preliminaries) The directory consists of an Introduction with general information on the Soviet Union. The next section entitled "Survival" is divided into chapters on preparations, money, travel, food, and phones. The focus then shifts to doing business with a broad range of information on law, joint-ventures, cooperatives, imports and exports, taxation, and bureaucratic problems. A list of essential goods and services and one of restaurants is included. The business telephone directories and the city map round out the volume.

107. ——, **Where in Moscow**. 1st ed. Waitsfield, Vt.: Russian Information Services, 1991. 1 v. (various pagings) ISBN: 1880100011. Includes index.

"Where in Moscow is a comprehensive directory to goods and services in Moscow and includes a four color map, as well as organized telephone directory with more than 2500 listings, as well as hard-to-find information." (back cover) The book has four sections: essential goods and services, Moscow restaurant list, Moscow business telephone directory, and Moscow city map.

108. Rose, Clive, **The Soviet Propaganda Network: A Directory of Organizations Serving Soviet Foreign Policy**. New York: St. Martin's Press, 1988. xxi, 314 p. ISBN: 0312028133. Includes index.

This directory contains so-called "front" organizations of the Soviet propaganda machine. After an introduction that describes the role of propaganda and Soviet foreign policy, Rose divides his directory into five main sections: Soviet-controlled organizations, Soviet-influenced organizations, national organizations, and Soviet matrix organizations. Each entry includes information on membership, information relating to its internal affairs, and relationships with other bodies.

109. **The Soviet Union and Eastern Europe**, edited by George Schopflin. New York: Facts on File, 1986. xvii, 637 p. *Handbooks on the Modern World*, ISBN: 0816012601. Includes bibliographies and index.

A handbook covering historical, economic, and social development in the Soviet Union and Eastern Europe since World War II. This second edition was prompted by the increasing amounts of information available on the area. The collected essays attempt to provide both basic information and analysis of events. The volume is divided into broad subject categories: historical, political, economical, and social. The opening section is comprised of introductory essays on each country including biographical sketches on major political figures and a section on comparative statistics for the region. Each of the later essays includes a brief bibliography of materials for further reading. In the sections on historical, economic, and social themes, there are no essays on specific East European countries, rather topical essays that deal with the entire area. There are a number of essays on the situation in the Soviet Union.

110. Vronskaya, Jeanne, and Vladimir Chuguev, **A Biographical Dictionary of the Soviet Union 1917-1988**. Munich: K.G. Saur, 1989. xii, 525 p. Includes index.

A biographical source with some 5,000 entries, covering people from all walks of life. Entries include birth and death dates, occupation, a biographical sketch, publications by the subject, if any, works about the subject, if any. Entries are grouped in a final index by profession. Information for the entries was drawn from many sources including archival materials and printed sources.

111. Weeks, Albert Loren, **Brassey's Soviet and Communist Quotations**. Washington, DC: Pergamon-Brassey's, 1987. xxii, 387 p. ISBN: 0080344887. Includes index.

The 2117 quotations are arranged here under seventeen broad subject areas including capitalism and socialism; class and class warfare; democracy, freedom, and equality; foreign policy; Marxist-Leninist ideology; revolution; war and defense capability; and others. The compiler intended "to create a single document that gathered all of the words that reflect and have shaped the world view of the Soviet Union." (p. xi) The index is divided by chapters and provides access to the material gathered in each chapter.

Libraries, Archives and Museums

112. Bakhmeteff Archive of Russian and East European History and Culture, **Russia in the Twentieth Century: The Catalog of the Bakhmeteff Archive of Russian and East European History and Culture, the Rare Book and Manuscript Library, Columbia University.** Boston: G.K. Hall, 1987. xi, 187 p. ISBN: 081610462. Includes index.

The Bakhmeteff Archive at Columbia University has four focal areas: 1. materials pertaining to prominent literary figures of Russian emigration; 2. archives of institutions or organizations, mostly émigré benevolent and professional organizations, church organizations, and some political parties of revolutionary and prerevolutionary Russia; 3. historical materials that lay at the origin of the Russian emigration; and 4. materials pertaining to Eastern Europe. The catalog is arranged alphabetically by name or organization. Each entry includes a physical description as well as a summary of the holdings. An index of names and subjects facilitates access to the main listing.

113. **The Study of Russian History from British Archival Sources**, edited by Janet M. Hartley. New York: Mansell, 1986. ix, 184 p. ISBN: 0720117844. Includes bibliographies.

"Long standing contacts between Britain and Russia have resulted in the accumulation of extensive archival material in Britain, which unlike archives in the USSR itself, is readily available for research by scholars in many fields." (back cover) This volume presents several papers resulting from a conference held on "The Study of Russian History from British Archival Sources." Contributors include some of the foremost experts on Russian archives. Essays cover a variety of topics: projects to publish a survey of British documents and produce a Union catalog of British archival sources, description of specific archives such as those in Leeds and Aberdeen, sources on 18th century Anglo-Russian relations, sources in Britain on prerevolutionary Russian political emigration in Britain, and foreign collections on Soviet archives.

114. Hoover Institution on War, Revolution and Peace, **Guide to the Collections in the Hoover Institution Archives Relating to Imperial Russia, the Russian Revolutions and Civil War, and the First Emigration**, compiled by Carol A. Leadenham. Stanford, Calif.: Hoover Institution Press, Stanford University, 1986. xx, 208 p. *Hoover Press Bibliographical Series*, v. 68. ISBN: 081792681X. Includes index.

This excellent guide provides descriptions of 676 archival collections at the Hoover Institution relating to Imperial Russia, the Russian revolutions, civil war and the first emigration. The descriptions are arranged according to thirteen topics within this broad area. Each description includes either the author or collector of the archive, a designation of the type of material, the language of the material, extent of the material, a brief abstract of the contents, and indication of the access available for the archive, and method of acquisition. Within each subject area the entries are arranged alphabetically. Access to these descriptions is provided by a subject and name index. In addition, an alphabetical listing of the main entry of each collection is also provided.

115. International Conference of Slavic Librarians and Information Specialist, **Books, Libraries and Information in Slavic and East European Studies**, edited by Marianna Tax Choldin. New York: Russica Publishers, 1986. 530 p. *Russica Bibliography Series*, no. 8. ISBN: 0898301976. Includes bibliographies.

The essays collected here resulted from the Second International Conference of Slavic Librarians and Information Specialists held in 1985 in Washington, DC. Virtually every area of Slavic librarianship is briefly discussed. The volume is divided thematically with sections on the development of Book Studies in the Soviet Union, Book Studies in Eastern Europe, the History of Slavic Book Trade, Polish "Solidarity" Publications, East European Emigre Publications, Government in Publishing in the USSR, Slavic and Eastern European Archives, Bibliographic Projects, Databases Useful in the Slavic and East European Field, Information on the East-West Technology Transfer, National Bibliographies in Slavic Studies, and a large section on International Book Exchanges.

116. Stuart, Mary, **Aristocrat-Librarian in Service to the Tsar: Aleksei Nikolaevich Olenin and the Imperial Public Library**. Boulder, CO.: East European Monographs (Columbia University Press), 1986. ix, 245 p. *East European Monographs*, no. 211. ISBN: 0880331099. Includes index and bibliography (p. 191-234).

A study of the life of A.N. Olenin, first director of the Imperial Public Library in the Russian Empire. "His diverse achievements outside the library in art, literature, scholarship, and the central administration of the government, seemed closely connected to his striking success in the library. An examination of Olenin's activities in these other areas illuminates not only his role in the library, but also the social context of the library's founding and rapid development." (p. vii) The book is chronologically and topically organized with discussions on the founding of the national library, the history of the library in eighteenth century

Russia, and the library as a center of learning. Numerous illustrations are provided. Review: *Slavic and East European Journal* 31:4:634-45 (Winter 1987).

Description and Travel

117. Benjamin, Walter, **Moscow Diary**, edited by Gary Smith, translated by Richard Sieburth. Cambridge, Mass.: Harvard University Press, 1986. 150 p. ISBN: 067458743X. Includes bibliographical references and index.

German author Walter Benjamin stayed in Moscow from early December 1926 to the end of January 1927. He financed his trip by advances he had received to complete some writing assignments upon his return to Germany. Although he did complete four pieces relating to his trip, his diary was not part of that corpus. The honesty of the diary is noteworthy, as well as his description about the conditions prevailing in Moscow at that time and about the people, mostly Jewish intellectuals of the opposition, that he met there.

118. Goncharov, Ivan Aleksandrovich, **The Frigate Pallada**, translated by Klaus Goetze. New York: St. Martin's Press, 1987. xx, 649 p. ISBN: 0312005997.

Goncharov was invited by the Russian government to accompany Admiral Putyarin on a round-the-world journey aboard a three masted schooner, the Pallada. The purpose of the journey was to open up Russian trading. Written between 1852 and 1856, it has become a classic of Russian trading literature. The journey was a failure, the frigate abandoned and Goncharov put ashore to make his way home in winter—an 8,000 mile journey. Although it is ostensibly a travel book, it is as much an autobiography.

119. Iroshnikov, Mikhail Pavlovich, et al., **Before the Revolution: St. Petersburg in Photographs, 1890-1914**, with foreword by James H. Billington, and introduction by Dmitry S. Likhachov. New York: Harry N. Abrams Publishers, 1991. 310 p. ISBN: 0810938138.

A photographic record of St. Petersburg in the period just before the revolution. The chapters reflect different aspects of the city: St. Petersburg as the "Venice of the North"; historical events of the period, 1890-1914; St. Petersburg as capital city; the typical day in the city; and St. Petersburg as an artistic and educational center. Many photographs appear here for the first time. The original negatives are held at the Central State Archive of Cinema and Photo Documents in Leningrad. Most photographs are accompanied by explanatory text.

120. Schecter, Jerrold L., and Leona Schecter, **Back in the U.S.S.R.: An American Family Returns to Moscow**. New York: Scribner, 1988. ix, 468 p. ISBN: 0684189968. Includes index.

This is more than a travel book. The Schecter family initially spent several years in the 1960's working as correspondents in Moscow. In 1987, they returned, now with grown children who had formerly attended special school #47 in Moscow in the 1960's. The book is a series of vignettes written by all members of the family. It provides a fascinating examination of the everyday reality that existed in Moscow in 1987. Review: *New York Times Book Review* 14-15 (February 12, 1989).

121. Taubman, William, and Jane Taubman, **Moscow Spring**. New York: Summit Books, 1989. 301 p. ISBN: 0671677314.

The Taubmans describe intellectual and cultural life in Moscow in 1988. As a memoir is provides a well-written inside examination of Moscow Spring, a name intended to encompass the wide-ranging Gorbachev reforms that built to a crescendo in mid-1988. Reviews:

Slavic and East European Journal 34:1:130-31 (Spring 1990). *Orbis* 34:1:142 (Winter 1990).

122. Thubron, Colin, **Where Nights Are Longest: Travels by Car through Western Russia**. New York: Atlantic Monthly Press, 1987. 211 p. ISBN: 0871131676.
A highly praised account of a Westerner's encounters with Soviet citizens as he traveled across Western Russia by car. In his journey he travels through Belorussia, Ukraine, Russia, the Baltics, and Armenia. He traveled in all areas left open to him and he was allowed to purchase a higher octane fuel than is available to the Soviet citizenry, facilitating his travels. His trip was made in 1981.

ANTHROPOLOGY AND FOLKLORE

123. **Shamanism: Soviet Studies of Traditional Religion in Siberia and Central Asia**, edited by Marjorie Mandelshtam Balzer. Armonk, NY: M.E. Sharpe, 1990. xviii, 197 p. ISBN: 0873326245. Includes bibliographical references.
A collection of Soviet essays on shamanism which present a more balanced approach to the traditional religious practice than was displayed in earlier Soviet literature. Still the essays present a range of views, some viewing shamanism as suffering from "neuropsychological illness." others seeing the shaman's trance as culturally patterned behavior. The essays cover general questions about the nature of shamanism, as well as looking at specific types of shamanism: Turkic, Buryat, and Siberian. The bibliography, with few exceptions, includes only Russian language materials.

124. Dragadze, Tamara, **Rural Families in Soviet Georgia: A Case Study in Ratcha Province**. London: Routledge, 1988. xii, 226 p. *International Library of Anthropology*, ISBN: 0415006198. Includes index and bibliography (p. 210-221).
"This is a case study of a regional enclave of traditional culture which has retained its character despite the impact of the ideology, economics, and politics of the Soviet Union of which it is a part." (p.1) The author's anthropological approach stresses kinship, social and economic organization of family units, and socialization in her study. She believes that Soviet policies may actually have forged a sense of ethnic identity. The volume is thematically arranged with chapters on the environment the Soviet government has created for the Georgian villagers, the structure of family units, kinship, marriage, growing up in rural Georgia, gender, age, and kin distinctions, and changes in the family unit. The book includes a glossary of kinship terms of address. Reviews: *Anthropological Quarterly* 63:4:189-90 (October 1990). *Slavic Review* 49:3:478-79 (Fall 1990). *Russian History* 17:1:107-09 (Spring 1990). *Armenian Review* 43:1:115-18 (Spring 1990).

125. **Crossroads of Continents: Cultures of Siberia and Alaska**, edited by William W. Fitzhugh and Aron Crowell. Washington, DC: Smithsonian Institution Press, 1988. 360 p.
A collection of essays by American and Soviet scholars reflecting on the materials displayed in an exhibition of the same title. "We propose no final solutions to the problem of Siberian-American culture links; our intent has been simply to document, as fully and currently as possible, the diversity of and interrelationships between Siberian and American cultures." (p. 15) The exhibition of North Pacific ethnographic artifacts is discussed and

illustrated in this volume which is arranged topically. Following the introductory essays is a section on the peoples of each area. The next two sections discuss cultural contacts. This is followed by a lengthy section of essays on specific themes such as linguistics, economics, religion, and art. The final section discusses the lives of the contemporary natives of each area. Three appendices include an exhibition checklist and a discussion of beads and the bead theme of the North Pacific. Review: *Arctic* 43:3:298 (September 1990).

126. Miller, Frank J., **Folklore for Stalin: Russian Folklore and Pseudofolklore of the Stalin Era**. Armonk, N.Y.: M.E. Sharpe, 1990. xiv, 192 p. *Studies of the Harriman Institute*, ISBN: 0873326687. Includes index and bibliographical references.

Professor Miller looks at the origins and manifestations of the brand of Soviet folklore generated during the Stalin era. This "folklore" consisted of works composed to spread Stalin's propaganda. "The main body of this study examines the development of this new folklore, its relation to traditional folklore and its fate after the death of Stalin. The appendices contain synopses of the works discussed in this study as well as translations of representative works." (pp. xii-xiv) The second chapter focuses on the "noviny" of particular composers/singers such as M.S. Kriukova, P.I. Riabinin-Andreev, and M.R. Golubkova. Chapter three examines folktales by I.I. Kovalev and G.I. Sorokovikov. A scholarly study with the text of several works offered in English.

127. **Riddles of the Russian People: A Collection of Riddles, Parables and Puzzles**, collected by D. Sadovnikov and translated with an introduction by Ann C. Bigelow. Ann Arbor, MI: Ardis, 1986. xxiv, 556 p. ISBN: 0882339877. Includes bibliographical references and index.

An unusual collection of prerevolutionary riddles and parables gathered by D.N. Sadovnikov primarily in the Stavropol district of Samara Province and originally published in 1876. That collection contained some 2500 riddles. The later Soviet editions of his work omitted some 500 entries that are included in this translation. The compiler had hoped to arrange the riddles so as to elucidate peasant life. The volume is organized by subjects such as dwellings, heat and light, furnishings, etc. Entries within each category are related to objects that fall within these categories. The translator has added helpful notes explaining obscure usages, the origins of the riddle and in some cases giving comparative data on the riddles from other sources. Particularly heavily drawn on are the comments of V.P. Anikons from the Soviet edition. The introduction provides useful information on other sources of riddles as well as on Sadovnikov's life. The "alphabetical" arrangement is maintained reflecting Cyrillic alphabet order. However, the index is organized around the Latin alphabet. Reviews: *Slavic Review* 46: 3-4:641-42 (Fall-Winter 1987).

128. **Russian Exploration in Southwest Alaska: The Travel Journals of Petr Korsakovskiy (1818) and Ivan Ya. Vasilev (1829)**, edited and with an introduction by James W. VanStone. Fairbanks: University of Alaska Press, 1988. vii, 120 p. *Rasmuson Library Historical Translation Series*, vol. 4. ISBN: 0912006277. Includes index and bibliography (p. 111-115).

This is one of a series of studies dealing with the culture of the Yupik-speaking Eskimos who live in the Nushagak River region of southwest Alaska. These two travel journals provide a unique and early perspective on this particular population, which was not studied in more depth until the 1960s and 1970s. Notes are provided by the editors to elucidate obscure references in the main text. Review: *Arctic* 43:2:195 (June 1990).

THE ARTS

General Studies

129. **The Slavic World and Scandinavia: Cultural Relations**, edited by Kjeld Bjornager, Lene Tybjarg Schacke, and Eigil Steffensen. Aarhus: Aarhus University Press, 1988. 191 p. ISBN: 8772881739. Includes bibliographical references.

A 1984 symposium in Copenhagen produced the essays in this volume which cover a broad range of topics on cultural relations between Scandinavia and the Slavic world in the 19th and 20th centuries. The essays focusing on Russia include a Russian art show in Malno, Sweden, Soviet-Scandinavian artistic relations, the reception in Denmark of Gogol's "Inspector General," Norwegian translations of Russian literature, northern influences on Lermontov, reception of Chekov in Sweden, Russian literature in Norwegian newspapers, Kovaleskaia as "cultural monitor," and Moller as an interpreter of Turgenev.

130. Borisova, Elena Andreevna, and Girgory Sternin, **Russian Art Nouveau**. New York: Rizzoli, 1988. 400 p. ISBN: 0847809943. Includes index.

In the late 1890s to early 1900s art nouveau was at its height in Russia. This volume not only looks at the fine arts in isolation but examines the cultural and social context. Covered here, therefore, are the role of periodicals, churches, wooden buildings, ironwork, townhouses and apartments, applied arts, metalwork, graphic and plastic art and architectural illustrations. Review: *Russian Literature Triquarterly* 23:425 (1990).

131. Cerwinske, Laura, **Russian Imperial Style**, with the cooperation of A la Vieille Russie; with photography by Anthony Johnson. 1st ed. New York: Prentice Hall, 1990. 223 p. ISBN: 0137848102. Includes bibliographical references and index.

A portrayal of the lifestyle of the Russian aristocracy through illustrations of the decorative arts as well as narrative. Jewelry, furniture, palaces, table settings and costumes, many designed by Europe's leading artists, are represented here. "A fascinating historical narrative by Laura Cerwinske provides a vivid insight into the social and cultural life during this period, and the superb photographs draw together a portrayal of Russian life as never seen before." (book jacket) The book is divided into five chapters each devoted to one aspect of material life: fashions, palaces and furniture, objet d'art, table settings and painting. The book includes a chronology of Russian rulers.

132. Golomshtok, Igor, **Totalitarian Art: In the Soviet Union, the Third Reich, Fascist Italy and the People's Republic of China**. London: Collins Harvill, 1990. xv, 416 p. ISBN: 0002728060. Includes index and bibliography (p. 387-394).

A comparison of totalitarian art under four regimes intended to expose the characteristics common to all the regimes and specific to totalitarianism. Socialist realism from 1932 to 1956 and the art of the Third Reich from 1933 to 1945 are used to demonstrate "classic" elements of the style. "The aim of this book is to show how, with the appearance of the totalitarian political systems of the twentieth century, there came into being a particular cultural phenomenon with its own specific ideology, aesthetics, organization, and style." (p. xv) The book is divided into two parts, one dealing with the processes that gave rise to the style, the second focusing on the product. Individual chapters are arranged in both a thematic and, when appropriate, a chronological fashion. Besides the large number of illustrations interspersed with the text, the book contains an "Album of Totalitarian Art" with some sixty pages of reproductions. Although only recently published, the book was originally written in Russian in the glasnost period. The author's references to present day Russia refer to that time.

133. **The Culture of the Stalin Period**, edited by Hans Gunther. New York: St. Martin's Press, 1990. xxi, 291 p. ISBN: 031203993X.

A collection of essays which grew out of a conference of the same title held at the University of Bielefeld, West Germany in October of 1986. The purpose of the conference was to use an interdisciplinary approach to analyze Stalinist culture. It was felt that, to some extent, the culture of the Stalinist period was becoming extremely obscure and that it should not be forgotten as it comprises a significant part of Russian culture. Some of the topics discussed include lower strata of culture, popular culture and the use of nationalism, authoritarian and folkloristic tradition in Stalinist art, fate of utopian thought, carnivals, and the relationship between high and popular culture. The works of artists such as Eisenstein, Zholtovsky, Bulgakov, and Zoshchenko are discussed in detail.

134. Khan-Magomedov, Selim Omarovich, **Alexander Vesnin and Russian Constructivism**. New York: Rizzoli, 1986. 220 p. ISBN: 0847807738. Includes bibliography.

The multifaceted career of Aleksandr Vesnin is the subject of this book. His career is traced from his childhood to his death in a chronological presentation of his work as architect, set designer, printer, and graphic designer. The volume is illustrated with numerous reproductions of examples of his work. His central role in the artistic world as new styles defined themselves in the Soviet period is carefully examined. A great deal of archival material was used in compiling this work. The volume includes in its appendices a brief biography, a list of major works, and a list of his exhibitions and publications.

135. Leach, Robert, **Vsevolod Meyerhold**. Cambridge: Cambridge University Press, 1989. xiv, 223 p. *Directors in Perspective*, ISBN: 0521267390. Includes index and bibliography (p. 216-218).

A study of the consistencies in the works of the Russian director Vsevolod Meyerhold. The author sees Meyerhold as a pedagogue—a teacher, researcher, and practitioner. "This book attempts to show why and how these three strands were interdependent, and what are the implications for theatre—now as much as then." (p. xiii) The arrangement is topical first giving an overview of Meyerhold's life and then turning to specific aspects of his work, his view of the actor, rhythm and meaning in his work, etc. The book includes two appendices, a chronology of the director's work, and a list of his productions.

136. Sarabianov, Dmitrii Vladimirovich, **Russian Art: from Neoclassicism to the Avant-garde, 1800-1917: Painting — Sculpture — Architecture**. New York: H. N. Abrams, 1990. 320 p. ISBN: 0810937506. Includes index and bibliographical references.

A history of nineteenth century Russian art. The author's goal is to show the roots of early 20th century avant-garde art in the world of its nineteenth century predecessors. Many of the plates have never been seen outside the Soviet Union making the work of interest even to specialists. The study includes a discussion of development of architecture and some of the applied arts as well as painting and sculpture. The bibliography cites many English language works on the subject.

137. **Street Art of the Revolution: Festivals and Celebrations in Russia 1918-33**, edited by Vladimir Tolstoy, et al. London: Thames and Hudson, 1990. 240 p. ISBN: 0500235627. Includes bibliographical references (p. 231-233) and index.

This volume is a translation of a 1984 Soviet publication on popular revolutionary art. The authors have tried to compile a representative sample of various kinds of art used in the celebration of revolutionary festivals from 1918-1933. The volume includes numerous illustrations and lengthy discussions of the significance of the art used in such festivals as the anniversaries of the revolution, May Day celebration, street carnivals, and the Second

Congress of the Third International. Many of the photographs and sketches were reproduced for the first time in this book. There are also reminiscences of some of the artists who took part in the festivals. The development of festival art though this period is depicted in the chronological arrangement of material.

Architecture

138. **Reshaping Russian Architecture: Western Technology, Utopian Dreams**, edited by William C. Brumfield. Cambridge: Cambridge University Press, 1990. xvii, 222 p. *Woodrow Wilson Center Series*, ISBN: 052139418X. Includes bibliographical references and index.

A collection of essays which originated as presentations at the Kennan Institute on Modern Russian Architecture. The six essays discuss various aspects of Russian architectural development in the twentieth century. The architectures of Moscow and Leningrad are examined as is the Russian perception of American architecture. The use of Western technology and architects to accomplish the Russian ideal in architecture is also discussed.

139. Cracraft, James, **The Petrine Revolution in Russian Architecture**. Chicago: University of Chicago, 1988. xxvi, 372 p. ISBN: 0226116646. Includes index and bibliography (p. 357-364).

Using architecture as an example, Professor Cracraft looks at some of the broader issues reflected in its development. "Yet if today historians can agree that the reign of Peter I 'the Great' (1682-1725) marked the decisive onset of 'europeanization' in Russia, meaning by the term a political and economic as well as a cultural process, there is no clear consensus as to how and why this took place and with what specific results, especially in the field of culture. The overall purpose of this book is to provide a case study of cultural Europeanization in seventeenth and eighteenth century Russia in just such concrete terms." (p. 1) The author traces Russian architectural development up to Peter I's reign. He then describes the changes introduced by the tsar and their evolution as they spread to the provincial areas. The author is primarily a historian, not an architect. However, he hopes his lack of technical knowledge will be balanced by a more general, and perhaps more readable discussion. The book has numerous illustrations. Reviews: *American Historical Review* 95: 868-69 (June 1990). *Journal of Modern History* 62:4:891-94 (December 1990). *Russian History* 17:3:344-45 (Fall 1990). *Slavic Review* 49:2:316-18 (Summer 1990).

140. Massie, Suzanne, **Pavlovsk: The Life of a Russian Palace**. 1st ed. Boston: Little, Brown, 1990. xx, 394 p. ISBN: 0316549703. Includes bibliographical references (p. 367-378) and index.

This book describes the design, construction, destruction and restoration of the Pavlovsk Palace. The book is divided into two parts. The first traces the history of the palace from its inception to the years of the Bolshevik revolution. Part two traces its history in this century discussing at length its destruction during World War II, the reconstruction that has been ongoing since and those responsible for its renewal. The book has numerous photographs, a list of those involved in the restoration, and plans of the palace.

141. Schmidt, Albert J., **The Architecture and Planning of Classical Moscow: A Cultural History**. Philadelphia, PA: American Philosophical Society, 1989. xiii, 218 p. *Memoirs of the American Philosophical Society*, v. 181. ISBN: 0871691817. Includes index and bibliography (p. 202-208).

A description of the development of classicism in Russia using Moscow's architecture as the model. "This book attempts to explain Russia's, specifically Moscow's appropriation and adaptation of European classicism as its badge and gives plausibility to the thesis that classicism became a vehicle for incipient nationalism." (p. x) The book is arranged chronologically beginning with a description of the city before classicism and then tracing its evolution from its beginnings in 1762 to the plans for rebuilding Moscow after 1812 and its development. The book includes numerous illustrations.

Fine Arts

142. **Pskov Icons: 13th-16th Centuries**, with introductory articles by Mikhail Alpatov and Irina Rodnilova. Leningrad: Avrora, 1991. 318 p. Includes bibliographical references (p. 316-19).

Some of the finest examples of Pskov icon painting are reproduced in this volume. The special characteristics of the Pskov school are highlighted through the selections depicted here spanning the 13th through the 16th centuries. Over 150 icons are reproduced with extensive notes describing the subject of the icon, its type, and analogies in other schools of icon painting. The volume also includes two lengthy introductory essays on Pskov icons by Mikhail Alpatov and Irina Rodnilova. The bibliography cites numerous works, but may be misleading if the notes are not closely read since most titles, although cited in English, are actually in Russian.

143. **Russia, the Land, the People: Russian Painting, 1850-1910: From the Collections of the State Tretyakov Gallery, Moscow and the State Russian Museum, Leningrad**, translated from the Russian by Nicholas Berkoff with assistance from Karen E. Anderson and Sally Hoffmann. Washington, DC: Smithsonian Institution Traveling Exhibition Service, 1986. xviii 141 p. Includes index and bibliography (p. 140).

The editors have selected more than "sixty canvasses by distinguished artists from the second half of the nineteenth century and the beginning of the twentieth drawn from two major museums of the USSR the State Tretyakov Gallery in Moscow and the State Russian Museum in Leningrad." (foreword) They were selected to present to the American people Russia's land, people, history, spiritual life, and enduring cultural heritage. The canvasses, each of which is annotated, are preceded by an introductory essay on Russian art. Review: *Canadian Slavonic Papers* 29:4:432-33 (December 1987).

144. **Russian and Soviet Paintings, 1900-1930: Selections from the State Tretyakov Gallery, Moscow and the State Russian Museum, Leningrad**. rev. ed. Washington, DC: Smithsonian Institution Press, 1988. 238 p. ISBN: 0874744954. Includes bibliography (p. 233-238).

This exhibition contains paintings from the State Tretyakov Gallery in Moscow and the State Russian Museum in Leningrad that were produced between 1900 and 1930. Besides the plates of the paintings exhibited, the catalog contains an introductory essay by E.V. Basnev and A.P. Gusarova, an essay on early 20th century Russian art by John Bowlt and annotations on each of the paintings.

145. **Russian Art of the Avant-Garde: Theory and Criticism, 1902- 1934**, edited and translated by John E. Bowlt. rev. and enl. ed. New York: Thames and Hudson, 1988. xvl, 371 p. ISBN: 0500610118. Includes index and bibliography (p. 309-358).

This is a collection of published statements by artists and critics. "The aim of this volume is to present an account of the Russian avant-garde by artist themselves in as lucid and as balanced a way as possible." (p. vii) The essays are presented in six parts: Symbolism and the intuitive, neoprimitivism and cubofuturism, nonobjective art, the revolution and art, constructivism and the industrial arts, and toward socialist realism. Review: *ARTnews* 89:2:101-03 (February 1990).

146. Barnett, Vivian Endicott, **Kandinsky and Sweden**. Stockholm: Moderna museet, 1988. 220 p. *Malno Konsthall Catalog/Moderna Museet Cataloge*, no. 134/no. 231. ISBN: 9177040376. Includes bibliographical references.

The years of World War I and the development of the works of Vasilii Kandinsky are the subject of the exhibition documented in this volume. Along with 65 plates displaying the artist's works, created while he was in Sweden, the book also includes over one hundred pages of text and photographs describing his development at that time.

147. Bowlt, John E., et al., **Russian Samizdat Art: Essays**. New York: Willis Locker & Owens Pub., 1986. 210 p. ISBN: 0930279042. Includes index and bibliography (p. 196-201).

As difficult as it is to define samizdat art, we can at least agree with Charles Doria, who writes in the preface that, "most of the best samizdat art seems rooted in negative capability: an inability to accept things as they are, in this case Soviet-style reality, accompanied by an earnest desire for change and renewal, but in what direction, into what untried realms of thought and ideation, remains resolutely unclear." (p. 2) This collection contains three essays that explore this specific brand of dissident art. The first, by John Bowlt, examines the art of the book and the Russian avant-garde. The second, by Szyman Bojko, looks at three waves of emigration and their art. The final essay, by Rimma and Valery Gerlovin, by far the largest essay, assesses a whole range of recent samizdat art and artists. A list of artists' work in the 1920s and 1930s is included in an appendix.

148. **Tradition and Revolution in Russian Art**, edited by Susan Causey. Manchester: Cornerhouse Publications in association with the Olympic Festival, 1990. 199 p. ISBN: 0948797266. Includes bibliographical references (p. 194).

Exhibitions of materials from Leningrad museums sponsored by Siemens for the Olympic festival of 1990 form the basis of the illustrated materials used in this volume to trace the history of Russian artistic development during the Soviet period. Six themes and their relationship to the events of 1917 are explored: St. Petersburg, street art in Petrograd, Bolshevik posters, Russian faces, Russian Lubok, and the posters of perestroika. The volume includes numerous reproductions and a brief chronology of Russian-Soviet history.

149. Decter, Jacqueline, **Nicholas Roerich: The Life and Art of a Russian Master**, with the assistance of the Nicholas Roerich Museum. Rochester, VT: Park Street Press, 1989. 224 p. ISBN: 0892811560. Includes bibliography (p. 220).

Decter presents the life and work of Roerich, a wondrously prolific painter and set designer. "Trained not only as an artist but also as a lawyer, he wrote extensively in legal matters, the arts, ethics, and their links to a more general law of the universe." (preface) Roerich traveled widely and died in India in 1947. Review: *Dance Chronicle* 13:3:401-12 (1990-91).

150. Elliott, David, **New Worlds: Russian Art and Society 1900-1937**. London: Thames and Hudson, 1986. 160 p. ISBN: 0500013977. Includes index and bibliography (p. 158).

The author traces the upsurge and decline of one of the most creative periods in Russian art. Some of the most radical movements in Russian art are traced as they developed. Numerous reproductions are supplied with the text including photographs of many of the artists.

151. **100 Years of Russian Art: 1889-1989: From Private Collections in the USSR**, edited and with introductions by David Elliot and Valery Dudakov. London: Lund Humphries, 1989. 152 p. ISBN: 0853315493. Includes bibliography (p. 79).

Companion volume to the British exhibition of Russian art from private collections in Russia and held at the Barbican Art Gallery. The review of the work presented here was intended to give Westerners the opportunity to analyze the development of Russian Modern Art. "The largest part of the exhibition is focused on the years 1905 to 1940 when in painting, sculpture, the graphic and applied arts, modernism became synonymous with a radical political programe." (back cover) The works of numerous artists are included such as: Altman, Bogomazov, Chagall, Deneica. Filonov, Goncharova, Jawlensky, Kabakov, Latrionov, Malevich, Nikritin, Petrov-Vodkin, Rabin, Sarian, Tatlin, Vasnetov, Zakharov, and many others. Biographies of these artists are also available.

152. Gray, Camilla, **The Russian Experiment in Art, 1863-1922**. Rev. and enl. ed. London: Thames and Hudson, 1986. 324 p. ISBN: 0500202079. Includes bibliography (p. 313-319) and index.

One of the first Western works to treat the avant garde period of Russian Art. The author drew heavily on Russian archival sources. Originally this volume was published in 1962. This revised and enlarged edition is described as "...the most compact, accurate, and reasonably priced survey of sixty years of creative dynamic activity that influenced the progress of Western art and architecture." (back cover). The author has been accused by some as having a Marxist bias. The book is arranged chronologically and is intended for anyone with an interest in the history of western art as well as the specialist. Reviews: *Naval War College Review* 41:3:115-18 (Summer 1988). *Wilson Quarterly* 12:2:149-50 (Spring 1988).

153. **Russian Painting: Portraiture**, selected by Galina Ivashevskaia, translated by Inna Sorokina. Leningrad: Aurora Art Publishers, 1991. ISBN: 5730002246.

This is an enchanting album of Russian portraiture from the end of the seventeenth century to 1922. There is a short historical introduction to Russian portraiture that precedes the plates.

154. Lavrentev, Aleksandr Nikolaevich, **Vavara Stepanova, the Complete Works**, edited and translated by John E. Bowlt. 1st MIT Press ed. Cambridge, Mass.: MIT Press, 1988. 190 p. ISBN: 0262121352. Includes index and bibliography (p. 188-189).

Stepanova (1894-1958) was an "amazon of Russian art" during the avant-garde period in the 20s and 30s. Included in this volume are essays, reproductions, letters, and remembrances, and articles by and about Stepanova.

155. Lissitzky, El, **El Lissitzky, 1890-1941: Architect, Painter, Photographer, Typographer**, compiled by Jan Debbaut ... et al. Eindhoven: Municipal Van Abbemuseum, 1990. 220 p. ISBN: 0500973938. Includes bibliographical references (p. 214-216).

El Lissitzky (1890-1941) played and important role in the development of the Russian avant-garde. This work not only includes reproductions from the many genres in which he worked, travel sketches, figurines, photography, architecture, typographic designs, etc., but also nine essays dealing with Lissitzky and his work.

156. Solomon, Andrew, **The Irony Tower: Soviet Artists in a Time of Glasnost**. 1st ed. New York: Knopf, 1991. xxiv, 310 p. ISBN: 0394585135. Includes index.

Personal impression of the artistic community in the Soviet Union during the changes brought on by perestroika. The book is less a discussion of artistic style and more a general discussion of the ideologies behind the artists' works. The drawings included were supplied by the artists whom the author interviewed. The book is organized like a travel account. Reviews: *Foreign Affairs* 70:4: 181 (Fall 1991). *New York Times Book Review* 5-6 (July 28, 1991).

157. Stepanova, Varvara Fedorovna, **The Rodchenko Family Workshop**, compiled by Varvara Rodchenko and Aleksandr Lavrentiev, edited by Chris Carrel, Katya Young, et al. London: Serpentine Gallery, 1989. 86 p. ISBN: 0906474892. Includes bibliographical references (p. 83).

Catalog of the exhibit of works mainly by Aleksanr Rodchenko and Varvara Stepanova. The exhibit was first shown in Glasgow in 1989, later in London (1989-90). The volume includes letters from A. Rodchenko to Varvara Stepanova, excerpts from Stepanova's diary, an essay on "the workshop of the future" by Aleksandra Lavrientiev, and biographical sketches on Rodchenko and Stepanova.

158. Valkenier, Elizabeth Kridl, **Ilya Repin and the World of Russian Art**. New York: Columbia University Press, 1990. xiv, 248 p. *Studies of the Harriman Institute*, ISBN: 0231069642. Includes bibliographical references.

Valkenier had four purposes in writing this book: "to tell the story of Repin's eventful career; to rescue his art from the neglect it has fallen into outside Russia; to free him from the distortions of Russian historiography; and to draw attention to some distinctive features of Russian artistic culture." (p. xiii) The book is amply illustrated and manages to weave together biography, art criticism, and cultural history.

159. White, Stephen, **The Bolshevik Poster**. New Haven: Yale University Press, 1988. vii, 152 p. ISBN: 0300043392. Includes index and bibliography (p. 144-148).

White intends to present more posters to the public than previous Soviet editions of the same material have done and also in the text "to outline and explain the emergence, flowering and subsequent decline of the Soviet civil war poster, examining the changing subject matter of the posters, the people who prepared and distributed them, their impact upon contemporaries, and their subsequent evolution into the Soviet poster of more recent years." (p. vii) Review: *Soviet Union* 15:2-3:284-85 (1988).

160. Yablonskaia, Minda, **Women Artists of Russia's New Age, 1900- 1935**. New York: Rizzoli, 1990. 248 p. ISBN: 0847810909. Includes bibliographical references and index (p. 237-238).

An examination of several major and minor women artists working in the first third of the century. "The author principally considers the period 1900-1935 during which, she argues, women artists conceived a new role for themselves. Adopting a contextual approach for the discussion of their work, the author sketches in their individual temperaments, highlights the most important and exciting aspects of their creativity and observes their developments against the rapidly changing background of their times." (p. 7) The artists discussed are Rozanova, Lybov Popova, Alexandra Exter, Varvara Stepanova, Nadezhda Vdaltsova, Antonina Sofronova, Eva Rosenlolts-Levina, Nova Simonovich- Efimova, Sarra Lebedeva, and Vera Mukhina. Bibliographies and chronologies on each artist are also included. There are numerous illustrations.

161. Zaletova, Lidya, et al., **Revolutionary Costume: Soviet Clothing and Textiles of the 1920s**. 1st English Language ed. New York: Rizzoli, 1989. 1 v. ISBN: 0847810534.

Throughout the essays and plates that make up this book the publisher's desire to emphasize the cultural aspects of Soviet clothing in the 1920s is realized. The book consists of several essays concerned with various aspects of Soviet textile design and fashion, including ones on Vkhutemas, an art school in Moscow that concentrated on textile design, and the Russian Academy of Artistic Science. It also includes about seventy pages of color plates and translations of manifestoes and articles from the period. The result is a wonderful source book of information, both verbal and pictorial, on clothing and textiles of the 1920s. A short section giving brief biographies of well-known textile designers is especially useful.

162. **Tatlin**, edited by Larissa Alekseevna Zhadova. New York: Rizzoli, 1988. 533 p. ISBN: 0847808270. Includes indexes and bibliography (p. 524-517).

Originally published in Hungarian, this ambitious work tries to cover the many facets of the works of Vladimir Tatlin, an inventor, painter, architect, and stage designer. To do this the editors have structured the work into three parts. The first covers works about Tatlin's many talents and draws on the expertise of art historians, theater historians, and literary historians. The second presents translations of many of Tatlin's own writings and the third contains writings of Tatlin's contemporaries to 1940. The appendixes contain biographical data, a list of Tatlin's works for theater, and a selected bibliography. Review: *Slavic and East European Journal* 34:1: 129-30 (Spring 1990).

Music

163. Campbell, James Stuart, **V. F. Odoyevsky and the Formation of Russian Musical Taste in the Nineteenth Century**. New York: Garland Pub., 1989. x, 424 p. *Outstanding Dissertations in Music From British Universities*, ISBN: 0824001885. Includes bibliography (p. 413-424).

Prince Odoyevsky was best known as a writer of prose fiction, but he was also a civil servant, played piano and organ, and wrote prolifically on Russian music. He had, according to Campbell, "a powerful behind-the-scenes influence on musical life and musicians." (p. ix) Campbell presents an overview of Odoyevsky's life and works and then devotes individual chapters to Odoyevsky as a writer on music, music education, and the Russian Musical Society, Odoyevsky and Russian composers, Odoyevsky's views on music by composers of other nationalities, and Odoyevsky and Russian folk and church music.

164. Milstein, Nathan, and Solomon Volkov, **From Russia to the West: The Musical Memoirs and Reminiscences of Nathan Milstein**. 1st ed. New York: H. Holt, 1990. vi, 282 p. ISBN: 0805009744.

The memoirs of Russian violinist Nathan Milstein concerning his development as a musician in Russia. He describes his memories of Rachmaninoff and his friends Vladimir Horowitz and Gregor Piatigorsky.

165. Morosan, Vladimir, **Choral Performance in Pre-Revolutionary Russia**. Ann Arbor, MI: UMI Research Press, 1986. xx, 376 p. *Russian Music Studies*, no. 17. ISBN: 0835717135. Includes index and bibliography.

This work seeks to fill a gap in the literature by addressing the question of choral performance and its development in Russia. Because of its ties to the Church, choral music has been largely ignored by Soviet scholars. The author hopes this work will be of interest to the scholar and performer. He begins with a history of choral music trying to trace its origins in Russia. Part two discusses choral voice training and conducting. The book traces the development of choral music up to the revolution.

166. Orlova, Aleksandra Anatolevna, **Glinka's Life in Music: A Chronicle**. Ann Arbor, MI: UMI Research Press, 1988. xxiv, 823 p. *Russian Music Studies*, no. 20. ISBN: 0835718646. Includes indexes.

A translation of Alexandra Orlova's chronicle, based on original documents, of the life of 19th century Russian composer Mikhail Glinka. The author works in this genre in the hope of providing new perspectives on the artist's works that have the additional advantage of being based on fact, not conjecture. The author has relied on materials contemporary with the subject, with the exception of memoirs. This work was written in two parts. The first covering Glinka's life through 1843 was originally published in the Soviet Union in 1978. The second was completed after the author's emigration. An index of Glinka's works is included.

167. Roccasalvo, Joan L., **The Plainchant Tradition of Southwestern Rus'**. Boulder, CO: East European Monographs, 1986. x, 185 p. *East European Monographs*, no. 202. ISBN: 0880339053. Includes index and bibliography (p. 171-179).

Roccasalvo investigates the "sources of Carpatho-Ruthenian plainchant as found in their basic chant book, the *Tserkovnoje Prostopinije* (Plain Chants of the Church)." (p. ix) In the first part of her study, she examines the history and culture of the Rusyns. In the second part, she analyzes the structure of melodies, the Koran, the 1709 Irmologion and the other chants. Several appendices provide additional information about the 1709 Irmologion. A glossary of technical terms is also included.

168. Ryback, Timothy W., **Rock Around the Bloc: A History of Rock Music in Eastern Europe and the Soviet Union**. New York: Oxford University Press, 1990. xii, 272 p. ISBN: 0195056337. Includes index.

The growth of the popularity of rock and roll music and the significance this had on the changing East European and Soviet societies are the subjects of this study. "The following account of Soviet-Bloc rock should dispel the Western impression that rock music is new to Eastern Europe and the Soviet Union. Further, it should challenge assumptions about everyday life under socialism, about the relationship between the state and the individual, and ultimately, about the nature of these societies." (p. 5) The chronological arrangement begins in 1946 and traces the growth in popularity of rock music in each Eastern European country and the official attempts to stop its spread. The book contains a chronology.

169. Troitskii, Artemii, **Back in the USSR: The True Story of Rock in Russia**. Boston: Faber and Faber, 1988. 160 p. ISBN: 0571129978.

"This book is the first attempt by a Soviet writer to analyze the social revolution that has been slowly unfolding in the USSR since the end of World War Two. It is a description and interpretation of a series of overlapping youth cultures, each of which presented its own challenge to the bewildered, surly and often cruel monolith of the Soviet Communist State." (p. 7-8).

170. Walsh, Stephen, **The Music of Stravinsky**. London: Routledge, 1987. 317 p. *Companions to the Great Composers*, ISBN: 0415001986. Includes index and bibliography (p. 293-306).

This biography of Stravinsky concentrates on two important themes in his life, his Russian roots and his work as a concert artist. The author follows a chronological arrangement beginning with a discussion of the firebird and Stravinsky's years in Russia. Sections of numerous scores are reproduced. A list of Stravinsky's works is included.

Dance

171. Danilova, Alexandra, **Choura: The Memoirs of Alexandra Danilova**. 1st ed. New York: Knopf, 1986. 213 p. ISBN: 0394505395.
Memoirs of the Russian prima ballerina Alexandra Danilova. The memoirs also cover the history of the ballet in Europe in the twentieth century. Review: *New York Times Book Review* 4:13 (January 1987).

172. **A Century of Russian Ballet: Documents and Accounts, 1810- 1910**, selected and translated by Ronald John Wiley. Oxford: Oxford University Press, 1990. x, 444 p. ISBN: 0102164167. Includes indexes and bibliographical references.
A documentary of the Russian ballet. The compiler has chosen documents based on their significance, rarity, authority, and lack of availability to the English reader. The libretti of a dozen ballets are included. "As the libretti are expressions of style, they would by themselves produce an accurate outline of the balletic conventions in nineteenth century Russia: from Diderot's dramatic pantomime to Tagloon's romantic and back again with Perrot, from Petipa's oriental extravaganzas to the sumptuous fairy tales of his later years and on to Fokine." (p. vii) Additional documents describe the technique of stagecraft, the social setting of ballet, its national components and identity, the rise of criticism and the life of its artists. Numerous illustrations are also included.

Film

173. Eisenstein, Sergei, **Eisenstein, Selected Writings**, general editor, Richard Taylor. Bloomington: Indiana University Press, 1988. 3 v. ISBN: 0253350425 (v. 1). Includes bibliographical references and index.
This collection of Eisenstein's writing, planned for three volumes, is arranged in chronological order. Volume 1 includes his theoretical essays from 1922 to 1934. Volume 2, entitled *Towards a Theory of Montage*, contains Eisenstein's sometime fragmentary and often unfinished writings from the 1930s and 1940s. Volume 3 contains other essays published from 1935 to his death in February 1948. The documents here have been chosen "not merely to record the development of his aesthetic ideas but also to illuminate the context in which that development occurred." (p. ix).

174. Galinchenko, Nicholas, **Glasnost—Soviet Cinema Responds**, edited by Robert Allington. 1st ed. Austin: University of Texas Press, 1991. x, 142 p. ISBN: 029272747x. Includes bibliographical references (p. 129-131) and index.
Three essays and biographical information on contemporary directors make up this exploration of the effects of glasnost on the Soviet cinema and its artists. The first essay provides a historical context within which the changes in Soviet cinema have taken place. In particular, the work of Soviet director Mikhail Romm is discussed. In the second essay, the theme of youth is analyzed as it has appeared in contemporary cinema. The third essay looks at the "philosophical dimension" of Soviet cinema. The final section, the "filmography... is a guide to the works of some of the most significant contemporary Soviet directors and to the effects that glasnost and perestroika have had on their lives and their art." (p. x) The filmography does not provide basic biographical data but rather focuses on information on the careers of each director. Some thirty-three directors are included.

175. Golovskoy, Valery S., **Behind the Soviet Screen: The Motion-Picture Industry in the USSR, 1972-1982**, with John Rimberg. Ann Arbor, MI: Ardis, 1986. 144 p. ISBN: 0882339702.

This collection includes eleven essays, translated from the Russian, about the Soviet film industry. Covered here are such topics as Goskino in Moscow, Soviet feature film studios, the unions, distribution, exhibition and film audiences, film promotion and film criticism, and a description of a typical week in the life of a film magazine editor. It also contains several appendices of excerpts from documents, and most importantly, a who's who in Soviet film criticism. Reviews: *Film Quarterly* 40: 4:36-40 (Summer 1987). *Slavic Review* 46:3-4:662-62 (Fall-Winter 1987).

176. **Post New Wave Cinema in the Soviet Union and Eastern Europe**, edited by Daniel J. Goulding. Bloomington: Indiana University Press, 1988. xii, 317 p. ISBN: 0253345596. Includes indexes and bibliography (p. 285-293).

A collection of essays on the contemporary cinema in the Soviet Union, East Germany, Poland, Hungary, Bulgaria, and Yugoslavia. The essay on the USSR is by Anna Lawton who surveys the policy changes introduced by glasnost and perestroika as they have affected the cinema.

177. Mayne, Judith, **Kino and the Woman Question: Feminism and Soviet Silent Film**. Columbus: Ohio State University Press, 1989. ix, 211 p. ISBN: 0814204813. Includes bibliographical references (p. 193-205).

Mayne concentrates on five films made between 1925 and 1929: Eisenstein's "Strike;" Ermler's "Fragment of an Empire;" Vertov's "Man with a Movie Camera;" Pudovkin's "Mother;" and Room's "Bed and Sofa." Her "primary focus will be on how the narrative, aesthetic, and ideological projects of Soviet silent film are shaped, subverted, or otherwise complicated by representations of women." (p. 1) Review: *Russian History* 17:1:123-25 (Spring 1990).

178. **Inside the Film Factory: New Approaches to Russian and Soviet Cinema**, edited by Richard Taylor and Ian Christie. London: Routledge, 1991. xviii, 256 p. *Soviet Cinema*, ISBN: 0415049512. Includes bibliographical references (p. 217-247) and index.

A collection of essays by Western and Soviet authors intended to examine a variety of questions on Soviet and Russian cinema. It is one volume in a series on Soviet cinema. "The continuing aim of the series will be to situate Soviet cinema in its proper historical and aesthetic context, both as a major cultural force in Soviet politics and as a crucible for experimentation that is of central significance to the development of world cinema culture." (p. xvi) The essays look at early Russian cinema, Kuleshov's work on acting, the origins of Soviet cinema, Soviet Yiddish cinema, the directors Boris Barnet and Alexander Medvedkov, and the use of cinema for ideological purposes.

179. Zorkaia, Neia Markovna, **The Illustrated History of the Soviet Cinema**. Bryn Mawr, Pa.: Hippocrene Books, "Published by arrangement with Novosti Press Agency Publishing House, Moscow, U.S.S.R.," 1988. 320 p. ISBN: 0870525603. Includes index and bibliography (p. 309-312).

The purpose of Zorkaia's book is "to conduct a brief survey of the history of the Soviet cinema from the vantage ground of the 1980s and the approaching world cinema centennial in 1995." (p. 8) In her survey, Zorkaia treats the cinema as art and judges it accordingly, taking into consideration the sociological, historical, and cultural aspects of film as well.

Theater

180. Hoover, Majorie L., **Meyerhold and His Set Designers**. New York: P. Lang, 1988. x, 258 p. *American University Studies, Series XX, Fine Arts*, vol. 3. ISBN: 0820405795. Includes index and bibliography (p. 233-235).

"This book aims to study the variety and continuity of design in Meyerhold's many official and experimental productions of opera and both classic and contemporary plays.... More attention than usual [is] given to the first, less known part of the director's work between the Russian revolution of 1905 and the Soviet revolution of 1917." (p. viii) In addition the author has provided three informative appendices: 1) chronological list of Meyerhold's productions; 2) twenty productions with Golarin; and 3) a glossary of terms. Reviews: *Slavic and East European Journal* 34:3:404-05 (Fall 1990). *Slavic Review* 49:4:685-687 (Winter 1990).

181. Worrall, Nick, **Modernism to Realism on the Soviet Stage: Tairov—Vakhtangov—Okhlopkov**. Cambridge: Cambridge University Press, 1989. xviii, 238 p. *Directors in Perspective*, ISBN: 0521247632. Includes index and bibliography (p. 224-225).

After an informative introduction that sets the Russian theater and its development in context, Worrall devotes long chapters to the directors Tairov, Vakhtangov, and Okhlopkov. Each chapter assesses the work of each artist and relates his activities and productions to the events of Soviet theater history. A table of historical and theatrical events accompanies the text. Reviews: *Canadian Slavonic Papers* 32:1:97-99 (March 1990). *Slavic and East European Journal* 34;1:113-14 (Spring 1990). *World Literature Today* 64:2:328 (Spring 1990). *Russian Review* 49:3: 333-34 (July 1990).

THE ECONOMY

General Studies

182. **A Study of the Soviet Economy**, prepared by the staffs of the International Monetary Fund, the World Bank, and the Organization for Economic Co-operation and Development, and by consultants to the designated President of the European Bank for Reconstruction and Development. Paris, France: Organization for Economic Co-operation and Development, 1991. 3 volumes ISBN: 9264134689. Includes bibliographic references (v. 3, p. 391-408).

This study was undertaken as a result of the Houston Economic Summit of July 1990. In order to make "a detailed study of the Soviet economy, make recommendations for its reform, and establish criteria under which Western economic assistance could effectively support such reforms." (p. ix) The main findings were published separately. These three volumes contain the background papers that were used in preparation of the summary report. The report covers economic developments and reform, macroeconomic policies and reform, systemic policies, sectional issues, and the medium-term outlook.

183. Buck, Trevor, and John Cole, **Modern Soviet Economic Performance**. New York: B. Blackwell, 1987. viii, 192 p. ISBN: 063114417X. Includes index and bibliography (p. 180-187).

This examination of Soviet economic performance tries to strike a stylistic middle ground between other books that, on the one hand, are either too journalistic, or, on the other hand, too academic for the layman. The authors try to analyze economic performance using a conceptual framework suggested by the Hungarian economist Janos Kornai. Such a framework claims that the hardness or softness of constraints that reward or penalize industrial enterprises for their performance can provide an explanation of the comparative performance of different systems. The authors' analysis includes an overall description of the Soviet economic system plus individual chapters devoted to fairness, allocation and production, excess demand and inflation, unemployment, investment, innovation, economic growth, living standards, and soft budgets. Review: *Slavic Review* 48:3:507-08 (Fall 1989).

184. Buick, Adam, and John Crump, **State Capitalism: The Wages System Under New Management**. Basingstoke: Macmillan, 1986. ix, 165 p. ISBN: 0333367758. Includes index and bibliography (p. 154-58).

This book challenges the conventional wisdom that free market forces shape the economies of the capitalist world while the economies of the socialist and communist countries are planned. They argue that capitalism and socialism cannot coexist on a world economic scale and that in spite of the type of economy within an individual state, that state has to act and compete with rivals in a world (capitalist) market. In these countries the state actually becomes the capitalist. Their argument is explained in six chapters: What Is Capitalism?; State Capitalism in the West; The Revolutionary Road to State Capitalism; The Capitalist Dynamic of State Capitalist Economies; The Ideology of State Capitalism; and The Alternative to Capitalism.

185. Desai, Padma, **The Soviet Economy: Problems and Prospects**. Oxford, UK: Blackwell, 1987. viii, 281 p. ISBN: 063115227X. Includes index.

The essays contained in this volume have been published previously and are here brought together into a coherent framework. Only chapter one, on the causes and consequences of Soviet growth retardation, was written especially for this volume. The central theme of the collection is Soviet economic growth retardation. Essays are grouped under six sub-themes: the general aspects of the Soviet economic slowdown, diminishing returns and declining technical change, allocative inefficiency, foreign resources and foreign trade, agriculture (weather, yield variability and imports), and a concluding chapter on foreign economic relations, including the Third World. Most of the essays are highly technical and assume knowledge of econometric models and techniques.

186. Domar, Evsey D., **Capitalism, Socialism, and Serfdom: Essays**. Cambridge: Cambridge University Press, 1989. xxi, 294 p. ISBN: 0521370914. Includes bibliographical references and index.

A collection of essays by Evsey Domar spanning the years from 1957 to the present. The first three sections contain essays with the general theme of the "comparative performance of different economic systems, particularly of American capitalism and Soviet socialism." (p. xi) The final section includes essays on the history of serfdom. Numerous tables and figures are included.

187. Gregory, Paul R., **Restructuring Soviet Economic Bureaucracy**. New York: Cambridge University Press, 1990. xii, 181 p. *Soviet Interview Project Series*, ISBN: 0521363861. Includes bibliographical references.

In this study based on interviews with former Soviet economic bureaucrats, Gregory aims to describe how the Soviet economic bureaucracy works above the enterprise level. Specific questions addressed are: how do they make decisions; what are their goals; how are promotions within this bureaucracy effected; what are the various interactions among various levels of the bureaucracy; is there an independent auditing authority within the bureaucracy; and what are the relationships between state and party organizations? Gregory readily admits that his study lacks statistical validity vis a vis the population of economic bureaucrats surveyed. His work should be seen rather as that of an ethnographer who interviews representatives of a specific society or culture to see how things work.

188. Gregory, Paul R., and Robert C. Stuart, **Soviet Economic Structure and Perform-ance**. 3rd ed. New York: Harper & Row, 1986. xiii, 447 p. ISBN: 0060425075. Includes bibliographies and index.

This third edition of Gregory's and Stuart's basic text on the Soviet economy is arranged in four parts. Part one provides an in-depth description of Russian economic history from tsarist times to 1985. In part two, the authors describe how the Soviet economy operates, focusing on planning, pricing, markets, resource allocation, and the special areas of agriculture and foreign trade. Part three analyzes economic growth and performance with an additional emphasis on military power, technology, and the environment. Part four presents prospects for reform and change, material written at the beginning of Gorbachev's tenure.

189. Kronenwetter, Michael, **Capitalism vs. Socialism: Economic Policies of the USA and the USSR**. New York: F. Watts, 1986. 103 p. *Economic Impact Book*, ISBN: 0531101525. Includes index and bibliography (p. 97-98).

This book serves as a primer to introduce the two major economic systems in the world today, capitalism and socialism. The author successively gives a brief history of the forerunners of capitalism, its emergence, the response of socialism to it, contacts between the two systems, and a chapter each devoted to a description of the two countries where these systems are most highly visible today, the U.S. and the Soviet Union. A concluding chapter portrays other economic systems and a discussion of the world economy. This book is intended only as a brief introduction to the topic.

190. Libbey, James K., **American-Russian Economic Relations: A Survey of Issues and References**. Claremont, CA: Regina Books, 1989. xiii, 202 p. *Guides to Historical Issues*, no. 4. ISBN: 0941690350. Includes bibliographical references.

A survey of the changing economic relationship between Russia and America over the last 200 years. Only the first chapter deals with earlier centuries. The rest of the text is devoted to the twentieth century. One of the most important features of the book is the nearly 50 page bibliography. The text is organized chronologically with thematic subdivisions on agriculture, technology transfer, lend-lease, Comecon, and the Soviet command economy. There are numerous tables.

191. Millar, James, **The Soviet Economic Experiment**, edited and with an introduction by Susan J. Linz. Urbana: University of Illinois Press, 1990. xv, 297 p. ISBN: 0252016572. Includes bibliographical references.

A collection of essays by Professor Millar written over a twenty year period tracing the problems and accomplishments of the Soviet economic system. The essays are divided into three parts. Part one focuses on the role of agriculture in the Soviet economy and its development since 1917. Part two analyzes financial resources as they have been used by the Soviets. The final part examines central management and the possibility of change in the Soviet Union. "The essays collected in this volume span the major theoretical and policy issues that have confronted all Soviet leaders. ...Although the focus is primarily economic, political and social dimensions are explored in nearly every chapter." (p. xv).

192. Nove, Alec, **Socialism, Economics, and Development**. London: Allen & Unwin, 1986. 243 p. ISBN: 0043350542. Includes bibliographies and index.
These are previously published essays by Nove, republished here under common thematic rubrics. The thirteen essays are arranged in four parts. In part one, development, he looks at the Chilean economy in the seventies, and offers some insights on microeconomics. Part two deals with problems of Marxist and Soviet economics, part three on the contemporary Soviet economy and part four on politics and law in which he looks at Soviet constitutional theory and the class nature of the Soviet Union. Review: *Review of Radical Political Economics* 19:2:89-91 (Summer 1987).

193. ———, **Studies in Economics and Russia**. New York: St. Martin's Press, 1990. vii, 375 p. ISBN: 0312045093. Includes bibliographical references and index.
Alec Nove has collected together twenty-four essays that he has published in books, journals, collections, and occasional papers or which he has presented at conferences. They are unevenly divided into four broad areas in which Nove has expressed a long-term interest. Part I (2 essays) focuses on the lives and ideas of four prerevolutionary Russian economists. Part II (7 essays) covers Russian economic history from war Communism through Russian modernization in the mid 1980s. Part III (eight essays) looks at economic theory and policy in the East as well as the West. Part IV (7 essays) deals with the contemporary USSR and touches on such topics as growth, labor incentives in the kolkhozy, defense, and possibilities for reform.

194. Poznanski, Kazimierz Z., **Technology, Competition, & the Soviet Bloc in the World Market**. Berkeley: Institute of International Studies, University of California, Berkeley, 1987. ix, 226 p. *Research Series*, no. 70. ISBN: 0877251703. Includes index and bibliography and (p. 211-221).
A discussion of the place of the centrally planned economies in the world economy. In particular, the author focuses on the recent changes in those economies and the question of whether or not those changes will allow the Soviet Bloc countries to compete not only with the Western economic systems but also with the newly industrialized nations of the world. As is indicated in the title one aspect of economic development in particular will be the focus, technology. "It is our contention that technological strength—the ability to generate new inventions and to implement them in production—is the most important factor involved; here we agree with the main thrust of the neo- technological theories of trade." (p. 2) The analysis covers the years 1970 to 1985 and is divided into three sections: the effect of economic reforms on the technological sector; the measurement of technological performance and the factors affecting the performance of the centrally planned economies. The author concludes that it is the centralization of these economies that caused them to fail in the competition for world markets.

195. Scrivener, Ronald, **USSR Economic Handbook**. First edition. London: Euromonitor Publications, 1986. 246 p. ISBN: 0863381561. Includes index.
This handbook is designed for the Western entrepreneur who intends to do business in Russia or with Russian firms. It includes individual chapters on Soviet economic history and growth, resources and planning, industrial growth and production, transport and communications, agriculture, forestry and fisheries, foreign trade and tourism, finance and banking, and the USSR as a market for consumer goods. The volume also includes several appendices that contain statistical and directory-types of information about foreign trade.

Statistics

196. **Statistics for a Market Economy**, edited by Derek Blades. Paris: Organization for Economic Co-operation and Development, 1991. 199 p. ISBN: 9264134867. Includes bibliographical references.

One in a series of volumes published by the Centre for Co-operation with Soviet Economies in Transition examining the changes in those countries moving from a centralized to a market economy. Many topics related to statistical analysis are included. There is a chapter on Soviet agricultural statistics.

197. **The Impact of Gorbachev's Policies on Soviet Economic Statistics: A Conference Report**. Washington, DC: Central Intelligence Agency, 1988. v, 81 p. Includes bibliography (p. 65-67).

This volume contains a summary of a conference held in December 1987 on the impact of Gorbachev's policies on Soviet economic statistics. It also includes the texts of four papers presented at the conference. The participants focused on four questions relating to the influence of glasnost: 1. have the revelations recently made public increased our understanding of the failings of Soviet economic statistics, particularly regarding economic growth; 2. have the revelations increased the availability of statistics; 3. have glasnost and anti-corruption campaigns improved the quality of recent statistics or corrected past distortions; and 4. what are the implications of glasnost for estimates of economic growth and resource allocation?

198. Kushnirsky, Fyodor I., **Growth and Inflation in the Soviet Economy**. Boulder, CO: Westview Press, 1989. xi, 319 p. *Westview Special Studies on the Soviet Union and Eastern Europe*, ISBN: 0813377005. Includes index and bibliography (p. 304-310).

Soviet statistical problems in the context of measuring economic growth is the subject of this book. The author covers a variety of issues including price regulation, the effects of the Soviet distribution system, and inflation. The first part discusses economic planning in terms of physical commodities. Microeconomic models are emphasized. The second part deals with estimation of real and inflationary growth in the machine building and metal working sector, specifically the automotive, electrotechnical, energy and power machinery industries. The study is technical, requiring knowledge of economic analysis. Reviews: *Annals of the American Academy of Political and Social Science* 508:221-22 (March 1990). *Southern Economic Journal* 57:2: 584 (October 1990).

199. Ryan, Michael, **Contemporary Soviet Society: A Statistical Handbook**, compiled and with a translation by Michael Ryan. Aldershot, England: E. Elgar Pub., 1990. ix, 283 p. ISBN: 1852783494. Includes index.

A valuable reference source containing statistical data extracted largely from journals published in late 1989 and early 1990. The author has sought to present comparative statistics where possible. He has also presented the data in such a way as to give breakdowns by Union republics and urban centers wherever possible. His layout, in some cases, differs from that of his source material. This has been done to make the data more readily understandable to the reader. Statistics are offered on population, urbanization, births, deaths, marriages, divorces, families, ethnic composition, education, environment, crime, income support, women, life expectancy, diseases and accidents, mortality, and a special section on public opinions. The volume includes some of the newly published statistics on infant mortality and disease.

Economic History

200. Ball, Alan M., **Russia's Last Capitalists: The Nepmen, 1921- 1929**. Berkeley: University of California Press, 1987. xvii, 226 p. ISBN: 0520057171. Includes index and bibliography (p. 209-216).

The Nepmen, large-scale urban traders, manufacturers, financiers, speculators, smaller-scale merchants, and artisans, who operated legally in the Soviet Union in the 1920s, are the subject of this history by Alan Ball. After the advent of Bolshevism, socialism did not immediately follow on its heels. There was tremendous difficulty in distributing the essential consumer goods to the population. With the hope for the immediate transition abandoned, the Soviets legalized private business. NEP (New Economic Plan) was born. Ball examines the Nepmen themselves from two vantage points: from the perspective of the Bolsheviks themselves and the arguments in which they engaged over permitting private enterprise; and from the perspective of the Nepmen themselves, describing their business activity, social origins, and their reactions to the official policies. Reviews: *Russian History* 17:4:460-61 (Winter 1990). *Canadian-American Slavic Studies* 24:2:242-44 (Summer 1990). *American Historical Review* 94:4:1139-41 (October 1989). *Russian Review* 48:2:214-15 (April 1989).

201. Boettke, Peter J., **The Political Economy of Soviet Socialism: The Formative Years, 1918-1928**. Boston: Kluwer Academic, 1990. xxi, 246 p. ISBN: 0792391004. Includes bibliographical references (p. 203-217) and index.

An economic history of the first ten years of the Bolshevik system. The author believes that the Soviet experience has been misunderstood. Based on Western analysis, he proceeds in his chronological analysis from two basic criticisms of the existing literature "First, the standard economic history literature does not treat Marxism seriously enough as a system of thought. Second, the standard literature does not recognize fully the economic coordination problem that any society, let alone a Marxian economic system, would have to confront." (p. 6) The book contains a review of the literature and then moves on to an analysis of economic history of Bolshevik policy from 1918 to 1928. There is also a discussion of the debates that took place as Stalinist economics began to arise.

202. Bradley, Joseph, **Guns for the Tsar: American Technology and the Small Arms Industry in Nineteenth-Century Russia**. DeKalb, Ill.: Northern Illinois University Press, 1990. xi, 274 p. ISBN: 0875801522. Includes bibliographical references (p. 237-265).

In this unique study, Bradley examines the history of the small arms industry in Russia prior to 1890. Up to the Crimean War, the Russians were self-sufficient in arms manufacturing. By the 1870s, however, they were forced to borrow the machine method of making firearms from the United States. Facing this seeming paradox, Bradley poses and answers two questions. First, why was there a need to import a foreign technology when they had been self-sufficient prior to 1855? Second, why did Russia's native technology "fail to reproduce itself" and keep up with foreign developments? In answering these questions, Bradley examines the general question of small arms in an industrial age, the development of small arms in an industrial age, the development of small arms in pre-reform Russia, the Russian small arms industry and related issues of labor and management in the Russian factory. A concluding chapter pulls all these strands together by seeing how the state, technology, and labor each played their part.

203. **From Tsarism to the New Economic Policy: Continuity and Change in the Economy of the USSR**. Ithaca, N.Y.: Cornell University Press, 1991. xx, 417 p. ISBN: 0801426219. Includes bibliographical references (p. 385-403) and indices.

The collection of essays given in this book represent several years of joint writing and discussions among the collaborators. Acknowledging that few economic historians specialize in both prerevolutionary and Soviet economic history, the contributors realized that they had inadequate data from which to draw meaningful comparisons. They set out, therefore, to examine in detail both the tsarist economy on the eve of the revolution and the Soviet economy in the mid-1920s. They meant to discover continuities and differences between them. The book has an introduction summarizing their findings and eleven chapters in five distinct parts. Part I deals with the social background, socio-economic differentiation, and unemployment. Part two examines various aspects of agriculture; Part III various parts of industry; and Part IV other sectors of the economy such as railways, research and technology, and foreign trade. Part V looks at national income.

204. Davies, Robert W., **The Soviet Economy in Turmoil, 1929-1930**. Cambridge, Mass.: Harvard University Press, 1989. xx, 601 p. *Industrialization of Soviet Russia*, v. 3. ISBN: 0674826558. Includes indexes and bibliography (p. 551-570).

This volume, a companion to Davies' two previous works on this time period, *The Socialist Offensive, 1929-1930* and *The Soviet Collective Farm, 1929-1930*, examines in detail the crucial period of 1929-1930 when Soviet leaders realized that the New Economic Policy would not allow the much needed rapid industrialization to take place. While his two former works dealt with agriculture, this one focuses entirely on the industrial economy. Its thirteen chapters guide the reader through a brief overview of the Soviet economy in the 1920s, the expansion of industry, the social and intellectual contexts in which rapid industrialization took place, the party debates, or lack thereof at the XVI Party Congress in the summer of 1930, the economic difficulties at the end of 1930 that led to conflict within the party, and the role of national defense and the armaments industry in industrialization. A concluding chapter ties all these strands together into a concise summary that points out the complexity and paradoxes of the social and economic transformation of the first dozen years of Soviet rule. Review: *Journal of Economic History* 50:3:744-45 (September 1990).

205. Fenin, Aleksandr I., **Coal and Politics in Late Imperial Russia: Memoirs of a Russian Mining Engineer**, translated by Alexandre Fediaevsky, edited by Suzan P. McCaffray. DeKalb, Ill.: Northern Illinois University Press, 1990. xxii, 228 p. ISBN: 0875801536. Includes bibliographical references and index.

Fenin, a mining engineer, witnessed both the 1905 and 1917 revolutions and supported the anti-Bolshevik forces in the Civil War. His memoir "offers an intimate, astute, and often witty portrait of the many problems that accompanied the industrialization of Russia." (p. xi).

206. Gatrell, Peter, **The Tsarist Economy, 1850-1917**. New York: St. Martin's Press, 1986. xvi, 288 p. ISBN: 0312821913. Includes bibliography (p. 273-279).

Gatrell's examination of the tsarist economy is not meant to be a comprehensive treatment of the subject. Instead, he concentrates on several significant issues. Those which he looks at are those considered to be significant by three ideological traditions that were active at the time: liberal, populist, and Marxist-Leninist. He shows, in his critical examination of these traditions how problems for one school of thought were solutions for others. He first looks at Russian economic development from the perspective of these three schools of thought. He then proceeds in five chapters to examine the dimensions of poverty and economic growth, population growth, social change and the labor market, the agricultural sector and the manufacturing sector, capital, and credit. In his conclusion he carefully shows how certain assumptions about the tsarist economy no longer hold. Review: *Journal of Economic History* 47:2:538-39 (June 1987).

207. Hughes, James, **Stalin, Siberia, and the Crisis of the New Economic Policy**. Cambridge: Cambridge University Press, 1991. xiii, 260 p. *Soviet and East European Studies*, vol. 81. ISBN: 0521380391. Includes bibliographical references (p. 246-254) and index.

A thematically arranged, scholarly analysis of the failure of Lenin's NEP. This study takes a regional perspective, that of Siberia, focusing on the pressures exerted from Soviet society. Several areas are examined "These include Party-peasant relations, the Kulak question, Stalin's patron-client network in the provinces, the regional impact of the grain procurement crisis and the use of emergency measures to overcome the crisis. The author concludes that Stalin's experience of economic conditions which were unique to Siberia, accelerated his negative reappraisal of the NEP and initiated the descent into the cataclysm of his 'revolution from above' in late 1929." (p. i) The book includes a statistical appendix and a glossary of terms.

208. Kahan, Arcadius, **Russian Economic History: The Nineteenth Century**, edited by Roger Weiss. Chicago: University of Chicago Press, 1989. xii, 244 p. ISBN: 0226422429. Includes bibliographies and index.

This is the third collection of Arcadius Kahan's social and economic historical writings. These essays had either been published previously or presented at conferences. Topics covered include a brief history of the Russian economy 1860-1913, government policies and the industrialization of Russia, serfdom, social protest by the agrarian population, education, and literacy. Review: *Business History Review* 64:3:579-80 (Fall 1990).

209. **The Economic History of Eastern Europe, 1919-1975**, edited by M. C. Kaser. Oxford: Oxford University Press, 1985. 3 v. ISBN: 0198284446 (v. 1). Includes bibliographical references and indexes.

This history covers the period from the Treaty of Versailles in 1919 through the Final Act of the Helsinki Conference in 1975. "Its function also is to chart the transformation of the region into industrialized and predominantly urban states." (vol. 1, p. 1) Volume 1 covers economic structure and performance between the two wars; volume 2 examines interwar policy, the war and reconstruction; and volume 3 focuses on institutional change within a planned economy.

210. Kuromiya, Hiroaki, **Stalin's Industrial Revolution: Politics and Workers, 1928-1932**. Cambridge: Cambridge University Press, 1988. xviii, 364 p. ISBN: 052135157X. Includes index and bibliography (p. 324-351).

Kuromiya's broad topic is the industrial transformation that took place in the Soviet Union between 1928-1932, the period of the first Five Year Plan. Stalin's strategy was to "pump out" resources from the agrarian sector of the economy and transfer these resources to a growing industrial sector. This would provide the leap to industrialized socialism. More specifically, Kuromiya focuses on how the political leadership made the mobilization of these resources politically possible. The key to the strategy was the establishment of class war atmosphere, labeling NEPmen, kulaks, and other bourgeois enemies of socialism. His book examines the social, economic, and institutional contexts of this mobilization from the perspective of the period itself. Reviews: *Russian History* 17:4:463-65 (Winter 1990). *Contemporary Sociology* 19:2:224-45 (March 1990). *Slavic Review* 49:3:456-57 (Fall 1990).

211. Macey, David A. J., **Government and Peasant in Russia, 1861-1906: The Prehistory of the Stolypin Reforms**. DeKalb, Ill.: Northern Illinois University Press, 1987. xviii, 380 p. ISBN: 0875801226. Includes index and bibliography (p. 339-367).

Macey presents a prehistory of the 1906 Stolypin agrarian reforms. His book is arranged in four parts. Part one is background and broadly sketches the emancipation and its aftermath, 1861-1900. Part two examines the revolution in perceptions of the agrarian question and the role played by the Finance Ministry and the Interior Ministry. Part three covers the revolution in policy for 1905 to 1906, and part four describes the new agrarian policy put forth in the last half of 1900. Reviews: *Canadian Journal of History* 23:3:435-37 (December 1988). *Canadian Slavonic Papers* 30:2:265-66 (June 1988). *Russian History* 15:2-4:265-66 (Summer-Fall-Winter 1988). *Agricultural History* 62:3:211-12 (Summer 1988).

212. Ward, Chris, **Russia's Cotton Workers and the New Economic Policy: Shop-Floor Culture and State Policy, 1921-1929**. Cambridge: Cambridge University Press, 1990. xvi, 394 p. *Soviet and East European Studies*, no. 69. ISBN: 0521345804. Includes bibliographical references (p. 275-290).

Ward investigates the development of the cotton industry and the effect on its workers from 1921-1929. His study is arranged in four parts. Part one investigates the New Economic Policy and the role that the cotton industry and its workers had in it. Part two focuses on the mill itself, the machines, skills, and workers' cooperatives. Part three examines the economic crisis of 1923 on the cotton industry and its consequences, including the rise of Taylorism. Part four deals with the crisis of 1927 and its consequences on the shop floor and the end of NEP.

213. White, Colin M., **Russia and America: The Roots of Economic Divergence**. New York: Croom Helm, 1987. 268 p. ISBN: 0709952465. Includes index and bibliography (p. 230-260).

A comparative economic history tracing the development of the twentieth century economies of Russia and America. The book is divided into four parts, the first of which is an introduction detailing the basic elements of economic development in the two countries. The two middle sections examine the role of the national environment in economic development in Russia and America. The final chapter takes a broader perspective looking at the model of an uncertain world in economic analysis. Reviews: *Journal of Comparative Economics* 14:1:166-67 (1990). *International Historical Review* 10:3:512-14 (August 1988). *Journal of Economic History* 48:4:984-85 (December 1988).

Economic Theory and Planning

214. Bergson, Abram, **Planning and Performance in Socialist Economies: The USSR and Eastern Europe**. Boston: Unwin Hyman, 1988. xii, 304 p. ISBN: 0044451156. Includes index.

These previously published essays by Bergson all concentrate on the relative economic merit of the socialist and capitalist systems. His conclusion is that "socialist economic performance tends to be undistinguished by Western standards." (p. 1) The thirteen essays are divided into four parts: 1) productivity and welfare, 2) growth, 3) planning, and 4) problems of measurement. Review: *Comparative Economic Studies* 32:4:107-09 (Winter 1990).

215. Hewett, Edward A., **Reforming the Soviet Economy: Equality Versus Efficiency**. Washington, DC: Brookings Institution, 1988. 404 p. ISBN: 0815736045. Includes index.

In this well documented study Hewett first examines the strengths and weaknesses of the current economic system and the institutions that allow it to operate. Then he analyzes past and present efforts to reform the system. In his eight chapters Hewett first covers the analytical framework that he has used in the study. Then he proceeds to assess Soviet economic performance, the formal system as it was designed to operate and the de facto system. He then covers various reform programs including Khrushchev's Sovnarkhoz reforms, the 1965 reforms, the 1973 Industrial Reorganization and the July 1979 decree. He identifies common elements among these reforms. He describes the debates over the economic system that occurred during the brief tenures of Andropov and Chernenko and then proceeds to examine the early Gorbachev reforms of 1985-1986. In conclusion he speculates on the possible outcomes of Gorbachev reform activity. Reviews: *Slavic Review* 49:1:119 (Spring 1990). *Journal of International Affairs* 42:2:487-88 (Spring 1989). *Orbis* 33:1:126 (Winter 1989). *Journal of Comparative Economics* 13:2:350-51 (June 1989). *Southern Economic Journal* 56:2:553-55 (October 1989). *Soviet Union* 15:1:108-09 (1988).

216. **Economics and Politics in the USSR: Problems of Interdependence**, edited by Hans-Hermann Hohmann, Alec Nove, and Heinrich Vogel. Boulder, CO: Westview Press, 1986. xii, 306 p. ISBN: 0813303346.

The 14 papers in this volume, updated from the proceedings of a conference held in November 1984 and organized by the Bundesinstitut für ostwissenschaffliche und internationale Studien, are multidisciplinary in nature. The authors are specialists in Soviet history, political science, philosophy, and economics. They attempt to evaluate the political impact of the unprecedented decline perceived internally by elites. How is the decline to be managed? Is reform of the system possible? How would potential reformers be thwarted? Can old taboos be discarded in the interests of higher efficiency? These and other relevant questions are thoroughly examined from several disciplinary perspectives. Reviews: *Soviet Union* 14:1:199-20 (1987). *Russian Review* 46:3:343-44 (July 1987). *Slavic Review* 46:1:139-40 (Spring 1987).

217. Smith, Graham, **Planned Development in the Socialist World**. New York: Cambridge University Press, 1989. v, 106 p. *Cambridge Topics in Geography, Second Series*, ISBN: 0521305462, 0521269466 (pbk.). Includes index and bibliography (p. 103-105).

This book, intended for geographers, is an introduction to the social and economic development of the socialist world and the Soviet Union in particular. Smith intends to show, in a historical and systemic way, "how various strategies of development are conceived and how they are bound up with the territorial organization of society and with the nature of regions, cities and the countryside and with the lives of the people who inhabit these places." (p. v) Chapter one sets the stage for what follows by describing alternative development strategies in other socialist countries, in China, Kampuchea, and Hungary. Chapter two deals with the Stalinist model of development. In chapters 3-6 the author examines other aspects of contemporary development such as urbanization, regional policy and development, development of the non-Russian periphery, and rural development. A concluding chapter summarizes the points made throughout the book and questions whether perestroika is a new beginning.

218. Sutela, Pekka, **Economic Thought and Economic Reform in the Soviet Union**. Cambridge: Cambridge University Press, 1991. x, 197 p. *Cambridge University Paperbacks*, no. 5. ISBN: 0521380200, 052138902X (pbk.). Includes bibliographical references (p. 192-194) and index.

This clearly written monograph for the most part is an historical overview of political economy in the Soviet state. Soviet economic thinking began on the basis of a form of Marxian ideology and was, for all intents and purposes, barren of relevant policy advice. It was primarily managerial in nature. The entrenched economic ideology met several challenges over the years, the strangest being that of linear optimization and other mathematical methods. Reforms enacted under Khrushchev were partly successful, but reformers, an ever increasing number of whom were non-economists, kept up the pressure. Description of economic thought occupies the first five chapters. In the last, sixth chapter, Sutela compares East European reform concepts with Soviet ones against a framework designed to answer the question posed at the beginning of the book: "is the Soviet economic profession capable of meeting the challenge posed by recent perestroika reform efforts." (p. 5) He concludes by stating that the transition to a market economy can only be undertaken by a strong government, "following consistent policy guidelines and enjoying popular support." (Ibid.).

219. **The Soviet Economy on the Brink of Reform: Essays in Honor of Alec Nove**, edited by Peter Wiles. Boston: Unwin Hyman, 1988. vii, 256 p. ISBN: 004350631. Includes bibliographies and index.

This festschrift for Alec Nove contains articles that the editor hopes will be read and used. They include essays on Trotsky and democratic control, Soviet investment criteria, allocation of investment, production and sales fluctuations, the CIA's Soviet Economic indices, Soviet second economy, Soviet agriculture, and economic policies under Andropov and Chernenko.

Perestroika

220. **Revisiting Soviet Economic Performance Under Glasnost: Implications for CIA Estimates**. Washington, DC: Document Expediting (DOCEX) Project, Exchange and Gift Division, Library of Congress, 1988. ix, 23 p. Includes bibliographical references.

"This paper assesses the implications of recent glasnost-inspired critiques of the USSR's official economic statistics for CIA's estimates of Soviet economic performance. The CIA estimates, although predicated on the belief that Moscow's macroeconomic measures are unreliable, are based on a variety of official Soviet data. In particular, the paper focuses on what the recent criticisms have to tell us about the accuracy of CIA's estimates for the growth and structure of Soviet gross national product (GNP)." (p. iii).

221. Aganbegyan, Abel Gezevich, **The Economic Challenge of Perestroika**, edited by Michael Barratt Brown; introduced by Alec Nove; translated by Pauline M. Tiffen. Bloomington, Indiana: Indiana University Press, 1988. xxvii, 248 p. *Second World*, ISBN: 0253320933. Includes index.

This work by the noted Soviet economist A. Aganbegyan is about "perestroika of the economy, its problems and the tasks involved." (p. xxv) The changes described and proposed here are not a short term campaign he reminds us, but "a strategic, long-term economic policy." (p. xxv) Recognizing that perestroika of the economy is a complex, multifaceted affair, Aganbegyan devotes chapters to a historical overview and lessons learned from previous reform efforts, the importance of efficiency and technology, the necessity of managerial reform, a new investment policy, various social aspects of economic transition and the effects of an arms race on economic development. In conclusion, he predicts what he believes the Soviet economy will look like in the 21st century. Reviews: *Journal of Economic Literature* 28:1: 85-86 (March 1990). *Canadian-American Slavic Studies* 24:3:339-41 (Fall 1990). *Bulletin of the Atomic Scientist* 45:4:47-48 (May 1989). *Slavic Review* 48:1:120-21 (Spring 1989). *Russian Review* 48:3:328-30 (July 1989).

222. ———, **Inside Perestroika: The Future of the Soviet Economy**. New York: Harper & Row, 1989. vi, 241 p. *"A Cornelia & Michael Bessie Book,"* ISBN: 0060390999.

Aganbegyan, head of the economic branch of the Academy of Sciences of the U.S.S.R. and chief economic advisor to Mikail Gorbachev, seems to aim this book at a general audience. His three chapters: (1) A New Stage in Perestroika-The Restructuring of Management in the USSR; (2) Is Perestroika Irreversible?; and (3) Will the Soviet Economy Open Up?, are all written in a chatty style with wide use of the first person. He poses questions such as a journalist would ask, e.g. How can we make people care about their work?, How does perestroika differ from the unsuccessful reforms?, or Will the rouble become convertible?, and then proceeds to answer them, often giving historical background, survey of present conditions, and prescriptions for the future. An afterword is a statistical review, in prose, of three years of economic reconstruction. Review: *New Republic* 202:10:34-38 (March 5, 1990).

223. Aganbegyan, Abel Gezevich, and Timor Timofeyev, **The New Stage of Perestroika**. New York: Institute for East-West Security Studies, distributed by Westview Press, 1988. 77 p. ISBN: 0813377374. Includes bibliographical references.

Two of the papers presented here, one by the Head of the Economics Branch of the USSR Academy of Sciences, A. Aganbegyian, and the other by General Secretary Mikhail Gorbachev's chief economic advisor, T. Timofeyev, address the relationship between domestic economic reform in the Soviet Union and the social aspects of the reform process. The volume, which is sponsored by the Institute for East-West Security Studies, is the third in a series of similar volumes on Soviet New Thinking. The volume has four parts. Part one consists of an essay by John Mroz on perestroika and economic security; part two, by Aganbegian, examines acceleration (uskorenie) and perestroika; part three by Timofeyev describes and analyzes the social aspects of perestroika; and part four is a translation of an article that originally appeared in *Pravda* on April 5, 1985 entitled "Principles of Restructuring: Revolutionary Nature of Thinking and Acting."

224. **Perestroika 1989**. New York: Charles Scribner's Sons, 1988. viii, 346 p. ISBN: 0684191172. Includes index and bibliography (p. 333-336).

This volume was intended to be the first volume of an annual publication devoted to chronicling the progress of perestroika in the Soviet Union. Perestroika is here conceived very broadly encompassing not only the economic sphere, but the cultural, social, and political spheres as well. All the articles are original with this volume and are written by Russians living through the experience of perestroika. Individual essays cover such topics as the political philosophy of perestroika, economic reforms, legal aspects, foreign economic relations, the theater, political leadership, summit meetings between the U.S. and the USSR, social forces working for and against perestroika and religious aspects.

225. Aslund, Anders, **Gorbachev's Struggle for Economic Reform**. Updated and Expanded Edition. Ithaca, N.Y.: Cornell University Press, 1991. xi, 262 p. ISBN: 0801426391, 0801499437 (pbk.). Includes bibliographical references (p. 242-253) and index.

Updated and expanded from the previous (1988) edition of this work, Aslund's book is a history of perestroika from March 1985 to January 1991. His purpose is to uncover the underlying forces that influence the Soviet leader's attitude towards systemic change in the economy and to explain recent developments in Soviet economic policy. In the nine chapters of this edition, Aslund describes the origins of the economic reform in the Soviet Union, recent alternative programs for economic revitalization, actual changes that have taken place in enterprise management and generally throughout the economy, new policies toward private enterprise and cooperatives, reforms in planning, supply allocation, press, foreign trade, and the role of the Party. In the most recently added chapters, he explains the causes and dimensions of the Soviet economic crisis in late 1988 and 1989, the abortive search for a solution and an evaluation of the new reform wave. Three appendices provide biographical information about the actors involved in the events described. Reviews: *New Republic* 202:10:34038 (March 5, 1990). *American Political Science Review* 84:4:1340-41 (December 1990). *Canadian Slavonic Papers* 32:4:500-01 (December 1990). *SAIS Review* 10:2:250-51 (Summer-Fall 1990). *New York Times Review of Books* 38:18:53-59 (November 7, 1991).

226. **Chronicle of a Revolution: A Western-Soviet Inquiry into Perestroika**. New York: Pantheon Books, 1990. vi, 266 p. ISBN: 039457706X.

Prior to Gorbachev's ascent to power, most Western observers of the Soviet scene assumed that the future of the Soviet Union simply meant "more of the same." Few, if any, Sovietologists conceived of the revolution from above. In this volume, both Western and Soviet commentators enter into a dialogue of sorts about the recent changes in the Soviet Union. In an introductory essay, Abraham Brumberg sets the stage for what is to follow by reviewing the assumptions from which most Sovietologists proceeded. This is followed in Part One by a group of eight essays covering many facets of the perestroika/glasnost phenomenon. In Part Two, Soviet commentators respond to those essays with comments and insights of their own. Topics covered include the political systems, economics, law, the nationalities and nationalism problems, and poetry.

227. Desai, Padma, **Perestroika in Perspective: The Design and Dilemmas of Soviet Reform**. Princeton, NJ: Princeton University Press, 1989. viii, 138 p. ISBN: 0691042438. Includes index and bibliography (p. 131-132).

Desai's book is based on a lecture given in the spring of 1988 at Michigan State University. Claiming that he has departed from the conventional treatment of perestroika, he has taken a broader view of that phenomenon by also examining the political and cultural elements, in addition to the economic aspects. The core of his analysis is economic, however. His nine chapters examine briefly the history of the Soviet planned economy, then moves to examining Gorbachev's blitzkrieg of decrees dealing with economic reform. Various aspects of the reforms are evaluated including introduction of markets, changing the superstructure, and foreign policy. Two appendices, one dealing with some technical aspects of the reform and the other on political structure and election procedures are also included. Reviews: *New Republic* 202:10:34- 38 (March 5, 1990). *Annals of the American Academy of Political and Social Science* 507:172-73 (January 1990). *Southern Economic Journal* 57:2:565-66 (October 1990). *Russian Review* 49:3:382-83 (July 1990).

228. Goldman, Marshall I., **Gorbachev's Challenge: Economic Reform in the Age of High Technology**. 1st ed. New York, N.Y.: W.W. Norton, 1987. xvii, 296 p. ISBN: 0393024547. Includes bibliographical references and index.

Marshall Goldman apologetically declares that this work is meant as a guidebook for Gorbachev himself, not only to describe the situation he faces, but also to suggest concrete steps he might pursue. Initially, Gorbachev's reforms were confined to increasing discipline and sobriety among workers. But then these measures were soon perceived to be insufficient in an economy where, for all intents and purposes, money had lost its meaning, and with it any incentive to work. Gorbachev faced two seemingly irreconcilable problems: 1. not to reform too fast, thereby stepping on many sensitive toes, and 2. not reform fast enough so that it can be shown that reforms will work. In his eight chapters, Goldman describes the situation about 1986-1987, shows the relevance of technology transfer to economic reform, portrays other roads to economic reform as they unfolded in Hungary and the GDR, and

China, and concludes with a smorgasbord of choices and obstacles that lie ahead. Reviews: *Antioch Review* 46:3:383- 89 (Summer 1989). *Commonwealth* 372-72 (June 17, 1988). *Bulletin of the Atomic Scientist* 44:3:52-54 (April 1988). *Perspective: Review* 17:1:30 (Winter 1988).

229. **Milestones in Glasnost and Perestroyka**. Washington, DC: Brookings Institution, 1991. 2 vols. ISBN: 0815736223 (v. 1), 081573624X (v. 2). Includes bibliographical references and indexes.

The essays in these two volumes are largely drawn from the journal *Soviet Economy*, which began publication in 1985, the same year Gorbachev was named General Secretary of the Communist Party of the Soviet Union. Volume one, devoted to the economy, is divided into four sections that roughly follow a chronological path. These parts are (1) the Emerging Reform, covering the first 2 years of Gorbachev's rule; (2) the Architects of Change, describing new economic proposals; (3) the Complexities of Transition; and (4) Entering the 1990s, which focuses on the events and proposals of 1989 and 1990. Volume two, devoted to politics and society, also in four parts, covers the (1) Early Years of the Gorbachev Era, (2) The Politics and Adversities of Change, (3) the Stirrings of Democratization, and (4) Mikhail Gorbachev as leader. The forty three essays in both volumes provide a broad but detailed picture of the many facets of glasnost and perestroika. Of particular reference value are the Chronology of Major Economic Reform Legislation, 1985-1991 in volume one and Chronology of Noteworthy Events, 1985-1991 in volume two. Review: *Current History* 90:558:346 (October 1991).

230. **Gorbachev and Perestroika: Towards a New Socialism?** Aldershot, Hants, England: E. Elgar Pub. Co., 1989. 234 p. *International Library of Studies in Communism*, ISBN: 1852781467. Includes bibliographical references.

These eleven essays all deal with perestroika. Perestroika, or restructuring, actually means an increase of efficiency in the economic sector. To be successful, however, it requires the participation of all the people engaged in the economic system, for all intents and purposes, the entire Soviet population. To make this participation possible, glasnost, the ability to speak one's opinion without fear of reprisal, is required. Aspects of perestroika covered here are Gorbachev as a political reformer, his legal reforms viewed historically and contemporaneously, glasnost and the debate in history, Gorbachev's personal policy, foreign policy, and the aftermath of the 19th Party Congress.

231. Hosking, Geoffrey A., **The Awakening of the Soviet Union**. Enlarged ed. Cambridge, Mass.: Harvard University Press, 1991. ix, 246 p. ISBN: 0674055519. Includes bibliographical references (p. 220-239) and index.

This book is based on the Reith Lectures that Hosking delivered for the BBC in the autumn of 1988. This enlarged edition is an update on these lectures. Hosking's purpose was to give a historical explanation of the various events that have come to be known as glasnost and perestroika. Review: *New York Times Review of Books* 38:18:53-59 (November 7, 1991).

232. Ioffe, Olimpiad Solomonovich, **Gorbachev's Economic Dilemma: An Insider's View**, edited by David A. Rome. St. Paul: Merrill/ Magnus Pub. Corp, 1989. ix, 317 p. ISBN: 1877927015, 1877927023 (pbk.). Includes bibliographical references (p. 287-300) and index.

Ioffe has spent his career analyzing, interpreting, and writing civil and economic law in the Soviet Union. After leaving the Soviet Union in 1981, he has continued to monitor economic policy in his former homeland. His book focuses on Gorbachev's economic reforms in which he has found more appearance than substance. Here he singles out those reforms that have the potential for effecting concrete results and describes their limitations. In Ioffe's view, Gorbachev was trying to save the socialist economy by introducing private economic constructions. But at the same time, Gorbachev seems to want to preserve the socialist economy. Ioffe can only predict two essential outcomes: rejection of the socialist economy or return to a strong centrally planned economy. Review: *Foreign Affairs* 69:2:181 (Spring 1990).

233. **Perestroika and the Economy: New Thinking in Soviet Economics**. Armonk, N.Y.: M.E. Sharpe, 1989. xxi, 277 p. ISBN: 0873325699. Includes bibliographical references.

This collection of 19 essays by Soviet economists covers several troublesome issues presently confronting the Soviet Unions. Published previously in the translation journal *Problems of Economics*, these essays provide an excellent sampling of new Soviet thinking on economics. There are six main topics covered. Five essays focus on general economic issues such as restructuring, management, competition, and worker participation in management. Another group of five essays discuss the plan and markets. The next three sections on price reform, labor incentives, and property and social justice all lead up to the final section on barriers to reform. Reviews: *Southern Economic Journal* 57:1:256-57 (July 1990). *Canadian Slavonic Papers* 32:4: 501-02 (December 1990).

234. **Perestroika: How New Is Gorbachev's New Thinking?: The Challenge by Mikhail Gorbachev; Responses by Zbigniew Brezinski ... [and others]**, edited by Ernest W. Lefever and Robert D. Vander Lugt. Washington, DC: Ethics and Public Policy Center, 1989. xiv, 245 p. ISBN: 0896331334, 0896331342 (pbk.). Includes index and bibliography (p. 237-238).

These essays, all written before the historic Party conference in June 1988, are concerned with evaluating Gorbachev's policies of glasnost and perestroika and whether they will bring about fundamental, systemic change. The essays were written by statesmen, scholars, journalists, and Soviet dissidents.

235. **Reorganization and Reform in the Soviet Economy**, edited by Susan J. Linz and William Moskoff. Armonk, N.Y.: M.E. Sharpe, 1988. x, 147 p. ISBN: 0873324722. Includes bibliographical references.

After sixty years of central planning experience, with thirty years of sustained growth and thirty years of significant slowdown, Soviet society came to recognize the necessity of reform. These seven essays portray the Soviet economic bureaucracy in its attempts to deal with Gorbachev's reform proposals. These proposals, a result of compromise, were marked by ambiguity. Various aspects of the problem are examined. A historical perspective on the economic bureaucracy is followed by comparisons with other countries' reform efforts, evaluation of the Gorbachev reform program, detailed analysis of the industrial and agricultural sectors, and an examination of economic reform and industrial performance from 1950 to 1984. Evidence from the Soviet Interview Project is offered in an attempt to explain the impact of recent Soviet economic reform and the seeming inevitability of abandoning the command economy and the role of the party.

236. Medvedev, Roy Aleksandrovich, and Giulietto Chiesa, **Time of Change: An Inside View of Russia's Transformation**. New York: Pantheon Books, 1990. xvi, 346 p. ISBN: 0394581512. Includes index and bibliographical references (p. 321-331).

This is a highly unusual chronicle, but a valuable one. The book is in four parts, each corresponding to a year from 1986 to 1989. Within each part are separate chapters that cover specific periods within the year or specific topics that seemed to dominate the year, e.g. foreign policy in 1986 and 1988. Each chapter is then divided into two sections. In the first section specific events are described and evaluated. Excerpts from speeches and newspapers are cited in order to drive points home. In the second section of each chapter Chiesa poses a series of questions or problem statements to which Medvedev, an inside observer of these events, responds. The final chapter addresses the final months of 1989 and poses the question "Can the center hold?" A highly abbreviated chronicle of events an outline of the changing composition of the Politburo from 1976 to 1988 are included as appendices.

237. Shmelev, Nikolai Petrovich, and Vladimir Popov, **The Turning Point: Revitalizing the Soviet Economy.** 1st ed. New York: Doubleday, 1989. xvii, 330 p. ISBN: 0385246544. Includes bibliographical references and index.

Shmelev and Popov, two leading Soviet economists, set about to understand the sources and meaning of perestroika. They explore how the Soviets got to where they were economically in 1988, provide a critique of the existing situation, and draw attention to both the advances and mistakes made during perestroika. They conclude with suggestions for further development. In the system existing in 1988 they identify three built-in defects: the monopoly of producers, resulting in chronic shortages, industrial enterprises that have little or no interest in scientific progress and inadequate incentives for hard work. Committed to socialism, they see in Lenin's New Economic Policy (NEP) the workings of a truly socialist market economy. Perestroika must now face the same questions faced at the end of the 1920s when NEP was crushed by Stalin. Their eight chapter work includes an enlightening discussion of Soviet economic statistics as well as their prescription for what is needed now. Reviews: *New Republic* 202:10:34-38 (March 5, 1990). *National Review* 42:1:49- 53 (January 22, 1990).

238. Spulber, Nicolas, **Restructuring the Soviet Economy: In Search of the Market.** Ann Arbor, MI: University of Michigan Press, 1991. 315 p. ISBN: 047210229X. Includes bibliographical references and index.

The ways in which the Soviet Union's centrally administered economy can be changed to a mixed or market-directed economy is the focus of this book. Spulber thoroughly examines restructuring attempts from 1985 on in order to see how the main problem of efficient allocation of resources can be solved. His book consists of 14 chapters, divided into four parts. Part one examines the basic principles of adjusting the economy with which Soviet economic architects deal. Part two is concerned with the reshaping of the directive center: capital, manpower, fiscal, monetary, and credit management. Part three looks at the sectoral arrangements and interconnecting of agriculture, manufacturing, domestic, and foreign trade. Part four evaluates the possible courses of action open. Spulber concludes by emphasizing that elimination of the ownership of the means of production by the state is the first great step needed for a growth oriented economy. Review: *Foreign Affairs* 70:5:199 (Winter 1991-92).

239. **Socialism, Perestroika, and the Dilemmas of Soviet Economic Reform.** Boulder, CO: Westview Press, 1990. xix, 239 p. ISBN: 0813380170. Includes bibliographical references and index.

The eleven essays in this volume are the result of a conference held at Radio Free Europe/Radio Liberty in 1989. There are two themes. The main one is that fundamental changes, not just incremental refinements, are needed to effect genuine change and improvement in the economic system. The second theme is that other issues such as a multiparty system, a democratic legislature, and private ownership must go hand in hand with the economic reforms. Individual essays examine redefining socialism in the USSR, ownership issues, the emergence of Soviet cooperatives, privatization of Soviet agriculture, industrial innovation, prospects for commodity and financial exchanges, retail price reform, the consumer, and social entitlements.

240. Yavlinsky, G., and et al., **500 Days: Transition to the Market**, English translation edited by David Kushner. New York: St. Martin's Press, 1991. xxi, 234 p. ISBN: 0312073968. Includes index.

This book is a translation of the full text of the so-called Shatalin plan which was named after a working group, headed by S. Shatalin, that met between August 2 and August 31, 1990. After an introductory summary, the core of the report is split into five parts. Part one is the general concept of the program for the transition to a market economy. Part two describes the basic blocks of the transition program, devaluation and development of competition, finance, and pricing. The labor market and the shadow economy are both covered. Part three is concerned with structural policy and organization. Part four describes the legislative and organizational support for economic reform. Part five is a supplement consisting primarily of tables.

Agriculture

241. Chaianov, Aleksandr Vasilevich, **A.V. Chayanov on the Theory of Peasant Economy**, edited by Daniel Thorner, Basile Kerblay, and R.E.F. Smith; with a foreword by Theodore Shanin. Madison, Wis.: The University of Wisconsin Press, 1986. ISBN: 0299105741. Includes index.

Chaianov's works "On the Theory of Non-Capitalist Economic Systems" and "Peasant Farm Organization" are presented here in translation. Chaianov's theories have a direct bearing on understanding not only the Russian peasant family economy, but also any developing agricultural society. Three major questions face both: 1. How can a poor rural society be transformed to eliminate the misery of the people; 2. How can you get the peasants to modernize their agricultural and farming technique; and 3. How can the transformation and modernization be carried out to aid the development of the national economy? Chaianov's message is prefaced by three essays. The first, by T. Shanin, discusses Chaianov in relation to contemporary development theory. The second, by B. Kerblay, examines Chaianov's concept of the peasant economy. The third, by B. Kerblay, presents Chaianov's life, career, and works.

242. **Soviet Agriculture: Comparative Perspectives**, edited by Kenneth R. Gray. 1st ed. Ames: Iowa State University Press, 1990. xiii, 284 p. *A Special Study of the Kennan Institute for Advanced Russian Studies, Woodrow Wilson International Center for Scholars*, ISBN: 0813804884. Includes bibliographical references and index.

The fourteen essays in this volume are divided into two sections: 1) organization and performance of Soviet agriculture, and 2) borrowing from foreign agricultural systems. Part one focuses on such topics as comparative agricultural trends, agricultural growth and development, food imbalances, agricultural policy and pricing under Gorbachev, rural housing, and dry land farming and soil conservation. Section two covers such topics as technical information concerning agriculture, the Bulgarian experience for centrally planned agriculture, private agriculture in socialist countries, and lessons from Hungarian and Chinese agriculture.

243. **Perestroika in the Countryside: Agricultural Reform in the Gorbachev Era**. Armonk, N.Y.: M.E. Sharpe, 1990. xiii, 135 p. ISBN: 0873327675.

This collection of seven essays examines the failure of Soviet agriculture to feed its people adequately. There is inadequate production, an inefficient and wasteful distribution system, and partly as a result of these two, a woefully unbalanced diet, which lacks sufficient milk, meat, eggs, vegetables, and fruit. These problems can all be traced, the authors believe, to the hierarchical command system that tells farmers what and how much to produce. Several aspects of the problem are analyzed. A historical perspective, comparing Gorbachev's and Stolypin's policies, is given. Various types of reform measures are discussed, including farm finances, equity, family and lease contracts, and agricultural trade liberalization. A final essay examined Hungarian agricultural reform for the lessons that it may give to Soviet agriculture.

Industry, Management, and Manufacturing

244. Beissinger, Mark R., **Scientific Management, Socialist Discipline, and Soviet Power**. Cambridge, Mass.: Harvard University Press, 1988. viii, 363 p. *Russian Center Studies*, v. 84. ISBN: 0674794907. Includes bibliographical references and index.

Maintaining that in communist systems central planning is the basic principle of social organization within society, Beissinger analyzes one political aspect of central planning — overbureaucratization. He examines how it has affected the evolution of national politics in the Soviet-style systems and how bureaucrats try to assert control over far-flung activities of society. The main danger of overbureaucratization is rigidity. Two strategies used by Soviet leaders to respond to organizational rigidity are scientific management, and discipline by coercion. The first four of his eight chapters are devoted to these administrative strategies to overcome rigidity from the revolution to the death of Stalin. The final four chapters cover the period from the death of Stalin to the mid-1980s. He ends with a comparison of Soviet patterns with analogous phenomena in other communist countries. Reviews: *Slavic Review* 49:3:471-72 (Fall 1990). *Political Science Quarterly* 104:4:732-34 (Winter 1989-90).

245. Berliner, Joseph S., **Soviet Industry from Stalin to Gorbachev: Studies in Management and Technological Progress**. Ithaca, N.Y.: Cornell University Press, 1988. xi, 306 p. *Studies in Soviet History and Society*, ISBN: 0801421705. Includes index.

Berliner's essays, written between 1950 and 1987, are collected into two sections, the management of enterprise and technological progress. In the first he covers subjects such as monetary planning, informal organization of the firm, and a comparison of US and Soviet managerial incentives and decision making. In section two, he explores such topics as statistics, efficiency, bureaucratic conservatism and creativity, and aspects of technological progress.

246. Chung, Han-ku, **Interest Representation in Soviet Policymaking: A Case Study of a West Siberian Energy Coalition**, with foreword by Peter Reddaway. Boulder, CO: Westview Press, 1987. xvii, 192 p. *Westview Special Studies on the Soviet Union & Eastern Europe*, ISBN: 0813373174. Includes index and bibliography (p. 177-188).

This is a case study of pressure group politics in Soviet policy formation. Dr. Chung's focus is on a policy coalition in the West Siberian oil fields. The coalition was composed of petroleum specialists, local Party officials, and government officials associated with the West Siberian region. This coalition gained Politburo backing of its views of the current priorities on energy development. Reviews: *Russian Review* 48:4:438-40 (October 1989). *Canadian-American Slavic Studies* 22:1:99-101 (Spring 1989).

247. Ioffe, O. S., and Peter B. Maggs, **The Soviet Economic System: A Legal Analysis**. Boulder, CO: Westview Press, 1987. ix, 326 p. *Westview Special Studies on the*

Soviet Union and Eastern Europe, ISBN: 0813372224. Includes bibliographies and index.

Ioffe and Maggs provide a comprehensive analysis of the Soviet economic system from a legal perspective. In discussing the Soviet theory of legal regulation of economic activity and the formal structure of economic legislation, the authors maintain that the Soviet regulatory system is characterized by two contradictory tendencies: reform and retreat from reform. They also examine labor law and the legal aspects of technology transfer. They emphasize the way economic legislation is developed and applied in practice. Reviews: *Texas International Law Journal* 23:3:521-22 (Summer 1988). *Canadian Slavonic Papers* 30:2:273-75 (June 1988). *Soviet Union* 14:3:368-69 (1987).

248. **The Great Market Debate in Soviet Economics: An Anthology,** edited by Anthony Jones and William Moskoff. Armonk, NY: M.E. Sharpe, 1991. xix, 408 p. *USSR in Transition,* ISBN: 087332868X, 0873328698 (pbk.). Includes bibliographical references and index.

This anthology of translated articles originally appeared in the translation journal *Problems of Economics.* Their intent is to try to find a way back to the market economy. Indeed, the debates that took place at the end of the 1980s and 1990 were reminiscent of the great industrialization debates of the 1920s. At that time, as now, the concern is how to catch up with the industrialized countries. The debate centers on two questions. First, what form should market institutions take? Second, what are the most effective strategies for reaching the goals specified? Included are excerpts from the actual texts of the Ryzhkov plan, the Shatalin plan, and the compromise Gorbachev plan.

249. Rumer, Boris Z., **Soviet Steel: The Challenge of Industrial Modernization in the USSR.** Ithaca: Cornell University Press, 1989. viii, 251 p. *Studies in Soviet History and Society,* ISBN: 0801420776. Includes index.

Rumer's aim is "to present several tightly argued and closely focused analyses of these problems most pertinent to an allocation of shortfalls in Soviet steel production." (p. 5) It covers the dynamics and peculiarities of steel consumption, qualitative achievements of Soviet steel production, descriptive features of Soviet steel plants, capacity utilization, iron-ore resources, and investment.

250. ZumBrunnen, Craig, and Jeffrey P. Osleeb, **The Soviet Iron and Steel Industry.** Totowa, NJ: Rowman and Allanheld Publishers, 1986. xvii, 237 p. ISBN: 0865981582. Includes index and bibliography (p. 213-221).

The authors have developed a "highly spatially disaggregated non-linear dynamic model" of the Soviet iron and steel industry. Their work is presented in five chapters. In chapter one they provide a background for the study and explain the nature of their investigation. Chapter two presents the SISEM (Soviet Iron and Steel Evaluation Model). Chapter three examines data availability, limitations and assumptions. Chapter four gives the results in terms of production and flow patterns. Chapter five contains a summary and conclusions.

Labor and Trade Unions

251. Arnot, Bob, **Controlling Soviet Labour: Experimental Change from Brezhnev to Gorbachev.** Basingstoke: Macmillan, 1988. xv, 305 p. ISBN: 0333434021. Includes indexes and bibliography (p. 274-295).

Experiments in labor policy and planning preceded the Gorbachev reforms. Arnot explains why these experiments were necessary and he analyzes several of them focusing on the Shchekivo experiment. In doing so he points out how these are illustrative of the distinctive nature of the Soviet political economy. Part One deals with the social relations of production and general economic problems in the USSR and part two with experimental initiatives.

252. Filtzer, D. A., **Soviet Workers and Stalinist Industrialization: The Formation of Modern Soviet Production Relations 1928-1941**. London: Pluto, 1986. vi, 338 p. ISBN: 0745301576. Includes index and bibliography (p. 316-322).

The rapidly changing position of Soviet workers during the first three five-year plans is the topic of Filtzer's book. It is not a "comprehensive account of working-class work, but focuses on the major historical determinants of the modern system of Soviet production relations." (p. 2) Part one covers the New Economic Policy, forced industrialization and the contradictions of Stalinist industrialization. Part two deals with the control over the labor process between 1933 and 1941, Stakhanovism, managerial concessions over wages and norms, and responses to the labor laws of December 1938 and June 1940. Reviews: *Contemporary Sociology* 16:4:495-97 (July 1987). *Slavic Review* 46:2:308-9 (Summer 1987). *Canadian Slavonic Papers* 29:2-3:323-24 (June-September 1987).

253. **Labour and Employment in the USSR**, edited by David Lane. New York: New York University Press, 1986. viii, 280 p. ISBN: 0814750192. Includes bibliographies and index.

In these essays, originally presented at a conference at the University of Birmingham in 1984, employment is considered from the perspective of history, sociology, economics, and politics. They reflect various ideological perspectives. Arranged in four parts, they cover historical background, the economics of full employment, socio-economic problems, and labor and the law. Review: *Slavic Review* 46:1:144-45 (Spring 1987).

254. Teague, Elizabeth, **Solidarity and the Soviet Worker: The Impact of the Polish events of 1980 on Soviet Internal Politics**. London: Croom Helm, 1988. 378 p. ISBN: 0709943504. Includes index and bibliography (p. 347-361).

This is a study of the impact the success of the Solidarity movement in Poland had on the Soviet worker. The author has focused primarily on policy relating to the work force in order to discover how the Soviet leadership viewed and managed the working class. Most source material dates from the pre-Gorbachev era. The author examines official trade unions in the USSR and past attempts to establish unofficial unions. She then turns to methods used to "ward off the 'Polish infection' " (p. 17) in the official trade unions, public opinion, and changes in the priorities of the five year plans. An examination of unofficial sources follows in order to indicate the effect of the Polish union movement on the general public. Next, the author turns to the tightening of internal policies and an examination of the ideological debates initiated by the events in Poland. The final chapter looks to the future under Gorbachev.

Unemployment

255. Porket, J. L., **Work, Employment, and Unemployment in the Soviet Union**. New York: St. Martin's Press, 1989. xv, 250 p. ISBN: 0312030959. Includes bibliographical references.

In theory at least, socialism was supposed to have abolished unemployment. This feat is just one of the ways in which socialism is supposed to be different from capitalism. Porket takes issue with this theoretical formulation. In part one he discusses different types of economic systems and unemployment in them. In part two he presents a history of the Soviet case, devoting individual chapters to the first decade of Soviet rule, the Stalin era, and the post-Stalin era. In the third and final part he analyzes the Soviet case and examines unregistered unemployment, overmanning, the use of educational qualifications, labor supply and demand, and prospects for the future.

Resources and Their Utilization

256. Bergensen, Helge Ole, et al., **Soviet Oil and Security Interests in the Barents Sea**. London: Pinter, 1987. xv, 144 p. ISBN: 086187689X. Includes bibliographies and index.
"The main purpose of this study is to analyze the prospects for Soviet petroleum production in the Barents Sea." (p. xiii) He examines Soviet oil exploration, petroleum and military strategy, and Soviet options in the Barents Sea.

257. Blanchard, Ian, **Russia's 'Age of Silver' Precious-Metal Production and Economic Growth in the Eighteenth Century**. London: Routledge, 1989. xvi, 431 p. ISBN: 041500831X.
Blanchard describes and analyzes Russia's world role in precious metal production and economic development in the 18th century. In part one the author covers international precious metal production and distribution form 1670-1770. Of specific interest here is the South and Central American mining crisis and the European producer's response to it. In part two he deals with Russian precious metal production, the money supply, and economic growth. In part three he concludes with a chapter on Russian silver and international specie markets in the 18th century. Review: *Journal of Economic History* 50:2:477 (June 1990).

258. Dellenbrant, Jan Ake, **The Soviet Regional Dilemma: Planning, People, and Natural Resources**, translated by Michel Vale. Originally published in Swedish as Sovjetunionens regionala dilemma. Armonk, N.Y.: M.E. Sharpe, 1986. ix, 218 p. ISBN: 087332384X. Includes bibliography (p. 195-203).
In a previous study by the author, covering the period between 1956 to 1973, Dellenbrant demonstrated that absolute differences remained unchanged for the three regions of the USSR: Central Asia, Siberia, and European USSR. This present study is concerned with the broad spectrum of regional development, regional differences, and regional policy in the Soviet Union. The differences in labor resources, natural resources, and other factors present immense problems for the political leadership. In eight chapters covering the remaining years of Brezhnev's rule and Andropov's brief interregnum, the author succinctly poses the problem of regional development, expounds his theoretical premises, provides a systematic literature review of the subject using both Western and Soviet research, and then proceeds to describe and analyze internal debates, decisions, and policies and their outcomes, before providing a review summary of his study.

259. Gustafson, Thane, **Crisis Amid Plenty: The Politics of Soviet Energy Under Brezhnev and Gorbachev**. Princeton, NJ: Princeton University Press, 1989. xxv, 362 p. ISBN: 0691078351. Includes bibliographical references.
In analyzing Soviet energy policy under Brezhnev and Gorbachev, Gustafson begins his book with an introductory chapter on the Soviet energy crisis and the problem of reform. He then takes a long term view of the evolution of Soviet energy policy from 1970 to 1988, looks in more detail at the origins of the first Soviet oil crisis, 1970-1982, the second oil crisis, 1982-1988, the gas campaign 1970-1988, the intervention of domestic policy and import strategy, the slow move to conservation, and Soviet energy exports. In a concluding chapter, he explains the Soviet energy crisis in terms of the system and political leadership. Reviews: *Foreign Affairs* 69:4:191 (Fall 1990). *Current History* 89:549:333 (October 1990).

260. Jentleson, Bruce W., **Pipeline Politics: The Complex Political Economy of East-West Energy Trade**. Ithaca, N. Y.: Cornell University Press, 1986. 263 p. *Cornell Studies in Political Economy*, ISBN: 0801419239. Includes index and bibliography (p. 247-255).

The book's primary objective is to examine the question of whether and under what conditions the United States and its NATO allies should trade with the Soviet Union. In particular Jentleson focuses on East-West energy trade and its history. The author's work also seeks to answer two perennial questions of political science: what constitutes power and how is influence achieved? He devotes more than half of the book to the history of East-West energy trade and the remainder focusing on the debate over the Siberian natural gas pipeline and the interaction of politics and economics in East-West energy trade. Review: *Journal of American History* 74:3:1103-4 (December 1987).

261. Kelly, William J., Hugh L. Shaffer, and J. Kenneth Thompson, **Energy Research and Development in the USSR: Preparations for the Twenty-First Century.** Durham, NC: Duke University Press, 1986. xvi, 417 p. *Duke Press Policy Studies*, ISBN: 0822306042. Includes indexes and bibliography (p. 356-397).

This volume is not only addressed to the Western scientific community and those conversant with the technical details of energy research and development, but also to Sovietologists who are interested in international affairs. It "discusses energy research and development (R & D) efforts under way in the Soviet Union and attempts to provide the reader with an understanding of the major technical, economic, geographic, and social factors that are motivating, or at least, influencing Soviet R & D activities in the energy area." (p. xi).

262. Sagers, Matthew J., and Milford B. Green, **The Transportation of Soviet Energy Resources**. Totowa, NJ: Rowan & Littlefield, 1986. xvi, 177 p. ISBN: 0847675041. Includes indexes and bibliography (p. 154-166).

The size of energy resources alone do not allow a country to avoid energy problems. Efficient transportation of energy resources is also mandatory. "This monograph analyzes the transportation of Soviet energy resources. The purpose is to determine the general pattern of movement for each of the main forces of energy (gas, crude petroleum, refined products, coal, and electricity), to identify constraints in the transportation system that inhibit efficient flows, and to evaluate the prospects for future developments, based upon this analysis of the system." (p. xiii) Review: *Slavic Review* 46:2:319 (Summer 1987).

263. Schiffer, Jonathan R., **Soviet Regional Economic Policy: The East-West Debate Over Pacific Siberian Development**. Basingstoke: Macmillan in association with the Centre for Russian and East European Studies, University of Birmingham, 1989. 384 p. *Studies in Soviet History and Society*, ISBN: 0333459539. Includes index and bibliography (p. 340-345).

This monograph began as the author's doctoral dissertation, completed in 1986. In it he combines elements of economic geography, political sociology, political economy, and economic theory to examine and "analyze selected aspects of Soviet central governmental decision-making processes concerning spatial resource allocation and investment patterns." (p. 1) He first examines spatial resource allocation within its administrative and financial context. Then he highlights the debates over industrial location in general, using the ferrous metallurgy and chemical and petrochemical sectors as examples. He follows this with a review of the debates over machine building and metal working sector. Finally, he analyzes the varying interpretations and calculations of regional inequality. He concludes by placing the discussion in an international, geopolitical framework.

Business and Entrepreneurial Activity

264. Berliner, Joseph S., **Soviet Industry from Stalin to Gorbachev: Studies in Management and Technological Progress**. Ithaca, N. Y.: Cornell University Press, 1988. xi, 306 p. *Studies in Soviet History and Society*, ISBN: 0801421705. Includes index.

A collection of essays by economist Joseph Berliner spanning almost forty years of issues in Soviet economics. In his foreword Holland Hunter notes that each of those essays is relevant to understanding the economic changes taking place today in the Soviet Union. The subjects covered are certainly of interest, including military planning, business administration, managerial incentives, planning and management, international aspects of technological progress, the effects of bureaucratic conservatism on creativity, pricing policy and technological progress, and management from Stalin to Gorbachev. The effects of Gorbachev's changes on the system and the future of the system can be carefully reviewed in reading these essays.

265. Carvounis, Chris C., and Brinda Z. Carvounis, **U.S. Commercial Opportunities in the Soviet Union: Marketing, Production, and Strategic Planning Perspectives**. New York: Quorum Books, 1989. xii, 192 p. ISBN: 089930351X. Includes index and bibliography (p. 179-185).

This book is written for the American corporate executive. It tries to answer the question "What new commercial opportunities are now available to the firm by doing business with the Soviets?" (p. x) It examines an overview of opportunities and constraints, various aspects of trade, the environment and form of joint enterprises, and an analysis of debt, competition, and world systems. Review: *SAIS Review* 10:1:189-91 (Winter-Spring 1990).

266. Center on Transnational Corporations (United Nations), **Joint Ventures as a Form of International Economic Cooperation.** New York: United Nations, 1988. vi, 210 p. ISBN: 9211042941.

The material included here was originally presented at a seminar held in Moscow in March of 1988. It includes both papers and documents relating to specific characteristics of the Soviet economy and the lack of experience with international cooperative business relationships. Its aim is to assist those who wish to explore joint ventures in the USSR. Topics include negotiations for joint ventures, joint venture policies, arrangements between joint venture partners, and model guidelines for the preparation of joint venture project studies.

267. Christians, F. Wilhelm, **Paths to Russia: From War to Peace**, translation from the German by Joachim Neugroschel. New York: Macmillan, 1990. xv, 236 p. ISBN: 0025252410.

The account of a German banker's experiences in Russia. The author recounts the experiences of his recent trips and makes note of the effects his previous contact, as a German soldier in World War II, have had on him. He pleads for aid to Russia as a way of ensuring reform. The book contains a chronology of important dates.

268. **Red Multinationals or Red Herrings?: The Activities of Enterprises from Socialist Countries in the West**, edited by Geoffrey Hamilton. New York: St. Martin's Press, 1986. xi, 202 p. ISBN: 031266656X. Includes bibliographies and index.

Since the 1960s there has been a growing number of enterprises in Eastern bloc countries that have undertakings in the West and in developing countries. The essays in this book attempt to describe the nature and extent of these companies in order to determine whether they are multinational enterprises in the Western sense of the term. After an introduction that discusses the nature of multinationals, there follows several case studies of these enterprises in the United Kingdom, Ireland, Sweden, West Germany, Austria, and in developing countries. In concluding, suggestions for future research are offered. Review: *Orbis* 31: 1:154 (Spring 1987).

269. Kiser, John W., **Communist Entrepreneurs: Unknown Innovators in the Global Economy**. New York: F. Watts, 1989. x, 225 p. ISBN: 0531151107. Includes bibliographical references.

A discussion of the contributions of eleven entrepreneurs in the Soviet Union and Eastern Europe. They fall into two broad groups: inventors motivated by creativity, and reformers trying to change the system. The author uses their stories to develop four broader themes: 1) the challenge they represent to the stereotype of technological backwardness in communist countries; 2) the business opportunities for Westerners in the communist world; 3) the role of these entrepreneurs in perestroika; 4) the "commonality" of entrepreneurial behavior and political leadership. The book is topically arranged with discussions of computer use, chemical research, the effects of central planning, and welding techniques among many other diverse topics. A bibliography of English language sources is included. Review: *National Review* 42:1:48-49 (January 22, 1990).

270. Knight, Misha G., **How to Do Business with Russians: A Handbook and Guide for Western World Business People**. New York: Quorum Books, 1987. xiii, 311 p. ISBN: 0899302114. Includes index and bibliography (p. 301-306).

General information on a variety of problems relating to business transactions between Soviets and Westerners. A wide range of topics are covered including a general overview of the USSR's advertising practices. Part one discusses the way trade operates in the Soviet Union with discussions of business outlooks, setting up a business office in the USSR, trade fairs, contract negotiation, and Soviet customs. Part two deals with the structure of Soviet foreign trade operations and orders of a business transaction. Some of the topics covered include commercial letters, revision of prices, export license process, arbitration, and business conversations. Numerous figures and tables are provided.

271. McMillan, Carl H., **Multinationals from the Second World: Growth of Foreign Investment by Soviet and East European Enterprises**. New York: St. Martin's Press, 1987. xvi, 220 p. ISBN: 031255253x. Includes indexes and bibliography (p. 203-210).

A noted economist explores the role of COMECON foreign investments and COMECON enterprises in the West. Professor McMillan focuses on several issues: who and what are the enterprises that are being established; what challenges do they present to their host countries; could they undermine the national security of their host countries; and will direct investment abroad increase the power of the Soviet Union and East European countries. Although the countries involved claimed there was no profit motive in these enterprises, the author finds that to be their primary function. The volume is divided into three parts: introductory chapters: discussing broad policy issues, COMECON, and forms of organizations and foreign investment, investment decision making; discussion of investment in specific economic sectors: service sector, production facilities; and a final concluding chapter summarizing past policies and their implications for the future. Because of a lack of statistical data, the author relies on his own database for information, which is described in the appendix. There are numerous tables and an index of company names. Reviews: *Russian Review* 47:2:216-17 (April 1988). *Slavic Review* 47:1:142-44 (Spring 1988).

272. United Nations Centre on Transnational Corporations, **Joint Ventures as a Form of International Economic Cooperation.** New York: United Nations, 1988. vi, 210p. *"U.N. Pub. Sales"*, no. E.88.II.A.12. ISBN: 9211042941.

The material included here was originally presented at a seminar held in Moscow in March of 1988. It includes both papers and documents relating to specific characteristics of the Soviet economy and the lack of experience with international cooperative business relationships. Its aim is to assist those who wish to explore joint ventures in the U.S.S.R. Topics include negotiations for joint ventures, joint venture policies, arrangements between joint venture partners, and model guidelines for the preparation of joint venture project studies.

273. United Nations Conference on Trade and Development, Secretariat, **USSR, New Management Mechanism in Foreign Economic Relations.** New York: United Nations, 1988. ii, 22 p. ISBN: 9211122457.

A United Nations publication on their conference on trade and development, reflecting changes in the Soviet economic system. The information supplied, including statistics were provided by a consultant. Topics covered include perestroika in foreign economic relations, new mechanisms for foreign trade, joint ventures, and new trade policy instruments. A brief outline of the developing system in the USSR is included.

Finance and Credit

274. Newcity, Michael A., **Taxation in the Soviet Union.** New York: Praeger, 1986. xiii, 392 p. ISBN: 003056980. Includes index.

Newcity has prepared a detailed description and analysis of the Soviet tax system and the extent to which the Soviet system meets the requirements of Marxism with respect to taxation. After an overview of the Soviet tax system, he covers domestic taxation including taxation of enterprises, direct taxation of individuals, local taxes, and state duties. He then turns to taxation of foreign individuals and enterprises, the U.S.- U.S.S.R. Convention on Matters of Taxation, other tax agreements, and the dilemma of a Socialist system of taxation.

275. Pososhkov, Ivan Tikhonovich, **The Book of Poverty and Wealth**, edited and translated by A. P. Vlasto and L. R. Lewitter. London: Athlone, 1987. 440 p. ISBN: 0485112906. Includes bibliography (p. 401-430).

Pososhkov was an eyewitness to Peter the Great's Russia. This translation of his work on public finance is a classic. This English language edition is accompanied by an introductory essay and extensive notes in the text. Review: *Russian History* 17:1: 86-87 (Spring 1990).

276. Shelton, Judy, **The Coming Soviet Crash: Gorbachev's Desperate Pursuit of Credit in Western Financial Markets.** New York: Free Press, 1989. xviii, 246 p. ISBN: 002928581X. Includes index and bibliography (p. 225-238).

Shelton maintains that the main reason that the Soviets were seeking financial credits from the West in late 1988 was simply that they needed the money. Her case is made all the more convincing in light of the events occurring after December 1991. "One purpose of this book is to bring to light, by scrutinizing the statistical and accounting data published by the Soviet government, the real state of the Soviet domestic budget while tracing its impact on the internal financial system.... The other main purpose is to lay out the various ways in which Western financial capital is transferred to the Soviet economy." (p. xvii).

Dismantling of Command Economy

277. Geron, Leonard, **Soviet Foreign Economic Policy Under Perestroika**. New York: Council on Foreign Relations Press, 1990. x, 126 p. *Chatham House Papers*, ISBN: 0876090943. Includes bibliographical references (p. 81-95).
The development and changes in Soviet foreign economic policy are the subject of this volume. The author "scrutinizes the legislative and institutional basis for reform in order to determine whether reform will be taken to its logical conclusion—a break with the past command system and the introduction of a market economy." (back cover) The author examines Soviet domestic economic policy presenting statistical evidence for his conclusions. The presentation is thematic and includes several appendices with biographical information and statistical data. Review: *Current History* 90:558:346 (October 1991).

278. Kotkin, Stephen, **Steeltown, USSR: Soviet Society in the Gorbachev Era**. Berkeley, CA: University of California Press, 1991. xxx, 269 p. ISBN: 0520073533. Includes index.
Kotkin, an American historian of the Stalin era, initially went to Magnitogorsk in 1987 with the intention of studying the city's past during the Stalin era. He returned in 1988-89 in order to gather material for this book, the context of which covers 1985-1989. In interviews with many of the town's citizens and officials, he has produced a lively chronicle of Magnitogorsk life and its changes in the Gorbachev era. His book is divided into six chapters. In them he covers perestroika, glasnost, reformation of the party, the rise of informal groups, the effect of reforms in everyday life, elections, and the revival of historical memory. Reviews: *Foreign Affairs* 70:4:180 (Fall 1991). *Antioch Review* 49:4:607-09 (Fall 1991). *Orbis* 35:4:628 (Fall 1991).

279. **Soviet Conversion, 1991: Report and Recommendations of an International Working Group on Economic Demilitarization and Adjustment**, edited by John Tepper Marlin and Paul Grenier. New York: Council on Economic Priorities, 1991. xiii, 95 p. Includes index.
Conference proceedings from two projects, an academic conference and a business mission both held in late 1990. The subject is the conversion of a largely military economic system to peaceful uses. This is seen as one of the major problems in rebuilding the Soviet economy. The conference participants were both American and Soviet. This brief volume presents findings and recommendations along with the proceedings.

280. Winiecki, Jan, **Resistance to Change in the Soviet Economic System: A Property Rights Approach**. New York: Routledge, 1991. xvi, 111 p. ISBN: 0415042437. Includes bibliographical references (p.103-106) and index.
Winiecki analyzes the elements of resistance to change in the Soviet economic system using a property-rights approach. In chapter one he describes how apparatchiks and bureaucrats are the main economic beneficiaries of the status quo. Chapter two deals with rent dissipation at the enterprise level and its impact on reforms and change. Chapter three is concerned with industry as a prime rent-seeking area for apparatchiks and bureaucrats. In chapter four Winiecki explores what may seem like an irrational program of buyout proposal for bureaucrats and apparatchiks. Winiecki holds throughout to the thesis that economic change cannot go forward without a previous political change.

Foreign Economic Relations

281. **Joint Ventures in the USSR**. Moscow: Terra, 1991. 327, 39, 61, 9 p.
This reference work consists of four parts. Part one is a joint ventures listing and contains information about specific companies. Such information includes name, address, telephone, fax, telex numbers, director name, share capital, foreign and Soviet participants, and activities. Part two is an index of foreign participants; part three an index of Soviet participants; and part four an index of goods and services provided with a product-supplier cross reference.

282. Boguslavskii, M. M., and P. S. Smirnov, **The Reorganization of Soviet Foreign Trade: Legal Aspects**, edited and with a foreword by Serge L. Levitsky. Armonk, N.Y.: M.E. Sharpe, 1989. xiii, 210 p. ISBN: 0873325087. Includes bibliographical notations.
The material presented here "is a pragmatic, matter-of-fact account of the changes now being introduced in the USSR in doing business abroad and in managing both the foreign economic relations and the changes themselves." (p. xiii) The work covers in detail such topics as recent normative acts affecting foreign economic relations, the organization and legal forms of foreign economic relations, enterprises and their foreign trade companies, legal forms of relations between industry and foreign trade, and joint enterprises.

283. **The Post-containment Handbook: Key Issues in U.S.-Soviet Economic Relations**, edited by Robert Cullen. Boulder, CO: Westview Press, 1990. xii, 227 p. ISBN: 0813379784.
With a change in U.S. policy to assist the Soviet Union in entering the world economy comes the necessity of changing a whole series of laws, regulations and bureaucratic priorities that were aimed to inhibit such an integration. The present volume includes papers relating to the issues of banking and credit, COCOM, détente and trade, economic cooperation and the Helsinki process, information control, and documents, both American and Soviet, that relate to these topics.

284. Graziani, Giovanni, **Gorbachev's Economic Strategy in the Third World**. New York: Praeger, "Published with the Center for Strategic and International Studies, Washington, DC," 1990. xx, 116 p. *Washington Papers, 0278-937X*, v. 142. ISBN: 0275935388, 0275935396 (pbk.). Includes bibliographical references (p. 101-109).
"This volume contains Giovanni Graziani's interpretations of Mikhail Gorbachev's emerging new economic policy toward the Third World—an analysis backed by well-documented, sophisticated statistical analysis of Soviet economic assistance and trade." (p. xvii) Among the topics covered are the economics of Soviet policy in the Third World, Soviet economic assistance to developing countries, the geographical orientation of trade, the commodity composition of trade, trade balances and payment arrangements, new forms of economic cooperation, and obstacles and prospects for future Soviet strategy.

285. Hough, Jerry F., **Opening Up the Soviet Economy**. Washington, DC: Brookings Institution, 1988. 100 p. ISBN: 0815737475. Includes bibliographies and index.
Hough's purpose is to explore the foreign policy implications of economic reform. Responding to M. Gorbachev's statement made in 1985 that foreign policy is a continuation of domestic policy, he poses two major questions. First, how does Soviet foreign policy fit into Gorbachev's strategy of overcoming resistance to domestic reform? Second, what are imperatives of foreign policy form an economic point of view? The book consists of five chapters covering the economic and political contexts of reform, the strategies of reform,

foreign economic policy, including joint ventures, and suggested policy choices for the United States, encompassing business, societal, and government choices.

286. Hunter, David William, **Western Trade Pressure on the Soviet Union: An Interdependence Perspective on Sanctions**. New York: St. Martin's Press, 1991. xii, 163 p. ISBN: 0312062168. Includes bibliographical references (p. 139-153) and index.

Hunter has two objectives in this book. The first is "to analyze U.S. and Western European sanctions against the Soviet Union from an interdependence perspective." (p. 11) The second is to "provide a conceptual framework for distinguishing between the different types of sanctions available to sanctioning states and explain how the relative deprivation of a target state can be manipulated." (p. 11).

287. **Perestroika and East-West Economic Relations: Prospects for the 1990's**, edited by Michael Kraus and Ronald D. Liebowitz. New York: New York University Press, 1990. x, 356 p. *Geonomics Institute for International Economic Advancement Series*, ISBN: 0814746047. Includes index.

"Soviet reform policies and objectives, especially in the foreign economic sector, the questions they raise, their East-West implications, and the prospects for a major breakthrough in East-West economic relations form the focus of this volume." (p. 2) The essays printed here were originally presented in 1988 at a conference sponsored by the Geonomics Institute for International Economic Advancement and ISKAN (the Institute for the Study of the U.S.A. and Canada). Soviet and American authors focus on the political context of reform that influences the economic agenda, Soviet economic perestroika, the impact of perestroika on the CMEA, and East-West relations within a broad framework.

288. Mehrotra, Santosh K., **India and the Soviet Union: Trade and Technology Transfer**. Cambridge, England: Cambridge University Press, 1990. xvi, 242 p. *Soviet and East European Studies*, no. 73. ISBN: 0521362024. Includes index and bibliographical references (p. 226-235).

Mehrotra has conducted an analysis of economic relations between an industrialized planned economy and a developing market economy. His study has three objectives. The first is "to analyze Soviet economic interests in LDCs in general and India in particular." (p. 1) The second is to go beyond the stress in aid to India and focus more carefully on technology transfer. The third and final objective is to fill a gap in the literature "by examining Indo-Soviet trade between 1920 and 1985." (p. 2).

289. **Soviet-American Horizons on the Pacific**, edited by John J. Stephan and V.P. Chichkanov. Honolulu: University of Hawaii Press, 1986. xxii, 181 p. ISBN: 0824810201. Includes bibliographies and index.

These essays, written by Russians and Americans, proceed from the assumption that the United States, the Soviet Union and the Pacific Basin countries "have an opportunity to build mutually beneficial ties across the Pacific, ties based on geographical propinquity, a legacy of trade and cooperation, and contemporary economic complementarities."(p. xiii) The contributed essays explore such topics as the salient geographical features of the American Far West and Soviet Far East, the development of Soviet and American economic interests in the region, what are current economic trends in the region, how will these trends affect growth, and other related questions. Reviews: *Pacific Affairs* 60:1:95-96 (Spring 1987). *Slavic Review* 46:2:313 (Summer 1987).

290. **Soviet Foreign Economic Policy and International Security**, edited by Eric Stubbs. Armonk, N.Y.: M.E. Sharpe, 1991. xix 215 p. ISBN: 0873326660. Includes bibliographical references and index.

In 1988 the Center of Foreign Policy Development at Brown University sponsored a conference "to examine the economic and national security implications of U.S.-Soviet commercial relations." (p. ix) The seven essays presented here are arranged in three sections. Section 1 provides a historical overview of U.S. trade policy towards the Soviet Union. Section 2 delineates the economic issues such as new opportunities and concerns for East-West commercial relations, Soviet trade mechanisms and Soviet participation in International Economic Institutions. Section three focuses on export controls and technology transfer including options for policy reform, and a case study of East- West trade control joint research efforts.

EDUCATION AND CULTURE

General Studies

291. Kassow, Samuel D., **Students, Professors, and the State in Tsarist Russia**. Berkeley: University of California Press, 1989. xii, 438 p. ISBN: 05250057600. Includes index and bibliography (p. 417-427).

"This book is about government, professors, and students in Russia from 1899 until the Revolution of 1917. Most of the story will center on the student movement and its crucial role in defining the position of the universities in tsarist Russia." (p. 1) Kassow also includes two statistical appendices on university students and the professoriate. Reviews: *Social Science Quarterly* 17:4:872-73 (December 1990). *Canadian Slavonic Papers* 31:1:77-78 (March 1990).

292. Pearson, Landon, **Children of Glasnost: Growing Up Soviet**. Seattle: University of Washington Press, 1990. xv, 505 p. ISBN: 0295970901. Includes bibliographical references (p. 472-496) and index.

A study of the effects the changes of glasnost are having on the children of the Soviet Union. The book is divided into five sections which taken together give a well rounded description of Soviet children. Part one examines the historical, political, and ideological context in which a Soviet child grows up. Part Two focuses on the formative years and the daily circumstances of children in the USSR. Part Three analyzes the provisions the Soviet state has made for children with special needs. Part Four looks at the physical culture of children. The final section examines education for Soviet youth. The author, a Canadian educator and wife of the Canadian ambassador to the USSR, draws on her experience with children while living in the Soviet Union.

293. Richmond, Yale, **U.S.-Soviet Cultural Exchanges, 1958-1986: Who Wins?**, with foreword by Marshall D. Shulman. Boulder, CO: Westview Press, 1987. xvi, 170 p. *Westview Special Studies on the Soviet Union and Eastern Europe*, ISBN: 0813372755. Includes index and bibliography (p. 161-63).

An expanded and revised version of the author's 1984 publication. "This study, written for the general public as well as the foreign affairs specialist, is an attempt to explain how cultural exchanges with the Soviet Union began in the late 1950s, how they have evolved since their inception, and how they are conducted today." (p. xiii) The author has a strong belief in the value of cultural exchanges. He examines various aspects of cultural exchanges: performing arts, academia, public diplomacy, science and technology, sports and tourism.

The author also looks at U.S. evaluative procedures for Soviet proposals. The two appendixes include documents on U.S.-U.S.S.R. exchange agreements.

294. Seregny, Scott Joseph, **Russian Teachers and Peasant Revolution: The Politics of Education in 1905.** Bloomington, Ind.: Indiana University Press, 1988. x, 292 p. *Indiana-Michigan Series in Russian and East European Studies*, ISBN: 025335031X. Includes index and bibliography (p. 271-284).

Seregny characterizes this book as "a case study of the rise of a key profession in a traditional political culture and society undergoing a rapid transformation." (p. 7) In other words, he examines a professional group that was instrumental in rural modernization. In spite of the stereotype as a shy, ineffectual group, Seregny shows how these "zemstvo rabbits" emerged at the vanguard of a movement to mobilize the teachers profession. The All-Russian Teachers' Union was the result. The author examines teachers' gatherings and education for the decade prior to 1905, the emergence of a teacher's movement, teachers and politics on the eve of 1905, their role in revolutionary politics in the 1905 revolution, the aftermath and the ensuing reaction and its consequences for 1906-1914. Reviews: *Russian History* 17:1:93-95 (Spring 1990). *American Historical Review* 95:5:1589-90 (December 1990). *Russian Review* 49:3:345-346 (July 1990). *Canadian Slavonic Papers* 32:1:79-80 (March 1990). *Canadian-American Slavic Studies* 24:4:469-71 (Winter 1990).

295. **Soviet Politics and Education**, edited by Frank M. Sorrentino and Frances R. Curcio. Lanham, MD: University Press of America, 1986. vii, 417 p. ISBN: 0819151238. Includes bibliographies.

Sorrentino has assembled a group of readings on Soviet education and politics. It includes previously published articles and essays by political theorists, government officials, journalists, political scientists, and educators. The essays are arranged in four sections, preceded by an introductory essay by Sorrentino and Curcio. The essays deal with Soviet ideology, Soviet politics and culture, Soviet educational philosophy, and current practice and curricular emphasis in Soviet schools. Review: *Educational Studies* 18:4:571-75 (Winter 1987).

296. **The Red Pencil: Artists, Scholars, and Censors in the USSR**, edited by Marianna Tax Choldin and Maurice Friedberg; Russian portions translated by Maurice Friedberg and Barbara Dash. Boston: Unwin Hyman, 1989. xvii, 240 p. ISBN: 0044452039. Includes bibliography (p. 215-229) and index.

In May of 1983 a conference on "Soviet Direction of Creative and Intellectual Activity" was held at the Kennan Institute of Advanced Russian Studies in Washington, DC The essays, written by a dozen Western and Soviet émigré writers, are a result of this gathering. The authors' report on their first hand experiences with the Soviet system of censorship and information control. The contributions are arranged in four parts: Soviet censorship, the scientist's laboratory, literature and intellectual life, and the mass media. Each part is followed by a summary of the discussion of the papers presented. An annotated bibliography on the wide range of topics involving censorship is also included.

Mass Communications

297. **Culture and the Media in the USSR Today**, edited by Julian Grabby and Geoffrey Hosking. New York: St. Martin's Press, 1989. 168 p. ISBN: 0312034571. Includes bibliographical references.

A set of papers coming out of a "background briefing" held in 1988 at the School of Slavonic and East European Studies, University of London. There is no unifying theme to the papers. Various areas of the media are discussed including television, the press, the cinema, music, the theater, and the literary press. All essays do focus on the effects of glasnost and the media. Review: *Soviet Union-Union-Sovietique* 17:3:309-12 (1990).

298. McNair, Brian, **Images of the Enemy: Reporting the New Cold War**. London: Routledge, 1988. 216 p. ISBN: 0415006457. Includes index and bibliography (p. 210-212).

This volume reviews the treatment of the Soviet Union in the British media, particularly television news. The author demonstrates the effect biases have on the portrayal of events in the USSR; in perpetuating biases against the Soviets even in the age of glasnost. To do this, the author examines some specific cases: Chernobyl and the Korean Airlines disaster. The author stresses the effects of Gorbachev's policies on Western media coverage in his analysis. The author does see some evidence of change as the Soviet media becomes more open. Nevertheless, he concludes that the negative treatment of the Soviet Union in the Western media will persist. He does note that those who have aspired to objective coverage will have better raw material in the future.

299. Otto, Robert, **Publishing for the People: The Firm Posrednik, 1885-1905**. New York: Garland Pub., 1987. 251 p. *Modern European History*, ISBN: 082080602. Includes bibliographical references (p. 236-251).

"Posrednik, founded in 1884 through the efforts of Lev Tolstoi's disciple Vladimir Chertkov, was the first intelligent publishing firm to reach its intended audience in a significant fashion. This study treats the ideas behind the cause of publishing for the people; Posrednik's predecessors and why they failed; the founding of the firm; the reasons for the successful distribution of its publication; how the firm attempted to attract collaborators; the literature it produced; and, finally, the reaction its publications produced among people, the culturists at large, and the members of the tsarist regime." (p. 3-4) Review: *Slavic Review* 49:4:658-59 (Winter 1990).

300. Pozner, Vladimir, **Parting With Illusions**, with introduction by Brian Kahn. New York: Atlantic Monthly Press, 1990. 234 p. ISBN: 08711332877. Includes index.

Pozner, a Russian journalist, gives his views on Russian culture, perestroika, and other timely topics. Pozner was born in Paris, lived in America as a child, and then went to the Soviet Union where he became a highly respected journalist. His views are presented in the context of his fascinating biography.

301. Remington, Thomas F., **The Truth of Authority: Ideology and Communication in the Soviet Union**. Pittsburgh, PA: University of Pittsburgh Press, 1988. xv, 255 p. *Series in Russian and East European Studies*, no. 9. ISBN: 0822935902. Includes index and bibliography (p. 211-250).

After an introductory chapter describing the structure of ideology and communications, Remington then focuses on particular elements of oral propaganda and media and the groups that control them. Included here is a discussion of Aktiv and apparat political education, planning the news, party-media relations, and politics and professionalism in Soviet journalism. The final chapter concentrates "on the target of ideological work, the Soviet populace itself, and reviews existing data about how people use channels of information to meet their particular needs for information and opinion." (p. xiv) Reviews: *Journal of Communication* 40:1:175-77 (1990). *Slavic Review* 49:3:470-71 (Fall 1990).

302. Ruud, Charles A., **Russian Entrepreneurs**. Buffalo: McGill-Queen's University Press, 1990. x, 270 p. ISBN: 0773507736. Includes bibliographical references (p. 254-261) and index.

I.D. Sytin was an unlettered villager who became the premier publisher of the Russian empire. "This book interweaves the history of Sytin as a force for change with the histories of the two institutions that gave him his influence: his publishing house, Sytin and Co., and his Moscow daily *Russian Word*." (p. 3).

303. Smith, Ted J., **Moscow Meets Main Street: Changing Journalistic Values and the Growing Soviet Presence on American Television**, with an introduction by John Corry. Washington, DC: Media Institute, 1988. vi, 130 p. *Media in Society Series*, ISBN: 0937790370.

A discussion of the effects of the increasing visibility of Soviet journalists on American television. "Professor Ted J. Smith III argues that this trend is not merely a reflection of questionable news judgement — it is a manifestation of a change in journalistic values occasioned by the 'intellectualization' of elite journalists." (back cover) The author presents this view of television propaganda and how the "Sovietization" of American television is coming to pass. He uses the coverage of KAL flight 007 as an example of the effects of the "intellectualization of elite journalists."

304. Wilhelm, Donald, **Global Communications and Political Power**. New Brunswick (USA): Transaction Publishers, 1990. xiv, 172 p. ISBN: 0887383548. Includes bibliographical references (p. 155-166) and index.

The role of communication in the political reforms in Russia is examined in this book. The author first gives an overview of perestroika and discusses the difficulties of reforms. He then looks at the spread of the use of satellites for communication and their effect on cultural change. Changes in space programming in Russia and the strengthening of cross-cultural ties as well as the effects of mass communication on the political process are also discussed.

Special Studies and Physical Education

305. Black, Joseph Lawrence, **G. F. Muller and the Imperial Russian Academy**. Kingston: McGill-Queens University Press, 1986. xi, 290 p. ISBN: 0773505539. Includes index and bibliography (p. 267-279).

The first full length English language biography of G. F. Muller. This volume covers his whole life from his early years in Leipzig through his move to Russia to become one of the first members of the Imperial Academy. His many intellectual roles as historiographer, geographer, journalist, and explorer are all traced in this study. Since Muller was at the Academy for its first 58 years, a history of his career is in many ways also a history of that institution. The volume is chronologically arranged around Muller's career since the Russians and the Soviets have viewed Muller somewhat ambiguously, it remained for a more objective observer to analyze his role. Reviews: *Canadian Journal of History* 22:3:407-08 (December 1987). *Canadian Slavonic Papers* 29:2-3:296-97 (June-September 1987). *Slavic Review* 46:1:156 (Spring 1987).

306. Eklof, Ben, **Russian Peasant Schools: Officialdom, Village Culture, and Popular Pedagogy, 1864-1914**. Berkeley: University of California Press, 1986. xv, 652 p. ISBN: 0520051718. Includes index and bibliography (p. 591-627).

What was the response of the village community to the pressures of rapid social and economic change? This is the larger question that frames Eklof's study. He has a two-pronged focus: the first is the expansion and results of mass schooling. He investigates such questions as who sponsored education, providing the funding, labor, and support. What were the stages in the creation and evolution of schools? How did the peasants participate? What does their participation say about their view of the world? How was control exerted over rural schools? How was the conflict between secular and religious schools resolved? His second concern is what was the effect of schooling on village life? The book has four parts. The first examines institutions and sponsors; the second Russian teachers, the outsiders in the villages; the third peasant pedagogy and the emergence of a school system; and the fourth, the results of schooling. Reviews: *Agricultural History* 61:4:98-100 (Fall 1987). *Slavic Review* 46:3-4:605-6 (Fall-Winter 1987).

307. **In the Nation's Image: Civic Education in Japan, the Soviet Union, the United States, France, and Britain,** edited by Edgar B. Gumbert. Atlanta, Ga.: Center for Cross-Cultural Education, College of Education, Georgia State University, 1987. iii, 120 p. *Center for Cross-National Education Lecture Series,* vol. 6. ISBN: 0884062031 (pbk.). Includes bibliographies.

The authors of the essays in this volume address the question: "What and how do people in selected nations learn about their own nation and culture?" Explicit in their answers are, "What people think about citizenship and civic virtue; how they create and sustain feelings of self-awareness and common identity; and how they produce and reproduce their nation's distinctive political and cultural characteristics." (p. 3).

GEOGRAPHY AND DEMOGRAPHY

308. Kozlov, Viktor Ivanovich, **The Peoples of the Soviet Union,** introduced by Michael Kywkin and translated by Pauline Tiffen. London: Hutchinson, 1988. xi, 262 p. *Second World,* ISBN: 0253343569. Includes bibliography (p. 240-253).

Kozlov has based the data for this book on Soviet censuses and other official sources. It "presents an ethno-demographic and ethno-geographic survey of the population of the USSR." (p. 11) The five chapters include history and ethnic geography, geography and urbanization, demography and ethnic populations, ethnography and processes of ethnic transformation, and a conclusion, An appendix examines ethno-linguistic composition and ethnic distribution in 1897. Reviews: *Russian Review* 49:2:235-37 (April 1990). *American Political Science Review* 83:3:1058-59 (September 1989). *American Anthropology* 91:2:504-05 (June 1989). *Canadian Slavonic Papers* 30:4:520-21 (December 1989).

GOVERNMENT AND STATE

Bibliographies

309. Kavass, Igor I., **Soviet Law in English: Research Guide and Bibliography, 1970-1987.** Buffalo, NY: Willam S. Hein, 1988. vii, 653 p. ISBN: 0899416314.

A bibliographic handbook on Soviet legal sources in English. The work is intended for the specialist as well as the beginner with a lengthy section on "Researching Soviet Law" for the latter. The bulk of the volume is a subject bibliography with a shorter annotated bibliography by author. The work is selective but seems quite inclusive. The only difficulty is the lack of a general index although there is a checklist of authors. Reviews: *Slavic Review* 49:3:466-67 (Fall 1990). *Russian Review* 48:3:337- 38 (July 1989).

General Studies

310. **The Soviet Union: Opposing Viewpoints,** edited by Neal Bernards, et al. St. Paul, Minn.: Greenhaven Press, 1987. 251 p. *Opposing Viewpoints,* ISBN: 089908429X. Includes index and bibliography (p. 244-246).

Collection of articles, position papers, essays from numerous authors on five questions: 1) Does the Soviet Union seek world domination? 2) Does the Soviet Union guarantee human rights? 3) How strong is the Soviet economy? 4) What is the Soviet Union's role in Eastern Europe? 5) Is glasnost genuine? Papers within each section are purposefully arranged to represent different points of view. Discussion questions are provided at the end of each section. The purpose is to present a broad spectrum of opinion on each topic. Aimed at the general reader, the volume includes a list of organizations that might be of interest in pursuing various topics as well as a list of books and a selected list of periodicals with acquisition information.

311. Black, Cyril Edwin, **Understanding Soviet Politics: The Perspective of Russian History.** Boulder, CO: Westview Press, 1986. xi, 308 p. ISBN: 0813304024. Includes index.

In this collection of previously published essays, Black addresses three broad questions. In part one (ch. 1-4) he examines the discontinuities between the Russian Empire and the Soviet Union. In part two (ch. 5-8) he explores various aspects of modernization, that is the ways the prerevolutionary heritage of institutions and values has been adopted and adapted to carry out goals of political development, economic growth and social integration. In part three (ch. 9-12) he focuses on how relations between Russia/Soviet Union have been affected by modernization. A brief introductory essay introduces each part. Reviews: *Soviet Union* 14:1:158-50 (1987). *Slavic Review* 48:2: 309-10 (Summer 1989).

312. Bruchis, Michael, **The USSR, Language and Realities: Nations, Leaders, and Scholars.** New York: East European Monographs, 1988. iii, 393 p. *East European Monographs,* no. 250. ISBN: 088033147X. Includes bibliographies.

A scholarly study of problems facing nationalities in the Soviet Union. The author feels that Russification and denationalization have not only not diminished but are actually on the rise under Gorbachev. The volume is divided into four parts. The first deals with nationality policy as expressed in the Soviet constitution and by the Communist Party. Part two discusses the mechanisms that have been used to enforce the policy. The third part gives a specific example of the policy in Moldavia, and how the policy has manifestations in popular writings such as those of Ion Druta. The book closes with a review of the effects of the policy on nationalities. Review: *American Political Science Review* 84:2:683-84 (June 1990).

313. Campeanu, Pavel, **Exit: Toward Post-Stalinism.** Armonk, N.Y.: M.E. Sharpe, 1990. xiii, 169 p. ISBN: 0873325877. Includes bibliographical references (p. 157-162) and index.

The author analyzes the effects of destalinization on power in the Soviet bloc. The author believes that the very nature of power, formerly centralized in those that controlled the means of production, will change as other economic and social changes come into play. The book is organized around the concept of the "global regulator"—those forces that control power that were developed by Stalin. The author describes the development of this regulator, how it emerges as a global force, the social needs that create it, and how in its role as initiator of change it is destroying itself.

314. Carter, Stephen, **Russian Nationalism: Yesterday, Today, and Tomorrow**. New York: St. Martin's Press, 1990. 175 p. ISBN: 0312047649. Includes bibliographical references and index.

Rather than focus on Soviet nationalities policy, as many other Sovietologists have done, Carter examines the phenomenon of Russian nationalism and the effect it has on Soviet politics, especially in the late 1980s, an age of declining ideology. His study is historical, political, and sociological. He examines Russian nationalism through several distinct periods (origins, 1900-1917, Stalin, Khrushchev, Brezhnev) and also theories of Russian nationalism and Gorbachev's politics of Russian nationalism.

315. **Gorbachev's Agenda: Changes in Soviet Domestic and Foreign Policy**, edited by Susan L. Clark. Boulder, CO: Westview Press, 1989. xviii, 422 p. *Westview Special Studies on the Soviet Union and Eastern Europe*, ISBN: 0813377749. Includes bibliographical references.

This collection of essays is very broad in its scope, both in terms of its subject matter and its contributors. The latter comprise an international group of experts in politics, economics, foreign affairs, and Soviet domestic affairs from Europe, the United States, and Israel. In the former category are included essays on five areas: reform efforts under Gorbachev and the opposition to his policies, economic and trade reform, role of the military, Soviet-European interaction under Gorbachev, and a section on regional issues (Latin America, Japan, the Pacific, and Soviet-Israeli relations). Rather than seeking a unified approach, the editor has sought to bring a wide spectrum of issues and interpretations to the attention of the reader. Review: *Foreign Affairs* 69:2:180-81 (Spring 1990).

316. Hill, Ronald J., **The Soviet Union: Politics, Economics, and Society from Lenin to Gorbachev**. 2nd ed. London: Pinter, 1989. xxii, 256 p. *Marxist Regimes Series*, ISBN: 0861878000. Includes index and bibliography (p. 232-246).

An analysis of the basic elements of Soviet society. The author surveys such topics as party-state institutions, policy-making, foreign policy, policy questions in education, economics, and minority problems. The revised edition, discussed here, includes an updated list of office holders, updated glossary, sections on the effects of the 1988 Party Conference, among other changes. The book is directed at the general reader and student and is noted for its clarity and absence of jargon. The author believed that since the Soviet Union as a Marxist state was to become the model for so many other developing countries it was imperative to understand its development. The volume has five sections: history and political traditions, social structure, political system, economic system, and regimes' policies. It also contains a table of "basic data" with a wide variety of information on demographics, geography, administrative organization, trade, education and economy. A glossary is included at the opening of the volume.

317. Katsenelinboigen, Aron, **The Soviet Union: Empire, Nation, and System**. New Brunswick, NJ: Transaction Publishers, 1990. xx, 471 p. ISBN: 0887383327. Includes index and bibliographical references.

This volume is a translation of a collection of essays by the author. It is organized into two sections. The first deals with problems related to the Soviet political system. The author believes that the Soviet political system is not able to deal with the high level of development in Soviet technology. He sees Gorbachev as seeking to maintain an authoritarian system through the most flexible means available. The volume also contains a discussion of the role of anti-Semitism in maintaining Russian nationalism. In the second section the author draws on his first hand knowledge of Soviet economic analysis. The author believes that the only way the Russians can rid themselves of their highly centralized system is through the initiation of an indicative optimal plan. He uses examples of specific Soviet economic theorists to show how economic thinking has evolved. There are numerous tables.

318. Laird, Roy D., **The Politburo: Demographic Trends, Gorbachev and the Future**. Boulder, CO: Westview Press, 1986. xv, 198 p. *Westview Special Studies on the Soviet Union and Eastern Europe, 1063-6057*, ISBN: 0813371988. Includes index and bibliography (p. 187-89).

A systemic analysis of demographic changes in the politburo since its beginning. The author presents a catalog of data on each of the 83 members of the politburo in order to analyze policy change over time. The author analyzes difficulties arising in the post- Brezhnev era and demonstrates that Gorbachev will likely attempt major reforms in the late 1980s. The book is organized chronologically, taking each regime from Lenin on, in turn. The chronology of politburo members presented in the index gives a great deal of information on each member including family background, nationality, year into party, higher education, military experience, republic or region of secretariat, other political experience, travel outside bloc, why off politburo, and cause of death. Review: *Soviet Union* 13:3:1049-50 (1987).

319. **Leadership and Succession in the Soviet Union, Eastern Europe and China**, edited by Martin McCauley and Stephen Carter. London: Macmillan, 1986. xiii, 259 p. *Studies in Russia and East Europe*, ISBN: 0333386485. Includes index and bibliography (p. 230-289).

Papers from seminars held at the School of Slavonic and East European Studies, University of London, 1984 are presented here. The seminars focused on the problem of elderly leadership and no legitimate succession mechanisms prevalent in communist systems worldwide. Three studies of communist systems manifest this same problem: 1) the independent communist states: Soviet Union, China, and Yugoslavia; 2) communist states under Soviet influence: Poland, the GDR, Czechoslovakia, Hungary, and Bulgaria; and 3) Soviet-style states that display some independence: Romania and Albania. The essayists reached numerous conclusions jointly among them: 1) heads of the communist party in these countries are the central political figures; 2) the leadership of the party is a lifetime position; 3) there is no mechanism for removing an incompetent leader; 4) the party leader controls the military; 5) as the revolution ages, so does the leadership. The contributors are drawn from diverse backgrounds both scholarly and commercial.

320. Rigby, T. H., **Political Elites in the USSR: Central Leaders and Local Cadres from Lenin to Gorbachev.** Aldershot, Hants, England: E. Elgar, 1990. vii, 301 p. ISBN: 1852783036. Includes bibliographical references and index.

Rigby examines the leading party and state officials in order "to understand what kind of people they are, how they achieve office, and what factors determine their mutual relationships." (p. 1) Rigby proceeds historically, describing and analyzing political elites under Lenin, provincial cliques under Stalin, nomenklatura and patronage, Khrushchev and the resuscitation of the Central Committee, a comparative profile of the Politburo from 1951 to 1971, regional leadership under Brezhnev and central leaders and local cadres under Gorbachev.

321. **The Future of the Soviet Empire**, edited by Henry S. Rowen and Charles Wolf Jr. 1st U.S. ed. New York: St. Martin's Press, 1987. xx, 368 p. ISBN: 0312013477. Includes bibliographical references and index.

An assessment of the many facets of the Soviet Union with the goal of examining the future of that country. Divided into five broad parts, the editors hope to be as all encompassing as possible in their coverage. The five parts cover moral aspects, economics, the military, social conditions, and estimations of the future. Contributors have a wide range of backgrounds from broadcasting to economics, history and political science to the military. There is no unifying theme behind the directions predicted for the Soviet future. Individual essays cover a variety of topics, including political conditions in the Soviet empire, relations with Eastern Europe, the Third World, economic problems, resistance movements in the USSR, demographic trends, social progress, and implications of changes for the West.

322. Sakwa, Richard, **Soviet Politics: An Introduction**. London: Routledge, 1989. xvi, 356 p. ISBN: 0415005051. Includes bibliographical references.

A general study of Soviet politics intended for the general reader and the student of Soviet politics with an interest in history. The author hopes to provide an introduction to Soviet history and institutions by analyzing how the system functions. To do this he has divided the volume into three parts. The first, comprised of the first five chapters, focuses on the history of Soviet politics. Chapters six through ten make up his second section in which he deals with the institutions and social processes of the Soviet system. The final section, chapters eleven through fifteen, are case studies of the system at work. Throughout the author pursues three themes: change and continuity in Soviet politics, the tension between ideology and practice, and the interaction of politics and society. He covers a broad range of topics including local politics, policy-making, command economy, foreign policy, nationality politics, and dissent. Every chapter includes a select bibliography on its topics and the bibliography at the back of the volume covers general works. Review: *Canadian Slavonic Papers* 32:2:193-94 (June 1990).

323. Shlapentokh, Vladimir, **Soviet Intellectuals and Political Power: The Post-Stalin Era**. Princeton, NJ: Princeton University Press, 1990. xiv, 330 p. ISBN: 0691094594. Includes indexes and bibliographical references (p. 288-311).

Shlapentokh maintains that intellectuals and the political elite "exhibit dual and deeply contradictory attitudes towards each other. Indeed, it is this duality which determines the ambiguous place of the intellectuals in socialist society." (p. xii) In the first four chapters the author explores the place of intellectuals in Soviet society, their values and orientations, and their oppositional views and inconsistent political behavior. In the concluding five chapters he describes and analyzes the relations between intellectuals and the political structure during the 1960s and their reliance on liberal socialism, their response during a time of political reaction, the trend of Russophile ideology that rose to prominence in the 1970s, and finally the chosen land of the Gorbachev era.

324. Solzhenitsyn, Aleksandr Isaevich, **Rebuilding Russia: Reflections and Tentative Proposals**, translated and annotated by Alexis Klimoff. 1st ed. New York: Farrar, Straus and Giroux, 1991. 119 p. ISBN: 0374173427.

An essay by the well-known émigré author on how Russia should proceed is presented in this brief essay. The author draws on the thoughts of many Russian thinkers of the past. He discusses his views on the economy, education, system of government, nationalities, and many other issues. The translator has provided an appendix of brief biographical entries for the non- western thinkers mentioned in this book. Review: *New York Times Book Review* 9 (November 24, 1991).

325. **The USSR in 1989: A Record of Events**, compiled by Vera Tolz and edited by Melanie Newton. Boulder, CO: Westview Press, 1990. x, 740 p. ISBN: 0813380162. Includes indexes.

A useful reference tool in light of the tremendous amount of information coming out of the Soviet Union. The volume is organized by month with synopses of events and references to Radio Free Europe-Radio Liberty publications. The volume includes a subject and name index to assist in identifying important events. The work was based on the section "The USSR This Week" in Radio Liberty's publication *Report on the USSR.*

Law

326. **Law in the Gorbachev Era: Essays in Honor of Dietrich Andre Loeber**, edited by Donald D. Barry, editor in chief F.J.M. Feldbrugge. Boston: M. Nijhoff, 1988. xix, 426 p. *Law in Eastern Europe*, no. 39. ISBN: 9024736781.

A collection of essays compiled as a festschrift in honor of Dietrich Loeber. The purpose of each contributor was to assess the impact of changes in the Gorbachev era on Soviet law. A variety of topics are covered such as the place of the Communist Party, human rights, the awarding of honors, economic management, administration of enterprises, Soviet civil law, trade unions, legal status of international economic organization and arbitration procedures. A bibliography of Loeber's publications is included.

327. Boguslavskii, Mark Moiseevich, **Private International Law: The Soviet Approach**. Boston: Kluwer Academic, 1988. ix, 261 p. *Law in Eastern Europe*, no 35. Includes index and bibliography (p. 251-52).

A translation and update of the 1982 Soviet *Mezhdunarodnoe Chastnoe Pravo*. The book was originally intended as a textbook. New Soviet legislation on international treaty practice as of December 1986 has been incorporated into the text. Numerous international treaties to which the USSR is a party are included. Some of these cover legal issues such as rights of property, obligations arising in tort, questions on copyright, patent and family law, among others.

328. **Perestroika and International Law**, edited by W. E. Butler. Boston: Dordrecht, 1990. vi, 330 p. ISBN: 0792304837. Includes bibliographical references.

This collection of essays examine several aspects of international law from a unique perspective, "First, Soviet international lawyers have been invited to expound upon the 'new thinking' and international law by addressing the principal branches of the discipline systematically and suggesting new line of inquiry. ... Second, and uncharacteristically, English international lawyers have been asked to be 'future minded' with a view to identifying areas for approaches to restructuring international law, extending a domestic Soviet preoccupation quite legitimately to the international plane." (p. 3).

329. Ginsburgs, George, **The Soviet Union and International Cooperation in Legal Matters**, with the assistance of William B. Simons. Boston: Kluwer Academic Publishers, 1988. v. *Law in Eastern Europe*, no. 38. ISBN: 9024736773. Includes index.

The first part in a three volume set focusing on those rules between governments "whereby the legal organs of one will procure for the legal organs of the other procedural services designed to facilitate performance by the recipient party of its mission to 'administer justice.' " (p. xiii) The first volume focuses on arbitral agreements and foreign commercial arbitral awards. An article by Howard Hilton provides the pre-war background for the reader. The remaining three parts consider bilateral treaty practice, multilateral treaty practice, and the non-treaty setting.

330. Grzybowskii, Kazimierz, **Soviet International Law and the World Economic Order**. Durham, NC: Duke University Press, 1987. xii, 226 p. *Duke Press Policy Studies*, ISBN: 0822307340. Include index and bibliography (p. 215-222).

An update of the author's earlier work, *Soviet Public International Law and Domestic Practice*, published in 1970. However, this work differs from the original in that it treats the Soviet Union as part of one world economic system. The approach to international law taken here is policy oriented. The analysis is limited to Soviet diplomacy as it relates to the international community and other Socialist countries. Issues covered here include foreign service, technical and cultural cooperation, boundaries and territories, international law as it relates to population, and maritime law.

331. Hober, Kaj, **Joint Ventures in the Soviet Union**. Dobbs Ferry, NY: Transnational Juris Publications, 1989. 1 v. ISBN: 09291779137.

"The purpose of this book is to describe and discuss the provisions of the Joint Venture Decree and to analyze such provisions on the background of relevant parts of Soviet Law; the Joint Venture Decree is drafted in such a way as to make joint ventures dependent on the general rules of Soviet law." (p. 1) Translation of the text is included in the volume along with thorough discussions of later revisions. Numerous appendices include the texts of related laws. The book also presents practical information for those attempting to negotiate joint ventures.

332. Huskey, Eugene, **Russian Lawyers and the Soviet State: The Origins and Development of the Soviet Bar, 1917-1939**. Princeton, NJ: Princeton University Press, 1985. xii, 247 p. ISBN: 0691077061. Includes index and bibliography (p. 233-241).

Huskey examines the processes by which the bar in prerevoulutionary Russia "a legal institution of the old order dedicated to the representation of individual interests, has been integrated into the Soviet state, whose proclaimed commitment is to the furtherance of collective, or class interests." (p. xiii) After an introductory chapter on the emergence of the Russian legal profession, the author concentrates on the transformation of the bar from 1917 to 1939. Reviews: *Russian Review* 46:1:104-6 (January 1987). *American History Review* 92:2: 461 (April 1987). *Slavic Review* 46:2:317-18 (Summer 1987). *History: Reviews* 15:3:84-85 (January-February 1987).

333. Ioffe, Olimpiad Solomonovich, **Soviet Civil Law**. Boston: Kluwer Academic Publishers, 1988. ix, 382 p. *Law in Eastern Europe*, no. 36. ISBN: 9024736765. Includes index.

The author attempts a study of Soviet civil law in light of Gorbachev's reforms. "In other words, here is an attempt to create a work which can serve as a guide in the realm of civil law in the USSR." (p. 17) The book is divided into five parts each focusing on various aspects of the Soviet Civil Law Code: a general part, laws of ownership, laws of obligation, laws of creative activity (copyright, inventions, and discovery), and laws of inheritance. The introduction covers general questions on the definitions, sources, and system of Soviet civil law. Reviews: *Soviet Union* 15:2-3:276-77 (1988). *Russian Review* 48: 2:227-28 (April 1989).

334. **Soviet Civil Law**, edited by O.N. Sadikov. Armonk, N.Y.: M.E. Sharpe, 1988. xv, 543 p. ISBN: 0873324293. Includes index.

This work is an unabridged translation of the textbook *Sovetskoe Grazhdanskoe Pravo*, originally published in 1983. It includes contributions from nine Soviet scholars. The text book is divided into two parts: civil law and family law. The part on civil law covers general provisions, the law of property, the law of obligations, copyright and the law of inventions and the law of succession. Family law includes general provisions, marriage, parents and children and maintenance obligations. A Russian- English and English-Russian glossary of legal terms is also included. Review: *Russian Review* 48:2:227-28 (April 1989).

335. **The Impact of Perestroika on Soviet Law**, edited by Albert J. Schmidt. Norwell, Mass.: Kluwer Academic Publishers, 1990. xxvii, 558 p. *Law in Eastern Europe*, no. 41. ISBN: 079230621X. Includes bibliographical references and index.

Essays originally presented at a 1987 symposium at the University of Bridgeport. "... the papers focus in a preliminary way on the legal aspects of perestroika and glasnost, their role in the recurring cycles of law reform that have shaped Soviet legal history and the role assigned to law in facilitating economic and societal perestroika." (p. xxi) The essays are grouped topically covering historical perspectives, legislative process, legislation on socialist democracies, economic legislation on accelerating scientific and technical progress, legislation on social development and culture, and other issues.

336. Sipkov, Ivan, **The Codified Statutes on Private International Law of the East European Countries: A Comparative Study**. Washington, DC: Law Library, Library of Congress, 1986. 55 p. Includes bibliography (p. 52-55).

Sipkov compares the private international law of the East European countries that were under the control of the Soviet Union immediately after World War II. Private international law "is an independent and separate branch of the municipal law of a state." (p. 3) After a brief discussion of the science of private international law, Sipkov then examines conflicts of law rules among the various states. These include general rules as well as rules relating to legal capacity, property, contracts, family law, succession, labor law, copyright and inventions, international transport, and limitation of claims.

337. Stucka, P. I., **P.I. Stuchka: Selected Writings on Soviet Law and Marxism**, edited by Robert Sharlet, Peter B. Maggs, and Piers Beirne. Armonk, NY: M.E. Sharpe, 1988. xxii, 265 p. ISBN: 0873324730. Includes indexes and bibliography (p. 253-255).

These essays, originally written in Russian, are by one of "the principal architects of modern Soviet legal theory and of the Soviet legal system itself." The essays themselves were written from 1917 to 1931 and are divided into three sections: From "Bourgeois Law" to "Revolutionary Legality;" the Marxist Theory of Law; and Socialist construction and Soviet legality. The bibliography contains works cited by Stuchka in the essays.

338. Vaksberg, Arkady, **The Soviet Mafia**. New York: St. Martin's Press, 1991. x, 275 p. ISBN: 0312071353. Includes index.

An expose on organized crime in the Soviet Union covering its history and its contemporary operation. The author is a well- known journalist in the Soviet Union who was exposing government corruption even before glasnost. In this volume he traces government involvement in organized crime including the role played by Brezhnev. Gorbachev's attempts and failures to crackdown on the system are also described. Vaksberg asserts that the rising nationalism of the glasnost period is adding to the problem. In fact the author feels that almost everyone in positions of power in the Soviet Union is connected with the Soviet mafia.

339. Zumbakis, S. Paul, **Soviet Evidence in North American Courts: An Analysis of Problems and Concerns with Reliance on Communist Source Evidence in Alleged War Criminal Trials**. 1st ed. Wood Haven, NY: Americans for Due Process, 1986. ii, 168 p. Includes bibliography (p. 140-167).

This review was undertaken in order to ascertain whether American and Canadian courts could use Soviet produced evidence against persons accused of war crimes. Zumbakis examines various categories of communist source evidence, questions why it might be suspect, describes evidentiary problems with communist source evidence, ponders historical, political, and moral considerations in using communist source evidence, describes the

United States experience with communist source evidence and explores what damage might have been done to the American and Canadian law systems.

Politics and Government, Special Studies

340. Barghoorn, Frederick Charles, and Thomas F. Remington, **Politics in the USSR**. 3rd ed. Boston: Little, Brown, 1986. xiii, 530 p. *Little, Brown Series in Comparative Politics. A Country Study*, ISBN: 0316080918. Includes bibliographical references and index.

A structural-functional approach to the analysis of the Soviet political system. Although this book has had two previous editions, this third edition is completely revised. Chapters on Soviet foreign policy and Gorbachev have been added. The chapters on political culture and socialization, communications, social structure, and political subcultures, elite recruitment, policymaking and implementation, and rule adjudication have all been rewritten. The emphasis is on policymaking and implementation. Although Gorbachev had only been in office a short time, the authors saw him as a reformer with the ability to enforce the reforms he sought. The volume is arranged thematically using the categories of a structural-functional analysis such as political culture and interest articulation. An appendix with a diagrammatic presentation of the Soviet Communist Party and governmental organization is also included.

341. **Political Leadership in the Soviet Union**, edited by Archie Brown. Bloomington: Indiana University Press, 1989. xi, 245 p. ISBN: 0253312140. Includes bibliographical references.

These essays consider political leadership in the Soviet Union from 1917 to 1988. Individual essays focus on the Soviet political executive, the role of patronage in cooptation into Soviet leadership, political processes and generational change, policy outside and politics inside, and power and policy in a time of leadership transition, 1982-1988. Reviews: *Journal of Baltic Studies* 21:2:161-62 (Summer 1990). *Foreign Affairs* 69:2: 181 (Spring 1990).

342. Clark, William A., **Soviet Regional Elite Mobility after Khrushchev**. New York: Praeger, 1989. xi, 206 p. ISBN: 0275931242. Includes index and bibliography (p. 193-200).

This study focuses on the changes in the political system reflected in the movement of individuals through the political hierarchy. The author concentrates on the oblast level of political hierarchy in his analysis. The five chapters each cover a facet of elite mobility: changes in personnel and their reflection in the larger power structure; the identification of the independent variables that indicate political change; and changes in policy indicated by Soviet cadre policy. There are several appendices providing statistical data on the oblast level political structure. Review: *Soviet Union-Union Sovietique* 17: 1-2:161-63 (1990).

343. Daniels, Robert Vincent, **Is Russia Reformable?: Change and Resistance from Stalin to Gorbachev**. Boulder, CO: Westview Press, 1988. x, 141 p. ISBN: 08133075797. Includes bibliographies and index.

Daniels uses different methodologies—theoretical, narrative, and empirical—in each of his chapters. His goal is to answer the question posed in the title: Is Russia reformable? "Going beyond the intentions of the leader of the moment, which may be deep or shallow, enduring or transitory, what are the forces and circumstances that demand reform on the one hand and that operate to frustrate it on the other?" (p. vii) Reviews: *Russian Review* 48:3:330-31 (July 1989). *Orbis* 33:3:461 (Summer 1989).

344. Desjardins, Robert, **The Soviet Union Through French Eyes, 1945-85**. New York: St. Martin's Press, 1988. xiii, 188 p. ISBN: 0312020686. Includes index and bibliography (p. 161-184).

A guide to French studies of the Soviet Union. The author has been selective, concentrating on the most interesting and influential French writers. He also excludes studies of foreign policy and international relations. The first chapter is an overview of French Sovietology. The author then moves to discussions of particular interpretations beginning with those in the Marxist tradition including discussions of the work of Castoryadis, Naville, and Bettelheim. He then turns to totalitarianism and ideology, reviewing the ideas of Aron, Monnerot, Lefort, and Besancon. The fourth chapter discusses the works of Carrere D'Encausse and French theorizing in general. A lengthy bibliography is included. Review: *American Political Science Review* 84:1:334-35 (March 1990).

345. Gerner, Kristian, and Stefan Hedlund, **Ideology and Rationality in the Soviet Model: A Legacy for Gorbachev**. London: Routledge, 1989. xii, 455 p. ISBN: 0415021421. Includes index and bibliographical references.

A game-theoretical approach to the synthesis of the trends in economic, political and cultural development in the Soviet Union. Two topics normally related have been excluded from this study, foreign policy and the military. The book is divided into five parts, the first of which is a general introduction to the subject. The following sections take a roughly chronological approach with part two focusing on the Stalin era, and part three analyzing Khrushchev's attempts to alter the Stalinist model. Part four reviews the stagnation of the Brezhnev years, part five turns to the Gorbachev years "the real obstacle to reform will be sought in terms of the impact on the psychology of Soviet Man of seven decades of Bolshevik rule." (p. 28).

346. **The Soviet Empire: Its Nations Speak Out: The First Congress of the People's Deputies, Moscow, 25 May to 10 June 1989**, edited and translated by Oleg Glebov and John Crowfoot, with an introduction by Ernest Gellner. Chur, Switzerland: Harwood Academic Publishers, 1989. xxx, 189 p. *Soviet Studies, 1046-1809*, v. 1. ISBN: 3718650002.

Excerpts from speeches given at the May-June, 1989 Congress of People's Deputies. Selection was based on the clarity and importance of the statements. They are arranged chronologically for each geographical and cultural region of the USSR. "The present volume assembles the most interesting contributions made at the Congress and in the first sessions of the new Supreme Soviet on the nationalist issue." (p. xxv) Appendices are included on the recent history of the USSR, the national composition of the Soviet Union and data on the republics and largest autonomous regions. This volume is the first in a series on current informed opinion in the Soviet Union.

347. Hammer, Darrell P., **The USSR: The Politics of Oligarchy**. 3rd ed. Boulder, CO: Westview Press, 1990. xvi, 320 p. ISBN: 0813307805. Includes bibliographical references and index.

This is the third edition of this work and it updates the 1986 second edition to be current through 1990. It is a political analysis of the Soviet Union that emphasizes the historical tradition of authoritarian rule on Soviet political culture and on the bureaucracy. Dr. Hammer sees the bureaucracy as central to Gorbachev's success or failure. The book is divided into two parts. The first is an overview of Soviet political culture including a discussion of political theory related to authoritarian regimes and a review of Soviet institutions. The second part focuses on policy-making and policy problems. This updated edition includes detailed information on the constitutional changes that created the Congress of

People's Deputies and the reemergence of ethnic nationalism. Review: *Slavic Review* 46:2:317 (Summer 1987).

348. Hazan, Barukh A., **From Brezhnev to Gorbachev: Infighting in the Kremlin**. Boulder, CO: Westview, 1987. xii, 260 p. ISBN: 0813303680. Includes index and bibliography (p. 221-246).

A discussion of how the struggle for power in the Politburo changed since Khrushchev's term in office. Hazan relied almost entirely on primary sources. The author discusses the ideological view of succession and leadership in the Marxist world and how this has affected the shape of power in the Soviet Union. He contends that, particularly since Brezhnev, changes in leadership are motivated by death, passed from one individual to another, with rare flirtations with collective leadership, and approved only by the party leadership. He then discusses the succession process with each ruler since Brezhnev. The roles of other Politburo members are also discussed in detail. There are separate sections on Ustnov and Romanov. The book also includes an appendix listing indicators for ranking Soviet leaders. Reviews: *Slavic Review* 47:3:552-53 (Fall 1988). *Canadian Slavonic Papers* 30:1:145-47 (March 1988). *History: Reviews of New Books* 16:4:179 (Summer 1988).

349. Kelley, Donald R., **Soviet Politics from Brezhnev to Gorbachev**. New York: Praeger, 1987. 242 p. ISBN: 0275927326. Includes index and bibliography (p. 235-236).

An analysis of changes in the political system in the Soviet Union beginning with the Brezhnev era. Each chapter is devoted to the succeeding Kremlin leaders in turn: Brezhnev, Andropov, Chernenko, and Gorbachev. The final chapter discusses the changes proposed as of the 27th Party Congress. The author demonstrates the difficulty of the task before Gorbachev by describing how firmly entrenched the "Brezhnev" doctrine has become.

350. Krickus, Richard J., **The Superpowers in Crisis: Implications of Domestic Discord**. Washington, DC: Pergamon-Brassey's International Defense Publishers, 1987. xiii, 236 p. ISBN: 0080347053. Includes bibliographies and index.

This comparative study of the superpowers has three stated goals: "To identify the problems responsible for it [societal crisis in the USSR] and to discuss its capacity to destroy the Leninist regime, the Russian empire, or both, is a pivotal goal of this book.... A second goal is predicated on the proposition that the U.S. predicament is not as serious as the Soviet crisis but is capable, nonetheless, of threatening U.S. security.... The third goal of this book is to explore what impact the Soviet crisis and the U.S. predicament will have upon East-West relations on the First Front." (p. x) The author has structured the book to compare the two problems by devoting the first section to the Soviet crisis: its economy, the minority problem, and the role of Eastern Europe. He then moves to an analysis of the American "predicament" in Part Two, reviewing American liberalism and the conservative movement. His final section looks at both of these problems as they affect international relations. Review: *Foreign Affairs* 66:4:876 (Spring 1988).

351. Mitchell, R. Judson, **Getting to the Top in the USSR: Cyclical Patterns in the Leadership Succession Process**. Stanford, Calif.: Hoover Institution Press, 1990. xiv, 237 p. ISBN: 0817989218. Includes bibliographical references (p. 225-230) and index.

A study of the succession process particularly in relation to Gorbachev. The author begins by reviewing past struggles for power and describes a cycle that was in evidence before Brezhnev took power. He then turns to the Brezhnev era and the succession patterns that have emerged since his death. He believes that Gorbachev is relying on traditional institutions, the KGB, the army, and the Communist Party, for the consolidation of his party. The author describes Gorbachev's policies as "non-revolution from above."

352. **Religion and Nationalism in Soviet and Eastern European Politics**, edited by Pedro Ramet. rev. and expanded edition. Durham, NC: Duke University Press, 1989. vi, 516 p. *Duke Press Policy Series*, ISBN: 0822308541. Includes index.

A revised edition of the original volume that appeared in 1985 and contained papers from a conference on "Religion and Nationalism in the Soviet Union and Eastern Europe" held at UCLA and UC at Santa Barbara October 29-30, 1982. The updated edition has added essays on religious institutions in the Communist state, Jews in the USSR and Eastern Europe, religion and nationalism in Georgia and Armenia, revival of Lutheranism in East Germany, and Christianity among the Czechs. The volume is divided into four parts: an opening section of essays giving comparative studies; two regional sections—one on the Soviet Union and the other on Eastern Europe; and a concluding essay. Review: *East European Quarterly* 24:1:113-124 (Spring 1990).

353. **Politics and the Soviet System: Essays in Honour of Frederick C. Barghoorn**, edited by Thomas F. Remington. New York: St. Martin's Press, 1989. viii, 235 p. ISBN: 0312021232. Includes bibliographical references.

A collection of essays honoring Frederick Barghoorn. The essays demonstrate the development of Soviet studies since Barghoorn wrote as well as his influence on them. "This book also reflects Barghoorn's major research interests, in particular the study of Soviet communication, ideology and propaganda, and the study of Soviet policy." (p. 9) Other essays address such topics as religion and youth in the Soviet Union, glasnost, bureaucratic politics, and the arms race. A bibliography of Barghoorn's work is included.

354. Roeder, Philip G., **Soviet Political Dynamics: Development of the First Leninist Polity**. New York: Harper & Row, 1988. xviii, 456 p. ISBN: 0060455551. Includes bibliographies and index.

Professor Roeder has compiled numerous lectures that he has delivered in an attempt to cover a variety of topics in Soviet studies. These include historical development; socialization; political culture; policy making institutions; economic policy; nationalities policy; and national security policy. The author intends the work as a text and has structured it in such a way that topics can be read in an order other than the one used here. A number of different viewpoints are reviewed, and the author does have his own slant on the problems facing the Soviet Union. "I argue vigorously in these pages that the Soviet Union has been a rapidly changing society that should be understood against the background of the problems of modernization and development." (p. x).

355. Sakharov, Andrei, **Memoirs**, translated from the Russian by Richard Lourie. 1st American ed. New York: Alfred A. Knopf, 1990. xxi, 773 p. ISBN: 0394537408.

An abridged translation of the Russian edition. Sakharov's memoirs were written over a twelve year period. Aside from their value as the description of the life of one of the major figures of modern Soviet society, they also give the reader an insider's view of Soviet life. "Sakharov's narrative deals primarily with the events of his life and with his ideas, but his comments on the extraordinary cast of characters he encountered during his several careers bring the human texture of Soviet society to life in a way that no foreign journalist or scholar can match." (p. xvi) The book includes a bibliography of Sakharov's writings. The appendixes reproduce several of his writings including his statements on the theft of his manuscripts, his open letter to Sidney Drell on the dangers of nuclear war, the Sakharov-Carter correspondence, the 1973 anti-Sakharov Soviet press campaign and writings during the 1984 hunger strike.

356.   Shimotomai, Nobuo, **Moscow under Stalinist Rule, 1931-1934**. New York: St. Martin's Press, 1991. xii, 179 p. ISBN: 0312062125. Includes bibliographical references (p. 172-174) and indexes.

Shimotomai's study focuses on the cultural and political processes in Moscow and in the Moscow region, from 1931-1934. Moscow was a region where heavy industry was supplanting light industry during this period, and the social structure was not quite stabilized. The study traces the development in social structure and social interactions during this time when party bureaucrats were trying to cope with these changes. The author covers Moscow party organization and membership, decision making in the party, the governmental process in Moscow, the Party and social problems, industry, transport, energy and agricultural policy, management of the municipal economy, and supply and shortage.

357.   Smith, Gordon B., **Soviet Politics: Continuity and Contradiction**. New York: St. Martin's Press, 1987. xi, 388 p. ISBN: 0312007957. Includes bibliographical references and index.

The multifaceted world of the Soviet political system is the subject of this study. The author is concerned with the reasons for political conflicts and how those conflicts are expressed and resolved. "Through case studies and drawing on my personal experience in the USSR, I have attempted to go beyond the formal depiction of political institutions and their power in order to illustrate how the political system works in practice." (p. v) The author examines the historical and ideological background to the contemporary system with discussions on the revolution, Marxism, Leninism, and Stalinism. He then focuses on institutions such as the Communist Party, the government structure (regional and national), the legal system, the secret police, and the armed forces as they affect the political system. Next he looks at the role of the economy, education, science and the politics of culture in the changing political system. There is also a discussion of Gorbachev's reforms. The appendices contain the 1977 Constitution of the USSR and the Rules of the CPSU (approved by the Twenty-Seventh CPSU Congress). A bibliography is included with each chapter. Review: *Slavic Review* 48:2:312-13 (Summer 1989).

358.   Thompson, Terry L., **Ideology and Policy: The Political Uses of Doctrine in the Soviet Union**. Boulder, CO: Westview Press, 1989. viii, 220 p. *Westview Special Studies on the Soviet Union and Eastern Europe*, ISBN: 0813374634. Includes bibliographical references.

The role of ideology and its importance in determining public policy in the Soviet Union are examined in this study. The author believes that ideology plays an influential role in policy development since the politicians of the Soviet Union are heavily influenced by Marxist-Leninist theory during their training. He does not believe that ideology now or in the past has played a major role in motivating the common man. By examining a selected number of policies (labor incentives, nationalities, political participation, CPSU policy, and Sino-Soviet relations) the author addresses several issues. Matching ideology with specific policies, deciding if policy is motivated by or has motivated the ideology, and evolution of ideological debates are some of the major issues analyzed in this work. The author believes that the primary role of ideology in the Soviet Union is in communications among party leaders. The volume is organized around the policies to be examined with one chapter devoted to each topic. Within each chapter past ideological approaches and changes are estimated. There is also a final chapter on Gorbachev's approach to all of the policies previously discussed. Review: *Russian Review* 49:4:509-11 (October 1990).

359.   Tucker, Robert C., **Political Culture and Leadership in Soviet Russia**. 1st ed. New York: Norton, 1987. x, 214 p. ISBN: 039302489X. Includes bibliographies and index.

Customary ways of life, or cultures, can change through reform movements or through revolutions. But the new culture and society that result are dependent on the former way of life. Tucker's purpose in this book is to examine political culture and leadership in order "to produce a general interpretation of Russia's historical experience in the seventy-year aftermath of the revolutions of 1917." (p. vii) After an introductory chapter on culture, political culture and Soviet studies, he then focuses more specifically on culture and leadership in social movements, Lenin's Bolshevism, the breakdown of revolutionary culture between Lenin and Stalin, Stalinism, Stalin's legacy, and change under Gorbachev. Reviews: *Russian Review* 49:2:221-23 (April 1990). *Slavic Review* 47:4:730 (Winter 1988).

To 1917

360. Geyer, Dietrich, **Russian Imperialism: The Interaction of Domestic and Foreign Policy, 1860-1914**, translated from the German by Bruce Little. New Haven: Yale University Press, 1987. 385 p. ISBN: 0300037961. Includes index.
"The subject of this book is Russian imperialism between 1860 and 1914, between the emancipation of the serfs and the outbreak of the First World War. Of special concern is the connection between foreign and domestic policy—the internal workings of what we shall call 'Russian imperialism.' This is therefore not a history of diplomacy, but an account of the internal background to foreign policy." (p.1) Reviews: *Russian Review* 47:2:194-96 (April 1988). *Slavic Review* 47:2:328 (Summer 1988). *History: Reviews of New Books* 15:5:157-58 (July-August 1988).

361. Lieven, Dominic C. B., **Russia's Rulers Under the Old Regime**. New Haven: Yale University Press, 1989. xxii, 407 p. ISBN: 0300043716. Includes indexes and bibliography (p. 369-375).
Lieven has written a study of the Russian imperial ruling elite under Nicholas II. He examines the development of this elite and the interrelationships among the monarchy, the aristocracy, the gentry, and the bureaucracy. Several appendices, including men appointed to the State Council and a schematic diagram of Russian state institutions with explanatory notes, enhance material presented in the text. Reviews: *Journal of Interdisciplinary History* 21:1:150-51 (Summer 1990). *Russian Review* 49:3:343-44 (July 1990). *Canadian Journal of History* 25:2:286-87 (August 1990).

362. McCauley, Martin, **The Emergence of the Modern Russian State, 1856-81**. Totowa, NJ: Barnes and Noble, 1988. x, 218 p. ISBN: 0389207551. Includes index and bibliography (p. 213-216).
A collection of documents from the reign of Alexander II. These documents are selected from different subject areas: government, mechanism of control, rural life, urban expansion, society, foreign policy, education, culture, and nationalities. A lengthy introduction provides a context for the reader. "The volume is intended to provide a guide to contemporary perception of the difficulties facing Russia and the ways in which they might be solved, through a selection of documents." (p. ix).

363. Pearson, Thomas S., **Russian Officialdom in Crisis: Autocracy and Local Self-Government, 1861-1900**. Cambridge: Cambridge University Press, 1989. xx, 284 p. ISBN: 0521361273. Includes index and bibliography (p. 261-277).
"This book focuses on the Russian government's efforts to divert local self-government and its reform from its introduction in 1861 to its bureaucratization under the land captains and zemstvo counterreforms of 1889 and 1890. It seeks to answer two interrelated questions: Why did the Russian government introduce these counterreforms in local

self-government? and What does our case study of the administrative reasons for these counterreforms and the bureaucratic politics surrounding them tell us about the nature and viability of the imperial government on the eve of the twentieth century?" (p. ix) Reviews: *Russian Review* 49:3:342- 43 (July 1990). *Journal of Interdisciplinary History* 21:1:152-55 (Summer 1990).

364. Robbins, Richard G., **The Tsar's Viceroys: Russian Provincial Governors in the Last Years of the Empire**. Ithaca: Cornell University Press, 1987. xiv, 272 p. ISBN: 0801420466. Includes index and bibliography (p. 253-266).

Robbins concentrates his examination of Russia's governors to the period 1880-1914 and to those guberniias, "where zemstvos and other institutions of self-government were to be found." He "seeks to show who the governors were, how they functioned, and why they acted as they did." (p. ix) Reviews: *Russian History* 17:3:367- 68 (Fall 1990). *Canadian Slavonic Papers* 30:3:384-85 (September 1988).

365. Wcislo, Frances William, **Reforming Rural Russia: State, Local Society, and National Politics, 1855-1914**. Princeton, NJ: Princeton University Press, 1990. xviii, 347 p. *Studies of the Harriman Institute*, ISBN: 0691055742. Includes bibliographic references.

Wcislo "studies the repeated attempts of imperial bureaucratic elites to reform the civil administration of local rural society, perhaps the most critical mediating link between the autocratic state and the developing society that it ruled." (p. x) Included are the reforms of Loris-Melnikov in the 1880's, the revolution of 1905 and its antecedents, the Stolypin ministry, local reform, and bureaucratic reform on the eve of war.

1917 to 1984

366. Bialer, Seweryn, **The Soviet Paradox: External Expansion, Internal Decline**. 1st ed. New York: Knopf, 1986. ix, 391 p. ISBN: 0394540956. Includes index and bibliography (p. 379-386).

The Soviet paradox can be expressed by two domestic dilemmas faced by the leadership. First, military growth is perceived by the leadership as the supreme value, but military growth is one of the main sources of internal problems. Second, in order for the economy to be revitalized, power must be diverted to lower levels, yet from its beginning much of the energy of the leadership has been spent in centralizing and concentrating power. Bialer not only examines domestic politics since the death of Stalin, but also Russia's relationships with other communist states and the U.S. Reviews: *Parameters* 17:1:119-120 (Spring 1987). *Orbis* 30:2:393 (Summer 1986). *Society* 24:6:82-84 (September-October 1987).

367. **Soldiers and the Soviet State: Civil-Military Relations From Brezhnev to Gorbachev**, edited by Timothy J. Colton and Thane Gustafson. Princeton, NJ: Princeton University Press, 1990. xiii, 370 p. ISBN: 069102328X (pbk.), 0691078637. Includes index and bibliographical references.

"This book covers a twenty-five-year span, from the beginning of the Brezhnev era to the present, and it devotes separate chapters to the major factors affecting the civil-military relationship: politics, economics, technology, society, and foreign relations." (p. xi).

368. Conquest, Robert, **Stalin and the Kirov Murder**. New York: Oxford University Press, 1989. xiv, 164 p. ISBN: 0195055799. Includes index and bibliography (p. 157-160).

A prominent victim of the purges of 1937-1938 was reported to have said that they actually began on December 1, 1934, the day of the murder of Sergei Mironovich Kirov, the Leningrad party boss. Conquest explores the evidence and the past falsification of the evidence in order to render his guilty verdict for Stalin. In fact, he observes that the Kirov murder "was made the central justification for the whole theory of Stalinism and the necessity for the endless terror." (p. x) His study examines the art of the murder itself, the known assassin, Leonid Vasilevich Nikolaev, background information on Kirov, the various reputed "terrorist centers," the role of the police, and Stalin's role.

369. D'Agostino, Anthony, **Soviet Succession Struggles: Kremlinology and the Russian Question from Lenin to Gorbachev**. Boston: Allen & Unwin, 1987. xvi, 274 p. ISBN: 0044970439. Includes index and bibliography (p. 233-269).

An examination of the methods of analysis applied to the study of Soviet succession. In particular, the author focuses on two main approaches; first on that method that analyzes succession by examining the nature of Soviet society and the Soviet state or "Russian question." Then the author looks at the study of succession via an analysis of the distribution of power within the Soviet hierarchy. The author relies primarily on the works of émigré authors for his source material. He identifies a "pattern of alternance of party programs" shifting between Moscow and Leningrad. "Instead of producing a timeless model, then, I have had to be content to trace patterns of change connecting unique historical situations.... I hope, however, that an examination of alternance may contribute something to the demystification of the struggle for power and at least clarify some of its mechanics." (p. xiii) The book is arranged chronologically covering the years 1919 to 1982. Reviews: *American Historical Review* 95:1:214 (February 1990). *Historian* 51:4:672-73 (August 1989). *Nationalities Papers* 16:2:300-04 (Fall 1988).

370. Gill, Graeme J., **The Origins of the Stalinist Political System**. Cambridge: Cambridge University Press, 1990. xv, 454 p. *Soviet and East European Studies*, vol. 74. ISBN: 0521382661. Includes bibliographical references (p. 427-441) and index.

This is a study of the rise of Stalinism. The author feels that previous studies have focused either too exclusively on Stalin himself or peculiarities of the Soviet system. Central to this study will be the institutional and value structure of the Soviet system as they evolved from October, 1917 to June, 1941. The book is organized around the four political systems identified by the author—all forms of an oligarchy in different stages. The system that develops under Stalin is shown to be fundamentally different than that of the revolution.

371. Kagarlitsky, Boris, **The Thinking Reed: Intellectuals and the Soviet State, 1917 to the Present**, translated by Brian Pearce. London: Verso, 1988. x, 374 p. ISBN: 0860911985. Includes bibliographies and index.

Kagarlitsky was thrown into prison just after this book was completed. The manuscript circulated among his friends and eventually saw its way to the West, just before the author's release. As the author describes it: "This work is an attempt at an examination, as objective as possible, of some pressing problems of the cultural-political process in our country." (p. 3) Reviews: *American Historical Review* 95:4:1255-56 (October 1990). *Journal of International Affairs* 42:2:501 (Spring 1989). *Nation* 94-97 (January 23, 1989).

372. Khrushchev, Nikita Sergeevich, **Khrushchev Remembers: The Glasnost Tapes**, foreword by Strobe Talbott, translated and edited by Jerrold L. Schecter with Vyacheslav V. Luchkov. 1st ed. Boston: Little, Brown, 1990. xvi, 219 p. ISBN: 0316472972. Includes bibliographical references and index.

Two volumes of Khrushchev's memoirs have already appeared, one in 1970 and the other in 1974. Both of these were based on the tape recordings made by Khrushchev and smuggled to the West. But there were gaps in these narratives. In 1988, Khrushchev's son delivered unexpected tapes to the editors of this volume, so that previously withheld material could be made known. This volume contains new material only and is not repetitive of the earlier works.

373.   Laqueur, Walter, **Stalin: the Glasnost Revelations**. New York: Scribner's, 1990. xi, 382 p. ISBN: 0684192039. Includes bibliographical references (p. 333-367) and index.

This work was written in order to illuminate several areas of Stalin's rule, something not possible a decade ago. Laqueur uses materials that have recently been declassified and made available through the summer of 1989. Much more is to be found here about purges and terror than about five-year plans. Laqueur concludes by offering a forty year perspective on the Soviet leader. An appendix provides a translation and running commentary on transcripts from the purge trials of 1936—the first and second Zinoviev-Kamenev trials, the Radek-Piatakov trial, the trial against the Red Army Supreme Command, and the Bukharin trial.

374.   Medvedev, Roy Aleksandrovich, **Let History Judge: The Origins and Consequences of Stalinism**. Rev. and expanded ed. New York: Columbia University Press, 1989. xxi, 903 p. ISBN: 0231063504. Includes bibliographical references and index.

The first edition of Medvedev's book was published under the same title in 1972. This new edition can rightly be called a new book. It was not only translated by a different person than was the 1972 book, but new chapters have been added, whole sections deleted, and paragraphs added. Medvedev's monumental investigation of Stalin and the effects of Stalinism is considered by the author to be his life's work. He has taken many of the criticism addressed to his first book and responded to them. It's structure remains the same. There are four parts. The first describes Stalin's rise in the party, the second assesses Stalin's usurpation of power and the great terror, the third deals with the nature and causes of Stalinism, and the fourth evaluates some consequences of Stalin's personal dictatorship. Reviews: *Russian History* 17:2:233-35 (Summer 1990). *SAIS Review* 10:2:265-67 (Summer-Fall 1990). *Soviet Union-Union Sovietique* 17:1-2:170-71 (1990). *Canadian Journal of History* 25:3:444-48 (December 1990). *Orbis* 34:2:295-96.

375.   Rowney, Don Karl, **Transition to Technocracy: The Structural Origins of the Soviet Administrative State**. Ithaca, NY: Cornell University Press, 1989. xv, 236 p. *Studies in Soviet History and Society*, ISBN: 0801421837. Includes index and bibliography (p. 211-231).

This is a study of Russia's evolution to a technocratic administration in the Soviet era. The author believes that the huge bureaucracy of prerevolutionary Russia was replaced with a large technocratic organization. The specialists that make up that new administration are also the subject of this study. Thus, this is also a social history. "In certain respects, then, this study is broad and complex. The role of civil administration has been so intricately combined with the evolution of Russian society that it is impossible to study any important aspect of Russian civil administration without writing about segments of Russian society." (p. 2) The study is arranged chronologically and makes extensive use of statistical analysis. The author has tried to make this form of analysis accessible to the non-specialist. Review: *American Historical Review* 95:5:1592-93 (December 1990).

376. World Congress for Soviet and East European Studies, **Essays on Revolutionary Culture and Stalinism: Selected Papers from the Third World Congress for Soviet and East European Studies**, edited by John W. Strong. Columbus, Ohio: Slavica Publishers, 1990. 244 p. ISBN: 0893572101. Includes bibliographies.

All of these essays from the Third World Congress focus on Stalin and Stalinism. The first several essays concentrate on revolutionary culture and Soviet attempts to spread this culture abroad. The remaining contributions deal with topics directly related to Stalinism, trials, regional support for the dictator, mass politics, the bureaucracy, and peasants and the party.

1985 to Present

377. **The Gorbachev Generation: Issues in Soviet Domestic Policy**, edited by Jane Shapiro Zacek. 1st ed. New York, NY: Paragon House, 1989. xii, 281 p. "*A PWPA Book,*" ISBN: 0943852420. Includes bibliographical references.

The contributors to this volume presented their papers at a conference sponsored by the World Peace Academy in 1986. Each of the authors seeks to understand the "programs, the progress, and the prospects of Gorbachev's changes." (cover) Issues addressed include a historical background of the reform program, the renewal of party leadership, economic recovery, agriculture, nationalities, educational policy, culture, religion, law enforcement, party-military relations, and health care.

378. Bonner, Elena, **Alone Together**. 1st ed. New York: Knopf, 1986. 269 p. ISBN: 0394558359. Includes index.

This personal narrative by Elena Bonner, wife of Nobel Prize physicist Andrei Sakharov, was written in Newton, Massachusetts in 1986, during a leave of absence from her exile in Gorky. It tells of the house arrest of Sakharov and Bonner, their struggle with the Soviet regime, and her attempts to allow Sakharov to be freed from exile. Review: *Canadian Defense Quarterly* 17:1:60 (Summer 1987).

379. Gupta, Bhabani Sen, **The Gorbachev Factor in World Affairs: An Indian Interpretation**. New Delhi: B.R. Publishing Corp., 1989. xxvi, 507 p. ISBN: 8170185459. Includes index.

Gupta has collected together both his own published and unpublished writings on Gorbachev and his meaning for world affairs, as well as several documents related to this theme. "The focus of this volume is on internal reforms in the USSR, the impact of Gorbachev on the superpower relationship, regional conflicts with part nuclear emphasis on Afghanistan and South Asia, inter-communist relations, international and regional security, and on Gorbachev's New Thinking on foreign policy and the human condition." (p. v).

380. Hahn, Jeffrey W., **Soviet Grassroots: Citizen Participation in Local Soviet Government**. Princeton, NJ: Princeton University Press, 1988. xiii, 320 p. ISBN: 0691077673. Includes index and bibliography (p. 293-308).

Hahn's goal is "to provide an objective picture of what locally elected Soviet representatives do so that debate about the nature of citizen participation in Soviet politics will have a stronger basis in fact." (p. 6) After several introductory chapters giving the rationale for the study, the background of mass participation in local government and how local government is organized, chapters five and six come to the main problem. How do constituents communicate their problems and preferences to their deputy and what the deputy can do to respond to their needs?

381. **Elites and Political Power in the USSR**, edited by David Lane. Hants, England: Elgar, 1988. xii, 299 p. ISBN: 1852780444. Includes bibliographies and index.

A collection of essays which were the result of a conference held at the University of Birmingham in July 1987 is presented in this volume. "The changes in leadership, personnel, and the roles of elites which have accompanied the rise to power of Gorbachev will be examined in this book." (p. xi) The book is divided into four sections, each examining some aspect of political power in the USSR. Part one includes essays on the top political leadership. An appendix to this section provides biographical sketches on major political figures (it should be noted that Yeltsin is not included in this group as at the time he was not a major figure in the Communist Party). Part two examines questions on mobility in the party structures and recruitment policies. Part three turns to the role of institutions for the party leadership. Part four is concerned with the spatial relations between "centre and periphery." The contributors are scholars from various Western institutions.

382. Laqueur, Walter, **Soviet Union 2000: Reform or Revolution?** 1st ed. New York: St. Martin's Press, 1990. xx, 201 p. ISBN: 03120044259.

This book was written after the momentous events in Eastern Europe had taken place. It is a series of speculative essays on the future of the Soviet Union. The speculation is concentrated in eight essays. Topics of these essays include current trends in Soviet politics, future scenarios in Soviet politics, the future of economic reform, the fate of the nationalities, perestroika and the Soviet army, the Soviet grand strategy, and Sino-Soviet relations. Laqueur ties all these disparate strands by several authors into a concluding chapter.

383. **Limits to Soviet Power**, edited by Rajan Menon and Daniel N. Nelson. Lexington, Mass.: Lexington Books, 1989. xii, 230 p. ISBN: 0669132268. Includes index.

An interdisciplinary analysis of the significance and severity of the constraints on Soviet power. The method of analysis is one of focusing on domestic and foreign policy elements that serve to limit central power. In each essay of this collection, several assumptions are made, one that the Soviet Union is a world economic power with tremendous reserves. But also that the inefficiency inherent in the Soviet system is affecting the use of those economic assets. A similar argument is presented with regard to military resources. The book is divided into two parts, one examining internal limitations including economic, leadership, ethnic problems, and technology. The second part focuses on external constraints such as military intervention, Warsaw pact relations, and Third World relations. Generally, all the contributors feel that the Soviet system with all of its flaws is not disintegrating, just changing. Perestroika is viewed as a means to "reinvigorate" the Soviet Union and "reinforce the Communist Party."

384. Motyl, Alexander J., **Sovietology, Rationality, Nationality: Coming to Grips with Nationalism in the USSR**. New York: Columbia University Press, 1990. xii, 263 p. ISBN: 0231073267. Includes bibliographical references (p. 197-253) and index.

Motyl is interested in discovering the strengths and weaknesses of Sovietology as it is applied to current problems of theory and political analysis. In this book he examines nationalism in the Soviet Union in order to see the relation between contemporary Sovietology and to uncover new information about nationalism. He says: "This is, then, a study of not just nationalism, but of the way in which a critical investigation of nationalism can enrich our understanding of the Soviet Union." (p. x).

385. Ross, Cameron, **Local Government in the Soviet Union: Problems of Implementation and Control**. London: Croom Helm, 1987. 229 p. ISBN: 070994246X. Includes bibliography and index.

While many Western scholars have focused their efforts on the input side of policy making (the interest group/pluralist school), Ross turns his attention to implementation of policy once it has been formulated. He shows, for example, "that too much emphasis has been placed on group inputs and conflict, and that in the Soviet Union, groups are far more likely to mold and adopt policies in the implementation stage." (p. 3) In his study, Ross examines Party-state relations, local budgets, local Soviets and planning, planning of housing, and problems of implementation and control in Soviet local government. Review: *Slavic Review* 47:1:136-37 (Spring 1988).

386. **The Soviet Union and the Challenge of the Future**, edited by Alexander Shtromas and Morton A. Kaplan. 1st ed. New York: Paragon House, 1988. 4 vols. *"A PWPA Book,"* ISBN: 0943852293. Includes bibliographies and index.

This first volume in the series *The Soviet Union and the Challenge of the Future* resulted from the Second International Conference of the Professors for World Peace Academy in Geneva, Switzerland. It includes essays by a number of scholars. "In contrast to subsequent volumes, all of which concentrate on particular aspects of the Soviet system, the present volume is devoted to the discussion of the Soviet system as a whole. It starts with a debate on the Soviet system's nature, continues with the analysis of its present critical state, and then considers the prospects for transition to and, consequently, the possible character of an alternative non-Soviet and post-Soviet system." (p. x) The book's four parts cover these four topics. Most parts contain essays with greatly varying opinions. The appendix is an essay on American research and teaching on the Soviet Union in the literature.

387. Solovyov, Vladimir, and Elena Klepikova, **Behind the High Kremlin Walls**, translated by Guy Daniels in collaboration with the authors. 1st ed. New York: Dodd, Mead & Co., 1986. xxi, 248 p. ISBN: 0396087108. Includes index and bibliography (p. 223-228).

A thematically arranged analysis of power and politics in the Kremlin. The authors trace the Kremlin leadership since 1982. They are interested in explaining how power is obtained, controlled, and lost in the Kremlin. There is analysis of Andropov, Chernenko, and Gorbachev as well as other major figures in the Politburo. The authors also focus on the events that affected the political development of these men. The two Soviet authors hope to clear up some misconceptions of Western readers on these subjects. The book is written in a documentary style with a roughly chronological arrangement.

Political Parties

388. Narkiewicz, Olga A., **Soviet Leaders: From the Cult of Personality to Collective Rule**. Brighton, Sussex: Wheatsheaf, 1986. ix, 256 p. ISBN: 0745001963. Includes index and bibliography (p. 247-251).

Narkiewicz wrote this book because she believed there was a need to provide up-to-date biographies of recent Soviet leaders in concise form. Seven of her thirteen chapters are devoted to Khrushchev and Brezhnev, with two on Andropov and one each on Chernenko and Gorbachev. She also provides an introductory chapter on approaches to the Soviet leadership problem and some contextual background necessary to understand problems of leadership succession. Her approach throughout is to focus on the person rather than the myth and "to concentrate on the way in which the leaders' personalities interact with their duties, and impinge on the policies of the state." (p. ii).

389. **Developments in Soviet Politics**, edited by Stephen White, Alex Pravda, and Zvi Gitelman. Durham, NC: Duke University Press, 1990. xvi, 310 p. ISBN: 0822310848. Includes bibliographical references (p. 298-304) and index.

A collection of essays that focuses on the changes in the Soviet political scene since Gorbachev took office. A useful volume for students and scholars, the book is divided into four sections, each analyzing one area of political change. Each contains several essays on the topic. The four sections are "Historical and Cultural Context," "The Contemporary Political System," "The Making of Public Policy," and "The Future of the Soviet System." A guide to further readings on each topic is included as well as a full bibliography and index. Useful information on past Soviet leaders as well as those presently in power is provided.

390. Yanov, Alexander, **The Russian Challenge and the Year 2000**. Oxford: Basil Blackwell Inc., 1987. xvi, 302 p. ISBN: 0631153349. Includes index.

A discussion of Russian nationalism since the late 1970s. The author attempts to distinguish between various degrees of nationalism, separating that which can be called patriotism from that which is chauvinistic in nature by examining the varying ideological basis for different approaches. The book is divided into three parts. The first deals with the history of Russian nationalism as well as its perception in the West. The second examines present day aspects of the movement and what they may lead to. Finally, two concluding chapters discuss Fascism in the Soviet Union and the Western reaction to developments in the Soviet Union. The volume includes an appendix with numerous tables on data-ideology, results of past reformist attempts, as well as several graphics on Soviet government and society.

Communism, Communist Party

391. **The Challenges of Our Time: Disarmament and Social Progress**. New York: International Publishers, 1986. 216 p. ISBN: 0717806421.

Excerpts from the most significant speeches at the 27th Congress of the Communist Party of the Soviet Union. "Observers across the political spectrum agree that the 27th was no ordinary Congress. The aims it projected for the next fifteen years are indeed breathtaking." (publisher's note) The volume includes Gorbachev's Political Report, commentary from Vadim Zagladin, speeches by Ivan Frolov and Edward Shevardnadze, and the program put forward by the CPSU. Translated from the Russian.

392. Brezezinski, Zbigniew K., **The Grand Failure: The Birth and Death of Communism in the Twentieth Century**. New York: Scribner, 1989. x, 278 p. ISBN: 0684190346. Includes index.

The author traces the rise and decline of communism. He believes that it will totally disappear in the next century. "Prospering only where it abandons its internal substance even if still retaining some of its external labels, communism will be remembered as the twentieth century's most extraordinary political and intellectual aberration." (p. 1) The six part arrangement develops a picture of an ideology failing in practice. The first part examines the socioeconomic problems of the Soviet Union. Part two reviews current attempts to revitalize the party and concludes that they cannot succeed. Part three focuses on communism in Eastern Europe and its failure there. Part four turns to Chinese communism and argues its only success was in the maintenance of the trappings of communism while reforms rob it of its substance. The fifth part examines ideologies and the political decline of the system and the final section forecasts the demise of communism and its possible aftermath. The appendix shows the economic decline in communist countries.

393. Brucan, Silviu, **Pluralism and Social Conflict: A Social Analysis of the Communist World**, with foreword by Immanuel Wallerstein. New York: Praeger, 1990. xxx, 186 p. ISBN: 0275934756. Includes index and bibliographical references.

A Marxist's view of changes in Communist countries around the world. For example, the author interprets the "stagnation of the Brezhnev period" as a result of Brezhnev's unwillingness to sacrifice the preeminence of the working class to the rising technological workers. The book is divided into three parts: the evolution of classes and class policy, social struggles and the scientific technological revolution, and social conflict generated by reform. Although the Soviet Union is the focal point of the study, there are sections on Eastern Europe and China.

394. Campeanu, Pavel, **The Origins of Stalinism: From Leninist Revolution to Stalinist Society**, translated by Michael Vale. Armonk, NY: M.E. Sharpe, 1986. ix, 187 p. ISBN: 0873323637.

The driving question behind Campeanu's study is "How did it come to pass that the first great anti-imperialist revolution of the modern era ultimately gave birth to but another imperialism of a new kind?" (p. 3) He concentrates on various aspects of the Revolution including its antifeudal character, its anti-bourgeois character, and its anti-imperialist character. Review: *Orbis* 31:1:158-59 (Spring 1987).

395. Goudoever, Albert P. van, **The Limits of Destalinisation in the Soviet Union: Political Rehabilitations in the Soviet Union Since Stalin**, translated by Frans Hijkoop. New York: St. Martin's Press, 1986. 276 p. ISBN: 0312486804. Includes indexes and bibliography (p. 255-266).

With each successive leader after Stalin, some of those who were purged, persecuted, and imprisoned have been rehabilitated. Goudoever examines the concept of rehabilitation and various aspects of it including formal, public, and posthumous rehabilitation. He then moves from the theoretical and analyzes rehabilitations behind the scenes including the process of rehabilitation in Czechoslovakia and the Soviet Union and the role of the Communist Party. The largest chapter is devoted to public posthumous rehabilitations in the Soviet Union, the methods used, and the purposes served. He concludes with three individual case studies of persons rehabilitated. Several appendices provide additional factual and statistical information not easily incorporated into the text. Review: *Orbis* 30:4:750-51 (Winter 1987).

396. **The Transformation of Socialism: Perestroika and Reform in the Soviet Union and China**, edited by Mel Gurtov. Boulder, CO.: Westview Press, 1990. x, 258 p. ISBN: 0813379881. Includes bibliographical references.

Papers resulting from a conference held in Portland, Oregon in 1989 are compiled in this volume. The conference participants were from the Soviet Union, China, and the U.S. "The contributors assess the effects of the reforms in four key areas: the reinterpretation of history; the relationship between the communist party and the state; culture, intellectuals, and society; and the domestic and international economies. Additional chapters treat the Soviet and Chinese reforms comparatively, focusing on their international impact and on the formation of elites." (back cover).

397. Hill, Ronald J., and Peter Frank, **The Soviet Communist Party**. 3rd ed. Boston: Allen & Unwin, 1986. 177 p. ISBN: 0044970242. Includes index and bibliography (p. 159-172).

This work presents an analytical descriptive view of the Communist Party of the Soviet Union. Now in its third edition, the book covers the role of the Party in the Soviet system, the Party membership, structures, institutions, and personnel, the Party's functions and performance, Party-state relations, and the Party and nonstate institutions. Two appendices are included: the CPSU Politburo in March 1986 and key dates in the Party's history.

398. **Restructuring Soviet Society: An Appraisal of the New Programme of the Communist Party of the Soviet Union**, edited by Zafar Imam. New Delhi: Panchsheel Publishers, 1987. xiv, 312 p. ISBN: 8185197016. Includes bibliographies and index.

This series of essays by Indian scholars is the result of an All-India Seminar in the Revised Programme of the Communist Party of the Soviet Union, as adopted by the 27th Congress of the Party. The essays are arranged in four sections. In section one, four essays treat various aspects of the new programme in order to sketch out its general profile. Section two deals with economic issues and trends, including implications of perestroika and the relation between politics and economics. Section three identifies political, social, and cultural trends, and section four is devoted to issues and cultural trends in foreign policy, including the restructuring of Soviet Central Asia.

399. **The Workers' Revolution in Russia, 1917: The View from Below**, edited by Daniel H. Kaiser. Cambridge: Cambridge University Press, 1987. xiii, 152 p. ISBN: 0521341663. Includes bibliography (p. 142-146).

The papers collected here arose from a conference held at Grinnel College in the spring of 1984. The aim of the conferees "was not to introduce new research or talk to other specialists, but to synthesize their findings for a general audience and begin constructing an alternative explanation for the Russian Revolution." (p. ii) The authors attempt to give a more comprehensive examination of the revolution, emphasizing not just the revolutionaries themselves, but also the view from below—from factory workers and peasants, as well as the cultural and political forces that were simultaneously at work to produce this earth-shaking event.

400. Levine, Alan J., **The Soviet Union, the Communist Movement, and the World: Prelude to the Cold War, 1917-1941**. New York: Praeger, 1990. 189 p. ISBN: 0275934438. Includes bibliographical references (p. 175-182).

Levine describes and analyzes Russian internal and foreign policies and the role of Marxism, Leninism, and the Communist movement in them. After an introduction covering Marxism and Leninism as ideologies, he proceeds chronologically from the Revolution and Civil War and the hopes for world revolution, to the role of communist ideology through the Stalinist prism, the struggle for China, Europe, and East Asia.

401. Melograni, Piero, **Lenin and the Myth of World Revolution: Ideology and Reasons of State, 1917-1920**, translated by Julie Lerro. Atlantic Highlands, NJ: Humanities Press International, 1989. xiv, 161 p. ISBN: 0391306106. Includes bibliographic references.

Lenin did not intend to create a world revolution maintains the author. Instead "his objective was to create communist parties in the West that were totally loyal, disciplined, and subordinate to the needs of the Soviet State." (p. xiv) Melograni's book attempts to support this view with documentary and legal evidence.

402. Nation, R. Craig, **War on War: Lenin, the Zimmerwald Left, and the Origins of Communist Internationalism**. Durham, NC: Duke University Press, 1989. xviii, 313 p. ISBN: 0822309440. Includes bibliographical references (p. 289-303) and index.

The Zimmerwald Left, a group founded and led by Lenin, is the topic of Nation's book. He "seeks to interpret the experience of the Zimmerwald Left in a manner that takes into account its importance without surrendering to what recently have been the assumptions of official communist historiography." (p. xi) It offers a fascinating study of the failed promise of international socialism. Reviews: *Foreign Affairs* 69:4:191 (Fall 1990). *Canadian Slavonic Papers* 32:2:189-90 (June 1990). *Russian History* 17:2:228-29 (Summer 1990).

403. Norval, Morgan, **Red Star Over Southern Africa**. Washington, DC: Selous Foundation Press, 1988. xix, 217 p. ISBN: 0944273009. Includes bibliographies and index.

Norval, in this virulently anti-Soviet work, tries to show that "using Mongol tactics of terror, tribute collection, and choke-point control, the Soviets have mounted a massive assault on this area of essential importance to the Free World." (p. xviii) Reviews: *Global Affairs* 3:4:214-19 (Fall 1988). *Orbis* 33:2:314-15 (Spring 1989).

404. Parker, John W., **Kremlin in Transition**. Boston: Unwin Hyman, 1990. xvii, 475 p. ISBN: 004450990. Includes index.

This is one of a two-volume set attempting to analyze changes at the highest level of government in the USSR. The book traces Gorbachev's rise to power beginning with the death of Kulakov in 1978, the event that brought Gorbachev to Moscow. The book is not a contemporary history—the author makes no attempt to update his conclusion in light of changes in the Soviet Union. His goal is to trace the transitions in the Kremlin since 1978 and to explain them. The focus is on national security, domestic and foreign. The format is one of a standard chronology. The book is divided into parts covering the terms of each Soviet leader from Brezhnev on. This is a scholarly work focusing on the reaction to perestroika and glasnost at the highest level. The author drew heavily on media sources as a reflection of official reaction to various reforms.

405. Ra'anan, Uri, **Inside the Apparat: Perspectives on the Soviet System from Former Functionaries**. Lexington, MA: Lexington Books, 1990. xxviii, 281 p. ISBN: 10669242268 (pbk.), 0669219851. Includes bibliographical references and index.

This work is the result of an oral history project that interviewed Soviet émigrés who were former officials in the KGB and other powerful party organs. Through the interviews the author has attempted to find out information not available elsewhere. The analysis focuses on several topics: 1. careers, appointments, promotions, dismissals, and alignments; 2. foci of power; 3. exoteric and esoteric communications; 4. international relations decision making; 5. direct and indirect implementation of policy decisions; 6. coordination and control, and dissonance among Soviet allies; and 7. Soviet analysis and perceptions of international developments. This book includes brief identifications of persons mentioned in the text.

406. Rigby, Thomas Henry, **The Changing Soviet System: Mono-organisational Socialism from Its Origins to Gorbachev's Restructuring**. Brookfield, VT: E. Elgar Pub., 1990. vii, 256 p. ISBN: 1852783044. Includes bibliographical references and index.

A collection of articles written by the author some years ago and reissued here in a generally chronological order. The author believes Soviet society to be mono-organizational in structure and that the nature of this structure grew out of Bolshevism and has led to the crisis that prompted Gorbachev's reforms. Essays cover such topics as Stalinism, bureaucratization in Russia; the USSR, and mono-organizational socialism, among others.

407. Roberts, Paul Craig, **Alienation and the Soviet Economy: The Collapse of the Socialist Era**, with foreword by Aaron Wildavsky. 2nd rev. ed. New York: Holmes & Meier, 1990. xxvi, 123 p. *Independent Studies in Political Economy*, ISBN: 0841912475. Includes bibliographical references and index.

A volume dealing with communist political economy. The author attempts to demonstrate why the system failed. This is a revised edition of the 1971 original. The subjects discussed here include Marx's theory of alienation and central planning, "war communism," organizational structure of the market, and Oskar Lange's theory for socialist planning. The volume also includes an appendix critiquing other interpretations of Marxist alienation.

408. Ryan, Michael, and Richard Prentice, **Social Trends in the Soviet Union from 1950**. Basingstoke: Macmillan, 1987. xiii, 100 p. ISBN: 0333408462. Includes bibliographical references.

A reference work for the general reader supplying statistical data on societal change. The authors have limited themselves to the period from 1950 to 1987 since the post-war era marks the second phase of Soviet economic development. The organization of the book was influenced by that of the source most heavily drawn upon for data, *Naselenie SSSR (The Population of the USSR)*. Chapter one looks at broad changes in population structure. Chapters two through six look at specific aspects of Soviet demographics, urban and rural conditions, migration, child-bearing, family structure, and ethnic composition. Chapters seven and eight examine social service provisions. While some evaluative statements are included, the goal of the book is to present statistical data. Although a complete list of tables is included, the volume does not include an index. Review: *Contemporary Sociology* 17:3:319 (May 1988).

409. **Understanding Soviet Society**, edited by Michael Paul Sacks and Jerry G. Pankhurst. Boston: Allen & Unwin, 1988. xix, 268 p. ISBN: 0044450362. Includes index and bibliography.

Sociological essays on the changing Soviet Union make up this volume, originally intended as an update to the book *Contemporary Soviet Society*. The authors stress a comparative approach. They have attempted to avoid or, when possible, dispel stereotypes currently popular in both the scholarly and popular literature on the USSR. The book is divided into three parts. Part one includes essays on social stratification, including topics such as ethnic differences, movement through social classes, urban-rural society, and gender inequalities. The two essays in part two discuss the effects of the state and the Party on Soviet society. Part three contains essays on everyday life in the Soviet Union. The four essays in this section consider sociological aspects of religion, crime, labor utilization, and the military. Each essay includes a bibliography of titles related to its topic.

410. Shah, Rajiv, **New Horizons of Soviet Policies**. New Delhi: Patriot Publishers, 1987. viii, 103 p. ISBN: 8170500621.

A discussion of the changes in Marxism as practiced in the Soviet Union since the CPSU congress of 1986. The author argues that creative development in Marxist theory is what is behind the change in Soviet policies that have been introduced. The book is thematically arranged covering such topics as the "new thinking," nationalism, democratization, and intensification.

411. Thorniley, Daniel, **The Rise and Fall of the Soviet Rural Communist Party, 1927-1939**. Basingstoke: Macmillan in Association with Centre for Russian and East European Studies, University of Birmingham, 1988. xiii, 246 p. *Studies in Soviet History and Society*, ISBN: 0333385144. Includes bibliography and index.

Thorniley's purpose is to examine the role of the Communist Party in the Russian country-side during the interwar period. Special attention is given to its size, growth, membership, organization, and function. Several appendices concentrate on statistical information about the party with tables and explanatory notes. Reviews: *Slavic Review* 49:1:120-22 (Spring 1990). *Russian Review* 49:4:504-505 (October 1990). *Russian History* 17:4:461-63 (Winter 1990).

412. **Can the Soviet System Survive Reform?: Seven Colloquies about the State of Soviet Socialism Seventy Years after the Bolshevik Revolution,** edited and introduced by George R. Urban. London: Pinter Publishers, 1989. xix, 383 p. ISBN: 0861870018. Includes bibliographical references and index.

This collection of conversations with Soviet and Western officials, journalists, and scholars attempts to bring together the opinions of Westerners and first hand observers on the permanency of the changes in the Soviet Union. The editor, G. R. Urban, has discussions with Max Kampelman, Napolitano, and Milovan Djilas. A different topic is covered with each discussant, but each of the conversations also focuses on the chances for survival of the Soviet Union after reform. An appendix with information on Eurocommunism in 1978 is included.

413. Williams, Robert Chadwell, **The Other Bolsheviks: Lenin and His Critics, 1904-1914**. Bloomington, IN: Indiana University Press, 1986. 233 p. ISBN: 0253342694. Includes index and bibliography (p. 222-228).

This intellectual history of Bolshevism traces that movement from its beginnings in 1904 to the outbreak of World War I. By 1914 Lenin had taken over what was left of that movement. While recognizing the importance of Lenin, Williams focuses on the ideas and activities of the other Bolsheviks and in so doing shows that "Lenin was one revolutionary among many in a fractious, polemical, and divided political movement, not the undisputed leader of an obedient party." (p. 4) Although the author does not describe Lenin's rise to power in the years 1914 to 1917, he does include a final chapter on Lenin's debates with other Bolsheviks on the subject of syndicalism in 1920. Review: *Canadian Slavonic Papers* 29:4:438-39 (December 1987).

414. Wren, Christopher Sale, **The End of the Line: The Failure of Communism in the Soviet Union and China**. New York: Simon and Schuster, 1990. 352 p. ISBN: 0671638645. Includes bibliographical references (p. 317-338).

A journalist for the *New York Times* observes the decline of the Communist system in the Soviet Union and in China. The author believes that in both countries, the leaders realized change was essential, but neither Gorbachev nor Deng Xiaoping had a coherent plan for the future. He also believes that the failure of communism was inevitable. He tries to demonstrate the validity of these views by recounting his experience in both countries over many years.

Perestroika, Glasnost

415. **Implications of Soviet New Thinking: Summary Report of International Conference, St. Paul, Minnesota, October 9-11, 1987**. New York: Institute for East-West Security Studies, 1987. 93 p. *Special Report,*.

The 1987 conference that produced this summary was aimed at defining new ways to respond to the changes in the Soviet Union introduced by Mikhail Gorbachev. This volume was intended for a general American and European audience. The contributors consist of four public figures: Hans-Dietrich Genscher, Vice-Chancellor of the Federal Republic of

Germany; Harry Ottof, GDR, John Whitehean, U.S. Deputy Secretary of State, and Senator Bill Bradley. The intent of the volume is to stimulate debate on the question of how to respond to the policy changes in the USSR and, hopefully, plan some role in assisting in policy formulation. An executive summary of the conference proceedings is also included summarizing the conclusions reached. The book presents early perceptions of Gorbachev's policies and their long term implication. This group was urging cooperation. There is no index or bibliography.

416. Armstrong, G. Patrick, **Gorbachev, "Reform," and the USSR**. Toronto: Macken-zie Institute for the Study of Terrorism, Revolution and Propaganda, 1987. 32 p. *Mackenzie Paper*, no. 1. ISBN: 0921877005. Includes bibliographical references.
These two essays focus on both earlier initiatives and those of Gorbachev's early years. Two conclusions are reached. First, that the reforms initiated by Mikhail Gorbachev are intended to improve the existing system, not supplant it. That being the case, world peace is no closer. Second, the centralized system that allows the reforms to be initiated will prevent them from being taken to their logical conclusion. The author believes that the centralized power in the Soviet Union will be maintained and the reforms will only have a limited effect.

417. Aspen Strategy Group and the European Strategy Group in cooperation with the Aspen Institute Italia, **The Soviet Challenge in the Gorbachev Era: Western Perceptions and Policy Recommendations.** Lanham, MD.: University Press of America, 1989. xiii, 155 p. ISBN: 0819173991. Includes bibliographies.
One of a series of reports by the Aspen Strategy Group whose goal is to relate varying viewpoints on international security to current policy debates in the U.S. It is made up of individuals from different backgrounds drawing on the academic, policy, and business communities. This volume contains five brief reports on Soviet economics, international trade, Soviet-East European relations, Soviet military strategy, Soviet foreign policy, and arms control. The bulk of the volume is made up of four appendices on economic reform, Eastern Europe, Soviet military doctrine, and "new thinking." The consensus of the committee was that the reforms are in the interest of the West but their success or failure will depend upon internal forces of the Soviet Union.

418. **Politics, Society, and Nationality Inside Gorbachev's Russia**, edited by Seweryn Bialer. Boulder, CO: Westview Press, 1989. 255 p. *"An East-West Forum Publica-tion,"* ISBN: 0813305047. Includes bibliography.
A group of essays sponsored by the East-West Forum. These essays look at a number of problems facing Gorbachev as he attempts to establish his reforms. Political culture, the basis of reform, the problem created by Gorbachev's liberal supporters, the development of a civil society, nationality problems, and the 19th Party Congress are all essay topics. A bibliography of current publications on the Soviet Union is included.

419. **The Soviet Revolution: Perestroika and the Remaking of Socialism**, edited by Jon Bloomfield. London: Lawrence and Wishart, 1989. 285 p. ISBN: 0853157138. Includes bibliographical references.
A collection of essays by scholars and journalists, all of whom believe that the program, perestroika, could transform Soviet society under the direction of the Communist Party leadership. The contributors are directing their comments to the general reader as well as the specialist. "The essays in this collection chart the emerging process of change, and examine the main difficulties facing the reformers: problems of the economy, the institution of democracy and accountability, complex issues such as the question of nationalities, and the challenge of the international situation." (back cover) The essays are divided into four

sections: "Problems and Prospects, 1982-1985," "The Perestroika Offensive," "Making Perestroika a Reality," and "The International Context." The volume includes a glossary of Soviet names and a select chronology.

420. **Glasnost, Perestroika, and the Socialist Community**, edited by Charles Bukowski and J. Richard Walsh. New York: Praeger, 1990. xi, 176 p. ISBN: 0275931307. Includes bibliographical references and index.

A selection of essays that focus on the effect the Soviet reforms are having on socialist countries. No unifying theme guided the contributors. Each approached their area as they saw best. There are seven essays, each examining a different area. The first focuses on the effects of perestroika in Poland and Czechoslovakia. The others deal with the USSR, China, Cuba, Vietnamese-Soviet relations, Afghanistan, and Korea. The final essay assesses the impact of glasnost and perestroika. The volume seeks to focus attention on important areas of interest that have so far been largely ignored.

421. **Voices of Glasnost: Interviews with Gorbachev's Reformers**, edited by Stephen F. Cohen and Katrina vanden Heuvel. 1st ed. New York: Norton, 1989. 339 p. ISBN: 0393026256. Includes index.

Fourteen Soviet intellectuals of diverse backgrounds were interviewed by the editors. All were proponents of perestroika and glasnost but they sometimes have widely divergent views on how it should proceed. The contributors range in background from a Politburo member to a poet. They share a chronological background in that all began their careers in the post-Stalinist 1950s. The authors hoped to give Americans more direct access to the historical reforms in Russia through these interviews. Since the authors wanted to encourage the contributors to discuss their ideas, they did not challenge their statements.

422. Colton, Timothy J., **The Dilemma of Reform in the Soviet Union**. revised and expanded edition. New York: Council of Foreign Relations, 1986. v, 274 p. ISBN: 0876090145. Includes index and bibliography (p. 264-266).

This revised edition of the author's earlier work seeks to evaluate the possibility of reform in the Soviet Union and the obstacles to it. The author had felt that with Gorbachev's rise to power the possibility of moderate reforms existed in the Soviet Union, but that radical reforms, that is, fundamental changes of the political institutions, was not a real possibility. Nor did he feel it was Gorbachev's goal. To assess the possibility of future change the author begins by describing the legacy of the past, particularly the Brezhnev era. He then goes on to an assessment of economic obstacles to change in the current system. The next chapters deal with the succession struggle and options for reform. The final chapter moves to a wider context focusing on Soviet internal events and the outside world and the implications of change in the Soviet Union for the West. Review: *SAIS Review* 7:2:226-27 (Summer-Fall 1987).

423. Cooper, Leo, **Soviet Reforms and Beyond**. New York: St. Martin's Press, 1991. viii, 190 p. ISBN: 0312065043. Includes index and bibliographical references (p. 183-186).

This study seeks "to analyze in depth the nature and scope of the Soviet reforms, to look at them in the context of the expressed willingness of the USSR to become incorporated in the world economic system, and the implications of such a trend in Soviet policies for East-West relations." (p. 11) The author believes the reforms to have been economically motivated. He also believes those same economic factors affected Soviet military policy, creating the impetus for arms reductions. The book is thematically arranged with chapters covering the ideological context of reform, new military doctrine, agriculture, foreign trade, and the possibilities for the future.

424. Crouch, Martin, **Revolution & Evolution: Gorbachev and Soviet Politics**. New York: Prentice Hall, 1990. ix, 245 p. ISBN: 0137804854. Includes index and bibliography (p. 233-240).

A general study of domestic politics in the Soviet Union focusing on the causes and future of perestroika. The volume is based on two propositions. First, that the current reforms have evolved over time from the Soviet system and are producing revolutionary changes. Second, that the Soviet Union should be analyzed as any other country would be. The book is divided thematically into sections covering the history of domestic politics in the Soviet Union, ideology, the Communist Party, society, economics, and environment. Each chapter has a section of suggested English language readings. There is also a helpful chronology covering Soviet political events from 1985 to 1989.

425. Doder, Dusko, **Shadows and Whispers: Power Politics Inside the Kremlin from Brezhnev to Gorbachev**. 1st ed. New York: Random House, 1986. x, 339 p. ISBN: 0394549988.

This account by the former Moscow bureau chief for the *Washington Post* traces Gorbachev's rise to power. The coverage begins in 1978 when the author was first assigned to Moscow. It is a journalistic rather than historical account of events. Largely based on personal observations of the author it also draws on his interviews with those close to the center of power and intellectuals. The author intends to give an account of the beginning of the Gorbachev reforms and the events that led up to it.

426. **Gorbachev's Revolution: Economic Pressures and Defense Realities**, edited by Christopher Donnelly. Coulsdon, Surrey: Jane's Information Group, 1989. ix, 263 p. ISBN: 0710605900. Includes bibliographical references and index.

A collection of essays by Western writers attempting to analyze the problems of Gorbachev's reforms from a Soviet point of view. All essays rely on Soviet materials for their information. While not attempting to answer broad queries on the feasibility of Gorbachev's reforms and the seriousness of his intentions, this volume hopes to "...go some way towards helping readers to understand the complexity of issues facing Gorbachev as he attempts to solve the many problems which afflict the USSR, and how his internal problems drive his external policies." (p. 1) The contributors are primarily scholars of Soviet and East European studies. Essay topics include discussion of Soviet economic policy, Soviet technology policy, the reforms and Eastern Europe, economic burden-sharing in the Warsaw Pact, changes in Soviet military policy, etc. There are several appendices providing information on Politburo membership, statistics on technological development, East European defense spending, and tank versus anti-tank technological development.

427. **The Soviet Union Under Gorbachev: Prospects for Reform**. London: Croom Helm, 1987. 227 p. ISBN: 0709945191. Includes bibliographies and index.

This collection of essays is the result of an informal study group centered at the School of European Studies, University of Sussex. The four contributors, who met in the summer of 1986, addressed the question: What is the likely future of Gorbachev's Soviet Union? Their conclusions are interesting in retrospect. For example, they believed that Gorbachev would not question the basic assumptions of party rule; that although glasnost is a real break with the past, media openness would not bereave political openness; that Gorbachev would be pragmatic about private enterprise. They saw Gorbachev as a rationalizer and disciplinarian who realized that the economy was grossly overcentralized and who would bring the second economy out in the open. Finally, the flurry in arms-control activity, they believed, was motivated to a great degree by economic concerns. Review: *Fletcher Forum* 12:1:187-88 (Winter 1988).

428. **The Glasnost Reader**, compiled and edited by Jonathan Eisen. New York: New American Library, 1990. xvii, 445 p. *NAL Books*, ISBN: 0453006957. Includes bibliographical references.

This compendium of writings by Russians on a myriad of topics represents a sampling of the type of writing that has appeared during Mikhail Gorbachev's glasnost. By and large the items are drawn from a fairly small sampling of Soviet newspapers and periodicals with publication dates of 1988 and 1989. Topics covered a range from advertising, foreign aid and the black market to a transcript of Joseph Brodsky's trial. An appendix of major events from March 1985 through 1989 is also included.

429. Eklof, Ben, **Soviet Briefing: Gorbachev and the Reform Period**. Boulder, CO: Westview Press, 1988. 195 p.

An attempt to create a clear chronicle of events in the Soviet Union since 1987. The goal of the author is accuracy and clarity as opposed to originality. The books began as a personal effort to sort out the rapid flow of events. The author spent five years in the Soviet Union and draws on that experience and many secondary sources. He is aware of the limitations of these materials with their biases, but feels it would be impossible to cover all the primary sources available and present them in a clear fashion. He intends to focus on the four main aspects of Gorbachev's reforms: glasnost, perestroika, democratization, and new thinking. The book is organized into thematic chapters on the political aspects of reform, glasnost, legality in Soviet society, economy, popular views, environment, and ethnicity. The author has omitted foreign policy questions and therefore there is nothing on the situation in Eastern Europe. The author was trained as a historian and tries to keep a historical perspective in analyzing the events of the last few years. Reviews: *Slavic Review* 49:1:130-31 (Spring 1990). *Russian History* 17:2:249-51 (Summer 1990).

430. **The Soviet Union 1988-1989: Perestroika in Crisis?**, edited by the Federal Institute for East European and International Studies. Boulder, CO: Westview Press, 1990. xv, 410 p. *Westview Special Studies on the Soviet Union and Eastern Europe*, ISBN: 0812279520. Includes bibliographical references and index.

This volume evaluates the dramatic political and domestic developments in the USSR in 1988-89. The volume is divided into three parts each devoted to a major area in Soviet life: domestic policy, economics, or foreign policy. The goal is not to predict the future of perestroika. Rather, the authors present discussion of important factors in the process of reform and attempt to clarify the structure of remaining problems. The hope is that the long term nature of the reforms will be clear to the reader. Numerous topics are covered in the essays contained in this volume, but the authors agree on certain factors that will affect the progress of the reforms: the complexity of the problem to be solved; public resistance to change; the skepticism of the Soviet public; a value system which rejects entrepreneurial activities; and the lack of experience in democracy.

431. **Gorbachev—The Debate**, edited by Ferenc Feher and Andrew Arato. Atlantic Highlands, NJ: Humanities Press International, 1989. vi, 234 p. ISBN: 0391036394. Includes bibliographical references.

All essays in this collection address the question why reformism arose in the USSR. The contributors have different explanations, but they can be divided into four general categories: economics; internal problems (in particular demographic pressure and government corruption); cultural-political explanations; and external pressures. Thus, the authors reach widely divergent conclusions as to the causes of perestroika and its future direction. The volume includes an introductory essay summarizing the events that have taken place so far. Some essays include bibliographic notes.

432. **Glasnost—How Open?** Lanham, Md.: Freedom House, 1987. 130 p. *Perspectives on Freedom*, no. 8. ISBN: 0932088139.

The events of two conferences are included in this volume. The first held March 7, 1987, the second April 11, 1987. Both were sponsored by Freedom House. The first was comprised of participants all of whom were émigrés from the Soviet Union; the second by émigrés from East European countries. The participants in both cases were from widely varying backgrounds. They were being asked to assess the motivation behind the changes generated by perestroika and the seriousness of Gorbachev's intent. The editor notes that "glasnost" also means "cosmetic." At the time this was published the changes were coming quickly and it was felt that these recent émigrés could provide different views than the ones usually available to Westerners as to what was driving Gorbachev.

433. Goldman, Marshall I., **What Went Wrong with Perestroika**. 1st ed. New York: Norton, 1991. 258 p. ISBN: 0393030717. Includes bibliographical references (p. 239-248) and index.

This volume is something of a political biography of Mikhail Gorbachev, tracing his rise and fall and suggesting some explanations for the course events took. As such it goes back to the Brezhnev years tracking Gorbachev's early career and pointing to problems particularly with the Soviet economy that made the country ripe for change in 1986. The author also traces the events that made Gorbachev's fall inevitable as the new freedoms brought an intense anti-communist sentiment and a desire for a departure from the past to the fore. This volume traces Gorbachev's career as he became a hero in the West and continually more resented at home. The author draws on a wide range of sources to demonstrate his ideas from newspapers to in depth analysis. Finally, he presents some speculation on what is to come in the Soviet Union. Review: *New York Times Review of Books* 38:11:53-59 (November 7, 1991).

434. **The Second Revolution: Democratisation in the USSR**, edited by Eric Gonsalves. New Delhi: Patriot Publishers, 1989. 157 p. ISBN: 8170501075. Includes bibliographical references and index.

A collection of essays on various aspects of democratization and perestroika. General information on the historical context are included. New approaches to socialism are discussed as are problems related to resurgent nationalism, the Soviet media, and perestroika in Soviet Central Asia.

435. Gorbachev, Mikhail Sergeevich, **Perestroika: New Thinking for Our Country and the World**. 1st ed. New York: Harper & Row, 1987. 254 p. *"A Cornelia & Michael Bessie Book"*, ISBN: 006390859.

Gorbachev's presentation of his ideas and what they mean for the Soviet Union and the rest of the world. An explanation from the Soviet point of view of the causes of conflict areas in the world and suggestions for alleviating that conflict. Topics include initiating restructuring of the USSR, new economic policy, democratization, foreign relations, and disarmament. Reviews: *Foreign Affairs* 66:4:883 (Spring 1988). *National Interest* 12L157-75 (June 1988). *American Journal of International Law* 82: 4:878-86 (October 1988). *Orbis* 32:3:420-25 (Summer 1988). *Slavic Review* 47:4:716-25 (Winter 1988). *Naval War College Review* 42:1:151-53 (Winter 1989).

436. ———, **Speeches and Writings**. 2nd ed. New York: Pergamon, 1987. xii, 230 p. ISBN: 0080348653.

A collection of significant speeches and essays of Mikhail Gorbachev from June 1986 to May 1987. Includes the press conference at Reykjavik, a speech on glasnost at a Kremlin dinner for Margaret Thatcher, and his speech in Prague. Many others are included in this second volume as well as an appendix with the IBM treaty.

437. **The Soviet Union Under Gorbachev: Assessing the First Year**, edited by Arthur B. Gunlicks and John D. Treadway. New York: Praeger, 1987. x, 163 p. ISBN: 0275927016. Includes index.

A symposium at the University of Richmond on assessing the new regime in the Soviet Union provided the basis of this volume. The goal of that meeting and this volume was to provide a general university and metropolitan audience with an assessment of Gorbachev's first year. The authors also speculate on the future of U.S.-Soviet relations. A wide range of subjects are covered by the contributors: foreign policy, economics, social policy, culture, and the 27th Party Congress. The contributors range from members of congressional research staff to scholars at various universities. Review: *Canadian Slavonic Papers* 30:2: 277-78 (June 1988).

438. Hazan, Baruch A., **Gorbachev and His Enemies: The Struggle for Perestroika**. Boulder, CO: Westview Press, 1990. vii, 335 p. ISBN: 0813306264. Includes index and bibliographical references.

To some extent, this book is a study in the nature of power in the Soviet Union and how attitudes toward it have changed. The author, in analyzing the opposition to reforms, develops the argument that, at base, the differences between the various groups lie in their varying attitudes toward power. He describes the opposition to reform as having three main sources: inherent Russian conservatism, primitive economic structures, and vested interests in the continuation of the existing system. The book is organized into chapters focusing on the various groups opposing the reforms: the bureaucrats and apparatchiks, led by Ligachev, the army, the KGB, Yeltsin and other "opponents of the left" who feel that Gorbachev is moving too slowly, and nationalistic groups. Gorbachev does have a lack of unity among the opposition groups in his favor, but the author makes very clear the magnitude of the difficulties facing Gorbachev and his reforms.

439. Hazan, Barukh, **Gorbachev's Gamble**. Boulder, CO: Westview, 1990. x, 485 p. *Westview Special Series on the Soviet Union and Eastern Europe*, 0163-6057. ISBN: 081337779X.

The major documents of the 19th All-Union Party Conference are compiled here along with news reports of the time analyzing the events of the time. The importance of the conference as the power struggle between the supporters and opponents of perestroika gives these documents significance for historical analysis of the Gorbachev era. The conference served as a testing ground for perestroika. The author has compiled the documents, organizing them chronologically. There is also a lengthy introduction analyzing the events of the conference. The author also demonstrates the difficulties facing Gorbachev by assessing the compromises presented in the speeches for and against perestroika. One difficulty with this valuable collection is the absence of an index to the massive amount of material presented here.

440. **U.S.-Soviet Cooperation: A New Future**, edited by Nish Jamgotch. New York: Praeger, 1989. ix, 234 p. ISBN: 0275930823. Includes bibliographical references.

A collection of essays on the areas of the past and possible future cooperation between the U.S. and Soviet Union. The study grew out of work done over several years in the International Studies Association. The authors and editor also believe it fills a gap in the literature on U.S.-Soviet interaction which focuses on conflict as opposed to cooperation. Two themes run through all nine essays: first, that this area of study has been largely ignored and that there is a great deal to be learned by examining past successful cooperative projects in terms of present day foreign policy. The essays each focus on specific areas of coopera-tion, many on specific projects: in the area of cultural cooperation the U.S.-Soviet cultural agreement established in 1958 is reviewed. The advantages gained from the Antarctic Treaty (1959) are covered as an example of diplomatic cooperation. In ecology, the U.S.-Soviet 1972 Agreement on Environmental Protection is analyzed. There are also essays on cooperative efforts in trade, space, medicine, and security communications. The volume is intended for the general reader and includes a bibliography of English language publications.

441. **Gorbachev and Gorbachevism**, edited by Walter Joyce. London: Frank Cass, 1989. 160 p. ISBN: 0714633607. Includes bibliographies.
The results of a conference on political reform in the USSR since January 1987 are presented in this volume. The focus was to be on the Soviet Union since democratization was introduced. An international group of scholars considered a broad range of areas affected by the reform. The essays included here cover the electoral system, the CPSU, the media, problems of glasnost, economics, law, foreign policy, Europe, and the Soviet Union as well as two devoted to Gorbachev. Each essay includes bibliographic footnotes. The lack of an index may make this volume less useful for some purposes, but the wide range of subjects and scholars will make it valuable to many students.

442. Krasnov, Vladislav, **Russia Beyond Communism: A Chronicle of National Rebirth**. Boulder, CO: Westview Press, 1991. xxi, 355 p. *CCRS Series on Change in Contemporary Soviet Society*, ISBN: 0813383617. Includes bibliographical references and index.
Krasnov attempts to describe and analyze the demise of communism in the USSR and to speculate about the future that lies beyond. His purpose is to find "a solution to the current Soviet crisis before it degenerates into... an apocalyptic catastrophe." (p. xx) His book is arranged in five numbered chapters with an introduction and a conclusion. In chapter one he looks to Solzhenitsyn's proposed reforms as a possible solution. In chapter two, "Beyond Marxism-Leninism: Voices of Glasnost 1987-88," and in chapter three "Beyond Commu-nism: Voices of Glasnost 1989," he demonstrates how a stray intellectual alternative to one-party rule already exists and is developing. Chapter four, "Revolutions and Russia," examines a 1989 debate that intertwined four themes dealing with Russian history that focus on how to get out of the current crisis. Chapter five, "Toward a New Russia: Building an Infrastructure," attempts to examine alternatives for the future.

443. Kubalkova, V., and A. A. Cruickshank, **Thinking New About Soviet "New Thinking."** Berkeley, Calif.: Institute of International Studies, University of Cali-fornia, Berkeley, 1989. vii, 143 p. *Research Series, 0068-6093*, 74. ISBN: 0877251746. Includes bibliographical references.
This book was based on research that hypothesized that Soviet international behavior could be changed by changing international law. After an introduction explaining what is meant by "new thinking" in international relations, several chapters follow that explore new thinking in relation to Soviet ideology, to Marxism and Leninism, as a theory of interna-tional relations, as a foreign policy guide, and as a challenge to Western "old thinking." Review: *Foreign Affairs* 69:2:182 (Spring 1990).

444. Lane, David Stuart, **Soviet Society Under Perestroika**. Boston: Unwin Hyman, 1990. xv, 401 p. ISBN: 0044451660. Includes bibliographical references and index.
The structure of Soviet society as it has changed during the regime of Mikhail Gorbachev is the subject of this volume. "Following a discussion of the reform strategy of Gorbachev, its economic and political implications, we shall consider the relationship between major

social groups (classes and nationalities), forms of social welfare and control (education and the family), and the process of social change (the mass media and the rise of independent groups). By analyzing the social context in which Soviet politics takes place — the ways that politics constrains the social system and vice-versa — we shall understand better the changes and challenges the USSR faces." (p. 1-2) Several documents have been translated and reproduced here. Among them are Boris Yeltsin's election platform of March 1989, and the Constitution of the USSR (December 1989). Each section of the book includes a bibliography of English language sources.

445.   Laqueur, Walter, **The Long Road to Freedom: Russia and Glasnost**. New York: Scribner's, 1989. xviii, 325 p. ISBN: 0684190303.
In this volume Laqueur explores glasnost and its effects on Soviet social life and conditions. After giving some background about the state of Soviet society prior to 1985, he examines the effects of glasnost on writers, the rise of patriotism and fascism in the Russian right, alcoholism and other social evils, glasnost and the Soviet economy, the limits of glasnost, and the role glasnost will play in Russia's future. He was convinced at the time that this book was written that "the champions of glasnost have gone, I suspect, as so far as they feel they can go for the time being. It is easier to be more hopeful with regard to the distant future. In ten or twenty years, with the rise of yet another generation, there could be a new initiative to take glasnost beyond its present limits." (p. xvi) Reviews: *Orbis* 34:2:296 (Spring 1990). *Problems of Communism* 39:2:105-08 (March-April 1990). *Political Science Quarterly* 105:2:330-31 (Summer 1990).

446.   ———, **Soviet Realities: Culture and Politics from Stalin to Gorbachev**. New Brunswick, NJ: Transaction Publishers, 1990. xix, 231 p. ISBN: 0887377035. Includes bibliographical references.
This collection of essays, previously published in journals such as *Commentary*, *Foreign Affairs*, *The New Republic*, and *Encounter*, focuses on the Soviet political and cultural scene from Stalin to Gorbachev. The sixteen essays are arranged in four sections: "Glasnost and Its Future," describes glasnost and its probable limits. "Russians Right and Left" contains six essays that examine cultural politics through literature, film, and other means. "Before Gorbachev Came" explores internal bureaucratic politics and foreign policy. Finally, "Cloaks, Bombs, and Daggers" offers reflection on terrorism and espionage.

447.   **The Soviet Union 1988: Essays from the Harriman Institute Forum**, edited by Paul Lerner. New York: Crane Russak, 1989. iv, 219 p. ISBN: 0844816116. Includes bibliographies.
This collection of essays, originally published in the Harriman Institute Forum, covers a wide variety of topics from trade unions to religion. The one consistent theme is a focus on current trends in the Soviet Union and in-depth analysis. It is intended for general readers and scholars seeking serious analysis of current events. No one bias or theme is evident in the essays.

448.   Lewin, Moshe, **The Gorbachev Phenomenon: A Historical Interpretation**. Berkeley: University of California Press, 1988. xii, 176 p. ISBN: 0520062574. Includes index and bibliography.
The author attempts an analysis of recent events in the USSR within a historical context. He divides his study into two parts. The first traces the growth of urban centers in Russia. The second examines the changes Gorbachev is attempting as they affect ideology, politics, and the economic situation. "What distinguished such an account from a mere inventory of episodes and incidents—what makes it history— is that the events are observed as belonging to a process, a continuity that has some direction, passes through stages, and crosses

some thresholds." (p. vii) Reviews: *American Historical Review* 95:1:214-15 (February 1990). *Problems of Communism* 39:2:109-14 (March-April 1990). *Russian Review* 48:3:327-28 (July 1989). *Social Science Quarterly* 70:2:522-23 (June 1989). *Soviet Union* 15:1:128-30 (1988).

449. Mandel, Ernest, **Beyond Perestroika: The Future of Gorbachev's USSR**. New York: Verso, 1991. xvi, 240 p. ISBN: 086091223X. Includes bibliography (p. 219-240).

A revised edition of the author's 1989 publication. The author describes the reforms of the Gorbachev era, their background, and implications for the future of Soviet society. The topical arrangement covers the reemergence of public opinion, the economic reforms, political reforms, de-Stalinization, the changes in foreign policy, social democracy and the future of the reforms. "Mandel argues that, without broad popular involvement and a willingness to concede basic democratic rights like national self-determination, the whole project of reform will be doomed. However, he remains optimistic that a newly awakened workers' movement and public opinion may yet seize the initiative and drive the bureaucracy beyond perestroika." (back cover) Reviews: *Studies in Comparative Communism* 23:2:213-22 (Summer 1990). *Society* 28:1:85-87 (November-December 1990). *American Political Science Review* 84:4:1340-41 (December 1990).

450. **Gorbachev and Perestroika**, edited by Martin McCauley. New York: St. Martin's Press, 1990. xii, 222 p. ISBN: 0312045107. Includes bibliographical references and index.

A collection of essays most of which were delivered as papers at a conference held at the School of Slavonic and East European Studies at the University of London, July 7-8, 1988. The majority of the essays focus on the first four years of perestroika. Various aspects of Gorbachev's reforms are considered. "...This survey does not claim to be comprehensive; nevertheless it should provide the reader with an in-depth analysis of the most stunning political, economic, and social experiment in the Soviet Union since 1929." (p. ix) Each essay examines one aspect of Soviet society as it has been affected by perestroika. Thus the book includes essays on politics, industry, agriculture, foreign trade, employment, the labor system, nationalities, the armed forces, foreign policy, and the arts.

451. **The Soviet Union Under Gorbachev**, edited by Martin McCauley. Basingstoke: Macmillan in association with School of Slavonic and East European Studies, 1987. xii, 247 p. ISBN: 0333439112. Includes index and bibliography (p. 231-241).

A conference held in March 1986 generated the papers collected in this volume. The aim of the conference was to assess Gorbachev's first year in office. There were three basic considerations the contributors were mindful of in their analyses: the seriousness of the problems facing Gorbachev; progress so far and options for the near future; what are the probabilities of success. The eleven essays included here cover Gorbachev as leader, ideology, law, nationalities, economy, agriculture, foreign trade, labor, Eastern Europe, defense and security, and foreign policy. Contributors bring a European assessment to the reader. Reviews: *Russian Review* 48:3:321-25 (July 1989). *Orbis* 33:3:462-63 (Summer 1989).

452. **Perestroika in Action**, edited by Vladimir Mezhenkov and Eva Skelley. London: Collets, 1988. 453 p. *Soviet Scene 1988*, ISBN: 0569090938.

A collection of journalistic literature from the Soviet press. The editors hoped to give some sense of the degree of popular involvement in glasnost. To do so, they have chosen from a wide array of subject areas: party politics, economics, agriculture, science and technology, religion, Soviet youth, social conditions, health services, human rights, culture, joint ventures, and international opinion. The authors of these articles represent a broad spectrum of Soviet opinion ranging from Mikhail Gorbachev to Valentin Rasputin. A complete list of articles and a name index are included at the back of the volume. The collection offers a unique perspective on the changes of the last few years as they have affected virtually every area of Soviet society.

453. **Gorbachev at the Helm: A New Era in Soviet Politics?**, edited by R.F. Miller. New York: Croom Helm, 1987. viii, 251 p. ISBN: 0709955065. Includes bibliographies and index.

Several authors have contributed essays as a part of an early analysis of the changes proposed by Gorbachev at the 27th Party Congress. The goal these authors have set is to discover if the changes initiated at that Party meeting are substantial and can survive. The authors hope to identify general trends in the new political reforms. Particular areas have been examined to test the failure or success of the reforms. These include domestic politics, economic policy and administration, agriculture, ideology, and foreign policy. The volume is divided into three general sections. The first examines the political realm of policy making under Gorbachev. There follows an examination of the basic elements of economic policy. Finally, there is a section on foreign policy.

454. Mlynar, Zdenek, **Can Gorbachev Change the Soviet Union?: The International Dimensions of Political Reform**, translated by Marian Sling and Ruth Tosek. Boulder, CO: Westview Press, 1990. viii, 184 p. ISBN: 0813309344. Includes index and bibliographical references (p. 169-178).

This work was written in 1988 at the time of the nineteenth all-union conference of the communist party. The author hoped to describe the conditions necessary for the Soviet Union to carry out the changes proposed by Gorbachev and to suggest an optimal program for change. The author describes conditions peculiar to the Soviet Union which he feels will limit Gorbachev's actions. Basic institutions are the key to change in his view. The book is organized into three sections. The first describes past attempts at reform and the place reform has held in institutional processes. Part two defines those institutional characteristics that will either hinder or advance reform efforts. The concluding section discusses international factors that will play a role in reform in the Soviet Union. The book also includes a section added in 1989 to take stock of the current changes and their effects.

455. Naylor, Thomas H., **The Gorbachev Strategy: Opening the Closed Society**. Lexington, Mass.: Lexington Books, 1988. xi, 253 p. ISBN: 0669138312. Includes index and bibliography (p. 237-241).

An economist and business scientist analyzes the early years of the Gorbachev reforms. Professor Naylor believes the U.S. is failing to take advantage of the changes and is, in fact, operating under policies that work against our own self-interest. To explain his point and suggest some alternative courses, he begins with a description of the past Soviet system under Stalin and then goes on to describe Gorbachev's attempts at reform. He feels that the economic model for many of the changes is Hungary and describes the move in that country to a more decentralized, market-oriented system. He also spends some time discussing changes in the socialist system in China. He then turns to an analysis of Gorbachev's efforts in international trade and the Reagan response which he finds totally inadequate. He also spends some time discussing the difficulties that face Gorbachev if he is to succeed. The author uses "strategic analysis," a method used in business by corporations analyzing their competitors.

456. Novak, Michael, **Taking Glasnost Seriously**. Washington, DC: American Enterprise for Public Policy Research, 1988. xvi, 206 p. ISBN: 0844736422 (pbk.), 0844736414.

Novak, head of the U.S. delegation at the Bern conference, has collected and presented here the speeches he made at the conference (review conference on human contacts) in 1986. His speeches "explain how, by honoring the [Helsinki] accords, governments enrich the lives of their citizens and how, in betraying these commitments, governments impoverish the lives of persons, families, societies, and nations." (p. xiv).

457. Nove, Alec, **Glasnost in Action: Cultural Renaissance in Russia**. Boston: Unwin Hyman, 1989. xi, 251 p. ISBN: 004445340X.

A popular description of changes in "cultural" life in Russia since Gorbachev took office. The author uses the term culture in the broadest sense to include history, law, social sciences, and religion as opposed to just literature. The book is not intended as an analysis so much as a comparison of present and past standards. The author draws mainly on periodicals and some newspapers. Since he was trying to follow rapidly changing events he felt periodical literature would more quickly reflect the varied aspects of the reforms as opposed to books since the latter are so slow to be published. The volume is arranged in nine thematic chapters beginning with two that give the reader some background as to previous conditions. They go on to discuss the rehabilitation of history, the terrors, religion, nationalism, literature and the media, politics, economics, and then summarizes with some broad conclusions as to the permanence of the reforms. Reviews: *Problems of Communism* 39:2:105-08 (March- April 1990). *Russian Review* 49:4:511-12 (October 1990).

458. **Gorbachev's USSR**, edited by Uri Ra'anan and Igor Lukes, with a foreword by George R. Urban. New York: St. Martin's Press, 1990. xxi, 154 p. ISBN: 0312044925. Includes bibliographical references and index.

A strategic overview of the situation in the USSR in 1988. This collection of essays was the result of a conference held in Boston in 1988. The theme of the conference was to determine if the Soviet Union had actually reached the stage of systemic crisis. The participants came from widely varying backgrounds: scholars, government officials, and representatives from RAND corporation and Radio Free Europe/Radio Liberty. The diversity of their backgrounds lends equal diversity to their opinions. Several questions were considered that eventually formed the structure of the volume. The essays cover the following topics: general overview of the Soviet system, Sovietology, changes in the Soviet system, Gorbachev's struggle, nationalities problems, changes in decision-making, foreign policy, domestic problems, Eastern Europe, U.S. foreign policy, domestic problems, and U.S. foreign policy in light of changes in the USSR.

459. Sakharov, Andrei, **Moscow and Beyond 1986-1989**. New York: Knopf, 1990. xvii, 168 p. ISBN: 0394587979. Includes index.

The second volume of Sakharov's life covers his last years. This is the period of his growing political activity. It explains the changes in his intellectual interests after leaving exile from a focus on science to the political scene. His trips abroad and return to a Russia in upheaval are discussed. As a major influence on the Soviet public, this account of Sakharov's final years reflects much of the turmoil in Soviet politics. There are numerous photographs. Reviews: *Foreign Affairs* 70:2:191 (Spring 1991). *Antioch Review* 49:2:288-95 (Spring 1991). *Bulletin of the Atomic Scientists* 47:6:37-38 (July-August 1991). *New Republic* 204:8:29-36 (February 25, 1991).

460. Sakwa, Richard, **Gorbachev and His Reforms 1985-1990**. New York: Philip Allan, 1990. xiv, 459 p. ISBN: 0860034232. Includes index and bibliography (p. 421-439).

An analysis of Gorbachev's personal role in reform. While the author recognized the coincidence of events that have allowed for the changes that have been introduced, he feels that Gorbachev led the direction of reform in a personal way from the beginning. Therefore, the reforms reflect the breadth of his ideas and the limitations of his personality. He does see Gorbachev as someone who wishes to reform and improve the existing system rather than one in revolt against it. Professor Sakwa felt the time was appropriate for analyzing the new system of socialism put in place by the reformers. The book is organized thematically covering numerous topics including communism and reform, ideology, democracy, politics and party, civil rights, nationalism, economy, and foreign policy. While not glorifying Gorbachev, the author attempts to give an accurate picture of his role in the reforms. Reviews: *Russian Review* 48:4:425-26 (October 1989). *Russian History* 16:2-4:474-75 (1989).

461. Sallnow, John, **Reform in the Soviet Union: Glasnost and the Future**. New York: St. Martin's Press, 1989, 136 p. ISBN: 0312040768. Includes bibliographical references.

An analysis of the causes and motivations behind the reform movement. The author feels that while Gorbachev has played a significant role, he is the catalyst, not the cause. Change was a necessity if the Soviets were to maintain their world position. In this volume the author traces the Gorbachev era beginning with a profile of the legacy left by Brezhnev. He then goes on to describe the first steps of reform, glasnost, and perestroika and the opposition to it that arose in the form of nationalism. The next three chapters are devoted to foreign policy questions, specifically Soviet-European, Soviet-U.S., and Soviet-Asian relations. The final chapter describes the prospects for the future and discusses the possible fate of reform without Gorbachev. Review: *Soviet Union-Union Sovietique* 17:3:320-22 (1990).

462. Shevardnadze, Eduard, **The Future Belongs to Freedom**. New York: The Free Press, 1991. xx, 237 p. ISBN: 0029286174. Includes index.

This book is used by Shevardnadze as a forum to answer all his critics and the critics of the "new thinking." It is meant as a history of the ideas of perestroika. Some personal background is supplied to explain the former foreign minister's attitudes and approaches to the problem. The volume was originally intended as a collection of speeches but the author felt this would not give an accurate picture of the nature of the reforms. Reviews: *New York Times Book Review* (September 22, 1991). *Foreign Affairs* 70: 5:197 (Winter 1991-92). *New Republic* 205:21:40-45 (November 18, 1991). *National Review* 43:19:44-46 (October 21, 1991).

463. Shlapentokh, Vladimir, **Soviet Ideologies in the Period of Glasnost: Responses to Brezhnev's Stagnation**, written with the participation of Dmitry Shlapentokh. New York: Praeger, 1988. xiii, 211 p. ISBN: 0275926710. Includes index and bibliography.

The author examines the causes for Soviet stagnation in the early 1970s and the subsequent attempts to deal with the problem. In Shlapentokh's view there were several ideologies competing among one another for dominance in this period: conservation (Brezhnev), neo-Stalinist, and liberal Marxist. Special attention is paid to the third alternative, Gorbachev's liberal ideology and its evolution from neo-Stalinism. Attention is also paid throughout this book to the interaction of economic, social, political, and ideological forces.

Reviews: *Russian Review* 49: 3:381-82 (July 1990). *Contemporary Sociology* 18:3:316-9 (May 1989).

464. **Beyond Perestroika: Choices and Challenges Facing Gorbachev**, edited by Manohar L. Sondhi. New Delhi: Abhinav Publications, 1989. 156 p. ISBN: 8170172543. Includes bibliography (p. 135-148).

A collection of essays by Indian scholars directed primarily at the population of India. The authors feel that Sovietology in India has taken a rather singleminded approach, emphasizing only Indo-Soviet friendship. The essays here seek to present a more diverse set of opinions on the future of Indo-Soviet relations in light of Gorbachev's reforms. Topics covered include disarmament, Soviet enterprise, the future of reforms in the Communist Party, foreign relations, and the nationalities question.

465. **Gorbachev and Glasnost: Viewpoints from the Soviet Press**, edited by Isaac J. Tarasulo. Wilmington, Del.: SR Books, 1989. xxvi, 363 p. ISBN: 0842023372. Includes bibliographies and index.

Thirty-three articles have been translated from the Soviet press to give the Western reader a sample of the issues arising as glasnost evolves itself. The articles are grouped into categories: reinterpretation of history; economic reforms; unofficial groups and Soviet youth; national, religious and social issues; foreign and military issues; and party struggle and political reform. The editor has hoped to present the reader with a selection of materials on the most significant issues, not to identify the more provocative materials published by the press. The editor is a native of the Soviet Union now living in the United States. The volume contains a glossary of terms.

466. Thom, Francoise, and David Regan, **Glasnost, Gorbachev & Lenin: Behind the New Thinking**. London: Policy Research, 1988. 80 p. ISBN: 0951143611. Includes bibliography.

Two different approaches to a common theme are presented. Both authors feel glasnost will be crippled by its Leninist underpinnings. In the first essay, Thom, a Sovietologist, attempts to demonstrate the problems arising from Gorbachev's foundation in Leninism by examining Gorbachev's speeches and party policy over the last few years. The second essay examines Lenin's writings and actions to demonstrate the problems that arose with his own attempts at reform. By, extension, the author feels Gorbachev will be crippled in his own attempts if his ideological basis is the same as Lenin's.

467. **The Anti-Communist Manifesto: Whom to Help in Russia?**, edited by Lev Timofeyev, translated from the Russian by Vitaly Kisin and Oleg Glebov. 1st ed. Washington, DC: Free Enterprise Press, 1990. xvii, 96 p. *"A Project of the Referendum Foundation,"* ISBN: 0939571102.

This book is a product of the Referendum Foundation in Moscow which was organized "to serve as a rallying point for the establishment of free enterprise and private property rights." (p. iv) The contributors to this volume all feel the Soviet Union should not be given foreign aid to assist its development. This, they believe, will only keep the Communist system in place by bolstering existing structures. The essayists are all Russian writers discussing the reforms, inflation, conversion to a free market, the Russian black market, and Gorbachev. Their essays can provide the Western reader with insight into Russia's problems as it attempts its economic reforms.

468. **Gorbachev's Glasnost: Red Star Rising**, edited by Oliver Trager. New York: Facts on File, 1989. 215 p. *Editorials on File Book*, ISBN: 0816022208. Includes index.

A collection of newspaper materials covering issues related to Gorbachev's program of glasnost. The volume is divided into five thematic sections: changes within the Soviet Union, U.S.-Soviet relations, Eastern Europe, nationality issues, human rights, and religious freedom. An index allows ready access to specific subjects such as alcoholism, atomic weapons, business, labor, science and technology, etc.

469. White, Stephen, **Gorbachev in Power**. Cambridge, England: Cambridge University Press, 1990. viii, 268 p. *Cambridge Soviet Paperbacks*, no. 3. ISBN: 0521393248. Includes index and bibliographical references.

A critical analysis of the first five years of Gorbachev's tenure in office. Intended for the student and scholar, the author tries to analyze the "experience" of perestroika in all major policy areas, including foreign relations, economic reform, democratization, nationalities policy, and the political area. The author intended the work as an interim report at the time of its publication although he was well aware of the tenuous position Gorbachev occupied. The lengthy notes and index are helpful.

470. Woodby, Sylvia, **Gorbachev and the Decline of Ideology in Soviet Foreign Policy**. Boulder, CO: Westview, 1989. vii, 127 p. *Westview Special Studies on the Soviet Union and Eastern Europe*, ISBN: 0813377838. Includes bibliographical references.

In this volume changes in Soviet foreign policy are analyzed and translations of several of Gorbachev's speeches are supplied as examples of those changes in foreign policy and ideology. The first part of the book consists of an analysis of the role of ideology as it has affected and been affected by the Gorbachev reforms. One basic premise is that Gorbachev has abandoned the long established model of East-West conflict in foreign relations. This has meant that much of the past ideology must be reexamined. Reviews: *Russian History* 17:2:247-48 (Summer 1990). *Soviet Union-Union Sovietique* 17:1-2:191-93 (1990).

471. **Restructuring Soviet Ideology: Gorbachev's New Thinking**, edited by Sylvia Woodby and Alfred B. Evans. Boulder, CO: Westview Press, 1990. v, 226 p. *Westview Special Studies on the Soviet Union*, ISBN: 0813380286. Includes index.

A series of essays discussing the impact of Gorbachev's reforms in politics, economics, nationalities, foreign relations, national security, and socialism. "The discussions show that although Gorbachev insists the ideas he advocates are truly 'Leninist,' they actually challenge key Soviet political and social values in ways that could impair the traditional ideology's ability to continue functioning as a source of legitimacy for the regime." (back cover) The essays also show that the reforms had their beginning before Gorbachev took office and will continue after him.

472. Wright, Martin, **Soviet Union: The Challenge of Change**. Harlow, England: Longman, 1989. ix, 116 p. *Countries in Crisis*, ISBN: 0582051584. Includes index.

An unusual collection of essays that attempts to explain and analyze the "revolution" the authors feel Gorbachev is trying to achieve. The book is divided into two parts. The first provides the historical background to the Gorbachev era and then goes on to discuss major issues including perestroika, glasnost, nationalities question, Eastern Europe, and foreign affairs. The second part of the book consists of short journalistic essays on a variety of topics. The book is intended for the general reader. There are few references. The chronology of the Soviet Union provided in the first section is almost too brief, ignoring the reigns of some tsars such as Alexander I and Nicholas II altogether, but going into more detail for the Soviet period. There is a map and a reference section that includes general information on the structure of the Soviet government.

473. Zaslavskaia, T. I., **The Second Socialist Revolution: An Alternative Soviet Strategy**, with foreword by Teodor Shanin and translated by Susan Davies with Jenny Warren. Bloomington: Indiana University Press, 1990. xx, 241 p. *Second World*, ISBN: 025336860X. Includes bibliographical references and index.

A socialist view of the perestroika movement, its problems and future. This translation gives westerners an opportunity to view a socialist supporter's ideas on how perestroika arose, the inefficiencies in the Soviet economy, social policy under a Soviet system, the effects of perestroika on the social process, and what must change to accomplish democratization. The book ends with the events of 1989 and the crisis arising out of restructuring.

474. Zemtsov, Ilya, and John Farrar, **Gorbachev: The Man and the System**, edited by Yisrael Cohen. New Brunswick, N. J.: Transaction Books, 1989. xvii, 462 p. ISBN: 0887382223. Includes bibliography (p. 433-444).

At the time this volume appeared there were still many questions about Gorbachev's sincerity and motivation. Many scholars felt that while he was reform minded the reforms would be limited by his own devotion to the communist system that produced him. This volume is a study of Gorbachev's personality and his interaction with the Soviet system. The premise is that only by examining this crucial factor is it possible to understand the reforms, Soviet society, and its past and future. The volume is arranged thematically into four parts. The first covers topics related to internal policies: the economy, changes in leadership, society, and the arts. Part two is concerned with foreign policies: U.S.-Soviet relations, arms control, East European-Soviet relations, Sino-Soviet relations, and the Third World-Soviet relations. The third part deals with military doctrine, and the final section covers the author's conclusions. The book contains several appendices showing changes in government officials and a glossary of abbreviations, acronyms, and Soviet terms. Review: *Annals of the American Academy of Political and Social Science* 512:195-96 (September 1990).

Police Terror, Espionage, Propaganda

475. **Violations of the Helsinki Accords, USSR: A Report Prepared for the Helsinki Review Conference, Vienna, November 1986**. New York: U.S. Helsinki Watch Committee, 1986. xii, 343 p. *A Helsinki Watch Report*, ISBN: 0938579762.

This collection of human rights violations was prepared by the Helsinki Watch Committee. The violations are reported under eleven headings: human rights monitors, freedom of expression, contact with foreigners, freedom of movement, the Sakharovs, independent peace movement, workers rights and forced labor, political prisoners, extralegal harassment of dissenters, freedom of religion, and minority rights and national self-determination.

476. Amundsen, Kirtsten, **Inside Spetsnaz: Soviet Special Operations: A Critical Analysis**, edited by William H. Burgess III and with foreword by Robert C. Kingston. Novato, CA: Presidio Press, 1990. xx, 308 p.

The contributors to this volume have written highly enlightening case studies covering several aspects of Soviet special operations and spetsnaz forces. Specifically, they add to our knowledge of "the complexity of Soviet military thought, the underlying organizations that control special operations and special operations forces, and under whose policies, direction, and command these forces operate. This volume also offers several technical and operational lessons for Western nations in their conduct of special operations." (p. ix) An appendix giving biographical information about significant individuals in Soviet spetsnaz forces is also included.

477. Andrew, Christopher M., and Oleg Gordievsky, **KGB: The Inside Story of Its Foreign Operations from Lenin to Gorbachev**. 1st ed. New York: HarperCollins, 1990. xvii, 776 p. ISBN: 0060166053. Includes index and bibliography (p. 729-744).

A collaborative effort between Western writer Christopher Andrew and double agent Oleg Gordievsky has produced this history of the KGB. "Though this history has been written by Andrew, it is based on combined research, follows interpretations arrived at together in many detailed discussions, and represents the authors' joint conclusions. It draws on the secret archives of the KGB, on other source material in a wide variety of Western libraries and archives, and on Gordievsky's long experience of the FCD on KGB residence abroad." (p. 3) The book is chronologically arranged with several helpful reference sections such as the chart showing the evolution of the KGB and the appendices listing the KGB chairmen, heads of the chief directorate, and organization of the KGB. This book is written for the general reader.

478. **The New Image-Makers: Soviet Propaganda and Disinformation Today**, edited by Ladislav Bittman. McLean, VA: Pergamon-Brassey's International Defense Publishers, 1988. vii, 262 p. ISBN: 0080349390. Includes bibliographies and index.

The first research initiative of Boston University's Program for the Study of Disinformation, this collection of essays shows the uses of disinformation in Gorbachev's Russia. The essays are divided into three sections, the first on the new uses the Soviets have found for propaganda. Part two examines the Soviet propaganda apparatus focusing on its use of Radio Moscow and social science literature in the U.S. and the methods used for reaching the rural population of India. The last part examines specific cases of Soviet propaganda campaigns, specifically the campaign around Sakharov, the manipulation of religious circles, the treatment of AIDS in the press, and the disinformation disseminated on Greece. The book is intended for students, scholars, and journalists.

479. Broido, Vera, **Lenin and the Mensheviks: The Persecution of Socialists Under Bolshevism**. Boulder, CO: Westview Press, 1987. viii, 216 p. ISBN: 0813304784. Includes index and bibliography (p. 191-201).

Broido, whose parents were Mensheviks and with whom she shared their Siberian exile, examines the ways in which the Bolsheviks eliminated all non-Bolshevik parties. She places most emphasis on the persecution of the Mensheviks. Reviews: *Problems of Communism* 39:2:98-104 (March-April 1990). *Canadian-American Slavic Studies* 22:1:127-28 (Spring 1989). *Russian Review* 48:1: 69-79 (January 1989).

480. Conquest, Robert, **The Great Terror: A Reassessment**. New York: Oxford University Press, 1990. viii, 570 p. ISBN: 0195055802. Includes bibliographical references.

This is a revision of Robert Conquest's book first published some twenty years ago. The author makes use of the documents that have become available under Gorbachev's administration. These materials have largely served to verify his earlier work and have allowed him to expand his discussion of some topics, especially the Tukhachesvsky trial, the February Plenum, the fate of Yezhov, and the events of 1936. The volume is one of the few in-depth studies of the topic and has been translated and published serially in the Soviet journal *Neva*. Review: *Slavic Review* 49: 2:289 (Summer 1990).

481. Deriabin, Peter, and T. H. Bagley, **KGB: Masters of the Soviet Union**. New York: Hippocrene Books, 1990. xxiv, 466 p. ISBN: 0870528041. Includes bibliographical references and index.

The authors examine the actual internal structure of the KGB and the manner in which it exerts and retains power. They have separated their analysis into five parts: 1. the revolution defends itself; 2. high command of the internal war; 3. a look into the KGB; 4. methods of internal warfare; and 5. foreign dimensions of internal warfare.

482.   Dzhirkvelov, Ilya, **Secret Servant: My Life with the KGB and the Soviet Elite**. London: Collins, 1987. 398 p. ISBN: 0002175983. Includes index.

The life of "a reluctant defector" is recounted here. The author hopes to give Westerners an inside view of the Russian system as seen by someone who believed in the system. Indeed, the author explains he not only believed in it, but actively participated in that branch considered most repressive in the West. He describes his training as a spy and assassin, how decision-making proceeds, how the KGB operated at home and abroad, and his role as a journalist as well as his escape. Reviews: *Problems of Communism* 39:1:101-108 (January-February 1990). *Military Review* 70:4:89-90 (April 1990).

483.   Earley, Pete, **Family of Spies: Inside the John Walker Spy Ring**. New York: Bantam Books, 1988. 385 p. ISBN: 0553052837. Includes index.

Based on interviews with John Walker, this volume attempts to explain how the John Walker spy ring operated in the U.S. The reader will find some information on how the KGB operates as well. However, this is primarily the account of the John Walker ring. Review: *Orbis* 34:1:126 (Winter 1990).

484.   Ebon, Martin, **The Soviet Propaganda Machine**. New York: McGraw-Hill, 1987. viii, 471 p. ISBN: 0070188629. Includes index and bibliography (p. 433-439).

The complex topic of Soviet propaganda is the subject of this study. While the author examines many aspects of this topic including agitprop, overt and covert propaganda efforts, the use of the media, and Soviet tactics for the future, he makes no claim to a comprehensive treatment of the topic. Nevertheless, he has focused on many central issues while discussing Western propaganda in the USSR only peripherally. The author's years at the U.S. office of War Information, as a staff member of the Foreign Policy Association, and as a lecturer at New York University on Communist tactics give him a strong background for his study. It is based primarily on Western sources and he gives a list of relevant Western works in the bibliography. A readable introduction is provided for the general reader.

485.   **Psychological Operations: The Soviet Challenge**, edited by Joseph S. Gordon. Boulder, CO: Westview Press, 1988. ix, 216 p. *Westview Special Studies in International Relations*, ISBN: 0813373956. Includes bibliographies and index.

The eleven essays that comprise this book evolved from a panel at the annual meeting of the International Studies Association in 1983. The panel's and book's purpose was to describe and analyze the use of propaganda by the Soviet Union and its allies as an instrument of foreign policy and to assess the response of the United States to these efforts. Review: *Problems of Communism* 39:1:93-100 (January-February 1990).

486.   Hersh, Seymour M., **"The Target Is Destroyed": What Really Happened to Flight 007 and What America Knew About It**. 1st ed. New York: Random House, 1986. xii, 282 p. ISBN: 0394542614. Includes index.

A study of the tragic results when communications intelligence is abused, this account of the downing of KAL 007 really focuses on American intelligence and practices. It does call attention to the international results of intelligence abuses particularly as regards the Soviet Union with sections addressing propaganda campaigns against the USSR, American over-flights of Soviet territory, and other issues. Most of the information has been taken from conversations with American intelligence officers. Reviews: *SAIS Review* 7:1:225-28 (Winter-Spring 1987). *Progressive* 50:11:40-41 (November 1986). *National Review* 27:52-54 (March 1987). *Naval War College Review* 41:2:119-20 (Spring 1988).

487.   Knight, Amy W., **The KGB, Police and Politics in the Soviet Union.** Boston: Allen & Unwin, 1988. xx, 348 p. ISBN: 0044450354. Includes index.
A study of the political role of the KGB in an attempt to begin to fill the gap in analysis on this topic. "The central thesis of this book is that the political police has continued to this day to be an essential institution for the Soviet regime, despite the disavowal of terror after Stalin died and the substantial political reforms that have been promoted by leaders such as Khrushchev and Gorbachev." (p. xviii) The book is divided into three parts covering the history of the KGB, its structure, and its function, respectively. There are also five appendices providing a chronology of the KGB, a list of crimes under investigation, the leading KGB cadres, its central apparatus from 1954 through 1987, and key KGB posts. Reviews: *Conflict Quarterly* 10:2:59-60 (Spring 1990). *Problems of Communism* 39:1: 101-08 (January-February 1990). *Russian History* 17:4:487-89 (Winter 1990). *Slavic Review* 49:3:465-66 (Fall 1990).

488.   Lamphere, Robert J., and Tom Shachtman, **The FBI-KGB War: A Special Agent's Story**. 1st ed. New York: Random House, 1986. 320 p. ISBN: 0394541510.
A chronicle of the espionage war between the U.S. and the Soviet Union that went on from 1941 to 1955 as seen by one agent of the FBI. The author supplements his recollections with documentary evidence on such topics as the Rosenberg trial. The Western view of Soviet espionage and its effects are portrayed here. Reviews: *Journal of American History* 74:2:558-59 (September 1987). *Midstream* 33:4:63-64 (April 1987).

489.   Mastny, Vojtech, **Helsinki, Human Rights, and European Security: Analysis and Documentation**. Durham, NC: Duke University Press, 1986. xvi, 389p. ISBN: 0822306824. Includes index.
This volume compiles much of the documentation associated with the Helsinki Final Act, The Conference on Security and Cooperations in Europe. As speeches, draft proposals, and formal documents adopted are not available, contemporary accounts and particularly the accounts by Radio Free Europe/Radio Liberty are used. Since the focus is human rights and security, the documents have been chosen to reflect those debates most closely associated with these issues. Many documents have been edited to save space with the exception of the final document from the Belgrade, Madrid, Ottawa, and Budapest conferences, which are presented in their entirety. The editor has made a special effort to give a balanced picture by providing documents on the positions of all sides. The book is divided into three parts. The first deals with human rights and political security; the second with human rights, trade, and security; and the final section with human rights and the military. The emphasis in all sections is on concepts and policies as opposed to specific human rights cases. Review: *Strategic Review* 15:1:70-72 (Winter 1987).

490.   Richelson, Jeffrey, **Sword and Shield: The Soviet Intelligence and Security Apparatus**. Cambridge, Mass: Ballinger Pub. Co., 1986. xix, 279 p. ISBN: 0887300391. Includes bibliographies and index.
The Soviet intelligence system, foreign and domestic, is examined in this study. The author considers the widely held view that the Soviet intelligence mechanism is the greatest threat to Western security and sets out to analyze the validity of this claim. He also tries to point out where Soviet intelligence has wrongfully been accused of interfering in foreign government's activities (he cites the example of claims that the KGB was involved in nuclear freeze movements). The author tries to present real and imagined dangers of the

KGB and GRV. The book is arranged thematically with sections on all aspects of the KGB and GRV from their history and organization to their mechanisms for intelligence gathering. Numerous charts and tables are presented to explain organizational structures. Reviews: *Canadian Slavonic Papers* 29:1:92-94 (March 1987). *American Political Science Review* 81:3:1049-50 (September 1987).

491. Romerstein, Herbert, **Soviet Active Measures and Propaganda: "New Thinking" & Influence Activities in the Gorbachev Era**. Toronto, Canada: Mackenzie Institute for the Study of Terrorism, Revolution, and Propaganda, 1989. 54 p. *Media Report and Mackenzie Paper*, no. 17. ISBN: 092187717X. Includes bibliography (p. 38-43).

In this brief report the author assesses the propaganda mechanism of the Soviet Union. He contends that its operation is to some degree a measure of the sincerity of the Gorbachev regime. That is, the author believes that the context and frequency of active measures (influence operations) in the Soviet Union allow the West to measure the degree of sincerity behind the spoken policies of glasnost. This essay describes how influence operations have functioned in the past and continue to function in the Gorbachev era.

492. Rosenberg, Suzanne, **A Soviet Odyssey**. Toronto: Oxford University Press, 1988. 212 p. ISBN: 0195406540. Includes index.

Rosenberg here narrates her own biography, starting with her arrest, and then recalling the events that led up to it. Rosenberg and her mother had emigrated to Canada shortly after the revolution and then returned to the Soviet Union in the late 1920s. She was arrested in 1950 and released in June of 1953, having served part of a five year sentence in the gulag. Review: *Canadian Historical Review* 72:4:608-610 (December 1991).

493. Rummel, Rudolph J., **Lethal Politics: Soviet Genocide and Mass Murder Since 1917**. New Brunswick: Transaction Publishers, 1990. xvii, 268 p. ISBN: 0887383335. Includes index and bibliographical references (p. 245-57).

This book is part of a larger study that aims "to test the hypothesis that the citizens of democracies are the least likely to be murdered by their own governments; the citizens of totalitarian, especially Marxist systems, the most likely." (p. iv) Each chapter is devoted to a chronological period and is further subdivided into two parts. The first gives some background to the period and the genocide that occurred then. The second, in the form of appendices, provides statistical data and an explanation to support the first part.

494. Shipley, Peter, **Hostile Action: The KGB and Secret Soviet Operations in Britain**. New York: St. Martin's Press, 1990. ix, 224 p. ISBN: 0312041209. Includes bibliographical references.

Shipley examines "the use and development by the Soviet Union over the past twenty years of covert measures directed against Britain. [He asks] some basic questions about the Soviet Union's aims and objectives, the place of clandestine methods in Soviet strategy, how these methods have been put into effect, their extent and variety, ... and how they have evolved and what results they have achieved." (p. vii).

495. Ushakov, Alexander A., **In the Gunsight of the KGB**. 1st ed. New York: Knopf, 1989. xi, 273 p. "*A Borzoi Book,*" ISBN: 0394562844.

Alexander Ushakov, under virtual house arrest, escaped from Odessa on April 1, managed to get to the Soviet-Turkish border, obtained mountain climbing equipment and tents, and successfully crossed two mountain ranges and the border on his way to the West. His story is not only suspenseful, but gives an insider's view of what it is like to be hunted by the KGB and escape.

DIPLOMACY AND FOREIGN RELATIONS

Bibliographies

496. Bolkhovitinov, Nikolai Nikolaevich, **Russia and the United States: An Analytical Survey of Archival Documents and Historical Studies**, translated and edited by J. Dane Hartgrove. Armonk, N.Y.: M.E. Sharpe, 1986. viii, 79 p. *Soviet Studies in History*, vol. XXV, no. 2. ISBN: 0873324145. Includes bibliography (p. 66-78).
Bolkhovitinov is a senior research scholar at the Institute of General History of the USSR Academy of Sciences. His survey consists of two parts. The first "is a survey of documents on the history of relations between Russia and the United States (eighteenth century-1917)" (p. i) based on his research. The second part describes and evaluates works on the history of Russian-American sociopolitical, commercial, scientific, and cultural contacts. Also included in an appendix is a list of works by Soviet and foreign authors in Russian American relations, Russian discoveries in the North Pacific, and activities of the Russian American Company.

General Studies

497. **Superpowers and Revolution**, edited by Jonathan R. Adelman. New York: Praeger, 1986. xiv, 304 p. ISBN: 0275921662. Includes bibliographies and index.
A group of experts studying the phenomenon of superpower intervention have compiled this volume of essays. They feel that interventionist behavior has not been analyzed in terms of behavior evaluation and set out to look at various situations which confronted the U.S. and the Soviet Union. The volume is divided into three sections, an introduction, the U.S. and revolution, and the Soviet Union and revolution. The final section includes essays on Soviet dealings with Yugoslavia, Hungary, Czechoslovakia, Iran, Poland, and Afghanistan. The authors assess policy options as well as choices emphasizing both the content of the final policy and the decision making process that provided it. Three basic questions form the focus for the essays. 1) What determines interventionary policy with regard to revolution? 2) Is there a superpower policy that can be identified by examining the U.S. and Soviet approaches? 3) What elements of revolution affect super power policy in particular?

498. Ashby, Timothy, **The Bear in the Back Yard: Moscow's Caribbean Strategy**. Lexington, Mass.: Lexington Books, 1987. xii, 240 p. ISBN: 0669147680. Includes index and bibliography (p. 191-221).
"This book examines the Soviet's Caribbean policies, explores the USSR's strategy toward the area, and analyses the threat. It concludes that the Soviet Union is following a deliberate and increasingly sophisticated strategy in its penetration of the Caribbean region." (p. xi) After an introductory chapter that explores the historical Soviet interest in Latin America and the Caribbean, Ashby examines Cuba, Grenada, Nicaragua, El Salvador, Honduras, Jamaica, Guyana, and Surinam as parts of the overall Soviet strategy. Review: *Problems of Communism* 39:5:99-107 (September-October 1990).

499. Ashton, S. R., **In Search of Détente: The Politics of East-West Relations Since 1945**. Houndmills, Basingstoke, Hampshire: Macmillan, 1989. xii, 254 p. *Making of the 20th Century*, ISBN: 033343875. Includes bibliographical references.
A study of the relationship between the Soviet Union and the U.S. that has come to be called détente. This analysis is intended for the uninitiated reader, providing the historical background for the stalemate between the two superpowers. The author traces the relation-

ship from 1945 through 1987. He believes that détente is not so much a policy as a mood. The author also discusses Western Europe and China and their perceptions of détente. The book is one in a series dealing with the major issues of the twentieth century. A chronology is included.

500. **Learning in U.S. and Soviet Foreign Policy**, edited by George W. Breslauer and Philip E. Tetlock. Boulder, CO: Westview Press, 1991. xiv, 881 p. ISBN: 0813382645. Includes bibliographical references and index.

This volume, produced under the sponsorship of the National Research Council's Committee on International Conflict and Cooperation, analyzes the process of change in foreign policy making. This is accomplished by examining the conditions under which policy makers change their beliefs. Initially, various theories of learning are presented. The second and third sections are case studies of foreign policy in the U.S. and the Soviet Union. The section on the Soviet Union uses the examples arising from various foreign policy issues including strategic arms, Soviet-Western European relations, Sino-Soviet relations, Soviet-Mideast relations, and U.S.-Soviet relations. The final section includes essays that synthesize the earlier material. The volume is intended for students of learning theory as well as those who focus on international relations.

501. Buhite, Russell D., **Decisions at Yalta: An Appraisal of Summit Diplomacy**. Wilmington, Del: Scholarly Resources, 1986. xvii, 156 p. ISBN: 0842022462. Includes index and bibliography (p. 139-149).

A reexamination of the negotiations at Yalta and their resulting agreements. The author, a historian and author of several works on diplomacy during the mid twentieth century, believes that Yalta can be viewed as the first attempt at détente. The diametrical opposition of the viewpoints of the Soviets and the United States made future disagreement inevitable. He generalizes from the problems at Yalta to difficulties with Summit meetings in general in his discussion. The book is organized around each of the accords reached with a chapter on Germany, Poland, the United Nations, the Far East, Iran, Yugoslavia, and the Palestine problem. The author has drawn on numerous sources including U.S. state department documents, British foreign office, and Russian correspondence. The sources appear to be largely from the West. Review: *Journal of American History* 74:3:1097 (December 1987).

502. Clemens, Walter C., **Can Russia Change?: The USSR Confronts Global Interdependence**. Boston, Mass.: Unwin Hyman, 1990. xxix, 384 p. ISBN: 0044455364. Includes bibliographical references.

Gorbachev's reforms, particularly those in foreign policy, are the subject of this work. The author reviews Russia's past approaches to foreign policy and examines the motivation for change. The author believes a more democratic system will promote a more stable world situation. The book is divided into four parts. The first part examines the history of Soviet foreign policy from 1917 to 1985. Part two looks at some of the motivations for change, particularly arms control. Part three analyzes Gorbachev's "new thinking" and his recent actions. The final section discusses the possibilities for the future. A glossary of terms is included.

503. Dibb, Paul, **The Soviet Union: The Incomplete Superpower**. London: Macmillan, 1986. xxi, 293 p. *Studies in International Security*, ISBN: 0333362810. Includes bibliographical references and indexes.

An analysis of the position of the USSR in the world. "This book attempts to contribute to the current debate about the Soviet Union's future by presenting a perception of the world as seen from Moscow." (p. xvii) The author believes the Soviet Union is without real global influence economically, technologically, and ideologically. To demonstrate this thesis he examines first the domestic and then the global context of Soviet international behavior. There is also a final section discussing the future of "Soviet Power." The book includes a glossary and numerous tables.

504. **American and Soviet Intervention: Effects on World Stability**, edited by Karen A. Feste. New York: Crane Russak, 1990. v, 162 p. ISBN: 0844816310. Includes bibliographical references (p. 147-152).

Papers from a variety of contributors gathered at a conference on Superpower Intervention (1988) are presented in this volume. Contributors include U.S. policymakers, foreign scholars, and U.S. academic specialists. "The theme and major focus at this conference was two-fold. First to understand the determinants of American and Soviet involvement in domestic crises of sovereign states, and second, to compare the types of interventionary actions adopted by the superpowers." (p. 6) The papers in this volume are divided under eight topics: Effects on World Stability, Multiple Meanings of Intervention, Current Issues of Superpower Intervention in Europe, U.S. Intervention in Central America, Superpower Intervention in Asia, Competitive Intervention in the Mid-East and Africa, and the Future of Intervention.

505. Gorbachev, Mikhail Sergeevich, **The Coming Century of Peace**. New York: Richardson & Steiman, 1986. 300 p. ISBN: 093133250.

A collection of essays, speeches, press conferences, and addresses by the former chief of the Soviet Union. By and large, the works were all written or delivered in late 1985. These works present Gorbachev's vision for peace in the future, how it can be attained, and the benefits it will provide. Since the materials included are approximately half directed at the West and the other half directed to a Soviet audience, they present, as a whole, a balanced picture of Gorbachev's views on the subject.

506. Gupta, Rakesh, **Soviet Policies in the Eighties**. New Delhi: Patriot Publishers, 1987. xi, 188 p. ISBN: 8170500605. Includes bibliographies and index.

A socialist analysis of the Western view of the Soviet Union and how its (the West's) misconceptions have led to various problems over time. The author discusses several policy areas to make his point, such as foreign policy, disarmament, space policy, and policy towards Asia. The author believes that Westerners have consistently underestimated the dynamic elements of a socialist system, or simply failed to recognize them. This has led to an analysis based on a misperception, in the author's view, seeing the Soviet system as rigid and one that generates political alienation.

507. Hough, Jerry F., **The Struggle for the Third World: Soviet Debates and American Options**. Washington, DC: Brookings Institution, 1986. x, 293 p. ISBN: 0815737467. Includes index.

The description and "illumination" of Soviet foreign policy thinking is the primary goal of this book. The author also hopes to contribute to an understanding of U.S. policy toward the Soviets. The author believes that threats to national security via Third World entities have become the focus of foreign policy since they are seen as being the most likely source of nuclear threats. The author has attempted to be comprehensive in his coverage discussing all regions of the world relevant to his debate. He focuses on the period since World War II. His work is drawn from the Soviet literature on Soviet attitudes and perceptions. The book has both a topical and chronological arrangement. A wide range of subjects is discussed such as communist ideology, the role of communist parties in the Third World, post-Stalinist policy, military force in international relations, analysis of American policy, Gorbachev, and future policies. Reviews: *American Political Science Review* 81:2:674-75

(June 1987). *Orbis* 30:2:395 (Summer 1986). *Political Science Quarterly* 102:1:117-18 (Spring 1987).

508. **Soviet National Security Policy Under Perestroika**, edited by George E. Hudson. Boston: Unwin Hyman, 1990. xv, 343 p. *Mershon Center Series for International Security and Foreign Policy*, ISBN: 0044455321, 0044455356 (pbk.). Includes bibliographic references.

The papers contained in this volume were originally presented and critiqued at a seminar at Ohio State University that met four times between December 1986 and October 1987. The papers intend to answer the question: "How shall the United States respond to a USSR that seeks to diffuse some of the past elements of military competition and conflict, while at the same time charts new paths for its economic and political security?" (p. xiv) The papers are arranged in five parts: introduction, the context of change, the change agents, change in the elements of Soviet national security, and conclusions and implications.

509. **Soviet Foreign Policy: New Dynamics, New Themes**, edited by Carl G. Jacobsen. New York: St. Martin's Press, 1989. xv, 214 p. ISBN: 0312036078. Includes bibliographical references.

A number of specialists have contributed to this analysis of foreign policy in the early Gorbachev years. The attempts to reform and improve the economic situation at home have driven many changes in foreign policy. The book, thus, first focuses on domestic politics and its effects on foreign policy. The next section examines arms control in the Gorbachev era. This is followed by two essays on foreign economic policy. The final section is devoted to regional issues that not only examine relations with the Eastern Bloc countries, but also Sino-Soviet relations, the Iran-Iraq War, and security in the Arctic.

510. **The Strategic Triangle: China, the United States, and the Soviet Union**, edited by Ilpyong J. Kim. New York: Paragon Press, 1987. viii, 293 p. *"A PWPA Book,"* ISBN: 0943852218 (pbk.), 094385220X. Includes index.

A collection of papers, originally written for a 1985 conference on U.S.-Soviet-Chinese relations, held in Los Angeles sponsored by the Professors for World Peace Academy. These essays focus on the relations between the three superpowers in the 1980s with special attention to China's role in the triangle. Aside from theoretical analysis of the evolving relationship between the three nations, topics include Japan and the superpowers, the effect of the interrelationship of China, the U.S., and the Soviet Union on Korea and Indochina, and implications for Taiwan. These scholarly studies emphasize theoretical models of the future evolution of the interaction between the three superpowers. Review: *Towson State Journal of International Affairs* 22:1:55 (Fall 1987).

511. **The Third World and the Soviet Union**, edited by Zaki Laidi, translated from the French by A.M. Berrett. London: Zed Books, 1988. xiii, 125 p. ISBN: 0862327318 (pbk.), 086232730X. Includes bibliographical references and index.

Essays examining the perception of the Soviet Union by Third World countries are presented in this volume. Countries include Iraq, Syria, Turkey, Vietnam, India, Argentina, Brazil, the ASEAN states, and the Black African states. Authors are all specialists on the Third World.

512. **Soviet Foreign Policy**, edited by Robbin F. Laird. New York: Academy of Political Science, 1987. x, 276 p. *Proceedings of the Academy of Political Science*, vol. 36, no. 4. Includes bibliographical references and index.

A collection of papers delivered at a meeting of the Academy of Political Science that focuses on the changes in foreign policy since Gorbachev rose to power. They attempt to define the degree of real policy change behind the new diplomatic veneer. The volume is divided into five sections beginning with an overview of past policy and some of its limiting factors, such as the role of the military. The volume continues with eight essays on Soviet relations with the major powers of the world including the United States, Western Europe, Eastern Europe, Japan, and Asia. Next, Soviet relations with other areas of the world are discussed. These essays include discussions on the Third World, the Middle East, Afghanistan, and Central America. The concluding section looks at Gorbachev's term in power since 1985, with a final essay projecting things to come.

513.   Laird, Robbin F., **The Soviets, Germany, and the New Europe**. Boulder, CO: Westview Press, 1991. 212 p. ISBN: 0813380480. Includes bibliographical references and index.

Soviet-West German relations are analyzed as a case study of Soviet-West European relations. The author focuses on the Gorbachev era and discusses many of the disputes between conservatives and reformers in the Gorbachev administration, demonstrating the range of opinion prevalent from 1985-90. The first chapters of the book discuss general approaches in policy toward Western Europe as a whole in the past. The author then turns to a discussion of the Gorbachev era and how foreign policy changed. Chapters four through eight focus on relations with Germany from 1985 to 1990. The final chapter discusses possibilities for the future.

514.   **Soviet Foreign Policy in a Changing World**, edited by Robbin F. Laird and Erik P. Hoffman. Hawthorne, N.Y.: Aldine Publishing Company, 1986. xxiv, 969 p. ISBN: 0202241661. Includes bibliographies.

Drawing on the research of scholars and former government officials, the editors have collected a large number of essays on many aspects of Soviet foreign policy. Varying interpretations are presented to meet the needs of a broad audience from students of Soviet politics to businessmen. Most of the contributors are Americans. The first three parts of the volume include essays on issues, policymaking, and the role of military power in Soviet foreign policy. The remaining sections gather essays on Soviet relations with particular regions: the United States, Western Europe, Eastern Europe, the Far East, and the Third World. The final section contains essays on the potential for change in Soviet foreign policy. While there is a wealth of information in the volume. Reviews: *Slavic Review* 46:3-4:608-9 (Fall-Winter 1987). *Soviet Union* 14:1:149-52 (1987). *Canadian Slavonic Papers* 29:2-3:316-17 (June-September 1987).

515.   Light, Margot, **The Soviet Theory of International Relations**. New York: St. Martin's Press, 1988. vi, 376 p. ISBN: 0312018916. Includes index and bibliography.

This analysis focuses on the theoretical framework underlying Soviet foreign policy. Key aspects of that theory are identified, discussed, and critically reviewed. "Soviet policy makers and international relations specialists believe that Soviet foreign policy is scientific because it is based on a Marxist-Leninist theory of international relations. This is a story of the historical origins of the content of that theory." (back cover) The book is structured around geographical areas of major concern in Soviet foreign policy: relations with the capitalist countries, third world countries, and other socialist nations are considered in turn. A final section looks at changes in theory under Gorbachev. An extensive bibliography is provided. Review: *Journal of International Affairs* 42:2:493-94 (Spring 1989).

516.   **Sinews of Self-Reliance**, edited by Girish Mathur. New Delhi: Allied Publishers, 1987. ix, 223 p. Includes bibliographical references.

This collection of essays was compiled in commemoration of the fortieth anniversary of the establishment of Indian-Soviet relations. There are five sections into which the essays are divided. The first section consists of essays on the convergence of revolutionary processes in India and the USSR. The second section looks at the revolutionary process among the non-aligned nations. Section three deals with the cooperative efforts between the Soviet Union and India. Section four presents future prospects. The final section examines the history of the relationship between the two nations.

517. Medhurst, Martin J., and et al., **Cold War Rhetoric: Strategy, Metaphor, and Ideology**. New York: Greenwood Press, 1990. xv, 224 p. *Contributions to the Study of Mass Media and Communications*, no. 19. ISBN: 0313267669. Includes index and bibliographical references (p. 209-216).

Rhetoric is seen by the editors as "the central defining characteristic of the Cold War." (p. xiv) The essays are divided into four parts. Part one, "Strategy," includes a general discussion of rhetoric and the Cold War as well as analysis of Eisenhower's "Atoms for Peace" speech and Kennedy's 1962 speech on the resumption of atmospheric tests. Part two, "Metaphor," discusses theoretical and practical applications of the use of metaphor in Cold War rhetoric. Part three, "Ideology, " examines critical and classical theory of ideology criticism. Part four provides a conclusion to the foregoing essays.

518. **The Soviet Union in Transition**, edited by Kinya Niiseki, with contributions by Seweryn Bialer. Boulder, CO: Westview Press, 1987. ix, 243 p. *Westview Special Studies on the Soviet Union and Eastern Europe*, ISBN: 0813373751. Includes bibliographies.

The papers in this volume were originally developed at a symposium sponsored by the Japan Institute of International Affairs. "In this volume, prominent Japanese, U.S., and European experts examine changes within the USSR as well as Soviet reactions to changes in the rest of the world. They assess the immediate implications of change for such areas as technology, energy policy, and economic reform and deliver commentaries on current policy directions and historical backgrounds of Soviet policies." (frontispiece) Review: *Russian Review* 49:2:233-34 (April 1990).

519. Rees, David, **Peaceful Coexistence: Study in Soviet Doctrine**. Washington, DC: International Security Council, 1989. 77 p. *International Security Council Publications*. Includes bibliography (p. 76-77).

The policy of peaceful coexistence is examined as it has developed from Lenin to Gorbachev. Changes in the policy under each ruler of the Soviet Union are examined in individual chapters. The members of the council feel that the Soviet definition of peaceful coexistence has really been a struggle against the West. They discuss elements in Soviet ideology that verify this. When examining Gorbachev's "new thinking" it is interpreted as motivated by the crisis condition in the economy. No real change in attitude toward the West has been demonstrated in their eyes, and they discuss Gorbachev's actions as a reaffirmation of past policy.

520. Ruddy, T. Michael, **The Cautious Diplomat: Charles E. Bohlen and the Soviet Union, 1929-1969**. Kent, OH: Kent State University Press, 1986. ix, 219 p. ISBN: 0873383311. Includes index and bibliography (p. 197-211).

Charles Eustis Bohlen served in the State Department as a professional foreign service officer from 1929-1969. This is more of a intellectual history of Bohlen and the internal debates within the State Department regarding the Soviet Union than it is a biography of Bohlen himself. This work traces Bohlen's role and his views of Soviet-American relations during this crucial period. His opinions were not always popular within the department. Bohlen attempted to understand Soviet motives and develop from this an appropriate response for the United States. Ruddy refutes arguments by revisionist historians that blame the coming of the cold war on the United States. He shows that there was not a unanimity among American leaders solely to reconstruct a world where American capitalism could function as it saw fit. Ruddy's book, based on recently opened archival sources, examines the roots of Bohlen's image of the Soviet Union and the growth and sophistication of these perceptions. Reviews: *International Historical Review* 9:3:486-88 (August 1987). *History: Reviews of New Books* 15:4:121 (March-April 1987). *Journal of American History* 74:3:1085-86 (June 1987).

521. Smolansky, Oles M., and Bettie M. Smolansky, **The USSR and Iraq: The Soviet Quest for Influence**. Durham, NC: Duke University Press, 1991. xi, 346 p. ISBN: 0822311038. Includes index and bibliographical references (p. 333-340).

Soviet-Iraqi relations from 1958 to 1988 are discussed in this detailed analysis. The author follows a chronological arrangement focusing on areas of conflict between the two nations such as the nationalization of the oil industry, the Kurdish problem, the Iraqi communist party, Persian Gulf stability from 1968-80, and the Iran-Iraq war. The author is particularly interested in analyzing the attempts to establish influence relationships and views this work as a case study of such a relationship. He sees resource dependence as a continuing factor in international relations that will affect foreign policy between many nations. The authors were forced to rely on public sources as officials were not allowed to discuss the subject beyond the "official" line in either country. This is the authors' second work on Soviet-Mid Eastern relations. Review: *Foreign Affairs* 70:2:179 (Spring 1991).

522. **Public Diplomacy: USA Versus USSR**, edited by Richard F. Staar, with foreword by W. Glenn Campbell. Stanford, Calif: Hoover Institution Press, 1986. xvii, 305 p. *Hoover Press Publication*, no. 345. ISBN: 0817984518. Includes bibliographies and index.

Papers collected from a workshop held at the Hoover Institution at Stanford University. The essays give a profile of differences and similarities in foreign and domestic policy in the U.S.A. and the USSR. The first two sections deal with specific areas of the topic such as foreign policy and U.S. Soviet exchanges, giving examples of differences in how public policy is handled in various contexts. The final section focuses on the West European view of public policy for both superpowers.

To 1917

523. Esthus, Raymond A., **Double Eagle and Rising Sun: The Russians and Japanese at Portsmouth in 1905**. Durham, NC: Duke University Press, 1988. x, 265 p. ISBN: 0822307782. Includes index and bibliography (p. 247-256).

Based on archival records in the United States and Japan, Esthus gives the reader a detailed account of the events up to the Portsmouth Peace Conference, the various diplomatic and other maneuverings during it, and its outcome. Reviews: *Slavic Review* 49:2:286 (Summer 1990). *Canadian-American Slavic Studies* 24:4: 471-73 (Winter 1990). *Russian Review* 49:1:97-98 (January 1990). *Canadian Journal of History* 24:1:130-32 (April 1989).

524. Jelavich, Barbara, **Russian's Balkan Entanglements, 1806-1914**. Cambridge, England: Cambridge University Press, 1991. xi, 292 p. ISBN: 0521401267. Includes index and bibliographic references (p. 277-284).

"The purpose of this study is to examine the reasons for the Russian involvement in the Balkan Peninsula and to attempt, at least partially, to explain the connections that drew the Russian government into entanglements that were not only often in contradiction with its great-power interests, but contained emotional commitments that were difficult to control.

The emphasis is on the unique relationship that many Russian statesmen felt that they had with the Orthodox Balkan people, one that they believed was shared by no other state. At the same time, an explanation is offered about why Balkan national leadership did not reciprocate these feelings, but were extremely happy to exploit Russian willingness to come to their assistance." (p. ix).

525. Roberts, Ian W., **Nicholas I and the Russian Intervention in Hungary**. New York: St. Martin's Press, 1991. xi, 301 p. ISBN: 0312048971. Includes bibliographical references (p. 277-285) and index.

"The present work is an attempt to give an account of Russian foreign policy during the revolutionary years 1848 and 1849 which culminated in Nicholas I's decision to respond to an appeal of Francis Joseph for aid in restoring order in Hungary. It is based on a study of material from diplomatic archives (published and unpublished) and makes extensive use of the memoirs written by Russian officers who took part in the campaign in 1849." (p. ix).

526. Westwood, J. N., **Russia Against Japan, 1904-05: A New Look at the Russo-Japanese War**. Albany: State University of New York Press, 1986. ix, 183 p. ISBN: 0887061915. Includes index and bibliography (p. 173-177).

This history of the Russo-Japanese War relies on sources previously untapped in the English language accounts. The author notes that many previous accounts have used the British *Official History* as their basis. This source is limited to military aspects of the war and often "makes over-confident" use of both the Russian and Japanese sources. The author here has drawn on personal accounts as well as later official Russian histories that have never been translated. The volume is arranged chronologically and illustrated with photographs.

1917 to the Present

527. Chang, Gordon H., **Friends and Enemies: The United States, China, and the Soviet Union, 1948-1972**. Stanford, Calif.: Stanford University Press, 1990. ix, 383 p. *Modern America*, ISBN: 0804715653.

In the words of the author, "This study attempts to show how the Sino-Soviet alliance figured in the development of U.S. policy, especially toward China, from 1948 to Richard Nixon's historic journey to Beijing in 1972. It seeks to understand how the United States tried to undermine the alliance, and then how the United States tried to exploit the rupture when it came." (p. 3- 4).

528. **Western Perceptions of Soviet Goals: Is Trust Possible?**, edited by Klaus Gottstein with contributions by Karl Birnbaum. Boulder, CO: Westview Press, 1989. 455 p. *"A Publication of Research Unit Gottstein in the Max Planck Society,"* ISBN: 0813309697. Includes bibliographical references.

Papers resulting from an international workshop on "Western Perceptions of Long-Range Goals of Soviet Policy" held in 1987 are presented in this volume. As the focus of the topic takes in a wide range of subjects, many areas are covered including perestroika and ideology, long-term obstacles to establishing trust between East and West, culturally linked attitudes toward the Soviet Union, foreign relations, Soviet economic reform, education, and reform. An extensive select bibliography is included made up of Western language studies on numerous subjects related to mutual perceptions of East and West.

529. Harbutt, Fraser J., **The Iron Curtain: Churchill, America, and the Origins of the Cold War**. New York: Oxford University Press, 1986. xiv, 370 p. ISBN: 0195038177. Includes index and bibliography (p. 341-353).

A study of the origins of the Cold War from the European perspective. Most analyses of the topic view it from an American vantage point. The author hopes to begin filling the void with this study. It is also in some ways a biography of Churchill during the war years and post-war environment. The author has taken a "structural" view of the origins of the Cold War that will enlarge the scope of the subject and establish connections with other American historical patterns. "I hope to leave the reader with, at the biographical level, a fuller appreciation of the ubiquity of Winston Churchill, here engaged for a third time in guiding the United States through the British corridor toward confrontation with the threatening European power, and at the deeper level of world affairs where the play of power is so much more elusive, a renewed sense of the long-rooted character of modern diplomatic history." (p. xiv) The arrangement is largely topical. Reviews: *Bulletin of the Atomic Scientist* 43:4:47ff (May 1987). *Political Science Quarterly* 102:4:688-89 (Winter 1987-88). *Orbis* 30:4:743-44 (Winter 1987).

530. **MEMO 2: Soviets Examine Foreign Policy for a New Decade**, edited by Steve Hirsch. Washington, DC: Bureau of National Affairs, 1990. 322 p. ISBN: 0871796813.

This is the second collection of articles on Soviet foreign policy published cooperatively by the Bureau of National Affairs and MEMO, the Soviet Institute for World Economy and International Relations. These articles were carefully edited to ensure that they hold more than passing interest in the topic. The contributions are arranged in three parts: The Crisis of Socialism: What Next; International Relations in a Changing Role; and the USSR in the World Economy. The book succeeds in providing a wide panorama of Soviet specialists' views on various problems. Review: *Foreign Affairs* 70:3:175 (Summer 1991).

531. **MEMO: New Soviet Voices on Foreign and Economic Policy**, edited by Steve Hirsch. Washington, DC: Bureau of National Affairs, 1989. xiii, 639 p. ISBN: 0871796333.

MEMO is an acronym for the Russian equivalent of World Politics and International Relations. It is also a monthly journal issued by the Institute of World Economy and International Relations in Moscow. The three dozen articles chosen are meant to introduce the Western reader to new Soviet thinking in the areas of global economics and international relations. The selections, chosen from the journal over a two year period in the late 1980s, vary in format and subject content. They are grouped under five classifications: global context of perestroika, present day capitalism, U.S. problems, the USSR and the CMEA in the world economy, the new thinking in international relations, and the Third World. The final selection is a series of excerpts from the journal that were published over the past 30 years.

532. Kovalenko, I. I., and Rais Tuzmikhamedov, **The Non-Aligned Movement: The Soviet View**. New Delhi: Sterling Publishers, 1987. x, 176 p. ISBN: 8120707504. Includes bibliographical references.

In the words of the authors, they intend "to make a concise exposition of the Soviet view on the non-aligned movement. They give a historical account of, among others things, the rise and formation of the movement, explain its aims and principles, analyze the role and place of non-alignment in the system of international relations, and show its growing significance in the struggle to consolidate world peace and security." (p. vii).

533. **Soviet Foreign Policy Today: Reports and Commentaries from the Soviet Press**, compiled and edited by Gordon Livermore. Columbus, Ohio: Current Digest of the Soviet Press, 1989. 192 p. *"Selections from the Current Digest of the Soviet Press,"* ISBN: 0913601624.

Collection of materials originally published in the Soviet press and first appearing in translation in the *Current Digest of the Soviet Press* from September 1986 through June 1989. The articles are divided by subject area: Soviet World Outlook, U.S.-Soviet Relations, Arms Control, Europe, China and the Far East, Afghanistan, Middle East, and the Third World. The volume is intended as a source of supplementary readings for college courses. The articles appear in the same format as they would in the *Current Digest*, that is with no commentary or introduction.

534. Lynch, Allen, **The Soviet Study of International Relations**. Cambridge: Cambridge University Press, 1987. xii, 197 p. ISBN: 0521330556. Includes index and bibliography.

A scholarly examination of Soviet views on international relations as they have evolved since the Khrushchev era, "This work specifically seeks to test Zimmerman's findings that Soviet perspectives on international relations have tended to converge with many non-Marxist Americans (and other Western theories) in their view of the basic structure of the international system." (p. 5) Such issues as methodology, traditional Soviet views on international relations, and changes in these attitudes are central to the study. The authors then examine works by Soviet authors to identify indications of changes in perspective. Reviews: *Foreign Affairs* 66:5:1132 (Summer 1988). *American Political Science Review* 82:3:1041-42 (September 1988).

535. Medvedev, Roy Aleksandrovich, **China and the Superpowers**. Oxford: Blackwell, 1986. 243 p. ISBN: 0631138439. Includes bibliographical references and index.

Medvedev does not intend to present a comprehensive review of superpower relations, but rather to "attempt to discover a pattern in the complex picture of the past, and to trace possible tendencies for the future." (p. 3) His four chapters cover relevant historical events for the USSR, and China and the United States and China, changes in the strategic triangle during the 1980s, and prognosis and perspectives on the future.

536. Nogee, Joseph L., and Robert H. Donaldson, **Soviet Foreign Policy Since World War II**. 3rd ed. New York: Pergamon Press, 1988. vii, 378 p. ISBN: 0080358861 (pbk.), 0080358853. Includes index.

The authors trace Soviet foreign policy since World War II by first examining the overall Soviet approach to foreign policy and the various domestic influences in the making of foreign policy. They then cover the main foreign policy events starting with the origins of the Cold War during World War II and ending with Gorbachev and his struggle to restructure policy in the late 1980s.

537. O'Connor, Timothy Edward, **Diplomacy and Revolution: G.V. Chicherin and Soviet Foreign Affairs, 1918-1930**. 1st ed. Ames, Iowa: Iowa State University Press, 1987. xx, 250 p. ISBN: 0813803675. Includes index and bibliography (p. 195-232).

"Using Chicherin, commissar of foreign affairs from 1918 to 1930, as a case study, this book investigates the efforts of the Soviet government to establish diplomatic relations with foreign governments during the first decade after the Bolshevik Revolution." (p. x) Reviews: *Slavic Review* 48:1:112 (Spring 1989). *American Historical Review* 94:2:493 (April 1989).

538. Rubinstein, Alvin Z., **Soviet Foreign Policy Since World War II: Imperial and Global**. 3rd ed. Glenview, Ill.: Scott, Foresman, 1989. xv, 381 p. *Scott, Foresman/Little, Brown Series in Political Science*, ISBN: 0673398935. Includes bibliographies and index.

Rubinstein's third edition retains the basic structure of previous editions, but chapters one and fourteen are new. The book is divided into four parts. Part I (ch. 1-4) covers the historical foundations of Soviet foreign policy from tsarism through the eras of Lenin and Stalin. Part II (ch. 5-9) examines the regional dimensions of Soviet foreign policy, including relations with Eastern Europe, Western Europe, the Far East, the Third World, and the Middle East. Part III (ch-10-12) analyzes the instruments of Soviet diplomacy, an area that encompasses the military dimensions of Soviet foreign policy, the world communist movement, and the United Nations. Part IV (ch. 13-14) discusses the future of Soviet-American relations and speculates about Soviet strategy to the year 2000.

539. Staar, Richard Felix, **Foreign Policies of the Soviet Union**. Stanford, Calif.: Hoover Institution Press, Stanford University, 1991. xxxi, 351 p. ISBN: 0817991026. Includes bibliographical references (p. 319-338) and index.

An extensive analysis of Soviet foreign policy methods taking the point of view that many of the early Communist expansionist goals are still driving foreign policy activities. "The author identifies four instruments applied by the Soviet Union to its foreign policy endeavors, propaganda, intelligence and active measures, military power, and foreign trade." (back cover) The author examines Soviet activities in specific areas of the world: Eastern Europe, East Asia, Latin America, India, Sub-Saharan Africa, as well as the United States. The author focuses on the effect perestroika has had and its future role should the Soviet system survive. Reviews: *Journal of Baltic Studies* 22:4:374 (Winter 1991). *Current History* 90:558:346 (October 1991).

With the United States

540. Allen, Robert V., **Russia Looks at America: The View to 1917**. Washington, DC: Library of Congress, 1988. vi, 322 p. ISBN: 0844405930. Includes index and bibliography (p. 279-314).

This work is a scholarly treatment of the attitudes held in Russia towards America from the sixteenth century to 1917. It deals with Russia's perception of America in the broadest sense and includes topics such as views of American literature and film, agriculture, technology, education, and government. Allen was a librarian at the Library of Congress for many years and drew on his extensive knowledge of that collection for his research. The study is limited almost entirely to Russian language materials. The work is intended as a survey of the literature. In reviewing that survey the author finds many opinions about America, but his general sense is that they are more positive than negative. The author also notes a corresponding lack of knowledge of Russia on the American side. One brief note; the bibliography includes extensive annotations. Review: *Hayes Historical Journal* 9:2:45-49 (Winter 1990).

541. **Windows of Opportunity: From Cold War to Peaceful Competition in U.S.-Soviet Relations**, edited by Graham T. Allison and William L. Ury with Bruce J. Allyn. Cambridge, Mass.: Ballinger Pub. Co., 1989. xviii, 345 p. ISBN: 0887303490. Includes index.

A study group on crisis prevention has provided the papers included in this volume. Originally founded in 1978 as a study on crisis management, the focus was shifted to crisis prevention by the group of Soviet and American scholars, journalists, and government officials. This work brings together numerous views on international security. It is divided into three parts. The first examines the basis for peaceful coexistence, the Soviet and American views on risk reduction procedures, rules for peaceful competition, and agreed norms are presented. Part two examines the history of Soviet-American relations concerning specific problems like the Cuban missile crisis and general issues such as arms limitation. The final section looks to the future of U.S.- Soviet relations.

542. Ben-Zvi, Abraham, **The American Approach to Superpower Collaboration in the Middle East, 1973-1986**. Boulder, CO: Westview Press, Published for the Jaffee Center for Strategic Studies by the Jerusalem Post, 1986. 133 p. *JCSS Study*, no. 5. ISBN: 081330461X. Includes bibliography (p.118-133).

Ben-Zvi distinguishes between two types of foreign policy orientations: the bipolar-confrontal conception and the multipolar-accomodative conception. "Using this typology as a analytical tool, the work examines American peacemaking diplomacy as it unfolded since 1973." (p.1)

543. Beschloss, Michael R., **The Crisis Years: Kennedy and Khrushchev, 1960-1963**. 1st ed. New York: Edward Burlingame Books, 1991. xii, 816 p. ISBN: 0060164549. Includes bibliographical references (p. 709-788) and index.

The relationship between John Kennedy and Nikita Khrushchev is the subject of this work. The author is particularly concerned with the question, "Why did these two leaders, who both come to power with genuine hopes of reducing the harshness of Soviet-American relations, take humankind instead to the edge of nuclear disaster and into the most ferocious arms race in world history?" (p. vii) The author draws on many sources recently made available to scholars on the Kennedy era, as well as those made available in the Soviet Union through the new policies of openness. Reviews: *New York Times Book Review* 3 (June 16, 1991). *Bulletin of the Atomic Scientists* 47:10:41-42 (December 1991). *Foreign Affairs* 70:4:174 (Fall 1991).

544. ———, **MAYDAY: Eisenhower, Khrushchev, and the U-2 Affair**. 1st ed. New York: Harper & Row, 1986. xvi, 494 p. ISBN: 0060155655. Includes index and bibliography (p. 415-422).

An analysis of the U-2 incident, its causes and repercussions. "The U-2 episode deserves renewed attention because of the light it sheds on American-Soviet diplomacy and other battles being fought in our own day.... Western historians have largely shown new appreciation of Dwight Eisenhower's shrewdness and commitment to curbing the arms race. Some who once saw Nikita Khrushchev purely as the Butcher of Budapest... have come to view him as a man committed—however ambivalently—to reducing the harshness of the Cold War." (p. xi) The book draws on western sources including interviews, manuscripts, and published works. Reviews: *SAIS Review* 7:1:239-40 (Winter-Spring 1987). *Soviet Union* 13:3: 384-85 (1986).

545. **Gorbachev's Russia and American Foreign Policy**, edited by Seweryn Bialer. Boulder, CO: Westview Press, 1988. xvi, 510 p. ISBN: 0813307481.

The changing Soviet Union and American foreign policy is the subject of this group of essays sponsored by the East-West Forum. The essays are arranged in five thematic parts. Part one examines patterns of change. Part two describes economics, human rights, security issues, and foreign policy after Stalin. Part three focuses on Gorbachev's Russia. Part four deals with Russia and the West, and part five evaluates East-West relations from the perspective of Gorbachev and his relations with the U.S. Reviews: *U.S. Naval Institute Proceedings* 164-65 (October 1989). *Harvard International Review* 12:1:62-63 (Fall 1989). *American Political Science Review* 83:3:1007-79 (September 1989). *Orbis* 33:2:303-04 (Spring 1989). *Slavic Review* 48:4:662-64 (Winter 1989).

546. Bialer, Seweryn, and Michael Mandelbaum, **The Global Rivals**. 1st ed. New York: A.A. Knopf, 1988. 210 p. ISBN: 0394571940. Includes index.
This book is a companion volume to the television series "The Global Rivals." The authors believe that the next decade (1990s) holds the promise of being a calmer decade for Soviet-American relations. They explore the roots of the Soviet-American conflict, the possible difference Gorbachev would make, the past and future of the arms race, and several possible areas of conflict in the Third World, Europe, and the strategic triangle (relations among the Soviet Union, the United States, China, and Japan). In a concluding chapter, they speculate on the future of the rivalry.

547. Bowker, Mike, and Phil Williams, **Superpower Détente: A Reappraisal**. London: Published for the Royal Institute of International Affairs by Sage, 1988. ix, 277 p. ISBN: 0803980418. Includes bibliographies and index.
The authors explore détente in both its theoretical and practical aspects. After an introductory chapter in which they outline differing interpretations of détente, Bowker and Williams describe détente between the superpowers in several aspects, including the movement from Cold War to détente and the Middle East War of 1973, competition in the Third World, the influence of both American and Soviet domestic politics on détente, arms control, the strategic balance and the demise of détente, and the Afghan Conflict and the return of the Cold War.

548. Brzezinski, Zbigniew K., **Game Plan: The Geostrategic Framework for the Conduct of the U.S.-Soviet Contest**. 1st ed. Boston: Atlantic Monthly Press, 1986. xiv, 288 p. ISBN: 087113084X. Includes index.
An analysis of the U.S.-Soviet struggle for global control by a former presidential advisor. The chapters are topical in approach covering such subjects as vulnerabilities of both sides and threat assessments. "To stay in this historical game requires not only political will, but also a long term design. This volume seeks to outline the necessary trade-offs, given unavoidable budgetary constraints, and to provide the needed U.S. geostrategical game plan." (p. xiv) An appendix on U.S. defense forces is included. Review: *Military Review* 67:9:94-95 (October 1987).

549. Byrnes, Robert Francis, **U.S. Policy Toward Eastern Europe and the Soviet Union**. Boulder, CO: Westview Press, 1989. 218 p. ISBN: 0813309522. Includes bibliographical references.
Byrnes examines U.S. policy towards the Soviet Union and Eastern Europe over four decades. His book is divided into two parts. In part one Byrnes treats U.S. and Soviet policy toward Eastern Europe. This includes chapters devoted to the triumph of containment, Soviet and Chinese Communist relations with Yugoslavia, the insecure hegemony of the Soviet Union in Eastern Europe, U.S. policy in Eastern Europe before and after Helsinki and a concluding chapter on the present situation and current trends. In part two he deals with the Soviet Union and the West. Here individual chapters concern Russian and Soviet attitudes toward the West, post-Stalinist policy toward Western Europe, scholarly exchange with the Soviet Union, and the use of trade restrictions to influence Soviet policy. He concludes by offering suggestions as to how the West and East could bring about the "break-up or gradual mellowing" of the Soviet system.

550. **Citizen Summitry: Keeping the Peace When It Matters Too Much to Be Left to Politicians**, edited by Don Carlson and Craig Comstock. Los Angeles: J.P. Tarcher, 1986. 396 p. *"An Ark Communications Institute Book,"* ISBN: 0874774063. Includes index.

A collection of essays demonstrating what can be accomplished by individuals attempting to improve relations between the superpowers. Four types of citizen summitry are described in the essays — unofficial contact between individuals; "space bridges" (two-way television conversations); changes in individual perceptions of the adversary; and overcoming fatalism. "This book argues that, although we are now in serious danger, our civilization does not have to perish in a nuclear war." (p. 14) The essays demonstrate a variety of methods by which new levels of understanding between the opposing sides can be reached.

551. **The Cold War Debated**, edited by David Carlton and Herbert M. Levine. New York: McGraw-Hill, 1988. xviii, 355 p. ISBN: 007027990X. Includes bibliographies.

A study of the Cold War framed in the format of a debate. The book is in large measure an educational tool, with discussion questions and suggested readings provided at the end of each section. "The book is organized into five chapters: 1) Historical Issues, 2) The International System, 3) Goals, 4) Instruments of Power, and 5) Formal Constraints on Conflict." (p. xvii) The editors have limited the study in several ways. First, they are concerned with the conflict between the superpowers, not the struggles between any communist versus any capitalist nation. Second, they considered broad issues as opposed to specific problems; i.e. the arms race as a whole rather than difficulties with specific treaties. They begin their story with events from 1935 on. The contributors are policy makers, scholars, and journalists.

552. Clark, Dick, **United States-Soviet Relations: Building a Congressional Cadre**. Queenstown, MD: Aspen Institute for Humanistic Studies, 1988. iii, 40 p. ISBN: 089843078X. Includes bibliographical references.

The papers included in this volume were originally delivered at a conference in Jamaica in 1988, held for members of Congress. The papers and discussions are "designed both to enrich the members understanding of the background and context of United States-Soviet relations and to address issues of policy with which they have to deal but without simply recreating the ongoing debates in Washington." (p. 1) Individual papers focus on the education and progress of Gorbachev, the Soviet economy, glasnost, and foreign policy.

553. **Containing the Soviet Union: A Critique of U.S. Policy**, edited by Terry L. Deidel and John Lewis Gaddis. Washington, DC: Pergamon-Brassey's International Defense Publishers, 1987. ix, 251 p. ISBN: 0080349471. Includes index and bibliographies.

This volume is a collection of essays by many prominent specialists on "containment." All the articles deal, from various perspectives, with those policies and problems connected with limiting Soviet expansionism. The book is divided into two parts. In part one issues such as public opinion, economic policy, and world politics are examined in terms of containment as it has been practiced in the past. The second part looks at the future and explores alternatives to containment. Each section has its own endnotes.

554. Dmytryshyn, Basil, and Frederick Cox, **The Soviet Union and the Middle East: A Documentary Record of Afghanistan, Iran and Turkey, 1917-1985**. Princeton, NJ: Kingston Press, 1987. xiii, 708 p. ISBN: 0940670240. Includes bibliographical references.

A compilation of Soviet documents on the Middle East covering most of the twentieth century with accompanying commentary by two eminent scholars. A table of the documents is included, but, unfortunately, this lengthy volume does not include an index. The documents are arranged in four sections. The first includes fifteen documents on Soviet intentions in the Middle East as a whole, while the other three sections include documents on the individual Mid-Eastern nations. The volume also includes a general conclusion. The documents are intended to demonstrate Soviet policy objectives in the area. They reveal the Soviet intent to gain control in the area as they felt the area was of major importance in insuring Soviet national security. Soviet proximity makes their conclusion real enough that failure to take them into account means failure to find security solutions for the area. Review: *Slavic Review* 48:3:502-03 (Fall 1989).

555. Drew, Nelson S., and et al., **The Future of NATO: Facing an Unreliable Enemy in an Uncertain Environment**. New York: Praeger, 1991. xii, 206 p. ISBN: 0275938026. Includes bibliographical references (p. 185-197) and index.
Drew and his colleagues tackle the question: "How should the U.S. contribution to NATO; military strategy and force posture best be crafted to meet the requirements of Western European security as the post-World War II bipolar relationship fades into history." (p. ix) Review: *Army* 41:12:55 (December 1991).

556. Dukes, Paul, **The Last Great Game: USA Versus USSR: Events, Conjunctures, Structures**. New York: St. Martin's Press, 1989. xii, 209 p. ISBN: 0312032285. Includes index.
"The basic aim of the book is to argue for the necessity of the study of both superpowers together in the widest space-time dimensions." (p. xi) To do this, Dukes interweaves analysis of contemporary events with a historical perspective reaching back to the 19th century when Britain and Russia jockeyed for power.

557. Foreign Policy Institute, School of Advanced International Studies, John Hopkins University, **U.S.-Soviet Relations: An Agenda for the Future.** Washington, DC: John Hopkins University, 1988. v. *FPI Policy Briefs.*
A series of policy briefs produced as part of a project of the John Hopkins Foreign Policy Institute. The purpose of this project was "to assess the changing nature of U.S.-Soviet relations and devise an agenda for the future." (p. i) To accomplish this, experts in the field were asked to assess the development of U.S.-Soviet relations to the present and at the same time create new and innovative proposals for increasing cooperation between the two countries. The resulting 225 proposals have been used as a general pool. Of these, 20 were selected for development. Those are presented in this series and cover such topics as the development of safe nuclear reactors, a partially convertible ruble, Soviet special economic zones, exporting information technologies, military liaisons between NATO and the Warsaw Pact, an American college in Moscow, and U.S.-Soviet cooperation on terrorism. A complete list of topics is reprinted in each policy brief.

558. Garthoff, Raymond L., **Assessing the Adversary: Estimates by the Eisenhower Administration of Soviet Intentions and Capabilities**. Washington, DC: Brookings Institution, 1991. 52 p. *Brookings Occasional Papers*, ISBN: 0815730578. Includes bibliographical references.
This short pamphlet analyzes and evaluates the Eisenhower administration's policy of containment. It is divided into two parts, the post-Stalin years 1953-56 and the post-Sputnik years 1957-61. The author focuses on the U.S. assessment of Soviet intentions and capabilities.

559. ———, **Reflections on the Cuban Missile Crisis**. Washington, DC: Brookings Institution, 1987. 159 p. ISBN: 0815730527. Includes index.
Garthoff was a participant in the U.S. deliberations of the crisis. Here he "reflects on the nature of the crisis, its consequences, and its lessons for the future. He presents a number of facts for the first time and provides a unique combination of memoir, historical analysis, and political interpretation." (foreword) He also pays attention to the "afterlife" of the crisis

and the effect it had on both Soviet and U.S. subsequent policy making. Reviews: *American Political Science Review* 84:3:1056-57 (September 1990). *Current History* 87:533:429-30 (December 1988). *Diplomatic History* 12:4:463-81 (Fall 1988).

560. **U.S.-Soviet Security Cooperation: Achievements, Failures, Lessons**, edited by Alexander L. George, Philip J. Farley, and Alexander Dallin. New York: Oxford University Press, 1988. xi, 746 p. ISBN: 0195053982 (pbk.), 0195053974. Includes bibliographies and index.

A collection of essays that all have as their basic hypothesis the idea that it is in the best economic and security interests of the U.S. and the Soviet Union to minimize their rivalry. The contributors have written case studies on various areas of the world that demonstrate the advantages and problems of cooperation for the superpowers. This study, intended for the general reader as well as the policy maker, sets out to answer questions on the conditions necessary for cooperation, obstacles to cooperation, and problems of implementing cooperative programs. A prospectus with questions used to guide the specialists writing these essays is included in the appendix. The first part of the study explains its goals and methods. Parts two through five consist of case studies on security in Europe, cooperation on arms control, regional security crises, and analytical conclusions respectively. Review: *Fletcher Forum* 13:2:435-38 (Summer 1989).

561. Gorbachev, Mikhail Sergeevich, **Toward a Better World**. New York: Richardson & Steirman, 1987. 389 p. ISBN: 0931933439.

This is a collection of speeches delivered between February and December 1986. It touches on a variety of topics, both domestic and global, driven by a common idea: "We can no longer live and think as we have in the past." His overriding concern here, however, is that fear among nations cannot be allowed to continue. Only in peaceful conditions can the peoples of the world confront and solve the problems that trouble us all. The speeches include Gorbachev's press conference at Reykjavik, Iceland on October 12, 1986, speeches televised and three presented before the 27th Party Congress, his comments on the reactor accident at Chernobyl, as well as speeches to foreign dignitaries, including presidents Mitterand and Reagan.

562. **Mutual Perceptions of Long-Range Goals: Can the United States and the Soviet Union Cooperate Permanently?** Frankfurt am Main; Boulder, CO: Campus Verlag; Westview Press, 1991. 404 p. *"A Publication of Research Unit Gottstein in the Max Planck Society,"* ISBN: 3593344653 (Campus Verlag), 0813312299 (Westview Press). Includes bibliographical references (p. 372-393) and index.

The papers and discussions reproduced in this book were first presented at a meeting held in mid-1989 by Soviet and American scholars. The purpose was to have each side describe the perception in their own countries of developments in the other country and then discuss the proffered descriptions and assumptions. A summary chapter presents an analysis of the results of the conference.

563. **Breakthrough: Emerging New Thinking: Soviet and Western Scholars Issue a Challenge to Build a World Beyond War**, editors-in-chief, Anatoly Gromyko and Martin Hellman. New York: Walker, 1987. xx, 281 p. ISBN: 0802710158. Includes bibliography (p. 273-281).

A group of scientists, Soviet and Western, working with the group Beyond War have compiled these essays. They cover a variety of topics but are divided into three broad categories: inevitability, global thinking, and process of change. The focus of the volume is on the avoidance of nuclear war.

564. Halliday, Fred, **From Kabul to Managua: Soviet-American Relations in the 1980's**. 1st American ed. New York: Pantheon Books, 1990. vii, 198 p. ISBN: 0679726675 (pbk.), 0394573102. Includes index and bibliography (p. 190-191).

Soviet-American relations are examined in the context of the Third World. It is an analysis intended for the general reader. "It focuses on the varying policies and ideologies produced by each of the great powers to conduct that rivalry (in the Third World) and the illusions which these have generated." (p. 1) The author is highly critical of the policies of both the U.S. and the U.S.S.R. The structure of the book is roughly chronological. Four appendices are included containing the 1972 Agreement on Basic Principles Between the U.S. and U.S.S.R., the 1988 U.S. strategy for "low intensity conflict," the 1988 Afghanistan-Pakistan agreement on nonintervention, and Castro's 1988 speech on rectification and perestroika.

565. Henderson, Loy W., **A Question of Trust: The Origins of U.S.-Soviet Diplomatic Relations: The Memoirs of Loy W. Henderson**, edited and with an introduction by George W. Baer. Stanford, Calif.: Hoover Institution Press, 1986. xxx, 579 p. *Hoover Archival Documentaries*, ISBN: 0817983317. Includes index.

Loy Henderson was a U.S. diplomat in Eastern Europe during the 1920s and 1930s. He was a "central figure in the bitter debate over whether the United States should grant diplomatic recognition to the communist regime, and his memoir gives readers a unique look at this controversy." (p. xii) This book is an abridgment of his typewritten memoirs which are presently located at the Hoover Institution Library.

566. Homet, Roland S., **The New Realism: A Fresh Beginning in U.S.-Soviet Relations**. New York: Harper/Collins, 1990. xvi, 316 p. *"A Cornelia & Michael Bessie Book,"* ISBN: 0060391251. Includes bibliographical references and index.

A reassessment of U.S.-Soviet interactions in light of perestroika and the "new thinking" in foreign policy. The author has drawn on discussions held from 1984-1989 among American specialists on the Soviet Union, American policy makers, and correspondents. The discussions covered 27 different topics such as Soviet internal policies, resistance and support for reform, Soviet external policies, Soviet criteria for success, and many others. Most sources are limited to English language materials.

567. Hough, Jerry F., **Russia and the West: Gorbachev and the Politics of Reform**. New York: Simon and Schuster, 1988. 301 p. ISBN: 0671618393. Includes index and bibliography (p. 269-287).

A reanalysis of the Soviet Union and its relations with the West, returning to some earlier interpretations of the Bolshevik revolution. The author believes, with some earlier historians such as Nicholas Timasheff that the Bolshevik revolution of 1917 was a reactionary "Khomeni-like revolt and that Gorbachev represents a return to the progress generally being made before the revolution." (p. 2) He also feels that the U.S. must be prepared by understanding the new direction of the Soviet Union to protect its own interests. The book discusses such subjects as the nature of the Gorbachev generation—their level of education, their expectations—the Cold War, decision making in the Politburo, Kremlin politics before and after Gorbachev, Gorbachev's domestic and international policy, and U.S. policies with Russia. Review: *Problems of Communism* 39:2:109-14 (March-April 1990).

568. Huber, Robert T., **Soviet Perceptions of the U.S. Congress: The Impact on Superpower Relations**. Boulder, CO: Westview Press, 1989. vii, 197 p. *Westview Studies on the Soviet Union and Eastern Europe*, ISBN: 0813376033. Includes index and bibliography (p. 177-185).

"This study will provide an in-depth examination of contemporary Soviet perspectives on the role of Congress in U.S. foreign policy." (p. 14) It examines Soviet perspectives on the process of Congressional involvement in U.S. foreign policy, Soviet case studies on Congress, Soviet "Congress watchers," Soviet party and government interactions with congress, and leadership attitudes. Reviews: *Slavic Review* 49:1:124-25 (Spring 1990). *American Political Science Review* 84:2:719-20 (June 1990). *Orbis* 34:2: 293-94 (Spring 1990). *Soviet Union-Union Sovietique* 17:1-2:184- 86 (1990).

569. Hyland, William, **The Cold War Is Over**. New York: Times Books/Random House, 1990. 222 p. ISBN: 0812918711. Includes bibliographical references.
"What the Cold War was all about is the subject of this book, which also seeks to answer some of the related questions: who started it, whether is was unavoidable, and whether is could have been settled." (p. 5) The volume is chronologically arranged beginning with 1939 and continuing through the Gorbachev years to 1990. The author is the editor of *Foreign Affairs Quarterly* and has worked for the National Security Council.

570. ———, **Mortal Rivals: Superpower Relations from Nixon to Reagan**. New York: Random House, 1987. 271 p. ISBN: 0394557689. Includes index.
A memoir of the period of détente in Soviet-American relations written by a former member of the National Security Council Staff. Since this is written as a memoir there are no documentary sources. Rather, it is an individual's attempt to explain the events of the years he discusses. Reviews: *Orbis* 32:1:131 (Winter 1988). *Harvard International Review* 10:6:47 (August-September 1988). *SAIS Review* 8:1:242-43 (Winter-Spring 1988).

571. **East-West Conflict: Elite Perceptions and Political Options**, edited by Michael D. Intriligator and Hans-Adolf Jacobsen. Boulder, ÇO: Westview Press, 1988. xi, 210 p. *Studies in International Strategic Affairs Series of the Center for International and Strategic Affairs, University of California, Los Angeles.*
These papers, prepared jointly by American and German scholars, were written to understand U.S.-Soviet relations and U.S., Soviet, and Federal Republic views of the east-west conflict. They "analyzed perceptions both generally and in relation to specific decision maker perceptions with the goal of identifying policy implications and political options." (p. ix) Specific topics include learning in East-West relations, the superpowers as habit-driven actors, West German foreign policy and the bifurcation of the Western Security regime, and the potential for forging a U.S.-FRG policy consensus in the Soviet Union.

572. **Soviet-American Relations after the Cold War**, edited by Robert Jervis and Seweryn Bialer. Durham, NC: Duke University Press, 1991. vi, 356 p. ISBN: 0822310805. Includes bibliographical references and index.
The writers of these essays try to fathom and speculate on the type of relations the U.S. and the Soviet Union will have after the Cold War. Their essays are arranged in three parts. Part one (6 essays) is devoted to Soviet-American relations and domestic changes. Part two (7 essays) examines Soviet-American security under relaxed tensions and part three (3 essays) offers some policy choices. Review: *Foreign Affairs* 70:5:199 (Winter 1991-92).

573. **Dominoes and Bandwagons: Strategic Beliefs and Great Power Competition in the Eurasian Rimland**, edited by Robert Jervis & Jack Snyder. New York: Oxford University Press, 1991. viii, 299 p. ISBN: 01950662469. Includes bibliographical references.
"The contributors assess what statesmen in the United States and other great powers have believed about falling dominoes, whether their fears had any foundation, and the psychological and domestic political factors that may have contributed to those ideas. Essays on

the Soviet Union test for the first time whether the Soviets actually drew the inferences about American credibility that American domino thinkers anticipated. Historical essays examine whether only bipolar international settings give rise to domino thinking, and what kinds of strategic concepts are prevalent in systems of the multipolar variety, like the one which may be now emerging." (p. vii).

574. Johnson, Richard William, **Shootdown: Flight 007 and the American Connection**. 1st American ed. New York: Viking, 1986. xvi, 335 p. ISBN: 0670812099. Includes index and bibliography (p. 324-327).

Johnson explores the unanswered questions concerning the downing of civilian flight KAL 007. He believes that there is evidence to support the Soviet contention that the flight was involved in espionage. He draws on information about loading weight, airline procedures, U.S. surveillance capabilities etc. An appendix is included that reproduces the flight plan, flight release sheet, and weight and balance manifest. Reviews: *Progressive* 50:11:40-41 (November 1986). *American Academy of Political and Social Science Annals* 492:199 (July 1987).

575. **U.S.-Soviet Relations: The Next Phase**, edited by Arnold L. Horelick. Ithaca: Cornell University Press, 1986. 312 p. *"A Book from the Rand-UCLA Center for the Study of Soviet International Behavior,"* ISBN: 0801419123. Includes bibliographical references and index.

This collection of essays was a result of U.S.-Soviet Relations Conference of 1984. Rand-UCLA Center for the Study of Soviet International Behavior asked a group of prominent scholars to evaluate the issues raised at the conference. This volume reflects views of Soviet-U.S. relations at the beginning of the Gorbachev era, when his intentions were still unclear. The book is divided into four sections. The first set of essays deals with the history of U.S.-Soviet foreign relations in contemporary times. The next group deals with the effects of the domestic environment on foreign relations. A variety of issues are examined in the third section including nuclear arms, economics, and the Third World as they affect the interaction between the U.S. and the Soviet Union. Finally, possibilities for the future are discussed in the last set of essays. Throughout the volume two themes recur: 1) the nature of the Soviet Union as an adversary and 2) strategic approaches for dealing with that adversary. The book includes information on the contributors and an index.

576. **Old Myths and New Realities in United States-Soviet Relations**, edited by Donald R. Kelley and Hoyt Purvis, with foreword by J. William Fulbright. New York: Praeger, 1990. x, 181 p. ISBN: 0275934985. Includes bibliographical references and index.

This group of essays is the result of a symposium held under the auspices of the Fulbright Institute of International Relations of the University of Arkansas. The title echoes a book written in 1964 by Senator Fulbright in which he urged a new approach to U.S.-Soviet relations. With Gorbachev's rise to power, the contributors see the appropriateness of discarding old myths and proceeding to new realities. They offer a variety of perspectives, from academe, the diplomatic corps, and journalism.

577. Killen, Linda R., **The Soviet Union and the United States: A New Look at the Cold War**. Boston: Twayne Publishers, 1988. xv, 195 p. *Twayne's International History Series*, no. 3. ISBN: 0805779132. Includes index and bibliography (p. 179-183).

A topical and chronological study of how the Cold War developed. This volume is one in the Twayne International History Series which seeks to provide readable accounts of the post-World War II environment. The author of this volume, a professor of diplomatic history, stresses both a historical and global perspective in analyzing the years of the Cold War. The author uses the perspective of other peoples, the Yugoslavs and the Arabs, to show how East-West relations are viewed. The book includes a chronology and glossary to assist the reader.

578. Kovrig, Bennett, **Of Walls and Bridges: The United States and Eastern Europe**. New York: New York University Press, 1991. xiii, 425 p. *"A Twentieth Century Fund Book,"* ISBN: 0814746128. Includes index and bibliographical references (p. 401-410).

A study of relations between the United States and Eastern Europe with heavy emphasis on the role of the Soviet Union. The Soviet role in German reunification, in trade with Eastern Europe, and in Czechoslovakia are of special interest in this volume as well.

579. Leighton, Marian Kirsch, **The Deceptive Lure of Détente**. New York: St. Martin's Press, 1989. 260 p. ISBN: 0312028016. Includes index and bibliography (p. 235-251).

Leighton's examination of détente begins with an introductory chapter on the background of détente. She then examines arms control and "military détente," the trade bridge, European allies and détente, and the uses and misuses of détente. At the time this book was written, Dr. Leighton was employed by the Department of Defense. Review: *Fletcher Forum of World Affairs* 14:1:180-83 (Winter 1990).

580. Liska, George, **Rethinking U.S.-Soviet Relations**. New York: Blackwell, 1987. xi, 231 p. ISBN: 0631155112. Includes index.

A collection of essays, all previously published elsewhere, on U.S.-Soviet relations. All were written in the last ten years. The essays are grouped into five sections: Structures and Strategies; Issues and Interrogations; Reappraisals and Refinements; Communities and Civilizations; and Patterns of Thought and Policy Prescription. "Of special interest is the controversial status and the unevenly helpful use of historical analogy as a basis for projections from past to future, on which much of what follows rests. Equally pertinent, and a recurrent theme in the essays that follow, is the relationship between historic consciousness and conservatism as an intellectual outlook and the social and philosophical mindset...." (p. 1) An overview of the book is included at the beginning of the volume reviewing the themes and biases of the essays.

581. **Superpower Competition and Security in the Third World**, edited by Robert S. Litwak and Samual F. Wells. Cambridge, Mass.: Ballinger Pub. Co., 1987. xiv, 295 p. *"A Wilson Center Book,"* ISBN: 088730253X. Includes index.

A collection of essays emanating from a series of seminars on "The Third World and International Security: Competing East-West Perspectives and Policies" held at the Wilson Center in 1985. The contributors represent the academic world as well as government. "The first section explores how the foreign policies of the Western powers toward the Soviet Bloc have evolved during the post war period. The second section focuses on specific regional cases in which the outside powers have declared an interest and might be drawn into local conflicts. In pursuing this approach, the purpose is to integrate the perspectives and concerns of the regionalist and geopolitical approaches in order to provide a basis for more informed debate and policy choices." (p. xiv)

582. Mandelbaum, Michael, and Strobe Talbott, **Reagan and Gorbachev**. 1st ed. New York: Vintage Books, 1987. xi, 190 p. *"A Council on Foreign Relations Book.,"* ISBN: 0394747216. Includes bibliographical references.

This book emerged as the result of the authors' participation in a study group sponsored by the Council on Foreign Relations in 1986. It examines the political careers of both Reagan and Gorbachev within the context of their own domestic political climate and the prevailing global rivalry between the superpowers. It tries to assess the possibility of a breakthrough in U.S.-Soviet relations, especially in the wake of the superpower summit in Iceland. Review: *New York Times Book Review* 7 (January 25, 1987).

583. Mayers, David Allan, **Cracking the Monolith: U.S. Policy Against the Sino-Soviet Alliance, 1949-1955**. Baton Rouge: Louisiana State University Press, 1986. 176 p. *Political Traditions in Foreign Policy Series*, ISBN: 0807112879. Includes index and bibliography (p. 165-169).

The evolution of Sino-Soviet relations is explored from the American perspective. The study covers such factors as personalities involved in diplomacy, domestic policies, and the changing quality of Sino-Soviet relations. The study is limited to a consideration of the years 1949-1955, largely because China's stance toward the West was being formulated during this period and Soviet attitudes toward the West were characterized by a tremendous amount of cooperation. The book is arranged chronologically. Reviews: *Journal of American History* 74:1: 223-24 (June 1987). *Reviews of American History* 15:3:499-506 (September 1987).

584. McNamara, Robert S., **Out of the Cold: New Thinking for American Foreign and Defense Policy in the 21st Century**. New York: Simon and Schuster, 1989. 223 p. ISBN: 0671689835. Includes bibliographical references (p. 194-207).

A look at some of the possibilities for change in U.S.-Soviet relations made possible by the Gorbachev reforms. The author, a former Secretary of Defense, reviews the development of the Cold War, the "costs" of the relationship, financial and others, assesses Gorbachev's policy of "New Thinking," and proposes some Western responses to the changes.

585. Melville, Andrei, Alexander Nikitin, and Philip D. Steward, **Prospects for a New U.S.-Soviet Relationship: Perceptions of the Soviet Foreign Policy Community**. Jerusalem: Hebrew University of Jerusalem, 1989. 36 p. *Research Paper*, no. 72. Includes bibliographical references (p. 30-31).

A brief assessment of the changes in Soviet foreign policy that have resulted from Gorbachev's "New Thinking." Some statistical analysis is used although the authors note that the small size of their sample does not allow for great generalization.

586. Menges, Constantine Christopher, **The Twilight Struggle: The Soviet Union v. the United States Today**. Washington, D. C.: AEI, 1990. xix, 428 p. *AEI Studies*, no. 197. ISBN: 0844737011. Includes bibliographical references (p. 405-413).

An analysis of the Soviet and U.S. struggle for dominance of the Third World powers. The author sees these as battles to spread communist regimes throughout the world. The book begins with a review of the history of the Soviet "indirect aggression" and the Reagan Doctrine, formulated to counteract it. It then analyzes five countries where Soviets have been active—Afghanistan, Cambodia, Angola, Mozambique, and Nicaragua. Only Western sources are used in the analysis. The author was formerly a member of the Reagan Administration.

587. **Soviet-American Relations: Understanding Differences, Avoiding Conflicts**. Wilmington, Del: SR Books, 1988. xxix, 211 p. ISBN: 0842023003. Includes bibliographies and index.

The eleven essays gathered in this book arise out of a symposium held at the University of Kentucky in 1987. The contributors are experts from various fields such as law, theology, economics, sociology, political science, arms control and security, and literature. The purpose of the symposium was to develop a deeper understanding of the Soviets in order to avoid conflicts in the future. Topics included are reports from the Soviet Interview Project, religious faith in Soviet-American relations, health care, aging trends and policies, Gorbachev, arms control, interventionism in the Third World, and superpower relations with their allies.

588. Oberdorfer, Don, **The Turn: From the Cold War to a New Era: The United States and the Soviet Union, 1983-1990**. New York: Poseidon Press, 1991. 514 p. ISBN: 0671707833. Includes bibliographical references (p. 449-478) and index.

A chronological analysis of the Gorbachev years in foreign policy, as he changed the relationship between the Soviet Union and the West. "*The Turn* is a gripping narrative history of the most important international development of our time—the passage of the United States and the Soviet Union from the Cold War to a hopeful new era." (book jacket) The author was a diplomatic correspondent for the Washington Post and was able to use his connections to carry out interviews with all the major figures involved. The book includes an appendix with the text of the U.S. and Soviet proposals at Reykjavik. Reviews: *New York Times Book Review* 11-12 (October 27, 1991). *Military Review* 71: 12:98 (December 1991).

589. Payne, Richard J., **Opportunities and Dangers of Soviet-Cuban Expansion: Toward a Pragmatic U.S. Policy**, foreword by Roger Fisher. Albany, New York: State University of New York Press, 1988. xv, 261 p. ISBN: 0887067964, 0887067972 (pbk.). Includes index and bibliography (p. 237-246).

"This book rejects the fatalism characteristic of contemporary American relations with the Soviet Union and Cuba and suggests that through negotiating, deemphasizing ideology, and focusing on problems that provide opportunities for Soviet-Cuban involvement, the United States can have a pragmatic, workable, and efficient foreign policy in relation to Soviet-Cuban activities in the Third World." (p. xiv) After an introductory chapter in which he lays the groundwork for a pragmatic U.S. policy toward Soviet-Cuban relations, he then analyzes several problem areas such as the Horn of Africa, Afghanistan, Nicaragua, the Caribbean, and Southern Africa that could benefit from improved relations between the superpowers. Review: *Journal of International Affairs* 42:2:490-92 (Spring 1989).

590. **Superpower Politics: Change in the United States and the Soviet Union**, edited by Micheal C. Pugh and Phil Williams. Manchester, UK: Manchester University Press, 1990. xi, 208 p. ISBN: 0719032830. Includes bibliographical references.

This collection of essays deals with the changing conditions that the superpowers face in their quest for stability. The eleven essays focus on the Reagan-Bush years, the effect of Reaganomics on foreign policy, perestroika, Gorbachev's defense policy, and "new thinking" and Soviet foreign policy.

591. **Scorpions in a Bottle: Dangerous Ideas About the United States and the Soviet Union**, edited by Lissa Roche. Hillsdale, Michigan: Hillsdale College Press, 1986. xxvii, 96 p. ISBN: 0916308944.

These papers are the result of a seminar, convened by the Shavano Institute at Hillsdale College at the request of the State Department. The purpose was to discuss "moral equivalence" between the Soviet Union and the United States and to discover how prevalent this idea had become. Contributors are recognized authorities of the political right. Papers cover many aspects of the question including philosophical, semantic, and educational perspectives, examination of popular culture, the view from Europe, a view from the Third World, and speculation about the world in 2010.

592. Ryavec, Karl W., **United States Soviet Relations**. New York: Longman, 1988. xiv, 320 p. ISBN: 0582285879. Includes bibliographies and index.

Ryavec's purpose is to describe and analyze the main features of the Soviet-American relationship and to get a sense of the differing views and controversy that surround that relationship in the U.S. He sees the book as filling a gap in the literature by offering here a survey of the whole range of the Soviet-American relationship and its major topics. The work's nine chapters provide a historical perspective of the relationship and its nature, the elements that undergird each other's power such as geography, natural resources, economic power, national morale and the like, military aspects and arms control, rivalry in the Third World, trade, technology transfer, cooperative agreements and exchanges, and finally an examination of contrasting cultures, domestic politics, public opinion, and diplomacy.

593. Savigear, Peter, **Cold War or Détente in the 1980s: The International Politics of American-Soviet Relations**. Brighton: Wheatsheaf, 1987. xii, 196 p. ISBN: 0745002927 (pbk.), 0745001238. Includes bibliography and index.

Savigear assesses "the fate of the United States and the Soviet Union in the face of predominant trends in international relations. [He attempts] to show how the superpowers have been affected by the events and developments" of the years 1980-1986. (p. 1) One question to which he returns is "whether the term 'superpower' retains any meaning as a result of the changes that have taken place in international relations." (p. 1) Reviews: *Political Science Quarterly* 103:3:550-51 (Fall 1988). *Slavic Review* 47:2:335-36 (Summer 1988). *Orbis* 32:2:328-29 (Spring 1988).

594. Sestanovich, Stephen, **Coping with Gorbachev's Soviet Union**. Washington, DC: Center for Strategic and International Studies, 1988. vii, 55 p. *Significant Issues Series*, v. 10, no. 9. ISBN: 0892061219. Includes bibliographies.

The four essays in this volume answer questions "about precisely what the United States can and should seek from the Soviet Union in terms of its international behavior and the bilateral relationship." (p. vii) Topics include an introductory examination about U.S.-Soviet relations in a new environment, managing nuclear arms control with Moscow, managing competition in the Third World, and the role of Europe in superpower relationships.

595. **The Superpowers, Central America, and the Middle East**, edited by Peter Shearman and Phil Williams. 1st ed. Washington, DC: Brassey's Defense Publishers, 1988. xix, 240 p. ISBN: 0080358144. Includes index.

"One of the main objectives of this volume is to compare Soviet and U.S. policies in Central America and the Middle East in order to illuminate the dynamics of decision making towards different Third World regions prone to conflict, instability, and change." (p. xiv-xv) The individual chapters are arranged in three sections; Part I deals with the making of U.S. and Soviet policies focused on this region. Part II moves beyond the policy formulation and implementation stages and examines the impact of these policies. Part III evaluates superpower regional competition and U.S.-Soviet relations.

596. **Mutual Security: A New Approach to Soviet-American Relations**, edited by Richard Smoke and Andrei Kotunov; with prefaces by Cyrus Vance and Georgiy Arbatov. New York: St. Martin's Press, 1991. xxvii, 403 p. *"A Joint Study by the Center for Foreign Policy Development at Brown University and the Institute for U.S.A. and Canada of the Soviet Academy of Sciences,"* ISBN: 0312048041, 0312050354 (pbk.). Includes bibliographical references.

Mutual security changes the meaning of "victory" and allows competition to achieve security, not at the expense of its adversary, but along with it. This book is centered on how the U.S. and the Soviet Union can achieve mutual security. It consists of chapters written by both Soviets and Americans, who organized themselves into several working groups. These working groups focused in turn in different areas of problems: principles and criteria, Europe, Persian Gulf, North Pacific, nuclear and conventional arms reductions, and future scenarios. Review: *Foreign Affairs* 70:2:179 (Spring 1991).

597. **Western Europe and the Crisis in U.S.-Soviet Relations**, edited by Richard H. Ullman and Mario Zucconi. New York: Praeger, 1987. viii, 123 p. ISBN: 0275925846. Includes bibliographies and index.

These papers were originally presented at a conference held in Naples in 1985. Their purpose "is to explore the roots and the manifestations" of U.S. and European tensions over policy toward the Soviet Union and Eastern Europe, especially in the 1980s. A final chapter is an attempt at a summary by coalescing various comments by the contributors on the topic.

598. Van Tuyll, Hubert P., **Feeding the Bear: American Aid to the Soviet Union, 1941-1945**. New York: Greenwood Press, 1989. xii, 200 p. *Contributions in Military Studies*, no. 90. ISBN: 0313266883. Includes index and bibliography (p. 183-196).

The role of the U.S. Lend-Lease program in the Soviet campaign against the Germans is the subject of this study. The author discusses the problems in extending the Lend-Lease Act to the Russians in the U.S. He also examines the Soviet view of the program and the impact its implementation had on Soviet military campaigns. Numerous tables are provided giving data on materials supplied to the Russians. Reviews: *Russian History* 17:4:475-76 (Winter 1990). *Russian Review* 49:4:505-06 (October 1990). *Soviet Union-Union Sovietique* 17:1-2:156-57 (1990).

599. Weihmiller, Gordon R., **U.S.-Soviets Summits: An Account of East-West Diplomacy at the Top, 1955-1985**, with epilogue by Dusko Doder and foreword by David D. Newsom. Lanham, MD: University Press of America, 1986. xv, 211 p. *Institute for the Study of Diplomacy, Georgetown University*, ISBN: 0819154423. Includes bibliography (p. 209-211).

The prefatory phases and outcomes of ten summit meetings are reviewed by retired naval officer Gordon Weihmiller. Dusko Doder discusses the Reagan-Gorbachev summit of 1985. The emphasis in the study is on specific aspects of preparation particularly, timing and circumstances; setting the dates and location; the issue of any preconditions; and setting the agenda. While many other aspects of summit preparation are considered, these four points are considered "primary elements of the process." The appendix to the volume makes up approximately half the book and includes summaries of each summit and any final communiqués or statements issued at the end of the summit. Reviews: *Canadian Slavonic Papers* 29:2-3:319-20 (June-September 1987). *Canadian-American Slavic Studies* 21:1-2:145-46 (Spring-Summer 1987).

600. Whelan, Joseph G., **The Moscow Summit, 1988: Reagan and Gorbachev in Negotiation**. Boulder, CO: Westview Press, 1990. xvi, 141 p. *Westview Special Studies in International Relations*, ISBN: 0813379296. Includes bibliographical references.

The Reagan-Gorbachev summit of 1988 is examined in detail in this study originally prepared under the auspices of the Congressional Research Service. It "reviews pre-summit trends, the agenda, goals and expectations of both sides; surveys and analyzes the activities of each day from the end of the opening of the summit until the President's departure from Moscow and arrival in Washington...; and analyzes the results and significant aspects of the meeting as a case study in Soviet-American negotiations." (p. 1).

601. ———, **Soviet Diplomacy and Negotiating Behavior, 1979-88: New Tests for U.S. Diplomacy**, study prepared by Senior Specialists Section, Office of Research Coordination, Congressional Research Service, Library of Congress. Washington, DC: U.S. G.P.O., 1988. xxxiii, 876 p. *Special Studies Series on Foreign Affairs Issues*, v. 2. Includes bibliographical references and index.

This is a continuation and expansion of a similar study completed in 1979. It "examines Soviet negotiating behavior at a number of negotiating fora during the 1979-88 period, including the Vienna Summit, which concluded the Strategic Arms Limitation Talks (SALT II) agreement, summits between President Reagan and Gorbachev, the Intermediate Nuclear Forces (INF) and Strategic Arms Reductions Talks (START) negotiations, and various economic, scientific, commercial, and cultural negotiations." (p. iii)

With Western and Third World Countries

602. Albright, David E., **Soviet Policy Toward Africa Revisited**, foreword by Helen Kitchen. Washington, DC: Center for Strategic and International Studies, 1987. vii, 68 p. *Significant Issues Series*, v. 9, no. 6. ISBN: 0892061065. Includes bibliography (p. 54-68).

"This study focuses on the Soviet approach to Africa that has emerged in the 1980's and seeks to delineate both the nature and causes of the revisions in policy.... [It] sets forth a base line for analysis of the shifts [in policy] by assessing Soviet strategy in Africa in the 1970's. Next it lays out the various schools of thought that have taken shape in the 1980's about what strategy on the continent should be.... Then it looks at the impact that absence of endorsement by the top leadership of a single school of thought has had on Soviet behavior in Africa." (p. vii-viii)

603. Allison, Roy, **The Soviet Union and the Strategy of Non-Alignment in the Third World**. Cambridge: Cambridge University Press, 1988. vi, 298 p. ISBN: 0521355117. Includes index and bibliography (p. 276-287).

This work examines the rationales behind Soviet policy toward the non-aligned nations of the Third World and the consequences of that policy. The first two chapters analyze the means by which Moscow had sought to reap positive results from its relationships with the various Third World nations. Chapter three studies the methods by which the Soviets have sought to neutralize the influence of the nonaligned nations. This is done by examining specific situations in Southeast Asia, the Persian Gulf, the Mediterranean, and Afghanistan. Chapter four focuses on Soviet policy towards military alignment in the Third World. Reviews: *Canadian Slavonic Papers* 32:1:84-85 (March 1990). *Russian Review* 49:3:317-320 (July 1990). *Political Science Quarterly* 105:3:495-96 (Fall 1990). *American Political Science Review* 84: 4:1343-45 (December 1990). *Studies in Comparative Communism* 23: 1:89-99 (Spring 1990).

604. Amstutz, J. Bruce, **Afghanistan: The First Five Years of Soviet Occupation**. Washington, DC: National Defense University Press, 1986. xxvi, 545 p. Includes index and bibliography (p. 501-526).

Amstutz, U.S. charge d'affaires in Kabul from 1977 to 1980, begins his treatment of the first five years of Soviet occupation with an historical overview of several years of Russian meddling in Afghan affairs. He follows this account with a first-hand report of the 1979 invasion, then analyzes that intervention from political, military, and economic perspectives. Among the important issues Dr. Amstutz discusses are the numerous Afghan political factions — pro-Soviet and resistance, their leaders, the human rights and refugee problems, diplomatic efforts to settle the conflict, and Soviet measures to repress and indoctrinate the

Afghans." (p. xvii) The volume contains numerous illustrations and appendices providing information on Afghan leaders, resistance leaders, and a history of the resistance. A lengthy English language bibliography is provided. Review: *Problems of Communism* 36:5:69-76 (September-October 1987).

605. **Afghanistan: The Forgotten War; Human Rights Abuses and Violations of the Laws of the War Since the Soviet Withdrawal**, edited by Asia Watch Committee and Human Rights Watch. New York: Human Rights Watch, 1991. 145 p. *Asia Watch Report*, ISBN: 09296920.

Violations of human rights by both Soviet forces and its puppet government is the subject of this report. The report is divided into three sections, the first "describes violations of the laws of war by Afghan government forces and by certain hidden majahidin forces.... The second part discusses the reforms undertaken by the Najibullah government in the context of continuing war, the protections provided by these reforms, and the measures which still need to be taken to guarantee full freedom of expression and association and the rights to due process and fair trial. The third part discusses human rights abuses by the resistance forces in areas controlled by the majahidin." (p. 4)

606. **The Soviets in the Pacific in the 1990s**, edited by Ross Babbage. Rushcutters Bay, Australia: Brassey's Australia, 1989. xiv, 143 p. ISBN: 0080371590. Includes bibliographical references and index.

A collection of essays focusing on the effects of changes in the Soviet Union on its relations with the countries in the Pacific. The authors feel the Soviets will be trying to maintain their position as a super power and this aim will color their interaction with the nations of the Pacific. The essays deal with a variety of subjects: domestic constraints on economic change; national security issues; modernization of the Soviet navy; and Soviet prospects in each area of the Pacific: Northeast Asia, Southeast Asia, and the South Pacific.

607. Barany, George, **The Anglo-Russian Entente Cordiale of 1697-1698: Peter I and William III at Utrecht**. New York: Columbia University Press, 1986. 101 p. *East European Monographs*, no. 207. ISBN: 0880331046. Includes bibliography (p. 76-101).

A brief scholarly study of the text of a document, the existence of which was previously questioned. The document is a speech by Peter the Great given on the occasion of his first meeting with William III at Utrecht. "After a critical scrutiny of the newly found text, this study will examine the broader military-political and economical background of the Utrecht encounter, turning subsequently to its implications in Central Europe and indeed in the global alliance systems existing in the clair-obscur of the transition from one general European confederation to two military conflicts..." (p. 3)

608. **The Red Orchestra: Instruments of Soviet Policy in Latin America and the Caribbean**, edited by Dennis L. Bark. Stanford, Calif.: Hoover Institution Press, Stanford University, 1986. 3 v. *Hoover Press Publication*, 308. ISBN: 0817980822. Includes bibliographies and index.

The purpose of these volumes was to examine "the Soviet strategy of synchronizing and orchestrating proxy assets as a means of destabilizing its enemies as a means of advancing Soviet influence in the First and Third worlds." (p. ix) The volumes devote attention both to discussions about the use of policy instruments and case studies in the regimes covered. Review: *Pacific Affairs* 63:3:425-27 (Fall 1990).

609. Behbehani, Hasim S. H., **The Soviet Union and Arab Nationalism, 1917-1966**.
New York: KPI, 1986. 252 p. ISBN: 0710302134. Includes index and bibliography
(p. 237-247).

Behbehani examines the Russian stance toward Arab nationalism and the resulting foreign
policy with Arab states. The author begins his analysis with Lenin and his theories and then
follows five decades of Soviet-Arab relations, giving particular emphasis to the Soviet's
recognition of Israel, the Suez and Lebanese crises, and other key elements.

610. Bennigsen, Alexandre, and et al., **Soviet Strategy and Islam**. New York: St.
Martin's Press, 1989. x, 182 p. ISBN: 0312024819. Includes bibliographical references and index.

This work is in two parts. The first examines the Soviet Islamic establishment as a strategic
instrument and how the Soviets have used Islam as a instrument of foreign policy both prior
to and after Afghanistan. The second part deals with how the Soviets have dealt with Islamic
nations in the Middle East and Africa. In short, "this study examines the origins and
evolution of the Soviet view of the Islamic World as a unique set of geo-strategic problems
requiring special tactics; and Soviet efforts to design and put into operation these tactics in
hopes of realizing their short and long-term political objectives." (p. 3) Reviews: *Foreign
Affairs* 69:2:183 (Spring 1990). *Middle East Journal* 44: 3:511-512 (Summer 1990).

611. Berner, Orjan, **Soviet Policies Toward the Nordic Countries**. Lantham, MD:
University Press of America, 1986. xii, 192 p. ISBN: 0819153826 (pbk.),
0819153818. Includes bibliography (p. 187-192).

Berner's book, a shorter version of which was published in Sweden in 1985, focuses
primarily on military relations between the Soviet Union and its Nordic neighbors. He has
divided his analysis into three chapters. Chapter 1, War Diplomacy, covers Soviet-Nordic
relations from 1800 to the end of World War II. Chapter 2, Tension, Accommodation, and
Restraint, brings the story up through the early 1960s. Chapter 3, Relaxation, Stability, and
Tension, describes the past twenty years.

612. Bhatia, Vinod, **Indira Gandhi and Indo-Soviet Relations**. New Delhi: Panchsheel
Publishers, 1987. x, 141 p. ISBN: 8185197024. Includes bibliographies.

A study of Indira Gandhi's role in the development of Indo-Soviet relations. These relations
are viewed as having been mutually beneficial and a natural outgrowth of India's nonalignment policy. "However, Indira Gandhi raised Indo-Soviet relations to commanding heights,
leading ultimately to the Indo-Soviet Treaty because she realized that these relations had
proved to be of substantial national interest, particularly with regard to India's security and
development." (p. x)

613. **The October Revolution & 70 Years of Indo-Soviet Relations**, edited by Vinod
Bhatia. New Delhi: Panchsheel Publishers, 1987. xiv, 184 p. ISBN: 8185197008.
Includes bibliographies.

A collection of essays compiled in honor of the seventieth anniversary of the October
Revolution. The essays focus on Indo-Soviet relations from their earliest establishment to
the present. Topics covered include early contact between India and the Soviet Union,
Soviet disarmament, Soviet attitudes toward nonalignment, the Indo-Soviet Treaty, the
Delhi Declaration, and economic cooperation between the two countries. Contributors
include scholars and government officials.

614. Bhatt, G. D., **Indo-Soviet Relations and Indian Public Opinion**. New Delhi: Pacifier Publications, 1989. vi, 245 p. Includes index and bibliography (p. 197-233). This chronologically arranged study is intended to fill a gap in the existing literature. The author believes that most studies see Indo-Soviet relations as having a Soviet bias. "The study indicates that the equidistance from the superpowers is neither possible nor desirable, and Indo-Soviet relations are not based on mere sentiments but are the natural culmination of our peculiar historical circumstances, economic, strategic, and diplomatic compulsions." (p. vi) The author has consulted a number of official documents from parliamentary reports to newspapers in compiling sources.

615. Blasier, Cole, **The Giant's Rival: The USSR and Latin America**. Rev. ed. Pittsburgh, Pa.: University of Pittsburgh Press, 1987. xx, 240 p. *Pitt Latin American Series*, ISBN: 0882254001 (pbk.), 0822935767. Includes Index and bibliography (p. 191-194).
Blasier examines the Soviet presence in Latin America by looking at several aspects of Soviet activity. He examines ways in which they have built diplomatic networks, their trade with the region, their aid to national liberation movements, and their relations with Cuba. This is all set against the U.S.-Soviet rivalry in the region. Reviews: *Foreign Service Journal* 66:2:17-18 (February 1989). *Slavic Review* 48:4:665-66 (Winter 1989).

616. Breslauer, George W., **Soviet Strategy in the Middle East**, with contributions by Galia Golan. Boston: Unwin Hyman, 1990. xvi, 320 p. *"A Book of the Berkeley-Stanford Program in Soviet Studies,"* ISBN: 0044452322. Includes bibliographical references and index.
A collection of materials largely resulting from a conference on Soviet policy in the Middle East held at Berkeley in 1986, with updates of the material to 1989. "The purpose of this volume is more limited: it offers new fundamental research and analytical perspectives on the nature and sources of Soviet strategy in the region, and particularly toward the Arab-Israeli conflict." (p. xv) The volume is divided into three parts. The first focuses on interpreting Soviet strategy. While the focus is largely on the Arab-Israeli conflict there are chapters on the Lebanon War and the Iran-Iraq War. The second part examines the sources of the Soviet strategy with emphasis on consensus and conflict in the decision making process. Part three looks to the future and the possibility of superpower cooperation.

617. Brigot, Andre, and Oliver Roy, **The War in Afghanistan: An Account and Analysis of the Country, Its People, Soviet Intervention and the Resistance**, translated by Mary and Tom Bottomore. Brighton: Wheatsheaf, 1988. vii, 157 p. ISBN: 0745004318 (cased), 074500342 (pbk.). Includes bibliography and index.
This book intends to explore the military and political facets of the Soviet intervention in Afghanistan and attempts to explain why that intervention was unsuccessful. It provides a context for the analysis by giving a chapter on the history of the country prior to 1978. It then devotes subsequent chapters to the conflicts, the resistance, and the consequences of the conflict.

618. Brun, Ellen, and Jacques Hersh, **Soviet-Third World Relations in a Capitalist World: The Political Economy of Broken Promises**. New York: St. Martin's Press, 1990. x, 35 p. ISBN: 0312040709. Includes bibliographical references (p. 301-322) and index.

A study of the Soviet Union from a "leftist" point of view. The authors take four approaches. The first examines Soviet views of the Third World in a Marxist context. Next the development of Soviet attitudes to the capitalist world is analyzed. Third, a study of the development of internal structures in the USSR is presented. The fourth approach makes up part two of the book and is comprised of a discussion of Soviet-Third World relations.

619.   Buszynski, Leszek, **Soviet Foreign Policy and Southeast Asia**. London: Croom Helm, 1986. 303 p. ISBN: 0709932219. Includes index and bibliography (p. 278-293).

"This book is an attempt to assess the aims of and the underlying motives behind Soviet policy towards Southeast Asia since 1969. Moreover, it seeks to identify regional reactions to Soviet policy in the context of enhanced great power interest in Southeast Asia since 1978." (p. 1)

620.   Campbell, Kurt M., **Soviet Policy Towards South Africa**. New York: St. Martin's Press, 1986. xii, 223 p. ISBN: 0312748531. Includes index and bibliography (p. 201-217).

In attempting to discern current Soviet policy toward South Africa, Campbell examines the historical and current political context from which current policy arose. He begins with Russian involvement in South Africa and the Anglo-Boer War, the growth of resistance politics in South Africa, Soviet diplomatic relations with South Africa from 1942-1956, the influence of mineral resources, Soviet espionage, and the contemporary political situation.

621.   **Gorbachev's Third World Dilemmas**, edited by Kurt M. Campbell and S. Neil MacFarlane. London: Routledge, 1989. xvi, 270 p. ISBN: 0451500487X. Includes index.

Papers drawn from a 1986 conference, held at Harvard, on the Soviet dilemmas in the Third World. Contributors were asked to examine elements of foreign policy reflecting continuity and change. "Gorbachev has inherited an activist foreign policy in the developing world from his gerontocratic predecessors. Some of these previous commitments and objectives stand in stark contrast to the new tenets of Gorbachev's foreign policy. The dilemma that Gorbachev and the Soviets face in the Third World are the central issues of inquiry addressed by the contributors to this collection." (p. xv) Besides reviewing past Soviet policy objectives and Gorbachev's changes, the military in the Third World, nuclear nonproliferation, crisis prevention, and policy in the Caribbean, South Africa, and Afghanistan are all topics of discussion.

622.   Carbonell, Nestor T., **And the Russians Stayed: The Sovietization of Cuba: A Personal Portrait**. New York: Morrow, 1989. 384 p. ISBN: 0688072136.

This is Carbonell's memoir of his experiences from January 1, 1959, with the fall of Batista, to 1989. The author was a Cuban citizen whose family was well known in Cuban history. His focus is on the Soviet military buildup in Cuba, and Castro's communist activities around the world.

623.   Clarke, Joseph Calvitt, **Russia and Italy Against Hitler: The Bolshevik-Fascist Rapprochement of the 1930's**, foreword by Clifford Foust. New York: Greenwood Press, 1991. xvii, 218 p. *Contributions to the Study of the World History*, no. 21. ISBN: 0313274681. Includes bibliographical references (p. 201-207) and index.

Clarke has written "a close study of the diplomatic and commercial ties binding Stalin's Russia and Mussolini's Italy in 1933 and 1934." (p. ix) The chapters are arranged in two parts. In part one, Clark describes the background to the Italo-Soviet rapprochement of 1933 and 1934. In part two, he analyzes the ideological, economic, and political aspects of that rapprochement. Review: *Historian* 54:1:115-16 (Autumn 1991).

624. **East-West Rivalry in the Third World: Security Issues and Regional Perspectives**, edited by Robert W. Clawson. Wilmington, Delaware: Scholarly Resources Inc., 1986. xxv, 348 p. ISBN: 0842022368. Includes bibliographical references and index.

A collection of essays focusing on superpower competition in the Third World. The volume is divided into two parts. Each is a gathering of essays by various scholars of political science and history to focus on specific security issues in part one and regional perspectives of the East-West rivalry in part two. Essays specifically pertaining to the Soviet Union include a historical overview of Soviet Bloc security issues, analysis of Soviet military presence in the Third World, Soviet occupation of Afghanistan, NATO-Warsaw pact rivalry over Africa, the Mid-East, Latin America, and Southeast Asia. While the authors vary in their analysis, several general conclusions do emerge. One is that neither side was seen to be winning the competition for the Third World. This was generally attributed to the inability of either side to deal with the diversity of the area. It has also been generally recognized that neither side has been able to cope with the rising nationalism, partially developing in response to the foreign incursions in the area. Last, neither side has been able to develop a coordinated approach to the Third World.

625. **The Western Community and the Gorbachev Challenge**, edited by Armand Clesse and Thomas C. Schelling. Baden-Baden: Nomos, 1989. 408 p. ISBN: 3789017892. Includes bibliography (p. 407-408).

Papers resulting from a 1988 conference of the same title, held at Harvard University, are presented here. The papers cover three areas of study: Soviet domestic policy, economic policy changes, and foreign policy changes. The volume also incudes a "conversation between John Kenneth Galbrath and Leonid I. Abalkin" on capitalism and socialism and a round table discussion on the status of Soviet Studies in the West. Individual essays cover a wide range of topics and there is no attempt at maintaining a unified approach. Indeed, the variety of opinion presented in the volume is indicative of the changes taking place in the Soviet Union as many of the scholars expressing these varied views are Soviet. Topics include the effect of perestroika on the nationality question, the ideology of reform, constitutional reform, pricing policy, foreign economic dependency, Gorbachev and Eastern Europe, East-West security problems, military dimensions of security, and many others.

626. **Asia in Soviet Global Strategy**, edited by Ray S. Cline, James Arnold Miller, and Roger E. Kanet. Boulder, CO: Westview Press, 1987. viii, 193 p. *Westview Special Studies on the Soviet Union and Eastern Europe*, ISBN: 0813374812. Includes bibliographies and index.

A collection of essays originally delivered as papers for the Soviet Global Strategy project between 1983-1985. The authors believe that the Soviet foreign policy has not deviated from its original Leninist goals of world domination. They also feel that the Soviets have followed a two-tiered approach: first trying to expand their military, political, and economic influence in those countries still aligned with the West and also trying to strengthen those states that are already Communist. The essays discuss issues affecting all of Asia such as Soviet global strategy, military power, Soviet economic relations in Asia, and specific countries such as Japan, Korea, Australia, New Zealand, Oceania, and the Persian Gulf States. Review: *Pacific Affairs* 61:2:325-26 (Summer 1988).

627. **Reassessing the Soviet Challenge in Africa**, edited by Michael Clough with contributions by Paul B. Henze, Martin Lowenkopf, and John Marcum. Berkeley: Institute of International Studies, University of California, 1986. xi, 105 p. *Policy Papers in International Affairs*, no. 25. ISBN: 0877255253. Includes bibliography (p. 97-105).

American relations with the Soviet Union have had for some time to be filtered through regional environments. The essays in this volume explore the problems of Soviet-American relations in Africa and focus on Angola, Ethiopia, and Mozambique.

628. Collins, Joseph J., **The Soviet Invasion of Afghanistan: A Study in the Use of Force in Soviet Foreign Policy**. Lexington, Mass.: Lexington Books, 1986. xv, 195 p. ISBN: 0669112593. Includes index and bibliography (p. 177-190).

"The work which follows will analyze the Soviet use of force in Afghanistan. More specifically, this work — subject to the limitations imposed by the available, unclassified sources — will attempt to answer the following questions: 1. What were the Soviet motives for invading Afghanistan?; 2. How was the invasion conducted and how have subsequent military operations been prosecuted?; 3. How does the Soviet invasion of Afghanistan fit the commonly accepted propositions that describe how and under what conditions the Soviets have previously used force in support of their foreign policy?; 4. What conclusions may be drawn from the Soviet invasion of Afghanistan regarding changing trends in Soviet foreign policy?" (p. xiii-xiv) The work is arranged chronologically with several chapters devoted to Russian/Soviet-Afghan relations from 1838-1979. The bibliography includes numerous English language sources on Soviet-Afghan relations. Review: *Problems of Communism* 36:5:69-76 (September-October 1987).

629. Cronin, Audrey Kurth, **Great Power Politics and the Struggle Over Austria, 1945-1955**. Ithaca, NY: Cornell University Press, 1986. 219 p. *Cornell Studies in Security Affairs*, ISBN: 0801418542. Includes index and bibliography (p. 202-211).

"This book is an analysis of one unusual and intriguing episode in post-war international relations, the agreement of Britain, France , the United States, and the Soviet Union at the height of the Cold War to terminate their ten year military occupation of Austria and leave the country unified and neutral." (p. 9)

630. **Britain and the First Cold War**, edited by Anne Deighton, with a foreword by Lawrence Freedman. New York: St. Martin's Press, 1990. x, 301 p. ISBN: 0312040202. Includes bibliography (p. 291-297).

The essays printed here are from a conference held at King's College, London in the spring of 1988. The contributors "focus more narrowly on the first years of the cold war, in order to encourage a reassessment of the existing historiography in the cold war and Britain's role within it." (p. vii)

631. Deporte, A. W., **Europe Between the Superpowers: The Enduring Balance**. 2nd ed. New Haven; London: Yale University Press, 1986. xvi, 256 p. *Council of Foreign Relations Book*, ISBN: 0300037589. Includes bibliography and index.

An in-depth study of European reaction to and involvement with the superpowers since World War II, through the Cold War years. The author believed that the Atlantic alliance system and the division of Europe between East and West were likely to survive. These two factors are seen as playing major roles in shaping European interaction with East and West.

632. Duncan, Peter J. S., **The Soviet Union and India**. London: Routledge, 1989. vii, 150 p. *Chatham House Papers*, ISBN: 0415002125. Includes bibliography (p. 139-150).

India has been one of the few non-communist nations with which the Soviet Union has maintained stable relations over a relatively long period. Duncan examines this relationship from 1971 to the present. After several chapters detailing the context of this relationship, he explores economic, military, and other issues, as well as the role of Soviet propaganda. Review: *Soviet Union-Union Sovietique* 17:1-2:189-91 (1990).

633. Duncan, Walter Raymond, and Carolyn McGiffert Ekedahl, **Moscow and the Third World Under Gorbachev**. Boulder, CO: Westview, 1990. xvi, 260 p. ISBN: 0813305187. Includes index and bibliographical references (p. 241-243).

A study of changes in foreign policy since Gorbachev came to power. Specifically. this work assesses the rationale for and the implication of foreign policy changes toward the third world. The authors draw on a variety of sources including policy statements, official communiqués, and press commentary. Various other analyses of Gorbachev's policies are reviewed. The authors believe that Gorbachev is attempting to better serve interests in national security, economics, and protection of political sovereignty. With this as their basic focus, the authors examine past policy in the Third World and outline the changes of recent years. They then turn to an examination of various areas: Afghanistan, South Asia, Middle East, Asia, Sub-Saharan Africa, and Latin America. The concluding section is developed to examine prospects for the future. The volume includes seven appendices on arms dealings in the Third World. There are numerous tables and maps.

634. Duner, Bertil, **The Bear, the Cubs, and the Eagle: Soviet Bloc Interventionism in the Third World and the U.S. Response**. Brookfield, VT: Gower, 1987. 204 p. *Swedish Studies in International Relations*, v. 22. ISBN: 0566056313. Includes bibliographies and index.

A survey of Soviet military intervention in the Third World since 1970. The author seeks to expose patterns of interventionism and the ideological and behavioral underpinnings that drive it. The book is divided into three parts. The first covers Soviet intervention beginning with a survey of Soviet actions. This is followed by several chapters on Soviet relations with its allies. The author turns to the special role of Cuba and then to the situation in Afghanistan. Part two deals with the U.S. response. The book closes with a brief look at the future.

635. **Superpowers and Client States in the Middle East: The Imbalance of Influence**, edited by Moshe Efrat and Jacob Bercovitch. New York: Routledge, 1991. xv, 272 p. ISBN: 041500490X. Includes bibliographical references and index.

"This book analyses the nature of superpower involvement in the Middle East, paying particular attention to the relations between the United States, the Soviet Union, and their small regional allies." (p. 2) The essays contained in this volume are arranged in three parts. Part one presents a theoretical framework, part two examines the case of U.S.-Israel relations, and part three analyzes the case of Soviet-Syrian relations.

636. El Hussini, Mohrez Mahmoud, **Soviet-Egyptian Relations 1945-1985,** with foreword by Abd Halim Abu Gazala and preface by Admiral Ali Gad. Houndsmills: Macmillan, 1987. xix, 276 p. ISBN: 0333383575. Includes index and bibliography (p. 261-271).

A study of the evolution of Soviet relations with Egypt from the time Egypt recognized the USSR through the mid 1980s. "This book is an intensive case study focused primarily on two issues: the impact of the naval facilities question on the evolution of Soviet-Egyptian relations; and the influence of action-reaction between the two superpowers on the political-decision-making process in Cairo." (p. xix) The book is divided into three parts. The first discusses the basis of superpower policies in the Mediterranean area. The second analyzes Soviet-Egyptian relations from 1945 to 1970. The final section examines the more recent history of Soviet-Egyptian relations. An appendix showing patterns of Soviet Naval visits in the region is included. The author is a Commodore of the Egyptian Navy and represents the views of his government. Review: *Russian Review* 48:2:203-04 (April 1989).

637. Eliot, Theodore L. Jr, et al., **The Red Army on Pakistan's Border: Policy Implications for the United States**. Washington, DC: Pergamon-Brassey's, 1986. vii, 88 p. ISBN: 0080344879.

This special study of four essays was prompted by the Soviet invasion of Pakistan and the ensuing policy implications for the United States. The authors assume that maintenance of good relations with Pakistan and provision of assistance to the Afghan freedom fighters is the best way of containing Soviet expansionism in that part of the world. The essays examine the problem from several perspectives. First, the Soviet threat to Pakistan is described and assessed. This is followed by an evaluation of Pakistan's capabilities to meet the Soviet threat from Afghanistan. Relations between India and Pakistan are then examined. The series is concluded with an overview of U.S. policy toward Pakistan. An appendix contains "An Agreement of Cooperation Between the Government of the United States of America and the Government of Pakistan."

638. Emadi, Hafizullah, **State, Revolution, and Superpowers in Afghanistan**. New York: Praeger, 1990. 156 p. ISBN: 0275934608. Includes bibliographical references.

While the focus of this volume is Afghanistan, it examines that country's development in the context of the struggle between the U.S. and USSR to expand their spheres of influence. That is, the author looks at the development of Afghanistan as a conflict among various socio-political forces that led to a use of force. The author draws on both primary and secondary sources. The book is organized as follows: chapter one deals with the background of nation-state formations in Afghanistan. Chapter two focuses on development since World War II and the role of the superpowers in the fall of the monarchy. Chapter three examines the elements, internal and external, that resulted in the 1978 coup, U.S.-Soviet reactions at the time and Soviet interference in 1979. Chapter four focuses on opposition political parties in Afghanistan that aligned themselves with the U.S. The final chapter summarizes and synthesizes the previous arguments and suggests some possible future prospects for Afghanistan.

639. Floridi, Alexis Ulysses, **Moscow and the Vatican**. Ann Arbor, MI: Ardis, 1986. 279 p. ISBN: 0882336479. Includes bibliography (p. 275-279).

Floridi traces the development of foreign relations between the Soviet Union and the Vatican. He analyzes many aspects of the Vatican's "Eastern policy" and concludes that "this policy is the consequence of a complete failure to comprehend the goals and nature of the system that governs the totalitarian world — a system directed above all against man as the being and likeness of God." (p. 7) Review: *National Review* 58 (July 17, 1987).

640. **The West and the Soviet Union: Politics and Policy**, edited by Gregory Flynn with Richard E. Greene and a foreword by Thomas L. Hughes. New York: St. Martin's Press, 1990. xiv, 266 p. ISBN: 0312040970. Includes bibliographical references and index.

Foreign relations with the West is the subject of this collection of essays. Each essay focuses on relations between the Soviet Union and one specific Western nation, covering Anglo-Soviet, Franco-Soviet, Italio-Soviet, Japanese-Soviet, and U.S.-Soviet relations. Two essays on general aspects of Soviet foreign relations are also included. The emphasis in each essay is on the role of domestic factors in determining Western policy toward the USSR.

The authors are also interested in exploring how differences in each country's attitudes toward the Soviet Union have affected conflicts between Western countries in settling on a policy for dealing with the changes in the USSR. This book is the result of a project growing out of a conference held in Versailles in 1987.

641. Ford, Robert A. D., **Our Man in Moscow: A Diplomat's Reflections on the Soviet Union**. Toronto: University of Toronto Press, 1989. xii, 356 p. ISBN: 0802058051. Includes index.

Ford was a Canadian diplomat who spent most of the period 1946-1980 in the Soviet Union. He is the only Western diplomat who dealt with all of the Soviet leaders since the end of the war. His memoir of sixteen chapters is in four parts: In Stalin's Shadow and After; The Russian Face to the West; Russia's Problems; and The Rise and Fall of Détente. Review: *Canadian Historical Review* 71:3:411-12 (September 1990).

642. Freedman, Robert Owen, **Moscow and the Middle East: Soviet Policy Since the Invasion of Afghanistan**. Cambridge, England: Cambridge University Press, 1991. xii, 426 p. ISBN: 0521359767 (pbk.), 0521351847. Includes bibliographical references (p. 399-415) and index.

Freedman "provides an exhaustive account of Soviet policy in the Middle East from the invasion of Afghanistan in December 1979 to withdrawal from the country ten years later.... [He] examines policy motives and outcomes in a broadly chronological approach. Specific and detailed attention is paid to Soviet policy toward the Iran-Iraq War, the Arab-Israeli conflict, and intra-Arab policies." (front piece) Review: *Foreign Affairs* 70:4:184 (Fall 1991).

643. ———, **Soviet Policy Toward Israel Under Gorbachev**. New York: Praeger, 1991. xvi, 141 p. *Washington Papers*, no. 150. ISBN: 0275939936. Includes index and bibliographical references (p. 129-135).

Freedman's chronological focus is the period 1985 to 1990. After a brief introduction, Freedman analyzes the Soviets' efforts to improve relations with Israel from 1985-1986, especially under Gorbachev's leadership. He then describes Soviet-Israeli relations for 1987-1988, calling it a new beginning. Finally, he examines Soviet-Israeli relations from 1989-1990, seeing it as the start of a new relationship.

644. Gnatiuk-Danilchuk, Aleksander, **Tagore, India, and Soviet Union: A Dream Fulfilled**. 1st ed. Calcutta: Firma KLM, 1986. x, 410 p. Includes indexes and bibliography (p. 389-401).

A biography of the Indian poet and thinker Rabindranath Tagore with special emphasis on the poet's interest in Russia. "He foresaw with prophetic eyes how fruitful and creative the collaboration between the peoples of India and the Soviet Union could be." (p ix) The book is chronologically arranged. The author is a Soviet scholar of Indian studies.

645. Golan, Galia, **Soviet Policies in the Middle East: From World War Two to Gorbachev**. Cambridge: Cambridge University Press, 1990. vii, 319 p. *Cambridge Soviet Paperbacks*, v. 2. ISBN: 0521358590 (pbk.), 0521353327. Includes index and bibliographical references (p. 298-309).

"This study examines the evolving interests of the Soviet Union in the Middle East and the pursuit of these interests since World War Two. Focusing on Soviet relations with the various actors in the region, up to the rise of Gorbachev in Moscow, particular attention is given to the crises within the Middle East and the often critical decisions connected with them." (p. 2) Not surprisingly, almost one-half of the book focuses on problems involving Israel.

646. Golan, Galia, **The Soviet Union and National Liberation Movements in the Third World**. Boston: Allen and Unwin, 1988. 374 p. ISBN: 0044451113. Includes bibliographies and index.

Golan analyzes Soviet policies toward national liberation movements around the world. His book is divided into two parts. In part one, "Toward a Soviet Theory of National Liberation," he examines the origins of national liberation movements, their composition, leadership and organization, ideology, strategy and tactics. In part two he explains the Soviet policy toward national liberation movements by analyzing patterns of Soviet behavior. Reviews: *Annals of the American Academy of Political and Social Science* 507:142 (January 1990). *American Political Science Review* 84:1:358-61 (March 1990). *Slavic Review* 48:4:667-69 (Winter 1989). *Political Science Quarterly* 104:3:539-41 (Fall 1989).

647. Goodman, Melvin A., **Gorbachev's Retreat: The Third World**. New York: Praeger, 1991. xii, 206 p. ISBN: 0275936961. Includes bibliographical references (p. 189-194) and index.

A study of the changes in foreign policy under Mikhail Gorbachev that have led to the withdrawal from involvement in the Third World. The author feels Gorbachev's decisions were directly responsible for the decline in Soviet military presence in the Third World. He covers many topics and people including Edward Shevardnadze's resignation and the significance of the choice of his replacement, Bessmertnykh. Other topics discussed range from a discussion of Soviet involvement in Afghanistan to a description of crisis management under Gorbachev. There are lengthy discussions of the role "New Thinking" has played in Soviet relations with Africa, Asia, China, the Middle East, and the Korean Peninsula. A serious study based on many current sources.

648. **Agenda for Action: African-Soviet-U.S. Cooperation**, edited by Anatoly A. Gromyko and C. S. Whiter. Boulder, CO: L. Rienner Publishers, 1990. xii, 290 p. ISBN: 1555871968. Includes bibliographical references.

This work focuses on possibilities for joint U.S.-USSR cooperation in Africa. Areas examined for possible inclusion in cooperative activity include the agrarian sector, the environment, debt and development, mineral resources, communications, health and epidemics, nuclear non-proliferation, arms transfers, and security concerns.

649. Gupta, Surendra K., **Stalin's Policy Towards India, 1946-1953**. New Delhi: South Asian Publishers, 1988. viii, 293 p. ISBN: 8170030935. Includes index and bibliographical references.

The early years of Indo-Soviet relations are the subject of this study. This period has previously been treated in only a cursory way in the literature. The author also feels this is a particularly significant period in the development of Indian foreign policy. "After all, it was during this period that the first encounters between Moscow and New Delhi took place at several international forums, including the United Nations, and in their direct dealings with each other. It was also under Stalin that Moscow evolved its policy towards non-alignment...." (p. v) The volume is arranged chronologically.

650. **Gorbachev and Europe**, edited by Vilho Harle and Jyrki Iivonen. New York: St. Martin's Press, 1990. xi, 213 p. ISBN: 0312042469. Includes bibliographical references and index.

This volume contributes to the analysis of the new role of Western Europe in Soviet foreign relations. The ten essays focus on: general background (chapters 1-4), recent European issues in Soviet foreign policy (chapters 5-7), and economic interaction (chapters 8-10).

651. **Afghanistan and the Soviet Union: Collision and Transformation**, edited by Milan Hauner and Robert L. Canfield. Boulder, CO: Westview Press, 1989. xi, 219 p. ISBN: 0813375754. Includes bibliographical references and index.

These essays were written to "draw attention to the wider structural conditions that set the context of decision making— specifically, with regard to the military and security conditions in the region, which could eventually intensify the clash between the Islamic interest groups on the one hand and the two forms of alien modernization, Western and Soviet, on the other." (p. 4) The essays are grouped into two parts. Part one is the human factor, which explores topics of the conflict of political evolutionary processes and Islamic ideology, the Mujahedin and the preservation of Afghan culture, and the Sovietization of Afghanistan. Part two is the geopolitical infrastructure, which discusses regional position and economic integration, Afghan resources and Soviet policy, transport infrastructures, and the Soviet geostrategic dilemma. Reviews: *Russian Review* 49:3:364-66 (July 1990). *Middle East Journal* 44:3:506-07 (Summer 1990). *Canadian Slavonic Papers* 32:1:87-88 (March 1990).

652. Hilton, Stanley E., **Brazil and the Soviet Challenge, 1917-1947**. Austin: University of Texas Press, 1991. xvi, 287 p. ISBN: 0292707839. Includes bibliographical references (p 261-171) and index.

Although the Soviet Union and Brazil had formal diplomatic relations for only a short time of the period under study in this volume, the author feels the Soviets played a critical role in shaping Brazilian government. He believes that the authoritarian system which developed in Brazil can to some extent be considered a reaction to the threat of communism presented by the Soviet government. "The analytical focus is, thus, a dual one: the images of the USSR, particularly of its policies and goals, held by the Brazilian foreign policy elite, and the transformation of those images into a program of anti-Communist actions." (p. x) The study is chronologically arranged with the focus being on the years 1925-1940.

653. **The Soviet Union, Eastern Europe, and the Third World**, edited by Roger E. Kanet. Cambridge: Cambridge University Press, 1987. xvi, 233 p. ISBN: 052134459X. Includes bibliographies and index.

Articles resulting from papers presented at the Third World Congress for Soviet and East European Studies held in Washington, DC from October 30 to November 4, 1985. This volume examines specific aspects of the changes in Soviet policy toward the Third World since Khrushchev's reign. The study is organized into three parts. The first deals with general aspects of Third World policy including such subjects as an overview of Soviet policy goals, the effects of revolutionary changes on policy, and national liberation movements. The second section deals with Eastern European economic involvement in the Third World. The final chapters consist of two case studies, one on Syria, the other on India. Reviews: *Russian Review* 49:3:317-20 (July 1990). *Orbis* 33:1:139-40 (Winter 1989).

654. Karsh, Efriam, **Soviet Policy Towards Syria Since 1970**. New York: St. Martin's Press, 1991. ix, 235 p. ISBN: 031205310X. Includes bibliographical references (p. 221-229) and index.

Karsh attempts to answer several questions about the Soviet-Syrian relationship, including Soviet motivations and what methods have been used to achieve Soviet goals. His book is divided into two parts. "The first part focuses on the structure of the Soviet-Syrian relationship and analyzes the nature and characteristics of its main three components: the political, the military and the economic.... Part II sets out to trace the evolution of Soviet policy towards Syria during the past two decades and seeks to discern the elements of continuity and change in this policy from Brezhnev to Gorbachev." (p.7)

655. Katz, Mark N., **Russia and Arabia: Soviet Foreign Policy Toward the Arabian Peninsula**. Baltimore: John Hopkins University Press, 1986. xvi, 279 p. ISBN: 080182897X. Includes index and bibliography (p. 255-267).

The importance of the Arabian Peninsula to the world's oil reserves is obvious. Katz examines the strategic importance of this area and the Soviet policy toward this region. He devotes separate chapters each to North Yemen, South Yemen, Oman, Saudi Arabia, and a composite chapter to Kuwait, the United Arab Emirates, Bahrain, and Qatar. Reviews: *Slavic Review* 46:3-4: 613-25 (Fall-Winter 1987). *Orbis* 29:4:844-45 (Winter 1986). *Political Science Quarterly* 102:1:141-43 (Spring 1987). *Problems of Communism* 36:5:77-84 (October 1987).

656. **Neither East nor West: Iran, the Soviet Union, and the United States**, edited by Nikki R. Keddie and Mark J. Gasiorowski. New Haven: Yale University Press, 1990. ix, 295 p. ISBN: 0300046588 (pbk.), 0300046561. Includes bibliographical references.

"This book deals with the relations of Iran, the United States, and the Soviet Union between 1945, when the Cold War began, and 1988-89, when it was dramatically attenuated." (p.1) It is divided into four sections: the view from Tehran, Iran and the Soviet Union, Iran and the United States, and the Fateful Triangle.

657. Keeble, Curtis, **Britain and the Soviet Union, 1917-89**. New York: St. Martin's Press, 1990. xiv, 387 p. ISBN: 0312036167. Includes bibliographical references and index.

Keeble has written a study of British policy toward Soviet Union. He proceeds in essentially chronological order from Britain's response to the 1917 revolution to suggestions for a new policy for the 1990s. Much of it is written from Keeble's perspective as Britain's ambassador to the Soviet Union from 1978 to 1982. Three appendices help keep the myriad facts in some reasonable order. These are: a chronology of British-Soviet relations, British and Soviet leadership from 1917-1989, and British and Soviet diplomatic representatives.

658. Kempton, Daniel R., **Soviet Strategy Toward Southern Africa: The National Liberation Movement Connection**. New York: Praeger, 1989. 261 p. ISBN: 0275931188. Includes index and bibliography (p. 241-256).

Three case studies of Soviet behavior toward National Liberation Movements are presented in this volume: the African National Congress, the Movimento Popular de Liberacao de Angola, and the Zimbabwe African People's Union. The author believes this type of analysis will fill a gap in the existing literature which is confined to studies that examine Soviet behavior of the Third World or studies that examine Soviet attitudes toward national liberation movements. "The specific research question this study attempts to answer is what strategy, if any, has the Soviet Union pursued in its relations with NLM's?" (p. 3) The book is divided into five chapters, the first an overview of national liberation movements and Soviet strategy, the next three on the individual cases to be considered, and, finally, a chapter of general conclusions.

659. Kitchen, Martin, **British Policy Towards the Soviet Union During the Second World War**. London: Macmillan, 1986. viii, 309 p. ISBN: 0333398777. Includes bibliography and index.

A history of the events that shaped the British policy, particularly the alliance, with the Soviets during World War II. The arrangement is largely chronological with an opening chapter covering the history of Anglo-Soviet relations. The author believes the alliance was a product of the unique circumstances of the time and sets about proving this point. Review: *New York Times Review of Books* 11:44-50 (June 1987).

660. **The Limits of Soviet Power in the Developing World**, edited by Edward A. Kolodziej and Roger E. Kanet. Baltimore, MD: Johns Hopkins University Press, 1989. xx, 531 p. ISBN: 0801837626. Includes index and bibliography (p. 463-513).
The editors posit two objectives for this volume: "to evaluate Soviet penetration of the developing world and to identify the implications of Soviet success and failure for U.S. security and foreign policy." (p. xiii) The sixteen essays are arranged in a global perspective in the Soviet Union and the Third World. In part two, contributors focus on regional perspectives from Latin America, East and Southeast Asia, South and Southwest Africa, Middle East and North Africa, and Sub-Saharan Africa. In part three they synthesize the material presented and draw conclusions. Reviews: *Canadian Slavonic Papers* 32:1:84-85 (March 1990). *Russian Review* 49:3:317-20 (July 1990). *Conflict Quarterly* 10:2:67-69 (Spring 1990). *American Political Science Review* (84:4:1343-45 (December 1990).

661. **The Soviet Union and the Third World: The Last Three Decades**, edited by Andrzej Korbonski and Francis Fukuyama. Ithaca: Cornell University Press, 1987. xvi, 318 p. *"A Book from the RAND/UCLA Center for the Study of the Soviet International Behavior,"* ISBN: 0801494540 (pbk.), 0801420326. Includes index.
This publication includes papers originally presented at a conference held in 1985 and sponsored by the RAND/UCLA Center for the Study of Soviet International Behavior. Topics covered include a history of Soviet foreign policy in the Third World from 1955 to 1985, general studies on military and economic aspects of Soviet strategy, as well as papers focused on specific areas; Eastern Europe, Cuba, Southwest Asia, the Middle East, South Asia, and Sub-Saharan Africa. "The authors of the individual chapters have sought to place the current situation in the broader context of Soviet policy in the past three decades and to see if larger historical patterns are at work which might help us predict future Soviet behavior." (p. xi)

662. Korn, David A., **Ethiopia and the United States and the Soviet Union**. London: Croom Helm, 1986. xviii, 199 p. ISBN: 0709931166. Includes index and bibliography (p. 190-191).
A diplomat's account of the events in Ethiopia, particularly from 1982 to 1985, that turned Ethiopia to the Soviet Union. Although the author is giving the Western view of events in Ethiopia, he is aware of importance of the Soviet role there and tries to recount as fully as possible the history of the development of their relationship. The book has a chronological arrangement with opening chapters giving background information on events in Ethiopia form 1974 to 1982. Appendices are included on the press release on Socialist Ethiopia (1985), U.S. emergency assistance to Ethiopia 1984-85, and total emergency assistance for the same period.

663. Laidi, Zaki, **The Superpowers and Africa: The Constraints of a Rivalry, 1960-1990**. Chicago: University of Chicago Press, 1990. xxv, 232 p. ISBN: 0226467813. Includes bibliographical references (p. 219-226) and index.
"The purpose of this book is to show, in a historical perspective, how the dialectical relationship between the superpowers and African actors has evolved." (p. xx) Thus, the author covers decolonization in Africa from 1960-1964, the marginalization of Africa from 1965-1974, and Angolan crisis, and the roles of the United States and the Soviet Union in these events.

664. Laird, Robbin F., and Susan L. Clark, **The USSR and the Western Alliance**, with contributions by Hannes Adomeit, et al. Boston: Unwin Hyman, 1990. 269 p. ISBN: 0044453922. Includes bibliographical references.

"This book assesses Soviet analyses and perceptions of the nature of the Western Alliance, particularly those elements of its security policy most directly relevant to the military challenge. Within this broad framework, the security policies of the key West European members of the Western Alliance are examined and the East European factor in Soviet policy toward the alliance is assessed." (p. 1)

665. **Vital Interests: The Soviet Issue in U.S. Central American Policy**, edited by Bruce D. Larkin. Boulder, CO: L. Rienner Publishers, 1988. ix, 500 p. ISBN: 1555871127 (pbk), 1555871119. Includes index and bibliography (p. 471-483).

"The object of this volume is to bring together representative statements that Managua's policies and dispositions threaten security, assessments and critiques of that claim, and evidence of the Soviet and Cuban activity and capabilities from which the reader may better judge the charges and countercharges." (p. 1) The essays are arranged under four rubrics: the Claim, Critiques and Assessments of the Claim, Soviet and Cuban Activities in Central America, and resolution of long-term tensions in the region. Reviews: *Military Review* 70:1:106 (January 1990). *Slavic Review* 49:3:463-64 (Fall 1990).

666. Leonhard, Wolfgang, **The Kremlin and the West: A Realistic Approach**, translated by Houchang E. Chenabi. New York: W. W. Norton, 1986. xii, 228 p. ISBN: 0393023729. Includes bibliographical references and index.

An exploration of the possibility of reform in the Soviet Union by one of its former government officials. The author examines the power structure within the system, domestic policies and problems, Soviet foreign policy, and the role of the West in the liberalization process. The author feels his background gives him a unique advantage over other Soviet analysts, "A knowledge of the inner mechanisms of the system, the ability to imagine what forms the changes might take, and above all, a certain empathy for the people in Communist-ruled states." (p. x) The author sees his own biases as placing him in the same camp as Sakharov — i.e., someone seeing liberalization of the existing system. Reviews: *Eastern Europe Quarterly* 22:1:126-27 (Spring 1988). *Foreign Service Journal* 64:4:14-15 (April 1987). *Freedom at Issue* 101:32-34 (March-April 1988).

667. Makinda, Sam, **Superpower Diplomacy in the Horn of Africa**. London: Croom Helm, 1987. 242 p. ISBN: 0709946627. Includes index and bibliography (p. 225-234).

This examination of U.S. and Soviet diplomacy in the Horn of Africa covers issues and contexts, the regional equation, evolution of superpower policies, rivalry in a changing order, 1974-76, the 1977-78 Ogaden War, American reassertion of force, and Soviet policy 1979-86. Two appendices contain the U.S.S.R.-Somali Treaty and the U.S.S.R.-Ethiopian Treaty.

668. Malcolm, Neil, **Soviet Policy Perspectives on Western Europe**. London: Royal Institute of International Affairs, 1989. viii, 117 p. *Chatham House Papers*, ISBN: 0415039010. Includes bibliography (p. 113-117).

A brief study of the Soviet Union's European policy and prospects for the future based on an analysis of Soviet writings on the subject. "The conclusion of this paper is that Gorbachev's policy towards Western Europe arises logically from the new overall Soviet perspective on international relations, which stresses bridge-building and interdependence, rather than conflict and defense isolationalism." (p. vii)

669. **Soviet-American Relations with Pakistan, Iran, and Afghanistan**, edited by Hafeez Malik. New York: St. Martin's Press, 1987. xiii, 431 p. ISBN: 0312002408. Includes bibliographies and index.

These papers were originally presented at a seminar at Villanova University in 1984. They explore relations of the U.S. and the Soviet Union with Iran, Afghanistan, and Pakistan from a variety of different perspectives. Reviews: *Orbis* 32:1:151 (Winter 1988). *American Academy of Political and Social Science Annals* 498:133-36 (July 1988).

670. Manning, Robert A., **Asian Policy: The New Soviet Challenge in the Pacific**. New York: Priority Press Publications, 1988. vi, 150 p. *"A Twentieth Century Fund Paper,"* ISBN: 0871782444 (pbk), 0870782452. Includes bibliography (p. 141-146).

Manning "traces, with great skill and insight, the ramifications for U.S. policy of Soviet initiatives. Underlying his analysis is the assumption that these initiatives not only present an opportunity for the United States to redefine its current posture in East Africa — which is now based on a loose, informal network of bilateral alliances, a quasi-alliance with China, and the now eroded ANZUS alliance—but also provide the opportunity for greater super-power cooperation in the region." (p. vi).

671. Maprayil, Cyriac, **The Soviets and Afghanistan**. 1st Indian ed. New Delhi: Reliance Publishing House, 1986. xii, 117 p. ISBN: 8185047073. Includes bibliographies and index.

"This book surveys and analyzes some of the important relationships between Afghanistan and the Soviet Union since the revolution in 1917. Some considerations which might have relevance to the working out of a peaceful settlement in the region are presented here." (p. xii)

672. Menon, Rajan, **Soviet Power and the Third World**. New Haven: Yale University Press, 1986. ix, 261 p. ISBN: 0300035004. Includes bibliographical references and index.

In examining Soviet military policy in the Third World, Menon covers the Soviet view of East-West competition in that region, interventions in Angola, Ethiopia, and Afghanistan, and Soviet arms transfers. In conclusion, he assesses Soviet perceptions, power, and, performance. Reviews: *Political Science Quarterly* 102:2:330-31 (Summer 1987). *Russian Review* 46:3:337-38 (July 1987). *American Political Science Review* 81:2:674-75 (June 1987). *Slavic Review* 46:2:311-13 (Summer 1987).

673. Miller, Nicola, **Soviet Relations with Latin America, 1959-1987**. Cambridge: Cambridge University Press, 1989. ix, 252 p. ISBN: 0521351936. Includes index and bibliography (p. 226-244).

A general analysis of the policies and economic factors that have shaped Soviet-Latin American relations from 1959-1987. The author reviews overall trends in policies and the ideological underpinnings of these policies in the first two chapters. The focus then shifts to a case-study analysis of relations with Cuba, Chile, and other major Latin American powers. "The chapters explore the hypothesis that Soviet foreign policy towards Latin America is determined primarily by political and economic variables, which act as constraints on the realization of the maximum ideological/strategic goals so often emphasized in the literature." (p. 2) An appendix giving statistics on Soviet trade with Latin America is provided. Reviews: *Problems of Communism* 39:5:99-107 (September-October 1990). *American Political Science Review* 84:4:1346-47 (December 1990). *Foreign Affairs* 69:2:177 (Spring 1990).

674. Miner, Steven Merritt, **Between Churchill and Stalin: The Soviet Union, Great Britain, and the Origins of the Grand Alliance**. Chapel Hill: University of North Carolina Press, 1988. 319 p. ISBN: 0807817961. Includes index and bibliography (p. 301-307).

"This book examines Anglo-Soviet relations during two critical years, 1940-42, from the early days of the Nazi-Soviet Pact to the Anglo-Soviet Treaty.... It is, above all else, a story of how British leaders chased a diplomatic mirage, trying to gain Stalin's confidence by acceding to his early demands, only to discover that by doing so they had undermined their ability to resist Soviet expansion later in the war." (p. 1-2) Reviews: *Reviews in American History* 18:1:112-17. *Russian Review* 49:2: 228-30. *American Historical Review* 95:4:1168-69 (October 1990).

675. Mitrokhin, Leonid Vasil'evich, **Lenin and Indian Freedom Fighters**. New Delhi: Panchsheel Publishers, 1988. xiii, 88 p. Includes bibliographical references.

A study of Lenin's influence on 20th century Indian political development. The book is divided into three parts. The first deals with the first contacts Indian political thinkers had with Lenin in Moscow. Part two focuses on the developing interests in the Indian press in Lenin's theories. The final part discusses the influence Lenin had on Nehru and Gandhi.

676. **The USSR and Latin America: A Developing Relationship**, edited by Eusebio Mujal-Leon. Boston: Unwin Hyman, 1989. xxviii, 408 p. ISBN: 0044451652. Includes index.

The contributors to this volume have approached Soviet-Latin American relations from various perspectives. They "aim to elucidate the way the region fits into Soviet global concerns and the degree to which the USSR has been successful in employing various instruments in pursuit of its objectives in Latin America." (xxvii) The essays are divided into two parts. Part one focuses on Latin America in Soviet Third World strategy. Part two examines Soviet perspectives in Latin America and the ways in which their strategy had been implemented. Reviews: *Problems of Communism* 39:5:99-107 (September-October 1990). *American Political Science Review* 84:4:1346-47 (December 1990).

677. **Asian Dimension of Soviet Policy**, edited by D. D. Narula and R. R. Sharma. New Delhi: Patriot Publishers, 1986. xiv, 240 p. ISBN: 8170500265. Includes bibliographical references and index.

A collection of essays examining the meaning and implications of the changes proposed by Mikhail Gorbachev at the 27th Party Congress. The essays are organized into two groups: The Asian Viewpoint and the Soviet Viewpoint. Economic and foreign policy changes are of particular interest. The question of nuclear disarmament and its effect on Asian security are also a special focus.

678. Nelsen, Harvey W., **Power and Insecurity: Beijing, Moscow, and Washington, 1949-1988**. Boulder, CO: Lynne Rienner Publishers, 1989. xii, 178 ISBN: 1555871623 (pbk.), 1555871615. Includes index and bibliography (p. 166-173).

"This book is an explanation of the Sino-Soviet dispute from its origins through its militarization to the current phase of détente between Beijing and Moscow. It is an attempt to systematically interpret the history of the dispute in national security terms." (p. x) The analysis is divided into three parts. In part one he examines the decade 1950-1960, which began with a Sino-Soviet alliance and ended with Sino-Soviet animosity. In part two he devotes attention to the 1960's, and in part three, to the period 1970-1988, when the U.S. began playing a more active role. Reviews: *Pacific Affairs* 63:2:237 (Summer 1990). *Conflict* 10:3:277-79 (July-September 1990). *Orbis* 34:1: 154 (Winter 1990).

679. Nissman, David B., **The Soviet Union and Iranian Azerbaijan: The Use of Nationalism for Political Penetration**. Boulder, CO: Westview Press, 1987. ix, 123 p. *Westview Special Studies on the Soviet Union and Eastern Europe*, ISBN: 0813373182. Includes index and bibliography (p. 109-113).

A chronologically arranged analysis of the Soviet attempt to gain a foothold in Iran using a nationalistic movement of the Iranian Azeris. The author carefully examines the numerous Soviet sources on the subject. "He also surveys the development of the political relationship between the Azeris of the Soviet Union and those of Iran — who originated the spread of Bolshevism among Iranian Azeri oil workers in 1905 — and examines the legacy of this movement today." (p. iii) Two appendices are included: a chronology and a few biographical sketches. Reviews: *Armenian Review* 40:3:71-73 (Fall 1987). *American Academy of Political and Social Science Annals* 497:191- 93 (May 1988).

680. Patman, Robert G., **The Soviet Union in the Horn of Africa: The Diplomacy of Intervention and Disengagement**. Cambridge: Cambridge University Press, 1990. xvii, 411 p. ISBN: 0521360226. Includes index and bibliographical references (p. 375-396).

Soviet policy in the Horn of Africa is riddled with paradox, especially with regard to Somalia and Ethiopia. The book is divided into four parts. After an introductory part that establishes the theoretical framework, the second part describes and analyzes Soviet-Somali ties and their 1974 treaty, the Ethiopian revolution of 1974-1976, and realignment and enforcement of proletarian internationalism. The final part offers an assessment of Soviet behavior and speculations about the future.

681. Prakash, Arvind, **Non-Alignment and Indo-Soviet Relations,** with foreword by Bishwanath Singh. Allahabad, India: Chugh Publications, 1990. xx, 188 p. ISBN: 8185076995. Includes bibliographical references (p. 183-188).

The role of non-alignment in Indo-Soviet relations is the subject of this study. "The present study is devoted to the analysis of not only the changing pattern of non-alignment but also to the attempts made to create the 'New International Economic Order' through the non-aligned movement." (p xvi) The arrangement is roughly chronological with an introductory chapter on non- alignment as a policy. The author's methodology consists of studying the published government records and other materials.

682. **Soviet-British Relations Since the 1970s**, edited by Alex Pravda and Peter J.S. Duncan. Cambridge, England: Cambridge University Press, 1990. xii, 263 p. ISBN: 0521370944.

This collection of essays describes and analyzes various aspects of Soviet-British relations since 1920. Included are essays covering pre-perestroika patterns, a historical perspective, the security dimension, political and diplomatic aspects, cultural contacts, and trade and commercial relations. The editors conclude with an essay on Soviet-British relations under perestroika.

683. Prizel, Ilya, **Latin America Through Soviet Eyes: The Evolution of Soviet Perceptions of Latin America During the Brezhnev Era, 1964-82**. Cambridge, England: Cambridge University Press, 1990. xiii, 253 p. ISBN: 0521373034. Includes bibliographical references (p. 203-244).

The changing Soviet perception of Latin America during the USSR's rise to a position of global power is the subject of this book. The author is interested in those aspects of diplomacy that might reflect a more subtle approach to the Latin American world as the Soviets become more knowledgeable of their culture. The author analyzes three components of Soviet perceptions: "...the changing Soviet perception of Latin America's domestic politics; the new role of Latin America in the international arena and the ability of the United States to influence regional events; and emerging Soviet-Latin American relations." (p. ix) The author has drawn primarily on Soviet academic journal articles since he believes the authors of these works play a fairly significant role in policy making unlike their Western counterparts. The book is structured topically covering the Soviet's perception of Latin America's global role, perceptions of Latin American social structure, case studies on Mexico, Chile, Brazil, and Argentina, and general conclusions.

684. Rahul, Ram, **Afghanistan, Mongolia, and USSR**. New Delhi: Vikas, 1987. viii, 97 p. ISBN: 0706937198. Includes index and bibliography (p. 91-93).

A brief survey of the histories of Afghanistan and Mongolia and the development of their relationship with the USSR. A bibliography of English language materials is included. The approach is pro-Soviet in orientation. Appendices contain the earliest and latest treaties between Afghanistan and the USSR to demonstrate the evolution of the relationship between the countries.

685. Rai, S. S., **The Red Star and the Lotus: The Political Dynamics of Indo-Soviet Relations**. Delhi: Konark Publishers, 1990. xi, 347 p. Includes bibliographical references and index.

A study of the political factions affecting the seventy year relationship between India and the Soviet Union. The author emphasizes the fact that the differences in political ideology between the two nations have not affected the dynamics of their foreign policies toward one another. The work is very current with an essay covering the period 1977-1989.

686. Ramet, Pedro, **The Soviet-Syrian Relationship Since 1955: A Troubled Alliance**. Boulder, CO: Westview Press, 1990. xiv, 290 p. *Westview Special Studies in International Relations*, ISBN: 0813377692. Includes bibliographical references.

Ramet analyzes the Soviet-Syrian system from 1955 to the mid-1980s. Special emphasis is on economic, military, and political ties.

687. Ray, Hemen, **The Enduring Friendship: Soviet-Indian Relations in Mrs. Gandhi's Days**. New Delhi: Abninav Publications, 1989. xii, 227 p. ISBN: 8170172497. Includes bibliography (p. 207-221).

A study of the mutually beneficial relations between the Soviet Union and India during Indira Gandhi's tenure in office. The book is organized chronologically. The emphasis is on the Indo-Soviet relationship as a response to Western activity in the region.

688. Read, Anthony, and David Fisher, **The Deadly Embrace: Hitler, Stalin, and the Nazi-Soviet Pact, 1939-1941**. 1st American ed. New York: Norton, 1988. xxi, 687 p. ISBN: 0939025284. Includes index and bibliography (p. 667-674).

The authors trace the diplomatic history of the Nazi-Soviet Pact and Stalin's betrayal by Hitler in 1941. Reviews: *Problems of Communism* 39:6:106-11 (November-December 1990). *Russian History* 17:2:237-38 (Summer 1990). *Journal of Military History* 54:2: 239-40 (April 1990). *American Historical Review* 95:2:492-93 (April 1990).

689. Ree, Erik van, **Socialism in One Zone: Stalin's Policy in Korea, 1945-1947**. New York: St. Martin's Press, 1989. xv, 299 p. ISBN: 0854962743. Includes bibliographical references (p. 281-296).

"This is a case study of Soviet foreign policy in the formative years of the Cold War, 1945 to 1947. It concerns Soviet policy in Korea, opening with the military operations in August 1945 which resulted in the occupation of the part of the peninsula north of the 38th parallel by the Red Army." (p. 1) The book is divided into four parts: The War in the East; The Northern Zone; Diplomacy; and Conclusions. Review: *Journal of Asian Studies* 49:3:670-71 (August 1990).

690. Rezun, Miron, **The Soviet Union and Iran: Soviet Policy in Iran from the Beginning of the Pahlavi Dynasty Until the Soviet Invasion 1941**. Boulder, CO: Westview Press, 1988. xi, 425 p. *"A Westview Encore Edition,"* ISBN: 0813376165. Includes index and bibliography (p. 397-419).

Rezun's main purpose is "to describe the extent to which ideological considerations were subordinates to national security interests and to show how, and under what circumstances, a general, ideologically-based, policy receded further and further into the background as the USSR's unique political relationship with Iran evolved." (p. i) Reviews: *Russian Review* 49:1:111-13 (January 1990). *Strategic Review* 17:4:62-64 (Fall 1989).

691. Robertson, Myles Leonard Caie, **Soviet Policy Towards Japan: An Analysis of Trends in the 1970s and 1980s**. Cambridge: Cambridge University Press, 1988. xvii, 234 p. *Cambridge Studies in International Relations*, v. 1. ISBN: 0521351316. Includes index and bibliography (p. 223-232).

In analyzing Soviet policy towards Japan, Robertson has focused on four areas: "Soviet ideology and Japan, Soviet-Japanese economic relations, the Soviet military and Japan, and Soviet policy toward Japan. A short introductory section outlines some important traditional and historical influences relevant to understanding Soviet approaches to Japan. There is also a small appendix on Japanese fishing." (p. x) Reviews: *Orbis* 34:4:616 (Fall 1990). *Annals of the American Academy of Political and Social Science* 507:146 (January 1990). *Pacific Affairs* 63:3:393- 95 (Fall 1990). *Russian History* 17:2:243 (Summer 1990). *Russian Review* 49:2:234-35 (April 1990). *Slavic Review* 49:3:462-63 (Fall 1990).

692. Roy, Arundhati, **The Soviet Intervention in Afghanistan: Causes, Consequences, and India's Response**. New Delhi: Associated Pub. House, 1987. viii, 140 p. ISBN: 8170450063. Includes index and bibliography (p. 132-137).

Strategically situated, Afghanistan has long been the focus of power intrigues. The purpose of this book is "to analyze the Soviet Union's policy in Afghanistan as it slowly developed through the period and gradually took a definite shape with the December intervention of 1979." (p. v)

693. Rubinstein, Alvin Z., **Moscow's Third World Strategy**. Princeton, NJ: Princeton University Press, 1988. xi, 311 p. ISBN: 0691077908. Includes index and bibliography (p. 295-302).

The behavior of the Soviet Union in the Third World is the focus of this book. The aims and goals of this behavior are rarely, if ever, discussed by the Soviets. Rubinstein tries to discuss what their motives are from their behavior. He does this by examining in turn several key variables to the Soviets' Third World behavior. There are types of involvement, the backing of liberation movements, intervention, surrogates and surrogate relationships, the management of vulnerabilities, and observable impact on the Third World behavior. He concludes by offering prospects for the future, with a preliminary assessment of Gorbachev. Reviews: *Conflict Quarterly* 10:2:67-69 (Spring 1990). *American Political Science Review* 84:4:1343-45 (December 1990). *Military Review* 70:1:103 (January 1990). *Naval War College Review* 43:3:143-44 (Summer 1990).

694. Sahai, Shri Nath, **The Delhi Declaration: Cardinal of Indo-Soviet Relations: A Bibliographical Study**. 1st ed. New Delhi: Mittal Publishers, 1990. xix, 334 p. ISBN: 8170992265. Includes bibliographical references and index.

A study of the events leading up to and consequences of the signing of the Delhi Declaration. The book covers the period from November 1986 to December 1988. Appendices include the text of the Declaration as well as the 1971 Treaty of Peace, Friendship, and Cooperation and a table of the Soviet-Indian Summit Meeting from 1955 to 1988. The remainder of the book is taken up with excerpts from various newspapers and official sources on a range of topics. These include various aspects of Indo-Soviet cooperation, disarmament, and culture.

695. **The Soviet Withdrawal from Afghanistan,** edited by Amin Saikal and William Maley. Cambridge: Cambridge University Press, 1989. 177 p. ISBN: 0521375886 (pbk.), 0521375770. Includes bibliographies and index.

These essays were originally presented at an international symposium held in Australia in 1988. Their aim is to examine the consequences of the withdrawal of Soviet forces from Afghanistan. It covers several aspects of the withdrawal, its antecedents and its aftermath including the Geneva Accords of 1988, the regional politics of the Afghan crisis, the conflict and Soviet domestic politics, and the Afghanistan "settlement" and the future of world politics. Reviews: *Strategic Review* 18: 1:68-70 (Winter 1990). *Russian Review* 49:4:516-17 (October 1990).

696. Saivetz, Carol R., **The Soviet Union and the Gulf in the 1980's.** Boulder, CO: Westview Press, 1989. xi, 139 p. *Westview Special Studies in International Relations,* ISBN: 0813370728. Includes index.

The central focus of this study is Soviet policy toward the Iran-Iraq War. Saivetz also "discusses Soviet interpretations of the Iranian revolution and evaluations of the potent impact of the fundamentalist revival for Moscow's clients in the region." (p. 5) The author also explores the effect Gorbachev has had on Soviet policy toward the Gulf.

697. **The Soviet Union and the Third World,** edited by Carol R. Saivetz. Boulder, CO: Westview Press, published in cooperation with the Harvard Russian Research Center, 1989. ix, 230 p. *John M. Olin Critical Issues Series,* ISBN: 081337692. Includes bibliographical references and index.

A collection of essays covering theoretical and policy issues on the Soviet Union and the Third World. Papers cover national liberation movements, Soviet policy in the Mid-East, comparison of Soviet policy in Latin America and other regions, including Afghanistan, sub-Saharan Africa, Northeast Asia, and protection of the evolution of Soviet policy in the Third World. "The contributors to this volume were asked to assess the Kremlin's successes and failures in several Third World areas, as well as to analyze the trends and prospects for Soviet involvement in the developing world." (p. 210)

698. Sand, Gregory W., **Soviet Aims in Central America: The Case of Nicaragua,** foreword by Lewis A. Tambs. New York: Praeger, 1989. xii, 126 o. ISBN: 0275930505. Includes index and bibliography (117-121).

An examination of Soviet foreign policy goals in Nicaragua from 1959 to 1989. A topical approach is used covering such subjects as the Sandinistas, Western strategy, and the history of Soviet foreign policy. Two appendices are included, one containing maps and a second reprinting a Sandinista strategy. Reviews: *Russian Review* 49:4:514-15 (October 1990). *American Political Science Review* 84:4:1346-47 (December 1990).

699. Segal, Gerald, **The Soviet Union and the Pacific.** Boston: Unwin Hyman, 1990. 236 p. ISBN: 0044458142 (pbk.), 0044458134. Includes bibliographical references.

Segal's study "focuses on changes in several major dimensions of Soviet regional foreign policy, rather than adopting the conventional strategy of taking each country or subregion in turn—an approach that would fail to show how Soviet policy increasingly concerns groups of states rather than individual nations." (p.2) In adopting this regional perspective, Segal examines the Soviet Pacific setting, the historical background, ideology and culture, military issues, the economic dimension, and hopes for the future.

700. Shultz, Richard H., **The Soviet Union and Revolutionary Warfare: Principles, Practices, and Regional Comparisons**. Stanford, Calif.: Hoover Institution Press, Stanford University, 1988. x, 283 p. *Hoover Press Publication*, no. 371. ISBN: 0817987126 (pbk.), 081798118. Includes index and bibliography (p. 253-271).

A study intended for the general reader and the policymaker on the Soviet Union's opportunistic advances in Third World countries. "This survey by Richard H. Shultz, Jr. traces trends since World War II that show how Soviet-sponsored and/or supported insurgencies have integrated political, economic, military, social, and psychological instruments into strategies and tactics." (p. vii-viii) The author uses four case studies to demonstrate his point: Vietnam, the Mid-East, Angola/Namibia, and Central America. The author was the only non-Department of Defense member of the Pentagon's Special Operations Advisory Group. Reviews: *Slavic Review* 49:3:461-62 (Fall 1990). *Studies in Comparative Communism* 23:1:89-90 (Spring 1990).

701. Sicker, Martin, **The Bear and the Lion: Soviet Imperialism and Iran**. New York: Praeger, 1988. 156 p. ISBN: 0275931315. Includes index and bibliography (p. 145-150).

Russia's longstanding interests in Iran as a buffer to Western controlled countries in the region is the subject of this study. The author feels the Soviets maintained the same imperialistic policies as their tsarist predecessors. "This book is primarily concerned with the examination of the context and character of the current Soviet interest in Iran, particularly from the perspective of the global implication of that interest. In pursuing the question, the book will also present a study in the continuity of Russian imperialist policy with respect to Iran from Peter the Great to the present." (pp 2-3) The study is chronologically arranged beginning with the eighteenth century up to 1988. The sources cited in the bibliography are Western and Iranian with no reference to Russian materials. Review: *Soviet Union-Union Sovietique* 17:1-2:168-70 (1990).

702. **Superpower Détente and Future of Afghanistan**, edited by Jasjit Singh, et al. New Delhi: Patriot Publishers, 1990. 183 p. ISBN: 8170501199. Includes index.

Papers resulting from a seminar at the Indian Center for Regional Affairs are collected in this volume along with several diplomatic documents reprinted in the appendices. Various aspects of settlements to the Afghan conflict are examined. One of the premises of the seminar was that the signing of the General Accords might lead to a political solution to the conflict. The essays tend to be brief and most are under ten pages so that although there are fifteen essays, almost half the book is devoted to the appendices.

703. Singh, Nihal S., **The Yogi and the Bear: Story of Indo-Soviet Relations**. London: Mansell, 1986. vii, 324 p. ISBN: 0720118182. Includes bibliographical references and index.

"This is an historical narrative of Indo-Soviet relations from Indian independence in 1947 to the present day, with a brief speculative look at the future." (p. vii) The author was a foreign correspondent in Pakistan and the Soviet Union, and he has relied on a wide array of Pakistani, Chinese, Indian, Soviet, and American sources. The title's echo of an icon of American popular culture is accidental.

704. Singh, Sukeshar Prasad, **Political Dimensions of India-USSR Relations**. New Delhi: Allied Publishers, 1987. iv, 302 p. Includes index and bibliography (p. 283-292).

An analysis of the development of Indo-Soviet relations from Nehru's term in office to the present. The book is divided into six parts covering various phases of that relationship chronologically. Such subjects as Sino-Indian border conflicts, Sino-Soviet polemics, and the Bangladesh crisis are covered in detail. The sources are largely Indian and Western although some standard Soviet sources are included (for example, *Pravda, Izvestiia*, and the materials from Party Congresses). The book is based on the author's dissertation.

705. Stavrakis, Peter J., **Moscow and Greek Communism, 1944-1949**. Ithaca, NY: Cornell University Press, 1989. xvi, 243 p. ISBN: 080142125X. Includes index and bibliography (p. 221 -231).

An analysis of Soviet conduct during the Greek Civil War in an attempt to elucidate Soviet conduct in the Cold War. "The study of the Greek Civil War, because it draws on virtually every factor important in the explanation of Soviet foreign policy generally, can illuminate the extent to which the Soviet Union was driven by ideological rather than pragmatic considerations; Soviet willingness to pursue objectives within the existing state system; the relative importance to the Soviets of subordinating all Communist parties to the Soviet state...." (p. x) The study is largely in chronological order and includes an appendix discussing the approach used in this study. Reviews: *Foreign Affairs* 69:4:194 (Fall 1990). *American Historical Review* 95:5: 1582-83. *Annals of the American Academy of Political and Social Science* 512:206-07 (November 1990).

706. Taylor, Alan R., **The Superpowers and the Middle East**. 1st ed. Syracuse, NY: Syracuse University Press, 1991. xiii, 212 p. *Contemporary Issues in the Middle East*, ISBN: 0815625421, 081562553X (pbk.). Includes bibliographical references (p. 201-204) and index.

"The major theme of this book is that despite the vastly superior strength of the United States and the Soviet Union, both countries have had difficulty in dealing advantageously with their respective interests in the area." (p. xii) Taylor deals with this theme in five chapters in which he sets the context, describes the confrontation, analyzes the Soviet and American policies, and looks toward a transition to increased cooperation.

707. **The Soviet Union as an Asian Pacific Power: Implications of Gorbachev's 1986 Vladivostok Initiative**, edited by Ramesh Thakur and Carlyle A. Thayer. Boulder, CO: Westview Press, 1987. vi, 236 p. ISBN: 081337457X. Includes bibliographies and index.

The focus of this volume is Gorbachev's speech in Vladivostok on July 28, 1986. In it, he touched on a whole range of domestic and foreign policy issues, but most importantly championed more cooperation with the United States, especially in Asia. The papers that appear in this volume analyze the so-called Vladivostok Initiative and its implications. A text of the speech is included in an appendix. Reviews: *Studies in Comparative Communism* 23;1:89-90 (Spring 1990). *Slavic Review* 48:1:115-17 (Spring 1989). *American Political Science Review* 83: 3:1007-79 (September 1989). *Naval War College Review* 42:1:154-55 (Winter 1989).

708. **The Soviet Union and the Asia-Pacific Region: View from the Region**, edited by Pushpa Thambipillai and Daniel C. Matuszewski. New York: Praeger, 1989. ix, 217 p. ISBN: 0275932125. Includes bibliography (p. 207-209).

"Collectively, the chapters in this volume provide a broad portrait of the state of current Soviet relations with the countries of the region, perspectives of the Soviet role, and prospects for change." (p. viii) Essays cover topics such as the Soviet reforms and the Asia-Pacific challenge, Sino-Soviet relations in the 1990s, individual studies covering Japan, South Korea, Indonesia, Malaysia, Philippines, Singapore, Thai, Vietnam, Australia, New Zealand, the Pacific Islands, and Soviet fishery initiatives.

709. Vanneman, Peter, **Soviet Strategy in Southern Africa: Gorbachev's Pragmatic Approach**. Stanford, Calif.: Hoover Institution Press, 1990. xi, 142 p. ISBN: 10817989021 (pbk.), 0817989013. Includes bibliographical references and index.
An analysis of Soviet behavior in Southern Africa based on the assumption that Soviet strategy has remained consistent. The author begins from the premise that Soviet interests in the area have been and will remain intense given the political instabilities of the region. The individual chapters focus mainly on particular areas: South Africa, Namibia, Angola, Mozambique, and the non-aligned nations.

710. **Soviet-East European Relations as a Problem for the West**, edited by Richard D. Vine. London: Croom Helm, 1987. 262 p. *An Atlantic Institute for International Affairs Research Volume*, ISBN: 0709951132. Includes bibliographies and index.
This collection of essays looks at changes in the Soviet-East European Bloc and how those changes may affect Western policy. The volume is divided into four sections. The first reviews the history and evolution of Western policy toward the Eastern Bloc. The second focuses on the changes in Eastern Europe. Western policy goals—specific, economic, and military—are examined. The final section attempts to synthesize the conclusions of all the earlier chapters. "The examination of the issues throughout the book stresses the factors in both East and West that tend toward immobility as well as those that stimulate change." (p. 5)

711. Wettig, Gerhard, **Changes in Soviet Policy Towards the West**. London: Pinter, 1991. 193 p. ISBN: 0861871588. Includes index.
A variety of issues are discussed as a means of examining how the changes in the Soviet Union have come about and what they will mean for the rest of the world. Such areas as domestic motivation for the changes, examination of approaches to international security, new policies toward Western Europe, and the changing relationship between the Soviet Union and Eastern Europe are analyzed. The inadequacy of the Brezhnev "doctrine" is discussed. The author points out the interesting dichotomy in Brezhnev's approach that sought to conquer imperialism, but so threatened the economic survival of the Soviet Union that it was impossible to achieve the goals it had set itself. The author believes that the spontaneous changes that have arisen since Gorbachev took office have set in motion many of his reforms and have complicated the situation further. One chapter is devoted to German reunification and the problems that are associated with it. Review: *Foreign Affairs* 70:4:181 (Fall 1991).

712. ———, **High Road, Low Road: Diplomacy and Public Action in Soviet Foreign Policy**. 1st ed. Washington: Pergamon Press, 1989. ix, 165 p. *A Special Study From the Kennan Institute for Advanced Russian Study*, ISBN: 0080367259. Includes index.
"The fundamental topic of this study is the political contest between the Soviet Union and the North Atlantic Treaty Organization (NATO) over crucial issues of international security that determine their mutual relationships. Analysis focuses on the role played by West Germany." (p. vii)

713. Whelan, Joseph G., and Michael J. Dixon, **The Soviet Union in the Third World: Threat to World Peace?** Washington: Pergamon-Brassey's International Defense Publishers, 1986. xvvii, 486 p. ISBN: 0080339999.
The third in a series of studies carried out by the Congressional Research Service. The previous studies concluded that the USSR was actively committed to the Third World and that it holds an important place in the Soviet world view. "The principal purposes of this current study are to analyze Soviet activities in the Third World during 1980-85 and to determine whether these generalizations are still valid. The study, subdivided into six parts,

is structured around four basic questions: trends in the Soviet experience, the rationale and instrumentalities of Soviet policy, the meaning of its involvement, and the implications for U.S. foreign policy." (p. ix) The volume includes maps of projected expansion of Soviet influence and territorial growth since 1961. There are also extensive bibliographies on each area that the student will find useful. Review: *Political Science Quarterly* 102:3:511-13 (Fall 1987).

714. Williams, Andrew J., **Labour and Russia: The Attitude of the Labour Party to the USSR, 1924-1934**. Manchester, UK: Manchester University Press, 1989. vi, 264 p. ISBN: 0719029245. Includes bibliographical references.

An analysis of how the Soviet Union was viewed by members of the British Labor Party and how its actions affected the development of that party. The viewpoint is from the West, i.e., the author is interested in how the Soviets were viewed, not necessarily what they were doing. The study is limited to the early period 1924-1934, with particular emphasis on the period after 1927. The book is a study of the Labour Party first and foremost and examines Soviet actions in this light alone.

715. World Congress for Soviet and East European Studies, **The Soviet Union: Party and Society**, edited by Peter J. Potichnyj. Cambridge: Cambridge University Press, 1988. xvii, 253 p. ISBN: 0521344603. Includes bibliographies and index.

Papers given at the Third World Congress for Soviet and East European Studies are collected in this volume. The essays selected revolve around domestic policy. The volume has three sections. The first consists of essays on the party apparat with specific attention focused on various levels of party organization. The second section is entitled "Socialization and Political Discourse." The five essays in this section discuss the uses of political discourse, its evolution, and how it reflects policy mandates such as those related to the nationality question. There is also a general essay on political socialization and one describing the political evolution of the local Soviets. The final section contains essays on various aspects of social policy: full employment, social security, abortion, nationality policy and social stratification, and Russian nationalism. The contributors were scholars of political science from all over the world.

With Communist Countries

716. **Soviet-East European Relationship in the Gorbachev Era: The Prospects for Adaptation**, edited by Aurel Braun. Boulder, CO: Westview Press, 1990. 240 p. *Westview Special Studies on the Soviet Union and Eastern Europe*, ISBN: 0813377994. Includes bibliographical references.

A collection of essays focusing on the nature of change in the Soviet Union and in the Eastern Bloc. The essays are divided into three sections; the first on Soviet perspectives, the second on East European concerns, and the final section on the future of the Socialist Bloc as a whole. The CMEA nations are considered along with the USSR — i.e., Bulgaria, Hungary, Czechslovakia, Romania. Poland, and the German Democratic Republic. "The contributors assess not only the nature of the relationship but also the possibility of more 'organic' linkages in the region.... Focusing on the key areas of political/ideological, economic, military and sociocultural relations. The book uses a double- entry system that allows experts on Soviet policy and on Eastern Europe to examine the same issues and collectively provide a comprehensive analysis." (back cover)

717. Carrere d'Encausse, Helene, **Big Brother: The Soviet Union and Soviet Europe**, translated by George Holoch. New York: Holmes & Meier, 1987. xii, 332 p. ISBN: 084191043X. Includes index and bibliography (p. 323-326).

This is a translation of the original 1983 French publication *Le Grand Frere*. The author sees the Soviet Union as the controlling force in Eastern Europe's destiny for the last thirty years and believes it is seeking to further entrench itself in Europe's future. "What is of first importance are Soviet plans and actions to force a unified space running from the Baltic to the Adriatic, to confront conflicts, and to impose the ideas and the instrumentalities by which this world is to be integrated. The intent of this book is to follow the USSR step by step in this European adventure of the last four decades." (p. xii) The book is arranged topically in three parts. The first describes the creation of the twentieth century Soviet empire. Part two looks at the divisive elements in the Soviet empire. An afterword, not included in the original, has been added, to take account of the changes since Gorbachev rose to power. Reviews: *Problems of Communism* 39:3:99-103 (May-June 1990). *Studies in Comparative Communism* 23:1:101-08 (Spring 1990). *Journal of Baltic Studies* 20:1:89-90 (Spring 1989).

718. Dean, Jonathan, **Meeting Gorbachev's Challenge: How to Build Down the NATO-Warsaw Pact Confrontation**. New York: St. Martin's Press, 1989. xviii, 445 p. ISBN: 0312032668. Includes bibliographical references.

An arms control adviser gives his views on how disarmament can proceed in Europe. Specifically, the author deals with how C.F.E. negotiators can proceed with the then ongoing task at the Vienna meetings. How both sides could cut back, which weapons to limit and the problem of verification are dealt with. Another theme of the book is the defense of Europe after such a cut back. The author foresees future policy of the Warsaw Pact and NATO organizations as continuing. Other related topics such as the INF Treaty, existing relations between East and West, and Gorbachev's reforms make up a large part of the discussion. The book also includes several appendices providing data published by the alliances, data published by the Institute of Strategic Studies, air strength, ground forces, unilateral withdrawals from Eastern Europe, documents from various meetings of the two alliances, and a table of reductions proposed in this book. A detailed study of a complex topic. Reviews: *New York Times Book Review* 30 (January 28, 1990). *Foreign Affairs* 69:2:169 (Spring 1990).

719. Durman, Karel, **Lost Illusions: Russian Policies Towards Bulgaria in 1877-1887**. Stockholm: Uppsala University, 1988. 184 p. *Uppsala Studies on the Soviet Union and Eastern Europe*, 1. ISBN: 9155421539. Includes index and bibliography.

"Challenging the myth of Russo-Bulgarian 'eternal friendship,' the study examines Russian efforts to establish and uphold hegemony over Bulgaria in the crucial formative period of her statehood (1877-1878). The author used the hitherto largely unexplained Russian press and English and German diplomatic sources to prove that behind the highly contradictory, reckless, and, as a consequence, increasingly counter-productive Russian policies lay predominantly the pressures of the military and the 'Moscow' Panslav-nationalists on the St. Petersburg government." (verso of t.p.)

720. Felkay, Andrew, **Hungary and the USSR, 1956-1988: Kadar's Political Leader-ship**. New York: Greenwood Press, 1989. 334 p. *Contributions in Political Science*, 0147-1066; no. 227. ISBN: 0313259828. Includes index and bibliography.

Felkay analyzes Soviet-Hungarian relations over the period form 1956-1988. In addition, it also is a study of Kadar's political leadership. Felkay believes that, "Hungary's rapid recovery from the ruins of 1956 is the direct result of Kadar's ability to overcome the alienation of his compatriots without incurring the displeasure of the Soviet Union." (p. 2) Review: *Journal of Baltic Studies* 21:2:162-64 (Summer 1990).

721.   Garver, John W., **Chinese-Soviet Relations, 1937-1945: The Diplomacy of Chinese Nationalism**. New York: Oxford University Press, 1988. vii, 301 p. ISBN: 0195054326. Includes index and bibliography (p. 278-294).

Garver examines "the relationship between the Soviet Union and Chinese nationalism during a critical period in the latter's formation." (p. 3) He covers such topics as the Sino-Soviet Alliance of 1937-1939; the revolution in China and Soviet national security; China and the Soviet-Axis alignment; the Chinese Communist Party and the Soviet-Axis alignment; and China, the Chinese Communist Party, and World War II. Reviews: *Historian* 52:2:329-30 (February 1990). *American Political Science Review* 84:3:1057-58 (September 1990).

722.   Gati, Charles, **The Bloc That Failed: Soviet-East European Relations in Transition**. Bloomington: Indiana University Press, 1990. xiv, 226 p. *Midland Book*, no. MB561. ISBN: 0253325315. Includes index and bibliography (p. 220-222).

The author analyzes the changes in relations between the Soviet Union and Eastern Europe by focusing on a number of questions. First, the author considers those factors related to Soviet policy in Eastern Europe. Specifically, such questions as how Moscow will define the limits of its tolerance for East European reform; what influence will Moscow be able to exert on Eastern Europe; will changes in Eastern Europe create a demand for greater reform in the Soviet Union; and will the reforms fail if Gorbachev fails are discussed. The author then turns his attention to questions related to the prospects for Eastern Europe. Here he focuses on the following problems: 1) the possibility of the resurgence of the KGB in Eastern Europe; 2) problems in the success of the emerging economies; 3) the possibility of old national rivalries resurfacing; and 4) the effects of the breakdown of the Warsaw Pact. Finally the author will also consider the role of the West in security, economically and specifically as it relates to the reunification of Germany. The book is divided into three sections. The first deals with past Eastern Europe-Soviet relations from Stalin to Chernenko. Part two focuses on the early years of reform 1985-88. Part three deals with the revolutions in Eastern Europe. The volume includes an appendix with a statement of Moscow's policy on Eastern Europe. There is also a bibliographic essay with suggested readings.

723.   ———, **Hungary and the Soviet Bloc**. Durham, NC: Duke University Press, 1986. 244 p. ISBN: 0822307472. Includes index and bibliography (p.233-237).

"The purpose of this book is to illustrate Moscow's problems of empire by explaining Soviet relations with successive postwar Hungarian regimes. What I offer here is a series of interpretations and reinterpretations, which place specific Hungarian issues in the broader context of Soviet foreign policy, bloc politics, and East-West relations.... The connecting issue is my attempt to come to grips with the reasons why, even in the best of times, the mighty Soviet Union experiences difficulties in taming its small communist neighbor." (p. 2-3) The book is divided into three parts. The first recounts the events of 1944-48 and the development of the Hungarian Communist Party. Part two examines Hungary in the turbulent 1950s. The third part looks to Hungary's future. The bibliography includes Western language materials only. Reviews: *Political Science Quarterly* 102:4:718-719 (Winter 1987-88). *Orbis* 30:4:749 (Winter 1987).

724.   Heller, Agnes, and Ferenc Feher, **From Yalta to Glasnost: The Dismantling of Stalin's Empire**. Cambridge, Mass: B. Blacksell, 1991. vii, 288 p. ISBN: 0631177728. Includes index and bibliographical references.

The eleven essays that comprise this volume were written between 1979 and 1989. They trace the demise of the system set up at the Yalta conference turning control of Eastern Europe over to the Soviets. The authors focus on such pivotal events as the Hungarian Revolution of 1956, the "Prague Spring" of 1968, and the thaw under Khrushchev. The volume is written by two Hungarian émigrés whose views are colored by their personal experiences. The book is divided into five parts: an introduction; Hungary 1956; post-1956 world of Eastern Europe; Soviet strategy before Gorbachev; and the Gorbachev years. Soviet foreign policy in Eastern Europe is presented from an Eastern European perspective. Reviews: *Orbis* 35:2:307 (Spring 1991). *Reason* 22:11:49-51 (April 1991). *Political Science Quarterly* 106:4:751-752 (Winter 1991-92).

725. Jones, Robert A., **The Soviet Concept of "Limited Sovereignty" from Lenin to Gorbachev: The Brezhnev Doctrine**. New York: St. Martin's Press, 1989. ix, 337 p. ISBN: 0312028164. Includes bibliographical references.

Jones' study examines the Soviet concept of socialist sovereignty and its effect on Soviet foreign policy. He does this by exploring the Soviets' essentially dualistic perspective on international relations, the dynamics of doctrinal change in Soviet policy, and finally the Soviets' use of verbal strategies in international relations. Examples from crisis in Poland, Hungary, Czechoslovakia, and Afghanistan illuminate the author's discussion.

726. **The USSR and Marxist Revolutions in the Third World**, edited by Mark N. Katz. New York: Woodrow Wilson International Center for Scholars and Cambridge University Press, 1990. ix, 153 p. *Woodrow Wilson Center Series*, ISBN: 0521392659. Includes bibliographical references and index.

The editors note that several of the papers presented here have been revised several times since their initial presentation at a conference at the Kennan Institute. This was required due to the rapidly changing environment in Eastern Europe and the Soviet Union. The purpose of these contributions generally was "to explore the relations between the USSR and Marxist revolutionaries in the Third World when these revolutionaries were attempting to come to power and later in those case where they succeeded in doing so." (p. 2) The four essays more specifically cover successes and failures in Soviet policy toward Marxist revolutions in the Third World, Soviet military support for Third World Marxist regimes, Gorbachev and revolution, and Gorbachev's policies toward the Third World.

727. Low, Alfred D., **The Sino-Soviet Confrontation Since Mao Zedong: Dispute, Détente, or Conflict**. Boulder, CO: Social Science Monographs, 1987. xii, 322 p. "Continuation of my book *The Sino-Soviet Dispute, An Analysis of the polemics... 1976*" (pref.), ISBN: 0880339586. Includes bibliography (p. 302-322).

This sequel to the author's 1976 work on the same topic takes the view that both countries are highly nationalistic and that nationalism is imperialistic in nature. The study is intended for students of the area and the general reader and, thus, includes an overview of the history of Sino-Soviet relations. The book is divided into five sections: an historical overview, an examination of major areas of dispute, Soviet Union as portrayed in the Chinese press, the CPR in the Soviet press, and general conclusions. Review: *Canadian-American Slavic Studies* 22:1:110-11 (Spring 1989).

728. Phillips, Ann L., **Soviet Policy Toward East Germany Reconsidered: The Postwar Decade**. Westport, Conn.: Greenwood Press, 1986. xii, 262 p. *Contributions to Political Science*, no. 142. ISBN: 0313246718. Includes index and bibliography (p. 233-256).

"This study analyzes Soviet political and economic policies toward East Germany from 1945 to 1955, focusing on the transition in Soviet policy from ambivalence to support."

(p. 3) Phillips believes that the Soviet Union pursued an ambivalent policy towards East Germany during the period 1945-1955. This was evident in a mix of political and economic goals that were often incompatible with one another. Reviews: *Slavic Review* 46:3-4: 612-13. *German Studies Review* 10:3:622-23 (October 1987).

729. Pike, Douglas Eugene, **Vietnam and the Soviet Union: Anatomy of an Alliance**. Boulder, CO: Westview Press, 1987. xvi, 271 p. ISBN: 0813304709. Includes index and bibliography (p. 249-255).

An attempt to fill the gap in the literature on the history of Soviet-Vietnamese relations. This chronologically arranged study focuses on the perspectives of Vietnam rather than the USSR. The author sees the basic motivation behind the relationship between the USSR and Vietnam to be one of self-interest. He also believes that the relationship is still in a formative stage and that it had serious problems stemming from its very inception. The Hanoi leaders believe that Vietnamese interests are of little importance in Moscow and could be sacrificed at any time. Ideological problems are a constant source of contention. All of these ideas are developed in the study as the author traces the earliest contacts between the Vietnamese and French socialists, to Ho Chi Minh's years in Moscow. Many topics are covered in this volume including the Indochinese Communist Party, the Vietnamese War, the Sino-Soviet dispute and its effect on relations with Vietnam, a lengthy discussion of Soviet-Vietnamese economic relations with an appendix of USSR foreign projects in Vietnam and the Sino-Vietnamese War. Reviews: *Studies in Comparative Communism* 23:1:89-99 (Spring 1990). *Slavic Review* 47:4:747-48 (Winter 1988). *Journal of Asian Studies* 47:4:947-48 (November 1988). *Orbis* 32:1:152 (Winter 1988).

730. Rozman, Gilbert, **The Chinese Debate About Soviet Socialism, 1978-1985**. Princeton, NJ: Princeton University Press, 1987. xi, 396 p. ISBN: 0691094292. Includes index.

Rozman's primary goal is to convey Chinese views on the Soviet Union, especially during the period 1978-1985. He relies for the most part on articles published in Chinese newspapers and periodicals. The organization of the book allows separate chapters to examine the four social classes into which socialist societies can be divided: peasants, workers, intelligentsia, and officials. With a companion book on Soviet views of China it is possible "to draw comparisons and to examine the interrelationships between changing perceptions and developing relations between Bejing and Moscow." (p. ix) Reviews: *Social Science Quarterly* 69:1:227-28 (March 1988). *Pacific Affairs* 61: 2:322-33 (Summer 1988). *Political Science Quarterly* 103:4:760-61 (Winter 1988-89). *American Academy of Political and Social Science Annals* 496:151-52 (March 1988). *Journal of Asian Studies* 47:2:359-60 (May 1988). *Orbis* 32:2:324 (Spring 1988).

731. Sodaro, Michael J., **Moscow, Germany, and the West from Khrushchev to Gorbechev**. Ithaca, NY: Cornell University Press, 1990. xiv, 423 p. *Studies of the Harriman Institute*, ISBN: 0801425298. Includes index.

"This book presents a comparative analysis of Soviet and East German policy and policy making with respect to West Germany during a clearly demarcated era in East-West relations. It begins with Soviet and East German efforts to maintain Germany's division in the aftermath of the construction of the Berlin Wall; it ends with the failure of those efforts—and of the wall itself—in the final cataclysmic months of 1989." (p. 7)

732. **Dominant Powers and Subordinate States: The United States in Latin America and the Soviet Union in Eastern Europe**, edited by Jan F. Triska. Durham, NC: Duke University Press, 1986. xi, 504 p. *Duke Press Policy Studies*, ISBN: 0822306867. Includes index and bibliography (p. 471-498).

These papers were originally presented at a seminar at Stanford University in January 1986. Their purpose is to compare the United States and the USSR as regional powers, the former in Latin America, the latter in Eastern Europe. The essays are grouped into five parts. After a lengthy introduction, part one examines the history of the two regions and provides justification for comparative analysis. Part two lays out various concepts and theories concerned with the dominant- subordinate relationships, sphere of interest behavior, and bargaining. Part three explores behavior of dominant powers in general, including strategy and military behavior. Part four turns to similar themes in subordinate states. Part five analyzes the evolution of spheres of influence and the future of dominant-subordinate systems. Review: *American Political Science Review* 81:3:1051-52 (September 1987).

733. Urban, Joan Barth, **Moscow and the Italian Communist Party: From Togliatti to Berlinguer**. Ithaca, N.Y.: Cornell University Press, 1986. 370 p. ISBN: 080141321. Includes index and bibliography (p. 355-361).

Six decades of interaction between the Soviet Union and the Italian Communist Party are the subject of this book. While much of the work focuses on Italy and its Communist Party, the guiding affect of the Soviets on one of Europe's largest communist groups is of interest in the study of Soviet foreign policy. The book is divided into four sections. The first discusses the Italian Communist Party of the 1920s and the characteristics it developed that put them at odds with Stalin. Part two examines the period from 1929 to 1944 and the adoption of the "ultrasectarian line" imposed by Moscow. Part three focuses on the post-war years, and the final chapter describes the rift between Moscow and the Italian Communist Party that began in the mid-1970s. Reviews: *Political Science Quarterly* 102:1:171-73 (Spring 1987). *Slavic Review* 46:3-4:617-18 (Fall-Winter 1987). *Orbis* 30:2:398-99 (Summer 1986).

Breakup of East European Satellites

734. **Continuity and Change in Soviet-East European Relations: Implications for the West**, edited by Marco Carnovale and William C. Potter. Boulder, CO: Westview Press, 1989. viii, 238 p. ISBN: 0813375266.

This book is a result of a conference on Soviet-East European relations held in 1985. The essays analyze the topic from various points of view. The contributors include Andrzej Korbowski, William C. Potter, Wolfgang Pfeiler, Eberhard Schultz, Keith Crane, Donato D. Gaetano, Marco Carnovale, Joachim Krause, and Wolfgang Berner. The book is directed at anyone interested in how Soviet-East European relations have developed and what possibilities are on the horizon. Topics include German-Soviet foreign relations, East-West German relations, Soviet-East European economic policy, the role of the West in Soviet and East European economic reform, the future of the Warsaw Pact, Soviet-East European military and the Third World countries, and the past effects and future of Comecon.

735. **The Rise of Nations in the Soviet Union: American Foreign Policy and the Disintegration of the USSR**, edited by Michael Mandelbaum. New York: Council on Foreign Relations Press, 1991. viii, 120 p. ISBN: 0876091001. Includes index.

With the disintegration of the Soviet Union, each of the former republics has attempted to assert its sovereignty; nationalism, once suppressed by the omnipresent Soviet state, exploded and gave rise to several difficult foreign policy problems. The five essays in this volume describe how the Soviet Union came to this critical juncture and what should be done about it in the future. The essays cover the linkage between foreign policy and nationality policy, totalitarian collapse, imperial disintegration and the rise of the Soviet

West, the Soviet South, and the implications of the "nationality front" for U.S. foreign and security policy. Review: *Foreign Affairs* 70:5:198 (Winter 1991-92).

HISTORY

Bibliographies, Encyclopedias, Source Materials

736. **A Researcher's Guide to Sources on Soviet Social History in the 1930s**, edited by Sheila Fitzpatrick and Viola Lynne. Armonk, N.Y.: M.E. Sharpe, 1990. xii, 296 p. ISBN: 0873324978. Includes bibliographic references and index.

This collection of 17 essays, bibliographies and directories is designed to provide the advanced researcher with all the information needed to investigate Soviet social history in the 1930s. Social history is interpreted widely. Individual contributions focus on archival resources, annual reports of industrial enterprises, document series on collectivization and industrialization, laws and administrative acts, statistical sources, newspapers and journals, city directories, Soviet computerized databases, Soviet memoir literature, émigré and dissident memoir literature and military sources.

General Studies, Readers

737. Acton, Edward, **Russia: Present and the Past**. London: Longman, 1986. xiii, 342 p. ISBN: 0582493234 (pbk.), 0582493226. Includes index and bibliography (p. 315-328).

A social history of Russia that attempts to analyze the current changes in that country in light of its past. The author has concentrated on five themes: Moscow's central role in Russian history and how it developed; the relationship between Russia's international situation and her domestic policies; why Russia was the site of the Bolshevik revolution; Russia's backwardness in its political, economic, social, and cultural development; and the dominant role of the state. "It is the relationship between State and society, between the power-coercive administrative, legal, cultural, and economic- at the disposal of the Tsar or Politburo and the social body at large, which provides the guiding thread of my analysis." (p viii) The arrangement is selectively chronological, that is, since the author wished to keep the work brief, not all events are covered in depth. The bibliographical essay is useful in identifying literature on specific topics in Russian history.

738. Blakely, Allison, **Russia and the Negro: Blacks in Russian History and Thought**. Washington, DC: Howard University Press, 1986. xv, 201 p. ISBN: 088251465. Includes index and bibliography (p. 182-189).

Blakely has written a social and cultural history of blacks in Imperial Russia and the Soviet Union. In part one she covers negroes of the Black Sea Region, negro servants in Imperial Russia, Russia and Black Africa, negro immigrants and visitors and the Russian response, and the negro in Russian art. In part two, devoted to Soviet Russia, she examines Black Sea negroes in Soviet society, the Soviet perception of the American "negro question," the USSR and Black Africa and the negro in Soviet art. Her study also provides for comparisons between the Russian experience and that of the U.S. and other western nations.

739. **The Soviet Union Today: An Interpretive Guide**, edited by James Cracraft. 2nd ed. Chicago: University of Chicago Press, 1988. xiii, 382 p. ISBN: 0226116611. Includes index and bibliography (p. 365-371).

An updated edition of the original work which first appeared in 1983. As with the first edition, this book is addressed to the general reader. Although this is not intended as a textbook it does cover a broad array of topics with sections on history, politics, the military, physical environment, science and technology, culture, and society. The essays within each broad subject category are arranged chronologically. The suggested readings at the back of the volume are divided into the same topical sections with titles for those who wish to pursue specific subjects. There is also a brief section at the back of the volume with some titles that might be of interest to those thinking of traveling to the Soviet Union. The individual essays are self-contained works and there is no unifying theme to the book. The work has been updated to include the impact of Gorbachev's early reforms where appropriate.

740. **Reform in Russia and the U.S.S.R.: Past and Prospects**. Urbana, Ill.: University of Illinois Press, 1989. 318 p. ISBN: 0252016122. Includes index.

These fifteen essays were originally presented at a conference held in April 1986 at the University of Michigan. Their aim was to study reform in Russia and the Soviet Union assuming that this would shed light on the "present contours of politics in the USSR." In doing so they further hoped that this study would suggest "the conditions under which the Soviet system of government ... might undergo significant change." (p. 2) The earliest period studied was that of the reign of Ivan IV. It also includes study of the government crisis of 1730, reform under Catherine II, the age of the great reforms, 1855-1894, reform during the 1917 revolutions and three essays on Khrushchev. A speculative essay on the potential for reform under Gorbachev covers most recent Soviet history.

741. **The World of the Russian Peasant: Post-Emancipation Culture and Society**, edited by Ben Eklof and Stephen Frank. Boston: Unwin Hyman, 1990. vi, 234 p. ISBN: 0044454783. Includes bibliographical references.

A collection of essays on the material life, society, and culture of the post-emancipation peasantry. "With carefully edited selections, this timely volume is designed to serve as a basic introduction to the Russian peasantry for undergraduate and graduate courses in the history of Imperial Russia, peasant studies, and rural sociology." (back cover) Essay topics include peasant commune life, the life of peasant women, peasant migration, and family patterns, peasantry in the military, religion, popular justice, peasant art and the peasant movement of 1905-07. All essays originally were published in journals or other books and are brought together here, in edited form, to create a more complete picture of peasant society in the late nineteenth century.

742. Herlihy, Patricia, **Odessa: A History, 1794-1914**. Cambridge, Mass: Harvard Ukrainian Research Institute, 1986. xiv, 411 p. *Monograph Series of Harvard Ukrainian Research Institute*, ISBN: 0916458083. Includes index and bibliography (p. 361-394).

The creation of a city, indeed one of the leading cities of the Russian empire, is the subject of this volume. The author uses a variety of records from statistical reports to travelers accounts to reconstruct the development of this city. The history ceases with the beginning of the First World War, since this marks the close of an era for Odessa whose expansion and development reached its height in the nineteenth century. The book follows basically a chronological approach with chapters on special topics such as the merchant class, the development of Odessa's hinterland, ethnic communities in Odessa, government and finance in the nineteenth century, architecture, and urban design. Throughout the work the author emphasizes those elements that allowed Odessa to grow quickly into a leading trading city, its location, agricultural development, and ethnic diversity. She also notes that many of these same elements, stagnating in a backward empire would stunt the city's development in the twentieth century. Review: *Business Historical Review* 61:4:670- 71 (Winter 1987).

743.   Pallot, Judith, and Dennis J. B. Shaw, **Landscape and Settlement in Romanov Russia, 1613-1917**. Oxford: Claredon Press, 1990. vi, 318 p. ISBN: 0198232462. Includes bibliographical references (p. 277-313).

" 'Place' is a central concept to the geographer and for the historical geographer it is past places which matter. It is perhaps nowhere more necessary to understand the importance of place than in the case of Russia, especially European Russia." (p. 4) The authors of this work consider the processes of change in Russia in the context of political, economic, and social developments on a local scale. Their analysis includes chapters on the Central Black Earth Region, Voronezh, and the Eastern Steppe. They also look at larger problems as they were affected by the geographical conditions unique to Russia: the commune in 19th Century Russia, land reform, peasant manufacturing, and cities during the Romanov period. This is a scholarly, specialized study with numerous tables and figures.

744.   Pipes, Richard, **Russia Observed: Collected Essays on Russian and Soviet History**. Boulder, CO: Westview Press, 1989. v, 240 p. ISBN: 0813307880. Includes index and bibliographies.

Several of Pipes' essays on Russia are gathered in this volume. All deal with some aspect of Russian political thought and practice. The specific topics include continuities in Russian political history, Russian liberal conservatism, the Jewish policies of Catherine II, Russian populism, Max Weber and Russia in contemporary times, Alexander I and the military colonies, and the nationality problem of the Soviet Union. Reviews: *Canadian Slavonic Papers* 32:4:524-25. *Fletcher Forum of World Affairs* 14: 1:212-13 (Winter 1990). *Russian History* 17:2:227-28 (Summer 1990).

745.   Pushkarev, Sergei Germanovich, **Self-government and Freedom in Russia**, translated by Paul Bannes, with an introduction by Nicholas V. Riasanovsky. Boulder, Colo: Westview Press, 1988. xiii, 158 p. *CCRS Series on Change in Contemporary Soviet Society*, ISBN: 0813374766. Includes index.

Written "to remind the reader of the historical beginnings of political freedom and social initiative in Russia," (p. xv) Pushkarev's history of Russia from ancient Rus' to the end of the Civil War in 1922 "gives important insights into the mind of the historian who approaches Russian history from a patriotic position." (p. viii) His thesis is that throughout their history Russians have been searching for individual liberty and the right to self-government. His approach clarifies the historical background of the process at work in Russia today. Reviews: *Russian Review* 49:2:204-05 (April 1990). *Slavic Review* 49:3:446 (Fall 1990).

746.   Raeff, Marc, **Russia Abroad: A Cultural History of the Russian Emigration, 1919-1939**. New York: Oxford University Press, 1990. viii, 239 p. ISBN: 0195056833. Includes bibliographical references (p. 199-220) and indexes.

The author discusses the contributions of the Russian émigré communities to the various countries they settled in as well as their attempts at the preservation of their native culture. Professor Raeff describes the context in which Russian émigré culture developed. His purpose is to give a general picture of Russian cultural life abroad. Certain areas have not been treated here as they have received in depth analysis elsewhere. Raeff limits his discussion to the émigré experience in education, publishing, preservation of Russian culture, religion, and history.

747. **Soviet Historians and Perestroika: The First Phase**, edited by Donald J. Raleigh. Armonk, N.Y.: M.E. Sharpe, 1989. xvi, 291 p. ISBN: 0873325540. Includes bibliographical references.
A collection of articles reflecting the changes in historical writings since perestroika. The editor selected articles on broad historical topics deliberately to give a sense of "how the historical profession first responded to the new climate." (p. xiii) The volume is divided into five parts. The first section includes articles demonstrating the early responses within the profession to perestroika. The second section reflects responses to directives from party leadership. Part three examines the treatment of the revolution. The fourth part examines the work of publicism, challenging historians to reevaluate their work. The final part contains selections from a roundtable discussion on the changes with several Soviet historians as participants. Contributors to the volume include I.U. Afanasev, S.L. Tikhvinskii, V.A. Kozkov, F.N. Smykov, V.G. Veriaskin. I.I. Mints, V. Seliunin, and F. Burlatskii.

748. Richardson, William, **Mexico Through Russian Eyes, 1806-1940**. Pittsburgh, PA: University of Pittsburgh Press, 1988. xi, 287 p. *Pitt Latin America Series*, ISBN: 0822938243. Includes index and bibliography (p. 261-280).
Richardson presents views of Mexico as seen by Russian visitors and diplomats. He proceeds chronologically covering the earliest accounts by Wrangell and employees of the Russian-American Company, the age of Porfirio Diaz, the 1920s, Eisenstein, and Trotsky.

749. **Russian Colonial Expansion to 1917**, edited by Michael Rywkin and with a foreword by Syed Z. Abedin. London: Mansell, 1988. xvi, 274 p. *Institute of Muslim Minority Affairs Monograph Series*, no. 1.
A collection of eleven essays examining Russia's drive, primarily to the East, as it built its colonial empire. Because so many of the nations conquered by the Russians were Muslim states, there is quite a bit of discussion of the effect of the conquest on Islam. Nevertheless the focus remains the policy of colonial expansion itself. The essays provide an overview of the development of the Russian empire, as well as discussions of the central colonial administration; Russia's first expansion to the far North; the conquest of Kazan, Astrakhan, Siberia, Ukraine, the Caucuses; and the administration of the Crimea, Turkestan, and Central Asia as a whole.

750. Stites, Richard, **Revolutionary Dreams: Utopian Vision and Experimental Life in the Russian Revolution**. New York: Oxford University Press, 1989. xii, 307 p. ISBN: 0195055365. Includes index and bibliography (p. 257-296).
The Utopian traditions of the Russian intelligentsia, the state and the people are the focus of this study of Utopianism and social experimentation at the time of the revolution. The first chapter provides a discussion of Utopianism, in general. Chapter 2 examines the authoritarian aspects of the Bolshevik experimentation. Chapters 3 through 7 describe the independent experiments in life and culture building that were part of the Utopia-building of the 1920s. Chapters 8 through 10 turn to the attempts at construction of ideal societies during the 1920s. The final chapters explain how Stalinism supplanted revolutionary utopianism. "I have written a book about the dream of human liberation and about the pathos of remaking society and mankind in the heat of revolution because I believe it is a process of thought, feeling, and action that is both eternal and relevant to our times." (p. 9) The book includes numerous illustrations. Reviews: *American Historical Review* 95:4:1251-52. *New York Times Review of Books* 37:19:60-67 (December 6, 1990). *Orbis* 34:2:296- 97 (Spring 1990). *Russian Review* 49:2:183-87 (April 1990).

751.   Ward, Charles A., **Moscow and Leningrad: A Topographical Guide to Russian Cultural History**. New York: K. G. Saur, 1989. 3 v. ISBN: 3598108338. Includes bibliography.

Volume one of this three volume set is a catalogue of the main architectural monuments of Moscow and Leningrad. Because they were the capital cities of the Russian empire and because of the unusual concentration of power in the Russian state it was felt that the main architectural patterns would be represented in the buildings of these two cities. The catalog covers the earliest times to 1915. For the most part Soviet constructions have not been included. The buildings chosen were the major architectural monuments of the cities. Each entry includes the building name in English and Russian, the address, date of construction, and the architect, if known. Entries are listed chronologically. Descriptions of each building are also included with information on the architect. Types of material used in construction are not included. Such a volume could be useful in following trends in architectural styles. The volume also includes topographical indexes for each city and maps identifying the locations of the buildings described.

Historiography and Archaeology

752.   Cox, Terry, **Peasants, Class, and Capitalism: The Rural Research of L.N. Kritsman and His School**. Oxford: Clarendon Press, 1986. xii, 271 p. ISBN: 0198780141. Includes index and bibliography (p. 251-268).

The focus of Cox's book is on capitalist development in Russian peasant society and "the attempts of Russian social researchers to understand the nature of the relationships between capitalism and the peasantry." (p. 1) The author also describes and analyzes the debates over the question "whether capitalist development does or does not undermine peasant agriculture and promote the differentiation of the peasantry." (p. 1) This Russian research tradition culminated in the work of L. N. Kritsman and his school, the Agrarian Marxists, who were at the height of their influence in the 1920s. Cox begins with chapters in Marxist theory and Russian peasant society, traces the development of the Agrarian Marxist perspective, devotes four chapters to various stages of research of Kritsman and his colleagues, and ends with an assessment of the research of the Agrarian Marxists and the modern relevance of their research.

753.   Davies, R. W., **Soviet History in the Gorbachev Revolution**. Bloomington, Ind.: Indiana University Press, 1989. viii, 232 p. ISBN: 0253316049. Includes bibliographical references (p. 206-223) and index.

After an introductory chapter giving a brief overview of how history and historiography was used and abused after Stalin until Gorbachev came to power in 1985, Davies deals with the role of history in more detail and from various perspectives. The remaining fourteen chapters are divided into four parts. In the first part (ch. 2-9), The Mental Revolution, he gives an account of new information that has been published and new approaches that have emerged in the press and the media since 1986. In part two (ch. 10-11), he examines the effect of the historical debates in the attitudes of Soviet leaders towards history. Part three (ch. 12-15) traces the consequent upheaval in the history profession and in the teaching of history. In part four (chapter 14-15) he tries to put this all in context, assess truth and bias in the new history and speculates how this will all have an effect on the reconstruction of Soviet society. Reviews: *Foreign Affairs* 69:2:182 (Spring 1990). *Russian History* 17:2: 255-56 (Summer 1990). *Soviet Geography* 31:3:222-23 (March 1990). *Soviet Union-Union Sovietique* 17:1-2:186-87 (1990).

Pre-Petrine Muscovy/Russia

754. Allsen, Thomas T., **Mongol Imperialism: The Policies of the Grand Qan Mongke in China, Russia, and the Islamic Islands, 1251-1259**. Berkeley: University of California Press, 1987. xvii, 278 p. ISBN: 0520055276. Includes bibliography (239-261).

A study of Mongol expansion during the reign of Mongke. The author is hoping to view events from the viewpoints of the Mongols and will, therefore describe their expansion and methods of control in Russia, China, and Islam. "This work will defend the thesis that the Mongols succeeded in creating the largest contiguous land-based empire in human history because they were able to mobilize effectively the human and material resources of the areas under their control." (p. 7) The first four chapters discuss aspects of Mongol society that allowed for this expansion: their political system, consolidation of power, concentration of power, and economic reforms. Chapters five through eight deal with specific aspects of resource mobilization in specific regions: census taking, tax collection, issuance of currency, and military recruitment. The author was able to draw on Chinese, Russian, and Persian sources in the original and works from translations of many other sources.

755. Crummey, Robert O., **The Formation of Muscovy, 1304-1613**. London: Longman, 1987. xv, 275 p. *Longman History of Russia*, ISBN: 0582491533 (pbk.), 0582491525. Includes index and bibliography (p. 242-254).

One volume in the Longman History of Russia. "This book is a short history of Muscovite Russia from 1304 to 1613. It is a work of historical synthesis, designed above all, for students and the educated general reader." When this volume was published, there was only one other similar English language work in Presniakov's *Tsardom of Muscovy*. That book was originally written in Russian and focused on the 16th and 17th centuries. This volume, written for a Western audience, is not as compressed and does not concentrate on the later period. It is arranged chronologically and contains numerous maps. Review: *Modern Greek Studies Yearbook* 4:331-33 (1988).

756. Gopal, Surendra, **Indians in Russia in the 17th and 18th Centuries**. New Delhi: Indian Council of Historical Research, 1988. 322 ISBN: 8185109737. Includes index and bibliography (p. 281-283).

A collection of documents translated from the Russian volumes *Russko-Indiiskiye Otnosheniie v XVII v.* (Russo-Indian Relations in the 17th Century) and *Russko-Indiiskiye Otnosheniie v XVIII v.* (Russo-Indian Relations in the 18th Century). The documents chosen for inclusion in this volume reflect Indian life in Russia. Life in numerous cities is described including Astrakhan, Saratov, Yaroslav, Kazan, Moscow, Baku, Krasnodar, Tsaritslov, and St. Petersburg. The documents are presented chronologically. Several appendices are included: one listing abbreviations, another listing Russian rulers, a third listing rulers of Persia, another describes a Hindu place of worship in Baku.

757. Halperin, Charles J., **The Tatar Yoke**. Columbus, Ohio: Slavica Publishers, 1986. 231 p. ISBN: 089357161X. Includes bibliography (p. 217-231).

Halperin's objective is to analyze how the medieval Russian sources present the Tatars. After an introductory chapter concerning general Russian-Tatar relations, he analyzes "text by text, the presentation of the Mongols in the medieval Russian sources, beginning with the first Russian encounter with the Tatars in 1223 and ending with the 'formal' liberation of Russia in 1480." (p. 1)

758. Kollmann, Nancy Shields, **Kinship and Politics: The Making of the Muscovite Political System, 1345-1547**. Stanford, Calif.: Stanford University Press, 1987. x, 324 p. ISBN: 0804713405. Includes index and bibliography (p. 289-308).

A detailed study of the relationship between the boyars and the Grand Prince in Muscovy. The author believes that most studies since the 1950s have focused on the role of the Grand Prince as an autocratic ruler and that is a somewhat one-sided view of the political system. She also feels that while comparisons with European systems are interesting, some fundamental differences are ignored. She sees the system in Russia as characterized by cooperation and integrity. Methodologically the analysis demanded identifying as much information on the boyars as possible. The author was forced to rely on primary source material. The book begins with the founding of the Muscovite Grand Duchy and continues into the early 14th century. The first chapter presents these early events. The following chapters are arranged thematically rather than chronologically covering such topics as political recruitment, political hierarchy, and political associations. The study emphasizes family and affinitive relationships. Reviews: *Slavic Review* 47:1:111-12 (Spring 1988). *American Historical Review* 93:2:460-61 (April 1988). *Historie Sociale-Social History* 21:41:183-85 (May 1988).

759. Levin, Eve, **Sex and Society in the World of the Orthodox Slavs, 900-1700**. Ithaca, NY: Cornell University Press, 1989. xiv, 326 p. ISBN: 081422604. Includes index and bibliography (p. 303-318).

A study of sexuality in medieval Slavic societies, Russia, Bulgaria, and Serbia. The author has not limited her study to the role of the Church in shaping sexuality. She tries to examine sexuality apart from the family structure and the status of women. The focus is on the nature of sexuality. The book looks at the ecclesiastical image of sexuality first and then marriage. The remaining chapters discuss incest, illicit sex, rape, and sex and the clergy. Major sources of information were found in the records of ecclesiastical courts, law codes, and penitential writings.

760. Martin, Janet, **Treasure of the Land of Darkness: The Fur Trade and Its Significance for Medieval Russia**. New York: Cambridge University Press, 1986. x, 277 p. ISBN: 0521320194. Includes index.

Martin describes an elaborate trade network formed to transport fur from northwestern Siberia and northeastern Russia to Europe and the Muslim world. She draws on a variety of disparate sources, including travelers' accounts, diplomatic records, ethnographic studies, and others to document the characteristics of this trade route, "to substantiate the existence of a relationship among the changes in the trade patterns, political control over critical elements of the fur trade network, and the more general political development of the region of the Rus and the mid-Volga lands during this period," (p. 2) and to assess the economic importance of the fur trade.

761. Shanin, Teodor, **Russia, 1905-07: Revolution as a Moment of Truth**. New Haven: Yale University Press, 1986. xvi, 379 p. *The Roots of Otherness: Russia's Turn of Century*, v. 2. ISBN: 0300036612. Includes indexes and bibliography (p. 317-365).

This book is a sequel to the author's earlier work, *Russia as a Developing Society*. "It begins with the revolution's build up and its major strands: the struggle in the cities for political freedom and/or socialism and the struggle of the villages for land and for liberty understood from the peasant's perspective. It is followed by an analysis of the interdependence of these struggles and of its main social actors. The last two chapters are devoted to the conceptual revolutions." (p. xiii) The author believes that the revolution followed a course unexpected by both its supporters and adversaries. It offered new and surprising aspects of their society, causing both groups to review their positions. The topical analysis is followed by a postscript which examines general issues in historical sociology and social history.

762. Skrynnikov, Ruslan G., **The Time of Troubles: Russia in Crisis, 1604-1618,** edited and translated by Hugh F. Graham. Gulf Breeze, FL: Academic International Press, 1988. xv, 325 p. *Russian Series*, vol. 36. ISBN: 0875690971. Includes bibliographical references and index.

Skrynnikov is a research professor of history at Leningrad State University. He has written widely on 16th and 17th century Russian history. This book covers the period when the False Dmitry, whom Skrynnikov shows was a defrocked monk Grigorii Otreper, enters the Kremlin with the aid of Prince Vasilii Golitsyn and popular support and ends in 1618 when the civil war and foreign intervention ceased.

763. **The Nikonian Chronicle**, edited, introduced and translated by Serge A. Zenkovsky. Princeton, NJ: Kingston Press, 1984- . v. ISBN: 0940670003 (v. 1). Includes bibliographical references.

This annotated five volume translation is includes a glossary of Russian and Byzantine terminology, genealogical tables of the first Russian dynasty, and a lengthy critical introduction to the work.

Imperial Russia

764. **Russia in the Age of the Enlightenment: Essays for Isabel de Madariaga**, edited by Roger Bartlett and Janet Hartley. New York: St. Martin's Press, 1990. x, 253 p. ISBN: 0312040685. Includes bibliographical references and index.

This volume of essays in honor of Isabel de Madariaga covers a wide range of 18th century topics including foreign relations, literature, female rule, navigation, legal history, serfdom, philanthropy, Old Believers, and Catherine the Great.

765. Brennan, James F., **Enlightened Despotism in Russia: The Reign of Elisabeth, 1741-1762**. New York: P. Lang, 1987. 295 p. *American University Studies, Series IX, History*, v. 14. ISBN: 0820402621. Includes bibliography (p. 271-295).

The author argues that enlightened despotism begins in Russia, not with the reign of Catherine the Great as is usually claimed, but with that of Elisabeth from 1741-1762. To establish this point, the author reviews government, culture, religion, nationalities policy, the economy, the military, and serfdom during Elisabeth's reign. He demonstrates that many of the policies associated with enlightened despotism, such as expanding education and abolition of the death penalty, were introduced under Elisabeth. This scholarly work is organized topically and draws on numerous primary and secondary sources. Review: *Russian Review* 48:2:200-01 (April 1989).

766. Brower, Daniel R., **The Russian City Between Tradition and Modernity, 1850-1900**. Berkeley: University of California Press, 1990. xiv, 253 p. ISBN: 0520067649. Includes index and bibliography (p. 237-247).

"This history of Russian cities examines the transformation of urban life in the late tsarist period. Specifically, it looks at the changes under way in European Russia in the decades between the reforms of Alexander II and the Revolution of 1905.... It incorporates economic, political, social, and cultural perspectives on the Russian city and attempts an interdisciplinary interpretation of the history of Russia in those years." (p. 1, 4)

767. **Between Tsar and People: Educated Society and the Quest for Public Identity in Late Imperial Russia**, edited by Edith W. Clowes, Samuel D. Kassow, and James L. West. Princeton, NJ: Princeton University Press, 1991. ix, 383 p. ISBN: 0691008515 (pbk.), 0691031533. Includes index and bibliographical references.

A collection of essays exploring various aspects of the emergence of an identity for educated society in Imperial Russia. "Each essay examines some element of late imperial social dynamics, institutional structure or cultural and artistic creativity that either symbolized or presaged the development in Russia of a stable and prosperous middle, yet each demonstrates the precariousness and fragility of that process." (p. 14) The essays are grouped into seven sections. Part one contains essays discussing the emergence of a middle as reflected in language and intellectual writing. Part two examines the place of Russia's entrepreneurs in society. Part three looks at the entrepreneur's attempt to gain social legitimacy through art patronage. Part four focuses on the rise of institutions that support a civil society. The fifth part includes essays on the development of the intelligentsia into the modern professional organization. Part six examines the development of social consciousness. Part seven focuses on the myths and symbols of the emerging middle class.

768. Connaughton, Richard Michael, **The War of the Rising Sun and the Tumbling Bear: A Military History of the Russo-Japanese War, 1904-05**. London: Routledge, 1989. xi, 300 p. ISBN: 0415009065. Includes index and bibliography (p. 290-292).

Connaughton introduces his topic with several chapters describing the events leading up to the declaration of war and characteristics of the two opponents. He then examines the naval and military events as well as the operational and logistical plans relating to these events. In the appendix he "provides a small exercise for those interested in comparing the Russian and Japanese adherence to the principles of war." (p. ix)

769. **Civil Rights in Imperial Russia**, edited by Olga Crisp and Linda Edmondson. Oxford: Clarendon Press, 1989. xvi, 321 p. ISBN: 0198228678. Includes bibliographical references and index.

Essays taken from a 1985 London conference on the question of civil rights in Russia during the last half of tsarist rule make up this volume. The essays can be divided into two categories: those that treat the general question of civil rights in Russia and those that focus on specific aspects of civil rights. No specific point of view is adopted overall. Some of the topics included are land tenure and civil rights, popular protest and civil rights, national minorities and their rights, women's rights, and the definition of civil rights. The editors feel they are approaching the topic differently from past studies by separating civil rights from the study of government and law. "In doing so, we not only begin to appreciate the connections between the civil rights theme and a host of problems which hitherto have not appeared to be closely related to it (land tenure, for example or popular protest); we are also forced to question certain assumptions which have been made about the nature of civil rights and citizenship in an autocratic state." (p. vii) Review: *Russian Review* 49:3:378-79. (July 1990).

770. Daly, John C. K., **Russian Seapower and the "Eastern Question," 1827-41**. Annapolis, Md.: Naval Institute Press, 1991. xvii, 314 p. ISBN: 1557507260. Includes bibliographical references (p. 261-291) and index.

A history of the development of Russia's Black Sea Fleet in the mid-nineteenth century and its effect on Russia's relations with its mid-Eastern neighbors. This has been a little studied area until now. The study is chronological covering the Greek Revolt, Russian Black Sea Trade, the Egyptian Revolts, and the First Turkish War. There are five appendices containing specific information on the construction of the Black Sea Fleet, its maintenance, and losses during military encounters. This scholarly study includes a lengthy bibliography.

771. De Madariaga, Isabel, **Catherine the Great: A Short History**. New Haven: Yale University Press, 1990. vii, 240 p. ISBN: 0300048459. Includes index and bibliographical references (p. 219-224).

This popular history of Catherine II is designed to bring the more recent scholarly work on Catherine to a wider audience than can be achieved by more specialized publications. The focus is primarily on her reign with only the briefest attention paid to her pre-imperial period. De Madariaga covers political, cultural, and military aspects of her reign and concludes with an assessment of Catherine's place in Russian and world history.

772. Durova, Nadezhda Andreevna, **The Cavalry Maiden: Journals of a Russian Officer in the Napoleonic Wars**, translation, introduction, and notes by Mary Fleming Zirin. Bloomington: Indiana University Press, 1988. xxxvii, 242 p. *Indiana-Michigan Series in Russian and East European Studies*, ISBN: 0253313724. Includes index and bibliography (p. 233-238).

A translation of the 1836 edition of Nadezhda Durova's memoirs recounting her experiences in the Tsar's army during the Napoleonic Wars. "Her pages reflect the fervor, idealism, and disillusion that swept Russia during the Napoleonic era. Today *The Cavalry Maiden* stands also as a unique record of the outlook and emotions of one of the rare Russian women of her time who managed to create an autonomous life outside the patriarchal confines of home and family." (p. x) The work has two main parts, the childhood years and the military years. The volume includes two appendices, one containing documents related to Durova's commission in the Hussars and the other containing Denis Davydov's comments on Durova. There is also a selected bibliography, a lengthy introduction providing a historical context for the work, and notes within the text. Reviews: *Social Science Journal* 27:4:475-76 (1990). *Russian History* 17: 1:88-89 (Spring 1990). *Slavic Review* 48:3:490-92 (Fall 1989).

773. Freeze, Gregory L., **From Supplication to Revolution: A Documentary Social History of Imperial Russia**. New York: Oxford University Press, 1988. xv, 331 p. ISBN: 0195043723. Includes index and bibliography (p. 317-324).

A collection of translated documents from the Catherinian Era, the Era of Great Reforms, and the Era of the 1905 Revolution. "These three junctures are the precise points which major social groups obtained, or usurped, the right to assert their complaints and hopes before the state. The documents they left behind provide an extraordinary opportunity both to hear how the voices changed over time and harmonized — or clashed violently with one another." (back cover) The book is meant as a complementary volume to general histories of Russia. The documents expose the reader to the views of noblemen, artisans, professionals, laborers, merchants, women, Jews, and peasants. A bibliography of each period and social group is included.

774. **The City in Late Imperial Russia**, edited by Michael F. Hamm. Bloomington: Indiana University Press, 1986. vii, 372 p. *Indiana-Michigan Series in Russian and East European Studies*, ISBN: 0253313708. Includes bibliography, p. 355-359.

Most of the papers presented in this volume were presented at conferences in 1982 and 1983. Their purpose is "to explore in detail the nature and consequences of growth and change in the Empire's burgeoning cities." (p. ix) Cities examined in this volume include Moscow, St. Petersburg, Kiev, Warsaw, Riga, Odessa, Tiflis, and Baku. One final essay analyzes the urban revolution in the late Russian Empire. Review: *American Historical Review* 92:5:1238-39 (December 1987).

775. Hoch, Steven L., **Serfdom and Social Control in Russia: Petrovskoe, a Village in Tambov**. Chicago: University of Chicago Press, 1986. x, 220 p. ISBN: 0226345831. Includes index and bibliography (p. 193-212).

The social system that developed among serfs is examined in this volume. The author has chosen to focus on one estate held by the Gargarin family. There exist good records for the life of the serfs on this estate. The number of serfs held demanded that the author, working within the structures of Soviet libraries and archives, limit his analysis to the serfs residing in the largest settlement of the estate. The same village has been analyzed by Soviet scholars, but the restrictions of Marxist-Leninist ideology have so colored the results of that research as to merit another study. The book begins with a discussion of the material life of the serfs and how it affected their performance. The second chapter focuses on the relationship between the size of the household and the maintenance of authority. The last three chapters deal with various aspects of social control. The author attempts to demonstrate that the serfs' behavior and attitudes were a response to ecological limitations on society. The key element to the more negative side of their lives was the authoritarian structure that placed serf over serf. Review: *Canadian Slavonic Papers* 29:4:340-32 (December 1987).

776. Hughes, Lindsey, **Sophia, Regent of Russia, 1657-1704**. New Haven: Yale University Press, 1990. xvii, 345 p. ISBN: 0300047908. Includes index and bibliographical references (p. 313-328).

A biography of the seventeenth century ruler. This work traces "the rise, regency and fall of the first woman effectively to rule Russia, against the background of Russian culture and society in the latter half of the seventeenth century." (p. xvii) This chronological study is divided into three parts: the early years of her development, the period of her regency (1682-1689), and her downfall as Peter the Great came to power. The volume includes several helpful features, a glossary of Russian terms, a family tree, and a chronology of events. The work gives fuller treatment to a historical figure largely unexamined in the West.

777. **Peasant Economy, Culture, and Politics of European Russia, 1800-1921**, edited by Esther Kingston-Mann and Timothy Mixter with the assistance of Jeffrey Burds. Princeton, NJ: Princeton University Press, 1990. xvii, 443 p. ISBN: 0691055955. Includes index.

A 1986 conference on the history of the Russian peasant generated the essays collected in this volume. The essays are divided into three subject areas: peasant economy, peasant culture, and peasant politics. Specific topics include peasant communes, social control of peasant labor, Russian peasant women, traditional healers, serf opposition to the gentry's economic reforms, and migrant agricultural workers. The conference brought together scholars who had studied a variety of regional peasant institutions and this volume reflects that variety. A glossary of terms is included.

778. LeDonne, John P., **Absolutism and Ruling Class: The Formation of the Russian Political Order, 1700-1825**. New York: Oxford University Press, 1991. xvii, 376 p. ISBN: 01906805X. Includes bibliographical references (p. 353-370) and index.

A study of the development of political institutions in pre- revolutionary Russia. The author believes that there was a ruling class that played a definitive role in the growth of those political institutions and that their role has heretofore been largely ignored. The author draws heavily on the Collection of Laws of the Russian Empire and other Russian sources. The book is divided into five parts. Part I examine Russian society of the eighteenth century and its constituent elements. Part II focuses on state institutions describing the changes in central and local administration from Peter the Great to Alexander I. Part III analyzes the role of the police. Part IV examines penal and civil laws. The final section is devoted to issues of state finance.

779. Lincoln, W. Bruce, **The Great Reforms: Autocracy, Bureaucracy, and the Politics of Change in Imperial Russia**. DeKalb, Ill.: Northern Illinois University Press, 1990. xxi, 281 p. ISBN: 0875805493 (pbk.); 0875801552. Includes bibliographical references and index.

The reforms of the Russian government in the 1860s were an attempt to renovate both Russia's society and economy. They would restructure the courts, free the serfs, and reform censorship. Professor Lincoln has written a focused analysis of these historic changes. "A synthesis based on archival materials and the latest monographic literature to appear in the Soviet Union and the West, W. Bruce Lincoln's book examines the origins and significance of the Great Reforms and evaluates their results in the context of Russia's experience between the Crimean War and the Revolution of 1905. This invaluable study explains why the legislation assumed the shape that it did and estimates what the Great Reforms ultimately accomplished." (jacket)

780. Long, James W., **From Priviledged to Dispossessed: The Volga Germans, 1860-1917**. Lincoln: University of Nebraska Press, 1988. xv, 337 p. ISBN: 0803228813. Includes index and bibliography (p. 291-321).

This in-depth analysis focuses on the Volga Germans during a crucial period of change in Russian history. Examining the political, economic, and social history of the Volga colonies, the author attempts to demonstrate the role of the Volga Germans as traditional peasants. This is contrary to other works on the subject that have presented them as agents of change. The work is topically arranged. Some of the subjects covered include the effects of the loss of government protection, participation in the zemstvos, the change from subsistence to commercial farming, and social stratification. This scholarly study draws on oral interviews, archival materials and many secondary sources. Reviews: *Immigration Migration Review* 24:1:172-73 (Spring 1990). *Russian Review* 49:2:200-01 (April 1990).

781. **Imperial Russia, 1700-1917: State, Society, Opposition: Essays in Honor of Marc Raeff**, edited by Ezra Mendelsohn and Marshall S. Shatz. DeKalb, Ill.: Northern Illinois University Press, 1988. xiv, 316 p. ISBN: 0875801439. Includes bibliography (p. 289-313).

A collection of essays focusing on three areas of study: ruling Russia, the society of imperial Russia, and the opposition to the state during the Imperial period. The essays are contributed by a number of historians. Specific topics include the legal system, Catherine the Great and the fine arts, systems of governance, the military, women in Kiev, Mikhail Bakunin, Jewish socialism, and V.M. Eikhenbaum. The volume includes a bibliography of Raeff's works. Reviews: *Russian Review* 49:3: 338-39 (July 1990). *Journal of Modern History* 62:4:889-90 (December 1990). *Slavic Review* 49:4:649-50 (Winter 1990).

782. Miller, Martin A., **The Russian Revolutionary Émigrés, 1825- 1870**. Baltimore: Johns Hopkins University Press, 1986. xii, 292 p. *Johns Hopkins University Studies in Historical and Political Science*, 104th ser., vol. 2. ISBN: 0801833035. Includes index and bibliography (p. 271-284).

The chronological limits of this study are defined by an act of the Russian government in 1825, when Nikolai Turgenev was declared the first émigré and the death of Alexander Herzen in 1870, which coincided with the emergence of a populist revolutionary movement. Miller introduces his subject with a chapter on emigration in 19th century Europe. This general introduction is followed by a series of biographical chapters on the most important émigrés who "are analyzed within the overall context of a social movement in formation." (p. xi) Reviews: *Slavic Review* 46:3-4:598-99 (Fall-Winter 1987). *International History Review* 9:4:653-54 (November 1987).

783. Myles, Douglas, **Rasputin: Satyr, Saint, or Satan**. New York: McGraw-Hill Pub., 1990. 330 p. ISBN: 0070442398. Includes bibliographical references (p. 309-310). Myles examines the life of Grigori Rasputin, the Russian holy man who ended up exerting such a tremendous influence on Tsaritsa Alexandra. Myles' approach is based on fact and his own imagination as he tried to recreate what went on in Rasputin's mind from his youth to his death.

784. Offord, Derek, **The Russian Revolutionary Movement in the 1880s**. Cambridge: Cambridge University Press, 1986. xviii, 213 p. ISBN: 0521327237. Includes index and bibliography (p. 197-207).
The Russian revolutionary movement in the 1880s has not received sufficient attention from historians, claims Offord. The decade is often perceived as a final decadent phase of revolutionary Populism that had its roots in the revolutionary groups of the 1860s and 1870s and a precursor to the emergence of social democracy that gained ascendancy in the 1890s. Indeed, the decade is characterized as a period of failure and despondency in the ranks of the revolutionaries. Here Offord examines the course that the revolutionary movement took in Russia in the 1880s. His four chapters are devoted to Russian revolutionary populism before March 1, 1881, Narodnaia Volia after March 1, 1881, Populists, Militarists, Conspirators, and other groups in the 1880s, and the beginnings of Russian social democracy. His examination ceases in 1889. He focuses on both their thinking and their activity as well as the various groups' interrelationships. Reviews: *Canadian Slavonic Papers* 29:4:434-35 (December 1987). *Russian Review* 46:2:227-28 (April 1987).

785. Ragsdale, Hugh, **Tsar Paul and the Question of Madness: An Essay in History and Psychology**. New York: Greenwood Press, 1988. xviii, 266 p. *Contributions to the Study of World History, 0885-9159*, no. 13. ISBN: 0313266085. Includes index and bibliographical references (p. 247-262).
Ragsdale's book has three aims: 1) "to describe the mentality of Paul in the context of the two most important influences which formed it, the thought of the European Enlightenment and the culture of Russian society of the time;" 2) "to examine that long-standing controversy in the historiography of Russia: was Paul really mad?;" and 3) to examine how "psychology/psychiatry [is] to be used judiciously and appropriately in the study of history." (p. xi, xv) Reviews: *American Historical Review* 95:2:547-48 (April 1990). *Historian* 52:4:643-44 (August 1990).

786. Ransel, David L., **Mothers of Misery: Child Abandonment in Russia**. Princeton: Princeton University Press, 1988. xiv, 330 p. ISBN: 069105522x. Includes index and bibliography.
A study of foundling homes in prerevolutionary Russia and the problems that provided the impetus for their construction, child abandonment. The author uses his analysis of the problem to uncover changes taking place within Russia's peasant class. The topical arrangement covers such topics as infanticide, illegitimacy, sex ratios of abandoned children, the Beskoi system, the fosterage system and its geography, and social and medical consequences. An appendix supplies statistics on admissions and deaths in the St. Petersburg and Moscow foundling homes from the late 1700s to the time of the First World War. Reviews: *Journal of Modern History* 62:3:670-71 (September 1990). *Journal of Social History* 24:1:190-93 (Fall 1990). *Ukrainian Studies* 14:1-2:198-201 (June 1990). *American Historical Review* 95:1:208-09 (February 1990).

787. **Russia and the World of the Eighteenth Century**, edited by Karen Rasmussen. Columbus, Ohio: Slavica Publishers, 1988. viii, 680 p. ISBN: 0893571865. Includes bibliographies.

A collection of the papers delivered in Bloomington, Indiana in 1984 at the Third International Conference of the Study Group on Eighteenth Century Russia. The theme of this conference was Russia's position in the world. The papers covered such topics as national identity, religion, learning, science, public welfare, visual arts, literature, freemasonry, government, rural order, and commerce. Each section includes three or more papers and commentary by discussants.

788. Riehn, Richard K., **1812, Napoleon's Russian Campaign**. New York: McGraw-Hill, 1990. ix, 525 p. ISBN: 0070527318. Includes index and bibliographical references (p. 511-513).

A military analysis of Napoleon's 1812 campaign on Russia, its prelude and consequences. The author examines the military establishment in the allied countries as well as in France. Although France is the focal point of this study, the author examines the effect of the Napoleonic Wars in a more general way. Detailed analysis of the Russian military is offered. A number of appendices offer statistical data on the Russian army in 1812 and show changes throughout the course of the campaign.

789. Roosevelt, Priscilla R., **Apostle of Russian Liberalism: Timofei Granovsky**. Newtonville, Mass.: Oriental Research Partners, 1986. xiv, 234 p. *Russian Biography Series*, no. 21. ISBN: 892501609. Includes bibliography and index.

Granovsky (1813-1855) was professor of world history at Moscow University. He served as a model for Dostoevsky's character Stepan Trofimovich Verkhansky, an incurable idealist. Scholar Leonoid Shapiro had called him "perhaps the most brilliant star of the period of the Remarkable Decade. Roosevelt's goal is to explain how two such divergent opinions of the same individual might arise." (p. xii) Reviews: *Slavic Review* 47:1:122-23 (Spring 1933). *Russian Review* 47:2:190-91 (April 1988). *American Historical Review* 93:2:463-64 (April 1988).

790. Rothstein, Andrew, **Peter the Great and Marlborough: Politics and Diplomacy in Converging Wars**. London: Macmillan, 1986. xi, 247 p. ISBN: 0333398785. Includes bibliographical references and index.

A discussion of the complex relationship which developed between England and Russia as each was embroiled in a war, the War of the Spanish Succession and the Russo-Swedish War in the early eighteenth century. The author draws on the papers of Marlborough and Peter the Great and the memoirs and correspondence of their contemporaries. The period saw the first prolonged contact between England and Russia. It resulted in the establishment of limits on the expansionist plans of both nations. Review: *History; Reviews of New Books* 15:4:114 (March-April 1987).

791. Saul, Norman E., **Distant Friends: The United States and Russia, 1763-1867**. Lawrence, KS: University Press of Kansas, 1991. xvi, 448 p. ISBN: 0700604383. Includes index and bibliographical references (p. 407-430).

The first in a three volume work on the history of U.S.-Russian relations. The author intends the work to be comprehensive but not exhaustive. He has drawn on archival sources from both countries as well as secondary materials. This first volume takes the study up to the sale/purchase of Alaska. This is a period of particularly positive and fruitful relations between the two nations culturally and economically. "Although credit must go to the two governments and their leaders, more must be given to the individuals, both Russian and American, who devoted their lives, or at least a substantial portion, to the furtherance of the relationship." (p. 401) The book is chronologically arranged with appendices listing the ministers to each country and numerous illustrations. It is a scholarly work for the student of the history of foreign relations.

792. Shatz, Marshall, **Jan Waclaw Machajskii: A Radical Critic of the Russian Intelligensia and Socialism**. Pittsburgh: University of Pittsburgh Press, 1989. xvi, 251 p. *Russian and East European Studies*, ISBN: 082293602X. Includes bibliographical references.

Shatz's book has three purposes: 1) "to provide a comprehensive biography of Machajskii and a history of Makhaevism; ... 2) to examine the identity and the historical significance of the Russian intelligentsia in the light of Machajskii's views; ... and 3) to identify Machajskii's contribution to the history of the concept of the 'new class.' " (p. xiv-xv) Review: *Russian Review* 49:3:349-51 (July 1990).

793. Surh, Gerald Dennis, **1905 in St. Petersburg: Labor, Society, and Revolution**. Stanford, Calif.: Stanford University Press, 1989. xvii, 456 p. *Studies of the Harriman Institute*, ISBN: 0804714991. Includes index and bibliography (p. 429-448).

Surh intends his work to be revisionist. In his mind the Soviet approach has "generally failed or refused to evaluate the political development of the labor movement apart from its relationship to the Social Democratic Party, particularly the Bolshevik faction." (p. xiv) Here Surh concentrates on the workers themselves and the various forces that influenced their behavior prior to the 1905 revolution. The two appendices are devoted to the industrial crisis and St. Petersburg labor and the Petersburg Printers. Reviews: *International Labor and Working Class History* 38:68-80 (Fall 1990). *Russian Review* 49:3:346-47 (July 1990). *Canadian Slavonic Papers* 32:2:185-86 (June 1990). *Russian History* 17:3:362-63 (Fall 1990).

794. Thurston, Robert W., **Liberal City, Conservative State: Moscow and Russia's Urban Crisis, 1906-1914**. New York: Oxford University Press, 1987. viii, 266 p. ISBN: 0195043316. Includes index and bibliography (p. 244-259).

A scholarly study of Moscow from 1904-1914 as an example of the crisis in Russian urban centers. The author feels that the urban areas were centers of the revolution of 1917. He focuses on "institutional modernization" in an attempt to demonstrate the obstacles to change inherent in urban administration in pre-revolutionary Russia. He directs his study to the analysis of the major factors affecting the lower classes, the intelligentsia "society," and central government. The volume includes several appendices on the conditions in Moscow during this period. It also includes a lengthy bibliography and detailed index. Since the nature of this study is such as to include social, political, and urban history there are sections that could be useful in a wide variety of areas such as the chapters on education, police activity, and municipal services.

795. Verner, Andrew M., **The Crisis of Russian Autocracy: Nicholas II and the 1905 Revolution**. Princeton, NJ: Princeton University Press, 1990. x, 372 p. *Studies of the Harriman Institute*, ISBN: 0691047731. Includes index and bibliography (p. 353-364).

"This book not only hopes to contribute to an understanding of autocratic theory and practice under Nicholas II, but also takes its place in the long standing historical and historiographical controversy that dates back to the 1905 revolution itself." (p. 6) It contains a glossary of terms to aid the reader.

796. **Politics and Society in Provincial Russia: Saratov, 1590-1917,** edited by Rex A. Wade and Scott J. Seregny. Columbus: Ohio State University, 1989. x, 468 p. ISBN: 0814204945. Includes index and bibliographical references (p. 427-454).

This collection of essays was a result of a conference held at the University of Illinois in 1985. The contributors came together "to examine the social and political movements that developed in this Volga province and to explore how these can shed light on the broader trends of Russian history, especially the last half-century of the Old Regime." (p. 1) A glossary of frequently used Russian terms is included.

797. Westwood, J. N., **Endurance and Endeavour: Russian History, 1812-1986.** London: Oxford University Press, 1987. xiv, 551 p. *Short Oxford History of the Modern World,* ISBN: 0198821452 (pbk.), 0198221460. Includes index.

This new edition of Westwood's book takes Russia's history up to 1986, on the eve of Gorbachev's reforms.

798. World Congress for Soviet and East European Studies, **Imperial Power and Development: Papers on the Pre-Revolutionary Russian History: Selected Papers of the Third World Congress for Soviet and East European Studies,** edited by Don Karl Rowney. Columbus, Ohio: Slavica Publishers, 1990. 189 p. ISBN: 0893572098. Includes bibliographical references.

All of these essays were originally presented at the Third World Congress for Soviet and East European Studies and cover a broad range of topics. "They share, however, two main themes: the emergence of modern Russia and the importance of perspective to understanding the history of this emergence." (p. 9) The essays fall into the following four groups: 1. exploration and profiteering in the eighteenth century; 2. foreign policy and diplomacy on a shifting power base; 3. industrialization, social, legal, and economic change; and 4. continuation of the historiographical debate about the Kurbskii-Groznyi Apocrypha.

799. Zimmerman, Judith E., **Midpassage: Alexander Herzen and European Revolution, 1847-1852.** Pittsburgh, PA: University of Pittsburgh Press, 1989. 305 p. *Russian and East European Studies,* no. 10. ISBN: 0822938278. Includes index and bibliography (p. 283-294).

"The major concern of this work is to explore the process by which Herzen became an effective political actor." (p. xii) Zimmerman accomplishes her task by tracing Herzen's intellectual and personal development during the years immediately preceding and following the 1848 revolution, while Herzen was in Paris and Geneva. Reviews: *American Historical Review* 95:5:1526-27 (December 1990). *Russian Review* 49:3:340-42 (July 1990).

Revolution and Civil War

800. Agursky, Mikhail, **The Third Rome: National Bolshevism in the USSR,** with a foreword by Leonard Shapiro. Boulder, CO: Westview Press, 1987. xvii, 426 p. ISBN: 0813301394. Includes index and bibliography (p. 384-405).

"This book presents an entirely new interpretation of the Bolshevik revolution by examining its geopolitical context in addition to its domestic aspect. Dr. Agursky argues that in the early 1900s Lenin's revolutionary strategy was to outpace the 'competitive' German revolution; German social democracy had its own formula to bring social revolution to Russia; and Lenin wanted to consolidate Bolshevik power in order to bring 'his' revolution to Germany. The author concludes that by 1917 Russian intellectuals well understood the deep-rootedness of Bolshevik nationalism, and, although Bolshevism had ostensibly been loyal to Marxism, on a political level, it was now in fact a rebellion against it." (p. iii) The author discusses the various European revolutionary movements as competing groups and examines their struggle from 1871 to Stalin's consolidation of power. The author, a former Soviet citizen, draws on a wide range of sources. Reviews: *Canadian-American Slavic Studies* 24:2:245-47 (Summer 1990). *Problems of Communism* 39:6:96-105 (November-December 1990). *Geographical Review* 80:2:186-88 (April 1990). *Slavic Review* 48:4:670-71 (Winter 1989). *Canadian Review of Studies in Nationalism* 16:1-2:333-34 (1989).

801. Ascher, Abraham, **The Revolution of 1905**. Stanford, CA: Stanford University Press, 1988. 2 v. ISBN: 0804714363. Includes index and bibliography (p. 383-397). "My aim in this volume is to conclude my account of the Revolution of 1905 by describing developments from early 1906 until June 3, 1907, the day on which the autocracy inflicted the fatal blow on the opposition that reduced it to virtual impotence." (p. 1) The author's first volume discusses the 1905 revolution when the opposition was facing concession from the old regime. The years 1906-1907 saw the tsarist regime's response. Ascher feels this later period is too little examined given the long term effects of the government's actions. The book follows a roughly chronological arrangement with quite a lot of attention focused on the significance of the rise in political terror and lawlessness. Reviews: *American Historical Review* 95:2:550-51 (April 1990). *Historian* 52:4:653-54 (August 1990).

802. Babine, Alexis Vasilevich, **A Russian Civil War Diary: Alexis Babine in Saratov, 1917-1922**, edited by Donald J. Raleigh. Durham, NC: Duke University Press, 1988. xxiv, 240 p. ISBN: 0822308355. Includes index and bibliography (p. 227-233).
Babine was a Russian who came to America and received bachelor's and master's degrees from Cornell University. He worked there in the library and subsequently at Indiana, Stanford, and the Library of Congress before returning to Russia to live in 1910. His diary of the revolutionary years in Saratov, from 1917 to 1921, offers a rare glimpse of the effects of that event in the provinces. Review: *Russian History* 16:2-4: 471-72 (1989).

803. Baum, Ann Todd, **Komsomol Participation in the Soviet First Five-Year Plan**. Houndmills, England: Macmillan, 1987. 62 p. ISBN: 0333439147. Includes index and bibliography (p. 56-57).
A brief analysis of the development and role of the Communist youth organization the Komsomol. The author contends that the organization developed with a traditional military structure and was used by Stalin to support and contribute to the success of the first Five Year Plan. "The underlying assumption is that Stalin provided Russian youth with a compelling ideology so convincing that it appealed to their still impressionable logic, and so exciting that his goals became theirs with an intensity that neared fanaticism." (p. 6) The book is thematically organized covering such topics as the history of the Komsomol, industrialization, education, and collectivization. Reviews: *Slavic Review* 48:3:499 (Fall 1989). *Russian Review* 48:1:103-04 (January 1989).

804. Benvenuti, Francesco, **The Bolsheviks and the Red Army, 1918-1922**. Cambridge: Cambridge University Press, 1988. viii, 264 p. *Soviet and East European Studies*, ISBN: 0521257719. Includes index.
A translation of the 1982 Italian study on the political and institutional aspects of the Red Army. "Attention has been focused on the changes that the internal Red Army regime underwent, on its institutional position within the Soviet state, and on how the Bolsheviks themselves perceived these issues. To borrow from the Soviet vocabulary an expression that was in common use at the time, this book is concerned with the 'military policy' (voennaia politika) of the Russian communist party (Bolsheviks, RVCP) during the Civil

War. It is my contention that this policy was much less clear-cut, unswerving, and consistent than contemporary Soviet and Western studies tend to suggest." (p. 1) The topical organization includes examinations of the history of the Russian Army, the formation of the Red Army, opposition to the existence of a standing army, military policy of the 8th Party Congress, and political tensions growing out of the military policy of the government to name but a few topics. Reviews: *Soviet Union-Union Sovietique* 17:1-2:178-79 (1990). *American Historical Review* 95:5:1591-92 (December 1990). *Slavic Review* 49:4:654-55 (Winter 1990). *Historian* 52:4:655-66 (August 1990). *Russian History* 17:4:452-53 (Winter 1990).

805. **Dear Comrades: Menshevik Reports on the Bolshevik Revolutions and the Civil War,** edited and translated by Vladimir N. Brovkin. Stanford, Calif.: Hoover Institution Press, Stanford University, 1991. xxii, 275 p. *Hoover Press Publication, Hoover Archival Documentaries,* no. 398. ISBN: 081798982X. Includes bibliographical references (p. 247-252) and index.

A collection of translated documents from the Boris I. Nicolaevsky archival collection at the Hoover Institute Archives. The documents selected for inclusion in this volume do not record a history of the Menshevik Party. They are reports by Mensheviks on events during the revolution and civil war describing conditions in urban industrial centers. "The documents focus on workers' material conditions, aspirations, and political views and their involvements in politics, elections, strikes, and protest actions." (p. xv) There are three types of documents in the book: reports of local Menshevik organizations or individuals on specific events, reports of the party leadership, and personal letters of leading Mensheviks. The documents are chronologically arranged.

806. Burbank, Jane, **Intelligentsia and Revolution: Russian Views of Bolshevism.** New York: Oxford University Press, 1986. viii, 340 p. ISBN: 0195040619. Includes index and bibliography (p. 315-326).

A scholarly study of the early reaction to the Bolshevik government by the Russian intelligentsia. The views of various intellectual groups are presented and analyzed. Many of those presented were at odds with one another as well as with the Bolsheviks, such as the autocrats and the social revolutionaries. But each brings a different perspective on the emerging Bolshevik power. The volume covers 1917-22, the years when dissenting opinions were still tolerated. There are lengthy sections on many of the major figures of the time including Iulii Martov, Paul Axelrod, Viktor Chernov, Petr Kropotin, Paul Miliukov, Peter Struve, and Nikolai Berdaev. There is an extensive bibliography and detailed index. Review: *Canadian Slavonic Papers* 30:1:141-42 (March 1988).

807. Burdzhalov, Edward Nikolaevich, **Russia's Second Revolution: The February 1917 Uprising in Petrograd,** translated and edited by Donald J. Raleigh. Bloomington: Indiana University Press, 1987. xxii, 388 p. *Indiana-Michigan Series in Russian and East European Studies,* ISBN: 0253350379, 0253204402 (pbk.). Includes index.

Burdzhalov's book appeared in 1966 and immediately engendered harsh criticism. "Burdzhalov dealt directly with division and confusion within the Bolshevik leadership over tactics, chronicling the lack of coordination among Bolshevik organisations in Petrograd.... Ignoring criticism to which he had been subjected since 1956, Burdzhalov depicted the revolution as an essentially spontaneous affair in which the workers themselves occupied the forefront, assisted by the garrison." (p xvii-xviii) Reviews: *Soviet Union-Union Sovietique* 17:3:312-13 (1990). *Canadian-American Slavic Studies* 24:2:231-32 (Summer 1990). *Problems of Communism* 39:2:98-104 (March-April 1990). *Canadian Slavonic Papers* 30:4:534 (December 1989).

808. Connaughton, Richard Michael, **The Republic of the Ushakovka: Admiral Kol-chak and the Allied Intervention in Siberia, 1918-1920**. London: Routledge, 1990. ix, 193 p. ISBN: 0415051983. Includes bibliographical references (p. 183-184) and index.

The second volume in a regional trilogy, the first of which covered the events of the 1918-1920 revolution and the final volume of which will discuss the Japanese invasion of China. This volume is devoted to Admiral Kolchak and the Allied intervention. While the author describes the work as an historical story, he does touch on broader issues. Specifically, he is interested in the long term effects of the intervention, which he feels determined the nature of Soviet-Western relations. "Herein therefore lies an important lesson in the potential political and spiritual penalties which can arise as a legacy of intervention in another state's internal affairs." (p. vii) The narrative is chronologically arranged with numerous illustrations and an appendix containing an excerpt from President Wilson's aide-memoir.

809. Fiddick, Thomas C., **Russia's Retreat from Poland, 1920: From Permanent Revolution to Peaceful Coexistence**. New York: St. Martin's Press, 1990. xiv, 348 p. ISBN: 0312039980. Includes index and bibliographical references (p. 328-336).

A history of the causes and results of the Soviet-Polish War of 1920. The author investigates the internal politics of both countries before and during the war. He also examines the ideological basis for the war and West European involvement. A note on historiography and a chronology of events are provided along with nine appendices containing various documents pertinent to the analysis. The volume is structured in such a way that each chapter focuses on a central figure related to some specific aspect of the war. Included are Leonid Krasin, Karl Radek, Leon Trotsky, George Chicherin, Lenin, M. N. Tukhachevsky, Leo Kamenev, Lloyd George, Felix Dzerzhinsky, and Sergei Kamenev.

810. Figes, Orlando, **Peasant Russia, Civil War: The Volga Countryside in Revolu-tion, 1917-1921**. Oxford: Clarendon Press, 1989. xvii, 401 p. ISBN: 0198228988. Includes index and bibliographical references (p. 363-388).

This study is "the first detailed non-Soviet history of the peasantry during 1917-21 [and] examines the social forces behind the consolidation of the Bolshevik dictatorship in the countryside." (p. 9) This consolidation of the peasantry behind the Bolsheviks helps explain their victory in the Civil War. The author has also included a glossary of Russian terms used in the text. Review: *Russian History* 17:4:453-456 (Winter 1990).

811. Galili y Garcia, Ziva, **The Menshevik Leaders in the Russian Revolution: Social Realities and Political Strategies in the Russian Revolution**. Princeton, NJ: Princeton University Press, 1989. xviii, 452 p. *Studies of the Harriman Institute*, ISBN: 069105567X. Includes index and bibliography (p. 417-429).

The author intends to take a closer look at the various problems surrounding revolution and democracy in 1917. In her book she seeks "to clarify the stages and chronology of the process of social and political polarization and thereby outline the 'geography' of political opportunities that existed at each stage as well as those that had been missed.... Throughout this study, the emphasis is on the interaction between workers and employers and, more generally, between labor and the commercial-industrial class." (p. 7)

812. Geller, Mikhail, and Aleksandr Nekrich, **Utopia in Power: The History of the Soviet Union from 1917 to the Present**, translated by Phyllis B. Carlos. New York: Summit Books, 1986. 877 p. ISBN: 0671462423. Includes bibliography (p. 820-845).

Russian émigré historians Geller and Nekrich present a thoroughly researched history of the Soviet Union from 1917 to 1985.

813. Got'e, Iurii Vladimirovich, **Time of Troubles, the Diary of Iurii Vladimirovich Gote: Moscow, July 8, 1917 to July 23, 1922**, translated, edited, and introduced by Terence Emmons. Princeton, NJ: Princeton University Press, 1988. xix, 513 p. ISBN: 0691055203. Includes indexes.

This diary of Got'e, a Moscow University history professor and associate director of the Rumiantsev Museum, was kept from July 8, 1917 to July 23, 1922. Got'e turned his diary over to Frank Golden, an American professor of history who was, among other things, collecting materials for the new Hoover library at Stanford. The diary provides a fascinating personal assessment of the turbulent years of revolution and civil war in and near Moscow. Reviews: *American Historical Review* 95:1:211-12 (February 1990). *Russian Review* 49:2:223-24 (April 1990). *Journal of Modern History* 62:3:672-74 (September 1990).

814. Haimson, Leopold H., **The Making of Three Russian Revolutionaries: Voices from the Menshevik Past**, in collaboration with Ziva Galili y Garcia and Richard Wortman, introduction by Leopold H. Haimson, notes by Ziva Galili y Garcia. Cambridge: Cambridge University Press, 1987. ix, 515 p. ISBN: 0521263255. Includes index.

Interviews with three Mensheviks taped between 1960 and 1965 as part of an interuniversity project make up this volume. The material provides a unique view of "Menshevik political culture and the radical intelligentsia of which it was a part." (p. vii) The original interviews comprised thousands of typed pages. What is presented here is an edited version. In editing the manuscript, preference was accorded to reminiscences of early youth and early political careers, repetition was eliminated, digressions were omitted, as were follow-up questions. The individuals included here, Lydia Dan, Boris Nicolaevsky, and George Denicke, originally intended to write their own history of the Menshevik Party. The editors feel these interviews not only contribute to the available information on the Party but, "First and foremost the evidence that these three life histories provide of the evolution of these informants' attitudes toward the world about them... challenged traditional explanations of the mentality of the Russian intelligentsia as an example of psychological 'alienation.' " (p. 44) The extensive introduction and notes provide the reader with background information and a context for some of the more obscure references.

815. Hardy, Deborah, **Land and Freedom: The Origins of Russian Terrorism, 1876-1879**. New York: Greenwood Press, 1987. xiii, 212 p. *Contributions to the Study of World History, 0885-9159*, no. 7. ISBN: 0313255962. Includes index and bibliography (p. 195-202).

Hardy reassesses the roots of Russian terrorism by examining the efforts of revolutionaries' work among the peasantry in 1876, efforts that led up to the formation of Narodnaia Volia, Russia's leading terrorist organization. Hardy attempts to demonstrate that "many 'villagers' or propagandists... did not regard themselves as unsuccessful in the countryside, From the beginning, their plans had involved several stages of development before any revolutionary attempt was forthcoming, and according to their schedule they were moving forward toward their goal." (p. xii) Reviews: *Canadian Slavonic Papers* 30:2:266-67 (June 1988). *Canadian Journal of History* 23:3:434-35 (December 1988).

816. Heenan, Louise Erwin, **Russian Democracy's Fatal Blunder: The Summer Offensive of 1917**. New York: Praeger, 1987. xv, 188 p. ISBN: 0275928292. Includes index and bibliography (p. 177-182).

A thorough discussion of a previously unexplored topic—the June offensive of the Provisional Government in 1917. The author believes it was a pivotal event in terms of the Bolshevik revolution of October 1917, alienating the troops and population as a whole from a government unable to win at war or provide for its people. The book is thematically arranged beginning with a review of the events of the war up to January of 1917 and then proceeding to later conferences planning the offensive, and discussions of conditions at the fronts. It then turns to the offensive itself and its aftermath. The author has drawn on personal memoirs as well as historical documents. An appendix includes some documents describing conditions at the front. Reviews: *Russian Review* 49:1:90-92 (January 1990). *Perspective: Reviews of New Books* 17:3:119-20 (Summer 1988).

817. Husband, William, **Revolution in the Factory: The Birth of the Soviet Textile Industry, 1917-1920**. New York: Oxford University Press, 1990. viii, 227 p. ISBN: 0195064356. Includes bibliographical references (p. 203-218) and index.

An analysis of the revolutionary movement among one specific group of the proletariat, textile workers of the Central Industrial Region, from 1917-1920. The author feels that the textile workers, although demonstrating a certain amount of enthusiasm for the revolution, really demonstrated more of a local than national solidarity. Other evidence the author explored when studying Soviet archival materials, previously unavailable, indicate that the importance of Party membership has been exaggerated. A glossary of terms is included.

818. **Storming the Heavens: Voices of October**, edited and introduced by Mark Jones. London: Pluto Press; Atlantic Heights, NJ: Paul & Company, 1987. lxiv, 186 p. *Soviet Studies*, ISBN: 1853050253, 1853050202 (U.S.). Includes bibliography (p. 184-186).

Jones has gathered together eighteen brief memoirs about the Russian revolution. Some of these are by principals in the event, such as Lenin, Krupskaia, and Trotsky. Others are by journalists or other observers. The memoirs are introduced with a lengthy introduction by Jones which puts the entire period in context.

819. Kazantzakis, Nikos, **Russia: A Chronicle of Three Journeys in the Aftermath of the Revolution**, translated by Michael Antonakes and Thanasis Maskaleris. Berkeley, CA: Creative Arts Book Company, 1989. xvi, 271 p. ISBN: 0887390722.

The travel record of Greek author Nikos Kazantzakis as he journeyed through Russia after the revolution of 1917. The author was sympathetic to socialism and to the efforts being made by the Bolsheviks to transform their society. In the introduction, Kazantzakis' predilection for "imaginative" portrayals of some events is evident, as he was often carried away by the drama of the events he was witnessing. The book is of interest to those . devotees of travel literature as well as historians.

820. **Party, State, and Society in the Russian Civil War: Explorations in Social History**, edited by Diane P. Koenker, William G. Rosenberg, and Ronald Grigor Suny. Bloomington, Ind.: Indiana University Press, 1989. xiv, 450 p. *Indiana-Michigan Series in Russian and East European Studies*, ISBN: 0253332621, 0253205417 (pbk.). Includes bibliographical references.

This collection of twenty-four essays is intended to contribute to a deeper understanding of the social history of the Russian Civil War. One theme to which the writers consistently return is the question "to what extent were responses and political choices of the Civil War years the product of social and economic circumstances, to what the independent exercise of conscious political will?" (p. xi) The essays are arranged in six sections: The Civil War and Social Revolution, The Social and Demographic Impact of the Civil War, Administration and State Building, the Bolsheviks and the Intelligentsia, Workers and Socialists, and the Legacy of the Civil War. A bibliographic essay on a guide to further reading is appended. Reviews: *Soviet Union-Union Sovietique* 17:1-2:163-66 (1990). *Canadian Slavonic Papers* 32:4:493-94 (December 1990).

821. Koenker, Diane, and William G. Rosenberg, **Strikes and Revolution in Russia, 1917**. Princeton, NJ: Princeton University Press, 1989. xix, 393 p. ISBN: 0691055785. Includes index and bibliographical references (p. 351-375).

A study of labor activism in Russia. "What began as a modest attempt to systematize the available evidence on strikes soon developed into a major effort to record, to analyze, and most compellingly, to integrate strike phenomena into an understanding of the broader processes of Russia's revolutionary conjuncture." (p. xv) The study is of interest to Russian historical scholars as well as those interested in the process of social revolution in general. The volume includes numerous tables and figures as well as a substantial appendix explaining the statistical aspects of the methodology used. The book is chronologically arranged, but the authors also wished to focus on specific themes. "We have therefore tried to weave thematic material, such as a consideration of the issue of strike demands, the role of management, and the questions of perception and leadership together with the broader narrative framework." (p. 2) Review: *Russian History* 17:4:443-44 (Winter 1990).

822. Lih, Lars T., **Bread and Authority in Russia, 1914-1921**. Berkeley: University of California Press, 1990. xvii, 303 p. *Studies on the History of Society and Culture*, ISBN: 0520065840. Includes index and bibliographical references (p. 275-289).

The breakdown of economic and political institutions in the period before the consolidation of Bolshevik power is the subject of this analysis. In particular, the author is interested in the breakdown of food supply and distribution and its effect on the stability of the government. The author views the period 1914-1921 as a "time of troubles" similar in some ways to the seventeenth century era of the same name. He characterizes the period as one of uncertainty, full of political rhetoric, and where the overriding question was to continue or discontinue the monarchy. The author takes a chronological approach.

823. Lincoln, W. Bruce, **Passage through Armageddon: The Russians in War and Revolution**. New York: Simon and Schuster, 1986. 637 p. ISBN: 0671557092. Includes index and bibliography (p. 581-613).

A description of the events of World War I as they affected Russia and the Russian revolution, valuable to both the scholar and the uninitiated reader. The numerous personal accounts included give the reader a picture of the devastation caused by these two pivotal events in Russian history. Professor Lincoln describes the stages of the revolution that would inevitably lead to the Civil War. The volume has numerous illustrations and maps. It is the second in a three part series covering the establishment of the Soviet power in the Soviet Union.

824. ———, **Red Victory: A History of the Russian Civil War**. New York: Simon and Schuster, 1989. 637 p. ISBN: 0671631667. Includes bibliographical references.

In this third volume of the trilogy on the establishment of Bolshevik power, the years of the Civil War are the focus. The pivotal role played by the Civil War in shaping the institutions of the future Soviet Union is emphasized. The volume is rich in detail and contains some features especially useful for the non- specialist such as a list of major characters. As with earlier volumes in this series, it is arranged chronologically and is focused on major events of the period. Lincoln has deliberately omitted some subjects such as the inner workings of the Bolshevik Party and the nationalities question. It is a serious, yet highly readable treatment of the period.

825. Mally, Lynn, **Culture of the Future: The Proletkult Movement in Revolutionary Russia**. Berkeley: University of California Press, 1990. xxix, 306 p. *Studies on the History of Society and Culture*, ISBN: 0520065778. Includes bibliographical references and index.

A new study of the revolutionary cultural movement called the Proletkult. The author tries to move beyond the focus of many other studies of this movement, the Lenin-Bogdanov debate. "In this book I examine the Proletkult as a complicated social and cultural movement with many conflicting programs....Using the archival records and publications of both local and central organisations, I try to show the complex interaction between official pronouncements and their implementation." (p. xxiv) This work focuses on the years 1917 to 1922. The last chapter deals with the decline of the organization from 1923-1932. The work is topically arranged covering such areas as the origins of Proletkult, class in a mass organization, membership, leadership, and the role of the Proletkult in the arts.

826. Mawdsley, Evan, **The Russian Civil War**. Boston: Allen & Unwin, 1987. xvi, 351 p. ISBN: 0049470248. Includes index and bibliography (p. 312-343).
A chronological history of the Civil War for the general reader. The author limits himself to the topic of the Civil War, touching on the development of the socialist state and foreign reaction to the revolution only as needed. Numerous maps are provided.

827. McAuley, Mary, **Bread and Justice: State and Society in Petrograd, 1917-1922**. Oxford: Clarendon Press, 1991. xviii, 461 p. ISBN: 0198219822. Includes bibliographical references (p. 441-454) and index.
A study of the construction of the Soviet state from 1917 to 1922. The author focuses on describing the features of the new Bolshevik state that grew out of the Revolution and its relationship to its people. This social history focuses on Petrograd as the Russian state in microcosm. The volume can be read on a variety of levels. "It is for those who are interested in the emergence of new states out of revolutions, and in the Soviet state in particular; it is for those concerned with creating a democratic socialist order. It is also simply a story of a city and its people as the battering ram of history struck them, rocking the old Tsarist capital on its foundations." (p. 7) The first three parts give a generally chronological account of the city in revolution and its aftermath to 1920. Parts four and five examine the state's attempts to control industry, goods, and services. Part six focuses on problems related to class conflicts. The final parts examine the social and political crises faced by the government in 1921 and 1922. Two appendices on leading Bolsheviks and the Petrograd Committee (RKPO) are included as well as numerous plates and tables. The bibliography contains Russian language sources almost exclusively.

828. Merridale, Catherine, **Moscow Politics and the Rise of Stalin: The Communist Party in the Capital, 1925-32**. New York: St. Martin's Press, 1990. xv, 328 p. ISBN: 0312047991. Includes bibliographical references (p. 306-315) and index.
The Communist Party in Moscow is examined as a part of the Stalinist machine and simply as a local institution. The first theme of Stalinism occupies the first part of the book. The author looks at the rise of Stalin's supporters among the Moscow elite and how they came to prevail. The second part of the book examines the effectiveness, membership, and role of the Moscow Communist Party. "The relationship between central and local politics and the contribution to Soviet political history of ordinary party members are central themes of the book, which uses local party reports and archives to build a unique picture of Moscow's Communist Party at a turning point in history." (book jacket)

829. Mstislavskii, Sergei, **Five Days Which Transformed Russia**, translated by Elizabeth Kristofovich Zelensky, and introduced by William G. Rosenberg. Bloomington: Indiana University Press, 1988. xi, 168 p. *Second World*, ISBN: 0253324823.
"Written in 1918 and now published in English for the first time, *Five Days Which Transformed Russia* is a dramatic firsthand account of the five critical events of the 1917

Revolution: the February uprising, the founding of the Provisional Government, the arrest of Nicholas II, the October Revolution, and the disbanding of the Constituent Assembly." (back cover) The book is arranged chronologically and is part of the "Second World Series" which attempts to present Russian views of their history and culture. A glossary of terms is included, along with several illustrations. Reviews: *Canadian Slavonic Papers* 30:4:535-36 (December 1988). *Nationalism Papers* 16:2:298-300 (Fall 1988). *Russian History* 16:2-4:468-69 (1989).

830. Pearce, Brian, **How Haig Saved Lenin**, foreword by Evan Mawdsley. New York: St. Martin's Press, 1987. xii, 138 p. ISBN: 031200754X. Includes index and bibliography (p. 126-134).

An analysis of the role of World War I in the success of the Russian Revolution. Specifically, the author examines the effects of the allies' role in war, defeating the Germans but failing to protect the Eastern front. The course of the war, with its emphasis on protecting the Western front is viewed as an integral part of the success of the Bolshevik Revolution. The book is arranged chronologically, following key events of 1918, and includes a chronology of 1918. Review: *Orbis* 32:3:461-62 (Summer 1988).

831. Pipes, Richard, **The Russian Revolution**. 1st ed. New York: Knopf, 1990. xxiv, 944 p. ISBN: 0394502418. Includes bibliographical references (p. 915-919) and index.

Pipes' monumental history of the Russian Revolution is a continuation of the work begun in his *Russia under the Old Regime*. The present work, taking up where his previous one left off, begins with the disturbances at the universities in 1899. For Pipes this was the beginning of the revolution, which broadly defined, can be said to have lasted almost a century, to 1991. In this work, however, Pipes ends with the consolidation of power by the Bolsheviks at the end of the Civil War. A subsequent work, *Russia under the New Regime*, will carry the story on through the final year of Lenin's dictatorship. The book is divided into two parts, "The Aging of the Old Regime" and "The Bolsheviks Conquer Russia," with a total of eighteen chapters. Appendices include a glossary of transliterated vernacular terms used and a detailed chronology of events from 1899 to December 1919.

832. Raleigh, Donald J., **Revolution on the Volga: 1917 in Saratov**. Ithaca, NY: Cornell University Press, 1986. 373 p. ISBN: 0801417902. Includes index and bibliography (p. 337-361).

The 1917 revolution is examined in the context of a provincial city in this scholarly study. The author felt Saratov a good choice as it was home to a large peasant problem and housed an army garrison. These elements along with its large working class gives it a social geography reflecting the concerns common all over Russia. The author hopes to begin filling the existing gap in studies of the revolution in the provinces of Russia. The study is chronological in structure, includes an appendix of election results to the constituent assembly, and contains maps of both Saratov province and the city of Saratov. Reviews: *Russian Review* 46:3:335-36. *American History Review* 92:1:178-79 (February 1987). *Canadian Slavonic Papers* 29:2-3:302-03 (June-September 1987).

833. Read, Christopher, **Culture and Power in Revolutionary Russia: The Intelligensia and the Transition from Tsarism to Communism**. New York: St. Martin's Press, 1990. xii, 266 p. ISBN: 0312036817. Includes bibliographical references (p. 253-261) and index.

An examination of the development of the Russian intelligentsia in the years immediately following the revolution. The author believes, contrary to many other studies of the subject, that government policy toward the intelligentsia was already formed by 1922. "Consequently, this book is devoted to substantiating this view and demonstrating that NEP was not so much based on a relaxed attitude to culture but on increasingly systematic control of intellectual life." (p. x) The author provides a chapter on the intelligentsia in prerevolutionary times and then goes on to examine their evolution chronologically focusing on specific areas such as Narkompros, Proletkult, and Party evaluation. These points of special focus were largely determined by the sources available to the author.

834. Reichman, Henry, **Railwaymen and Revolution: Russia, 1905**. Berkeley: University of California Press, 1987. xv, 336 p. ISBN: 0520057163. Includes index and bibliography (p. 313-328).

A historical study of the role of railwaymen in the 1905 revolution. "The principal task of this study is to recount and analyze the interrelations between economic and political struggle and between professional mobilization and class consciousness among railroad workers in 1905...." (p. 9) The author also seeks to explore railwaymen as a part of the work force. The book is divided into two parts. The first looks at the situation of the railway worker before the revolution: labor policy, recruitment, wages, hours, working conditions, and day-to-day life. Part two is a study of the railway worker as a participant in the revolution. The author draws on numerous primary and secondary sources. Reviews: *International Labor and Working Class History* 38:68-80 (Fall 1990). *Russian Review* 49:2: 207-08 (April 1990). *Slavic Review* 47:4:735-36 (Winter 1988). *Canadian Journal of History* 23:2:286-87 (August 1988).

835. Reiman, Michael, **The Birth of Stalinism: The U.S.S.R. on the Eve of the "Second Revolution,"** translated by George Saunders. Bloomington: Indiana University Press, 1987. xii, 188 p. *Indiana-Michigan Series in Russian and East European Studies*, ISBN: 0253311969. Includes index and bibliography (p. 155-181).

Stalin's rise to power from 1927 to 1929 is the subject of this study, originally published in German in 1979. Reiman examines many issues including the strengths and weaknesses of the opposition, the effects of economic crises on political decision making, the growing role of the security police, and Stalin's cult of personality. In Reiman's view, Stalinism, "as an all-embracing system, evolved as a gradual response to deepening crises, at one and the same time a product of Stalin's mentality and the natural outcome of Soviet Russia's early development dating back to the October Revolution." (p. viii) The chronological analysis includes appendices of selected documents with letters from Stalin to the Central Committee and other documents. Reviews: *American Historical Review* 93:4:1092-93 (October 1988). *History: Reviews of New Books* 16:2:87 (Winter 1988). *Slavic Review* 47:1:129-30 (Spring 1988). *Canadian Slavonic Papers* 30:2:271-72 (June 1988).

836. Riaboff, Alexander, **Gatchina Days: Reminiscences of a Russian Pilot**, edited by Von Hardesty. Washington, DC: Smithsonian Institution Press, 1986. 183 p. ISBN: 087474802X. Includes bibliography (p. 182-183).

Riaboff, a young military pilot during WWI, offers a unique perspective on the revolution and the civil war. The narrative begins with the year 1914 when Riaboff found himself in the Great War and ends in 1920, when he escaped to China. Besides his eyewitness accounts of the revolution and civil war, he also offer a unique personal perspective on early Russian aeronautics.

837. Rice, Christopher, **Russian Workers and the Socialist-Revolutionary Party Through the Revolution of 1905-07**. Basingstoke: Macmillan Press in association with the Centre for Russian and East European Studies, University of Birmingham,

1988. xiv, 272 p. *Studies in Soviet History and Society*, ISBN: 0333409159. Includes index and bibliography (p. 258-268).

An analysis of the little-studied Socialist Revolutionary Party drawing on materials only recently made accessible, as well as more traditional sources. The author is particularly interested in the role of the peasant worker as revolutionary. "More broadly, we examine the nature of SR activity in the urban and industrial centre, the social location of the Party's support, its organizational structure and overall relationship with the working population." (p. 3) The book is arranged topically examining the SR party program and agitational activities up to 1905. There is also a case study of the SR's in Petersburg and organizational profiles of the SR's in Baku, the North-West Oblast, the Mal'tseu District of Bryansk, Sevastopol, and the Urals Oblast. Reviews: *International Labor and Working Class History* 38:68-80 (Fall 1990). *Slavic Review* 49:4:656-58 (Winter 1990). *Russian Review* 48:2:197-99 (April 1989).

838. **The German Revolution and the Debate on Soviet Power: Documents, 1918-1919: Preparing the Founding Congress**, edited by John Riddell. 1st ed. New York: Anchor Foundation, 1986. xx, 540 p. *Communist International in Lenin's Time*, ISBN: 0937091006. Includes index and bibliography (p. 528).

While the first part of this two part volume emphasizes the development of the German communist party, the second part is devoted to those documents that describe the preparations for the Communist International. Chapter seven focuses on the debates between Lenin and the German Karl Kautsky. Chapter eight includes debates on Bolshevism from the international conferences held in Bern in February 1919. The final chapter follows the Bolshevik's work preparing for the New Communist International. Aside from the articles on Lenin, many of the documents compiled here have never been available in English before. Commentary by the editor is provided at the beginning of each section to incorporate relevant historical background into the text. Besides the chronology and glossary, an appendix is included containing the Program of the Russian Communist Party of 1919.

839. Sakwa, Richard, **Soviet Communists in Power: A Study of Moscow During the Civil War, 1918-21**. Basingstoke: Macmillan, 1988. xxi, 342 p. *Studies in Soviet History and Society*, ISBN: 0333398475. Includes index and bibliography (p. 321-333).

The city of Moscow and the enormous political and economic changes that took place there during the Civil War are the subject of this study. The author is using Moscow as an example of the kinds of changes going on all over Russia during this period. Thus, this is not meant to be a history of the city in general. Rather, it is a case study of the evolution of Soviet communism from a revolutionary movement to a system of government. "It was in this period that the main outlines of the Soviet system of power were established, and it is the belief of this work that detailed study of a single city helps us to understand the processes which determined the forms that this took." (p. xx) The thematic arrangement analyzes the relationship between the developing Leninist regime and society at large. The author then examines the government-society relationship in the context of the economy, labor relations, the Party, and society. He also discusses the growth of the centralized state in a local context. A scholarly study for the specialist or student of Russian history. Reviews: *Slavic Review* 49:3:454-56 (Fall 1990). *Problems of Communism* 39:2:98-104 (March-April 1990). *American Historical Review* 95:3:873-74 (June 1990).

840. Salzman, Neil V., **Reform and Revolution: The Life and Times of Raymond Robins**. Kent, Ohio: Kent State University Press, 1991. xiv, 472 p. ISBN: 0873384261. Includes bibliographical references (p. 441-456) and index.

A study of the life and work of Raymond Robins, one of the first Americans to support positive political relations with the Soviet government in 1917. The book traces Robins' life, from his early years prospecting, to his years in the Chicago settlement houses. The second half of the book is taken up with his life in Russia. The author sees Robins as something of a visionary, who realistically assessed the situation looking for the course of action that would best serve American interests. He assesses the revolution at the grass roots level. The appendix includes a letter to his wife on the revolution.

841.   Sanders, Jonathan, **Russia, 1917: The Unpublished Revolution,** with foreword by Vitaly Korotich. New York: Abbeyville Press, 1989. 260 p. ISBN: 089659775X. Includes index and bibliography (p. 255-256).

After a brief introduction setting the 1917 Revolution within the context of Russian history, the rest of the book is devoted to photographs, arranged chronologically from January to December 1917. The photographs themselves were culled from Russian archives and made available for publication with permission. They chronicle the fall of the monarchy, the February revolution, the October revolution, and the triumph of communism. Review: *Foreign Affairs* 69:3:185 (Summer 1990).

842.   Schleifman, Nurit, **Undercover Agents in the Russian Revolutionary Movement.** New York: St. Martin's Press, 1988. xvii, 222 p. ISBN: 0312000774. Includes index.

"This study concentrates on the agents in the SR party, and not on those indirectly connected to it like Gapon or Bogrov. Its intention is not primarily to draw attention to any specific secret agent, but to the question as a whole by describing and analysing it in a single party." (p. xii) Reviews: *American Historical Review* 95:3:872 (June 1990). *Slavic Review* 49:3:450- 51 (Fall 1990). *Russian Review* 48:4:421-22 (October 1989).

843.   Service, Robert, **The Russian Revolution, 1900-1927.** 2nd ed. Atlantic Highlands, NJ: Humanities Press International, 1990. x, 101 p. *Studies in European History*, ISBN: 0391037277. Includes bibliographical references (p. 84-90) and index.

A popular chronological study of the Russian Revolution. The author attempts to integrate economic, political, and social factors that contributed to the revolution. The author covers a longer time period than usual also to give the reader more of the historical context of the event. This second edition of the original 1986 publication includes an afterword assessing the treatment of the revolution in Soviet writings since 1985. "The assessment of continuities and disruptions is a prime objective. Another aim is to strike a path away from traditional narrative treatments.... A further intention is to show how aspects of political and social life in today's USSR have their origins in the Soviet historical experience." (p. ix) The book is one in the Studies in European History series which emphasizes changes in the historical literature of Europe, often presenting very new interpretations of historical events. Review: *American Historical Review* 93:4:1090-91 (October 1988).

844.   **The Blackwell Encyclopedia of the Russian Revolution**, edited by Harold Shukman. Oxford: B. Blackwell, 1988. xiv, 418 p. ISBN: 0631152385. Includes bibliographical references and index.

"The purpose of this Encyclopedia is to describe and analyse the events of 1917 in Russia, as well as their background and origin, and to show how they affected the political, economic, social, and ethnic structures of the old empire and gave rise to the new order. The Encyclopedia does not attempt to cover Russian society in its totality; it includes studies of revolutionary organizations, but not of those parties and bodies whose programs and tactics were based on negotiation, reconciliation and evolution, rather than revolution. The period of reform beginning in the 1860s is taken as a starting point, and the coverage terminates roughly with the end of the Civil War in 1921, by which time the Bolsheviks had eliminated any serious threat from their internal political enemies. The multi-national character of the Russian empire and the Soviet Union emerged with unprecedented (and unsurpassed) force during the events of 1917-1921, and this is acknowledged in the wide-ranging treatment of the revolution in the borderlands. Depth can be added to the evolution of ideas and institutions, as well as the playing out of events, by the study of the lives of individual figures. A series of biographies has been included in the Encyclopedia, covering characters from all parties, as well as a number of leading figures of the old regime (such as Nicholas II, Rasputin, Stolypin, Witte) whose activities compel their inclusion in a work devoted to the Revolution." (p. vi) Reviews: *Canadian Slavonic Papers* 32:4:525-26 (December 1990). *Russian Review* 49: 3:351-52 (July 1990).

845. Shulgin, V. V., **Days of the Russian Revolution**, edited, translated and with an introduction by Bruce Friend Adams. Gulf Breeze, FL: Academic International Press, 1990. xx, 251 p. ISBN: 0875691153. Includes bibliographical references (p. 212-244) and index.

This account of the Russian Revolution is unusual in that it was written by a supporter of the tsarist government and a Russophile. The author worked at the paper *Kievlianin*, founded by his father. He was also a government official serving as a zemstvo representative and on the Second State Duma in 1907. He was, therefore, at the center of the government in the early days of the Revolution. The translator has intended this work for students and non-specialists and has added explanatory notes to the text. The book is organized around the establishment and dissolution of the constitution. The readers should be aware that the author was anti-semitic, as well as being a Russophile and his account is strongly colored by these biases. The translator notes that it does present an interesting contrast to the numerous Bolshevik accounts of the period.

846. Slusser, Robert M., **Stalin in October: The Man Who Missed the Revolution**. Baltimore: Johns Hopkins University Press, 1987. xi, 281 p. ISBN: 0801934570. Includes index and bibliography (p. 269-276).

Stalin was absent, or at least inactive during the October 1917 revolution. Robert Slusser writes about why this was so and in the process provides a historical context for this unusual fact. For it was unusual given the claims in Stalin's famous "short course" of Soviet history. Among Slusser's claims are that the purges in the 1930s were carried out in part to silence those who knew the truth about Stalin's inactivity in 1917. His book consists of seven chapters, the first six of which present and interpret evidence month by month from March through October of 1917. The last chapter summarizes the foregoing and attempts to answer why Stalin missed the revolution. Review: *Russian History* 17:4: 446-47 (Winter 1990).

847. Swan, Jane, **The Lost Children: A Russian Odyssey**. 1st ed. Carlisle, Pa.: South Mountain Publishers, 1989. xiv, 224 p. ISBN: 0937339032. Includes index.

The story of the journey of some eight hundred school children across the world. These children were sent by their parents from Petrograd in May 1918 on what was intended to be a summer vacation. Their parents hoped to spare them some of the hardships and dangers of the city during the Revolution and Civil War. The author relies on the diaries of those involved in this journey for her information. The account tells how a summer vacation was turned into a journey around the world by necessity. Review: *Russian History* 17:2:231 (Summer 1990).

848. Tirado, Isabel A., **Young Guard!: The Communist Youth League, Petrograd, 1917-1920**. New York: Greenwood Press, 1988. xii, 264 p. *Contributions to the Study of World History*, no. 9. ISBN: 0313259224. Includes bibliography (p. 255-260) and index.

The early years of the Komsomol, the Communist Youth League in Petrograd, and its evolution are the focus of this study. The book is divided into two parts, the first dealing with the origins of the Communist youth organization and the second with its consolidation during the Civil War. The two chapters of part one "describe the membership, goals and internal deliberations of the youth organization." (p. 6) The four chapters in part two examine various aspects of Komsomol's consolidation, especially its social composition, educational activities, economic work and relationship to the Communist Party until 1920. Several appendixes are included such as the charters of various early youth organizations and the different charters of the Komsomol. Reviews: *Journal of Baltic Studies* 21:2:180-82 (Summer 1990). *American Historical Review* 95:3:872-73 (June 1990). *Slavic Review* 49:1:119-20 (Spring 1990). *Canadian Slavonic Papers* 30:4: 501-02 (December 1988). *Russian Review* 48:2:215-26 (April 1989).

849. Von Hagen, Mark, **Soldiers in the Proletarian Dictatorship: The Red Army and the Soviet Socialist State, 1917-1930**. Ithaca, N.Y.: Cornell University Press, 1990. xviii, 389 p. *Studies of the Harriman Institute/Studies in Soviet History and Society*, ISBN: 08014208. Includes bibliographical references and index.

The changing role of and attitudes toward the Red Army are the central concerns of this study. The author is using the Army as mechanism for examining the many changes in Russian society at large that were taking place during those years. "My aim is to weave together important moments in the institutional history of the Soviet state at the level of 'high politics,' in the social history of the early postrevolutionary years, and in the far more intangible evolution of political culture and mentalities." (p. 4) The chronological study examines civil-military relations, origins of the first socialist army, the social and political status of soldiers in post revolutionary society, and socialist and military values in the Soviet political culture.

850. Wood, Anthony, **The Russian Revolution**. 2nd ed. London: Longman, 1986. x, 98 p. *Seminar Studies in History*, ISBN: 0582355591. Includes index and bibliography (p. 91-95).

This book is a part of a series that includes studies that are "more substantial than a textbook chapter, but less formidable than the specialized full-length academic work." (p. vii) Wood's aim is to sketch what he calls the strange dialogue between intellectual theory and political action that eventuated in the Revolution and its aftermath. His study begins with the setting in imperialist Russia, continues through the 1905 revolution and ends with the revolution and its aftermath.

RSFSR and USSR

851. Alekseeva, Liudmila, and Paul Goldberg, **The Thaw Generation: Coming of Age in the Post-Stalin Era**. 1st ed. Boston: Little, Brown, 1990. 339 p. ISBN: 0316031461. Includes bibliographical references (p. 323-326).

This memoir by a long-time dissident chronicles her experiences from her childhood to the present day. It is especially interesting in its description of how she came to disbelieve the lie she had been taught in school and her struggles, both external and internal after Stalin's death.

852. Andreyev, Catherine, **Vlasov and the Russian Liberation Movement: Soviet Reality and Émigré Theories**. Cambridge: Cambridge University Press, 1987. xiv, 251 p. *Soviet and East European Studies*, ISBN: 0521305454. Includes index and bibliography (p. 224-239).

A study of the Russian Liberation Movement and the man so often associated with it, Andrei Vlasov. Two main questions form the focus of this book. First what exactly was Vlasov's role , was he a traitor or opportunist? Second, how should the Russian Liberation Movement be viewed in the context of Soviet history? The author points out the difficulty of analysis on this topic since it was a forbidden subject for researchers in the Soviet Union. The author of this work operates from the hypothesis that Russian émigrés after 1917 should be treated as part of the social history of the Soviet Union; thus opening the lines of research sources for herself. This scholarly study is organized around the life of Andrei Vlasov as he developed his ideas on the subject. Review: *Soviet Union* 15:1:82-83 (1988).

853. Andrle, Vladimir, **Workers in Stalin's Russia: Industrialization and Social Change in a Planned Economy**. Sussex: St. Martin's Press, 1988. xii, 243 p. ISBN: 0312023901. Includes index and bibliography (p. 233-236).

"This is a book about Soviet factory workers and the social organization of their labor during the 1930s. It examines the circumstances in which a new working class was formed in the course of that eventful decade, and in which there was established a pattern of interaction between politically instigated campaigns for industrial efficiency on the one hand, and a structure of labor-management relations on the other." (p. ix) The author hopes to shed light on the purges by approaching them from the standpoint of labor. The book is thematically arranged starting with a chapter outlining the major events of the 1930s for the general reader. He then turns to such topics as the changing position of the laborer in Soviet society, the relationship between management and political control, shopfloor interaction and the Stakhanovite movement. Reviews: *Slavic Review* 49:3:456-57. (Fall 1990). *American Historical Journal* 95:3:874 (June 1990). *Russian Review* 48:3:351-52 (July 1989).

854. Bazhanov, Boris, **Bazhanov and the Damnation of Stalin**, translation and commentary by David W. Doyle. Athens: Ohio University Press, 1990. xv, 285 p. ISBN: 0821409484. Includes bibliographical references.

The memoirs of Stalin's assistant and secretary to the Politburo from 1923 to 1925. Bazhanov was also one of the first Soviet defectors, leaving Russia in 1928. He, therefore, was the first to give the West a picture of the new Soviet government, its operations, and its leadership. The book was originally published in a shorter form in 1930. In 1979 Bazhanov provided a longer manuscript, elaborating points that had previously been left vague to protect his friends still in the Soviet Union. The translator notes the value the book still has in the introduction: "The principal value of Bazhanov's work is in the 'feel' that he gives the reader of what the power struggle in the Kremlin was like as Stalin carefully prepared the 'spicy dish' ... that would carry him to the top over the bodies of his semihypnotized competition." (p. xii) The book has extensive notes and a list of the Party Congresses from 1898 to 1986.

855. Danilov, V. P., **Rural Russia Under the New Regime**, translated and introduced by Orlando Figes. Bloomington: Indiana University Press, 1988. 351 p. *Second World Translation Series*, ISBN: 0253350751. Includes index and bibliography (p. 307-342).

A translation of the Russian edition. This is to be the first of a three volume set by Russia's foremost expert on its own peasantry. "*Rural Russia Under the New Regime* is a systematic effort, based on original data, to establish the nature of the Russian peasantry before collectivization. The book centers on land and property in relation to labor and population, making explicit (and claiming) the comparability of post-revolutionary rural Russia to the 'developing societies' of today." (book jacket) The book is organized into three parts: rural population and their economic and social conditions in the 1920s, the characteristics of peasant land and developments in the peasant economy under NEP. The book includes a lengthy introduction by Orlando Figes and a glossary of terms. Reviews: *Agricultural History* 63:3:116-18 (Summer 1989). *Russian History* 16:2-4:476-77 (1989).

856. De Jonge, Alex, **Stalin, and the Shaping of the Soviet Union**. New York: Morrow, 1986. 542 p. ISBN: 0688047300. Includes index and bibliography (p. 493-526).
An examination of the terror used by Stalin to run the Soviet Union. The author considers Stalin to have been a master at using this technique to his own advantage. He notes that Stalin was able to expand the Soviet Empire to its greatest lengths during his tenure. The author traces Stalin's development beginning with his life in Georgia. He has drawn heavily on many sources, but found the British embassy sources to be a particularly rich source, offering a unique perspective on the Stalin years. He feels that much of the analysis of Stalin and the popular reaction to him has been viewed by Westerners as something totally foreign and may be more understandable when viewed from a corporate point of view.

857. Dobson, Christopher, and John Miller, **The Day They Almost Bombed Moscow: The Allied War in Russia, 1918-1920**. 1st ed. New York: Atheneum, 1986. 288 p. ISBN: 0689117132. Includes index and bibliography (p. 277-278).
A history of the Allied intervention in Russia during World War I. The authors attempt to go beyond the biases of both sides and focus on the motivation behind the intervention. A general history of military actions is also provided beginning with the battles of Murmansk and Vladivostok. The book is arranged chronologically. Much of the material was gleaned from the family papers of Western soldiers and émigrés, British war records as well as a limited amount of material made available in the Soviet archives. Review: *Journal of American History* 74:1:208-09 (June 1987).

858. Dziak, John J., **Chekisty: A History of the KGB**, foreword by Robert Conquest. Lexington, Mass.: Lexington Books, 1988. xx, 234 p. ISBN: 066910258X. Includes index and bibliography (p. 207-217).
A history of the Soviet secret police from their creation as the Cheka to the present. The author is concerned with their domestic activities since this book is primarily a "history of the Soviet Union as a counterintelligence state." (p. xvi) The author draws on traditional sources of information in an attempt to present a general study of a subject rarely covered in the literature. The author provides several appendices on the structure and leadership of the KGB. He attempts to show the pervasive influence of the KGB in Soviet society. He includes foreign activities of the KGB only in so far as they affect domestic policies. He sees the secret police as a branch of the Party that allowed for the success of the revolution. Reviews: *Problems of Communism* 39:1:101-08 (January-February 1990). *Journal of Military History* 53:2:203-04 (April 1989).

859. Haigh, R. H., D. S. Morris, and A. R. Peters, **Soviet Foreign Policy, The League of Nations and Europe, 1917-1939**. Totowa, NJ: Barnes & Noble Books, 1986. x, 138 p. ISBN: 0389206113. Includes index and bibliography (p. 129-132).
The role of the Soviet Union in the events leading to World War II is examined in this brief study. The authors focus on how the Soviets, at the time of the revolution and defiantly cut off from the West, came to support the Western Alliance. The book is arranged chronologically, divided into four chapters. The first covers the longest period, 1919-33, tracing the shift in Soviet policy from a revolutionary, isolationist government to a power whose policy was peaceful coexistence. Chapter two follows the events that led up to Soviet membership

in the League of Nations from 1933 to 1955. "Collective security" is tested as Hitler begins his challenge in Abyssinia, the Rhineland, Austria, and Czechoslovakia in 1935-38. The final chapter discusses the motivation behind the Molotov-Ribbentrop Pact. The authors believe that much of what guided the Soviets was their mistrust of the West and their aggressive ideology.

860. Hindus, Maurice Gershon, **Red Bread: Collectivization in a Russian Village,** with foreword by Ronald Grigor Suny. 1st Midland Book ed. Bloomington: Indiana University Press, 1988. xix, 372 p. ISBN: 0253349532. Includes bibliographical references.

A firsthand account of the effects of collectivization originally published in 1931. Hindus believes that the extremes of collectivization, brutal though they were, permitted Russia to industrialize in time to meet the Nazi challenge. The style is that of the personal narrative relying on numerous anecdotes. It is unique in that it draws on direct observations, and in that its author had lived in the village he describes as a young man. Reviews: *Agricultural History* 63:3:110-11 (Summer 1989). *Russian History* 16:2-4:481-82 (1989).

861. **The Policies of Genocide: Jews and Soviet Prisoners of War in Nazi Germany,** edited by Gerhard Hirshchfeld and with an introduction by Wolfgang J. Mommsen. London: Allan & Unwin, 1986. xiii, 172 p. ISBN: 0049430459. Includes bibliographies and index.

The five essays collected in this volume attempt to analyze not only the historical-political motivation behind the murder of 5-1/2 million Jews and 3 million Soviet prisoners of war. They also examine the social and socio-psychological factors that allowed for such genocide. One goal of the volume is to remind the public of what certain types of political systems are capable of. The authors also hope to stimulate debate on the topic. The five essays discuss the German army and its role in the polices of genocide, the ideological work against the Soviet Union, attitudes in the concentration and extermination camps, Hitler's final solution, and its realization. Several appendices are included: a chronology of the holocaust, several maps, and a chart of comparative officer ranks. Reviews: *International Historical Review* 9:3: 479-81 (August 1987). *Slavic Review* 46:2: 310-11 (Summer 1987). *American Historical Review* 92:4:990-91 (October 1987).

862. Hughes, Gwyneth, and Simon Welfare, **Red Empire: The Forbidden History of the USSR,** with an introduction by Robert Conquest. New York: St. Martin's Press, 1990. 200 p. ISBN: 0312052952.

This volume is the printed form of a British program that focused on all the information that was suppressed or distorted during the Soviet regime. The book is chronologically arranged and has numerous photographs.

863. Kochina, Elena I., **Blockade Diary,** translated and introduced by Samuel C. Ramer. Ann Arbor, MI: Ardis, 1990. 112 p. ISBN: 0875010652. Includes bibliographical references (p. 110-112).

A translation of the diary of an ordinary citizen of Leningrad as she and her family tried to survive the first winter of the German blockade of Leningrad, 1941-1942. The diary presents the problems faced by the average individual during that time. It is a unique source of information on Soviet society. The diary was originally published in Russian from 1979-1981 in *Pamiat': Istoricheskii Sbornik.* The translation has provided notations to explain terms and supply contextual information on some statements.

864. Kort, Michael, **The Soviet Colossus: A History of the USSR**. 2nd ed. Boston: Unwin Hyman, 1990. xv, 355 p. ISBN: 0044457626. Includes bibliographical references (p. 331-334) and index.

A popular history of the Soviet system. The author traces the development of the USSR chronologically, beginning with its roots in the tsarist system it replaced. The chapters discuss the development of a highly centralized bureaucracy of the Soviet government and the reasons for its existence. This revised second edition contains long sections on Andropov, Chernenko, and Gorbachev. The author has been necessarily selective in his choice of focus, omitting lengthy discussions of foreign policy. He believes that domestic conditions were of primary significance in shaping the Soviet system. There is also relatively little attention focused on Stalin and the crimes of his regime. This is due to the lack of hard evidence available for historical analysis at the time of his writing. This is not to say that a discussion of that period is lacking, only that it is not the primary focus of the book.

865. Laloy, Jean, **Yalta: Yesterday, Today, Tomorrow**. 1st ed. New York: Harper & Row, 1988. vi, 153 p. ISBN: 0060391057. Includes index and bibliography (p. 147-148).

A brief discussion of the factors that determined the agreement at Yalta. The author believes that some misconceptions have colored the perception of what took place between Stalin, Churchill, and Roosevelt. This book argues that it was Roosevelt's attempts to preserve the agreement he had reached with the Soviet Union earlier that determined the results at Yalta. The book is arranged chronologically, discussing those events that led up to the Yalta conference. Two appendices include the text of the communiqué of the Yalta Conference and the correspondence between Roosevelt and Stalin in April 1945 and Churchill and Stalin in the same period.

866. Leonhard, Wolfgang, **Betrayal: The Hitler-Stalin Pact of 1939**, translated by Richard D. Bosley. 1st ed. New York: St. Martin's Press, 1989. xix, 215 p. ISBN: 0312028687. Includes bibliography (p. 207-215).

The consequences of the Hitler-Stalin Pact and in particular its secret protocol are the subjects of this study. The author discusses the role the pact had in initiating World War II. He also analyzes the division of Eastern Europe agreed upon in the Secret Protocols. A great deal of detail on specific aspects of the pact is provided.

867. **Khrushchev and Khrushchevism**, edited by Martin McCauley. Basingstoke: Macmillan in association with the School of Slavonic and East European Studies University of London, 1987. xii, 243 p. *Studies in Russia and East Europe*, ISBN: 0333434447. Includes index.

A collection of papers originally prepared for a conference in March of 1985. "The object of this volume is to provide an overview of the Khrushchev period for the general reader. Contributors were asked to consider the legacy of the Stalin period, then to analyze the period between 1953 and 1964 and then to asses the legacy, if any, of the Khrushchev years." (p. 2) While the work does not claim to be comprehensive in its coverage, essays discuss state and ideology, industry, science and technology, agriculture, labor problems, social policy, relations with Eastern Europe, foreign policy, and defense. Review: *Slavic Review* 49:2:291-92 (Summer 1990).

868. McClellan, Woodford, **Russia: A History of the Soviet Period**. Englewood Cliffs, NJ: Prentice-Hall, 1986. xi, 387 p. ISBN: 0137844557. Includes bibliographies and index.

McClellan's history of the Soviet period also includes social history discussing "work, leisure time, the arts, education, religion, national minorities, manners and morals, youth, women, science, computers, and automation..." as well as other aspects of contemporary life. (p. ix) Review: *Slavic Review* 46:1:118-22 (Spring 1987).

869. Mulligan, Timothy, **The Politics of Illusion and Empire: German Occupation Policy in the Soviet Union, 1942-43**. New York: Preager, 1988. xiv, 206 p. ISBN: 0275928373. Includes index and bibliography (p. 189-197).

This study examines the problem of the Nazi occupation of the Soviet Union, and why it was unable to capitalize on the population's dissatisfaction with Stalin as Western scholars had expected. This study looks at the situation from the German point of view examining the problems facing the Axis coalition and the strategic problems facing Germany in its multi-front war. The author has attempted to merge a topical and chronological approach. Certain regions of the occupation have been omitted because they did not fall under the German "Eastern Policy." They include Bialystok, Bukovina, Bessarabia, Transnistria, Karelia, and Western Ukraine. Reviews: *Slavic Review* 49:4: 659-60 (Winter 1990). *Journal of Baltic Studies* 21:1:59-62 (Spring 1990).

870. **Battle for Moscow: The 1942 Soviet General Staff Study**, edited by Michael Parrish. Washington, DC: Pergamon-Brassey's, 1989. xi, 210 p. ISBN: 0080359779. Includes index and bibliographical references.

This is a translation of a document in the U.S. national archives. "This is a survey of the battleground as seen by the Red Army's frontline troops, junior commanders, and all the others who suffered the brunt of the fighting. Thus, these pages are not about grandiose battles, but about how to fight in the trenches, in the cold, in rough terrain, and about which weapons to use." (p. x) The volume has been edited to make the text more readable. It includes maps, bibliographic references in the "editor's introduction" and two appendices on the battle.

871. Pethybridge, Roger William, **One Step Backwards, Two Steps Forward: Soviet Society and Politics in the New Economic Policy**. Oxford: Clarendon Press, 1990. xi, 453 p. ISBN: 019821927X. Includes bibliographical references (p. 421-443) and index.

Lenin's New Economic Policy of 1922 and 1926 are the focus of this study. The author believes that by concentrating on the events in provincial areas during this period a new view of the period will emerge. His approach is unusual in that he begins by describing the geography, economy, and society of the provincial areas and then turns to a discussion of aspects of communication and control by the central government. The views of the leading thinkers in Moscow and Petrograd are reviewed next. Linking institutions between center and periphery are then described. The final chapters describe life in Smolensk, Tver, and Kazakhstan. The emphasis in this work is on society, not politics. A chronology is included at the beginning of the book.

872. Rancour-Laferriere, Daniel, **The Mind of Stalin: A Psychoanalytic Study**. Ann Arbor, MI: Ardis, 1988. 161 p. ISBN: 0875010539. Includes index and bibliography (p. 144-154).

A psychoanalyst looks at certain aspects of Stalin's behavior. The author does not attempt to present a biography of Stalin or explain his personality. Rather, he looks at specific aspects of Stalin's mentality; such as the source of his paranoia, his attitudes toward women, feelings concerning homosexuality, the role of mimicry in his life, to name a few. The study is based largely on secondary sources. Reviews: *Russian Review* 49:1:109-10 (January 1990). *Slavic Review* 49:3:458-59 (Fall 1990). *Canadian-American Slavic Studies* 24:4:483-85 (Winter 1990).

873. Rees, E. A., **State Control in Soviet Russia: The Rise and Fall of the Workers' and Peasants Inspectorate, 1920-1934**. Basingstoke: Macmillan, 1987. xv, 315 p. *Studies in Soviet History and Society*, ISBN: 0333436032. Includes bibliography and index.

"The purpose of this study is to examine the political development of the Soviet regime—the growth of the party-state apparatus, the management of policy making, the conduct of factional struggles within the party—through the work of this agency. (Rabkrin—the People's Commissariat of Workers' and Peasants' Inspection)." (p. xiii) This scholarly analysis has drawn heavily on the works of other Western historians. It differs from them in its vantage point, that is, its focus on a previously little examined organization. The volume contains numerous tables and plates and also includes several appendices with information on Rabkrin such as its departmental heads. There is also a glossary of Russian terms, and the study is chronological. Review: *Slavic Review* 47:4:741-42 (Winter 1988).

874. Roberts, Geoffrey K., **The Unholy Alliance: Stalin's Pact with Hitler**. London: Tauris, 1989. xviii, 296 p. ISBN: 1850431272. Includes bibliographical references.

A study of the causes of the Nazi-Soviet Pact. The author "argues that Stalin's decision to temporarily ally himself with Hitler can only be understood in the context of the Soviet Unions failure to force an anti-fascist alliance with the Western democracies." (inside book jacket) The book's chapters can be divided roughly into three sections. The first section is a review of the treatment of the pact in the Soviet literature. Next, the author turns to the historical background of the treaty, examining events from 1917-39 that affected the decision for the alliance. Finally, the author focuses on the events during the years of the pact, 1939-41. There are several appendixes supplying documentary information on the alliance. The author has drawn heavily from the Soviet archival material. There is also a chronology of events from 1933-41 presented before the text of the volume. Reviews: *Soviet Union-Union Sovietique* 17: 1-2:146-49. *Russian Review* 49:3:379-80 (July 1990). *German Studies Review* 13:3:569-70 (October 1990). *Canadian Slavonic Papers* 32:4:494-95 (December 1990).

875. **Battle for Stalingrad: The 1943 Soviet General Staff Study**, edited by Louis C. Rotundo. 1st ed. Washington, DC: Pergamon-Brassey's, 1989. vii, 340 p. ISBN: 0080359744. Includes bibliographical references.

"A concise and thorough operational analysis of the key points of one of the decisive battles of history... the Red army appears in this narrative devoid of its present-day rhetorical trappings" (back cover) The Soviet General Staff's description of this battle focuses on tactics. This is a translation of a document in the U.S. archives. The volume includes maps supplied by the editor as the original maps were not included with the archival copy. The editor has also included an appendix supplying biographical information on the contributors and statistical data on the battle.

876. Siegelbaum, Lewis H., **Stakhanovism and the Politics of Productivity in the USSR, 1935-1941**. Cambridge: Cambridge University Press, 1988. xv, 327 p. *Soviet and East European Studies*, ISBN: 052134580. Includes index and bibliography (p. 309-320).

Finding previous Western and Soviet analyses of Stakhanovism to be lacking, the author has set out to investigate this Soviet method of stimulating productivity. The author does not try to be comprehensive in his analysis and focuses on Stakhanovism in industry. "Hence, the central issue that this study addresses is not whether or to what extent

Stakhanovism increased production but how the issue of raising productivity was handled. This question is treated multidimensionally." (p. 11) The book is arranged topically, beginning with a general discussion of the development of Stakhanovism. The author then treats a variety of issues: the impact on management, sociological aspects of the movement, ideology of Stakhnovism and the fate of the movement, and Stakhanovites after the Great Purges. Three types of sources were used: official documents, biographical accounts, and studies of technology. This is a highly specialized, scholarly account of a complex topic. Reviews: *American Historical Review* 95:2:554-555 (April 1990). *Canadian-American Slavic Studies* 24: 4:481-83 (Winter 1990). *Russian Review* 48:2:2-4-05 (April 1989). *Russian History* 16:2-4:482-83 (1989).

877. Smith, Bradley F., **The War's Long Shadow: The Second World War and Its Aftermath: China, Russia, Britain, America**. New York: Simon and Schuster, 1986. 319 p. ISBN: 0671524348. Includes index and bibliography (p. 303-308).

The relationship between the political, economic, and social mobilization of World War II and the post war environment are the focus of this study. Using a chronological approach, the author analyzes the events in China, Britain, the Soviet Union, and America before and immediately after the War looking for the roots of the redistribution of power which took place at that time. The author believes that the wartime experience of each nation sets the limits within which it would later be forced to function. He also feels that attention to ideological issues has drawn the focus away from the real motivation behind the Cold War. The author has written numerous works on World War II.

878. **The Soviet Takeover of the Polish Eastern Provinces, 1934- 41**, edited by Keith Sword. New York: St. Martin's Press, 1991. xxiii, 318 p. ISBN: 0312055706. Includes bibliographical references and index.

Polish and Western scholars contributed essays to this volume based on papers delivered at a 1989 conference held at the University of London to mark the fiftieth anniversary of the Soviet takeover of Eastern Poland. The essays cover numerous topics related to the takeover but not all areas or viewpoints are covered. This volume is intended "...both to draw attention to the nature and consequences of the Soviet takeover and to encourage others to look at the events in more detail." (p. xx) Essays are included on the Polish-Soviet War of 1939, the situation of the refugees, sociological, economic, and cultural aspects of the takeover. The new openness afforded by glasnost is evidenced by the contribution of Polish scholars. Three appendices are included. One on world press reaction to the takeover, a second on Soviet accounts of the Red Army in Poland, and the last contains numerous documents on mass deportations.

879. Walker, Martin, **The Waking Giant: Gorbachev's Russia**. 1st American ed. New York: Pantheon Books, 1987. xxviii, 298 p. ISBN: 0394552393. Includes index and bibliographical references.

Walker, a British journalist for the *Guardian*, went to Moscow in 1984 as that paper's third resident Moscow correspondent. His narrative is an intensely interesting portrayal of the Moscow of the mid 1980s, especially after Gorbachev came to power. He covers virtually every aspect of Soviet life from the party and the leadership, the KGB, economics, and the technological revolutions to changing lifestyles, the status of Soviet women, and Chernobyl.

MILITARY AFFAIRS

Handbooks, Encyclopedias, Bibliographies

880. **The Voroshilov Lectures: Materials from the Soviet General Staff Academy,** edited by Graham Hall Turbiville, Jr., with an introduction by Raymond L. Garthoff. Washington, DC: National Defense University Press, 1989. 2 v. Includes index.

Colonel Ghulam Dastagir Wardak, an Afghan military officer in attendance at the Voroshilov General Staff Academy, managed to transcribe and smuggle out the lectures presented there. They focus on theory and practice, relating to strategy, operations, and tactics. This edition provides the English speaking reader with invaluable insight into Soviet military education and policy.

General Studies

881. Adelman, Jonathan R., **Prelude to the Cold War: The Tsarist, Soviet, and U.S. Armies in the Two World Wars**. Boulder, CO: L. Rienner, 1988. viii, 287 p. ISBN: 1555871232. Includes index and bibliography (p 261-176)

Adelman, "explores, in a comparative framework, the military histories of the armies of the two future superpowers in World Wars I and II. This allows him to incorporate the military in the discussion of the origins of U.S.-Soviet tensions, a discussion more typically denumerated by political, economic, and diplomatic approaches." (p. 287)

882. **The Soviet Union and Northern Waters**, edited by Clive Archer. London: Routledge for the Royal Institute of International Affairs, 1988. xvii, 261 p. ISBN: 0415004896. Includes bibliographical references and index.

A collection of essays by a 1985 International Colloquium on increased Soviet activity in Northern Waters held at the University of Aberdeen. The contributors are both policymakers and academics. "This book is about the presence of the Soviet Union in Northern Waters. After a general overview (chapter 2) it covers the legal aspects (chapters 3 and 4), resource questions (chapter 5), and the strategic implications of that presence (chapters 6 and 7). Also examined are the responces of the major Western states with interests in the area (chapters 8, 9, 10, and 11)." (p. 2)

883. Brement, Marshall, **Reaching Out to Moscow: From Confrontation to Cooperation**, foreword by Claiborne Pell. New York: Praeger, 1991. ix, 191 p. ISBN: 027594073X. Includes bibliographic references (p. 179-183) and index.

Brement describes how the military-industrial complexes of both the U.S. and the former Soviet Union should be dismantled, at least in part in order to get "rid of the American threat in the Soviet Union and the Soviet threat in this country." (p. vii) The author "sets forward a grand strategy for its accomplishment, encompassing political, military, economic, and diplomatic fronts." (p. vii)

884. **The Soviet Military Power in a Changing World**, edited by Susan L. Clark. Boulder, CO: Westview Press, 1991. xiv, 324 p. ISBN: 081338379X. Includes bibliographical references and index.

The contributors to this volume explore many of the issues and problems facing the Soviet military in a changing security environment. Some of the topics include the crisis in Soviet military reform, military acquisition, defense conversion, the military personnel system, and ethnic tensions in the armed forces.

885. Glantz, David M., **Soviet Military Operational Art: In Pursuit of Deep Battle**. London, England: F. Cass, 1991. xxiv, 295 p. *Soviet Military Theory and Practice*, ISBN: 071463347X. Includes index and bibliography (p. 267-289).
A study of Soviet operational thinking, tracing its development since 1917. The author has produced other works on this topic and lectures on Soviet military topics. "This book represents a distillation of Colonel Glantz's research and study of the evolution of Soviet operational techniques and force structure within the context of Soviet military art and science." (p. xvii) The format is both topical and chronological, allowing the reader to study the development of various aspects of the Soviet military. Numerous tables accompany the text. Review: *Military Review* 71:12:90-91 (December 1991).

886. Kintner, William Roscoe, **Soviet Global Strategy**. Fairfax, Va.: Hero Books, 1987. xv, 273 p. *A National Security Policy Paper*, ISBN: 0915979209. Includes bibliographies and index.
"This book outlines and addresses the total threat which Soviet Communism presents to democracy and political freedom around the globe. The first three chapters trace the development of Soviet strategy. Chapter IV summarizes the Soviet record of intrusion and expansion into every region of the world, with particular emphasis placed on the last decade. From this record the general parameters of Soviet strategy are then deduced in chapter V. The final chapter forecasts Soviet strategic options for the rest of this century—which may prove to be the most crucial years of this tumultuous century." (p. xiv)

887. Macgregor, Douglas A., **The Soviet-East German Military Alliance**. Cambridge: Cambridge University Press, 1989. xi, 178 p. ISBN: 0521365627. Includes bibliographical references (p. 138-61).
"This book is about the nature and political consequences of institutionalized military cooperation between the East German and Soviet States in Central-East Europe." (p. ix) He examines the origins of cooperation prior to WWI, Nazi-Soviet collaboration, the East German rise to military prominence from 1956-1969, their collaboration in the post-1968 period, and the military alliance and Poland. An appendix includes nine data tables dealing with events, military capabilities, trade, defense expenditures, GNP, and manpower.

888. MccGwire, Michael, **Military Objectives in Soviet Foreign Policy**. Washington, DC: Brookings Institution, 1987. xiv, 530 p. ISBN: 0815755511 (pbk.), 081575552X. Includes bibliographic references and index.
"Rather than viewing the Soviet military posture from the perspective of the West, Michael MccGwire focuses on the Soviet viewpoint and way of thinking. He shows how the need to plan for the contingency of world war has shaped Soviet policy, resulting in a force structure often perceived as far in excess of legitimate defense needs." (p. vii) His book is divided into three parts. In part one, he describes and analyzes the genesis of Soviet strategic objectives. In part two, he examines the operational plans in various regions (Euro-Atlantic, Asian-Pacific, and Indo-Arabian). In part three, he explores contemporary concerns such as military objectives in the Third World, arms control, and the changing international environment. Four appendices dealing with the December 1966 decision over change in strategy, naval rules, and strategic rocket forces are also included. Reviews: *Airpower Journal* 2:1:83-84 (Spring 1988). *International Security* 12:3:203-14 (Winter 1987-88). *JPMS* 16:1:117-21 (Spring 1988). *American Academy of Political and Social Science Annals* 497:177-78 (May 1988).

889. **The Impoverished Superpower: Perestroika and the Soviet Military Burden**, edited by Henry S. Rowen and Charles Wolf, Jr. San Francisco, Calif.: ICS Press, 1990. xiv, 372 p. ISBN: 155815-668. Includes bibliographical references and index.
The effects of the shrinking Soviet economic base on the Soviet military is the subject taken up by the contributors to this collection of essays. The authors believe this puts perestroika and the impetus for reform in a new light. Essays focus on the Soviet national income, interpreting statistics, military spending, Soviet weapons acquisitions, research and development in the Soviet Union among numerous other topics.

890. Scott, Harriet Fast, and William F. Scott, **Soviet Military Doctrine: Continuity, Formulation, and Dissemination**. Boulder, CO: Westview Press, 1988. ISBN: 081330671X (pbk.), 0813306566. Includes indexes and bibliography.
Soviet military doctrine is analyzed here as "the military policy of the Communist Party." (p. x) The book is divided into four parts. The first traces the history and development of Soviet military policy from 1917 through the mid 1980s. This part also includes a chapter on the laws of war. Part two looks at the roles of the Communist Party and the government in the formulation of military policy and at the dissemination of that policy. There are several appendices on military members of the Central Committee, military holidays, official books, etc.... The authors have drawn primarily on Soviet sources in their analysis. Review: *Naval War College Review* 42:4:119-22 (Autumn 1989).

891. Van Dyke, Carl, **Russian Imperial Military Doctrine and Education, 1832-1914**. New York: Greenwood Press, 1990. xvi, 193 p. *Contributions in Military Studies*, no. 105. ISBN: 0313272492. Includes bibliographical references (p. 165-179).
"The purpose of the present work is to document the evolution of the military-theoretical tradition at the Nicholas Academy of the General Staff during a century fraught with tremendous technological innovation, wars in an increasingly tense international arena, and governmental reform in the face of growing social, economic, and political unrest throughout the Empire." (p. xv-xvi)

892. Vigor, Peter Hast, **The Soviet View of Disarmament**. New York: St. Martin's Press, 1986. vii, 189 p. ISBN: 0312749163. Includes index and bibliography (p. 173-182).
An analysis of disarmament in an era without détente. The author, viewing the poor relations between the U.S. and USSR during the Reagan administration evaluates the effect this will have on Soviet attitudes toward disarmament. He assumes that Soviet disarmament policy has in the past been one based on self- interest, as one would expect. The two major factors are Soviet security and the national liberation struggle. The book traces Soviet disarmament policy from 1917 through 1980. It is divided into two parts. The first provides a general introduction to the theory of Soviet disarmament. The second details Soviet attitudes toward general, complete, and partial disarmament as they have developed since 1917 and been affected by World War II and the introduction of nuclear weapons. The author does not try to justify the policies described, only to present their evolution. Review: *Naval War College Review* 40:4:116 (Autumn 1987).

893. Wirtschafter, Elise Kimerling, **From Serf to Russian Soldier**. Princeton, NJ: Princeton University Press, 1990. xix, 214 p. ISBN: 0691044858. Includes index and bibliographical references (p. 199-208).
"This study represents the first attempt to write a social history of the common soldier based on extensive archival research. The first task is to describe concretely the social condition of the lower ranks, to identify the basic parameter of the soldier's daily life.... The second task is to define the norms of 'military society,' explore the mental characteristics of the

soldier—his attitudes, expectations, and behavioral patterns. Finally... this study provides insights into the relationship between the state and society, especially the problem of modernization in the context of a traditional, though highly fluid social structure." (p. xv-xvi)

To 1917

894. McNeal, Robert Hatch, **Tsar and Cossack, 1855-1914**. New York: St. Martin's Press, 1987. 262 p. ISBN: 0312821883. Includes index and bibliography (p. 227-256).
"Despite their diversity, to which this book cannot do justice, the Cossacks in the later Russian Empire were all part of a single system. This is a book about that system, and anachronistic military-civil-economic order that emerged in its final form in the last half of the nineteenth century and struggled on, increasingly beset by the travails of modernization, until the crisis of the First World War." (p. 22) Reviews: *American Historical Review* 93:3:738-39 (June 1988). *Russian Review* 47:2:188-89 (April 1988). *History: Review of New Books* 15:5:157 (May-June-July-August 1987). *Slavic Review* 47:4:733-34 (Winter 1988).

895. Nightingale, Florence, **"I have done my duty": Florence Nightingale in the Crimean War, 1854-56**. Manchester: Manchester University Press, 1987. 326 p. ISBN: 0719019605. Includes index and bibliography (p. 305-306).
Of the three hundred letters that survive from the 18 months Florence Nightingale spent in the Crimea at Balclava and on the Bosphorus at Scutari, editor Sue Goldie has reprinted approximately one hundred here. The collection is presented in eight chapters that include letters linked together chronologically and contextually by extensive editorial comments. Together they portray very vividly what life in any hospital was like during the Crimean War. A document by David Fitzgerald, Purveyor to the Forces, describes the nursing system in the Crimea, from its inception in January of 1855 to at least the autumn of that year.

1917 to Present

896. **Main Front: Soviet Leaders Look Back on World War II**, foreward by Marshal of the Soviet Union Sokolov; commentary by John Erickson. 1st English Language ed. London: Brassey's Defense Publishers, 1987. 330 p. ISBN: 0080312179. Includes bibliography (p. 329-330).
This is a book of abstracts from published war memoirs, all written by Soviet generals and other military leaders. Each of them recounts a major battle in the war, including the defense of Moscow, Stalingrad, the Leningrad siege, the fall of Berlin, and the campaigns in the Far East.

897. **Contemporary Soviet Military Affairs: The Legacy of World War II**, edited by Jonathan R. Adelman and Christann Lea Gibson. Boston: Unwin Hyman, 1989. viii, 193 p. ISBN: 044450311, 0044450516 (pbk.). Includes bibliographical references.
The contributors to this volume attempt to understand the effects of World War II on contemporary Soviet military affairs. Their essays are arranged in three parts. Part I, "Relevance of History," looks at military history, the experiences of the Great Patriotic War, and Soviet staff structure and planning. Part II, "World War II and the Present," examines Soviet risk taking in major post-war crises, economic and military mobilization, the Soviet defense industry, and wartime decision making and control. Part III, "Implications

for the Future," evaluates the impact of World War II on our contemporary Soviet military theory.

898. Bocharov, Gennadii Nikolaevich, **Russian Roulette: Afghanistan through Russian Eyes**. 1st ed. New York: Harper Collins, 1990. 187 p. *"A Cornelia and Michael Bessie Book,"* ISBN: 0060391103. Includes index.

A Russian journalist, long stationed in Kabul, describes the Afghan War. The author's "articles showed a consistent disregard for official recommendations and were celebrated as among the few sources of genuine information about the Afghan war." (p. 1)

899. Cooper, Leo, **The Political Economy of Soviet Military Power**, with foreword by Murray Wolfson. Basingstoke: Macmillan, 1989. xi, 263 p. ISBN: 0333472799. Includes index and bibliography (p. 241-254).

The author maintains that "war and preparations for war involve the allocation of economic resources." (p. viii) With this premise Cooper proceeds to introduce the reader to the political economy of the arms race, the theory and practice of Soviet military thought, economic power and national security, the assessment of Soviet military resources, technology transfer, the propaganda war and the influence of glasnost and perestroika. In all he manages to depict with clarity the relationship between the economic and political and military institutions.

900. **Soviet Military Doctrine and Western Policy**, edited by Gregory Flynn. London: Routledge, 1989. xi, 418 p. ISBN: 0415004888. Includes bibliographical references and index.

Analysts of the Soviet system have always argued about Soviet policy and the rationales underlying those policies. This book "has attempted to understand both the origins and nature of the controversy over Soviet military doctrine, as well as how the West should attempt to relate Soviet thinking to its own military and arms control planning." (p. x) Review: *Foreign Affairs* 69: 2:169 (Spring 1990).

901. Gareev, Makhmut Akhmetovich, **M.V. Frunze, Military Theorist**. 1st ed. Washington, DC: Pergamon-Brassey's, 1988. xiii, 402 p. ISBN: 0080351832.

This translation from the Russian traces the development of Frunze's military theories. More importantly it, "...is especially noteworthy not because of its historical value, but, rather, because of the insight it provides on current Soviet military thinking." (p. vii) Chapters cover topics such as the elaboration of Soviet military doctrine, contributions to the theory of military art, organizational development of the armed forces, military indoctrination, and Lenin's influence on Frunze.

902. Hansen, James H., **Correlation of Forces: Four Decades of Soviet Military Development**. New York: Praeger, 1987. xix, 236 p. ISBN: 0275926575. Includes index and bibliography (p. 205-211).

This book is a database, covering the years 1946-1986, of factual data points. These data points include: milestones of Soviet military development, leadership and organization, economic-technical base and military industrial developments, geopolitical events, U.S./NATO developments and Soviet-U.S. encounters, data on weapons and forces, doctrine, and field training exercises. In addition, the author has analyzed several key years of particular significance. Review: *US Naval Institution Proceedings* 114:12:139-41 (1988).

903. Kumar, Lal Chand, **The Soviet Union and European Security**. New Delhi: Radiant Publishers, 1987. ix, 329 p. ISBN: 8170271053. Includes index and bibliography (p. 289-318).

Kumar's purpose is to examine the Soviet attitude toward European security. After presenting the framework of theoretical and historical antecedents, he covers the early phase (1946-1965) of the Soviet attitude to European security, the 1966 Budapest proposals, events leading up to and including the Conference on European Security, and post-Helsinki Europe.

904. Lee, William Thomas, and Richard F. Staar, **Soviet Military Policy Since World War II,** with foreword by William R. Van Cleave. Stanford, Calif.: Hoover Institution Press, Stanford University, 1986. xxii, 263 p. *Hoover Press Publication,* no. 330. ISBN: 0817983015. Includes index and bibliography (p. 249-258).

Lee and Staar explain the basis of Soviet military policy since W.W. II. "The basic thesis of this book is that official military doctrine and strategy clearly state both the reasons for and the objectives of the USSR military build up. The essence of Soviet military policy is to attain the forces required by its doctrine and strategy, the final objectives of which are to be prepared to fight and win war at all levels, including a nuclear war." (p. 2) The authors include an appendix on SALT. Reviews: *Political Science Quarterly* 102:1:134-35 (Spring 1987). *Slavic Review* 46:1:137-38 (Spring 1987). *American Academy of Political and Social Science Annals* 494:174-75 (November 1987).

905. **Soviet Military Policy: An International Security Reader,** edited by Sean M. Lynn-Jones, Steven E. Miller, and Stephen Van Evera. Cambridge, Mass.: MIT Press, 1989. xiii, 374 p. ISBN: 0262121425. Includes bibliographic references.

This series of essays by various authors provides up to date analysis on the foreign policy context of Soviet military policy, nuclear weapons, and Soviet doctrine, and Soviet conventional weapons strategy.

906. Moynahan, Brian, **Claws of the Bear: The History of the Red Army from the Revolution to the Present.** Boston: Houghton Mifflin, 1989. xx, 468 p. ISBN: 0395510767. Includes bibliographical references and index.

A serious analysis of the Soviet military. The book has a chronological arrangement beginning with the revolution and the birth of the Red Army. There is a lengthy discussion of the Soviet military as it functioned during World War II and the role of the military in more recent times in Hungary, Germany, Czechoslovakia, Poland, and Afghaninstan. The current state of the military is the subject of one of the final sections, analyzing all branches of the military, the use of spies by the army, and the strength of the Warsaw Pact.

907. Rhodes, Benjamin D., **The Anglo-American Winter War with Russia, 1918-1919: A Diplomatic and Military Tragicomedy.** New York: Greenwood Press, 1988. xii, 156 p. ISBN: 0313261326. Includes index and bibliography (p. 145-149).

Rhodes chronicles the weak Anglo-American intervention at Archangel, Russia in 1918-1919. As the author notes it was "unusually inept as it was based upon misinformation, profound geographical and political misconceptions, and a generous supply of wishful thinking." (p. ix) The intervention was viewed by the British as a way of opening up the eastern front against Germany. It failed. Rhodes provides an enlightening account of both the military and diplomatic aspects of this unfortunate debacle. Reviews: *American Historical Review* 94:5:1349 (December 1989). *International Historical Review* 11:3:568-69 (August 1989).

Navy

908. Amundsen, Kristen, **Soviet Strategic Interests in the North**. New York: St.
Martin's Press, 1990. 153 p. ISBN: 0312041896. Includes bibliographical
references.

Amundsen believes that "there is sufficient dissonance between continuing Soviet force
levels, military concepts and activity levels on the one hand and encouraging expressions
of defense and détente from Soviet leaders on the other, at least to raise a few doubts about
how readily and quickly the West should respond to demands at home and abroad for a
reduction in its current defense spending and force levels. ... [The book] acts as a valuable
corrective to increasingly fashionable views amongst Western analysts and politicians
about the rapid disappearance of any real Soviet threat." (p. ix)

909. Da Cuhna, Derek, **Soviet Naval Power in the Pacific**. Boulder, CO: L. Rienner,
1990. xii, 284 p. ISBN: 1555871763. Includes index and bibliographical references
(p. 259-273).

"This book focuses on just one geographic component of the naval branch of the Soviet
military institution. It is a book on the changing nature of Soviet naval power in the Pacific
since the late 1970s; and it contends that over the last decade the mission priorities of the
Soviet Pacific Fleet have been restructured from those demonstrated as late as 1975." (p.
x)

910. **The Sources of Soviet Naval Conduct**, edited by Philip S. Gillette and Willard C.
Frank, with a foreword by Ronald J. Kurth. Lexington, Ma: Lexington Books, 1990.
xiv, 295 p. ISBN: 066210730. Includes bibliographical references.

These essays were originally presented at a conference at Old Dominion University in May
1987. "This book examines the broader and enduring contexts, mind-sets, and tendencies
that, whether Gorbachev succeeds or fails, will likely combine with developments and
innovation to reform future Soviet naval conduct." (p. xv)

911. **Superpower Maritime Strategy in the Pacific**, edited by Frank C. Langdon and
Douglas A. Ross. London: Routledge, 1990. xvii, 295 p. ISBN: 0415043875.
Includes bibliographical references.

The contributors to this volume focus on the issues engendered by the confrontation of the
two superpowers in the Pacific area. The essays are grouped under the headings Soviet
issues and concerns, American issues and concerns, and regional issues and concerns. The
editors conclude with a chapter on alliance changes in the Gorbachev era.

912. Leitenberg, Milton, **Soviet Submarine Operations in Swedish Waters, 1980-
1986**, foreword by Lawrence Freedman. New York: Praeger Publishers, 1987. xi,
199 p. *Washington Papers*, no. 128. ISBN: 027592842X (pbk.), 0275928411.
Includes index.

Leitenberg examines the issues surrounding the discovery of a Soviet Whisky-class submarine in Swedish waters in 1981. He details the overall incidence of violations from
1970-1986, analogous events in other countries, events in Sweden, and a geopolitical
analysis of the incursions.

913. Ranft, Bryan, and Geoffrey Till, **The Sea in Soviet Strategy**. 2nd ed. Basingstoke:
Macmillan, 1989. xviii, 284 p. ISBN: 0333440293. Includes index and bibliography
(p. 267-276).

This new edition of *The Sea in Soviet Strategy* has attempted to incorporate the changes in
foreign policy since Brezhnev's death and Admiral Chernarvin's accession to the position

of Commander and Chief of the Soviet Navy. The topical arrangement covers aspects of the sea in Soviet military strategy from the foreign policy implications to a discussion of the makeup of the Soviet Navy. The development of the Navy from the time of the revolution is also described. "We have tried in this relatively short book to show how the Soviet Union's maritime policies have emerged from the country's general political and ideological background to analyze the specialized research in a way which we hope will enable the readers to clarify for themselves the issues already raised and to identify the most important future developments to watch for." (p. xiv) There are numerous illustrations of Soviet naval vessels and a lengthy bibliography of primarily Western language sources.

914. **Soviet Seapower in Northern Waters: Facts, Motivation, Impact, and Responses**, edited by John Kristen Skogan and Arne Olav Brundtland. New York: St. Martin's Press, 1990. 198 p. *Studies in Contemporary Maritime Policy Strategy*, ISBN: 0312041799.

These essays examine Soviet seapower and its effects on its neighbors. The essays are grouped into four sections. "In the first section of the book, the growth and motivation of Soviet seapower are explored. In the second section, its impact on some of the states of North West Europe is addressed. In the third section, some of the Western responses are discussed." (p. viii)

915. **The Future of the Soviet Navy: An Assessment to the Year 2000**, edited by Bruce W. Watson and Peter M. Dunn. Boulder, CO: Westview Press, 1986. xvii, 157 p. *Westview Special Studies on the Soviet Union and Eastern Europe, 1063-6057*, ISBN: 0813371708. Includes bibliographies and index.

Several experts have contributed essays to this analysis of the future development of the Soviet Navy. Topics covered include Soviet submarine development, aircraft carriers in the Soviet Navy, small Soviet naval combatants, naval mine warfare, and the evolution of naval strategy. "This volume addresses whether the Soviet Union will continue naval expansion and what directions technological development will take in the future." (p. iii)

916. **The Soviet Naval Threat to Europe: Military and Political Dimensions**, edited by Bruce W. Watson and Susan M. Watson. Boulder, CO: Westview Press, 1989. xix, 383 p. *Westview Special Studies on the Soviet Union and Eastern Europe*, ISBN: 0813376645. Includes bibliographical references.

The purpose of this book is to provide an accurate assessment of the Soviet naval threat to Europe. The essays are arranged in five sections: 1. strategy; 2. hardware; 3. operations; 4. the threat to Northern Europe; and 5. the threat to Southern Europe. The contributors are from both sides of the Atlantic. In order to clarify the discussion, the editors have included several appendices that contain order of battle information for several fleets to which all contributors make reference. Reviews: *Fletcher Forum of World Affairs* 14:1:209-11 (Winter 1990). *Soviet Union-Union Sovietique* 17:1-2:187-89 (1990).

917. **The Soviet Navy: Its Strengths and Liabilities**, edited by Bruce W. Watson and Susan M. Watson. Boulder, CO: Westview Press, 1986. xv, 333 p. *Westview Special Studies on the Soviet Union and Eastern Europe*, ISBN: 0865317674. Includes index and bibliography (p. 300-314).

A collection of essays by academics and naval analysts intended to provide a profile of the Soviet navy as it has developed and the possibilities for its use in the future. "This book offers a detailed assessment of every major aspect of the Soviet Navy, from fleet structure and training to command and control procedures and warfare and intelligence collection capabilities." (p. iii) The essays are divided into five groups covering the topics of tradition and personnel, equipment, operational capabilities, operations, and future developments. There are numerous tables and illustrations as well as a selected bibliography.

Special Studies

918. **The Changing U.S.-Soviet Strategic Balance: January 24-26, 1990, Moscow, USSR**, co-sponsored by the International Security Council and the Academy of Sciences of the USSR; in collaboration with the Central Committee of the CPSU and the General Staff of the Armed Forces of the USSR. Washington, DC: International Security Council, 1990. 19 p.

This pamphlet contains summaries of discussions between American and Soviet military experts. On the American side, these experts were primarily retired military officers. On the Soviet side, the participants were active duty military personnel. The discussions took place outside of Moscow in January 1990 and provide insights into mutual perceptions about the capabilities and strategies of both sides.

919. **Combat in Russian Forests and Swamps**. Facsimile ed. Washington, DC: Center of Military History, U.S. Army, 1986. vi, 39 p. *CMH Publications*, no. 104-2.

One in a series of U.S. government reports, compiled by the military using information from a committee of former German generals. Besides the information provided on military tactics to be used in certain areas under specific conditions in Europe, many of the attitudes of the German military toward the Russians are also revealed. An effort was made to maintain the tone of the German's original report and many of their attitudes are apparent in the text.

920. **Military Improvisations During the Russian Campaign**. Facsimile ed. Washington, DC: Center of Military History, U.S. Army, 1986. vi, 110 p.

One of a series of reports issued by the U.S. military, drawing on the experiences of a committee of former German generals. A preface by a representative of the U.S. military is provided. The remainder of the study reflects the prejudices of the German military. "The present study lays no claim to comprehensiveness, but even this fragmentary account may show the main characteristics of German improvisations and the part they played in military operations. The many separate examples are presented along functional lines, and the material is subdivided into tactical, logistical, technical, and organizational improvizations." (p. 3).

921. **Terrain Factors in the Russian Campaign**. Facsimile ed. Washington, DC: Center of Military History, U.S. Army, 1986. 60 p. *CMH Publication*, no. 104-5.

One of a series of reports issued by the U.S. military, drawing on the experiences of a committee of former German generals. A preface by a representative of the U.S. military is provided. The remainder of the report reflects the prejudices of the German military. A detailed description of the Russian terrain along with descriptions of tactics and accompanying maps make up this study of the German's attempt to deal with the difficult Russian terrain.

922. Adams, James, **Secret Armies: Inside the American, Soviet and European Special Forces**. New York: Atlantic Monthly Press, 1988. 440 p. ISBN: 0871132230. Includes index and bibliography (p. 417-420).

The rise of the role of special forces units is the subject of this book. Soviet special forces are not the main focus of this work, however several topics of interest to the student of Soviet armies are treated. Soviet policies on special forces' use, strategy, training, and specific examples of their use are all discussed. The author also analyzes the effects of interaction between the special forces of various countries. A list of several operations is provided in the appendix. A glossary and definition of terms is also included.

923. Almquist, Peter, **Red Forge: Soviet Military Industry Since 1965**. New York: Columbia University Press, 1990. xi, 227 p. ISBN: 0231070667. Includes index and bibliographical references (p. 201-219).

Almquist examines the Soviet defense industry since 1965. Gorbachev had touted the Soviet defense industry as a model for efficiency, quality, and mission research. Many of his civilian economic sector appointments were made by choosing from Soviet defense industry leaders. The author describes and analyzes the organizational context and work of the defense plant manager, the weapons scientist and the designer, and the defense industrial ministry. Appendices provide additional information about defense ministries and the personnel who work in them.

924. Baxter, William, **Soviet Airland Battle Tactics**. Navato, CA: Presidio Press, 1986. v, 269 p. ISBN: 0891411607. Includes bibliographies and index.

"The purpose of this book is to describe how the Soviet army thinks about itself, and how it intends to perform on the battlefield. The motivation is to make Soviet tactics comprehensible from a Soviet point of view." (p. 1) Baxter covers tactical theory, the relation of the soldier and the state, command and staff, offense and defense, supporting operations, force support, logistics, prognosis, and predictions. Review: *Military Review* 67:3:94-95 (March 1987).

925. Bluth, Christoph, **New Thinking in Soviet Military Policy**. New York: Council on Foreign Relations Press, 1990. 118 p. *Chatham House Papers*, ISBN: 0876090862. Includes bibliographical references.

Bluth examines all aspects of Soviet military doctrine, the sources of Soviet security policy, strategic arms policy, Soviet strategic defense, theater nuclear weapons, conventional force planning, and the future of East-West relations.

926. Center of Military History, **Effects of Climate on Combat in European Russia**. Washington, DC: Center of Military History, 1986. v, 81 p. *Historical Study, CMH Publication*, no. 104-6.

One of several government studies drawing on the experiences of German generals during World War II. This study focuses on the role of climate in determining combat strategies and techniques. "To this end the climate of the various regions is described together with its effects on men and equipment, combat and supply. Parts two, three and four are concerned with European Russia south of the Arctic circle; part five treats European Russian north of the Arctic Circle. The study emphasizes the lessons learned and improvisations employed to surmount difficult situations." (p. 1)

927. Cimbala, Stephen J., **Conflict Termination in Europe: Games Against War**. New York: Praeger, 1990. xxiv, 268 p. ISBN: 0027593592. Includes bibliographical references (p. 255-257) and index.

This theoretical study poses the question: How may an armed conflict in Europe be stopped? In answering this question for the present day, the author examines the various issues surrounding deterrence, preemption, military stability in general, Soviet war strategy for Europe, and mutual assured destruction. The author hopes that by "planning for war termination before the event begins may prevent a bad situation from getting worse." (p. xxi)

928. **Western Europe in Soviet Global Strategy**, edited by Ray S. Cline, James Arnold Miller, and Roger E. Kanet. Boulder, CO: Westview, 1987. vii, 166 p. *Westview Special Studies on the Soviet Union and Eastern Europe*, ISBN: 0813374804. Includes bibliographies and index.

The contributors to this volume "describe the USSR's land and sea targets in and surrounding West Europe, where the Soviet Union systematically engages its political, economic and military instruments of national power to expand its strength." (p. vii)

929. Cohen, Richard, and Peter A. Wilson, **Superpowers in Economic Decline: U.S. Strategy for the Transcentury Era**. New York: Crane Russak, 1990. xi, 276 p. ISBN: 0844816248. Includes index and bibliographical references (p. 260-266).

Cohen's thesis is that in the 1990s and early 21st century economic performance will cause radical alterations in the security environment of the United States. His task in this book, therefore, is to elucidate the parameters of the U.S. national security environment so as to produce approximate strategies for the 1990s. To do this, Cohen poses and answers several questions relating to the causes of the long-term economic decline of both superpowers, to the policies implemented in order to deal with the "economic dimension of security vulnerability" and to the effect of recent policies by Gorbachev and Reagan on each superpower's economic performance and security. He concludes by recommending the components and costs of "transcentury weapons" and the implications of rising costs for modern forces.

930. Collins, John M., **Green Berets, Seals and Spetsnaz: U.S. and Soviet Special Military Operations**. Washington, DC: Pergamon-Brassey's, 1987. xvi, 174 p. ISBN: 0080357466 (pbk.), 0080357474. Includes index.

Collins compares U.S. and Soviet priorities, establishments (high command and control, force postures), concepts and priorities (insurgency, cold war, counterinsurgency), and U.S. problems and options. The compendium "is intended as a tool to help U.S. policy makers and planners determine the optimum civilian/ military mix, size, structure, and characteristics of U.S. special operations forces, together with proper doctrines, strategies, and tactics, for their employment." (p.2)

931. **Soviet Strategic Deception**, edited by Brian D. Dailey and Patrick J. Parker. Stanford, Calif.: Hoover Institution Press, 1987. xx, 538 p. ISBN: 066913208X. Includes index.

This collection of essays explores several key areas where the Soviets practice deception for strategic purposes and the means used to effect that deception. The essays are arranged in six parts: 1. Soviet organizational structure for deception and active measures; 2. language, ideology, and diplomacy; 3. arms control and verification; 4. the Soviet military and maskirovka; 5. regional deception; and 6. deception and strategic planning.

932. Erickson, John, Lynn Hansen, and William Schneider, **Soviet Ground Forces: An Operational Assessment**. Boulder, CO: Westview Press, 1986. xix, 267 p. ISBN: 0891587969. Includes index and bibliography (p. 249-257).

Erickson and his authors assess "the methods by which the Soviet forces conduct operations and the standards they set for themselves." (p. xv) After an introductory assessment of Soviet ground forces the authors turn their attention to the evolution of Soviet ground forces 1941-85, Soviet operational procedures, norms, the air component, and speculations about the future of Soviet ground operations. Reviews: *Military Review* 67:6:90 (June 1987). *Parameters* 17:1:122-23 (Spring 1987). *Canadian Slavonic Papers* 29:2-3:321-22 (June-September 1987).

933. **Gorbachev and His Generals: The Reform of Soviet Military Doctrine**, edited by William C. Green and Theodore Karasik. Boulder, CO: Westview Press, 1990. viii, 239 p. ISBN: 08133789982. Includes index.

These essays are held together by a common theme: what effects have the changes occurring in Soviet society had on Soviet military doctrine and the conduct of military affairs? These domestic changes have been mirrored to some degree within the Soviet military itself. The conclusions of the various authors point to a change in U.S.-Soviet relations in general.

934. Herspring, Dale R., **The Soviet High Command, 1967-1989: Personalities and Politics**. Princeton, NJ: Princeton University Press, 1990. xv, 322 p. ISBN: 0691078440. Includes bibliographical references.

Herspring analyzes the relationship between Soviet politicians and Soviet generals. After two introductory chapters that deal with the methodological framework for the study and the legacy of Khrushchev, the author examines three eras in the Soviet high command. These are aptly named after the generals who led during these periods: Grechko 1967-1976, Ogarkov 1977-1984, and Akhromeyer 1984-1988. A final chapter examines Gorbachev and the Soviet high command and concludes that the West was confronted with a "relatively united national security apparatus in the Soviet Union," at the time of writing. (p. xi)

935. Kaufmann, William W., **Glasnost, Perestroika, and U.S. Defense Spending**. Washington, DC: Brookings Institution, 1990. x, 52 p. *Studies in Defense Policy*, ISBN: 0815748817. Includes bibliographical references.

Proposals for cutting the U.S. defense budget in light of the recent developments in the Soviet Union make up the central part of this book. Kaufmann lays out four proposed budgets for the year 1999. He makes the case that the U.S. can best support the new reforms by transferring its financial resources from military to civilian projects in the Warsaw Pact countries.

936. Macdonald, Hugh, **The Soviet Challenge and the Structure of European Security**. Aldershot, Hants, England: E. Elgar, 1990. ix, 318 p. ISBN: 1852780029. Includes bibliographical references.

An interpretation of the causes of and continuation of the Cold War. The author has divided his study into three parts. The first, chapters one and two, discusses origins of the Cold War. Chapters three through five deal with the "Soviet challenge to the Western powers" following World War II. The final section, chapters six through eight, analyzes the current attitudes on the Cold War and their source. The author describes the work as an attempt "to bring together the underlying tradition of sovereignty, an account of the strategic structure of security in Europe, and an estimation of some of the main forces of change in the present." (p. 11-12)

937. MccGwire, Michael, **Perestroika and Soviet National Security**. Washington, DC: Brookings Institution, 1991. xi, 481 p. ISBN: 0815755546. Includes bibliographical references and index.

In January of 1987 the long standing Soviet strategy of preparing for world war was replaced by the commitment to prevent such a war. MccGwire examines the reasons for this policy shift. He first puts the new policy in the context of the Soviets' evolving military requirements from 1945-1986, their policy on strategic weapons and arms control, and the climate of international relations from 1970 to 1983. He then devotes the remaining three-fourths of his book to the reappraisal of strategy in 1983-84, the ascent of Gorbachev and his implementation of perestroika, and the ensuing events in Eastern Europe. A final chapter speculates on the future.

938. Niepold, Gerd, **Battle for White Russia: The Destruction of Army Group Centre, June 1944**, translated by Richard Simpkin, foreword by Sir Robin Carnegie. 1st ed. London: Brassey's Defence, 1987. xix, 287 p. ISBN: 008033606X. Includes bibliography (p. 284-286).

The history of a pivotal confrontation is recounted in this book. It was this battle that defeated the Nazis on the eastern front. The author feels that some of the strategies and tactics used then have relevance for the defense of Europe today. The book is divided into three parts. The first gives an overview of the Soviet and German military situation and then describes the operational planning for the battle. Part two contains summaries of war diaries from June 22 through July 1944. Part three examines lessons for the present that can be learned from the battle.

939. **The Changing Western Analysis of the Soviet Threat**, edited by Carl-Christoph Schweitzer. New York: St. Martin's Press, 1990. 318 p. ISBN: 0312041845. Includes bibliographical references and index.

"The study concentrates on the analysis of threat perceptions by NATO itself ... by the United States, Great Britain, France, the Federal Republic of Germany, and the Netherlands.... The primary goal was to examine Western threat perceptions; that is, to explore the many-layered question of how the Soviet 'challenge' was judged in the individual states and by the Alliance." (p.2) The book's six parts are each devoted to the perspective of the individual countries in NATO.

940. Sherr, James, **Soviet Power, the Continuing Challenge**. New York: St. Martin's Press, 1987. xvii, 280 p. *RUSI Defence Studies Series*, ISBN: 0312748736. Includes index and bibliography (p. 269-275).

"The subject of this study is the way the military instrument combines with others to advance the purposes of the Soviet state and its Communist Party; it is also about the philosophy which shapes those purposes and the striking continuity manifested over the years in the Soviet way of war and politics." (p. xi) Sherr has only slightly modified his text for the second edition.

941. Suvorov, Viktor, **Spetsnaz: The Inside Story of the Soviet Special Forces**. New York: Norton, 1988. v, 21 p. ISBN: 0393026140. Includes index.

An account of the activities of the Soviet special forces by a former member of that group. The author gives some background and explanation for this branch of the army. He also discusses his views of how it was intended to be used. There is little or no documentary evidence to support this author's views presented in this volume. Several appendices are included with information on the structure of the organization.

942. **Military Basing and US-Soviet Military Balance in Southeast Asia**, edited by George K. Tanham and Alvin H. Bernstein. New York: Crane Russak, 1989. viii, 181 p. ISBN: 0844815772 (pbk.), 0844815764.

These papers were originally presented at a conference in Singapore in 1987 on military bases in Southeast Asia. The essays are arranged in four groups: 1. Soviet strategy and military presence; 2. internal communist threat (about the Philippine insurgency); 3. the U.S. military presence in Southeast Asia; and 4. the future (U.S.-Philippine relations).

943. U.S. Army Center of Military History, **Rear Area Security in Russia: The Soviet Second Front Behind the German Lines**. Washington, D. C.: Center of Military History, U.S. Army, 1986. 39 p.

One of a series of reports issued by the U.S. military, drawing on experiences of a committee of former German generals. A preface by a representative of the U.S. military is provided.

The remainder of the study reflects the prejudices of the German military. In this study, "Particularly striking examples have been selected which show most clearly the type of disturbances created by the Russians, the German counter measures taken against them and the lessons learned from experience." (p. 1)

944. Williams, E. S., **The Soviet Military: Political Education, Training and Morale**, with chapters by C.N. Donnelly and J.E. Moore, foreword by Sir Curtis Keeble. Basingstoke: Macmillan, 1987. xv, 203 p. *RUSI Defence Studies Series*, ISBN: 0333385616. Includes bibliography and index.

In attempting to understand the enigma of the Soviet soldier, the authors focus on the education of the Soviet soldier, an education "designed as much to prepare them for military service as to school them for life generally in the wider socialist community." (p. xiv) The book is in two parts. Part one deals with political education and training, the effectiveness of the Zampolit, and morale and other less tangible factors. Part two examines the three services. A concluding chapter describes some current aspects of morale.

Nuclear Arms

945. Adelman, Kenneth L., **The Great Universal Embrace: Arm's Summitry—A Skeptic's Account**. New York: Simon and Schuster, 1989. 366 p. ISBN: 0671672061.

Adelman, who was U.S. Arms Control Director from 1983 to 1987, provides a personal account of superpower summitry during those years. His narrative does not proceed chronologically, but does cover the period from the October 1986 conference at Reykjavik to the May-June 1988 summit in Moscow. Review: *SAIS Review* 10:2: 248-50 (Summer-Fall 1990).

946. Arbatov, Aleksei Greorgievich, **Lethal Frontiers: A Soviet View of Nuclear Strategy, Weapons, and Negotiations**, translated by Kent D. Lee and foreword by William G. Hyland. New York: Praeger, 1988. xvii, 296 p. ISBN: 0275930173. Includes index and bibliography (p. 277-284).

"Arbatov succeeds in illuminating from a Soviet perspective the last two decades of interaction between the United States and the Soviet Union on strategic affairs." (p. xii) Arbatov is a leading scholar at the Russian Institute for the Study of the USA and Canada. Review: *U.S. Naval Institute Proceedings* 124 (September 1989).

947. Bennett, Paul R., **The Soviet Union and Arms Control: Negotiating Strategy and Tactics**. New York: Praeger, 1989. xiv, 187 p. ISBN: 025931684. Includes bibliographical references and index.

The goal of Bennett's book "is to describe how the Soviets negotiate as accurately as possible and to explain why their bargaining behavior changes over time." (p. xiv) The five chapters are arranged in two sections. In the first section, "Theory," Bennett analyzes and describes Soviet decision making. In the second section, "Case Studies," he turns to an extensive analysis of SALT II, 1972-1974 and the Nuclear and Space Talks, 1985-1988.

948. Beukel, Erik, **American Perceptions of the Soviet Union as a Nuclear Adversary: From Kennedy to Bush**. London: Pinter, 1989. viii, 408 p. ISBN: 0861870336. Includes bibliographic references (p. 360-401) and indexes.

Beukel examines the "US government's perception of the Soviet Union as a nuclear armed adversary since the early 1960's, with special reference to elaborating relations between these views and the Soviet Union's position as a nuclear power as well as the domestic

American political system." (p. 28) After a thorough examination of the American perceptions over a thirty year period he provides conclusions and recommendations for future courses of action.

949. Blacker, Coit D., **Reluctant Warriors: The United States, the Soviet Union, and Arms Control**. New York: W.H. Freeman, 1987. xiii, 193 p. ISBN: 0716718626 (pbk.), 071678618. Includes index and bibliography (p. 179-184).

Blacker investigated the influence of nuclear weapon strategy in U.S.-Soviet relations. He covers from 1945 to 1985 in several chapters, each of which focuses on a ten-year span of events and developments.

950. Calingaert, Daniel, **Soviet Nuclear Policy Under Gorbachev: A Policy of Disarmament**. New York: Praeger, 1991. x, 180 p. ISBN: 0275937372. Includes bibliographical references (p. 167-171) and index.

This book "examines the interaction among the various political, economic, and military sources of Soviet behavior to identify the aims and priorities underlying the Soviet pursuit of nuclear disarmament." (p. ix) In its seven chapters it covers innovation in policy formation, the economic inducements for disarmament, new thinking in national security, changes in nuclear strategy, the diplomacy of arms control, and Soviet conduct of nuclear arms talks.

951. Catudal, Honore Marc, **Soviet Nuclear Strategy from Stalin to Gorbachev: A Revolution in Soviet Military and Political Thinking**. London: Mansell, 1988. 413 p. ISBN: 0720120004. Includes bibliography and index.

"This inquiry considers the interrelationship of Soviet ideological beliefs, political imperatives and calculation, military views and doctrine and their reconciliation in Soviet policy. Finally, it points up some important fundamental differences between Soviet and American strategic thinking which is still evolving — both at the level of value and the level of methods." (p. 14) Reviews: *Canadian-American Slavic Studies* 24:4:491-92 (Winter 1990). *Political Science Quarterly* 105:1:174-75 (Spring 1990). *Russian Review* 49:3:362-64 (July 1990). *American Political Science Review* 84:1:369-70 (March 1990).

952. Cimbala, Stephen J., **Rethinking Nuclear Strategy**. Wilmington, DE: SR Books, 1988. xxxi, 278 p. ISBN: 0842022945. Includes bibliographical references and index.

In rethinking previous nuclear strategy, Cimbala examines the near- and long-term issues of strategy and technology, the defense of Europe, problems and policy choices in U.S. Soviet Strategic Deterrence, "Intelligent" wars, and command/control challenges. Reviews: *Fletcher Forum* 13:1:171-73 (Winter 1989). *Social Science Quarterly* 70:2:526 (June 1989).

953. Committee on International Security and Arms Control, National Academy of Sciences, **The Future of the U.S.-Soviet Nuclear Relationship.** Washington, DC: National Academy Press, 1991. vii, 67 p. ISBN: 0309045827. Includes bibliographical references.

This work "offers a comprehensive synthesis of the major issues facing U.S. nuclear policy over the coming decades." (p. vii) It focuses on the changing political/military environment for U.S. nuclear weapons policy, new objectives for nuclear weapons policy, prospects for cooperative security arrangements and nuclear proliferation, nuclear forces, controlling strategic force operations, and a summary. It was prepared by the Committee on International Security and Arms Control, a standing committee of the National Academy of Sciences. These appendices present information relating to U.S. and Soviet strategic forces and START limits, target allocation issues and the sensitivity of strike results to preattack planning factors.

954. Evangelista, Matthew, **Innovation and the Arms Race: How the United States and the Soviet Union Develop New Military Technologies**. Ithaca, NY: Cornell University Press, 1988. xvi, 300 p. *Cornell Studies in Security Affairs*, ISBN: 0801421659. Includes index and bibliography.

"This book seeks to combine an evaluation of competing explanations of international relations with comparative historical case studies of Soviet and U.S. decisions on the basis of primary source material." (p. xi) The author's seven chapters are divided into two parts. In part one, he deals with technology and the arms race and addresses some key theoretical and policy issues. In part two, he analyzes the origins of tactical nuclear weapons, the role of the Academy in the arms race, and Star Wars. Reviews: *American Political Science Review* 84:1:355-56 (March 1990). *Naval War College Review* 43:1:136-39 (Winter 1990). *Orbis* 33:2:285-86 (Spring 1989).

955. Garthoff, Raymond L., **Deterrence and the Revolution in Soviet Military Doctrine**. Washington, DC: Brookings Institution, 1990. x, 209 p. ISBN: 081573056X. Includes bibliographical references and index.

The differences in Soviet and U.S. perceptions of the concept of "deterrence" and the ramifications of those differences are the subject of this study. The author also examines changes in Soviet military policy resulting from Gorbachev's New Thinking on the problem of preventing war. The author relied on the statement of Soviet political and military leaders, analysts, and commentators for this research. The author begins with a discussion of Soviet and U.S. views of the concept of deterrence. He then goes on to describe the consequences a policy of deterrence has had in political-military policy and on nuclear policy. An examination of Gorbachev's military policies is followed by a description of Soviet views on warfare. The final chapter examines implications for U.S. policy.

956. Gervasi, Tom, **The Myth of Soviet Military Supremacy**. 1st ed. New York: Harper & Row, 1986. xi, 545 p. ISBN: 0060155744. Includes index and bibliography (p. 495-532).

Gervasi believes that the United States is sufficiently well-armed not to require expansion of our weapons systems. In fact, he charges that Soviet military supremacy is a myth concocted by those who believe that we are not yet sufficiently armed. His book of 45 brief chapters is arranged in five parts: (1) myth and its role in the arms race; (2) the myth of Soviet strategic superiority; (3) the myth of Soviet nuclear superiority in Europe; (4) the myth of Soviet conventional superiority; and (5) creating the myth. Almost 200 pages of this 545 page book consist of interpretations of statistical data relating to his argument. Reviews: *Bulletin of the Atomic Scientist* 43:5:51-52 (June 1987). *Air University Review* 38:2:93-94 (January-March 1987).

957. Gormley, Dennis M., **Double Zero and Soviet Military Strategy: Implications for Western Security**. Coulsdon, England: Jane's Information Group, 1988. xx, 229 p. ISBN: 0710605633. Includes index and bibliography (p. 204-214).

Gormley has two objectives for his book. "It first assays the consequences for Soviet military strategy of elementary all ground-based ballistic and cruise missiles with ranges between 500 and 5,500 km—the so called "double zero" intermediate- nuclear forces (INF) agreement; it then turns to considering the implications of these consequences for Western security planning." (p. xi)

958. Gray, Colin S., **Nuclear Strategy and National Style**. Lanham, MD: Hamilton Press, 1986. xv, 363 p. ISBN: 081953346 (pbk.), 0819153338. Includes index and bibliography (p. 323-352).

A study of the effects of national culture and style on nuclear strategy in the U.S. and Soviet Union. "This book explores the merit in the proposition that there are distinctive U.S. and Soviet national styles in nuclear strategy, that those styles are comprehensive on the basis of historical and anthropological understanding, and that they may interact in actual armed conflict with possibly fatal consequences for the United States." (p. ix) This study largely focuses on consequences for the U.S., listing specific policy options for future U.S. nuclear policy in the penultimate chapter. Chapters are topically arranged covering geopolitics, national style of the U.S. and Soviet Union, deterrence, strategic stability crisis management, arms control, and strategic superiority. The author believes there is a fairly pervasive misinterpretation of the Soviet Union in the West. The author also feels that an anthropological approach has been neglected in policy analysis, and that it may be helpful in dealing with the Soviets. Review: *International Journal* 43:4:683-85 (Autumn 1988).

959. Green, William, **Soviet Nuclear Weapons Policy: A Research and Bibliographic Guide**. Westview replica edition. Boulder, CO: Westview Press, 1987. xv, 399 p. ISBN: 0865318174. Includes bibliographies and index.

This guide is intended for Sovietologists, strategic specialists, and the general reader interested in researching Soviet nuclear weapons policy. There are three main sections. Analytical essays on Soviet nuclear policy from 1945 to 1986 make up the first part. Part two consists of a bibliographic guide to the Western analysis on Soviet policy with abstracts for each entry. The final section covers primary Soviet sources on the subject. Reviews: *Slavic Review* 47:2:340-41 (Summer 1988). *Strategic Review* 16:1:66-68 (Winter 1988).

960. Haslam, Jonathan, **The Soviet Union and the Politics of Nuclear Weapons in Europe, 1969-87: The Problem of the SS-20**. Ithaca, NY: Cornell University Press, 1988. 227 p. *Cornell Studies in Security Affairs*, ISBN: 0801496160 (pbk.), 0801423945. Includes index and bibliography.

After a brief introduction that examines the roots of the problem from 1945-1969, Haslam covers SALT I and nuclear weapons in Europe, 1969-1972, China's impact on Soviet-American relations, SALT's side effects in 1973-1974. the SS-20 decisions, the reaction to these decisions in Western Europe from 1977-1979, the INF talks, 1980-1983, and renewal of negotiations and the Reykjavik Summit.

961. Honecker, Erich, et al., **The Results and Lessons of Reykjavik**. Berlin: Panorama DDR, 1986. 27 p. *Our Point of View, DDR*.

A collection of four official statements reflecting the official Eastern reaction to the events at Reykjavik. This includes the text of Gorbachev's speech on Soviet television on October 14, 1986.

962. **Strategic Power: USA/USSR**, edited by Carl G. Jacobsen. New York: St. Martin's Press, 1990. xxiii, 519 p. ISBN: 0312040865. Includes index and bibliographical references.

An international group of scholars have contributed to this volume which is intended to "compare and contrast United States and Soviet perceptions of and approaches to strategic realities." (p. xxii) The volume is divided into five sections. Each section contains essays contrasting U.S. and Soviet positions on specific issues. The five sections cover the place of strategic culture in theory and practice, strategical concepts such as deterrance, arms control, limited warfare, and crisis management; strategic processes including decision making in the realm of defense, economic aspects of defense, and defense industry; and the use of force and contemporary issues like Gorbachev's "New Thinking;" and naval power in the nuclear age. The work is intended for anyone interested in the subject area and is meant to be a "comprehensive reference source."

963. Kokeyev, Mikhail, and Andrei Androsov, **Verification: The Soviet Stance: Its Past, Present and Future.** New York: United Nations, 1990. vi, 125 p. ISBN: 9290450428. Includes bibliographical references.

The authors "have provided a detailed description and analysis of the evolution of the Soviet Union's policy towards verification from the early 1920s to the present. Examining the verification provisions of disarmament treaties and agreements in existence and under negotiation, they provide us with useful insights into official approaches to the subject. They conclude with a chapter exploring the USSR proposal to establish an international verification agency." (p. iii) The authors are with the USSR Ministry of Foreign Affairs.

964. **The Soviet Calculus of Nuclear War**, edited by Roman Kolkowicz and Ellen Propper Mickiewicz. Lexington, Mass.: Lexington Books, 1986. ix, 276p.; 24 cm ISBN: 0669115665. Includes bibliographies and index.

Several sources have yielded the contributions on the arms race and arms control collected in this volume. Some are taken from a special double issue of the journal *Soviet Union* published in 1983. Others are the results of several forums held in connection with the Consultation on International Security and Arms Control held between 1984-1985. These essays examine institutions, policy making and the motivation behind Soviet nuclear policy. Topics included are military policy and strategic planning, weapons procurement processes, arms control policymaking, the economics of the military machine and negotiating techniques of both sides. The goal of the authors was to mobilize the general public on these issues.

965. Krass, Allan S., and Catherine Girrier, **Disproportionate Response: American Policy and Alleged Soviet Treaty Violations.** Cambridge, Mass.: Union of Concerned Scientists, 1987. x, 92 p. *"A Report by the Union of Concerned Scientists."* Includes bibliographical references.

This Union of Concerned Scientists' report examines allegations of violations of Soviet nuclear arms control treaties. "This report analyzes the compliance policy of the Reagan administration, evaluates the major changes in its merits, assesses the strategic significance of the disputed activities, and explores the Soviet motivations underlying them. The study concludes that the Soviet Union has indeed pushed at the margins of arms control treaties and in one case has clearly exceeded them. However, the military significance of these activities has been minimal, and the reaction of the Reagan administration disproportionate and counter-productive." (p. vii)

966. Lindahl, Borje Ingemar Bertil, **The Soviet Union and the Nordic Nuclear-Weapons-Free-Zone Proposal,** with foreword by Vojtech Mastny. Basingstoke: Macmillan, 1988. xii, 227 p. ISBN: 0333436385. Includes index and bibliography (p. 214-217).

Bulgaria first proposed the concept of a nuclear-free zone for the Nordic countries in 1958. Lindahl examines this and subsequent proposals within the context of the political and military factors that had a bearing on the debate. He carries his analysis through to the 1980s.

967. **The Other Side of the Table: The Soviet Approach to Arms Control**, edited by Michael Mandelbaum. New York: Council on Foreign Relations Press, 1990. vi, 209 p. ISBN: 0876090714. Includes bibliographical references.

A collection of essays that examine the Soviet view of arms negotiations. "Rebecca writes about the negotiation for the cessation of nuclear tests between 1957 and the signing of the Limited Test Ban Treaty in 1963. Coit Blacker analyzes the Strategic Arms Limitation Talks (SALT) from the perspective of the first SALT accords in 1972 to the provisional agreement signed at Vladivostok in December 1974. Arthurs Goldbell's subject is the negotiations on intermediate-range nuclear forces (INF) in Europe.... A fourth essay, by Cynthia Roberts, traces the postwar evolution of the Soviet definition of strategic interests." (p. 2) While the intent is to discuss the Soviet approach, the lack of accessibility to Soviet sources requires that it still be described through Western eyes.

968. Mazarr, Michael J., **START and the Future of Deterrence**. New York: St. Martin's Press, 1991. viii, 257 p. ISBN: 0312053304. Includes bibliographical references (p. 221-251) and index.

A discussion of the policy of nuclear deterrence in the Gorbachev era. "...This volume contends [that] deterrence will evolve in the next century into a more defensive, co-operative form rather than traditional provocative offensive force structures and doctrines." (p. 2) A topical arrangement covers subjects such as the correct status of deterrence and requirements for its continued existence, stability in the nuclear community, and a survey of Soviet nuclear doctrine.

969. Myers, David B., **New Soviet Thinking and U.S. Nuclear Policy**. Philadelphia: Temple University Press, 1990. xvii, 295 ISBN: 0877227101. Includes bibliographical references (p. 283-292) and index.

An attempt to formulate policy options for the United States in light of the "New Thinking" in Soviet defense. The author makes the case that the Soviets must still be treated as a potential threat to U.S. security even in light of the recent reforms. Philosophical and strategic considerations are a central part of his analysis of nuclear policy. The topics covered include an overview of Soviet and U.S. nuclear strategies, tests for evaluating any new policy, nuclear deterrence, retribution policy, and rehabilitation policy. The author feels that there is a strong analogy to be drawn between defense policy and criminal correction theory, and this is reflected in the options he defines for U.S. nuclear policy. There are several appendices with critiques of the various policy options mentioned in the book.

970. Parrott, Bruce, **The Soviet Union and Ballistic Missile Defense**. Boulder, CO: Westview Press with the Foreign Policy Institute, School of Advanced International Studies, the Johns Hopkins University, 1987. xii, 121 p. *SAIS Papers in International Affairs*, no. 14. ISBN: 0813374294. Includes bibliography (p. 93-121).

One in a series of studies on "the military uses of space" funded by the Carnegie Corporation. The author focuses on the little-studied Soviet dimension in the debate on strategic defense. The six chapters begin by defining central issues of the problem including that of determining the Soviet aims based on public statements. Next, the author turns to the Soviets' view of the geopolitical situation today, followed by a description of Soviet policies as they have evolved towards ballistic missile defense. The author then turns to resource allocation in the USSR and possible Soviet responses to the U.S. strategic defense program. The final chapter presents some recommendations for dealing with the Soviet policies. Reviews: *Naval War College Review* 41:1:142-44 (Winter 1988). *Political Science Quarterly* 103:3:560-62 (Fall 1988). *Russian Review* 47:2:221-22 (April 1988).

971. Sherr, Alan B., **The Other Side of Arms Control: Soviet Objectives in the Gorbachev Era**. Boston: Allen & Unwin, 1988. xviii, 325 p. ISBN: 0044450613. Includes index and bibliography (p. 298-312).

An examination of arms control since the 1960s with a focus on the Gorbachev era. The author seeks to analyze the significance in the contradictions in certain recent developments. In particular, the contradiction between Gorbachev's desire to disarm and Soviet offensive military doctrine; between his idea of democratization and his commitment to the party. The book follows five basic principles: 1) Soviet motivation for arms control must be seen from a broad perspective; 2) Gorbachev's decisions are influenced by many factors including past policies and economic conditions; 3) There are no simple solutions to the problem; 4) Gorbachev is limited by other leaders in the Kremlin; 5) Whatever decisions are taken, they will be tempered by some irrational factors such as bureaucratic constraints. The author intends to show a policy development away from nuclear arms before Gorbachev's rise and how Gorbachev has continued this trend. Review: *Bulletin of the Atomic Scientist* 45:4:46-47 (May 1989).

972. Shimko, Keith, **Images and Arms Control: Perceptions of the Soviet Union in the Reagan Administration**. Ann Arbor, MI: University of Michigan Press, 1991. 277 p. ISBN: 0472102842. Includes bibliographical references (p. 251-270) and index.

Shimko examines the images of the Soviet Union held by the American policy makers and then relates these images to U.S. arms control policy. The book is divided into four parts. Part one looks at theoretical and methodological concerns. Part two conceptualizes the images held by the key decision makers. Part three analyzes the policy debates with the Reagan administration among these decision makers. Part four presents a conclusion and summary.

973. **A Game for High Stakes: Lessons Learned in Negotiating with the Soviet Union**, edited by Leon Sloss and M. Scott Davis. Cambridge, Mass.: Ballinger Pub. Co., 1986. xiii, 184 p. ISBN: 0887300723. Includes index and bibliography (p. 165-170).

These papers are an outgrowth of a series of seminars held under the auspices of the Roosevelt Center for American Policy Studies between May and July 1984. There were two goals. The first was to identify and discuss lessons learned from negotiating with the Soviets. The other was to explain negotiating behavior to the general U.S. public. Chapter one presents an overall summary of the lessons learned and conclusions presented in the papers that follow. Review: *Orbis* 30:1:217-18 (Spring 1986).

974. Snow, Donald M., **The Necessary Peace: Nuclear Weapons and Superpower Relations**. Lexington, Mass.: Lexington Books, 1987. vii, 147 p. ISBN: 066915332X. Includes index and bibliography (p. 133-143).

"The fundamental purpose of this book is to assert and defend the proposition that the truly revolutionary impact of nuclear weapons on international relations and, more specifically, U.S.-Soviet relationships has been their stabilizing and tranquilizing effect." (p. vii.) The book's three parts focus on the counterbalance, in which the present situation is described and analyzed, challenges to the balance, wherein Reagan's and Gorbachev's views on disarmament are proposed and a middle ground sought by the author, and the future where conditions for future stability are presented.

975. **The Soviet Far East Military Buildup: Nuclear Dilemmas and Asian Security**, edited by Richard H. Soloman and Masataka Kosaka. Dover, Mass.: Auburn House Pub. Co., 1986. xv, 301 p. ISBN: 0865691401. Includes bibliographical references and index.

A publication by the Japanese and American organization, The Security Conference on Asia and the Pacific. This particular study is an outgrowth of a conference held in 1984 on "reducing nuclear threats in Asia." "The issue of the growing Soviet nuclear presence in Asia—especially Moscow's deployment of SS-20 intermediate range 'theater' missiles and long range backfire bombers—was viewed as sufficiently important to warrant publication of this unique collection of analytical papers by a multinational group of defense and foreign policy experts." (p. viii) The book is divided into four parts: the Soviet military buildup in the region, views of the Soviet nuclear threat, areas of conflict in the region, the European experience with the Soviets and its lessons for Asia. An appendix lists nuclear forces in the region.

976. **Arms Control: Moral, Political, and Historical Lessons**, edited by Kenneth W. Thompson. Lanham, MD: University Press of America, 1990. xi, 149 p. *W. Alton Jones Foundation Series on Arms Control*, v. 15. ISBN: 0819176281, 081917629X (pbk.).

One in a series of short volumes on arms control. A traditional approach to foreign policy and defense is central to all five essays included here. "The underlying assumption of all the papers in this volume is that arms control can best be approached in relationship to the great traditional questions of international politics." (p. vii) The essays are divided between the three main concerns of the study; moral lessons, political lessons, and historical lessons.

RUSSIAN LANGUAGE

General Studies

977. **Language Planning in the Soviet Union**, edited by Michael Kirkwood. New York: St. Martin's Press, 1990. x, 230 p. ISBN: 0312041195. Includes bibliographical references and index.

Essays discussing various aspects of language planning by looking at historical as well as current issues are presented in this volume. Some of the areas explored include policy formation, planned language change, as well as language planning in specific republics: Uzbekistan, Georgia, the Baltics, Ukraine, Belorussia, and Moldavia. The relationship between language policy and nationality policy in general is a common theme.

Dictionaries and Glossaries

978. Scheitz, Edgar, **Dictionary of Russian Abbreviations: Containing About 40,000 Abbreviations.** Amsterdam: Elsevier, 1986. 695 p. ISBN: 0444995544.

This comprehensive dictionary contains approximately 40,000 entries for abbreviations in all fields, including science and technology. It devotes special attention to abbreviations and acronyms of Soviet political and governmental bodies, as well as to the various institutions of the Soviet and Republican academies of science. Dates of cessation and commencement of corporate bodies are provided when available. Items from earlier historical periods are also included. Furthermore, in scientific and technical entries, the SI units of measurement used in the standard specification of the USSR have been supplied as well. The dictionary is arranged in Russian alphabetical order with the full name of the abbreviation given in Russian alone. In cases where an abbreviation can be used in more than one subject area, a subject category indicator (fifty have been chosen) specifies which definition applies. The work is an improvement over the *Glossary of Russian Abbreviations and Acronyms* compiled by the Aerospace Technology Division of the Library of Congress in 1967 and the *Slovar' sokrashchenii russkogo iazyka*, third edition (1983). It is twice as long as either of these works and the other works fail to distinguish among various usages in different fields.

979. Zalucky, Henry K., **Compressed Russian: Russian-English Dictionary of Acronyms, Semiacronyms and Other Abbreviations Used in Contemporary Standard Russian, With Their Pronunciation and Explicit Correlates in Russian and Equivalents in English**. New York: Elsevier, 1991. xxvi, 880 p. ISBN: 0444987282.

A Russian-English dictionary of some 40,000 abbreviations, acronyms, semiacronyms, eponyms, typographical abbreviations, IDSC and graphicisms. The compiler has chosen to emphasize military technology, journalistic speech and writing, and slang contractions. The volume also emphsizes those abbreviations still in use in contemporary Russian. Entries include Russian and English explanations of the abbreviation. Where the same abbreviation is used with numerous expansions, separate entries are provided for each. The volume is intended for the reader or listener of Russian with or without a knowledge of English. The volume also has numerous tables in the back. Some contain fairly standard information such as the metric system, mathematical symbols, correlations of celsius and farenheit, and some more unusual such as a buying guide giving conversion of sizes between the U.S. and USSR and a caloric content chart.

980. Zimmerman, Mikhail, and Claudia Vedeneeva, **Russian-English Translator's Dictionary: A Guide to Scientific and Technical Usage**. 3rd ed. New York: John Wiley and Sons, 1991. 735 p. ISBN: 0471933163.

This dictionary is not one "of terms or idioms, but a collection of typical examples from scientific and technical sources and the words that make up the combinations that are usually common to a number of branches of science and technology. The remaining words of illustrative context are not so important since they are only meant as 'fillers' to link the combination elements together." (preface)

Textbooks and Grammars

981. Nakhimovsky, Alexander D., **Advanced Russian**. 2nd. rev. ed. Columbus, Ohio: Slavica Publishers, 1987. v, 262 p. ISBN: 0893571784. Includes index.

A text for advanced students of Russian with text, comments, analysis, and exercises. The text and comments have undergone the greatest revision with a reduction in the extreme colloquialism found in these sections in the first edition. The glossary has also been expanded. An appendix is now included with morphological specifications. Review: *Slavic and East European Journal* 33:1:495-96 (Fall 1988).

RUSSIAN LITERATURE

Bibliographies, Biographies, Encyclopedias

982. Kasack, Wolfgang, **Dictionary of Russian Literature Since 1917**, translated by Maria Carlson and Jane T. Hedges; bibliographical revision by Rebecca Atack. New York: Columbia University Press, 1988. xvi, 502 p. ISBN: 0231052421. Includes index.

A rich bio-bibliographical source concentrating on Russian literary figures whether émigré or Soviet. This work was intended to give more complete coverage to authors either overlooked in Soviet sources or inadequately described. This edition is a translation and expansion of the original 1976 German edition. It contains a total of 706 entries: 619 author entries and 87 subject entries. Authors were selected on the basis of the merit of their writing and critical recognition. Critics, literary scholars, and translators have largely been omitted. Author entries include basic information such as dates, full name, etc. They all include a bibliographical section, literary evaluation, and a selected bibliography. All bibliographic data were cross checked with Soviet sources, and émigré materials were verified with the authors themselves or their families. A great deal of information is included in each entry including membership in the Party and association with literary journals. Bibliographic material is grouped into primary and secondary sources. All entries are arranged chronologically. Review: *Slavic Review* 49:3:504-05 (Fall 1990).

983. Proffer, Carl R., and Ronald Meyer, **Nineteenth-Century Russian Literature in English: A Bibliography of Criticism and Translations**. Ann Arbor, MI: Ardis, 1990. 188 p. ISBN: 0882339435.

"*Nineteenth-Century Russian Literature in English* is the first encyclopedic and international bibliography devoted exclusively to this period. The bibliography, which catalogues items published from the 1890s through 1986, covers both general topics and 69 writers." (p. [8]) The bibliography covers books, dissertations, Festschriften, conference proceedings, chapters in monographs, and journal articles. Items are arranged either in one of a dozen general categories or under individual authors. There is no index.

General Studies and Histories

984. **Literature and History: Theoretical Problems and Russian Case Studies**, edited by Gary Saul Morson. Stanford, Calif: Stanford University Press, 1986. x, 332 p. ISBN: 0804713022. Includes index and bibliography (p. 297-320).

The essays in this volume all seek to understand the relationship between history and literary theory. The essays can be seen as a dialogue between Russian literary theory in the two decades following the revolution and contemporary American literary theory. The essays are arranged in three parts, each of which considers a central issue about the relation of literature to history. Part one, Literary Institutions, "considers the questions of how literary history develops and how best it can be described." Part 2, Controlling the Play of Meanings, focuses on "interpretative change, including its implications for criticism and the threat it may pose to all interpretative disciplines." Part 3, Narrative and the Shape of Events, "raises questions fundamental not only to literary narrative but also to all accounts of change." (p. 27-28) Reviews: *Slavic and East European Journal* 31:4:612-15 (Winter 1987). *Canadian Slavonic Papers* 29:1:109-10 (March 1987).

985. Andrew, Joe, **Women in Russian Literature, 1780-1863**. Basingstoke: Macmillan, 1988. vii, 210 p. ISBN: 0333331672. Includes index and bibliography (p. 203-206).

A reanalysis of some of the classic literary works of pre-Emancipation Russia from a feminist point of view. "It is the aim, then, of this book to look at key works of Russian literature, to see how they have 'led [us] to imagine ourselves,' to see to what extent they were an expression of hegemonistic, patriarchal culture in its nineteenth century, Russian variation." (p. 5) The texts analyzed in this work are Pushkin's *Evgenii Onegin*, Lermentov's *A Hero of Our Time*, Gogol's stories, several works by Turgenev including his second and third novels, and Chernyshevskii's *What Is to Be Done*. The bibliography is quite limited as the author wanted to approach these works from a fresh point of view. Reviews: *Poetics Today* 11:3:711-13 (Fall 1990). *Slavic Review* 49:4:674-75 (Winter 1990).

986. Barker, Adele Marie, **The Mother Syndrome in the Russian Folk Imagination**. Columbus, Ohio: Slavica Publishers, 1986. 180 p. ISBN: 0893571601. Includes index and bibliography (p. 163-170).

A psychoanalytical study of Russian folklore focusing on the mother-son theme. The epic songs or byliny are analyzed quite carefully since the mother-son relationship is so often central to these stories. The author is following a Freudian analysis and using Jung and the neo-Freudian as well. She believes that Russian folk tales show a variety of forms of strain in mother-son relationships and are well suited to this type of analysis. Such studies have been rare in the Soviet literature of the past. Reviews: *Slavic and East European Journal* 31:4:635-36 (Winter 1987). *Slavic Review* 46:3-4:356-58 (Fall-Winter 1987).

987. Bortnes, Jostein, **Visions of Glory: Studies in Early Russian Hagiography**. Atlantic Highlands, NJ: Humanities Press International, 1988. 303 p. *Slavica Norvegica*, no. 5. ISBN: 0391034901. Includes index and bibliography (p. 281-291).

The English translation of the original 1975 Norwegian text analyzes the development of Russian hagiography and the role it has played in modern literature. The book is intended for Slavic and Western students of literature in general. The author demonstrates the continuing role of hagiography in the works of such writers as Leskov, Turgenev, Dostoevsky, and Tolstoy. Most of the volume is concerned with the discussion and analysis of various medieval texts. The author traces the sources of the prototypes for the Russian lives of the Saints to their Western and Byzantine models. He also demonstrates how these prototypes were altered to fit the needs of the Russian condition. In the course of this analysis, he demonstrates that the changes in Russian hagiography do not represent an evaluation so much as a "combination or transformation of traditional conventions." The works of other writers in the field such as Dmitrii Likhachev, Roman Jakobson, Mikhail Bakhtin, and Iurii Lotman are also discussed. Review: *Slavic Review* 48:3:489 (Fall 1989).

988. Bristol, Evelyn, **A History of Russian Poetry**. New York: Oxford University Press, 1991. ix, 354 p. ISBN: 0195046595. Includes bibliographical references (p. 316-343) and index.

A chronological study of Russian poetry from medieval times to the present. The volume is arranged with sections on all major poetic movements: Classicism, Romanticism, Realism, Symbolism, Modernism, as well as a special section on émigré poetry. The author shows the continuity in the development of Russian poetic styles. The author also focuses on the significance of the role of Russian poetry in Russian culture as evidenced by its frequent suppression. There are brief sections on major poets including Karamzim, Lomonosov, Krylov, Pushkin, Tiutchev, Lermontov, Balmont, Sologub, Bunin, Bely, Akhmatova, Mandelstam, Mayakovsky, Pasternak, Esenin, Tvardovsky, Evtushenko, Brodsky, and many others. The volume includes appendices on metrical systems and a chronology.

989. Brodsky, Joseph, **Less Than One**. New York: Farrar, Straus, and Giroux, 1986. 501 p.

This is a selection of essays by Brodsky that were originally published elsewhere. They include the autobiographical sketches, as well as works on Russian literature and modern poetry. Review: *American Scholar* 56:2:298-301 (Spring 1987).

990. Brown, William Edward, **A History of Russian Literature of the Romantic Period**. Ann Arbor, Mich.: Ardis, 1986. 4 v. ISBN: 0882339389.

A scholarly and detailed study of Russian literature during its Romantic era, these volumes contain a great deal of information on major and minor figures of the day. The author believes that all European literature, including Russian, have the classics as their base. He sees a unity between the various nationalities of Europe and spends some time discussing interrelationships in these volumes. The work is, thus, directed at graduate students specializing in other areas of Russian literature and specialists of other European literatures. He feels that the Russian language works on this topic, while more comprehensive than his own, are not particularly readable given their ideological bent. The work is organized thematically covering such topics as tragedy, comedy, fables, verse satire, lyric poetry, archaists, journalism, travel sketches, adventure novels, and historical novels. Many literary figures are covered including Griboyedov, Krylov, Glinka, Karamazin, Kuchelbecker, Odoevsky, Narezhnyi, and many others. Review: *Slavic Review* 46:2:361-62 (Summer 1987).

991. Clowes, Edith W., **The Revolution of Moral Consciousness: Nietzsche in Russian Literature, 1890-1914**. DeKalb, IL: Northern Illinois University Press, 1988. x, 276 p. ISBN: 0875801390. Includes index and bibliography (p. 255-267).

The influence of Nietzsche on Russian literature is the subject of this work. The author believes that Nietzsche had a profound and lasting influence that can be discovered by examining the works of the turn of the century Russian authors such as Leonid Andreev, Aleksandr Kuprin, Anastasia Verbitskaia, Anatoly Kamensky, Dmitry Merezhkovskii, Viacheslav Ivanov, Aleksandr Blok, Andrei Belyi, Maksim Gorky, and Anatoly Lunachevsky. In each case she shows how Nietzsche affected the views and literary philosophies of these writers. She believes that Nietzsche had a unique influence in Russia, "Yet the popular cult and the mature literary myths that eventually emerged in Russia are revealing of a mentality that, although it partakes in European literary history, is specifically Russian. How writers imagined their future, their society, and their art gives us insight into the moral consciousness of a particular culture that brought itself to expect and even welcome cataclysm." (p. 13) The book is thematically arranged beginning with a discussion of Nietzsche's work on moral consciousness, suggesting ways in which it might have been interpreted by Russian readers. The author then examines the critical reception of Nietzsche's work in Russia. The next three chapters explore the variety of ways Nietzsche affected a spectrum of Russian writers. Reviews: *Russian Review* 49:3:329-40 (July 1990). *Russian Literature Triquarterly* 23:421-22 (1990).

992. **Studies in Russian Literature in Honor of Vsevolod Setchkarev**, edited by Julian W. Connolly and Sonia I. Ketchian. Columbus, Ohio: Slavica, 1986. 288 p. ISBN: 0893571741. Includes bibliographies.

A collection of essays on a variety of topics in Russian literature that were collected and presented in honor of Professor Vsevolod Setchkarev. Essays on Kozmin, Mandelshtam, Chekhov, Briusov, Akhmatova, and many others are included.

993. **New Studies in Russian Language and Literature**, edited by Anna Lisa Crone and Catherine V. Chvany. Columbus, Ohio: Slavica Publishers, 1986. 302 p. ISBN: 0893571687. Includes bibliographies and index.

A collection of essays dedicated to Dr. Bayara A. Aroutunova. A wide variety of topics and viewpoints are covered as there was no unifying theme to the volume other than to honor Dr. Aroutunova. In linguistics, research on departicipial adverbs, verbs of "teaching" in Russian, Slavic verbal systems, the preposition "iz," diminutive usage, and high frequency vocabulary is included. Some of the literary figures and works covered are Tolstoy, Tsvetaeva, Gogol, Bulgakov, Shklovskii, Nadezhda Mandelshtam's *Hope Against Hope*, Nabokov, and Zoshchenko's Lenin stories, to name a few. Review: *Canadian Slavonic Papers* 30:1:148-49 (March 1988).

994. Dunham, Vera Sandomirsky, **In Stalin's Time: Middleclass Values in Soviet Fiction**, with a new introduction by Richard Sheldon, introduction to the first edition by Jerry F. Hough. enl. and updated ed. Durham, NC: Duke University Press, 1990. xxix, 288 p. *Studies of the Harriman Institute, Columbia University*, ISBN: 0822310856. Includes bibliographical references (p. 280-283) and index.

This new edition of Vera Dunham's book has been enlarged and updated and includes a new introduction by Richard Sheldon. The focus of the book is popular fiction during the Stalinist period. "Both descriptive and analytical, Dunham's complex picture of 'high totalitarianism' both reveals insights into details of Soviet life and illuminates important theoretical questions about the role of literature in the political structure of Soviet society." (back cover) The original introduction by Jerry Hough is included as are two postscripts one of which discusses the changes in Soviet society since glasnost has been introduced.

995. Frank, Joseph, **Through the Russian Prism: Essays on Literature and Culture**. Princeton, NJ: Princeton University Press, 1990. xii, 237 p. ISBN: 0691068216. Includes bibliographical references.

A collection of essays by Joseph Frank. While all of them to some extent were inspired by his work on Dostoevsky, they cover a variety of topics including Bakhtin, Gogol, Leskov, Bakunin, Chernyshevsky, the "positive hero" in Russian literature, and many others. The book is divided into four parts. The first covers contemporaries, the second consists of essays on Dostoevsky, and the final sections consist of essays on radicalism in Russia. Most of the essays collected here appeared in other publications at an earlier point in time. The author has collected these studies to demonstrate how the Western influences on Russia return in altered form to affect the West.

996. **Literature in Exile**, edited by John Glad. Durham, NC: Duke University Press, 1990. xiii, 175 p. ISBN: 0822309874.

Writings issuing from a 1987 conference on writers in exile were the source for this volume. The general theme is not limited to the conditions the Soviet author in exile faces. However, several of the essays' authors and many of the discussion participants are former Soviets. Major themes discussed in the essays include the history of exile for writers, motives for leaving home countries, the émigré role in politics, what are the literary traditions of writers in exile, the effect of exile on language, what is the position of the émigré in his new society, what are the common problems of émigré writers, and money.

997. **Autobiographical Statements in Twentieth-Century Russian Literature**, edited by Jane Gary Harris. Princeton, NJ: Princeton University Press, 1990. xi, 287 p. *Studies of the Harriman Institute*, ISBN: 0691068186. Includes bibliographical references.

A selection of fifteen essays discussing the role of autobiography in 20th century Russian literature. Essays were chosen to demonstrate the varied role autobiography has played. Each essay discusses the work of one author. Those included are Alexei Remizov, Andrei Bely, Osip Mandelshtam, Boris Pasternak, Yuri Olesha, Mikhail Zoshchenko, Vladimir Nabokov, Edvard Limonov, and Andrei Sinyavsky. Selections are arranged chronologically. The book is intended for anyone interested in the place autobiography holds in literature in general. The extensive bibliography includes translations whenever possible.

998. Heldt, Barbara, **Terrible Perfection: Women and Russian Literature**. Bloomington: Indiana University Press, 1987. 174 p. ISBN: 0253358388. Includes index and bibliography (p. 161-171).

" 'Terrible perfection'—inequality guaranteed by idealization—is the organizing theme of Barbara Heldt's study of the impact of women in Russian literature. Heldt argues that the heroines of Russian women writers differ from those in the fiction of Russian men and are to be found outside that novelistic tradition, primarily in the genres of autobiography and lyric poetry." (book cover) To demonstrate this point, the author had divided the book into three parts, the first dealing with the images of women in the fiction of male writers, the second on women's autobiographies, and finally a section on women's poetry. Some of the authors discussed are Akhmatova, Anna Bonina, Princess Dashkova, Vera Figner, Sophia Parnok, Karolina Pavlova, Marina Shkapskaia, and Marina Tsvetaeva. Reviews: *Slavic Review* 47:4:771-72 (Winter 1988). *Canadian Slavonic Papers* 30:1:149-50 (March 1988).

999. **Discontinuous Discourses in Modern Russian Literature**, edited by Catriona Kelly, Michael Makin, and David Sheperd. Houndmills: Macmillan, 1989. xiv, 178 p. ISBN: 0333464990. Includes bibliographical references and index.

Papers presented at a 1984 conference at Oxford University are the basis of this volume. "The conference was intended to challenge some dominant trends in scholarship, Western and Soviet, on Russian literature and culture: an emphasis on the seamless continuity between authorial intention and text; a profound suspicion of the historical, political and ideological factors in literary production and reception; and a deeply entrenched belief in a 'high' culture whose transcendent aesthetic value is above interrogation." (p. xi) In challenging these traditional themes, three main ones are examined: theory, texuality, and sexuality. The eight essays included in the volume are arranged under these headings. The theories of Bakhtin are one focus of analysis.

1000. **Russian Futurism Through Its Manifestoes, 1912-1928**, edited by Anna Lawton, and translated by Anna Lawton and Herbert Eagle. Ithaca, NY: Cornell University Press, 1988. xiii, 353 p. ISBN: 0801418836. Includes index and bibliography (p. 333-339).

The first collection of Futurist documents, manifestoes, declarations, and essays on literature to appear in English. The editor hoped to provided a source of primary information for English speaking scholars of the avant garde and to generally make information on the movement more available. An overview of the history and development of the Futurist movement and a discussion of its effects on later genres of Russian literature are included in the introduction. Annotations and notes are provided with each document. A selected bibliography is also included in the volume.

1001. Lenhoff, Gail, **The Martyred Princes Boris and Gleb: A Socio-Cultural Study of the Cult and the Texts**. Columbus, OH: Slavica Publishers, 1989. 168 p. *UCLA Slavic Studies*, vol. 19. ISBN: 0893572047. Includes bibliographical references (p. 143-159) and index.

A protogeneric analysis of the texts related to Boris and Gleb. This type of analysis reviews the texts within the context of the culture that produced them. The volume is organized thematically. The first chapter reviews the existing literature and describes the premises for this study. The second chapter examines the early Kievan cult. The remaining chapters discuss the texts used in the veneration. Such texts as the *Saints Office* and *The Chronicles* are discussed, first examining past analyses and then using a socio-cultural approach to explain anomalies previously ignored. Reviews: *Slavic and East European Journal* 34:4:527-28 (Winter 1990). *Canadian Slavonic Papers* 32:1:90-91 (March 1990).

1002. Levitt, Marcus C., **Russian Literary Politics and the Pushkin Celebration of 1880**. Ithaca, NY: Cornell University Press, 1989. x, 233 p. *Studies of the Harriman Institute*, ISBN: 0801422507. Includes index and bibliography (p. 217-223).

This is not a study of Pushkin's works or even his place in Russian literature. It is a study of Pushkin's place in Russian culture at a particular point in time. "The focus here is on a special moment in Russian history when political and intellectual hopes for the nation's future became concentrated on the liberating role, and rightful place, of a free literature — personified in Pushkin — and on the unique convergence of forces which brought it about." (p. 3) The book focuses on the controversy within the Russian intelligentsia leading up to the monument, the organization of the celebration and the roles of such literary figures as Turgenev and Dostoevsky in the celebration. Reviews: *Russian Review* 49:4:489-90 (October 1990). *Slavic and East European Journal* 34:2:257-58 (Summer 1990). *Slavic Review* 49:4:676 (Winter 1990).

1003. Lowe, David Allan, **Russian Writing Since 1953: A Critical Survey**. New York: Ungar, 1987. 208 p. ISBN: 080442554x. Includes index and bibliography (p. 201-202).
A review of the changes that have taken place in Russian literature since Stalin's time and the social and political events that prompted them. The author begins with a general discussion of politics and its relationship with literature and then turns to an examination of each of the major genres: nonfiction, poetry, fiction, and drama. Each of these sections is further divided into brief discussions of other more specific genres: memoir literature, village prose, urban prose, science fiction, guitar poetry, scientists, absurdism, and realism. Many authors are briefly discussed and each section contains a historical survey of those elements chiefly affecting the development of the genre. Reviews: *Slavic Review* 47:3:578-80 (Fall 1988). *Canadian Slavonic Papers* 30:2:287 (June 1988). *World Literature Today* 62:4:681 (Autumn 1988). *International Fiction Review* 15:2:160-61 (Summer 1988).

1004. **From Pushkin to Palisandriia: Essays on the Russian Novel in Honor of Richard Freeborn**, edited by Arnold McMillin. New York: St. Martin's Press, 1990. xi, 255 p. ISBN: 0312046391. Includes bibliographical references and index.
A collection of essays gathered in honor of Richard Freeborn, former chair of Russian literature at London University. The essays cover a range of Russian authors and their work: Pushkin, Lermontov, Goncharov, Turgenev, Mariengof, Nabokov, Pasternak, Zinov'ev, and Sakorov. The volume includes a select bibliography of the works of Richard Freeborn.

1005. **The Cambridge History of Russian Literature**, edited by Charles A. Moser. Cambridge, England: Cambridge University Press, 1989. ix, 685 p. ISBN: 0521309948. Includes bibliography (p. 595-630).
This is a history of Russian literature from its beginnings (988) to 1980. Each of the ten chapters is written by a different author, but the editor had ensured that the coverage of material is adequate, in spite of the different approaches employed by each author. The chapters proceed chronologically with three devoted to the period prior to 1820, five to the period before 1925, and two to the Soviet period. Moser has appended a useful bibliography arranged by period and then by individual author.

1006. Porter, Robert C., **Four Contemporary Russian Writers**. New York: St. Martin's Press, 1989. viii, 184 p. ISBN: 0854962468. Includes index and bibliography (p. 177-180).
A study of the works of Valentin Rasputin, Chingiz Aitmatov, Vladimir Voinovich, and Georgii Vladimirov. The author has chosen these four because of their stature in Russia and abroad and because he hopes to give them a more extensive treatment than they have received to date in the Western critical literature. The book is also intended, through the discussion of the evolution of the works of these four authors, to present a picture of the development of Soviet literature in general from the 1960s to the 1980s. As such it touches on such topics as socialist realism, samizdat, human rights, and the changes under Gorbachev. Each author is treated in a separate section. Biographical sketches and brief

bibliographies are also supplied at the back of the volume, The work is intended for both the serious student of Soviet literature and the novice. Reviews: *World Literature Today* 64:1:144 (Winter 1990). *Russian Review* 49:3:331-32 (July 1990).

1007. **Problems of Russian Romanticism**, edited by Robert Reid. Brookfield, Vt.: Gower, 1986. ix, 224 p. ISBN: 0566050293. Includes bibliography (p. 215-217).
A study of the many facets of Romanticism in Russian literature. This collection of seven essays describes Romanticism in general terms as seen by the Russians and then continues to examine its manifestations in the works of six authors of the nineteenth century: Pushkin, Venevitinov, Bestuzhev-Marlinsky, Gogol, Lermontov, and Dostoevsky. These authors represent both the strictly programmatic view of romantic art and the more idiosyncratic interpretation of romanticism. The authors are hoping to illuminate the Russian romantic aesthetic in the past and today. Review: *Canadian Slavonic Papers* 29:4:448-49 (December 1987).

1008. Rowe, William Woodin, **Patterns in Russian Literature II: Notes on Classics**. Ann Arbor, MI: Ardis, 1988. 158 p. ISBN: 087501547. Includes bibliographies and index.
Rowe presents essays on Chekhov, Tolstoy, Dostoevsky, Turgenev, Gogol, Nabokov, Lermontov, and Pushkin. Reviews: *Canadian-American Slavic Studies* 24:4:462-64 (Winter 1990). *Russian Review* 49:1:103-05 (January 1990). *Slavic Review* 49:1:146-47 (Spring 1990).

1009. Russell, Robert, **Russian Drama of the Revolutionary Period**. Basingstoke: Macmillan, 1988. xi, 186 p. ISBN: 0333447581. Includes index and bibliography (p. 177-181).
The development of Russian drama during the turbulent years of the revolution and the 1920s is the focus of this book. The author limits himself to drama as opposed to theater although he acknowledges the difficulty of separating the two. The author also provides a brief background on earlier trends in Russian drama, particularly realism and conventionalism since they continue into the period of the revolution. He traces the changes in the artistic movements more generally to some extent following the development of the avant garde, the Bolshevik interest in proletarian art and the change from this varied artistic style to the rigid structure of socialist realism. Among the topics covered are the Civil War in Soviet drama, specific dramatic works of Mikhail Bulgakov, Nicholai Erdman, and Vladimir Mayakovskii. The use of satire in dramatic works of the period is also analyzed.

1010. **Russian Theatre in the Age of Modernism**, edited by Robert Russell and Andrew Barratt. New York: St. Martin's Press, 1990. xii, 269 p. ISBN: 0312045034. Includes bibliographical references and index.
"The essays collected here do not pretend to offer a comprehensive account of theatrical life in early twentieth-century Russia. Each is a self-contained study which may be read independently of the whole. Taken together, however, they provide a picture not only of the sheer diversity of the dramatic enterprise during these turbulent years but also of the central issues confronting the student who would wish to understand them better." (p. vii) Individual studies focus on Chekhov, Geyer, Pronin, Meyerhold, Andreyev, Kuzmin, Gumilev, Tsvetaeva, Evreinov, the Soviet audience, German expressionism and early Soviet drama, satire, and Bulgakov.

1011. Sherr, Barry P., **Russian Poetry: Meter, Rhythm, and Rhyme**. Berkeley: University of California Press, 1986. xvi, 366 p. ISBN: 0520052994. Includes indexes and bibliography (p. 329-355).

"The aim of this book is to present a general account of Russian versification in light of current research. I assume no previous study of the field and define all but the most basic terms. I have tried to provide explanations of Russian prosodic features that are not only clear and detailed but also up-to-date." (p. xii-xiii) The first chapter contains definitions of terms and a historical survey of Russian verse to the mid-eighteenth century. Chapter two examines the introduction of syllabo-tonic meters by Trediakovsky and Lomonosov. Chapter three focuses on other forms introduced in the twentieth century. Chapter four turns to rhyme and stanzaic forms. The final chapter looks at minor features of Russian verse. An annotated bibliography is provided at the back of the volume along with an index of poets and a subject index.

1012. Terras, Victor, **A History of Russian Literature**. New Haven: Yale University Press, 1991. x, 654 p. ISBN: 0300049714. Includes bibliographical references and index.

A general history of Russian literature from earliest times through the late Soviet period. The book is arranged chronologically with allowances for the reappearance of extremely influential figures in the literature. The author intended the volume for Western readers of Russian literature. He tries to present a view of Russian literature as the Russians see it. The focus in this volume in on "serious" literature, i.e., that literature directed at the educated elite of Russia. While the author recognizes the traditional view of Russian literature as a social literature his focus is on its aesthetic qualities. He sees three main sources for Russian literature: pre-Christian culture in its earliest stages; Byzantium during the medieval period; and Western influence during the modern period. The author believes that Russian literature cannot be understood without considering these basic sources. The volume contains some biographical information but only insofar as it relates to the understanding of an author's works.

1013. **The Search for Self-Definition in Russian Literature**, edited by Ewa M. Thompson. Houston, Tex.: Rice University Press, 1991. xiii, 216 p. ISBN: 0892633069. Includes index and bibliographical references (p. 187-207).

A collection of essays which arose from a conference held in 1989 on the role of literature as a medium for the expression of nationalist ideology. Only the theme in general terms runs through the volume — the essays vary in approach and interpretation. This topic is of particular interest in light of the rise of nationalistic feelings since glasnost. The essays are of significance to anyone with an interest in the national psychology of Russia. Review: *Canadian Slavonic Papers* 33:3-4:396-398 (December 1991).

1014. **Soviet Society and Culture: Essays in Honor of Vera S. Dunham**, edited by Terry L. Thompson and Richard Sheldon. Boulder, CO: Westview Press, 1987. xii, 290 p. ISBN: 0813305004.

"This book provides a wide-ranging, detailed view of economic, social, ideological, and literary aspects of the Soviet system leading to the Gorbachev era. The essays include both historical and contemporary perspectives in the sources of stability (and stagnation) in the post-Stalin years.... The contributors provide insights into the social and cultural motivations for Gorbachev's 'restructuring' policies." (front piece)

Anthologies

1015. **Balancing Acts: Contemporary Stories by Russian Women**, edited by Helena Goscilo. Bloomington: Indiana University Press, 1989. xxvii, 337 p. ISBN: 0253311349. Includes bibliography (p. 313-323).
A selection of writings by various women writers is presented here to help fill a gap in Western literature. The editor hopes to portray Russian women's self-perception as it is portrayed in literature. Many writers are represented including: Tatiana Tolstaia, Elena Makarova, Irina Velembovskaia, Maia Ganina, and many others. An addendum with the publication history of the stories is included as is a selection with substantial entries on each of the authors. Reviews: *World Literature Today* 64:3:486- 87 (Summer 1990). *Slavic and East European Journal* 34:4:538-40 (Winter 1990).

1016. **From Furmanov to Sholokhov: An Anthology of the Classics of Socialist Realism**, edited by Nicholas Luker. Ann Arbor, MI: Ardis, 1988. 508 p. ISBN: 0875010369.
Six works representing the communist politicization of art are collected in this volume. The first five are taken from the early Soviet period, the last originally published in 1956. All are officially considered excellent examples of this style. The editor has chosen Dmitrii Furmanov's "Chapaeu," Alexander Serafimovich's "The Iron Flood," Fydor Gladkov's "Cement," Alexander Fadeev's "The Rout," Nikolai Ostrovsky's "How the Steel Was Tempered," and Mikhail Sholokhov's "The Fate of a Man." The works have been abridged, but their original numbering is maintained. The editor hopes to make more readily available to teachers and students, the classic works of this genre in one volume. There is a substantial introductory essay on the doctrine of socialist realism.

1017. Mirsky, D. S. Prince, **Uncollected Writings on Russian Literature**, edited and with an introduction by G.S. Smith. Berkeley, CA: Berkeley Slavic Specialties, 1989. 406 p. ISBN: 0933884680. Includes bibliographical references.
A selection of essays intended for the serious student of Russian literature. All materials are either in English or Russian and none have been reprinted. Many were chosen to demonstrate Mirsky's development as a literary critic. There are, therefore, contradictions in Mirsky's opinions from one essay to another, but these were deliberately included. The English language essays cover such topics as Pushkin's writing, Russian prose 1910-1975, literature and politics 1917-25, Marina Tsvetaeva, the Eurasian movement, and Tolstoy. A bibliography of Mirsky's work is included in an appendix to the volume. Review: *Russian Review* 49:3:321-23 (July 1990).

1018. **An Age Ago: A Selection of Nineteenth-Century Russian Poetry**, selected and translated by Alan Myer; with foreword and biographical notes by Joseph Brodsky. 1st ed. New York: Farrar, Straus, Giroux, 1988. xix, 171p. ISBN: 0374104425.
This volume is an anthology of the works of V.A. Zhukovsy, N. Batiushkov, Prince P.A. Viazemsky, A.S. Pushkin, E.A. Baratynsky, N.M. Yazykov, M.L. Lermontov, F.I. Tiutchev, A.K. Tolstov, N.A. Nekrasov, and A.A. Fet, all active in the first half of the nineteenth century. It contains an insightful introduction and biographical notes on each poet, written by Joseph Brodsky.

1019. **Russian Literature of the Twenties: An Anthology**, edited by Carl and Ellendea Proffer. Ann Arbor, MI: Ardis, 1987. xvii, 566 p. ISBN: 088233820X. Includes bibliographies.

As Maguire says in his introduction, "the literature of the twenties offers not only a sociology of all the groups, classes, and professions, but also a grand tour of the territories belonging to the old Russian Empire... the twenties can be seen as the culmination of the process of opening up literature to new themes, characters, and locales that had only begun before the Revolution...." (p. i) This expansive anthology includes short stories, novellas (Bugakov's *Fatal Eggs*), novels (Zamiatin's *We*), poetry, drama (Mayakovsky's *The Bedbug*), nonfiction (Babel's *Diary: 1920*), and documents (*A Slap in the Face of Public Taste*; Mandelstam's *The Morning of Acmeism*). It offers an excellent selection of literature from the twenties, as well as a further guide to reading in English on the themes and writers represented.

1020. **The New Soviet Fiction: Sixteen Short Stories**, compiled by Sergei Zalygin. New York: Abbeville Press, 1989. 396 p. ISBN: 0896598810.
These sixteen short stories by Soviet writers are not meant to be a comprehensive collection, only a representative one of the best writers of the recent past. Brief biographical sketches of each of the writers are given at the end of the volume.

Critical Studies

1021. Bethea, David M., **The Shape of Apocalypse in Modern Russian Fiction**. Princeton, NJ: Princeton University Press, 1989. xix, 307 p. ISBN: 0691067465. Includes index and bibliography (p. 277-96).
Bethea provides close readings of Dostoevsky's *The Idiot*, Belyi's *Petersburg*, Platonov's *Chevengur*, Bulgakov's *The Master and Margarita*, and Pasternak's *Doctor Zhivago*. Each of these novels repeatedly alludes to *The Book of Revelation* and is concerned with the end of history, the eschaton. Bethea shows how these allusions "provide powerful models for structuring these works of fiction" and indicates "where this theme of apocalypse actually enters into the realm of narrative structure, where it takes on dynamic shape and expands into a moving picture of history in crisis." (p. xiv) His introduction traces the main features of Russian apocalyptic fiction.

1022. **Issues in Russian Literature Before 1917: Selected Papers of the Third World Congress for Soviet and East European Studies**, edited by J. Douglas Clayton. Columbus, Ohio: Slavica Publishers, 1989. 248 p. ISBN: 0893571997. Includes bibliographical references.
The essays contained in this volume were originally presented at the Third World Congress for Soviet and East European Studies in Washington, DC in November of 1985. "As a whole the papers tend to show that literature encodes and, indeed, attempts to resolve the problems facing the society that nurtures it." (p. 9) The papers focus on literary figures and motifs from the early 19th century through the Symbolists. Reviews: *Slavic and East European Journal* 34:4:524-26 (Winter 1990). *Canadian Slavonic Papers* 32:1:88-90 (March 1990).

1023. Emerson, Caryl, **Boris Godunov: Transpositions of a Russian Theme**. Bloomington: Indiana University Press, 1986. xi, 272 p. *Indiana-Michigan Series in Russian and East European Studies*, ISBN: 0253312302. Includes bibliographical notes and index.
Emerson investigates the transposition of the Boris Godunov tale in several genres. She begins with an introductory chapter on Boris Godunov, the false Dmitri, and the poetics of transposition. She then devotes lengthy chapters to Boris in history, focusing on Karamazin, Boris in drama, focusing on Pushkin, and Boris in opera, using Mussorgsky as the

springboard for discussion. Review: *Canadian Slavonic Papers* 29:4:445-46 (December 1987).

1024. **Bakhtin and Cultural Theory**, edited by Ken Hirschkop and David Sheperd. Manchester: Manchester University Press, 1989. 224 p. ISBN: 0719026148. Includes index and bibliography (p. 195-212).

These essays cover a wide range of scholarship on Bakhtin, including Bakhtinian theories of language, the notions of dialogism and heteroglossia, carnival and the treatment of the body, and other related topics.

1025. Mann, Robert, **Lances Sing: A Study of the Igor Tale**. Columbus, Ohio: Slavica Publishers, 1990. 231 p. ISBN: 089357208X. Includes bibliographical references (p. 224-231).

In this extensive study of Russia's medieval masterpiece, Mann explores several areas including the oral epic cycle about the conversion of Rus, the conversion cycle and the Slovo, wedding imagery, folklore parallels, literary influences, the Slovo and Zadonshchina, and oral formulas and the probability and authenticity of the Slovo. An old Russian text of the Slovo is also included.

1026. **Rethinking Bakhtin: Extensions and Challenges**, edited by Gary Saul Morson and Caryl Emerson. Evanston, Ill.: Northwestern University Press, 1989. 330 p. ISBN: 081010897. Includes index and bibliography (p. 261-304).

The essays in this volume attempt to address the confusion surrounding the interpretation of Bakhtin's work. In a long introductory essay the editors convincingly disprove the supposition that Bakhtin was the actual author of Valentin Voloshinov's *Marxism and the Philosophy of Language* and *Freudianism: A Critical Essay*, and of Pavel Medvedev's *The Formal Method in Literary Scholarship*. This introduction is then followed by essays that explore parody, dialogue, authority, Tolstoy, and the dangers of dialogue, all in relation to Bakhtin's theoretical writings. An appendix includes two of Bakhtin's prefaces to Tolstoy's works, one in the volume on drama, the other to the volume containing the novel *Resurrection*. Reviews: *Canadian Slavonic Papers* 32:1:92-94 (March 1990). *Slavic and East European Journal* 34:4:523-24 (Winter 1990). *Russian Review* 49:2:219-21 (April 1990). *Slavic Review* 49:3:502-04 (Fall 1990).

1027. Moser, Charles A., **Esthetics as Nightmare: Russian Literary Theory, 1855-1870**. Princeton, NJ: Princeton University Press, 1989. xxiv, 288 p. ISBN: 0691067635. Includes index and bibliography (p. 271-280).

Moser examines literary criticism and aesthetic theory from 1855 to 1970. His aim is "to trace the leading ideas in the controversies over art and literature in Russia from 1855 to 1870 in their various combinations and permutations, as formulated both by critics whose names are still writ large in Soviet and Western scholarship." (p. xv) The author begins with a chapter on the disputants and their journals and in subsequent chapters covers art in relation to rationality, morality, and reality. Reviews: *Canadian Slavonic Papers* 32:1:91-92 (March 1990). *Russian Review* 49:3:326-27 (July 1990). *Slavic and East European Journal* 34:2:259-60 (Summer 1990).

1028. **The Russian Short Story: A Critical History**, edited by Charles A. Moser. Boston: Twayne, 1986. xxiv, 232 p. *Twayne's Critical History of the Short Story*, ISBN: 0805790607. Includes index and bibliography (p. 196-219).

The aim of this book is to examine "the origins of the short story in Russia" and "the evolution of the genre from the reign of the romantics in the 1830s to the rise of the post-modernist writers in the 1970s." (jacket) Four contributors trace the development of the Russian short story in successive chronological periods. Reviews: *Studies in Short Fiction* 24:4:452-53 (Fall 1987). *World Literature Today* 61:3:465 (Summer 1987).

1029. Pachmuss, Temira, **Russian Literature in the Baltic Between the World Wars.** Columbus, Ohio: Slavica Publishers, 1988. 447 p. ISBN: 0893571814. Includes bibliographical references.

An anthology of the works of various Russian writers living in the Baltic between WWI and WWII. The volume is divided by country and each geographic section is subdivided by authors. Most of the authors included here have never been available in English before. It is the intent of the author to bring to the attention of Western readers a group of very gifted but little-known authors of Russian literature. A wide variety of genres is represented with examples of fiction, literary criticism, poetry, one-act plays, and travel notes. Bio-bibliographical essays accompany each entry. The anthology demonstrates the important role émigré authors have had in shaping Russian literary development. The volume is intended for a wide range of readers, not limited to students of Russian literature. All of the translations are presented here for the first time. Among the authors discussed in this book are Iurii Ivask, Igor Chinnov, Vera Bulich, Boris Nartissov, Karl von Hoerschelmann, Nikolai Belotsvetov, Leonid Zurov, Ivan Savin, and Boris Semenov. Reviews: *Slavic Review* 48:2:343-44 (Summer 1989). *Canadian-American Slavic Studies* 22:1-4:454-55 (Spring-Summer-Fall-Winter). *Slavic and East European Journal* 33:3:472 (Fall 1989).

1030. **The Human Experience: Contemporary American and Soviet Fiction and Poetry,** edited by the Quaker US/USSR Committee, with forewords by William Styron and Daniil Granin. 1st ed. New York: A. Knopf, 1989. xxiii, 357 p. ISBN: 0394570618.

According to the editors, this book represents what they feel is some of the best current Soviet and American writing. They also believe that it represents "the spirit that unites us in spite of cultural and political differences." (p. xiii) "The writings in this book are about everyday life, and the infinite worth of each human being which transcends national, political, and social differences." (p. xiv)

1031. **The Noise of Change: Russian Literature and the Critics (1891-1917),** edited and translated by Stanley Rabinowitz. Ann Arbor, MI: Ardis, 1986. 247 p. ISBN: 0882335251. Includes bibliographies.

Prose of the Silver Age of Russian Literature (1890-1917) is examined in twelve essays by critics of the time. Some of the essays have been abridged because of the repetitiveness and wordiness of the authors. Most focus on an individual author. Given individual treatment are Chekov, Gorky, Bunin, Sologub, Remizov, Briusov, Kuzmin, and Bely. Review: *Slavic Review* 46: 1:164-65 (Spring 1987).

1032. Shneidman, N. N., **Soviet Literature in the 1980s: Decade of Transition.** Toronto: University of Toronto Press, 1989. 250 p. ISBN: 0802058124. Includes index and bibliography (p. 235-242).

A general discussion and description of Soviet literature between 1978 and 1988. The survey is limited to officially published works, excluding samizdat. The author intends to give a general representation of the situation, therefore he has been selective in the authors he discusses. The authors are grouped in the text by theme, age, sex, or style. The first chapter gives an overview of the atmosphere in Soviet society affecting writers with emphasis on ideology, theory of literature, and literary practice. The next chapter discussed the literary evolution of the last decade. Valentin Kataev, Trifonov, and Vladimir Tendriakov, all of whom died in the 1980s, are the subject of chapter three. Chapters four through nine discuss specific themes in literature such as "countryside prose," war prose, the political novel, and women. The author intends the work for the student of Soviet literature and society.

1033. Simpson, Mark S., **The Russian Gothic Novel and Its British Antecedents**. Columbus, Ohio: Slavica Publishers, 1986. 110 p. ISBN: 0893571628. Includes bibliography (p. 107-110).

In studying the Russian Gothic Novel tradition, Simpson "answers questions about the prevalence of Gothic themes, motifs, characters, and situations in Russia's classic works of literature and music." He further "addresses the centrally important issue of Russian reliance upon and adoptation of Western trends, fads, and customs." (p. 7) After an introductory chapter on the Gothic tradition Simpson looks at Karamizin's *Bornholm Island*, Bestuzhov-Marlinsky's *The Cuirassier*, Pushkin's *The Queen of Spades*, Mel'nikov'-Pechersky's *Bygone Days*, and the examples of Gothic influence in other authors. Review: *Slavic and East European Journal* 31:4:618-19 (Winter 1987).

1034. Todd, William Mills III, **Fiction and Society in the Age of Pushkin**. Cambridge, Mass.: Harvard University Press, 1986. viii, 265 p. ISBN: 0674299450. Includes index and bibliography (p. 209-258).

Although separate chapters are devoted to Gogol, Pushkin, and Lermontov, Todd's aim "is to contribute to understanding and further study in several areas: literary theory, the social history of literature, cultural history, and literary interpretation." (p. vii) After two chapters dealing with Russian ideology and institution of literature, the author focuses specifically on *Eugene Onegin*, *A Hero of Our Time*, and *Dead Souls*. Reviews: *Slavic and East European Journal* 31:1:106-08 (Spring 1987). *Russian Review* 46:3:345-46 (July 1987).

Individual Authors

1035. Aitmatov, Chingiz, **Mother Earth and Other Stories**, translated by James Riordan. London: Faber, 1989. 314 p. ISBN: 0571152376.

A collection of short stories translated into English by the popular Soviet Kirghiz writer Chingiz Aitmatov. The purpose of the translation is to help fill the gap in the Soviet literature presently available to Westerners. In particular, the translator hoped to demonstrate for Westerners good literature of the Soviet period that is less ideological in nature. The first four stories represent the early stage of Aitmatov's work, while the final novella demonstrates his mature style.

1036. ———, **The Place of the Skull**, translated by Natasha Ward. London: Faber, 1989. 310 p. ISBN: 057114926X.

Another of Aitmatov's novels which is set in the Central Asian steppe. The lives of the wolves of the steppe and man are juxtaposed in this book which continues Aitmatov's style of including his Central Asian homeland as a focal point.

1037. ———, **The Time to Speak Out**. Moscow: Progress Publishers, 1988. 297 p. *Library of Russian and Soviet Literary Journalism*, ISBN: 501000459X. Includes bibliography (p. 295-298).

This collection includes essays on various topics, literary, cultural and political, by the well-known Soviet writer.

1038. Akhmadulina, Bella, **The Garden: New and Selected Poetry and Prose**, edited, translated, and introduced by F.D. Reeve. 1st ed. New York: Henry Holt and Co., 1990. xvii, 171 p. ISBN: 0805012494.

A selection of poems by the esteemed poetess Bella Akhmadulina. The poems chosen span her career from her earliest works appearing in the late 1960s to those from collections published in 1984. Many of the works are presented here for the first time in English. An introduction with references to other sources of the poet's works in English precedes the text. Three short stories are also included.

1039. **The Speech of Unknown Eyes: Akhmatova's Readers on Her Poetry**, edited by Wendy Rosslyn. Nottingham, England: Astra Press, 1990. 2 v. ISBN: 0946134162 (set). Includes bibliographical references.

Papers presented at a conferences held in 1989 at the University of Nottingham in honor of the centenary of Akhmatova's birth. The two volumes in this set of critical essays are divided into six sections. The first is made up of essays on her poem "Rekviem"; the second section is on the poem "Poema bez geroia"; the third section examines compositional and linguistic aspects of her work; the fourth deals with intertextuality of her work; the fifth is a set of essays taking a thematic approach to the poet's work and the final section contains essays on the theme of Akhmatova and England.

1040. Aksyonov, Vasilii Pavlovich, **In Search of Melancholy Baby**. New York: Random House, 1987. 227 p. ISBN: 0394543645.

In this book, the émigré Aksyonov writes of the experience of emigration. He has written one other book about America, *Non-stop Round the Clock*, which was published in the Soviet Union. That first account of his travels was written while he was still a Soviet citizen. In this book his view of America is altered by his own forced emigration. He is no longer a tourist; he now views the U.S. as his home and material for his future novels. A second novel is actually given in brief form between the chapters of *In Search of Melancholy Baby*.

1041. ———, **Our Golden Ironburg: A Novel with Formulas**. Ann Arbor, MI: Ardis, 1988. 254 p. ISBN: 0882335596.

This novel was written in 1972 and scheduled to be published in the journal *Yurist*. At the last moment it was pulled and only first published in France, and this English translation followed.

1042. ———, **Quest for an Island**. 1st ed. New York: PAJ Publications, 1987. 246 p. ISBN: 1555540201.

This volume presents a collection of works by the émigré author Vassily Aksyonov. A variety of genres are represented. The first offering is a short story published when the author was still in the Soviet Union, in 1979, in his journal *Metropol*. The second is an essay written in Moscow in 1980. The third is also a short story, but written in 1981 in the U.S. Another short story written from November 1977 to January 1978 on Ajaccio in Moscow follows. The final two works are plays, the first written in 1967 and the final one in 1979. The last is unusual in its inclusion of poetry within the work. A variety of translators worked on this volume.

1043. ———, **Say Cheese!** New York: Random House, 1989. 404 p. ISBN: 0394543637.

Aksyonov studied to be a doctor in Leningrad until 1956 and then worked as a doctor in various institutes in Moscow and Leningrad until 1960. He started writing in 1959. After coming under increased criticism for his views he emigrated to the U.S. in 1980.

1044. **Vasiliy Pavlovich Aksenov: A Writer in Quest of Himself**, edited by Edward Mozejko and co-edited by Boris Briker and Per Dalgard. Columbus, Ohio: Slavica Publishers, 1986. 272 p. ISBN: 0893571415. Includes bibliography (p. 255-268).

A series of articles on the prolific Soviet author Aksenov. "In preparing this volume the editors did not intend to impose any preconceived ideas, but tried to pursue one general goal: to cover the widest possible range of topics so that the reader might be guided through various aspects and stages of Aksenov's evolution as a writer and thereby develop some insights into his work." (p. 11) To accomplish this goal the editors have arranged the essays into four sections. The first deals with Aksenov the man and includes an interview with the writer and a brief biography. The second section is made up of general articles discussing such topics as Aksenov's drama, his early novellas, language, and his prose. Section three covers specific topics such as mystianic prose, travel writing and specific works by the author. The final section is an appendix with a bibliography by and about Aksenov.

1045. Aleshkovskii, Yuz, **Kangaroo**, translated by Tamara Glenny. 1st ed. New York: Farrar, Straus & Giroux, 1986. 278 p. ISBN: 0374180687.

Originally written in 1974-75, *Kangaroo* "is a kind of modern picaresque novel in which an old thief recounts his numerous experiences during a show trial in the late Stalin period. Stalin himself is even personally involved in the events." (Kasack, W. *Dictionary of Russian Literature Since 1917*, p. 12)

1046. ———, **The Hand, or, The Confession of an Executioner**, translated by Susan Brownsberger, with an introduction by Joseph Brodsky. 1st ed. New York: Farrar, Straus, Giroux, 1990. xii, 261 p. ISBN: 0374167702.

The Hand, in the words of the author, "is a novel about conversion, in the form of a protocol of a police interrogation. It is... a testimony, if you will — given not by the suspect, but by the case officer, by somebody very high up in the ranks of state security." (p. x-xi) It was originally written in 1980.

1047. Andreyev, Leonid, **Visions: Stories and Photographs**, edited and with an introduction by Olga Andreyev Carlisle. 1st ed. San Diego: Harcourt Brace Jovanovich, 1987. 325 p. ISBN: 0151939004.

Several short stories by the Russian writer Leonid Andreyev are presented in this volume. A lengthy introduction by his granddaughter with a great deal of biographical information is also included. Stories include "The Thought," "The Red Laugh," "At the Station," "The Thief," "The Abyss," "Darkness," and "The Seven Who Were Hanged." Numerous photographs are also scattered throughout the volume.

1048. Tucker, Janet G., **Innokentij Annenskij and the Acmeist Doctrine**. Columbus, Ohio: Slavica Publishers, 1986. 154 p. ISBN: 0893571644. Includes index and bibliography (p. 131-142).

Previous criticism has not determined the reasons for and nature of the tie between Annenskij and Acmeism. Tucker explores "those facets of Annenskij's work most closely related to the Acmeists' literary doctrine" and focuses "through thematic categorization of Annenskij's poetry and an analysis of his poetic devices, on his aesthetic and philosophical affinities with the younger poets." (p. 8)

1049. Ehre, Milton, **Isaac Babel**. Boston: Twayne Publishers, 1986. 168 p. *Twayne's World Authors Series*, ISBN: 0805766375. Includes index and bibliography (p. 159-164).

After an introductory chapter on Babel's life, Ehre discusses Babel's works individually "and in the context of the books or 'cycles' in which they appeared." (preliminaries) Review: *Studies in Short Fiction* 24:2:179-80 (Spring 1987).

1050. Sicher, Efraim, **Style and Structure in the Prose of Isaak Babel'**. Columbus, Ohio: Slavica Publishers, 1986. 169 p. ISBN: 0893571636. Includes bibliography (p. 137-169).

Sicher pays "the closest attention, as Babel did, to the language of his short stories," he analyzes the style and structure of Babel's prose, especially that written in the 1920s, because Sicher maintains that is the period for which the most evidence for Babel's stylistic development exists. Reviews: *Slavic Review* 46:3-4:646-47 (Fall-Winter 1987). *Studies in Short Fiction* 24:3:324-25 (Summer 1987). *Canadian Slavonic Papers* 29: 2-3:336-37 (June-September 1987).

1051. Bely, Andrey, **Spirit of Symbolism**, edited by John E. Malmstad. Ithaca, N.Y.: Cornell University Press, 1987. 375 p. *Studies of the Harriman Institute*, ISBN: 0801419840 (pbk.). Includes index.

This is less a collection of essays and more a collected monograph on Bely. The scholars whose contributions appear here met in 1984 at a conference to share these essays and discuss them over a five day period. Rather than have contributions in narrow, specialized topics, Malmstad had the ten contributors submit long essays "surveying Bely's major work in all genres, summarizing the present state of research, reassessing critical approaches, or offering fresh readings of major works." (p. 11)

1052. Berberova, Nina Nikolaevna, **The Accompanist**. New York: Atheneum, 1988. 94 p. ISBN: 0689119895. Translated from the Russian by Marian Schwartz.

A short novel written by the émigré literary scholar Nina Berberova. In this story a young girl is living with her mother in the years immediately following the revolution. The girl is an illegitimate child, the daughter of a piano teacher and her young lover. After her training as a pianist at the Conservatory in Petersburg, the girl is offered a position as an accompanist. It is the relationship between her and the singer she accompanies that is the focus of this story written in 1936.

1053. Sloane, David A., **Aleksandr Blok and the Dynamics of the Lyric Cycle**. Columbus, Ohio: Slavica Publishers, 1988. 384 p. ISBN: 0893571822. Includes index and bibliography (p. 342-379).

This book does much more than investigate lyric cycles in Blok. In the first chapter Sloane examines writings on the theory of the lyric cycle including definition, semiotics, reader competence, typology, plot cycles. Chapter two is devoted to a history of the cyclic tradition within Russian poetry and Blok's place within that tradition. Chapters three to five then analyze the various aspects of Blok's cycles. Review: *Slavic and East European Journal* 34:3:381-83 (Fall 1990).

1054. Borodin, Leonid, **The Story of a Strange Time**. London: Collins-Harvill, 1990. ix, 228 p. ISBN: 0002717689.

A collection of five early works by the Russian dissident Leonid Borodin. Borodin suffered under earlier regimes and was only released from prison by Gorbachev in 1987. He has been associated with Russian nationalists but tends to remain aloof from such extremist groups as Pamiat. His stories have been largely concerned with the truth that has arisen from the harsh daily experience of Russian life. This volume, translated by Frank Williams, includes "The Meeting," "On Time," "The Story of a Strange Time," "The Option," and "The Visit."

1055. Brodsky, Joseph, **Marbles: A Play in Three Acts**, translated by Alan Myers, with the author. 1st ed. New York: Farrar, Straus, Giroux, 1989. 87 p. ISBN: 0374202885.

Originally published in Russian under the title *Mramor* in 1984, this English translation of Brodsky's three act play takes place in a prison cell in the "second century after our era."

1056. ———, **To Urania**. 1st ed. New York: Farrar, Straus, Giroux, 1988. 173 p. ISBN: 0374172536.

This collection contains translations from the Russian of selected poems from *Chast' rechi* (Parts of Speech) and *Uraniia*. Review: *Partisian Review* 57:1:141-45 (1990).

1057. **Brodsky's Poetics and Aesthetics**, edited by Lev Loseff and Valentina Polukhina. New York: St. Martin's Press, 1990. xii, 211 p. ISBN: 0312045115. Includes index.

Studies of the works of Joseph Brodsky by a variety of contributors. The contributors are largely scholars of varying views, but one essay is contributed by a contemporary Russian poetess. The only common opinion among them is the importance of Brodsky's work. The contributions are also varied, several focus on individual works by Brodsky, several others discuss motifs in the poet's work. Two focus on specific problems of poetics: simile and rhyme. The volume also includes Brodsky's Nobel speech.

1058. Polukhina, Valentina, **Joseph Brodsky: A Poet for Our Time**. New York: Cambridge University Press, 1989. xx, 324 p. *Cambridge Studies in Russian Literature*, ISBN: 0521334845. Includes index and bibliographical references (p. 304-314).

This study seeks to identify the principles of organization in the poetry of Joseph Brodsky by analyzing the technical aspects of his work. Brodsky's interest in widening poetic language is of particular interest in this study. The first three chapters follow the author's literary development. The method of analysis is comparison with the works of ten other poets: Blok, Khlebnikov, Mayakovsky, Tsvetaeva, Pasternak, Akhmatova, Bal'mont, Dershavin, and Baratynsky. The third and fourth chapters discuss Brodsky's poetry in terms of grammatical structure, semantics and conceptual models. Chapters five and six focus on the poet's themes by analyzing his system of metaphors. Reviews: *Slavic and East European Journal* 35:3:447-48 (Fall 1991). *Russian Review* 50:3:358-59 (July 1991).

1059. Milne, Lesley, **Mikhail Bulgakov: A Critical Biography**. Cambridge: Cambridge University Press, 1990. xiv, 324 p. ISBN: 0521227283. Includes bibliographical references.

A scholarly biography tracing Bulgakov's career from his early years as a doctor, to his decision to become a writer in 1920, his popularity in the 1920s, and his decline during the Stalinist era. Although his work has become more popular since the Soviet publication of *Master and Margarita* in 1966-67, much biographical information was not available in the pre-glasnost period. "Leslie Milne traces through Bulgakov's career an ethical concept of the writer's role, his response to his time, and his search for and audience in and beyond that time." (frontispiece)

1060.   Chekhov, Anton Pavlovich, **Orchards: Stories**, plays by Maria Irene Fornes et al.
        1st ed. New York: Knopf, 1986. 175 p. ISBN: 0394745353 (pbk.), 0394553918.
Seven short stories of Chekhov's are presented in this anthology, followed by a play based
on the story. Each play was written by an American playwright especially for this volume.
The plays were commissioned by The Acting Company.

1061.   **Critical Essays on Anton Chekhov**, edited by Thomas A. Eekman. Boston, Mass.:
        G.K. Hall, 1989. 208 p. *Critical Essays on World Literature*, ISBN: 0816188432.
        Includes bibliographic references.
"Brought together in this volume are the views of eighteen essayists on Anton Chekov —
views of diverse personalities ranging from the Russian philosopher-essayist Leo Shestov
and the American poet and critic Conrad Aiken, writing at the beginning of this century, to
some present-day critics and literary scholars." (p. 1) Besides providing an opportunity to
understand Chekov and his works better, the essays also show how critical opinion of him
has changed over eighty years. Reviews: *Choice* 805 (January 1990). *Russian Review*
49:3:375-76 (July 1990).

1062.   Maegd-Soep, Carolina de, **Chekhov and Women: Women in the Life and Work
        of Chekhov**. Columbus, Ohio: Slavica Publishers, 1987. 373 p. ISBN:
        089357175X. Includes bibliography (p. 359-373).
Maegd-Soep's study is divided into two parts: Women in Chekhov's Life and Women in
Chekov's Work. The author provides an introduction to Chekhov as man and writer,
focusing on the woman reader, his attitude toward female students, working women, and
the female audience of his plays. Through archival sources and letters, she then explores
his relationship with various women, including the Kursistka sisters and women artists and
writers. In part two, the author follows a thematic approach covering marriage, women's
emancipation, and female types in both Chekhov's early and major works. Reviews:
Russian Review 48:1: 101-02 (January 1989). *Slavic and East European Journal* 33:4:
624-25 (Winter 1989). *Slavic Review* 48:2:335-37 (Summer 1989). *Canadian-American
Slavic Studies* 22:1-4:427-28 (Spring-Summer-Fall-Winter 1988).

1063.   Paperno, Irina, **Chernyshevsky and the Age of Realism: A Study in the Semiotics
        of Behavior**. Stanford, Calif.: Stanford University Press, 1988. viii, 305 p. ISBN:
        0804714541. Includes index and bibliography.
Paperno provides a detailed analysis of Chernyshevsky's novel *What Is to Be Done* in order
to answer the question: "Is it possible to trace the transformation of personal experience
into the structure of a literary text representative of a historical epoch and the text's reverse
influence on the experience of others?" (p. iii) In pursuing her goal Paperno introduces both
biographical and literary evidence. The book also includes an appendix with original
Russian quotations that were translated in the body of the book. Reviews: *Slavic Review*
49:3:499-500 (Fall 1990). *Philosophy and Literature* 14:2:433-34 (October 1990). *Poetics
Today* 11:3:711-13 (Fall 1990).

1064.   Chukovskaia, Lidiia Korneevna, **Sofia Petrovna**. Evanston, IL: Northwestern
        University Press, 1988. 120 p.
An English translation of *Opustelyi dom [The Deserted House]* recounting the effects of
the terror of the 1930 on one woman's life. The book has the unique characteristic of having
been written in the 1930s while the events recounted were fresh in the author's memory.
The volume also includes an excerpt from another of the author's works *The Process of
Expulsion*. This brief passage describes the treatment of this novel by the Soviets and the
effect it had on Chukovskaia's career.

1065. Davydoff, Marianna, **Memoirs of a Russian Lady: Drawings and Tales of Life Before the Revolution**, selected and translated by Olga Davydoff Dax. New York: Harry N. Abrams, 1986. 156 p. ISBN: 0810908395.

Life among the prerevolutionary nobility is depicted in the memoirs and the watercolors that accompany them. The author lived through turbulent times, leaving Russia during the Revolution for Odessa and Constantinople. Although her original diary and its illustrations were destroyed, the author reconstructed it after her emigration. It is that reconstruction that is presented here along with a family tree for the Davydoffs. Many traditional customs, clothing, as well as depiction of daily life for nobility and servants are recounted here.

1066. **Fyodor Dostoevsky**, edited and with an introduction by Harold Bloom. New York: Chelsea House, 1988. viii, 295 *Modern Critical Views*, ISBN: 1555462944. Includes index and bibliography (p. 275-285).

This collection gathers together a representative collection of the best criticism available in English on Dostoevsky. Like in other volumes of this series, the articles are presented in chronological order of their publication. Bloom's introduction gives readings of *Crime and Punishment* and *The Brothers Karamazov* to demonstrate both the strengths and weaknesses of this extraordinary novelist.

1067. Busch, Robert L., **Humor in the Major Novels of F.M. Dostoevsky**. Columbus, Ohio: Slavica Publishers, 1987. 168 p. ISBN: 0893571768. Includes index and bibliography (p. 161-164).

Busch focuses on Dostoevsky's five major novels, where the author's use of humor is most complex. In this critical study, Busch intends to "(1) test Bakhtin's thesis concerning parodic satellites for Dostoevsky's major characters; (2) to show in detail how these parodic satellites operate; (3) to point out and discuss Dostoevsky's satire...; (4) to give requisite attention to the special stylistic effects which Dostoevsky uses to achieve humorous nuances; (5) to bring out at length the final playoff characteristic of the polyphonic novel." (p. 19) Reviews: *Russian Review* 49:1:100 (January 1990). *Russian Language Journal* 44:147-49, 373-75 (Winter-Spring-Fall 1990).

1068. Catteau, Jacques, **Dostoyevsky and the Process of Literary Creation**. Cambridge: Cambridge University Press, 1989. xiv, 553 p. *Cambridge Series in Russian Literature*. Includes index and bibliography (p. 529-543).

A critical analysis of Dostoyevsky's works that was originally published in French in 1978. Reversing the usual critical procedure, the author works from Dostoevsky's notebooks. "The birth of the novel, the writer as artist, is the main subject of this book." (p. xi) The English edition differs from the French in that the text has been condensed, notes have been abbreviated and references have been standardized. The author believes that by examining the creative process he can better explore the finished novels. His approach is designed to correct a fault of much contemporary criticism, which tends to fragment the writer and his work into smaller units that can be more easily analyzed. Catteau aims for an integration of the author's works and the author's motivation. Reviews: *Modern Fiction Studies* 36:2:294-95 (Summer 1990). *Canadian Slavonic Papers* 32:1:92-94 (March 1990).

1069. Conradi, Peter J., **Fyodor Dostoevsky**. Houndmills, Basingstoke: Macmillan, 1988. xv, 147 p. *Macmillan Modern Novelists*, ISBN: 033407628. Includes index and bibliography (p. 136-139).

A brief study of the major works of Dostoevsky with the intent of relating them to the "post-romantic debates of the day" and to the modern novel. In particular, the author looks at Dostoevsky as a comic writer, focusing on this aspect of his four major and two minor novels: *Crime and Punishment, The Idiot, The Devils, The Brothers Karamazov, The*

Double, and *Notes from the Underground*. This work is one in the series *Macmillan Modern Novelists*, and "each volume in the series is intended to provide an introduction to the fiction of the writer concerned, both for those approaching him or her for the first time and for those already familiar with some parts of the achievement in question, and now wishes to place it in the context of the total oeuvre." (p. x) Due to the lack of space only brief biographical information is supplied. The book includes a chronology of Dostoevsky's life and a select bibliography of English language sources. Reviews: *Slavic and East European Journal* 34:2:253-54 (Summer 1990). *Russian Literature Triquarterly* 23:419-20 (1990).

1070. Lary, Nikita M., **Dostoevsky and Soviet Film: Visions of Demonic Realism**. Ithaca, N.Y.: Cornell University Press, 1986. 279 p. ISBN: 080148828. Includes index, bibliography (p. 265-267) and filmography (p. 268-271).
Lary explores the use of Soviet filmmakers have made of Dostoevsky's material. The author has used "film adaptations of Dostoevsky's works, two films about Dostoevsky, editing scripts, some literary scripts, a shooting script, film segments, adaptation exercises, theoretical and critical writings, and many autobiographical reminiscences." (p. 11) The book also contains twenty annotated photos and stills and appendices devoted to Eisenstain's notes on Ivan the Terrible. Reviews: *Slavic Review* 46:3-4:660-61 (Fall-Winter 1987). *Canadian Slavonic Papers* 29:2-3:332-33 (June-September 1987).

1071. Leatherbarrow, William J., **Fedor Dostoevsky: A Reference Guide**. Boston, Mass: G.K. Hall, 1990. xxxviii, 317 p. *A Reference Guide to Literature*, ISBN: 0816189412.
A bibliographic guide intended for students, scholars, and critics of Dostoevsky. This work covers publications issued between 1846 and 1988. It is a selective bibliography with works chosen that illustrate patterns to critical interest in Dostoevsky. The book is divided into four parts. The first is an introductory essay describing the reception of Dostoevsky's works in Russia and the West. The second section consists of a chronological list of Dostoevsky's major publications. The next section, the largest in the volume, is comprised of some 1,200 annotated entries arranged chronologically. Finally, two indexes, author and subject, are contained in the final section.

1072. **Critical Essays on Dostoevsky**, collected by Robin Freuer Miller. Boston, Mass.: G.K. Hall, 1986. vi, 270 p. *Critical Essays on World Literature*, ISBN: 0816188289. Includes bibliographies and index.
Miller presents here an outline of the critical response to Dostoevsky's literary works in a 20 page introduction. He then offers the reader a selection of such criticism that goes from Viacheslav Ivanov to Mikhail Bakhtin, or as he aptly puts it, "from biographical-historical, to formalist, to structuralist and reader-response criticism." (p. 17) An index aids access to the contents of the essays.

1073. Trace, Arthur S., **Furnace of Doubt: Dostoevsky and *The Brothers Karamazov***. Peru, IL: Sherwood Sugden, 1988. 178 p. ISBN: 0893850306.
The author examines Dostoevsky's philosophical and religious thought as it is expressed in earlier works and then proceeds to analyze *The Brothers Karamazov*. In Trace's eyes *The Brothers Karamazov* is the best novel of Dostoevsky and most fully expresses the author's religious and philosophical thinking. Reviews: *Russian Review* 49:4:486-87 (October 1990). *Russian Language Journal* 44:147-49:370-72 (Winter-Spring-Fall 1990).

1074. **Dostoevsky and the Human Condition After a Century**. New York: Greenwood Press, 1986. vi, 238 p. *Contributions to the Study of World Literature, 0738-9345*, no. 16. ISBN: 031325379X. Includes bibliographies and index.

Essays taken from papers given at Hofstra University on the centenary of the death of Dostoevsky. They are collected in three sections. The first group is comprised of ten essays dealing with issues of textual and conceptual interpretations. All of Dostoevsky's major works and some of his short stories are discussed by the various contributors. The second section is made up of just one essay; the key note address from the meeting. The final group presents eight essays in comparative and interdisciplinary studies. Review: *Slavic and East European Journal* 31:4:627-28 (Winter 1987).

1075.   Dovlatov, Sergei, **The Suitcase**. 1st ed. New York: Grove Wiedenfeld, 1990. 128 p. ISBN: 0802112463.
Dovlatov uses items in a suitcase to recall memories of his youth in the Soviet Union.

1076.   Laychuk, Julian, **Ilya Ehrenburg: An Idealist in an Age of Realism**. Bern: Peter Lang, 1991. 486 p. ISBN: 3261042923. Includes index and bibliography.
Laychuk attempts to present a balanced picture of the life and writings of Ehrenburg. "The method employed in the work is a combination of an analysis of virtually all Ehrenburg's writings from his first poetic efforts of 1910 to his death in 1967, and a discussion of his sundry activities and prolific travels against a backdrop of many of the momentous events that have shaped our century." (p. v)

1077.   Frantz, Philip, **Gogol: A Bibliography**. Ann Arbor, MI: Ardis, 1989. xvii, 360 p. ISBN: 0882338099.
The bibliography of some 8,418 entries covers almost all publications by and about Nikolai Gogol to 1980. Monographs and articles are included. The volume is divided into three sections: primary sources, secondary sources, and 1975-80 imprints (primary and secondary sources). All languages are included, making this an excellent source for those seeking translations as well as for those working with different editions of the same title. The index includes titles and names. The entries are not annotated. This is the most comprehensive source on Gogol to date.

1078.   **Nikolay Gogol: Text and Context**, edited by Jane Grayson and Faith Wigzell. Basingstoke: Macmillan Press in association with School of Slavonic and East European Studies, University of London, 1989. xiii, 130 p. *Studies in Russia and East Europe*, ISBN: 0333453093. Includes index.
Essays resulting from a 1986 conference at the School of Slavonic and East European Studies at the University of London. The studies either focus on textual or contextual analysis. The studies are intended for the general as well as the specialist reader. They cover such works as *Dead Souls* and *The Nose* along with many others. Reviews: *Russian Review* 49:2:212-14 (April 1990). *Russian Literature Triquarterly* 23:420 (1990).

1079.   Clowes, Edith W., **Maksim Gorky: A Reference Guide**. Boston, Mass: G.K. Hall, 1987. xxxvii, 226 p. *A Reference Guide to Literature*, ISBN: 0816187223. Includes indexes.
This guide is intended to cover the many works not cited in the numerous Soviet bibliographies on Gorky. The focus here is on Western and émigré publications. While there is a list of works by Gorky, it is not exhaustive. The volume is divided into four sections. The first section is made up of an introductory essay presenting the central issues in the study of Gorky. The second includes works by the author. The third, largest, section is made up of secondary works, arranged chronologically. All secondary titles include brief annotations. The fourth part is made up of two indexes: author and subject. Reviews: *Canadian Slavic Papers* 30:4:538 (December 1988). *Modern Fiction Studies* 35:4:836-39. *Canadian-American Slavic Studies* 22:1-4:463-65 (Spring-Summer-Fall-Winter 1988).

1080. Scherr, Barry P., **Maxim Gorky**. Boston: Twayne, 1988. 140 p. *Twayne's World Authors Series, Russian Literature*, no. 781. ISBN: 0805766267. Includes index and bibliography (p. 132-140).

Maxim Gorky, the literary pseudonym of Alexei Maximovich Peskov, became a writer of broad talents both before and after the revolution. His plays, novels, short stories, poetry, memoirs, and essays were all stamped with the experience and character of Gorky himself, as well as by the times in which he lived. Scherr's critical appraisal intends to demonstrate the worth of a larger part of Gorky's oeuvre than is generally known in the West. After a biographical first chapter, Scherr examines his short stories, novels, plays, autobiography, and memoirs in succeeding chapters. He then treats all of his past revolutionary writings before a brief concluding chapter.

1081. Pursglove, D. Michael, **D.V. Grigorovich: The Man Who Discovered Chekov**. Aldershot, Hants, England: Avebury, 1987. 133 p. ISBN: 0566053217. Includes index and bibliography (p. 112-115).

Pursglove presents the biography of Grigorovich, "a writer, and artistic bureaucrat, cultural mentor, and artistic socialite." (p. 111) Grigorovich (1822-1899) observed and participated in the great age of 19th century Russian literature.

1082. Iskander, Fazil, **Rabbits and Boa Constrictors**, translated by Ronald E. Peterson. Ann Arbor, MI: Ardis, 1989. 183 p. ISBN: 088233557X.

A novel by Abkhasian poet Fazil Iskander set in Africa. The story is allegorically portrayed. Review: *Choice* 1509 (May 1990).

1083. Davidson, Pamela, **The Poetic Imagination of Vyachelsav Ivanov: A Russian Symbolist's Perception of Dante**. Cambridgeshire: Cambridge University Press, 1989. xv, 319 p. *Cambridge Studies in Russian Literature*, ISBN: 0521362857. Includes index and bibliography (p. 303-311).

A scholarly study of the poet, philosopher, and critic Vyacheslav Ivanov. The central role held in the Symbolist movement provided the impetus for this analysis. The author focuses on Ivanov's creative method. In particular, the influence of religion on his self-expression is central to this study. The discussion centers around Ivanov's interpretation of Dante. The broader question of Western influence on Russia, particularly the influence of Catholicism, is also explored. This includes discussion of such topics as Solovyov's teaching on Sophia, Ivanov's view of classical religion. The second half of the book is devoted to textual analysis. All translations in the volume are by the author with the exception of that of the *Divine Comedy*. The author demonstrates the way in which the Symbolists sought substantiation of their own beliefs in other cultures without adopting those beliefs.

1084. **Vyacheslav Ivanov: Poet, Critic, and Philosopher**, edited by Robert Louis Jackson and Lowry Nelson, Jr. New Haven: Yale Center for International and Area Studies, 1986. xiii, 474 p. *Yale Russian and East European Publications*, no. 8. ISBN: 0936586087. Includes bibliographies.

This volume contains essays by notable specialists on four aspects of Ivanov. After two introductory essays on Ivanov and symbolism, sections are devoted to Ivanov as poet, critic, and classical scholar and philosopher. A final section contains reminiscences and a chronology of his life and works.

1085. Kaledin, Sergei, **The Humble Cemetery with Gleb Bogdyshev Goes Moonlighting,** translated from the Russian by Catriona Kelly. London: Collins-Harvill, 1990. 190 p. ISBN: 0002711176.

Two works by a controversial Soviet writer are presented here. These two represent the works that made Kaledin popular with the Soviet audience who had been unable to see this work until 1986. He has become very popular. The first study published in this volume, "The Humble Cemetery," deals with the afterlife which the author sees as being just as ridden with corruption and shortages as this life. The second selection, "Gleb Bogdyshev Goes Moonlighting," focuses on the black market and the underworld. In both Kaledin deals to some extent with subjects that have formerly been taboo in "Soviet official culture."

1086. **Daniil Kharms and the Poetics of the Absurd: Essays and Materials,** edited by Neil Cornwell. New York: St. Martin's Press, 1991. xvi, 282 p. ISBN: 0312061773. Includes bibliographical references (p. 266-277) and index.

Essays specially written for this volume by an international group of scholars. The volume is intended to make a significant contribution to the scholarly study of the writer Daniel Kharms. Some previously untranslated essays are included. Prose, theater, and poetry are discussed. The volume is not intended as a thorough treatment of Kharm's works and does not cover his children's literature, philosophical works or poetry as a whole. A chronology of the author's life is included in the introduction and a selected bibliography comprises the final essay.

1087. Khlebnikov, Velimir, **Collected Works of Velimir Khlebnikov,** edited by Charlotte Douglas. Cambridge, Mass.: Harvard University Press, 1987. 3 v. ISBN: 0674140451. Includes bibliographical references and index.

The prose, theoretical writings, and letters of the Russian futurist Khlebnikov are collected in these two volumes. The translations presented here are based on several Russian collections of the poet's works. Volume I includes a substantial introductory essay by Charlotte Douglas on Khlebnikov's life. The first two volumes of this three volume set present letters, theoretical writings, prose, plays, and supersagas. A third volume will include his poetry. Although Khlebnikov is not well known in the West, the translator feels his significant contributions to Russian poetic forms will be appreciated here. Reviews: *World Literature Today* 64:3:488 (Summer 1990). *Slavic and East European Journal* 34:4:540-42 (Winter 1990).

1088. **Velimir Chlebnikov (1885-1922), Myth and Reality,** edited by Willem G. Weststeijn. Amsterdam: Rodopi, 1986. x, 593 p. *Studies in Slavic Literature and Poetics,* vol. 8. ISBN: 9062037984. Includes bibliographical references.

Collection of papers given at a 1985 conference held in Amsterdam to commemorate the centennial of the poet's birth. The essays reflect a change in appreciation of the poet's work. In the past his works have not always been taken seriously, thus no scholarly collection of his work or biography existed at the time of this conference. The essay topics range from discussions of specific aspects of this poetry to more general discussions of his role in art. The majority of the essays are in English with a few titles in Russian, German, and French.

1089. Lvov, Arkadii, **The Courtyard: A Novel,** translated by Richard Lourie. 1st ed. New York: Doubleday, 1988. 682 p. ISBN: 38523133X.

Lvov wrote this novel between 1968 and 1972 in Russian, but it found its first success in French in 1979. The Russian edition was published after his emigration to the U.S. "*Dvor* depicts the variable, intersecting lives of some simple people in the courtyard of an apartment house in Odessa from 1936 to 1953.... Lvov concentrates on people who are severely hampered by the propaganda that permeates information." (Kosack, W., *Russian Literature Since 1917*, p. 229) He is planning a novel parallel to *The Courtyard*, where the intersection of peoples' fates is a Manhattan skyscraper.

1090. Isenberg, Charles, **Substantial Proofs of Being: Osip Mandelshtam's Literary Prose**. Columbus, Ohio: Slavica, 1987. 179 p. ISBN: 0893571695 (pbk.). Includes bibliography, p. 178-179.

Isenberg begins his study of Mandelshtam by examining Mandelshtam's verse and criticism "as the context in which the prose appears." (p. 13) He then goes on to devote separate chapters to the analysis of *The Noise of Time, The Egyptian Stamp,* and *"Fourth Prose"* and *"Journey to Armenia."* Review: *Slavic Review* 47:3:576 (Fall 1988).

1091. Mandelshtam, Osip, **The Eyesight of Wasps: Poems**, translated by James Greene; forewords by Nadezhda Mandelshtam and Donald Davie; introduction by Donald Rayfield; with Russian texts in the Appendix. Columbus, Ohio: Ohio State University Press, 1988. 141 p. *(A Sandstone Book)*, ISBN: 0814204783. Includes bibliography and index.

These new "faithful" translations of selected poems by Mandelshtam contain individual works from *Stone, Tristia,* and other posthumously published collections. The book also includes an insightful preface by the translator and a critical introduction. Review: *Choice* 955 (February 1990).

1092. ———, **Poems from Mandelstam**, translated by R.H. Morrison. Rutherford, NJ: Fairleigh Dickinson University Press, 1990. 118 p. ISBN: 83863382x. Includes index.

A selection of poems by the Russian poet Osip Mandelstam. Many have been published here in English because they are lesser known works by the poet. Others are included because they are considered major poetic works of the author. A lengthy introduction on Mandelstam by Ervin Brody is also included.

1093. ———, **The Prose of Osip Mandelstam: The Noise of Time**, translated with critical essays by Clarence Brown. San Francisco, CA: North Point Press, 1986. 249 p. ISBN: 0865472386. Includes index and bibliography (p. 243).

This reprint with additional comments by Brown on Mandelstam's prose is welcome. The first edition was published in 1973, long before Mandelstam had gained the reputation in the West that he now has.

1094. Stapanian, Juliette R., **Mayakovsky's Cubo-Futurist Vision**. 1st ed. Houston, TX: Rice University Press, 1986. ISBN: 0892632593. Includes bibliography: (p. 217-225).

"By an interdisciplinary approach called graphic scansion," the author hopes "to go beyond previous generalities about parallels of Mayakovsky's poems with painting and to detail the essential character of the poet's Cubo-Futurist 'vision.' " (p. 2) After an introductory chapter that explains graphic scansion, Stapanian examines several poems using the technique. Reviews: *Ararat* 28:3:53-55 (Summer 1987). *Canadian Slavonic Papers* 29:4:454-55 (December 1987). *World Literature Today* 61:1:125 (Winter 1987).

1095. Pachmuss, Temira, **D.S. Merezhkovsky in Exile: The Master of the Genre of Biographie Romancee**. New York: P. Lang, 1990. xvi, 338 p. *American University Studies, Series XII, Slavic Languages and Literature*, vol. 12. ISBN: 0820412546. Includes bibliographical references.

"This book is an informative survey of a long series of works written by Merezhkovsky in exile. It sets forth the essential context and points to the salient features of his 'biographies romancees,' which are not so much biographies, as philosophical treatises in disguise." (p. xii) The works studied here were all written in exile from 1919-1941.

1096. Barabtarlo, Gennady, **Phantom of Fact: A Guide to Nabokov's Pnin**. Ann Arbor, MI: Ardis, 1989. 314 p. ISBN: 0875010601. Includes bibliography (p. 309-314).
The essence of this book is an extensive commentary on Nabokov's novel *Pnin*. It includes much more such as a history of the text, chronology, cast, structure, thematic lines, theory, format, and principles. The five appendices (dramatic personae, chronograph, toponymy, flora and fauna, and chromatograph) provide access to the contents as no traditional index can. Reviews: *Modern Fiction Studies* 36:4:573-74 (Winter 1990). *Choice* 955 (February 1990). *Russian Review* 49:3:376-78 (July 1990). *Slavic and East European Journal* 34:2:268 (Summer 1990).

1097. Boyd, Brian, **Vladimir Nabokov: The American Years**. Princeton, NJ: Princeton University Press, 1991. xiv, 783 p. ISBN: 069106797X. Includes bibliographical references and index.
This second volume of Boyd's biography of Vladimir Nabokov deals with the second half of Nabokov's life. In spite of the title, *The American Years*, only part one deals with the time Nabokov lived in the U.S. Part two traces the later years of the author's life which were spent in Europe. Extensive discussion is devoted in this volume to Nabokov's autobiography, *Lolita*, *Pnin*, *Ada*, *Transparent Things*, and *Look at the Harlequin*. Professor Boyd continues to probe Nabokov's personality as a method of revealing the meaning behind his work and the motivation for his style. Reviews: *New York Times Book Review* (September 22, 1991). *Canadian Slavonic Papers* 33:3-4:383-85 (December 1991). *American Spectator* 24:10:36-37 (October 1991).

1098. ———, **Vladimir Nabokov: The Russian Years**. Princeton, NJ: Princeton University Press, 1990. xii, 607 p. ISBN: 0691067945. Includes bibliographical references (p. 533-583) and index.
The first of two volumes that explore the personality of Nabokov as a key to understanding his writings. Following the tumultuous life of the writer, Boyd examines various aspects of Nabokov's writing, the psychology behind it, the developing philosophy of the author, his strategies as a writer, and his searches for harmony in his own life. The first volume traces the author's development up to 1940 when he left Europe for America.

1099. Meyer, Priscilla, **Find What the Sailor Has Hidden: Vladimir Nabokov's Pale Fire**. 1st ed. Middletown, Conn.: Wesleyan University Press, 1988. v, 276 p. ISBN: 0819552062. Includes index and bibliography (p. 251-255).
"The three parts of this book are framed by *Lolita* (1955) and *Pale Fire* (1962); they illustrate the principle of cultural synthesis on which this book is based. The focus of *Lolita* is the Russian tradition; of *Pale Fire*, the English tradition. Each of Nabokov's cultures is exported to America; in this sense *Lolita* is the thesis and *Pale Fire* is the antithesis of Nabokov's art and experience, the synthesis of which maybe found in *Ada* (1969). The present book is itself a synthesis. It shows that the two novels are in close colloquy; the nine chapters between the Thesis and the Antithesis discover the methods, concerns, and materials that shape the dialogue between *Lolita* and *Pale Fire*" (p. 6).

1100. Nabokov, Vladimir, **Vladimir Nabokov: Selected Letters, 1940-77**, edited by Matthew J. Bruccoli. San Diego: Harcourt Brace Jovanovich, 1989. xxvi, 582 p. ISBN: 01516411900. Includes index and bibliographical references.
The collection includes letters that represent specific facets of Nabokov's character. Those selected "reflect one or more of the following facets of Nabokov: 1. His evolution as a writer and insights into the creative process; 2. His academic activity; 3. His passions: helicopters and chess; 4. Certain important details of his life; 5. His family relationships; 6. His artistic and personal morality; 7. The humor with which he composed everything."

(pp x-xi) The volume includes a chronology of Nabokov's life. The letters are intended to create a "direct and spontaneous portrait of the artist." Review: *Choice* 1152-53 (March 1990).

1101. Nabokov, Vladimir Vladimirovich, **The Enchanter**. New York: G. P. Putnam's Sons, 1986. 127 p. ISBN: 0399132112.
This volume represents a short story originally written by Nabokov in Russian in 1985. It was the precursor to the author's famous novel *Lolita*. The translator is the author's son and he attempted as faithful a translation as possible. The book includes a lengthy note from the translator on the work. Review: *New York Times Review of Books* 9 (March 12, 1987).

1102. Parker, Stephen Jan, **Understanding Vladimir Nabokov**. Columbia, S.C.: University of South Carolina Press, 1987. 160 p. *Understanding Contemporary American Literature*, ISBN: 0872484842. Includes index and bibliography (p. 144-155).
Parker, in consonance with other volumes in this series to which this work belongs, provides instruction in how to read Nabokov, "identifying and explicating [his] material, themes, use of language, point of view, structures, symbolisms, and responses to experience." (preface) After an introductory chapter, the author covers the Russian novels and the American novels in two separate chapters followed by a chapter in which he explicates Nabokov's other works and by a conclusion.

1103. Toker, Leona, **Nabokov: The Mystery of Literary Structures**. Ithaca, NY: Cornell University Press, 1989. xiv, 243 p. ISBN: 0801422116. Includes index and bibliography (p. 231-37).
An analysis of ten of Nabokov's novels. The author wishes to fill a gap in the critical literature on Nabokov by combining a study of his techniques and his humanistic themes. These two aspects of the author's work are usually considered separately. "Only a few [studies], most of them of limited scope, deal with the combination of formal refinement and poignant humanism in Nabokov's fiction. Precisely how this combination works is the subject of my inquiry." (p. ix) The ten works analyzed here are *Pnin, Mary, King, Queen, Knave, The Defense, Glory, Laughter in the Dark, Invitation to a Beheading, The Gift, Bend Sinister*, and *Lolita*. Four of the chapters appeared in earlier versions in other publications.

1104. Nagibin, Iurii, **Arise and Walk**, translated by Cathy Porter. London: Faber, 1990. 147p. ISBN: 0571154557.
Originally trained as a doctor, Nagibin then attended the Moscow Institute of Cinematography. He continues to write film scripts. Nagibin has described "the central theme of his creative work as the 'awakening of man,' that is, even perception of the environment, a more conscious relationship — one that had been altered in a positive way — to the next person and thereby to oneself." (Kasack, W., *Dictionary of Russian Literature Since 1917*, New York, Columbia University Press, 1988, p. 261).

1105. Nagibin, Iurii Markovich, **The Peak of Success and Other Stories**, edited by Helena Goscilo. Ann Arbor, MI: Ardis, 1986. 409 p. ISBN: 0882336916. Includes bibliography (p. 407-409).
These stories, selected with Nagibin's assistance, contain narratives from the 1950s, 1960s, and 1970s. The volume also contains a critical introduction and a biographical sketch of the author. Review: *World Literature Today* 61:2:311 (Spring 1987).

1106. Cornwell, Neil, **The Life, Times and Milieu of V.F. Odoyevsky, 1804-1869**. London: Athlone, 1986. xiv, 417 p. ISBN: 0485112795. Includes bibliography and index.

A thematic biography of V.F. Odoyevsky, focusing on the life and personality of this multifaceted figure of Russian 19th century culture. While the author recognizes the significant role of Odoyevsky in literature and spends some time discussing it, his aim is to present a fuller picture of Odoyevsky. Cornwell sees him as one striving for universalism and compares him to Goethe. This is the first study of Odoyevsky in English and is quite broad in its scope. The volume is divided into three parts: a biographical introduction, a section of Odoyevsky's creative work including separate studies of his work as a writer, musician, philosopher, and educator. The final section describes the historical and cultural background of the time. Besides description of the many historical movements of the time such as Decemberism and the reaction it spawned, the author spends a great deal of time discussing Odoyevsky's relationship to other prominent figures of Russian culture such as A.S. Griboyedov, A.S. Pushkin, F.M. Dostoevsky, and many others. Reviews: *Canadian Slavonic Papers* 29:2-3:329-31 (June-September 1987). *American Historical Review* 92:3:710 (June 1987). *Slavic Review* 46:2:36-61 (Summer 1987). *Russian Review* 46:3:346-47 (July 1987).

1107.   Peppard, Victor, **The Poetics of Yurii Olesha**. 1st ed. Gainesville: University of Florida Press, 1989. xi, 164 p. *University of Florida Humanities Monographs*, no. 63. ISBN: 0813009502. Includes index and bibliography (p. 147-157).

This study is meant to fill a gap in the existing literature on Yurii Olesha and his work. Until now, no comprehensive study of his poetics has been produced. This volume will explore features such as his imagery, narrative technique, thematics, dialogical quality and carnivalistic tenor. "The purpose of this study therefore is to demonstrate that there is in fact an identifiable set of interconnected poetic principles that governs Olesha's work and gives it artistic coherence." (p. 2) The book is organized primarily around topics that reflect major aspects of Olesha'a work. A selected bibliography is included. Reviews: *Modern Fiction Studies* 36:4:545-47 (Winter 1990). *Slavic and East European Journal* 34:4:542-44 (Winter 1990).

1108.   Barnes, Christopher J., **Boris Pasternak: A Literary Biography**. Cambridge: Cambridge University Press, 1989. v. ISBN: 0521259576. Includes bibliographical references (p. 460-476).

This volume of what will be a two volume biography of Pasternak takes a somewhat unusual approach in focusing much attention on the early years of the author's life. Barnes justifies this by pointing out Pasternak's strong sense of the importance of his childhood in molding his literary skills. Each chronologically arranged chapter begins with a translation of one of Pasternak's poems. While some literary interpretation is included the author has tried to limit himself to description. The volume has numerous illustrations. Reviews: *New York Times Review of Books* 38:9: 26-31 (May 31, 1990). *Choice* 1832 (July-August 1990).

1109.   Fleishman, Lazar, **Boris Pasternak: The Poet and His Politics**. Cambridge, Mass.: Harvard University Press, 1990. xi, 359 p. ISBN: 0674079051. Includes bibliographical references and index.

Although Fleishman does not touch on Pasternak's works, his primary interest is the author's life and the relation of it to the epoch in which he lived. He follows a chronological approach examining and reflecting on significant developments in Pasternak's life.

1110.   International Symposium on Pasternak, **Boris Pasternak and His Times: Selected Papers from the Second International Symposium on Pasternak**. Berkeley, CA: Berkeley Slavic Specialties, 1989. 423 p. *Modern Russian Literature and Culture, Studies and Texts*, vol. 25. ISBN: 0933884567. Includes bibliographical references.

A collection of selected papers originally delivered at an International Symposium held at Hebrew University in Jerusalem, May 19-24, 1984. The volume includes works in Russian and English. Some of the topics covered in the 15 English essays include Pasternak and his contemporaries, the poetic culture of Pasternak's time, Pushkin in the works of Pasternak and Briusov, Pasternak and Bukharin, and the poetics of *Dr. Zhivago*.

1111.   Levi, Peter, **Boris Pasternak**. London: Hutchinson, 1990. ix, 310 p. ISBN: 0091738865. Includes bibliography (p. 295-299).
A bibliography intended to elucidate Pasternak's poetry as well as inform the reader of the events of his life. The author has drawn on numerous interviews with Pasternak's family as well as the published sources. The author has included translations of several poems in an appendix. The book is chronologically arranged with a chapter devoted to *Doctor Zhivago*.

1112.   Livingstone, Angela, **Boris Pasternak: Doctor Zhivago**. New York: Cambridge University Press, 1989. xv, 118 p. *Landmarks of World Literature*, ISBN: 052132811X. Includes bibliographical references.
Livingstone devotes more than half of her book to an analysis of *Doctor Zhivago* itself. The other portion describes the reception, importance, and position of the novel, his life, work, and times prior to and after 1917, and a chapter devoted exclusively to the poems of Yurii Zhivago.

1113.   O'Connor, Katherine, **Boris Pasternak's My Sister—Life: The Illusion of Narrative**. Ann Arbor, MI: Ardis, 1988. 207 p. ISBN: 0882337785.
O'Connor presents an extensive analysis of Pasternak's work. Review: *Russian Review* 49:3:330-31 (July 1990).

1114.   Pasternak, Evgenii Borisovich, **Boris Pasternak: The Tragic Years 1930-1960**, translated by Michael Duncan, and the poetry of Pasternak translated by Ann Pasternak Slater and Craig Raine. London: Collins Harvill, 1990. xii, 278 p ISBN: 0002720450. Includes index and bibliography (p. 251-252).
A biography written by the author's son and based on family papers from Moscow and London. This work covers a period in Pasternak's life that has been sparsely described. There is also an analysis of some of his literary works, a chronology of his life, and a select bibliography. Given Pasternak's stature as a writer this work should be of interest to any one interested in 20th century literature as well as to those studying the intellectual world in Russia as it went through one of its most brutal periods.

1115.   **Alexander Pushkin**, edited and with an introduction by Harold Bloom. New York: Chelsea House Publishers, 1987. viii, 231 p. *Modern Critical Views*, ISBN: 1555462731. Includes index and bibliography (p. 219-222).
A selection of critical works on the work, of Pushkin presented in chronological order of their original publication. Essays cover such topics as the *Queen of Spades*, *Eugene Onegin*, *Boris Gogunov*, *Tales of Belkin*, as well as many others. The volume contains a chronology of Pushkin's life.

1116.   Driver, Sam N., **Pushkin: Literature and Social Ideas**. New York: Columbia University Press, 1989. xii, 143 p. ISBN: 0231068484. Includes index and bibliography (p. 137-140).
Driver examines the development of Pushkin's social ideas, primarily focusing on the period 1828-1837. In chapter one the author surveys the existing scholarship on Pushkin's political and social ideas. He does this in part because his view is so at odds with that corpus

of thought and writing. The second and third chapters examine the importance of Pushkin's aristocratic status and ethos and its relationship to his political views and how they were expressed in his literary works. He then examines Pushkin's dandyism and the relationship among dandyism, aristocratism, and politics. In the final chapter Driver treats two of Pushkin's fragments, *A Russian Pelham* and *Petronius* in regard to aristocratism and politics. Reviews: *Choice* 1152 (March 1990). *Russian History* 17:1:89-92 (Spring 1990).

1117. **Russian Views of Pushkin's Eugene Onegin**, translated with an introduction and notes by Sona Stephan Hoisington. Bloomington: Indiana University Press, 1988. xvii, 199 p. ISBN: 0253350670. Includes index.

A collection of essays, translated from the Russian, on Pushkin's literary masterpiece *Eugene Onegin*. The essays represent Russian literary criticism as it developed from the 19th through the twentieth century. Essayists include Vissarion Belinsky, Dmitry Pisarev, Fyodor Dostoevsky, Yuri Tynyanov, Yuri Lotman, Mikhail Bakhtin, and Sergei Bocharov. The book includes a glossary of proper names and a bibliography of critical works on *Eugene Onegin* in English.

1118. Sandler, Stephanie, **Distant Pleasures: Alexander Pushkin and the Writing of Exile**. Stanford, Calif.: Stanford University Press, 1989. ix, 263 p. ISBN: 0804715424. Includes index and bibliography (p. 249-257).

In 1820 Pushkin was sent into internal exile to the south of Russia for writing liberal poems that displeased the powers that be. Sandler examines Pushkin's literary activity during this period of exile, which lasted until 1826. Of particular interest is the idea of "distance" in Pushkin's lyrical voice and the poet's drama *Boris Godunov*. Review: *Russian Review* 49:4:484-86 (October 1990).

1119. Polowy, Teresa, **The Novellas of Valentin Rasputin: Genre, Language and Style**. New York: P. Lang, 1989. viii, 262 p. *Middlebury Studies in Russian Language and Literature*, vol. 1. ISBN: 0820406430. Includes bibliography (p. 247-255).

A study of several of the works of one of contemporary Russia's foremost writers. The author feels that there is a gap in the critical work on this author in that there are few detailed stylistic analyses of his individual works. In this volume the author discussed numerous works by Rasputin but focuses on *Dengi dlia Marii (Money for Maria)*. *Poslednii srok (The Final Hours)*, *Zhivi i pomni (Live and Remember)*, *Proshchanie i Materoi (Farewell to Matera)* from the period 1967-76, and *Pozhar* from his most recent works. The first chapter presents biographical and critical background on Rasputin while the next two chapters deal with general features of plot, structure, theme, and characterization in his work in general. Chapters four and five focus on the four earlier novellas analyzing them for elements of tragedy and myth as well as language and style. The author moves on to Rasputin's work in the eighties in the final chapter. The book is organized from general to specific topics. The author is seeking to place Rasputin in the broader context of Russia's literary tradition. Review: *Slavic Review* 50:2:462-63 (Summer 1991).

1120. Rasputin, Valentin Grigorevich, **Siberia on Fire: Stories and Essays**. DeKalb, Ill: Northern Illinois University Press, 1989. xxii, 230 p. ISBN: 0875801528. Includes bibliographical references (p. 229-230).

A collection of fiction and essays by one of Russia's greatest contemporary authors, Valentin Rasputin. The works of fiction span virtually his entire career, displaying his evolution from the village prose style and themes of his early years to his later focus on ecological problems. Most of the author's characters are based on individuals from Rasputin's own life. The essays reflect the author's interest in ethnography, history, environmental protectionism and literary criticism. The intent was to give the reader a well rounded view of this important author. An appendix is provided listing all Russian names cited in the book. Footnotes are also provided for clarification by the translators. The works of fiction include "Vasily and Vasilisa," "French Lessons," "Live and Love," "What Should I Tell the Crow?," "The Fire," and "Auntie Vlita." Essays include "Your Siberia and Mine," How Did They End Up in Irkutsk?," "Baikal," "What We Have," "Your Son, Russia, and Our Passionate Brother," and "The Truths of Alexander Vampilov." A bibliography of major works by Rasputin is also included. Reviews: *New York Times Review of Books* 37:4:26-27 (March 15, 1990). *World Literature Today* 64:3:488 (Summer 1990). *Slavic and East European Journal* 34:4:549-51 (Winter 1990).

1121. Ratushinskaia, Irina, **Beyond the Limit: Poems**, translated by Frances Padorr Brent and Carol J. Avins. 1st ed. Evanston, Ill.: Northwestern University Press, 1987. xvii, 121 p. ISBN: 0810107481, 081010749X (pbk.).
This collection, originally written as samizdat and smuggled out of prison, was received in the spring of 1985. The poems were written during Ratushinskaia's incarceration in a Soviet labor camp. Review: *Partisan Review* 55:3:497-500 (Summer 1988).

1122. ———, **Pencil Letter**. 1st American ed. New York, N.Y.: Knopf, 1989. 83 p. ISBN: 0394571703, 0679726004 (pbk.).
The first poem in this collection was written in November, 1982 in a KGB prison in Kiev as she was awaiting trial for charges of "anti-Soviet agitation and propaganda." She was released from prison on October 9, 1986. She now resides in the West.

1123. ———, **A Tale of Three Heads: Short Stories,** translated from the Russian, with a foreword and an afterword by Diane Nemec Ignashev. Tenafly, NJ: Hermitage, 1986. 123 p. ISBN: 0938920839.
This bilingual collection of short stories exhibits the broader talents of the author, who is primarily known for her poetry.

1124. **Aleksei Remizov: Approaches to a Protean Writer**, edited by Greta N. Slobin. Columbus, Ohio: Slavica Publishers, 1987. 285 *UCLA Slavica Studies*, vol. 16. ISBN: 0893571679.
The contributions here were originally presented at an international conference on Remizov. Because of this, seven of the nineteen papers are in Russian. The conference had two goals: "to provide a forum for sharing information and raising larger questions pertaining to the period; to examine existing presumptions and to begin working towards establishing a sound, methodological basis for the study of this writer, whose own claims and reputation for elusiveness need a careful critical reappraisal." (p.7)

1125. Rybakov, Anatolii Naumovich, **Children of the Arbat**, translated by Harold Shukman. 1st ed. Boston: Little, Brown and Co., 1988. 685 p. ISBN: 0316763721.
Originally published in the literary journal *Druzhba narodov* (1987: 4-6), this novel has gained wide acclaim for its depiction of life in the 1930s under Stalin's iron rule. Reviews: *Wilson Quarterly* 1:120-21 (New Year's 1989). *Hudson Review* 41:4:752-75 (Winter 1989). *Slavic Review* 48:3:484-85 (Fall 1989). *Orbis* 33: 3:459-60 (Summer 1989).

1126. Semyonov, Julian, **TASS Is Authorized to Announce**, translated by Charles Buxton. London: John Calder Ltd., 1987. 352 p. ISBN: 0714541026.
Semyonov's novel is set in three continents, in Moscow, in Africa, and in the U.S. It was originally published in the literary journal *Druzhba narodov* in 1979. It is typical of the author's other works where the plot is intense and the action adventurous.

1127. Shaginian, Marietta Sergeevna, **Mess-mend, Yankees in Petrograd**, introduced and translated by Samuel D. Cioran. Ann Arbor, MI: Ardis, 1991. 268 p. ISBN: 0882339710.

This 1923 novel is a suspenseful story of detective Michael Thingmaster and his fight to thwart a group of capitalists from overthrowing the young Soviet regime. The author wrote several novels as well as symbolist lyric poetry. This edition includes a lengthy introduction by the translator. Review: *New York Times Book Review* 12 (August 18, 1991).

1128. Sokolov, Sasha, **Astrophobia**. 1st ed. New York: Grove Press, 1989. vii, 385 p. ISBN: 0802110878.

A satirical novel set in the 28th century. Review: *New Republic* 202:1:39-42 (March 12, 1990).

1129. Greene, Diana, **Insidious Intent: An Interpretation of Fedor Sologub's The Petty Demon**. Columbus, Ohio: Slavica Publishers, 1986. 140 p. *Studies of the Harriman Institute*, ISBN: 089357158X. Includes index and bibliography (p. 119-136).

The Petty Demon was originally serialized in the journal *Voprosy zhizni*, but the journal ceased before the serialization was complete. Greene touches on all aspects of the novel, devoting separate chapters to reception, genre, character, plot, the pattern of Peredonovism, setting, narration, and its relation to the Symbolist movement. Reviews: *Slavic and East European Journal* 31:2:291-92 (Summer 1987). *Slavic Review* 46:1:160-61 (Spring 1987).

1130. Sollogub, Vladimir Aleksandrovich, **The Tarantas: Impressions of a Journey**, translated and with a commentary by William Edward Brown. Ann Arbor, MI: Ardis, 1989. 208 p. ISBN: 0875010458. Includes index.

Tarantas is the result of a journey made in 1839 by Sollogub and a friend from Moscow to Simbirsk by way of Kazan. It is part travelogue and part fiction. Sollogub manages to describe both the frivolous high society as well as petty officials and peasants. Review: *Slavic and East European Journal* 34:4:529-30 (Winter 1990).

1131. Solloukhin, Vladimir Alekseevich, **Scenes from Russian Life,** translated from the Russian and with an introduction by David Martin. London: P. Owen, 1988. 174 p. ISBN: 0720607124.

A collection of works by the Soviet writer of the "village prose" school, Vladimir Soloukhin. As with other writers of this genre, the author concentrates on themes of Russian village life. Themes in his work are conservation, concern for rural communities, love of villagers, and their humor. This volume of translation by David Martin includes seven stories: "Sentences: A Lyrical Documentary," "Tittle-Tattle," "The Fortieth Day," "A Winter's Day," "The Guest's Were Arriving at the Dacha...," and "A Little Girl by the Edge of the Sea." The introduction, by the translator, directs the reader to other works by the author.

1132. Marsh, Rosalind J., **Images of Dictatorship: Portraits of Stalin in Literature**. London: Routledge, 1989. xiii, 267 p. ISBN: 0415037964. Includes index and bibliography (p. 248-254).

"The aim of this study is, firstly, to develop a historical and theoretical framework within which literary portraits of major twentieth-century European historical figures can fruitfully be analyzed; and secondly, to discuss the depiction of Stalin in literature, particularly in the works of Russian writers living both within and outside the USSR." (p. ix) Reviews: *Choice* 1152 (March 1990). *Canadian Slavonic Papers* 32:1:99-100 (March 1990).

1133. Pontuso, James F., **Solzhenitsyn's Political Thought**. Charlottesville: University Press of Virginia, 1990. 272 p. ISBN: 081391280. Includes bibliographical references (p. 257-268) and index.

Novelist Aleksander Solzhenitsyn has also become known for his political and social views. While those in the West have tended to applaud his condemnation of the Soviet regime and its ideological underpinnings, they have been less willing to examine critically Solzhenitsyn's warnings to the West about its own lack of moral backbone. "This book argues that Solzhenitsyn's views on the West are neither inconsistent nor unappreciative. Quite the contrary, his principles derive from a deep understanding of the roots of Western culture." (p. 10) Pontuso examines Solzhenitsyn's views on the terror of the 1930s, Stalin, Lenin, Marx, the West and Solzhenitsyn's call for a revival of the spirit. Review: *American Political Science Review* 85:4:1451-1452 (December 1991).

1134. Solzhenitsyn, Aleksandr Isaevich, **The Love Girl and the Innocent with Victory Celebrations and Prisoners**. London: Faber, 1986. 365 p. ISBN: 0571133207.

These plays were originally conceived by the author in 1952-53 while Solzhenitsyn was in the gulag. *The Love Girl and the Innocent* reached dress rehearsal stage in Moscow but was banned before the opening curtain. It was produced by the Royal Shakespeare Company in London in 1981. The other two plays have not been publicly performed.

1135. Mersereau, John, **Orest Somov: Russian Fiction Between Romanticism and Realism**. Ann Arbor, MI: Ardis, 1989. 165 p. ISBN: 0875010334.

Somov (1793-1833) is a transitional figure in early 19th century Russian fiction between romanticism and realism. Mersereau examines this journalist-critic-writer to understand more fully the development of Russian prose fiction during this period. Reviews: *Slavic Review* 49:3:495-96 (Fall 1990). *Slavic and East European Journal* 34:3:376-77 (Fall 1990).

1136. Strugatskii, Arkadii Natanovich, and Boris Natanovich Strugatskii, **The Time Wanderers,** translated from the Russian by Antonina W. Bouis. New York: Kampmann & Co., 1986. 213 p. ISBN: 093193315.

A novel coauthored by two brothers. In the Soviet Union in the sixties these authors were "two of the best, most beloved writers of nonrealistic prose." (Kasack, W. *Russian Literature Since 1917*, p. 403) This novel is written in the form of a memoir of events in the year "99." Some chapters are constructed in documentary form.

1137. Terts, Abram, **Goodnight!: A Novel**. New York: Viking, 1989. xiv, 364 p. ISBN: 0670801658.

Terts, a pseudonym of Andrei Sinyavsky, is a literary critic and lecturer. He successfully wrote under his pseudonym, but was eventually arrested in 1965. As the editor comments, "nearly all of the book's contents describe actual events, except for the obvious flights of fantasy and the literary essays and plays inlaid within the text. But everything is arranged and held in a vision originating in the imagination." (p. ix) The novel is about his own complicity with the KGB and his arrest and trial. Since 1973 he has lived in Paris.

1138. **Bibliography of Works by and about F.I. Tiutchev to 1985**. Nottingham: Astra Press, 1987. vii, 114 p. *Astra Soviet and East European Bibliographies*, no. 7. ISBN: 0946134103.

A bibliography, largely of English language sources on one of Russia's greatest poets. As a thorough bibliography for Russian scholarship on Tiutchev already exists, this work was intended to present a guide to Western scholarship. The bibliography is divided into two main sections. The first includes works by Tiutchev. This section is subdivided into divisions on Russian editions, English editions, and publications on miscellaneous works. Part two consists of works about Tiutchev. This section includes subsections on monographs, English language materials, Russian language materials published outside Russia, and non-Russian language materials published during Tiutchev's lifetime. A section containing biographic data and a name index are also included.

1139. **Leo Tolstoy**, edited with an introduction by Harold Bloom. New York: Chelsea House Publishers, 1986. ix, 267 p. *Modern Critical Views*, ISBN: 0877547270. Includes index and bibliography (p. 259-260).

Bloom has brought together a representative selection of what he considers to be the best criticism of Tolstoy's works available in English. They are represented in chronological order according to their date of publication, 1920-1983, and cover a broad range of viewpoints.

1140. Courcel, Martine de, **Tolstoy: The Ultimate Reconciliation**, translated by Peter Levi. 1st American ed. New York: C. Scribner's Sons, 1988. 458 p. ISBN: 0684185695. Includes index and bibliography (p. 445-447).

Courcel wrote this biography of Tolstoy in order to understand why a man who was considered one of the greatest writers of his time abandoned his family and his home and finally succeeded "in dying as he would have wished to live." Although Courcel begins with Tolstoy's childhood and youth, he constantly keeps focused on the death of Tolstoy, hoping to discover some clue, some pattern that will explain his last days.

1141. Gustafson, Richard F., **Leo Tolstoy, Resident and Stranger: A Study in Fiction and Theology**. Princeton, NJ: Princeton University Press, 1986. xvi, 480 p. ISBN: 0691066744. Includes index and bibliography (p. 465-470).

"Based on a close reading of the fiction and the diaries as well as an original reconstruction of Tolstoy's theology seen in the light of Eastern Christian thought rather than under the influence of those Western thinkers many believe are formative, this book explores the relationship between Tolstoy's psychological life, his verbal icons, and his religious world view." (p. xiv) Reviews: *Canadian Slavonic Papers* 29:2-3:335-36 (June-September 1987). *Russian Review* 46:3:321-28 (July 1987). *National Review* 49-50 (July 31, 1987). *Slavic and East European Journal* 31:4:623-25.

1142. **In the Shade of the Giant: Essays on Tolstoy**, edited by Hugh McLean. Berkeley: University of California Press, 1989. viii. 193 p. *California Slavic Studies*, no. 13. ISBN: 0520064054. Includes bibliographies and index.

This collection of original essays on Tolstoy include specific aspects and characters in *Anna Karenina*, several short stories, and external influences on his fiction. Reviews: *Slavic Review* 49:4:67-79 (Winter 1990). *Russian Review* 49:4:488-89 (October 1990).

1143. Moller, Peter Ulf, **Postlude to the Kreutzer Sonata: Tolstoj and the Debate on Sexual Morality in Russian Literature in the 1890s,** translated from the Danish by John Kendal. Leiden: E.J. Brill, 1988. xviii, 346 ISBN: 9004083103. Includes index and bibliography (p. 314-339). Translation of *Efterspil til Kreutzersonaten*.

Tolstoy's *The Kreutzer Sonata* created an immense commotion when it first appeared in 1889 in St. Petersburg. Moller describes the ensuing debate about sexuality and places it in context with other Russian literature of the 1890s. Other writers examined include Chekhov, Gippius, Merezhkovskii, Briusov, Solovev and Rozanov. Reviews: *Slavic Review* 49:3:496-99 (Fall 1990). *Russian Review* 49:2:216-17 (April 1990).

1144. Morson, Gary Saul, **Hidden in Plain View: Narrative and Creative Potentials in War and Peace**. Stanford, Calif.: Stanford University Press, 1987. x, 322 p. ISBN: 0804713871. Includes index and bibliography (p. 275-301).

"The structure of the present study takes the form of a riddle, with the puzzle posed in Part I, and the answer advanced in the course of the extended analysis of Tolstoy's work in Parts II and III." (p. 5) Morson employs a Bakhtinian approach "with loopholes," and examines Tolstoy's war narrative and the novel in Part I, his approach to history and other systems in Part II, and selves and decisions in Part III. Review: *Canadian Slavonic Papers* 30:1:150-52 (March 1988).

1145. Rowe, William Woodin, **Leo Tolstoy**. Boston: Twayne Publishers, 1986. 143 p. *Twayne's World Authors Series, Russian Authors*, no. 772. ISBN: 0805766235. Includes index and bibliography (p. 137-140).

Recognizing the impossibility of discussing all of Tolstoy's writings in depth, the author took as his primary goal to "present a picture of Tolstoy the man, thinker, and writer as well as to offer careful readings of *War and Peace*, *Anna Karenina*, *Resurrection*, and some of his more important shorter works." (p. 1) Rowe's first chapter presents a brief biography of Tolstoy's life. Subsequent chapters are devoted to *Childhood, Boyhood, and Youth*, the novels named above, and *Confession*. A final chapter tries to present the full scope and significance of Tolstoy's vision, his values and his art.

1146. **Critical Essays on Tolstoy**, edited by Edward Wasiolek. Boston, Mass: G.K. Hall, 1986. vii, 200 p. *Critical Essays on World Literature*, ISBN: 0816188270. Includes index and bibliography (p. 193-198).

A demonstration of the variety of views on Tolstoy using a collection of essays from all over the world. The volume also includes reviews of his early stories, *War and Peace*, *Anna Karenina*, and the late novels. The essays on these same works are by such figures as V. I. Lenin, Virginia Woolf, Maxim Gorky, N.G. Chernyshevsky, I.S. Turgenev, Joseph Kirkand, Dmitri Merezhkovsky, E.M. Forster, Isaiah Berlin and many others. The editor hopes to display the many interpretations of Tolstoy's writing and the tremendous impact he had on the world — literary and philosophical.

1147. Wilson, A. N., **Tolstoy**. 1st ed. New York: Norton, 1988. xxviii, 572 p. ISBN: 0383025853. Includes index and bibliography.

This expansive critical biography of Tolstoy includes chapters devoted to several of his major works, as well as purely biographical chapters. A chronology of Tolstoy's life and times is a helpful reference aid for both the casual reader and the serious researcher.

1148. Taubman, Jane, **A Life Through Poetry: Marina Tsvetaeva's Lyric Diary**. Columbus, Ohio: Slavica Publishers, 1989. 295 p. ISBN: 0893571970. Includes bibliographical references (p. 275-295).

Taubman does not intend to provide us with a comprehensive overview of all of Tsvetaeva's artistic output, but instead "will study the most important aspect of Tsvetaeva's work, her lyric poems... and attempts to 'read' them... as a continuously unfolding, self referential diary." (p. 3) As a result of this plan of study, the examination of her poetry proceeds chronologically. Other works by Tsvetaeva will be treated only in so far as they can cast further light on her lyric diary. Reviews: *Choice* 122-23 (September 1990). *Canadian Slavonic Papers* 32:1:96-97 (March 1990).

1149. Tsvetaeva, Marina, **In the Inmost Hour of the Soul: Selected Poems of Marina Tsvetayeva**, translated by Nina Kossman. Clifton, NJ: Humana Press, 1989. xv, 108 p. *Vox Humana*, ISBN: 0896031373. Includes bibliographical references.

These poems were written between 1913 and 1934, when Tsvetaeva was in exile. They are, as the translator states "never calm and contemplative [but the] work of dynamism, strength, and a rapturous 'heathen' love of life." (p. viii) Review: *World Literature Today* 64:2:327 (Spring 1990).

1150. ————, **Selected Poems of Marina Tsvetayeva**, translated by Elaine Feinstein with literal versions provided by Angela Livingstone. New York: E.P. Dutton, 1987. 108 p. ISBN: 0525482830.

These poems were selected by the translator to give a broad range of the poet's abilities. Tsvetaeva left Russia for Prague in 1922 and lived there and in Paris for many years. She returned in the late 1930s after her husband, Sergei Efron, was accused of being a Soviet spy. Shortly after her arrival she and her family were suspected of working against the Soviet government. Her husband and daughter were arrested. She hanged herself in 1941. Feinstein is considered by many to be Tsvetaeva's best translator into English. Review: *World Literature Today* 62:4:683 (Autumn 1988).

1151. Costlow, Jane T., **Worlds Within Worlds: The Novels of Ivan Turgenev**. Princeton, NJ: Princeton University Press, 1990. 166 p. ISBN: 069106783X. Includes index and bibliographical references.

Costlow intends "to some extent to account for both the historicity and the aesthetic elegance of Turgenev's novels." The author provides close readings of *A Nest of Gentry*, *On the Eve*, and *Fathers and Sons*. She moves from examining Turgenev's language in *Rudin* to an analysis of the relationship "between his use of a specific literary genre and his political convictions in *Fathers and Children*."

1152. Knowles, A. V., **Ivan Turgenev**. Boston: Twayne, 1988. x, 144 p. *Twayne's World Authors Series: Russian Literature*, ISBN: 0805782419. Includes bibliography (p. 136-139) and index.

After a brief biographical sketch in chapter one, Knowles devotes six chapters to criticism of Turgenev's works starting with his early verse and prose in the 1840s and progressing through his early novels, *Fathers and Sons*, and ending with his last two novels, *Smoke* and *Virgin Soil*. After a chapter in which he discusses Turgenev's letters, he concludes with a general summary and assessment.

1153. Lowe, David Allan, **Critical Essays on Ivan Turgenev**. Boston, Mass.: G.K. Hall, 1988. 175 p. *Critical Essays on World Literature*, ISBN: 0816188424. Includes index.

Lowe has collected together twelve classic essays on Turgenev. His introduction consists of two parts: the first is a critical introduction to Turgenev and scholarship about him, and the second is a brief biographical sketch.

1154. Seeley, Frank Friedeberg, **Turgenev: A Reading of His Fiction**. Cambridge: Cambridge University Press, 1991. xvi, 380 p. *Cambridge Studies in Russian Literature*, ISBN: 052136521X. Includes bibliographical references (p. 335-368) and index.

Seeley focuses almost exclusively on Turgenev's fiction, with the exception of his first two chapters which explore Turgenev's life and reputation and how his poetry, plays, and criticism shed light on his prose. The remaining fifteen chapters offer a reading of his fiction, starting with his short stories, proceeding through the many novels and concluding with his *Senilia* or prose poems and final stories. Review: *Canadian Slavonic Papers* 33:3-4:394-96 (December 1991).

1155. Troyat, Henri, **Turgenev,** translated from the French by Nancy Amphoux. 1st American ed. New York: Dutton, 1988. vi, 184 p. ISBN: 052524746. Includes index and bibliography (p. 172-173).
Originally written in French, this biography of Turgenev follows a straightforward chronological approach to the author's life. It illuminates the social, cultural, and intellectual context surrounding the author's writings and explores in some depth the author's ideological journey.

1156. Vakhtin, Boris, **The Sheepskin Coat; and An Absolutely Happy Village.** Ann Arbor, MI: Ardis, 1988. 180 p. ISBN: 0882337866.
Vakhtin was a member of the unofficial group of writers in Leningrad called the "Urbanites." Born in 1930, he also was a sinologist and translator of Chinese literature. He died in 1981.

1157. Voinovich, Vladimir, **The Anti-Soviet Soviet Union**. 1st ed. San Diego: Harcourt Brace Jovanovich, 1986. xxv, 325 p. ISBN: 0151078408.
Soviet dissident Vladimir Voinovich presents a picture of life in the Soviet Union. The book is divided into three sections. The first contains short essays on Soviet life. The second deals with writers and literature and the final section with the "absurdities" of Soviet life. Review: *Orbis* 30:4:750 (Winter 1987).

1158. ———, **Fur Hat,** translated from the Russian by Susan Brownsberger. 1st ed. San Diego: Harcourt Brace Jovanovich, 1989. 122 p. ISBN: 0151391009.
Another novel from the popular author of *The Life and Extraordinary Adventures of Private Ivan Chonkin, The Ivankiad,* and *The Anti-Soviet Soviet Union.* Reviews: *New York Times Review of Books* 37:4:26-27 (March 15, 1990). *World Literature Today* 64:4:661-62 (Autumn 1990).

1159. ———, **Moscow 2042,** translated from the Russian by Richard Lourie. 1st ed. New York: Harcourt Brace Jovanovich, 1987. viii, 424 p. ISBN: 0151624445.
This novel, written in 1986, "combines experiences of emigration in Europe and the United States with a utopian depiction of life in Moscow after 20 years as a city where socialism has been realized." (Kasack, W. *Russian Literature Since 1917,* p. 459) Review: *Orbis* 32:1:155-56 (Winter 1988).

1160. Voznesenskii, Andrei, **An Arrow in the Wall: Selected Poetry and Prose**, edited by William Jay Smith and F.D. Reeve; poems translated by W.H. Auden ... et al.; prose translated by Antonina W. Bouis. 1st ed. New York: H. Holt, 1987. ISBN: 080500100X. Includes bibliography (p.325-344).
This collection includes poetry previously available, such as "Antiworlds" and "Nostalgia for the Present," some recent work gathered under the title poem "Release the Cranes," and two prose pieces which provide much of the background from which the poems have developed. The volume is devoted to the English reader, but the original Russian is included on facing pages for the poetry only. The editor has included end notes on each poem that give some background information and which elucidate uncommon allusions.

1161. Yevtushenko, Yevgeny Aleksandrovich, **The Collected Poems, 1952-1990**, edited by Albert C. Todd with the author and James Ragan. 1st ed. New York: Henry Holt, 1991. xxiv, 659 p. ISBN: 0805006966. Includes bibliographical references (p. 641-659).
Perhaps Siberia's most noted poet, Yevtushenko's heritage and the physical world of his youth and childhood play an important role in his poetry. This collection of his translated

poetry was selected by the poet himself and differs from the Russian edition of his collected works published in 1983-1984 and in three volumes issued in 1987. Some of the poems translated here have appeared in other translations. Some older poems are here translated for the first time. The poems are arranged in chronological sections of two or three years and within these sections are further arranged chronologically. Review: *New Republic* 204:18:33-37 (May 6, 1991).

1162. ———, **Fatal Half Measures: The Culture of Democracy in the Soviet Union**.
Boston: Little, Brown, and Co., 1991. xiii, 357 p. ISBN: 0316968838. Includes bibliographical references and index.

A collection of essays on current events, literary criticism, and the travel accounts by one of Russia's popular writers. Yevtushenko is most widely known as a poet, but he is also a photographer, film maker, representative to the Russian Congress, and a world traveler. The materials in this volume reflects his wide range of interests. Aside from his political beliefs, his views on Soviet life in general are represented. The theme of the essays is his belief that there is danger in doing things only half way.

1163. **Zamyatin's "We": A Collection of Critical Essays**, edited and introduced by Gary
Kern. Ann Arbor, MI: Ardis, 1988. 306 p. ISBN: 0882338048. Includes bibliography (p. 305-306).

A compilation of various critical works on Eugenii Zamyatin's *We*. The editor has included early Soviet criticism of the book as well as a variety of Western interpretations in the hope of providing a source book for anyone interested in interpretations of this work. The Western analysis is grouped under three headings. "The first 'mythic criticism' embraces the concerns of myth, religion and psychology. The second, 'aesthetics,' focuses on analysis of themes, structures and devices. The last, 'influence and comparisons,' explore influences on Zamyatin, coincidental expression on other writers and Zamyatin's influence on others." (p. 15) The editor has also included several writings by Zamyatin not previously published together. Review: *Russian Review* 48:4:433-34 (October 1989).

1164. Zinik, Zinovii, **The Lord and the Gamekeeper: A Novel**. London: Heinemann,
1991. 248 p. ISBN: 0434897310.

A novel centered around three Russian émigrés, all former Muscovites. The main characters are Felix, a person involved in the theater, Victor, a professional dissident, and Silva, a Turner scholar from the Pushkin museum. The story traces the lives of these three characters shifting between a focus on their Moscow past, to their present circumstances, living in 1984 on an estate with a Ukrainian benefactor. The author was born in Moscow and emigrated to London where he is now a theatrical critic and author.

1165. ———, **The Mushroom-picker: A Novel**. London: Heinemann, 1987. 282 p.
ISBN: 0434897353.

The story of an émigré, Konstantin, who has married a British woman and their difficulties living in England. The author, Zinovy Zinik emigrated from the Soviet Union to London where he works as a theatrical reviewer and writer.

1166. Zoshchenko, Mikhail, **A Man Is not a Flea: Stories**. Ann Arbor, MI: Ardis, 1989.
140 p. ISBN: 0875010237.

A selection of satirical stories by the Soviet writer Mikhail Zoshchenko. Among them are "Bathhouse," "A Dog's Nose," "The Charms of Civilization," "Firewood," and "What the Nightingale Sang About." A foreword by the translator with a brief chronology of Zoshchenko's life precedes the stories. Reviews: *World Literature Today* 64:4:662 (Autumn 1990). *Slavic and East European Journal* 34:3:389-90 (Fall 1990).

Special Studies, Censorship

1167. Baehr, Stephen Lessing, **The Paradise Myth in Eighteenth Century Russia: Utopian Patterns in Early Secular Russian Literature and Culture**. Stanford, Calif: Stanford University Press, 1991. xiv, 308 p. *Studies of the Harriman Institute*, ISBN: 0804715335. Includes bibliographical references (p. 271-292) and index.
A scholarly analysis of the use of the paradise myth in Russian literature. The volume covers the years 1682-1796. During this period images of an earthly paradise permeate Russian culture. The author views the central role of the paradise myth during this period as being generated by two of the most successful rulers in Russian history and the persistence of the "culture of consent." The paradise myth is seen as a propaganda tool used by the tsars. The author also feels that the characteristics of Russian literature he identifies place it much closer to European renaissance literature until the last third of the 18th century. Only then did it begin to reflect the values of the enlightenment. Many authors are discussed in this work including Mikhail Kheraskov, Pavel L'vov, Mikhail Lomonosov, Simeon Polotskii, Aleksander Pushkin, Aleksander Sumarokov, Vasilii Trediakovskii, and Gavril Derzhavin. The volume includes several appendices focusing on different aspects of the paradise myth. Review: *Canadian Slavonic Papers* 33:3-4:382-83 (December 1991).

1168. Bakhtin, Mikhail Mikhailovich, **Speech Genres and Other Late Essays**, edited by Michael Holquist and Caryl Emerson. Austin: University of Texas Press, 1986. xxii, 177 p. *University of Texas Press Slavic Series*, no. 8. ISBN: 0292720467. Includes bibliographies and index.
This collection includes the following essays by Bakhtin: "Response to a Question from the *Novy Mir* Editorial Staff"; "The Bildungsroman and Its Significance in the History of Realism"; "The Problem of Speech Genres"; "The Problem of the Text in Linguistics, Philology, and the Human Sciences: An Experiment in Philosophical Analysis"; "From Notes Made in 1970-1971"; and "Toward a Methodology for the Human Sciences." Michael Holquist, a noted Bakhtin scholar, provides an informative introduction to the critic's works. Review: *Canadian Slavonic Papers* 29:2-3:344-45 (June-September 1987).

1169. Garrard, John Gordon, and Carol Garrard, **Inside the Soviet Writers' Union**. New York: Free Press, 1990. xv, 303 p. ISBN: 0029113202. Includes bibliographical references and index.
There are two major considerations in this study, one is the context in which a Russian writer develops and works, and the other is the Soviet Writers' Union as an institution. The authors concern themselves with an analysis of the economic, social, and political environment of the Soviet writer. The Writers' Union is evaluated as an organization that creates a camaraderie among writers in order to accomplish its aims of using their talent to accomplish its ends. There is also an analysis of the effects that glasnost and perestroika have had on the literary world. An appendix with a variety of information on the Union is included at the back of the volume.

1170. Gutsche, George J., **Moral Apostasy in Russian Literature**. DeKalb, Ill.: Northern Illinois University Press, 1986. xii, 185 p. ISBN: 0875801188. Includes index and bibliography (p. 175-181).
A collection of the essays by the author on the theme of moral apostasy as it is portrayed in various works of Russian literature is presented here. The essays are arranged chronologically, that is in the order in which their subjects were written. The authors discussed are Pushkin, Turgenev, Tolstoy, Gorky, Pasternak, and Solzhenitsyn. One of the author's goals is to elucidate the moral values of the society that produced these works. Review: *Canadian Slavonic Papers* 29:4:450-51 (December 1987).

1171. LeBlanc, Ronald Denis, **The Russianization of** *Gil Blas*: **A Study in Literary Appropriation**. Columbus, Ohio: Slavica, 1986. 292 p. ISBN: 0893571598. Includes index and bibliography (p. 273-281).

An examination of Western influence on Russian literature. In particular, the author traces the novel *Gil Blas* by LeSage as it became known in Russia and shows how its main character was used as a model by two authors, Vasilii Narezhnii and Fadei Bulgarin. At the same time, he examines how a style of novel, the picaresque novel, was used in Russian literature. The author also discusses how this style lost popularity and why. Review: *Canadian Slavonic Papers* 29:2-3:337 (June-September 1987).

1172. Marsh, Rosalind J., **Soviet Fiction Since Stalin: Soviet Politics and Literature**. London: Croom Helm, 1986. 338 p. ISBN: 0709917767. Includes index and bibliography.

A study of the treatment of science and technology in Soviet literature in the post-Stalin era. The book is divided into three main parts. Part one examines socio-political problems related to science and technology. Part two focuses on general attitudes of Soviet writers toward science. Part three turns to the interaction between science, literature, and public policy. Samizdat publications have been included to serve as a measure of the degree of censorship in literature on this topic. Each chapter includes a summary of political and scientific factors which have influenced the treatment of some topics. These summaries are also intended to provide a context of the history of science. Such topics as the treatment of ecology, nuclear policy, automation, genetic engineering, and medicine are all discussed in this volume. Review: *World Literature Today* 61:1:123-24 (Winter 1987).

1173. McCarey, Peter, **Hugh Macdiarmid and the Russians**. Edinburgh: Scottish Academic Press, 1987. viii, 225 p. ISBN: 0707305268. Includes bibliography (p. 201-225).

A comparison of six authors with Hugh Macdiarmid; Fedor Dostoevsky, Vladimir Solovyov, Alexander Blok, Vladimir Mayakovsky, and Lev Shestov. The focus is on Macdiarmid and a knowledge of the works and the style of the Russian authors is assumed. The author sees Macdiarmid and the Russians as being on two sides of a "cultural divide." In order to study the commonalties between them, he presents them in the context of the European tradition they all hold in common. The first chapter compares Dostoevsky and Macdiarmid, followed by a chapter on Solovyov's philosophy, and a chapter on his poetry. The author then turns to a comparison with Blok, Mayakovsky, and Sheshtov. There is also a chapter on Macdiarmid's "Vision of Scotland."

1174. **The Russian Symbolists: An Anthology of Critical and Theoretical Writings,** edited and translated by Ronald E. Peterson. Ann Arbor, MI: Ardis, 1986. 223 p. ISBN: 0882337963. Includes bibliographies.

An unusual presentation of essays by Russian symbolists on symbolism. Many of these essays are well known and have been published elsewhere. They are gathered here in a chronological arrangement, not as a history of symbolism. They are meant rather to give the reader a clearer view of how the symbolists viewed their own art. The authors included are Sologub, Ivanov, Blok, and Ellis. The volume also includes translations of the introductions of some of the leading symbolist journals of the day. The editor is also responsible for all the translations in the volume. There is a useful "selected" bibliography, but no index. Reviews: *Slavic and East European Journal* 31:2:290-91 (Summer 1987). *World Literature Today* 61:1:124 (Winter 1987).

1175. Richardson, William, *Zolotoe Runo* **and Russian Modernism: 1905-1910**. Ann Arbor, MI: Ardis, 1986. 231 p. ISBN: 0882337955. Includes bibliography (p. 215-231).

A history of the publication *Zolotoe Runo*. The author feels it exemplifies Russian culture of the fin de siècle. The volume begins with a description of Russia's Silver Age and then goes on to describe the development and decline of *Zolotoe Runo*. It uses the journal as an example of the many movements in Russian culture: anarchism, realistic symbolism, and neo-primitivism. While the volume is rich in information on many of the cultural figures of the day, its lack of an index makes access somewhat difficult. Review: *Slavic Review* 46:3-4:656-57 (Fall-Winter 1987).

1176. **Russian Verse Theory: Proceedings of the 1987 Conference at UCLA**, edited by Barry P. Scherr and Dean S. Worth. Columbus, Ohio: Slavica Publishers, 1989. 514 p. *UCLA Slavic Studies*, v. 18. ISBN: 0893571989. Includes bibliographical references.

The essays in this volume cover a broad range of work on versification, comparative poetics, and folk verse and deal with bodies of material from the 18th to the 20th centuries.

Émigré Literature

1177. Beaujour, Elizabeth Klosty, **Alien Tongues: Bilingual Russian Writers of the "First" Emigration**. Ithaca, NY: Cornell University Press, 1989. xiv, 263 p. *Studies of the Harriman Institute*, ISBN: 0801422515. Includes bibliographical references.

The art of the bilingual writer is examined from both the literary and linguistic points of view in this study. The author begins with a review of the findings of neurolinguistics on bilingual writing. She then turns to individual writer's feelings about bilingual writing. The writers under consideration here are Nabokov, Triolet, Schakovsky, Yanovsky, Pozner, and Zoanevich. A control group was necessary to test whether the patterns she identified were peculiar to the Russian bilinguals or were universal. For this purpose, an appendix includes a study of Samuel Beckett's bilingual writings. The author believes that the bilingual writer is no longer a writer of one language or another but falls into a special category. Review: *Canadian Slavonic Papers* 32:2:205-207 (June 1990).

Folklore

1178. Ivanits, Linda J., **Russian Folk Belief**. Armonk, NY: M.E. Sharpe, 1989. xiv, 257 p. ISBN: 0873324226. Includes index and bibliography (p. 235-244).

Because ancient pagan folk beliefs have survived until recent times, Ivanits was able to write this book. Her book "covers paganism, Christian personages, the devil, house and nature spirits, and sorcery. The second part of the work contains her translations of a body of folk narratives about the supernatural." (p. x) The work is primarily descriptive. Reviews: *Choice* 806 (January 1990). *Canadian Slavonic Papers* 32:1:101-02 (March 1990). *Slavic and East European Journal* 34:1:127-28 (Spring 1990).

1179. Kelly, Catriona, **Petrushka, the Russian Carnival Puppet Theatre**. Cambridge: Cambridge University Press, 1990. xv, 292 p. *Cambridge Studies in Russian Literature*, ISBN: 0521375207. Includes bibliographical references.

Kelly explores many facets of Petrushka, the Russian equivalent of the Punch and Judy show. Maintaining that puppet theater is popular culture and not folklore, Kelly explains "how the Petrushka street theater tradition was caught in a pincer movement between economic and cultural reforms in the 1930s." (p. 7) She also provides its history and connections with the Western street glove-puppet theater, describes and analyzes its text and describes its audience and the circumstances under which it was performed.

PHILOSOPHY AND POLITICAL THEORY

General Studies

1180. Copleston, Frederick Charles, and Tunbridge Wells, **Philosophy in Russia: From Herzen to Lenin and Berdyaev.** Notre Dame, Ind.: Search Press, 1986. x, 445 p. ISBN: 0855325771. Includes index and bibliography (p. 413-430).
After a brief introductory chapter in which the authors set the context, they begin with Chadaev and devote individual chapters to him, Kireevsky, Kirov, Dostoevsky, and others. Several chapters focus on Marxism in Imperial Russia, during the time of Lenin, and in the Soviet period. Two final chapters are devoted to Russian philosophers in exile such as Lossky, Frank, Berdiaev, and Shestov. Reviews: *Russian Review* 46:4:460-61 (October 1987). *Canadian Slavonic Papers* 29:2-3:297-98 (June-September 1987).

1181. **Alexander Zinoviev as Writer and Thinker: An Assessment**, edited by Philip Hanson and Michael Kirkwood. New York: Macmillan, 1988. xv, 207 p. ISBN: 033432185. Includes bibliography and index.
A collection of critical essays on the works of Alexander Zinoviev whose goal is to broaden Western knowledge of this writer. Many aspects of his works are discussed, his language and art, ideology in his writings, and Stalinism. The various authors do not share a common view of Zinoviev's work. They all simply feel he should be better known and understood outside Russia. The final essay is a bibliography of Zinoviev's writings. The papers compiled here were parts of a 1986 conference held at the University of London. Reviews: *Russian Review* 49:4:491-92 (October 1990). *Slavic Review* 48:4:694-95 (Winter 1989). *Modern Fiction Studies* 35:4:836-39 (Winter 1989).

1182. Likhachev, Dmitrii Sergeevich, **Reflections on Russia**, translated by Christina Sever, with a foreword by S. Fredrick Starr. Boulder, CO: Westview Press, 1991. xxii, 191 p. *CCRS Series on Change in Contemporary Soviet Society*, ISBN: 0813377439. Includes bibliographical references and index.
Several works by the eminent Russian scholar and philologist are gathered in this volume. The bulk of this book is taken up with a work from which the volume draws its title. Much of the author's philosophy on the identity between culture and environment are presented here. Likhachev also presents his arguments against traditional nationalism, pleading for an openness he feels is necessary to healthy development. The other essays in the volume are "On National Feeling," "The Baptism of Rus' and the State of Rus'," "The Experience of a Thousand Years, " "Pangs of Conscience," "Memory Overcomes Time," and "Russia." There is also a substantial foreword tracing Likhachev's career and work by S. Frederick Starr.

1183. Trubetskoy, Nickolai Sergeevich, **The Legacy of Genghis Khan and Other Essays on Russia's Identity**, edited and with a postscript by Anatoly Liberman. Ann Arbor, MI: University of Michigan Press, 1991. v. *Michigan Slavic Materials*, no. 33. Includes index.

This volume is one of three selections to be issued by University of Michigan Press in honor of the 100th anniversary of the author's birth. The volume includes a postscript by Anatoly Liberman on the works of Trubetskoy. The essays included in this volume have, as with the earlier volume entitled *Philological Studies*, long been out of print. They include works written from 1920-1937, arranged chronologically. They cover everything from nationalism to Genghis Khan to the "decline of creativity."

1184. Tsipko, Aleksandr Sergeevich, **Is Stalinism Really Dead?** 1st ed. San Francisco: Harper & Row Publishers, 1990. x, 278 p. ISBN: 0062508717. Includes bibliographical references.

In writing about the changes taking place in Soviet society Tsipko searched for an engrossing point of view, a context in which to describe the philosophy of perestroika and the various changes occurring in Soviets' view of the world. He realized that the changes occurring came down "to the renunciation of Stalinism and its moral, political, and economic heritage.... [It would] provide penetrating insight into the causes, notions, and ultimate goals of the burgeoning moral revolution." (p. v-vi)

Non-Marxist Movements

1185. **The Origins of Nonviolence: Tolstoy and Gandhi in Their Historical Settings**. University Park: Pennsylvania State University Press, 1986. viii, 256 p. ISBN: 0271004398 (jacket); 0271004142. Includes index and bibliography (p. 245-253).

Green "studies the two men's lives [Gandhi and Tolstoy], showing how their ideas evolved from different starting points, and in different experiences, to come to a common climax." (p. vii) He focuses on the historical forces to which both men were reacting and draws parallels between both men's ideas about nonviolence and non-resistance.

1186. Cahm, Caroline, **Kropotkin and the Rise of Revolutionary Anarchism, 1872-1886**. Cambridge: Cambridge University Press, 1989. xii, 172 p. ISBN: 0521364450. Includes bibliographical references (p. 287-365).

"The present study, therefore, whilst endeavoring to show the continuity in the development of Kropotkin's life and career as a whole, concentrates on that period when he was most intimately and actively involved in the European anarchist movement, a period which began with this commitment to Bakuninism in 1872 and ended with his arrival in England in 1886...." (p. x) The book is divided into three parts: 1) Kropotkin and the development of the theory of anarchist communism; 2) Kropotkin and the development of anarchist ideas of revolutionary action by individuals and small groups (1872-1886); and Kropotkin and the development of anarchist views of collective revolutionary action (1872-1886). Review: *Russian History* 17:3:358-369 (Fall 1990).

1187. Ravindranathan, T. R., **Bakunin and the Italians**. Kingston, Ont.: McGill-Queens University Press, 1988. 332 p. ISBN: 0773506462. Includes index and bibliography (p. 309-324).

Mikhail Bakunin, well-known 19th century anarchist, was active all over Europe. "This is a study of his activities in Italy and his involvement with various Italian radicals who, through his influence were to become the earliest proponents of socialism in the peninsula." (p. ix) The main chronological focus of the book is the period 1864-77. Review: *American Historical Review* 95:5:1576-77 (December 1990).

1188. **Nietzsche in Russia**, edited by Bernice Glatzer Rosenthal. Princeton, NJ: Princeton University Press, 1986. xvi, 424 p. ISBN: 0691066957, 0691102090 (pbk.). Includes bibliographical references and index.

Nietzsche's impact on Russian literature and thought in the late 19th century in Russia was of great importance in intellectual and cultural historical assessments of that period. These essays, originally presented at a conference at Fordham in 1983, explore four major areas of Nietzsche's influence: Russian religious thought, Russian symbolists and their circles, Russian Marxism, and other, less-well defined areas such as the idea of the superman in neo-realist fiction. A bibliography of Nietzsche in Russia is included.

Marxism in Russia and in the USSR

1189. Campeanu, Pavel, **The Genesis of the Stalinist Social Order**. Armonk, NY: M. E. Sharpe, 1988. 165 p. ISBN: 087332420X. Includes bibliography (p. 161-164).

The purpose of this analysis is to identify the causes and factors that allowed Stalinism to develop and to prevent its reappearance through a perversion of the reforms of perestroika and glasnost. The author "...shall endeavor to describe the transformation of post revolutionary Russia into the Stalinist social order, and more specifically, the transformation of economically paralyzing, destabilized ownership into a global, ultracentralized monopoly with industrializing potential." (p. 5) A highly theoretical analysis. Reviews: *Russian Review* 49:3:356-57 (July 1990). *American Journal of Sociology* 95:4:1066-68 (January 1990).

1190. Graham, Loren R., **Science, Philosophy, and Human Behavior in the Soviet Union**. New York: Columbia University Press, 1987. xiii, 565 p. ISBN: 023106442X. Includes index and bibliography (p. 507-550).

In this expanded edition of his 1972 book, *Science and Philosophy in the Soviet Union*, Graham has added two new chapters on human behavior and he has revised the other chapters. His purpose is to illustrate the role Marxist ideology has played in all areas of Soviet science, including those areas, like physics, which were assumed to be immune from such influences.

1191. LeBlanc, Paul, **Lenin and the Revolutionary Party**, introduction by Ernest Mandel. Atlantic Heights, NJ: Humanities Press International, 1989. xxxiv, 399 p. ISBN: 0391036041. Includes bibliographical references and index.

A socialist account of Lenin's ideas on party organization. "The present study seeks to draw together a great revolutionary's own views on the organizational principles of the revolutionary party, utilizing substantial quotations so that he may speak for himself." (p. xi) Along with these quotations, the author tries to identify distortions of Lenin's ideas common in the literature. He elaborates the context of certain quotations and evaluates problems in Lenin's conceptions of Bolshevism. The work is loosely chronological in structure and includes a bibliography of sources for the general reader.

1192. Malhotra, Vinay Kumar, **Gorbachevian Revolution in the Soviet Union: Collapse or Renewal of Socialism**. New Delhi: Anmol Publications, 1991. xv, 147 p. ISBN: 817041535X. Includes index and bibliographical references.

"The scope of the present volume is to analyze the nature and magnitude of changes that are taking place in the mother country of contemporary socialism, in the Soviet Union." (p. x) The book is divided into six chapters. Chapter one explores the broad changes that occurred in the Soviet Union and Eastern Europe. Chapter two explains the key terms of glasnost and perestroika. Chapters three and four focus on the economic, political, and social changes occurring there. Chapter five explores the restructuring of foreign relations, and chapter six wrestles with the question whether these events signal a collapse or renewal of socialism.

1193. Sochor, Zenovia A., **Revolution and Culture: The Bogdanov-Lenin Controversy**. Ithaca, NY: Cornell University Press, 1988. x, 258 p. *Studies of the Harriman Institute, Studies in Soviet History and Society*, ISBN: 0801420881. Includes index and bibliography (p. 235-251).
A study of the Boleshevik's attempt to create a political culture and thus a study of the ideas of the leaders of the two main theorists of cultural transformation, Lenin and Bogdanov. The author examines the differences between the two schools of thought, the various schools of socialist thought common at the time which became the basis of the Soviet system. The author notes that there has been little published on Bogdanov in the West and attributes this, in part, to the complexity of his themes. This analysis reflects that complexity. It details the theoretical differences between Lenin and Bogdanov and the significance their theories had for the development of Soviet society. Reviews: *New York Times Review of Books* 37:19:60-67 (December 6, 1990). *Russian History* 16:2-4:140-41 (Spring 1989). *American Historical Review* 94:5:1441-43 (December 1989).

1194. Stojanovic, Svetozar, **Perestroika: From Marxism and Bolshevism to Gorbachev**. Buffalo, N.Y.: Prometheus Books, 1988. 167 p. ISBN: 0379754885. Includes bibliographical references.
Stojanovic carefully examines the crisis and fragmentation of Marxism over the past hundred years with a focus on recent developments in the Soviet Union. He concludes that as of the late 1980s, the Soviet Union was not moving towards democratic socialism, but simply towards reformed statism. His seven chapters analyze the development of Marxian dialectics as a tool for understanding societal development. In doing so, he shows how ideology has played an important role in both capitalism and statism. Finally, he applies his ideas to the current debates over perestroika showing the ideas upon which it was based.

1195. Trotsky, Leon, **Trotsky's Notebooks, 1933-1935: Writings on Lenin, Dialectics, and Evolutionism**, translated, annotated, and with introductory essays by Philip Pomper; Russian text annotated by Yuri Felshtinsky. New York: Columbia University Press, 1986. viii, 175 p. ISBN: 0231063024. Includes index and bibliography (p. 157-164).
Pomper's translations of Trotsky's notebooks are accompanied by an introductory essay on Trotsky and his life as well as two other essays that explicate Trotsky's notebooks and the context in which they were written. Reviews: *Slavic Review* 46:3-4:603-4 (Fall-Winter 1987). *American Historical Review* 92:4:1010 (October 1987).

Intellectual and Cultural Histories

1196. McDaniel, Tim, **Autocracy, Capitalism, and the Revolution in Russia**. Berkeley: University of California Press, 1988. xi, 500 p. ISBN: 0520055322. Includes bibliography (p. 472-491).
A sociological analysis of the Russian revolution. In keeping with this type of analysis, the focus is on labor and labor policy and comparisons with other countries. The book is divided into four parts. Part one reviews the basic characteristics of autocratic capitalist industrialization. Part II relates the failure of tsarist labor policy to autocratic capitalist industrialization. Part III gives an overview of the Russian labor movement. The final section looks at the possible outcomes generated by political and class relations in Russia of 1917.

Reviews: *International Labor and Working Class History* 38:68-80 (Fall 1990). *Canadian-American Slavic Studies* 24:4:473-75 (Winter 1990). *Historian* 52:3:495-96 (May 1990). *Soviet Union-Union Sovietique* 17:1-2:193-94 (1990). *Russian Review* 49:2:210- 22 (April 1990). *American Journal of Sociology* 95:1:234-36 (July 1989). *Russian History* 16:2-4:459-60 (1989). *American Academy of Political and Social Science Annals* 501:208-09 (January 1989).

1197. **Ideology and Soviet Politics**, edited by Stephen White and Alex Pravda. London: University of London, 1988. viii, 258 p. *Studies in Russia and East Europe*, ISBN: 0333434498. Includes index and bibliographical references.

A study of the role ideology has played in Soviet policy making over the years. This collection of essays is united by three goals: to review recent approaches to ideology and Soviet politics, to analyze the evolution and effect of ideology in policy making, and to show the dynamic aspects of Soviet ideology. The editors feel that Soviet ideology is only rarely examined as a serious component of change in Soviet politics. This volume attempts to clarify that role by discussing several areas of political life in terms of the changes in ideology including economic policy, the local Soviets, female roles, and the national question. The book is intended for the serious reader. The contributors include: Stephen White, Michael Waller, Alfred G. Meyer, Graeme Gill, Alfred B. Evans, David A. Dyker, Michael E. Urban, Mary Buckley, Peter Duncan, Stephen Shenfield, and Alex Pravda. Review: *Slavic Review* 50:1:188-89 (Spring 1991).

PSYCHOLOGY

1198. Benn, David Wedgwood, **Persuasion and Soviet Politics**. Oxford, UK: B. Blackwell, 1989. x, 243 p. ISBN: 0631156399. Includes index.

"This book sets out to explore some of the interconnections between persuasion and Soviet politics. It aims, more specifically, to examine the Soviet approach, both past and present, to the question of method in relation to propaganda, persuasion, and the influencing of public opinion. It also has two other purposes: to draw attention to specialist literature in this field which has appeared in the USSR over the years; and lastly, to explore, at least in a preliminary way, the relationship between two vast and extremely complex questions, namely the nature of Soviet beliefs and the nature of persuasion." (p. 1)

1199. Gluzman, Semon, **On Soviet Totalitarian Psychiatry**. 1st ed. Amsterdam: International Association on the Political Use of Psychiatry, 1989. 87 p. Includes bibliographical references.

A collection of papers on the abuse of psychiatry in the Soviet Union written by a Soviet psychiatrist. Dr. Gluzman was himself imprisoned for his failure to cooperate with the Soviet practice of imprisoning dissidents in psychiatric hospitals. The book also includes a case of one particular individual, General Grigorenko and a work written from the prison camp in Perm. "In this book, we present for the first time all the major papers written by Dr. Gluzman on the abuse of psychiatry for political purposes in the USSR, with all its complex aspects, but also its simple basic feature: the perversion of a science into a tool of repression." (p. 7)

1200. Joravsky, David, **Russian Psychology: A Critical History**. Oxford: Blackwell, 1988. xxii, 583 p. ISBN: 061163379. Includes index and bibliography (537-567).

Joravsky has set out to examine the tension that has existed between the study of the mind and the study of the brain in Russia. "Pluralism sets the problem: here are diverse groups of people claiming to achieve knowledge of human beings through incompatible modes of inquiry and self-expression." (p. xi) In approaching the problem he has cast his net wide, including not only neurophysiologists and philosophers, but also literary artists, and political ideologists. Reviews: *Russian History* 17:3:365-67 (Fall 1990). *Journal of Interdisciplinary History* 21:1:156-59 (Summer 1990).

1201. Koppers, Andre, **A Biographical Dictionary on the Political Abuse of Psychiatry in the USSR**. 1st ed. Amsterdam: International Association on the Political Use of Psychiatry, 1990. 180 p. ISBN: 9072657039. Includes bibliographical references (p. 177-179).

An attempt to document with more complete information the abuse of psychiatry as a means of interring political dissidents. This volume is divided into three parts: Psychiatrists, Hospitals, and Victims. In the first section the doctor's name, date of birth, place of work, academic credentials, biography, and a list of patients treated are listed. Part two includes information on the full name and address of the hospital, history of the institutions, sections, reputation of the staff, and a list of patients treated. The final part gives as much information on the victims as possible: name, date of birth, address, occupation, nationality, biography, and psychiatric history. The work is not comprehensive, but is intended by the author as a beginning to the documentation of the crimes of psychiatric abuse in the Soviet Union.

1202. Kozulin, Alex, **Vygotsky's Psychology: A Biography of Ideas**. Cambridge, Mass.: Harvard University Press, 1990. 286 p. ISBN: 0674943651. Includes bibliographical references and index.

A study of the life and significance of the work of Lev Vygotsky. The book traces Vygotsky's development from a student in Moscow during the revolution through his career as a psychologist. Much of the focus is on Vygotsky's work as a reflection of the development of 20th century psychology in general. Each chapter deals with one major area of Vygotsky; work beginning with his work on the psychology of art and tragedy. Next, his career as an academic psychologist along with an overview of his theory of cultural-historical development is discussed. His work as a mature researcher on language and the psychopathology of the handicapped follow. Finally, a chapter is devoted to the development of his ideas posthumously by such psychologists as Luria and Leontev concludes Kozulin's book. Each chapter has substantial notes, but there is no separate bibliography.

1203. Petrovskii, Arthur Vladimirovich, **Psychology in the Soviet Union: A Historical Outline,** translated from the Russian by Lilia Nakhapetyan. Moscow: Progress Publishers, 1990. 450 p. ISBN: 5010019906. Includes bibliographical references and index.

A translation of a Soviet work tracing the development of psychology in the Soviet Union. The author has not attempted an exhausting history. Rather he attempts "to trace a definite logic of the process of psychology's formation as a scientific discipline by its adopting the principle of material dialectics, and to highlight the historical path blazed by Soviet psychology for all other psychologists to follow." (p. 15) The book is arranged chronologically and includes a name index useful for identifying information on specific figures in Soviet psychology.

1204. Valsiner, Jaan, **Developmental Psychology in the Soviet Union**. Bloomington: Indiana University Press, 1987. x, 398 p. ISBN: 025331626. Includes index and bibliography (p. 336-386).

"The task of this book—an analysis of how developmental psychology in the U.S.S.R. has developed and reached its present state—constitutes a case history of the relationships between a science and its cultural-historical framework." (p. 1) The book discusses such figures as L. S. Vygotsky, Mikhail Basov, and others. It also includes an appendix consisting of a program for an interview with children for the study of their social knowledge. Review: *Slavic Review* 48:4:676 (Winter 1989).

1205.　**Soviet Psychiatric Abuse in the Gorbachev Era**, edited by Robert van Voren. 1st ed. Amsterdam: International Association on the Political Use of Psychiatry, 1989. 112 p. ISBN: 9072657012. Includes bibliographical references.

A collection of essays by seven members of the International Association on the Political Use of Psychiatry (IAPUP). The purpose of the study is to "analyze the history of 'Soviet political psychiatry,' its fundamentals, the opposition against these practices in both the Soviet Union and the West, the reaction of Western and international psychiatric bodies to those abuses and the effect Gorbachev's policy of glasnost and perestroika had on Soviet abuse of psychiatry for political purposes." (back cover)

RELIGION

General Studies

1206.　Baggley, John, **Doors of Perception: Icons and Their Spiritual Significances**. Crestwood, NY: St. Vladimir's Seminar Press, 1988. xii, 160 p. ISBN: 0881410713. Includes index and bibliography (p. 155).

An introductory work on the history and significance of icons in the Orthodox Church. The volume gives the historical background of the Orthodox Church presenting a framework for the development of iconography. The author tries to focus on those factors foreign to Westerners such as the visual orientation of orthodoxy as a means of explaining the significance of icons. The book also contains an appendix by Richard Temple of the Temple Gallery, London, with numerous color reproductions of icons and lengthy commentaries on each. The references and further readings provide a bibliography accessible to the English language reader.

1207.　Ellis, Jane, **The Russian Orthodox Church: A Contemporary History**. Bloomington: Indiana University Press, 1986. 531 p. ISBN: 0253350298. Includes index and bibliography (p. 508-509).

A study of the Russian Orthodox Church from 1965 to 1986 with an emphasis on the role of dissent. The author seeks in this volume to fill the gap of some earlier works, particularly Nikita Struve's *Christians in Contemporary Russia* and Dmitri Popielovsk's *The Russian Church under the Soviet Regime, 1917-1982*, which focus on the earlier years of the Church's existence. The author has drawn heavily on samizdat materials. The book is divided into two parts. The first discusses various issues affecting the church's development under the Soviet regime: dioceses, churches, parishes, clergy, theological education, monasticism, and church-state relations. The second part traces the history of the Orthodox dissent movement from its beginnings up to 1985. Reviews: *Slavic Review* 46:3-4:624-25 (Fall-Winter 1987). *Journal of Church and State* 29:3:542-43 (Autumn 1987). *Canadian Slavonic Papers* 29:4:439-40 (December 1987).

1208.　Forest, James H., **Religion in the New Russia: The Impact of Perestroika on the Varieties of Religious Life in the Soviet Union**. New York: Crossroad, 1990. xx, 217 p. ISBN: 0824510402. Includes index.

Religion and its history in Russia are the subject of this work. The author focuses on changes in the various religious communities since perestroika began. He also provides background to the situations faced by the different religions throughout the Soviet period. The book is arranged thematically, with each chapter devoted to a different religion: Orthodox, Old Believers, Catholics, Protestants, Jews, Muslims, and Buddhists. His last chapter examines some of the problems that remain to be solved.

1209. **Alaskan Missionary Spirituality**, edited by Michael Oleksa. New York: Paulist Press, 1987. ix, 406 p. *Sources of American Spirituality*, ISBN: 0809103869. Includes indexes and bibliography (p. 373-376).

A collection of documents from the history of the Russian Orthodox Church in Alaska. The materials gathered here date back to the eighteenth century and some of the earliest religious contacts with the Aleuts. The editor feels that while the focus is on the Aleut culture, the materials also describe Russians in their colonies in America. There are a range of documents: letters by various churchmen, extracts from diaries, and formal reports on the Russian Orthodox mission.

1210. Parsons, Howard L., **Christianity Today in the USSR**. 1st ed. New York: International Publishers, 1987. x, 199 p. ISBN: 0717806510. Includes bibliography (p. 189-192) and index.

This work, sponsored by the National Council of American-Soviet Friendship, was written in response to a perceived need in the United States for information about Christianity in the Soviet Union. It includes a brief chapter on the history of Christianity in the Soviet Union, chapters on various Christian denominations in the USSR today including the Russian Orthodox Church, the Armenian Apostolic Church, Roman Catholicism in Latvia, Evangelical Christians-Baptists, Lutheranism, and two chapters describing the views of Soviet scientists on Christianity and religion. It includes an appendix listing the rights and obligations of religious societies under the law. Reviews: *Occasional Papers on Religion in Eastern Europe* 8:2:40- 42 (May 1988). *Journal of Church and State* 30:2:367-68 (Spring 1988).

1211. **Christianity and Russian Culture in Soviet Society**, edited by Nicolai N. Petro. Boulder, CO: Westview Press, 1990. xi, 244 p. *CCRS Series on Change in Contemporary Soviet Society*, ISBN: 0813377420.

Two themes are reflected in this group of essays, originally presented at a conference at the Monterey Institute of International Studies in 1988. "One is the tension between the expression of Christian beliefs and the legal restrictions imposed by the Soviet State in professions of faith. The other is the growing importance of Christian culture to the process of perestroika." (p. vii) Contributors include scholars from Israel, Canada, Germany, Holland, England, the United States, and the Soviet Union.

1212. Pushkarev, Sergei, Vladimir Rusak, and Gleb Yakunin, **Christianity and the Government in Russia and the Soviet Union: Reflections on the Millennium.** Boulder, CO: Westview Press, 1989. xii, 166 p. *CCRS Series on Change in Contemporary Soviet Society*, ISBN: 081337524X.

Essays by three specialists on Soviet policy toward the Orthodox Church. "Exiled or imprisoned for their outspoken views, the authors share a remarkable unity of theme and spirit in their reflections on the millennium of Russia's adoption of Christianity in 988. They explain the role that religion has played in Russian history and offer valuable insight into why the 'religious question' continues to be so important in an officially atheist society." (back cover) The book is divided into three parts. The first reviewing the history of the Church, the second examining persecution by the Soviet regime, and the third looking to the future. A translator's bibliography is included.

1213. Ramet, Sabrina P., **Cross and Commissar: The Politics of Religion in Eastern Europe and the USSR**. Bloomington: Indiana University Press, 1987. x, 244 p. ISBN: 0253315751. Includes index and bibliography (p. 235-238).

This work analyzes church-state relations in the Soviet Union and Eastern Europe in order to develop a coherent theory about the interaction of those two institutions. The author looks at the place of the church in each of the Eastern European countries and the USSR to develop his theory. He considers such problems as the relationship between religion and nationalism, church-state relations, and the social functions of religion. The book is divided into four parts. Part I reviews religious policy in the region since World War II with particular emphasis on the relationship between religious and nationalities policies. Part II considers individual countries and their religious policies. Part III is devoted to developments in the region since 1978. The final part discusses theoretical conclusions the author draws from his analysis. The selected bibliography cites publications up to 1986 on each of the countries discussed in the text. Reviews: *Bulletin of the Atomic Scientist* 44:4:50-51 (May 1988). *Slavic Review* 47:3:561-62 (Fall 1988). *Canadian Slavonic Papers* 30:1:158-59 (March 1988). *Journal of Church and State* 30:3:571-72 (Autumn 1988).

1214. Steeves, Paul D., **Keeping the Faiths: Religion and Ideology in the Soviet Union**. New York: Holmes & Meier, 1988. 240 p. ISBN: 0841912599.

A volume in the "Beyond the Kremlin" series, which seeks to "enable Americans to assess more accurately the Soviet Union." (p. 9) Arranged topically, the book begins with an overview of the history of religion in Russia up to the revolution. The author then describes the numerous faiths existing in the Soviet Union and the competition between religion and Soviet ideology. Finally, he discusses the changes under Gorbachev and the effect they will have on religious practice. The book is made up of extensive quotations from various authors working in Soviet studies and commentary by the author. It includes a "reader's guide" as do all volumes in this series which supplies questions for discussion groups, telephone reference sources, educational projects and an annotated bibliography.

1215. ———, **The Modern Encyclopedia of Religions in Russia and the Soviet Union, Vol. I: Aaron-Annunciation**. Gulf Breeze, Fla.: Academic International Press, 1988. 241 p. ISBN: 0875691064. Includes bibliographical references.

According to the preface, this encyclopedia is planned as the most comprehensive work in any language and "is designed to serve the basic reference needs of the broad spectrum of users, with special concern for the needs of teachers in churches and synagogues, religious professionals, and students and teachers of high schools, junior colleges, universities, and theological schools. " (p. vii) "Entries in MERRSU generally fall into one of the following categories: biography, reign or administration, regulation or law, institution, denomination, ritual, ethnic group, custom, tradition, office, place, artistic creation, manufactured article, publication, church-state relations, and anti-religion." (p. viii) The length of articles varies from several lines to more than 500 words, and longer articles are usually signed. As was the case with *Encyclopedia of Russian and Soviet Literatures* or *Modern Encyclopedia of Russian and Soviet History*, some articles were originally written for this work while others are reprinted or translated articles from such sources as *Orthodox Theological Encyclopedia, Russian Biographical Dictionary*, and similar works usually published in Russian. Since this is the first volume, it is not known how many volumes will be in the entire set—we assume over 40. Bohdan S. Wynar

History

1216. House, Francis, **Millennium of Faith: Christianity in Russia, AD 988-1988**. Crestwood, NY: St. Vladimir's Seminary Press, 1988. X, 133 p. ISBN: 088141073x. Includes index and bibliography (p. 122-125).

This readable history of the church in Russia contains eleven chapters in two parts. Part one covers the Russian churches before the revolution, and part two examines Christians in the USSR. Two appendices are included: the Russian Orthodox Church and the Church of England, and Official Summary of the Rights and Obligations of Religious Societies. Review: *Journal for the Scientific Study of Religion* 29:1:132-33 (March 1990).

1217. Pospielovsky, Dimitry, **A History of Soviet Atheism in Theory and Practice, and the Believer**. London: Macmillan, 1987. 3 v. ISBN: 033434404. Includes bibliography.

"The main purpose of this study is a step-by-step presentation and analysis of the changing styles, strategies, and tactics of the never-ending Soviet attack on religion and on believers." (p. ix-x) It includes detailed accounts of specific persecutions beginning in February 1918 through 1964. It also includes a description of religious life in Russia. Each volume is devoted to a specific topic. Volume one is a history of Marxist-Leninist atheism and Soviet anti-religious policies. Volume two deals with anti-religious campaigns and persecutions, and volume three with Soviet studies on the Church and the believer's response to atheism. Reviews: *American Historical Review* 95:3:874-75 (June 1990). *Russian Review* 49:3:371-73 (July 1990). *Slavic Review* 48:1:124-25 (Spring 1989).

1218. Urry, James, **None But Saints: The Transformation of Mennonite Life in Russia, 1789-1889**. Winnipeg: Hyperion Press, 1989. 328 p. ISBN: 0920534805. Includes index and bibliographical references (p. 290-311).

Mennonites first settled in Russia in 1789 under the leadership of Deputy Jacob Hoeppner. This study, based on primary source documents, examines migration and settlement, the maintenance of community, commerce, education, dissent and division among the emigrants, and an emergent commonwealth by the end of the 19th century. Two appendices provide a charter of privileges awarded to the Mennonites on September 8, 1800 and information on Mennonite population growth in Russia.

Special Studies

1219. Berken, William Peter van den, **Ideology and Atheism in the Soviet Union**. Hawthorne, NY: Mouton de Gruyter, 1989. viii, 191 p. *Religion and Society*, vol. 28. ISBN: 0899253849. Includes index and bibliography (p. 177-186).

An analysis of the political and ideological aspects of Soviet Atheism. Originally published as a series of articles, the author felt that recent changes in the USSR made a publication of the series in one volume particularly relevant. The final two chapters update the earlier comments to include the effects of perestroika on Soviet religious policy. "The book is a socio-political study and contains a meta-ideological criticism of Soviet Atheism, which can be underwritten by adherents of Western philosophical Atheism and agnosticism." (p. 2) The five chapters examine the relationship between the state and ideology, between ideology and Weltanschauung, focus on the atheism of Soviet ideology, the relationship between atheism and the state, and the role of propaganda in Soviet atheism.

1220. **The Paterik of the Kievan Cave Monastery**, translated by Muriel Heppell and with a preface by Sir Dmitri Obolensky. Cambridge, Mass.: Harvard University Press, 1989. lii, 262 p. *Harvard Library of Early Ukrainian Literature, English Translations*, v. 1. ISBN: 091645827X. Includes indexes and bibliography (p. 231-241).

The Pecherskii Paterik is a collection of 11th and 12th century stories about monks who lived in the Kievan Cave Monastery. As Obolensky, the editor notes, the Paterik is a highly significant document for "it illustrates the early phases of Kievan monasticism by providing first-hand information on its ideals, organization, and relation with secular society...." (p. xv) It contains a detailed biography of Theodosus, a church leader who had great influence on church and society in medieval Rus'.

1221. Nichols, Aidan, **Theology in the Russian Diaspora: Church, Fathers, Eucharist in Nikolai Afanasev (1893-1966)**. Cambridge, Eng.: Cambridge University Press, 1989. xv, 295 p. ISBN: 0521365430. Includes index and bibliography.

Nichols focuses on the theology of Nikolai Afanasev, especially his writings on eucharistic ecclesiology. It is these writings, the author maintains, that will and have aided the rapprochement between Rome and the Eastern churches. Nichols also puts Afanasev's writings in context by comparing his ecclesiology with that of Berdiaev, Bulgakov and Florovskii.

1222. **Candle in the Wind: Religion in the Soviet Union**, edited by Eugene B. Shirley Jr. and Michael Rowe, foreword by Richard Schifter. Washington, DC: Ethics and Public Policy Center, 1989. xxvii, 328 p. ISBN: 0896331350. Includes bibliographical references.

This book grew out of and expanded upon research originally done for a documentary film of the same title. It is a study of how various traditional religions have adapted to survive under the Soviet system. The authors also hope to portray some part of Soviet life through an examination of the many religious beliefs that still survive there. Topics covered in the essays included here are church-state relations from 1917-1964, the rebirth of religion in Russia, and the effects of Gorbachev's reforms on religion. Analysis of specific religious groups in Russia is covered in essays on Islam, Buddhism, and Judaism. An appendix with drafts of the new law on freedom of religion of conscience is also included. Review: *Russian History* 17:1:114-15 (Spring 1990).

1223. Thompson, Ewa Majewska, **Understanding Russia: The Holy Fool in Russian Culture**. Lanham, MD: University Press of America, 1987. xi, 229 p. ISBN: 081916271X. Includes index and bibliography (p. 207-220).

The holy fools were considered to be saints and miracle workers, or by the more cynical, madmen. Thompson's book about them is in two parts. In part one, she describes and defines the holy fools and holy foolishness, evaluates mental illness and mental normalcy in relationship to the holy fools, describes their relationship to the church and compares holy foolishness and shamanism. In part two she illuminates the uses of holy foolishness in literature and culture at large. Reviews: *Social Science Journal* 25:2:242-44 (1988). *Slavic and East European Journal* 32:1:151-53 (Spring 1988). *Slavic Review* 47:2:320-21. *Canadian Slavonic Papers* 30:1:137-38 (March 1988).

SCIENCE, TECHNOLOGY AND RESEARCH

General Studies

1224. Ailes, Catherine P., and Arthur E. Pardee Jr., **Cooperation in Science and Technology: An Evaluation of the U.S.-Soviet Agreement**. Boulder, CO: Westview Press, 1986. xxviii, 334 p. *Westview Special Studies in Science, Technology, and Public Policy*, ISBN: 0813302048. Includes bibliography (p. 329-334).

The science and technology agreement established in May of 1972, and its resulting working group programs are evaluated in this study. The authors drew on numerous sources to evaluate the ten year program including assessment by chairmen, annual reports, working reports, protocols, trip reports, newsletter reports, Congressional studies, etc. The working group program ranged over a variety of subject areas: chemistry, microscopy, physics, science policy, earth science, polymer sciences, and scientific and technical information. The book is organized in three parts. The first part provides an introduction and supplies background on the subject as a whole and on the different working groups. Part 2 describes the individual working groups supported by the NSF. The success of the various working groups is evaluated in part three. The study does not cover broader policy issues such as East-West technology transfer or commercial relations. Numerous tables are provided in each section.

1225. **Technical Progress and Soviet Economic Development**. New York: B. Blackwell, 1986. 214 p. ISBN: 0631145729. Includes index.

The essays presented here were originally given as papers at a symposium on Soviet science and technology, held at Birmingham University in 1984. The technology gap between the Soviet Union and the West has been stated as problem number one by M. Gorbachev. These nine essays explore the various aspects of this recognized fact. The papers can be divided into two groups, those which focus on Soviet technological performance and those that explore the options that the Soviet government can choose to improve current performance. Sandwiched in between an introductory essay that surveys Soviet technological progress and economic development and a concluding essay that speculates on the prospects for the Soviet economy are papers that examine the defense industry, microprocessors and microcomputers, biotechnology, standards, the machine tool and electric motor industries, technology transfer, and technology flows within Comecon. Review: *Slavic Review* 46:1:145-46 (Spring 1987).

1226. Bailes, Kendall E., **Science and Russian Culture in an Age of Revolutions: V. I. Vernadsky and His Scientific School, 1863-1945**. Bloomington: Indiana University Press, 1990. xii, 238 p. *Indiana-Michigan Series in Russian and East European Studies*, ISBN: 0253311233. Includes index and bibliography (p. 225-231).

The development of Russian science is examined in this study of the life and work of V.I. Vernadsky and his scientific philosophy. The influence of Vernadsky, whose life spanned the last days of the imperial period and the establishment of the Soviet regime, has become a popular topic in Russia. His work as a geologist helped build the Soviet state. However, his attempt to maintain intellectual freedom under the Socialist regime has focused attention on him in the age of glasnost. "As Kendall Bailes shows in this book, he strove to develop an alternative philosophical viewpoint to the dogmatic Marxism that Soviet ideologists were propagating. Although Vernadsky was not a militant fighter for causes, he stoutly protested political incursions on academic freedom." (p. vi) The book follows a chronological arrangement tracing Vernadsky's developing career as his interests turned from the study of geology to the social and intellectual context in which that study took place.

1227. Balzer, Harley D., **Soviet Science on the Edge of Reform**, with an appendix by Stephen Sternheimer. Boulder, CO: Westview Press, 1989. xxi, 290 p. *Westview Special Studies on the Soviet Union and Eastern Europe*, ISBN: 0814477412. Includes bibliographical references.

Based on interviews with recent Soviet émigrés who worked in various aspects of Soviet science, this study examines the "enormous network of institutions in training scientific and technical specialists and conducting scientific and technical activity—basic and applied research, development and innovation." (p. i) After an introduction explaining the sample, the data, and various caveats, Balzer examines the training of the Soviet R & D community, the conduct of R & D in the USSR, Soviet military R & D, the strengths and weaknesses of the Soviet science system, and prospects for reform.

1228. Cochrane, Dorothy, Von Hardesty, and Russell Lee, **The Aviation Careers of Igor Sikorsky**. Seattle: University of Washington Press, 1989. 207 p. ISBN: 0295968427. Includes index and bibliographical references (p. 200-205).

"As a part of this centennial celebration, the National Air and Space Museum has produced this publication to address the major themes of Igor Sikorsky's life through historical narrative, photography, and documentary materials." (p. 11) Those themes include his role as a designer of airplanes, flying boats and helicopters. His early career was spent in Russia where he contributed designs such as that of the first four engine airplane which would become the first long-range bomber in World War I. In this country he is mainly noted for his work with flying boats and his early designs of the helicopter. This volume includes and appendix of design drawings and another of technical specifications.

1229. Fortescue, Stephen, **Science Policy in the Soviet Union**. London: Routledge, 1990. 230 p. ISBN: 0415023793. Includes bibliographical references (p. 217-225).

In the words of the author: "Scientific research, both theoretical and applied, is clearly of great importance to the Soviet economy but it is hampered by the USSR's economic and social structure. [This book] examines the major institutional and behavioral aspects influencing scientific research in the USSR. The book adopts the widespread view that Soviet science performs well below capacity, and then looks at the institutions and management in light of this assumption.... The author sees de-centralization as a potential solution, concluding with a commentary on Gorbachev—the obstacles he faces and his awareness of the need for change in the scientific sphere." (frontispiece)

1230. Judy, Richard W., and Virginia L. Clough, **The Information Age and Soviet Society**. Indianapolis, IN: Hudson Institute, 1989. 99 p. ISBN: 1558130292. Includes bibliographical references.

An introductory survey of the Soviet response to the development of computers and communication technology. The topically arranged chapters cover such topics as Soviet perceptions of the information age, personal computing in the USSR, the developing popular information culture, and Western views of the significance of the information revolution in the USSR. This brief study is intended as an introduction to the subject.

1231. Medvedev, Zhores, **The Legacy of Chernobyl**. 1st American ed. New York: W.W. Norton, 1990. xii, 352 p. ISBN: 039302802X. Includes bibliographical references (p. 322-344) and index.

Biologist Zhores Medvedev attempts an objective description of the events that led to the disaster at Chernobyl and the accident itself. He discusses the environmental, agricultural, and health impact of the accident and provides a history of the Soviet nuclear energy program and nuclear accidents in the USSR. The descriptions can be quite technical and the author includes a glossary of scientific terms, measurements, and abbreviations. There are also discussions of the global impact of the Chernobyl accident and the future of nuclear power in the Soviet Union.

1232. **USSR-India: The Path to Stars,** edited by Vladimir Shatalov. New Delhi: Vikas, 1986. viii, 188 p. ISBN: 0706927338.
This book discusses the joint space ventures of the USSR and India. Some background on each space program is provided.

1233. Todes, Daniel Philip, **Darwin Without Malthus: The Struggle for Existence in Russian Evolutionary Thought**. New York: Oxford University Press, 1989. 221 p. *Monographs on the History and Philosophy of Biology*, ISBN: 0195058305. Includes bibliographical references.
Todes explores the effect that Darwin's short hand expression of selection theory—"the struggle for existence"—had on Russian intellectuals of tsarist Russia. The author contends that "the critical reaction of Russian intellectuals to this metaphor and its conceptual implications had substantial consequences for Russian evolutionary thought." (p. 3) He pays particular attention to the effect on specific scientists, as well as a discussion of their ideas. Review: *Russian History* 17:3:364-65 (Fall 1990).

1234. Vucinich, Alexander, **Darwin in Russian Thought**. Berkeley: University of California Press, 1988. x, 468 p. ISBN: 0520062833. Includes index and bibliography (p. 425-453).
A scholarly study of the reception of Darwin's ideas in pre-revolutionary Russia. The author has arranged the book chronologically and topically. The first part of the book deals with the reaction to Darwin from 1860 through the early 1880s. Then the focus shifts to the formal attempts to develop anti-Darwinist arguments, specifically those by N. Ia. Danieleskii. This is followed by a description of the full acceptance of Darwin's ideas in Russia in the 1890s. Chapters 6-8 cover 1900-1917 again dealing with the debates between the defenders and declaimers of Darwin's work and also describing theoretical attempts to blend Darwin's ideas and biology. Chapter 9 gives an overview of the defining characteristics of Russian Darwinism. The concluding chapters deal with Darwinism and radical thought and the author's conclusion as to the effects of Darwinism on shaping Russian philosophical and scientific thinking.

Telecommunications

1235. **Spacebridges: Television and US-Soviet Dialogue**, edited by Michael Brainerd. Lanham: University Press of America, 1989. 115 p. ISBN: 0819174335 (pbk.), 0819174327. Includes bibliographical references (p. 113-115).
An analysis of the past and potential uses of two-way television linkages between the U.S. and the Soviet Union. The book provides discussions of the development of this medium and problems that have arisen such as simultaneous translation, imbalances in use in the U.S. and the U.S.S.R., and future uses of the medium. The appendices include resources for those interested in the technology used in spacebridges.

Computers

1236. Baranson, Jack, et al., **Soviet Automation: Perspectives and Prospects**. Mt. Airy, Md.: Lomond, 1987. xvi, 142 p. ISBN: 091233861X. Includes bibliographical references.

The six essays in this collection deal with different aspects of the Soviet efforts to automate industrial production. Recognizing that in order to compete globally in the economic sphere, and to keep their defense-related industries from falling behind in the West, Soviet planners have introduced over the past several years different types of automated systems, including computer aided design and computer aided manufacturing. The difficulties of introducing such automated systems, which inevitably effects changes in production methods and management systems, can be many in a centrally-planned economy. The chapters describe and analyze the political economy of automation, robotics, application of computer-aided design in Soviet enterprises, an example of industrial modernization program at the Voronezh Production Association imeni Kalinin, the role of the CMEA in Soviet automation efforts, and the prospects for future Soviet automation efforts in industry.

1237. Dizard, Wilson P., and S. Blake Swensrud, **Gorbachev's Information Revolution: Controlling Glasnost in a New Electronic Era**. Boulder, CO: Westview Press, 1987. vii, 99 p. *CBIS Significant Issues Series, 0736-7163*, vol. 9, no. 8. ISBN: 0813375195.

This volume discusses the problems and future of the communications industry under Gorbachev. The authors feel that Gorbachev is aware of the limitations placed on the development of the Soviet economy if there is no modernization of the communist system. This book discusses the reasons for past failures to modernize the system in both the Soviet Union and the West. It also describes the existing system, explaining what is necessary for change. It concludes with some discussions of the role of Western observations and Western observers of how information systems develop. While this volume does not include a bibliography, it does have several appendices that describe the state of Soviet communication, its organization, and some official views on computerization. Review: *Slavic Review* 48:2:315-16 (Summer 1989).

1238. McIntyre, Joan F., **Soviet Labor Requirements for the Information Era**. Washington, DC: Central Intelligence Agency, 1989. vii, 43 p.

"This paper examines the skill and educational requirements that will be needed as the USSR moves into its own version of the 'Information Era.' While the paper will focus on the demands on the labor force made by information technologies, other factors influencing the skill composition of the work force, such as intersectoral redistribution of employment and the economic policies and goals of the leadership, will be briefly examined." (p. i)

Environmental Protection

1239. Chernov, Iurii Ivanovich, **The Living Tundra**. Cambridge: Cambridge University Press, 1985. xiii, 213 p. *Studies in Polar Research*, ISBN: 0521253934. Includes index and bibliography (p. 197-200).

Chernov, a well-known Russian biogeographer and ecologist, "scrutinizes many problems of adaptation to subarctic living conditions and analyzes the structure of the fauna and flora as well as the interrelationships between groups of organisms in their special natural environment." (p. xi) Review: *Slavic Review* 49:3:471-72 (Fall 1990).

1240. Weiner, Douglas R., **Models of Nature: Ecology, Conservation, and Cultural Revolution in Soviet Russia**. Bloomington: Indiana University Press, 1988. xvi, 312 p. *Indiana-Michigan Series in Russian and East European Studies*, ISBN: 0253338379. Includes index and bibliography (p. 289-306).

A study of the conservation movements in the Soviet Union. While not underestimating the environmental damage done by the Soviet regime, the author focuses on the development of various ecological programs. The book is arranged chronologically. Two appendices are included both focusing on "virgin natural communities," some set aside since the 1920s. A list of acronyms and a glossary are also at the back of the volume. Reviews: *American Historical Review* 95:1:212-23 (February 1990). *Slavic Review* 49:3:457-58 (Fall 1990).

SOCIAL CONDITIONS AND SOCIOLOGY

General Studies

1241. Chamberlain, Lesley, **In the Communist Mirror: Journeys in Eastern Europe**. London: Faber, 1990. xii, 196 p. ISBN: 057114165x.

A personal account of one individual's reactions to life under the Communist regimes in Russia, Poland, Yugoslavia, Hungary, Banat, Romania, and East Germany. The author describes the economic situation, political system, art, and psychological conditions which were associated with each of the communist regimes. The work is set in an autobiographical framework, with each chapter devoted to a different country. The essays are also chronologically arranged. They cover a three year period.

1242. Connor, Walter, **The Accidental Proletariat: Workers, Politics and Crisis in Gorbachev's Russia**. Princeton, NJ: Princeton University Press, 1991. xv, 374 p. ISBN: 0691077878. Includes index.

One of the largest factors in the equation of economic development, the working class in the Soviet Union, is the subject of this study. The author traces their development from Stalin's death to the present. The volume is arranged both chronologically and topically, covering a wide range of topics: wages, welfare, the school reforms of 1984, populism, unions, labor authority and autonomy, and many others. The complex issue of the workers as a class is also discussed. The first chapter provides the historical context for the study. The second chapter traces the post war changes in the working class as levels of education rose. Chapter three examines the difficulties of recruitment to the working class as general expectations of the needs of the economy changed. Chapters four and five examine the material aspects of the workers' lives and their job satisfaction. Issues such as authority and worker control are a main focus of this discussion. In chapter six the role of the trade union is examined. The final chapter turns its attention to the Gorbachev era.

1243. Connor, Walter D., **Socialism's Dilemmas: State and Society in the Soviet Bloc**. New York: Columbia University Press, 1988. x, 299 p. ISBN: 0231066066. Includes index and bibliography (p. 263-299).

A collection of essays written from the mid-1970s to the mid-1980s. The first essay was the only one written for this volume and provides a general discussion of analytic categories and perspectives used by the author. Chapters 2-6 focus on the Soviet Union and cover the reemergence of dissent, class consciousness, the Soviet worker in modern times, and the social policies of the Gorbachev era. Chapters 7-11 cover Eastern Europe and problems such as social change, political culture, and dissent after the suppression of the Solidarity movement. "However socialism's dilemmas are resolved, the questions of class and inequality, social policy and popular demand, political culture, and dissent dealt with in the chapters to follow should figure importantly in their resolution." (p. 6) Reviews: *East Central Europe* 17:2:228-30 (Fall 1990). *Orbis* 34:1:143 (Winter 1990). *Canadian Journal of Political Science* 22:3:669 (September 1989). *Contemporary Sociology* 18:4:559-61 (July 1989).

1244. **Soviet Society Under Gorbachev: Currents Trends and the Prospects for Change**, edited by Maurice Friedberg and Heyward Isham. Armonk, NY: M.E. Sharpe, 1987. xiv, 159 p. ISBN: 0873324420. Includes index and bibliography.

Papers prepared for a conference sponsored by the Department of State in the fall of 1986 are collected here. The focus of the conference was Soviet domestic affairs. The papers cover such topics as the family, labor problems, alcoholism, Soviet nationalities, Soviet culture and the media. In all cases the authors have attempted to assess changes in each area since Gorbachev took power. Each article includes a bibliography of related or cited titles.

1245. Geller, Mikhail, **Cogs in the Soviet Wheel: The Formation of Soviet Man**. London: Collins Harvill, 1988. xx, 293 p. ISBN: 0394569261. Includes index.

An analysis of the transformation of the Russian population into unthinking parts of a machine. The author believed that Gorbachev's proposed reforms would remain no more than proposals, that Gorbachev used them as a ploy to gain the cooperation of a population which had stagnated during the Brezhnev years. The volume examines how the population was made to feel they were no more than "cogs" in a machine from Lenin through the Gorbachev era.

1246. Hope, Christopher, **Moscow! Moscow!** London: Heinemann, 1990. 190 p. ISBN: 043436713.

South African Christopher Hope shares his experiences during his repeated visits to Moscow in the late 1980s. He tries to experience Soviet life close up and then reflects on what he has seen, heard, and felt.

1247. Johnston, Robert H., **New Mecca, New Babylon: Paris and the Russian Exiles 1920-1945**. Kingston: McGill-Queen's University Press, 1988. ix, 254 p. ISBN: 0773506438. Includes index and bibliography (p. 231-247).

A history of the wave of refugees coming out of Russia after the 1917 revolution. The conditions they found in Paris in the interwar years and the means they found of dealing with their new life are a large part of this work. In particular, the author looks at their self image and the varying views held of their homeland. The book is topically arranged and includes a list of abbreviations and a glossary. Reviews: *Slavic Review* 49:4:655- 56 (Winter 1990). *American Historical Review* 95:3:841-42 (June 1990). *International History Review* 12:2:292-95 (May 1990). *Canadian-American Slavic Studies* 24:4:447-79 (Winter 1990).

1248. **Soviet Social Problems**, edited by Anthony Jones, Walter D. Connor, and David E. Powell. Boulder, CO: Westview Press, 1991. ix, 336 p. *John M. Olin Critical Issues Series*, ISBN: 0813376904. Includes index.

A collection of essays examining various social problems in Gorbachev's Soviet Union. "As the contributors to this volume show, the Soviet Union is facing a veritable explosion of social problems precisely at the time that a concentration of energies and resources is needed for the transition to a more effective economy, without which the future of society is very much in doubt." (p. 2) The essays focus on problems common to industrial societies such as ethnic problems, pollution, atomic energy, health care, drug abuse, aging and the elderly, education, youth problems, crime, and prostitution. This is the first text to consider a broad array of social problems. It is intended as a text for courses on Soviet society and for scholars. Review: *Contemporary Sociology* 20:5:659-70 (September 1991).

1249. Kerblay, Basile H., **Gorbachev's Russia,** translated by Rupert Swyer. 1st ed. New York: Pantheon Books, 1989. xii, 175 p. ISBN: 0394759710. Includes bibliographical references and index.

While recognizing that much attention had been paid to perestroika and glasnost, especially to these slogans, Kerblay also believes that more general societal effects are equally important. In fact, he says that he is "concerned primarily with the capacity for change on the main strata of Soviet society and with the processes that these reforms are likely to set in train at some time in the future." (p. ii) He begins by describing new trends in Soviet society, then moves on to considering the broad outlines of Gorbachev's policies, Soviet society and change, the pros and cons of economic development, social forces capable of producing change, and a concluding chapter, written six months after the rest of the book, that reconsiders his former predictions and opinions in the light of very recent events.

1250. Lourie, Richard, **Russia Speaks: An Oral History from the Revolution to the Present**. 1st ed. New York: Harper Collins, 1991. 396 p. *"An Edward Burlingame Book,"* ISBN: 0060164492. Includes index.

Noted author and translator Lourie narrates here a new kind of history. The narrative focuses "on a core of about a half a dozen people whose lives had been formed and deformed by Russia's century of faith and violence." (p. 11) The people whose stories are included here are not famous, with the exception of Andre Sakharov. The narrative begins in No. 6 Svotensky Boulevard and then proceeds chronologically from the revolution to the present day. Review: *New York Times Book Review* 19 (March 24, 1991).

1251. Perrie, Maureen, **The Image of Ivan the Terrible in Russian Folklore**. Cambridge: Cambridge University Press, 1987. x, 269 p. *Cambridge Studies in Oral and Literate Culture*, v. 14. ISBN: 0521330750. Includes index and bibliography (p. 254-261).

This study arose out of a concern with the topic of popular monarchism as seen in folklore, the folklore itself being a reflection of peasant attitudes and values about the tsar. Specifically, Perrie intends to explore the myth of the tsar as benevolent father of his people, concentrating on Ivan the Terrible. She initially reviews the controversies that have surrounded the folklore of Ivan the Terrible in Russian and Soviet folklorists. Then she turns to an examination of the major debates on related issues such as the historical basis for the folklore and the probable date of its first composition. An interpretation of the image of Ivan as presented in folksongs and tales is presented. Her analysis concludes with two chapters that examine the issues of when and how the folklore image developed. A second section of the book gives a series of annotated translations of selected folklore texts about Ivan. Reviews: *Slavic Review* 47:3:572 (Fall 1988). *Canadian Slavonic Papers* 30:1:135-36 (March 1988). *Russian History* 15:1:129-30 (Spring 1988).

1252. **The Soviet Empire: The Challenge of National and Democratic Movements,** edited by Uri Ra'anan. Lexington, Mass: Lexington Books, 1990. xvi, 254 p. ISBN: 0669246778. Includes bibliographical references and index.

A selection of essays which were originally delivered at a conference at Boston University's Institute for the Study of Conflict, Ideology, and Policy in 1989 are presented here. The theme of the conference was emerging national and democratic movements in various countries. The book is divided into three parts: the first is a group of essays focusing on the Soviet response to the problems posed by the democratic movement. Part two deals with the various problems raises by the national movements in the USSR, specifically Russian nationalism, nationalism in Belorussia and Ukraine, Baltic nationalism, and the national movements in Transcaucasia and Central Asia. The final part includes three essays on democratic and national movements in other communist regimes: Hungary, Poland, Czechoslovakia, and China.

1253. Rywkin, Michael, **Soviet Society Today**. Armonk, N.Y.: M.E. Sharpe, 1989. xii, 243 p. ISBN: 0873324447. Includes index and bibliography (p. 235).

A study of Soviet society examining social structure, state institutions, living conditions, working conditions, and social diversity. A section on perestroika and its feasibility is included. There is also a reading list for further study. The author does not attempt to project future developments of Soviet society but to describe its present state. Reviews: *Russian Review* 49:4:520 (October 1990). *Social Science Quarterly* 71:4: 874-75 (December 1990).

1254. Scott, Gini Graham, **The Open Door: Traveling in the U.S.S.R.** San Rafael, Calif.: New World Library, 1990. xviii, 211 p. ISBN: 0931432626.

A "citizen-diplomat's" view of Russia as she traveled through it in 1988. The author hopes to expand understanding of the Soviet Union by portraying day to day life and thus spent much of her tour meeting with Soviet citizens. The book is organized around the cities visited: Leningrad, Vilnus, Minsk, Moscow, and Kiev. The author presents the reader with sketches of law in the USSR, a visit to an artist's home, conversation with a black marketeer, and an encounter with a youth group. Much travel information is provided including statistics and what to expect while travelling. There is also an appendix of organizations working toward furthering Soviet-American relations.

1255. Shlapentokh, Vladimir, **Public and Private Life of the Soviet People: Changing Values in Post-Stalin Russia**. New York: Oxford University Press, 1989. 281 p. ISBN: 0195042662. Includes indexes and bibliography (p. 247-274).

A sociological examination of the differences between public and private behavior in the Soviet Union, "The goal of this book is to analyze the changing relationship between public and private spheres in Soviet society and to use this perspective to describe the life of the Soviet people in the post-Stalin period of the 1960s, 1970s, and early 1980s, especially during Brezhnev's regime when privatization spread across society with great rapidity." (p. 14) The author feels that privatization has played a particularly significant role in changing Soviet life. The first part of the book focuses on public behavior in the legal economy and political life. The second part studies aspects of private life such as the family, semilegal activities, the role of friendship, gangs, culture, bribery, and samizdat. The author draws on statistical data for his information in the first part of the book but relies on more impressionistic data in the second half on private life. Reviews: *American Journal of Sociology* 95:6:1613-14 (May 1990). *Global Economic Policy* 2:2:47-53 (Fall 1990).

1256. Siniavskii, Andrei, **Soviet Civilization: A Cultural History,** translated from the Russian by Joanne Turnbull with the assistance of Nikolai Formozov. New York: Arcade Publishing, 1990. xii, 291 p. ISBN: 1559700343. Includes index. Translation of *Osnovy sovetskoi tsivilizatsii*.

Looking through the eyes of Soviet literature Siniavskii explores Soviet civilization, "not so much as the history of civilization as the theory and even what [he] might call the metaphysics." (p. xii) In the study, he examines many aspects of Soviet society and civilization including Lenin, Stalin, the new man, Soviet language, and the revolution.

1257. Toscano, Roberto, **Soviet Human Rights Policy and Perestroika**. Cambridge, Mass.: University Press of America, 1989. x, 38 p. ISBN: 0819174084. Includes bibliographical references.

The author focuses only on the issue of human rights policy. Toscano traces the past system in the Soviet Union and how it has become an international issue. Noting some of the spectacular advances in human rights brought on by perestroika the author also points out some elements of the existing system. He believes it must change if human rights are to be guaranteed in the long run.

1258. Zaslavskaia, Tatiana I., **A Voice of Reform: Essays**, edited by Murray Yanowitch. Armonk, N.Y.: M.E. Sharpe, Inc., 1989. xix, 191 p. ISBN: 0873325052. Includes index.

Representative essays by Soviet sociologist Tatiana Zaslavskaia are collected in this volume. The essays reflect early reformist thinking in Soviet literature before the Gorbachev reforms. Essays in this volume cover economic sociology, economic behavior, social justice. An appendix is included on the formerly confidential Novosibirsk Report. Reviews: *Slavic Review* 49:2:293-94 (Summer 1990). *Contemporary Sociology* 19:1: 107-09 (January 1990). *Social Forces* 68:3:1008-09 (March 1990). *Journal of Economic Issues* 24:1:286-89 (March 1990).

Alcoholism and Drug Abuse

1259. Segal, Boris M., **The Drunken Society: Alcohol Abuse and Alcoholism in the Soviet Union: A Comparative Study**. New York: Hippocrene Books, 1990. xxiii, 618 p. ISBN: 0870523732. Includes index and bibliography (p. 539-606).

Segal examines drunkenness and its associated social effects in the Soviet Union. After an introductory chapter that provides historical background, he covers the emergence of the drunken society, Soviet drinking behavior, alcohol production, sales and consumption, sex, marriage and alcohol, alcohol and crime, alcohol-related accidents and suicides, economic losses due to alcohol abuse, alcohol research, treatment, and prevention, and causes and implications of Soviet and American drinking and alcoholism.

Medical Care and Social Welfare

1260. **The Disabled in the Soviet Union: Past and Present, Theory and Practice**. Pittsburgh, Pa.: University of Pittsburgh Press, 1989. vii, 303 p. *Series in Russian and East European Studies*, no. 12. ISBN: 0822936224. Includes bibliographies.

These twelve essays are an outgrowth of a conference held at Michigan State University in 1985. The participants all believed that the fate of the disabled in a society gives important clues to the inner directions of that society. These were the themes to which the conference participants addressed themselves. The first theme was a historical question: were the disabled recognized as a social problem prior to the Revolution and did the policy change after 1917? What was the effect of World War II on the treatment of the disabled? A second theme explored the actual experience of the disabled, the dimensions of the handicap problem, the bases for treatment of the disabled, and whether the Soviets have responded to the technological treatment of the disabled that has prevailed in the West since 1950. The third and final theme dealt with the attitudes towards the disabled and responses of the disabled towards societal conditions. Reviews: *Canadian Slavonic Papers* 32:4:502-03 (December 1990). *Slavic Review* 49:3:472-73 (Fall 1990).

Social Problems and Social Change

1261. Attwood, Lynne, **The New Soviet Man and Woman: Sex Role Socialization in the USSR**. Bloomington: Indiana University Press, 1990. x, 263 p. ISBN: 0253310741. Includes bibliographical references (p. 237-254) and index.

This is a scholarly study of the effects sex-role models have had in Soviet society. The author notes that while there have been many studies on women, this particular problem has not yet been addressed in relation to men. Attwood believes that the existing sex role models in the Soviet Union have made it impossible for there ever to be true equality between the sexes. In fact, the government has used sex role models to try to affect demographics. The author does not feel that this has changed with "perestroika." The volume begins with a discussion of Western studies of male and female personality differences. With this context established, the author turns to Soviet psychology as it relates to gender studies. The body of the book is devoted to a review of specific studies of sex differences. This is followed by an analysis of the practical application of studies of sex differences in the Soviet Union. Finally, a concluding chapter gives some predictions for the future with the author attempting to demonstrate the difficulty in establishing sexual equality given the existing role models.

1262. **Small Fires: Letters from the Soviet People to Ogonyok Magazine, 1987-1990**, selected and edited by Christopher Cerf and Marina Albee with Lev Gushchin, consulting editor, Lynn Visson, chief translator, Hans Fenstermacher, with an introduction by Vitaly Korotich. New York: Summit Books, 1990. 303 p. ISBN: 0671693972.

This is a remarkable collection of letters that were sent to the editors of *Ogonyok* magazine. Some of the letters appearing here were never published in *Ogonyok*. As the editor of *Ogonyok* says: "Only in a country where the government is ineffective can the editors of a weekly magazine receive so many letters." (p. 1) The letters are gathered under several rubrics: perestroika, glasnost, democratization, daily life, people and power, current issues (such as crime, punishment, drugs, AIDS and the environment), nationalities and the lessons of history. The "voices of the entire country" are represented here. They are eye-opening, sometimes depressing, sometimes inspiring, but always fascinating.

1263. Jones, Ellen, and Fred W. Grupp, **Modernization, Value Change, and Fertility in the Soviet Union**. Cambridge: Cambridge University Press, 1987. xvi, 420 p. *Soviet and East European Studies*, ISBN: 0521320348. Includes bibliographical notes and index.

The authors examine social change in a multi-ethnic, socialist state by analyzing "the way in which the social, economic, and political transformations, encompassed by modernization affect values and behaviors." (p. 1) They focus on values that affect family behavior and the relationship between the change of these values and fertility. They then examine the effect public policy has on those values and fertility trends. Reviews: *Canadian Slavonic Papers* 30:3:406 (September 1988). *Soviet Union* 14:3:373-74 (1987). *Slavic Review* 47:2:347-48 (Summer 1988). *Contemporary Sociology* 17:3:343-44 (May 1988).

1264. Matthews, Mervyn, **Patterns of Deprivation in the Soviet Union Under Brezhnev and Gorbachev**. Stanford, Calif.: Hoover Institution Press, 1989. xvi, 158 p. ISBN: 0817988319. Includes bibliographical references.

A subject taboo in the Soviet press is taken up in this volume that deals with the poor of the Soviet Union. Since the Soviets will not acknowledge the problem, little information has been available in the past. One study taken from data drawn from émigrés is presented in one of the chapters. The author has divided this work into four parts: 1) "Gorbachev's

Social Policies," covering fights against equal incomes, problems with job security, and the underprivileged; 2) "Soviet Living Standards and Consumer Reaction," discusses popular demand for better standards and the failure to satisfy consumer demands; 3) "Deprivation Among Soviet Families," is a presentation and interpretation of statistics drawn from the study of living conditions as portrayed by émigrés who have lived below the poverty line; and 4) "Poverty and Glasnost in the Press," which covers the effect of Gorbachev's policy of glasnost.

1265. ———, **Poverty in the Soviet Union: The Life-Styles of the Underprivileged in Recent Years**. Cambridge: Cambridge University Press, 1986. xv, 227 p. ISBN: 0521325447. Includes index and bibliography (p. 217-224).

This work takes up the neglected topic of poverty in the USSR. The author hopes that this work will stimulate further research on the area. The first three chapters give a factual overview of poverty in the Soviet Union: how it arose, who it affects, and what their living conditions are like. The remaining chapters are often more concerned with theory than fact, largely because of the scarcity of information on the topics covered such as poverty and education, medical facilities for the poor, and legal services for the poor. There is also a discussion of the social implications to labor, social security, and the exclusion of the poor from the political process. The author has supplemented his work with an appendix of "unofficial documents" including samizdat articles and an émigré survey on the subject. Sources of information include Soviet statistical works and secondary sources.

1266. **Toward a More Civil Society?: The USSR Under Mikhail Sergeeivich Gorbachev: An Assessment by the American Committee on U.S.-Soviet Relations**, edited by William Green Miller. New York: Ballinger, 1989. xxxiv, 366 p. ISBN: 0887302203. Includes bibliographical references and index.

This collection of essays attempts to assess whether perestroika, glasnost, democratization, and other Gorbachevian efforts will move the Soviet Union toward a more civil society. Includes essays on political reform, cultural reform, societal dynamics, economic reform, national security policy, and foreign policy. Fourteen contributors present mini-essay conclusions in a final chapter. It also includes two appendices. The first is a bibliographic essay on selected sources for research on the Soviet Union and the second a description of Soviet government structure as it existed in 1989.

1267. **Soviet Youth Culture**, edited by Jim Riordan. Bloomington: Indiana University Press, 1989. x, 148 p. ISBN: 0253354234. Includes bibliographies.

Six essays covering a broad range of perspectives on Soviet youth culture. The essays range from a general discussion of Soviet youth and subculture to the officially sanctioned Komsomol Youth organization, to rock music. Other topics include rural youth, the political education of the young and its effects, and gangs in Russia. Reviews: *Russian Review* 49:3:369-70 (July 1990). *Soviet Union-Union Sovietique* 17:3:317-18 (1990).

1268. Rosner, Lydia S., **The Soviet Way of Crime: Beating the System in the Soviet Union and the U.S.A.** South Hadley, Mass.: Bergin & Garvey Publishers, 1986. xvii, 140 p. ISBN: 0897890981. Includes bibliographies and index.

Using the Russian immigrant population that settled in Brighton Beach, the author examines criminal patterns that emerge within the group. She is particularly interested in determining if these criminal patterns differ from those seen in previous waves of immigration, made up largely of people of peasant origin. "The population will be considered as a possible example of a new type of immigrant who, coming from an already industrialized society, is urban, and has middle-class under pinnings and aspirations, but who is still engaged in crime. The social, political, and economic factors in the social structure of the homeland that may predispose the immigrants to crime there, and how they respond to similarities and difference in their homeland and new land with respect to criminal behavior will be examined." (pp. ix-x) The seven chapters cover criminal patterns in the USSR; the meaning of crime to the Soviet; American criminal values; Russian populations after immigration and the adaptation of values; differences between contemporary immigrant criminal behavior and previous immigrant populations; and reexamination of sociological theories on immigrants. Review: *Contemporary Sociology* 16:6:847-48 (November 1987).

1269.   Smith, Hendrick, **The New Russians**. New York: Random House, 1990. xxxi, 621 p. ISBN: 0394581903. Includes bibliographical references and index.
In this work, journalist Hendrick Smith returns to the Soviet Union to discover how deeply it has changed. He interviews many individuals from across the country. "What follows in this book are the stories of what it is like in the Soviet Union today; what it is like for individuals to live through a cultural convulsion, a wholesale change in their society and environment." (p. xxix)

1270.   **New Directions in Soviet Social Thought: An Anthology**, edited by Murray Yanowitch. Armonk, N.Y.: M.E. Sharpe, 2989. xxvi, 309 p. ISBN: 0873324951.
A collection of writings by Soviet reformist thinkers. The works presented are intended as a sample of the wide range of issues under review by these scholars. They also indicate the multi-disciplinary nature of reformist thinking. "The wide-ranging and multidisciplinary nature of more recent reformist currents is apparent in discussions of such themes as the 'democratization' of economic management and of the society at large, the problem of implementing 'social justice,' the need to transform long-established value-systems, and the urgency of fundamental reforms of this prevailing system of property ownership." The essays collected for this book cover these topics. No one point of view is held throughout. Several pre-1985 essays have been included to indicate the pre-Gorbachevian basis of the reforms.

Women

1271.   Bridger, Susan, **Women in the Soviet Countryside: Women's Roles in Rural Development in the USSR**. Cambridge: Cambridge University Press, 1987. xvii, 259 p. *Soviet and East European Studies*, ISBN: 0521328624. Includes index and bibliography (p. 245-253).
The economic and social roles of rural women in the Soviet Union are the subject of this study. "Women's roles in the workforce, the family and in culture are examined in order to assess whether the marginalisation of rural women which had occurred by 1960 has been reversed by greater access to education or, alternatively, intensified as mechanisation has increased." (p. 20) The volume is divided into three parts: women in the rural workforce, in rural families and in rural culture. The author believes that women as the primary workers in the subsistence farms hold an unrecognized financial role in the family. The importance of this role is further diminished by the government's reticence to recognize this work. The volume includes numerous tables and figures. Reviews: *Soviet Union* 15:1:89-90 (1988). *Slavic Review* 48:1:122 (Spring 1989).

1272.   Browning, Genia K., **Women and Politics in the USSR: Consciousness Raising and Soviet Women's Groups**. New York: St. Martin's Press, 1987. ix, 178 p. ISBN: 0312009534. Includes index and bibliography (p. 147-172).
This study examines the disparity between Soviet theory, which calls for sexual equality, and Soviet political practice which has kept women from the upper echelons of power. To

do so it focuses on the women's social group known as zhensovety. "The zhensovety will be looked at in two respects: how their aim to raise women's political consciousness is manifest; and whether they have the potential to act as autonomous consciousness-raising groups for women." (p. 3) The seven chapters cover a variety of topics beginning with a discussion of consciousness raising and women's political activity. It then moves to an overview of women's political participation in Soviet political institutions. This is followed by a description of opportunities for informal political activity in the USSR. The next four chapters are devoted to the zhensovety and their activities. A final chapter discusses the political future for Soviet women. Several appendices are included with data on women in political institutions and on the development of the zhansovety. Review: *Slavic Review* 48:1:117-18 (Spring 1989).

1273. Buckley, Mary, **Women and Ideology in the Soviet Union**. Ann Arbor, MI: University of Michigan Press, 1989. xiv, 265 p. ISBN: 0472094106. Includes index and bibliography (p. 234-253).

Buckley examines changes in official ideology concerning women and their role from just before the revolution through Gorbachev. She begins in an introduction discussing definitions and various theoretical aspects of ideology. She then explores in turn Marxist ideas on women, women's organizations in the early Bolshevik party, the putative solving of the women question under Stalin, Khrushchev, and women's political roles, the revival of the women question under Brezhnev, and finally women's issues under Gorbachev.

1274. Gray, Francine du Plessix, **Soviet Women: Walking the Tightrope**. 1st U.S. ed. New York: Doubleday, 1990. 213 p. ISBN: 0385247575. Includes bibliographical references (p. 209-213).

An impressionistic account of the lives and future of Soviet women. The author traveled to various parts of the Soviet Union focusing on the issues of interest to women, family, divorce, literature, work, and religion to name a few. The author tries to provide a picture of how Soviet women view their world, and what they aspire to in the future.

1275. Mamonova, Tatyana, **Russian Women's Studies: Essays on Sexism in Soviet Culture**, with the assistance of Margaret Maxwell. 1st ed. Oxford: Pergamon Press, 1989. xiv, 178 p. ISBN: 0080364810.

Russian feminism began in the 19th century with the establishment of higher education courses for women. Even through the 1920s modest strides were made in establishing de facto women's rights. Stalin effectively erased the memory of these early efforts when he declared the women's question solved. Mamonova intends "to rehabilitate Russian women's history and to trace its connection to the present-day situation of women in the Soviet Union, who are equal according to the law, but in fact live under conditions of constant exploitation and humiliation." (p. xiv) Reviews: *Women and Politics* 10:4:133-34 (1990). *Society* 27:4:108-10 (May-June 1990).

1276. Maxwell, Margaret, **Narodniki Women: Russian Women Who Sacrificed Themselves for the Dream of Freedom**. 1st ed. New York: Pergamon Press, 1990. xv, 341 p. ISBN: 0080374611 (pbk.), 008037462X. Includes index and bibliographical references.

"This book is not an analysis of the social, economic, and political condition of Russia in the half century preceding the 1917 revolution.... This book is history as story. Its purpose is to lift individual Russian revolutionary women out of the category of the usual one-or two-line references or complete omission in textbooks and monographs on Russian history from the 1870s through the 1917 Revolution." (p. xi)

Special Studies

1277. Conquest, Robert, **Tyrants and Typewriters: Communiqués from the Struggle for Truth**. Lexington, Mass.: Lexington Books, 1989. xiv, 208 p. ISBN: 0669212229. Includes bibliographical references.
The continued presence of unorthodox views in the Soviet state can be credited with its eventual downfall. This compendium of literary, historical, economic, and philosophical writing is, as the editor notes, "central to the understanding of the culture of tyranny." Conquest's selections are arranged in three parts. In part one, Witnesses, he has gathered voices from both within and without, such as Arthur Koestler, Milovan Djilas, Svetlana Alliluyeva, Andrei Sakharov, and Solzhenitsyn. In part two, Literature, we hear from the likes of Paternak, Mayakovsky, Ehrenberg, Tvardovsky, Orwell, and Vasilii Grossman. In part three, History and Pseudo-History, he offers us selections from Volksy (on Lenin), Preobraz Lensky, Roy Medvedev, Isaac Deutcher, and others. An epilogue is devoted to Solzhenitsyn.

1278. Friedgut, Theodore H., **Iuzovka and Revolution: Life and Work in Russia's Donbass, 1869-1924**. Princeton, NJ: Princeton University Press, 1989. xviii, 359 p. *Studies of the Harriman Institute*, vol. 1. Includes bibliography and index.
This work, the first in a two volume set, traces the socio-political development of Iuzovka as an example of the development of industrial capitalism in Russia. Originally, the author had sought to write a biography of Khrushchev but found the village in which Khrushchev grew up to be so fascinating that the original project was abandoned. The first volume focuses on an analysis of social relations in Iuzovka from its beginnings to the completion of its post-civil war reconstruction. The author believes that there was always a gap between political development and socio-economic development with the latter evolving more rapidly than the former. This creates a tension in the system as a whole. Friedgut has divided this volume into three parts: Part I gives an overview of the development of the Donbass into an industrial center. Part II covers social development including everything from diet to education. Part III traces economic development, the labor force and organization of labor. Review: *Canadian Slavonic Papers* 32:2:181-82 (June 1990).

1279. Hutchings, Raymond, **Soviet Secrecy and Non-secrecy**. Basingstoke: Macmillan, 1987. vii, 292 p. ISBN: 0333340205. Includes indexes and bibliography (p. 267-279).
Hutchings describes and analyzes various aspects of Soviet secrecy, including theoretical and general considerations, main features of Soviet secrecy, how secrets are kept, international comparisons, and the causes and consequences of secrecy.

1280. Klugman, Jeffry, **The New Soviet Elite: How They Think and What They Want**. New York: Praeger, 1989. x, 237 p. ISBN: 0275931528. Includes bibliography (p. 225-231).
Based on interviews with 20 former Soviet citizens the author tries to describe the process by which individuals obtain power in the Soviet Union. The first part of the book presents material from the interviews that describe the career building process. Part two examines the specific characteristics needed for success and their effect on interpersonal relations. Part three demonstrates that the information gained by studying career development can be used to elucidate the Soviet system as a whole. The final part looks at the relationship between individual psychology and institutional behavior. Two appendices are included. One deals with child rearing practices and education in the Soviet Union, and the other examines the "psychodynamics of career development." Review: *Annals of the American Academy of Political and Social Science* 512:195-96 (September 1990).

1281. Mills, Richard M., **As Moscow Sees Us: American Politics and Society in the Soviet Mindset**. New York: Oxford University Press, 1990. xi, 308 p. ISBN: 0195062604. Includes index and bibliographical references (p. 271-299).

"The aim of this book is to present a broad range of Americans with a comprehensive and comprehensible picture of how their politics and society are viewed from the perspective of a radically different culture." (p. vii) In eight chapters the author describes how Soviets perceive American politics, what classes make up American society, relations among the classes, how the Soviet intellectual context has shaped their perception of American politics and how their theories of class, pluralism, and elitism affect their view.

1282. Parchomenko, Walter, **Soviet Images of Dissidents and Nonconformists**. New York: Praeger, 1986. xv, 251 p. *"Praeger Special Studies-Praeger Scientific,"* ISBN: 0275920216. Includes index and bibliography (p. 213-243).

A study of the official presentation of the dissident in the Soviet Union. The author is attempting to demonstrate by means of several case studies, that during the Brezhnev era dissidents were presented in such a way as to blur the distinction between mild dissent and subversion. The author devotes some chapters to presenting his method of analysis and the research design used here. He also clearly states his own biases, describing himself as prodissident. The material used for this volume was originally drawn from his dissertation and covers the period up to 1984. The author includes several appendices on related topics including chronologies of the lives of both individuals used in the case studies, Vladimir Shelkov and Iurii Orlov, a list of political trials and documentation, a list of samizdat publications, and documents of the Moscow Helsinki Group. The author plans a second volume to continue research on his topic in different areas of the dissent movement.

1283. Robinson, John P., Vladimir G. Andreyenkov, and Vasily D. Patrushev, **The Rhythm of Everyday Life: How Soviet and American Citizens Use Time**. Boulder, CO: Westview Press, 1989. xiv, 148 p. ISBN: 0813375762. Includes index and bibliography (p. 143-146).

This book reports the results of a joint U.S.-USSR cooperative social science survey on the use of time by both employed and non-employed people in Pskov, Russia and Jackson, Michigan. It "identifies changes in time-use patterns of both cities during the last two decades." (p. 1) It goes beyond a simple documentation of changes, however, and explores many other aspects of daily life. Review: *Contemporary Sociology* 19:2:283-84 (1990).

1284. Rogers, Paul P., **Insurance in the Soviet Union**. New York: Praeger, 1986. xii, 210 p. ISBN: 0275922553. Includes index and bibliography (p. 201-205).

This book is addressed to two audiences. One is that which has little knowledge about the Soviet Union, but knowledge of the technical aspects of insurance. The other is that which knows little about the insurance industry, but is fairly knowledgeable about Soviet society. The book was written to answer the question "Why does a communist society have insurance?" The primary focus is Gosstrakh, the agency which deals with losses incurred by citizens and agricultural enterprises.

1285. Ruble, Blair A., **Leningrad: Shaping a Soviet City**. Berkeley: University of California Press, 1990. xxvi, 328 p. ISBN: 0520065344. Includes index and bibliographical references (p. 231-311).

Ruble's book on Leningrad was written to describe "how is it that today's Leningrad looks and feels the way it does." (p. xxiii) To do this he first examines the physical environment by describing Peter I's vision, the Romanov imperial legacy and Stalin's legacy, the postwar city (1945-66), and a new city plan (1966-1986). He then turns to the socioeconomic environment by analyzing the organization of the city's science and industry, the education of a new workforce and industrial sociology, and the search for effective urban management. Several appendices provide concise information on the structure of Leningrad's municipal administration, senior Leningrad officials from 1917-1987, and the city's urban planning institutions.

1286. Shlapentokh, Vladimir, **Soviet Public Opinion and Ideology: Mythology and Pragmatism in Interaction**. New York: Praeger, 1986. 256 p. ISBN: 0275925617. Includes bibliography and index.

The main purpose of this book, writes the author, "is to demonstrate that official ideology is a very complex and relatively flexible construction...." (p. xi) In pursuing his theme Shlapentokh develops a two-level structure theory of Soviet public ideology. Review: *Soviet Union* 14:1:157-58 (1987).

1287. Traver, Nancy, **Kife: The Life and Dreams of Soviet Youth**, with a foreword by Yuri Shchekochikhin. 1st ed. New York: St. Martin's Press, 1989. xvii, 252 p. ISBN: 0312029381. Includes index.

"Kife means catching a buzz, or having it all. When a Soviet has achieved kife, he's got it made." (p. xvi) Traver, who was a correspondent in Moscow, provides an in depth look at Soviet youth and their attitudes toward education, sex and marriage, the military, communism, and nationalism and other social topics. Reviews: *Commentary* 89:5:68-70 (May 1990). *World and I* 416-23 (April 1990).

Handicrafts

1288. Cheneviere, Antoine, **Russian Furniture: The Golden Age, 1780-1850**. New York: Vendome Press, 1988. 311 p. ISBN: 0865650993. Includes references (p. 304-308) and index.

An attempt to survey the most creative years in the history of Russian furniture making 1780-1890. The author notes that previous works have either been limited to the description of specific collections and are most often in Russian. Three phenomena in particular will be considered: development of technique, system of production, and development of national style. The volume is arranged chronologically and includes appendices of biographies of architects and artists and a description of the Palace of Pavlosk. The author notes the uneven coverage reflecting the differing amounts of information available for various topics. A special chapter on steelware from Tula has also been included. The volume is liberally provided with illustrations. Review: *Slavic Review* 49:2:316-18 (Summer 1990).

Chapter 12
NON-RUSSIAN REPUBLICS, JEWS,
AND OTHER MINORITIES

GENERAL STUDIES

1289. Bennigsen, Alexandre, and S. Enders Wimbush, **Muslims of the Soviet Empire: A Guide**. Bloomington: Indiana University Press, 1986. xvi, 294 p. ISBN: 0253339588. Includes index and bibliography (p. 251-278).
A reference guide on the Islamic peoples of the Soviet Union. The volume is divided into three sections. The first covers general issues affecting the Muslim population as a whole, its history, political dynamics that have affected it, domestic, and regional issues. Part two is divided first into broad geographical regions. Then each region is further divided into specific ethnic groups. The final section is a bibliography to direct the interested reader to literature on particular topics. The volume contains numerous tables and several maps. The census data used here is drawn from the 1979 census. It is important to point out that the authors include in the term "Muslim" any of those people who "belonged to the world of Islam" before the 1917 revolution. The bibliography does consist of many works in Russian, reflecting the authors' intent to be thorough. Review: *Canadian Slavonic Papers* 29:2-3:313-14 (June-September 1987).

1290. Bonkalo, Sandor, **The Rusyns**, translated by Ervin Bonkalo. Fairview, NJ: Carpatho-Rusyn Research Center, 1990. xx, 160 p. *Classics of Carpatho-Rusyn Scholarship: East European Monographs*, vol. 3. ISBN: 0880331909. Includes bibliographical references (p. 147-149) and index.
This is a general review of the literary, cultural, historical, and political history of the Rusyn people of Subcarpathian Rus. Originally written in Hungarian, the author treats the origins of Rusyn colonizations, the Rusyns during the Czech occupation, enormous teachings about the political history of Rusyns, the origins of Rusyns and their name, Rusyn ethnographic groups, Rusyn culture and literature, folk poetry, religion, and economic conditions. A statistical appendix of demographic data is also included.

1291. **The Last Empire: Nationality and the Soviet Future**, edited by Robert Conquest. Stanford, CA: Hoover Institution Press, 1986. xiv, 406 p. *Hoover Press Publication*, no. 325. ISBN: 081792515. Includes bibliographies and index.
This collection of sixteen essays found its origins at a conference held at the Hoover Institution in 1983. Nationalism is here examined from a variety of perspectives by a distinguished set of contributors. Essays cover, among other topics, the historical perspective of Russian nationalism, its role in Soviet politics, the anti-semitic component, a historical examination of minority nationalism, individual essays on Ukraine, the Baltic states, and the Muslim border lands. Nationality is also analyzed from the perspective of language, culture, religion and national awareness, social and economic aspects, and the demography of Soviet ethnic groups. Concluding essays cover Eastern Europe within the Soviet empire and nationalism in the USSR and its implications for the world. Review: *Political Science Quarterly* 102:2:331-32 (Summer 1987).

1292. Diuk, Nadia, and Adrian Karatnycky, **The Hidden Nations: The People Challenge the Soviet Union**. New York: Morrow, 1990. 284 p. ISBN: 068808849X.

A discussion of the nationalities question as the Soviet Union faces the changes of perestroika. The authors sketch the history of the problem from tsarist times to the present. They then turn to the economics of the situation. The remaining chapters focus on particular national groups or regions. Those discussed include Ukraine, the Baltic states, the Caucuses, Soviet Central Asia, and the Russians. An appendix gives statistical data on nationalities in the Soviet Union from 1979 and 1989.

1293. Fleischhauer, Ingeborg, and Benjamin Pinkus, **The Soviet Germans: Past and Present**, edited and with an introduction by Edith Rogovin Frankel. London: Hurst in association with the Marjorie Mayrock Centre for Soviet and East European Research at the Hebrew University, 1986. xi, 185 p. ISBN: 090583898X. Includes index and bibliography (p. 159-174).

A study of Soviet policy towards its German minority since the revolution. The five essays by Ingeborg Fleischhauer and Benjamin Pinkus comprise a chronological study of the Germans in Russia beginning with their role in tsarist Russia and continuing through Soviet times to the present. Essays cover the period between the revolution and World War II, the war years, Germans under Nazi rule, and conditions for Germans since 1945.

1294. Gleason, Gregory, **Federalism and Nationalism: The Struggle for Republican Rights in the USSR**, with a foreword by John N. Hazard. Boulder, CO: Westview Press, 1990. xiii, 170 p. *Westview Special Studies on the Soviet Union and Eastern Europe*, ISBN: 0813375525. Includes bibliographical references.

"In this analysis of Soviet federal development, Dr. Gleason outlines the organization of the USSR's federal system, exploring its institutions, principles and values. Detailing the close connection between the federal principle and ethno-nationalism in the USSR, Dr. Gleason provides insights into the underlying dynamics of the nationalist resurgence that has swept across the Soviet Union in recent years. He contends that the formal bureaucratic organizations of the Soviet party and state, originally designed to eliminate nationalism, have instead served to sustain and reinforce it." (back cover) The volume includes appendices supplying statistics on the republics and population growth, urban development, industrial workforce growth, and other information.

1295. **The Nationalities Factor in Soviet Politics and Society**, edited by Lubomyr Hajda and Mark Beissinger. Boulder, CO: Westview Press, 1990. vii, 331 p. *John M. Olin Critical Issues Series*, ISBN: 0814476890. Includes bibliographical references.

A collection of essays on various aspects of the nationalities problem in the Soviet Union. Essay topics include nationalities and political change; nationalities and the economy; nationalities and the military; Russification and Soviet nationalities; nationalities and Soviet religious policy. Several regions are considered extensively: the Baltic, Ukraine, Belorus, Transcaucasia, Moldavia, and Central Asia. Many of the essays analyze their subjects in terms of Gorbachev's proposed reforms and their effects on various national groups.

1296. Karklins, Rasma, **Ethnic Relations in the USSR: The Perspective from Below**. Boston: G. Allen & Unwin, 1986. xvi, 256 p. ISBN: 004320288. Includes index and bibliography (p. 241-251).

The author attempts to analyze the popular views and affects of ethnicity in the Soviet Union. "This is a study of the dynamics of Soviet ethnic relations and politics primarily from the point of view of the participating 'common man' in the non-Russian borderlands." (p. 1) The first chapter deals with how nationality is identified. Chapters 2-6 discuss specific elements of ethnic relationships: nationalism, ethnicity in the workplace, in schools, and ethnic intermarriage. Chapter 7 looks at particularism in cultural and religious life. The volume includes a statistical appendix. Reviews: *Soviet Union* 14:1:120-21 (1987). *Canadian Slavonic Papers* 29:2-3:311-12 (June- September 1987). *Slavic Review* 46:2:321-24 (Summer 1987).

1297. Nahaylo, Bohdan, and Victor Swoboda, **Soviet Disunion: A History of the Nationalities Problem in the USSR**. London: Hamish Hamilton, 1990. xvi, 432 p. ISBN: 0241135405. Includes bibliographical references (p. 412-417) and index.
Nahaylo and Swoboda trace the causes and effects of the so called "nationalities problem" from the February Revolution in 1917 to 1989. They illustrate how Russian expansionism incorporated by force many formerly autonomous peoples into the Soviet Union. They also analyze how the various nationalities attempted to retain their own unique character in the face of intense Russification. Their work serves as an excellent basis for understanding the various independence movements in the Soviet Union.

1298. **The Soviet Multinational State: Readings and Documents**. Armonk, N.Y.: M.E. Sharpe, Inc., 1990. xii, 605 p. ISBN: 0873323890. Includes bibliography (p. 597-599).
This collection of readings is arranged in ten chapters. Many of the readings are, in fact, primary source documents such as speeches or newspaper articles. It is an anthology of exclusively Soviet materials, aptly translated by the editors. Successive chapters examine official Soviet policy on the "national problem, " Soviet scholars and the study of the "national problem," party politics in the national regions, economic development, ethno-demographic trends, language training and nationality relations, literature and national culture, religion and national culture, patriotism and national exclusivity, and extensive coverage of nationality relations in conflict, focusing on the Baltics and Nagorno-Karabakh. It includes an appendix on nationalities of the USSR in 1979.

1299. Simon, Gerhard, **Nationalism and Policy Toward the Nationalities in the Soviet Union: From Totalitarian Dictatorship to Post-Stalinist Society**, translated by Karen Forster and Oswald Forster. Boulder, CO: Westview Press, 1991. xvii, 483 p. ISBN: 0813374944. Includes bibliographical references (p. 423-456) and index.
A study of the policies put in place by the Bolshevik government and those of later eras to control the various nationalities in the Soviet Union, and how these policies are now being used to assist in the breakup of the Soviet empire. The book takes a historical approach, with each chapter devoted to a period in Soviet development. The author believes that when the values of the Revolution failed, during and after World War II, they were replaced with a growing nationalism. In this volume the author traces the development of a nationality policy particularly in the 1930s, the war years, the affects of de-Stalinization, and the rise of the new nationalism. The volume contains an appendix with statistics on various national groups through 1979 and a list of abbreviations. Review: *Foreign Affairs* 70:5:197- 98 (Winter 1991-92).

1300. **The Nationalities Question in the Soviet Union**, edited by Graham Smith. New York: Longman, 1990. ix, 389 p. ISBN: 0582039533. Includes bibliographical references (p. 373-378) and index.
A reexamination of the nationalities problem since the Gorbachev reforms have been in place. This collection of essays was inspired by a need for a reassessment of the problem since the reforms had been enacted. The essays collected here demonstrate the variety of responses perestroika and glasnost have drawn from the various ethnic groups. The structure of the book provides first an historical overview of nationalities policy in the Soviet Union. This is followed by a special section on the Russians. The remaining chapters cover the major nationalities: Estonians, Latvians, Lithuanians, Ukrainians, Belorussians,

Moldavians, Kazakhs, Armenians, Azerbaiajanis, Georgians, Uzbeks, Turkmen, Kirgiz, Tadzhiks, Tatars, Buriats, Iakuts, Crimean Tatars, and Jews. While the volume does not cover all 140 nationalities it does cover the groups that made up nine-tenths of the Soviet population. The volume also has several maps, appendices showing the territorial claims of national groups, and giving population statistics. There is also a bibliography of English language sources.

BALTIC REPUBLICS

1301. Clemens, Walter C., **Baltic Independence and Russian Empire**. New York: St. Martin's Press, 1991. xxii, 346 p. ISBN: 031204868. Includes index and bibliographical references.

Clemens investigates Baltic autonomy and independence movements in the twentieth century, culminating with the fall of the Soviet empire in 1991. "The book's underlying hypothesis is that exploitative, zero-sum policies can net short-term gains..., but that they tend to backfire over time, creating greater burdens than profits for the exploiters." (p. xv) Reviews: *Foreign Affairs* 70:4:182 (Fall 1991). *Lituanus* 37:4:87-89 (Winter 1991).

1302. Kirby, David G., **Northern Europe in the Early Modern Period: The Baltic World, 1492-1772**. London: Longman, 1990. xii, 443 p. ISBN: 0582004101. Includes index and bibliographical references (p. 405-415).

This history of the early modern period in Northern Europe is presented against the background of Sweden's rise and fall. The Baltic is seen as the area of conflict between East and West. The focus is on Latvia and Estonia with less attention to Lithuania. The underlying theme in this work is the struggle for existence in a harsh environment. The author intends his work as a general introduction to the problems of the area. He views the area as one whose development has been determined largely by its responses to outside stimuli. The first part is an overview of conditions in the Baltic at the end of the Middle Ages. The next three parts, chronologically arranged, cover the major events in the Baltic's early history: the Livonian Wars, the years of Swedish ascendancy, and the rise of Russia. The volume includes several maps and a table of rulers of the area from 1500 to 1772.

1303. **Regional Identity Under Soviet Rule: The Case of the Baltic States**, edited by Dietrich Andre Loeber. Hackettstown, NJ: Institute for the Study of Law, Politics and Society of Socialist States, 1990. xxii, 470 p. ISBN: 0962490601. Includes bibliographical references.

Papers presented at the University of Kiel during a conference held in 1987 at which various aspects of regional identity under the Soviet government were discussed. Major areas for discussion included consciousness of regional identity and characteristics and manifestations of regional identity. The papers are arranged into sections on regionalism, regionalism and political integration, regionalism and social development, regionalism and cultural development, regionalism and economic development, comparative aspects of regionalism, and international aspects of regionalism. A section reprinting documentation is included containing numerous samizdat materials. The final bibliographic section of Soviet Baltic publications from 1956-1986 contains citations to materials made available to the participants before the conference. This was intended as a case study of this phenomenon under the Soviet regime.

1304.　**Fire and Night: Five Baltic Plays**, edited by Alfreds Straumanis. Prospect Heights, Ill.: Waveland Press, 1986. v, 386 p. ISBN: 088133216X.
This is the fourth anthology of Baltic drama compiled by Straumanis. Like the other volumes, the plays in this volume were selected according to some similarity in theme or plot. These plays were chosen because each of them depicts historical or legendary events or uses such events to create the dramatic action. All five, although belonging to three different generations, "focus their attention upon the prevailing myths of the people in specific developmental periods." (p. v)

1305.　Vizulis, Izidors Joseph, **The Molotov-Ribbentrop Pact of 1939: The Baltic Case**. New York: Praeger, 1990. vi, 176 p. ISBN: 027593456X. Includes index and bibliographical references.
The Molotov-Ribbentrop Pact, wherein Eastern Europe was divided into spheres of influence and the Baltic States were annexed by the Soviet Union, has had tragic consequences. This book analyzes the pact, "The course that led to its signing, its consequences, and today's challenge of the Soviet Union by the Baltic people for its repeal." (p. vii)

Estonia

1306.　Alexander, Tania, **Tania: Memories of a Lost World**. Bethesda, Md.: Adler & Adler, 1988. xviii, 168 p. ISBN: 0917561554. Includes index.
Alexander grew up in independent Estonia. Her memoir focuses on her life in the town of Kallijarv, as well as on her childhood adult friend Maxim Gorky and family friend H. G. Wells. Her memoir stops prior to WWII, just after she emigrated to London. Review: *Slavic Review* 49:3:459-60 (Fall 1990).

1307.　Raun, Toivo U., **Estonia and the Estonians**. 2nd ed. Stanford, Calif.: Hoover Institution Press, Stanford University, 1991. xvii, 313 p. *Studies of Nationalities in the USSR, Hoover Press Publication*, no. 351. ISBN: 081799131X, 0817991328 (pbk.). Includes index and bibliography (p. 277-302).
Raun traces the history of Estonia from prehistoric times to the present day. The emphasis is on ethnic Estonians, although other groups such as Baltic Germans are also included. His book is divided into four parts. Part one treats Estonia before 1710. Part two describes Estonia under Imperial Russia and includes the period to 1917. Part three examines independent Estonia from its emergence during the period 1917-1920 trough 1940. Part four deals with Soviet Estonia through the post-Stalin era. The second edition adds analysis of events leading to autonomy including the various independence movements in 1990. Reviews: *Russian History* 17:1:112-13 (Spring 1990). *Slavic Review* 47:4: 767-68 (Winter 1988). *Journal of Baltic Studies* 29:2:178-79 (Summer 1988).

Latvia

1308.　**Linguistics and Poetics of Latvian Folk Songs: Essays in Honour of the Sesqui-centennial of the Birth of Kr. Barons**, edited by Vaira Vikis-Freibergs. Kingston: McGill-Queen's University Press, 1989. xxi, 371 p. *McGill-Queen's Studies in Ethnic History*, vol. 4. ISBN: 0773506616. Includes index and bibliography (p. 343-356).
A collection of essays dealing with various aspects of Latvian folk literature. The essays were written in honor of Krisjanis Barons, the scholar who originally collated, classified, and published the huge collection of Latvian folk songs under discussion. The book is

divided into seven sections, the first on Kr. Barons and his work, the next on the theoretical framework within which the collection can be approached. Part three looks at Baltic mythology in general while parts four and five examine the prominent role of linguistics in the analysis of the folk songs. Part six discusses metrics and melodies as major areas of scholarship in the study of this literature. The final section examines the longer songs.

Lithuania

1309. Danys, Milda, **DP, Lithuanian Immigration to Canada after the Second World War**. Toronto: Multicultural History Society of Ontario, 1986. 365 p. *Studies in Ethnic and Immigration History*, ISBN: 0919045308 (pbk.), 0919045286. Includes index and bibliography (p. 352-353).

Danys' book is in three parts. Part one focuses of World War II and its aftermath. Most of the Lithuanians who emigrated were in DP camps. Part two deals with Canadian immigration policy and the various kinds of contracts—forestry, mining, domestic, and agricultural that enabled Lithuanians to settle in Canada. Part three describes the many ways in which the Lithuanian immigrants started their lives over again in Canada. The author uses both archival sources and oral histories to form her narrative. Reviews: *American Historical Review* 92:4:1058-59 (October 1987). *Lituanus* 33:1:74-75 (Winter 1987).

1310. Oleszczuk, Thomas A., **Political Justice in the USSR: Dissent and Repression in Lithuania, 1969-1987**. Boulder, CO: East European Monographs, 1988. viii, 221 p. *East European Monographs*, no. 247. ISBN: 0880331445. Includes bibliographical references and indexes.

Oleszczuk studies the legal treatment of dissidents in Lithuania from 1969-1987. In doing so, he examines the politicization of the judicial process, the determinants of sentencing and related factors. His conclusion deals with contemporary political justice and hopes for the future.

1311. Sabaliunas, Leonas, **Lithuanian Social Democracy in Perspective, 1893-1914**. Durham, NC: Duke University Press, 1990. xiii, 205 p. *Duke Press Policy Studies*, ISBN: 0822310155. Includes index and bibliographical references (p. 184-197).

Sabaliunas traces the history of the Lithuanian Social Democratic Party as it evolved from its Jewish and Polish precursors in the latter decade of the 19th century, through its aggressive development in 1904 and 1905 and its retreat during the years 1906-1914.

1312. Senn, Alfred Erich, **Lithuania Awakening**. Berkeley: University of California Press, 1990. 294 p. *Societies and Culture in East-Central Europe*, ISBN: 0520072700. Includes index and bibliographical references (p. 283-286).

A personal account of the events which took place in 1988 that freed Lithuania from the Soviet Union. The author is a historian of the area but for these events, due to their currency, he relies heavily on his memory of events observed and on interviews with participants. He intends to explain the importance of independence to the Lithuanians and discusses at some length the heroic actions of the members of the reform movement "Sajudis." He describes in some detail the events leading up to Lithuania's bid for independence including the mass rallies of 1988, the confrontation in Gedominas Square, and the removal of party secretaries. Several appendices are provided including a biographical section with brief mention of individuals involved in the Sajudis movement and a chronology of events from 1987 through 1988.

1313. Sesplaukis, Alfonsas, **Lituanica Collections in European Research Libraries: A Bibliography**. Chicago: Lithuanian Research and Studies, 1986. xvi, 215 p. ISBN: 0918920051. Includes indexes.

The title of this volume promises more than the book delivers. It does not describe all Lituanica collections in European research libraries, nor even the major ones, but in fact gives a glimpse of parts of four personal collections that have been deposited in four German and one French library. The bibliography is based on the collections of Vilius Gaigalaitis, Edward Hermann, Ernst Fraenkel, and Peter Klimas. The approximately 2,600 books selected are arranged alphabetically by author in seventeen major categories. Each citation indicates in which library the work is held. It includes publications in twelve languages other than Lithuanian.

1314. Vitas, Robert A., **The United States and Lithuania: The Stimson Doctrine of Nonrecognition**. New York: Praeger, 1990. 175 p. ISBN: 0275934128. Includes index and bibliographical references.

Vitas examines the diplomatic history surrounding the non-recognition of Lithuania after its occupation by Soviet forces and the installation of a puppet government. After a brief introduction, Vitas examines Lithuania's twilight of independence in 1939-1940, the Lithuanian situation in the context of international law, the genesis of the U.S. non-recognition policy, the political and legal effects of non-recognition, non- recognition and wartime politics, extended implementation of non- recognition, case studies in such problems and an epilogue that examines the policy as we enter the changed political climate of the 1990s.

UKRAINE

Bibliographies, Encyclopedias

1315. **Publications by Ukrainian "Displaced Persons" and Political Refugees, 1945-1954 in the John Luczkiw Collection Thomas Fisher Rare Book Library University of Toronto: A Bibliography**. Edmonton: Canadian Institute of Ukrainian Studies, University of Alberta, 1988. viii, 398 p. *Occasional Research Report*, no. 29.

This collection of the late John Luczkiw was recently acquired by the University of Toronto Library, and this bibliography provides descriptive listings of monographs, pamphlets, and some serial publications. The bibliography consists of three parts: alphabetical listing, subject listing, and serials. In most cases, bibliographic description is quite adequate, providing author, title, imprint and pagination. Two other collections of émigré materials are housed at the Ukrainian Free Academy of Arts and Sciences and the Shevchenko Scientific Society libraries, both in New York City. Bohdan S. Wynar

1316. Grimsted, Patricia Kennedy, **Archives and Manuscript Repositories in the USSR: Ukraine and Moldavia Book 1: General Bibliography and Institutional Directory**. Princeton, NJ: Princeton University Press, 1988. 1107 p. ISBN: 069105391X. Includes indexes.

The present volume is the third in the author's special series devoted to the study of archival collections throughout the Soviet Union. The first two volumes on *Archives and Manuscript Repositories in the USSR: Moscow and Leningrad* and *Manuscript Repositories in the USSR: Estonia, Latvia, Lithuania, and Belorussia* received excellent reviews in professional literature, and Dr. Grimsted presently is considered an international authority on Soviet archival institutions. The third volume, covering Ukrainian and Moldavian archival repositories, according to Grimsted, "is being issued in two parts: Book 1 and Book 2. Book 1 provides a bibliography of general reference literature relating to archives and other manuscript repositories... Book 2, to be published later, will present a historical survey of the development of archives and record-keeping practices in Ukraine and Moldavia." (preface, p. xviii) The present volume consists of three major sections: a general archival bibliography and reference aids for Ukraine and Moldavia; a directory of archives and manuscript repositories in the Ukrainian SSR, and a directory of archives and manuscript repositories in the Moldavian SSR. The appendices include materials on archival organizational structures and tables of geographical names for Ukraine and Moldavia. Reviews: *Slavic and East European Journal* 34:4:520-22 (Winter 1990). *American Archivist* 53:3:499- 501 (Summer 1990). *Libraries and Culture* 25:4:624-626 (Fall 1990). Bohdan S. Wynar

1317. Kardash, Peter, **Ukraine and Ukrainians**, edited by Brett Lockwood, with foreword by Professor Jaroslav Rudnyckyj. Melbourne: Fortuna Co., 1988. 220 p. Includes bibliography (p. 222-223).

Published on excellent paper, this handbook gives an impression of an elegant "coffee-table book," with over 40 brief articles, a selected bibliography of books in English pertaining to Ukraine, and hundreds of well-executed illustrations, all in color, covering different aspects of Ukrainian life and culture. There is no particular arrangement, and articles deal with such topics as architecture ("Saint Volodymyr and Saint Olha" by S. Hordynsky), religion ("Wasyl Lypkiskyj: Metropolitan of Kiev and Ukraine" by B. Stasyshyn), with several on major cities and regions (Chernihiv, Kharkiv, Odessa, as well as Bukovyna and Chernivtsi, Transcarpathia). Some older articles have been re-edited and translated into English, e.g. "Ukrainians Abroad" by V. Kubijovyc and V. Markus, "Bandura" by H. Kytasty, and a two-page article on "The Millennium of Ukraine" by M. Gojan. Bohdan S. Wynar

1318. **Encyclopedia of Ukraine: Volume 2: G-K**, edited by Volodymyr Kubijovyc. Toronto: University of Toronto Press, 1988. 737 p. ISBN: 0802033628. Includes bibliographies.

The *Encyclopedia of Ukraine* serves as a complementary volume for English-speaking people of *Entsyklopediia ukrainoznavstva*, a multivolume Ukrainian encyclopedia initiated some 40 years ago by the Shevchenko Scientific Society. *Entsyklopediia ukrainoznavstva* consists of two parts: a three-volume classified reference work arranged by broad disciplines or subjects ("Archaeology," "Economy," "Fine Art," etc.) and a projected ten-volume encyclopedia in dictionary arrangement covering all aspects of Ukrainian affairs. The first part was completed in 1952 with significant modification and updating, was published in English as the two-volume *Ukraine: A Concise Encyclopedia*. The present volume, one of a projected five-volume set, constitutes a revised and updated English version of the projected ten volumes of the alphabetical second part of *Entsyklopediia ukrainoznavstva*. Volume two contains approximately 3,000 entries, 450 black-and-white illustrations, 3 color photos, and 40 maps (4 in color). Some 100 scholars from around the world contributed articles. Most articles by deceased individuals were rewritten and significantly updated. Longer articles are signed and frequently contain bibliographies of relevant works published in several languages. Review: *Slavic Review* 48:2:318-19 (Spring 1989). Bohdan S. Wynar

1319. Luckyj, George S. N., **Keeping a Record: Literary Purges in the Soviet Ukraine (1930's): A Bio-Bibliography.** Edmonton: Canadian Institute of Ukrainian Studies, University of Alberta in association with Ukrainian Famine Research Centre, 1987. xli 50 p. *Occasional Research Report*, no. 17.

This interesting monograph consists of a comprehensive introduction to literary purges in Ukraine during the 1930s, a bibliography of important writings about this period, photographs of selected writers, and the main part—a bio-bibliographical guide listing 314 writers. The writers are divided into four categories: those who were arrested and/or exiled to perform forced labor, those who were rehabilitated during their lives or posthumously after 1956 and whose works were in part republished, and those who ceased to write or publish in the 1930s. The information is not always complete or of the same quality, but this register is a unique contribution to the study of Soviet mass terror in the 1930s, and was prepared by one of the recognized authorities in this area. Bohdan S. Wynar

1320. Magocsi, Paul Robert, **Carpatho-Rusyn Studies: An Annotated Bibliography**. New York: Garland, 1988. 143 p. *Garland Reference Library of the Humanities*, vol. 1, 1975-1984. ISBN: 0824012143. Includes index.

In his introduction, the compiler indicates that the marked growth in Carpatho-Rusyn studies during the 1970s is a result of two unrelated phenomena: 1) the consistent and long-time support of scholarly research by the Soviet regime, and 2) a new initiative on the part of individual scholars in the U.S. to study the Carpatho-Rusyn problem. The author has collected 649 publications (articles and books published in several languages) and arranged them by year of publication. Entries show full bibliographic citations and are accompanied by brief descriptive annotations. Reviews: *Our People*. P.W. McBride, *Nationalities Papers* 13:11150-51 (Spring 1985). A.B. Pernal. *Canadian Historical Review* 20:2:255-57 (August 1985). Bohdan S. Wynar

1321. Nordquist, Joan, **Glasnost: The Soviet Union Today: A Bibliography**. Santa Cruz, Calif.: Reference and Research Services, 1989. 60 p. *Contemporary Social Issues: A Bibliographic Series*, no. 13. ISBN: 0937855251.

Each bibliography contains approximately 500 selected entries covering books and journal articles. This rather expensive series ($15.00 for a small mimeographed pamphlet) is edited by a references librarian from the University of California at Santa Cruz. The present volume has nine chapters, e.g., a section on general works, economic policy, politics and government, foreign relations, the military, social policy, culture, the nationality problem, and bibliographies and resources. Bohdan S. Wynar

1322. **Ukraine: A Concise Encyclopaedia**, edited by Halyna Petrenko. Clifton, NJ: Ukrainian Orthodox Church of the U.S.A., 1987. 337 p. Includes bibliographies and index.

Prepared by Halyna Petrenko as editor, with a number of other individuals serving on the editorial board, this collection of articles is dedicated to the millennium of the baptism of Ukraine (988-1988) and was sponsored by the Ukrainian Orthodox Church of the U.S.A. and the United Ukrainian Sisterhoods of the U.S.A. There is a total of 29 articles on such topics as "People" by M.Smyk, "Language" by P. Odarchenko, "Geography" by I. Telsa, "Literature" (six articles by several authors), "Theater" by V. Revutsky, "Music" by O. Zalesky, "Fine Arts" by B. Pevenyi, "Folk Dress" by L. Burachynska, and "Economy" by N. Chymych. All in all, the articles are concise, popularly written, and are quite frequently accompanied by various black-and-white illustrations. An index concludes the volume, but as is unfortunately the case with most articles, there is no bibliography at the end—a serious deficiency in a work of this type. Bohdan S. Wynar

1323. Piaseckyji, Oksana, **Bibliography of Ukrainian Literature in English and French: Translations and Critical Works, 1950-1986**. Ottawa: University of Ottawa Press, 1989. xii, 386 p. *University of Ottawa Ukrainian Studies*, no. 10. ISBN: 0776602640. Includes bibliographical references.

This bibliography lists English and French translations of Ukrainian literature that were published between 1950 and 1986. The book is divided into several sections including General Anthologies of Translations, General Critical Works, Ukrainian Literature of Kievan Period, 13th-18th Centuries, and modern, Soviet, and Ukrainian literature of the diaspora. Under each, author works are listed in the original language (transliterated). Each listing also includes critical works about specific authors. Access is enhanced by an author and critical index.

1324. Tarnawsky, Marta, **Ukrainian Literature in English: Books and Pamphlets, 1890-1965: An Annotated Bibliography**. Edmonton: Canadian Institute of Ukrainian Studies, University of Alberta, 1988. 296 p. *Research Report of the Canadian Institute of Ukrainian Studies*, no. 19.

This bibliography lists 91 books and pamphlets published during 1890-1965 in the Soviet Union and abroad. Most items were examined *de visu* and unlike many other bibliographies published abroad, this author provides a complete bibliographic description for all the items plus intelligent and informative annotations. While describing anthologies and selected works of individual authors, Tarnawsky prepares detailed content notes, an extremely helpful feature for literary works of this type. In her introduction the author describes the scope and methodology utilized and gives some historical background about English translations of Ukrainian literary works. Bohdan S. Wynar

1325. Wynar, Bohdan S., **Ukraine: A Bibliographic Guide to English-Language Publications**. Englewood, CO: Ukrainian Academic Press, 1990. xiii, 406 p. ISBN: 0872877612.

Wynar's bibliography contains 1084 annotations of works written on all aspects of Ukrainian history, culture, and politics. It includes items published between 1950 and 1989, with a few exceptions. The annotations are arranged topically and within each topic, alphabetically by author and title. Each entry contains a full bibliographic citation, annotation, and, when available, citations to reviews. The combined author, title, and subject index offers additional access to the volume.

General Studies

1326. **Echoes of Glasnost in Soviet Ukraine**, edited by Romana M. Bahry. North York, Ont.: Captus University Publications, 1989. xvi, 236 p. ISBN: 092180105X. Includes bibliographical references.

A collection of papers from a symposium on "Glasnost in Soviet Ukraine" held at York University in Toronto, Canada, January 28-February 1, 1989. This volume "is unique not only because it is the first book on the subject, but also because the views expressed are not only those of academics and researchers, but also diplomats, dissidents, former political prisoners, journalists, artists, and musicians. As the first book on the subject its purpose is to capture the first views and overviews of glasnost and perestroika in Soviet Ukraine as they were expressed up to and including 1989." (p. vii) The essays are grouped into two sections, politics and literature and the arts. A wide range of topics are covered including uses of nuclear power, religious freedom, unofficial groups, Ukrainian diaspora, new poetry, Ukrainian cinema, and visual arts.

1327. Friedberg, Maurice, **How Things Were Done in Odessa: Cultural and Intellectual Pursuits in a Soviet City**. Boulder, CO: Westview Press, 1991. xii, 145 p. ISBN: 0813379873. Includes bibliographical references.

The basis for this study was the so-called Soviet third emigration in the second half of the 1970s. Of the 250,000 who did emigrate, about 10,000 of them came from Odessa. Friedberg personally interviewed 102 of these under the auspices of the Soviet Interview Project. The result is a fascinating study on "problems relating to the city's cultural and intellectual life as well as interethnic relations and religious observance." (p. x)

1328. Kordan, Bohdan S., **Land of the Cossacks: Antiquarian Maps of Ukraine. An Exhibition from the University of Alberta Map Collection, Ukrainian Cultural and Educational Centre and Private Collections**. Winnipeg: Ukrainian Cultural and Educational Centre, 1987. 56 p. ISBN: 921741006. Includes bibliography (p. 56).

The 24 maps reproduced in this collection cover the seventeenth and the first half of the eighteenth centuries, with the focus on the central lands of Ukraine. The title of this exhibition is taken from Sanson's 1674 map, which describes this region as "Ukraine—Land of Cossacks." In addition to satisfactory reproductions (in black-and-white), the reader will find brief descriptions of each map on a separate page (with text in English and Ukrainian), giving information on author and publisher, cartography, brief publishing history and, if pertinent, a summary of historical events. This catalog also includes two famous maps by Beauplan. Bohdan S. Wynar

History

1329. **Ethnicity and National Identity. Demographic and Socioeconomic Charac- teristics of Persons with Ukrainian Mother Tongue in the United States**. Cambridge, Mass.: Harvard Ukrainian Research Institute, 1986. 175 p. ISBN: 0916458148. Includes bibliographical references and index.

This is a collection of re-edited papers originally presented at the symposium on "Demo- graphic and Socioeconomic Characteristics of Persons with Ukrainian Mother Tongue in the United States, 1970" held at Harvard University on November 11-12, 1977. Review: A. Pawliczko. *The Ukrainian Quarterly* 43:3- 4:247-48 (Fall-Winter 1987). Bohdan S. Wynar

1330. Aster, Howard, and Peter J. Potichnyj, **Jewish-Ukrainian Relations: Two Soli- tudes**. New rev. ed. Oakville, Ontario: Mosaic Press, 1987. 92 p. ISBN: 0889622132. Includes index and biographical references.

The first edition of this work was published in 1983 (70 p.), and as indicated by Professor Bilinsky, "in their first essay the authors deplore the lack of mutual understanding between Jews and Ukrainians in the Ukraine, who have shared the same territory and many historical tragedies since the Middle Ages. Both peoples appear to be developing and cultivating stereotypes about each other rather than attempting the true historical record.... The second essay briefly sketches some trends in the development of Jewish and Ukrainian intellectual and political movements in the 19th and 20th centuries." (p. 373) This revised edition includes two new essays plus an index. As both authors indicate, this is a preliminary version of their work, and a more substantive discussion is to be found in *Jewish-Ukrainian Relations in Historical Perspective*. Bohdan S. Wynar

1331. Bohachevsky-Chomiak, Martha, **Feminists Despite Themselves: Women in Ukrainian Community Life, 1884-1939**. Edmonton: Canadian Institute of Ukrainian Studies, University of Alberta, 1988. 460 p. ISBN: 0920862578. Includes index and bibliography.

The present work is one of the most comprehensive treatments of this subject, not only in English but also in Ukrainian. The material is arranged in six chapters: "Ukrainian Women in the Russian Empire," "Ukrainian Women in the Austrian Empire," "The National-Liberation Struggle," "Western Ukrainian Women Between the Wars," "Ukrainian Women and International Feminism," and "Soviet Ukrainian Women." Notes, a bibliography, and an index conclude the volume. This study, based primarily on sources in the United States, Canada, Austria, Poland, and the Soviet Union, as well as numerous secondary sources in several languages, highlights important aspects of Ukrainian feminism in Eastern and Western Ukraine, concentrating on such well-known figures as Kobrynska, Kobylianska, Maria Bashkirtsev, Olena Pchilka, and many others. Bohdan S. Wynar

1332. **Ukraine During World War II: History and Its Aftermath: A Symposium,** edited by Yury Boshyk with the assistance of Roman Washuk and Andriy Wynny-ckyj. Edmonton: Canadian Institute of Ukrainian Studies, 1986. xviii, 291 p. *Canadian Library in Ukrainian Studies,* ISBN: 0920862365. Includes index and bibliography (p. 267-285).

This volume is based on papers and discussions from a symposium held in Toronto on March 2, 1985, for the purpose of examining several aspects of World War II and the Nazi occupation of Ukrainian territory. The first part deals with general problems under Nazi occupation and consists of six essays. The second part deals with the question that is now a matter of public debate, namely the process of investigation of war criminals in Canada and the United States. It consists of five essays written by scholars and journalists. Part 3 includes reproductions of 20 documents, covering the period 1926-1966, that provide historical background to previous essays in the volume. A chronology of major events, 1914-1945, a glossary, sources, and a bibliography conclude this interesting volume, which attempts to cover much territory in some 300 pages. Reviews: Boshyk, L.R. Wynar. *Canadian Slavonic Papers* 30:1:161-62 (March 1988). Bohdan S. Wynar

1333. **The Foreign Office and the Famine. British Documents on Ukraine and the Great Famine. British Documents on Ukraine and the Great Famine of 1932-1933,** edited by Marco Carynnyk. Kingston, Ont.: The Limestone Press, 1988. 493 p. *Studies in East European Nationalism,* no. 2. ISBN: 0919642314. Includes indexes and bibliography (p. 467-471).

The editors have uncovered contemporary descriptions of the famine (85 documents) relayed to the West in British diplomatic pouches. As indicated by Professor Marrus, "Largely ignored or suppressed at the time, and forgotten since, these urgent messages now constitute one of the most important sources we have of this colossal human tragedy. Much of the information in these papers comes from the simple accounts of a variety of observers—British diplomats and consular officials, of course, but also of relief workers, trade officials, newspaper correspondents, and the like. Much is also the *cri de coeur* of the starved and outcast, who managed to communicate their terrible experiences directly to outsiders who must have appeared to them as creatures from another planet." (p. xiv) Three editors wrote a very informative introduction to this selection of documents in an attempt to answer the basic questions: What did London know about the famine? What did London know about why the famine happened? How did London respond to the famine? Bohdan S. Wynar

1334. Commission on the Ukrainian Famine, **Investigation of the Ukrainian Famine 1932-1933: Report to Congress**. Washington, DC: Government Printing Office, 1988. xxv, 524 p.

Prepared by Dr. James E. Mace, staff director, this is a report of the Commission on the Ukrainian Famine established by Congress. The report was adopted by the Commission on

April 19, 1985 and submitted to Congress on April 22, 1988. It consists of six chapters: "Non-Soviet Scholarship on the Ukrainian Famine," "Post-Stalinist Soviet Historiography on the Ukraine," "Soviet Press Sources on the Famine," "Soviet Historical Fiction on the Famine," "The Famine Outside Ukraine," "The American Response to the Famine," "Summary of Public Hearings," and "Oral History Project." Appended to the report is a brief glossary of terms, and index to persons prominently mentioned in the text, and three appendices covering translations of selected oral histories and Italian diplomatic and consular dispatches. In comparison to *Ukrainian Famine of 1932 and 1933: Hearings Before the Committee on Foreign Relations* published in 1984, the Report of the Commission on the Ukrainian Famine is much more comprehensive and in most cases very carefully documented. Bohdan S. Wynar

1335. Conquest, Robert, **The Harvest of Sorrow: Soviet Collectivization and the Terror-Famine**. Edmonton: Alta University of Alberta Press in Association with the Canadian Institute of Ukraine Studies, 1986. 412 p. ISBN: 0195040546. Includes index and bibliography (p. 394-396).

By far, this is the best book on the famine of 1932-1933 inflicted by the Soviet government on the collectivized peasants of Ukraine, Kuban, Don, and Volga regions. This was accomplished, as Conquest indicates, "by methods of setting for them grain quotas far above the possible, removing every handful of food, and preventing help from outside—even other areas of the USSR—from reaching the starving. This action, even more destructive than those of 1929-1932, was accompanied by a wide-ranging attack on all Ukrainian cultural and intellectual centers and leaders, and on the Ukrainian churches. The supposed contumaciousness of the Ukrainian peasants in not surrendering grain they did not have was explicitly blamed on nationalism: all of which was in accord with Stalin's dictum that the national problem was in essence a peasant problem. The Ukrainian peasant thus suffered in double guise—as a peasant and as a Ukrainian." (p. 4) The volume consists of 18 chapters, among them "The Peasantry and the Party," "The Ukrainian Nationality and Leninism," "Revolution, Peasant War and Famine, 1917-1921," "Collision Course, 1928-1929," "The Fate of Kulaks," "Crash Course in Collectivization and Its Defeat, Jan.-March, 1930," "The End of the Free Peasantry, 1930-1932," along with chapters on Central Asia and the Kazakhs. All these chapters are in the first two sections of the book. The third section entitled "The Terror-Famine" consists of eight chapters dealing directly with the famine: "Assault on the Ukraine," "The Famine Rages," "A Land Laid Waste," "Kuban, Don and Volga," "Children," "The Death Roll, " "The Record of the West," and "Responsibilities." An epilogue, numerous notes, and a select bibliography of sources in several languages conclude the narrative. In his conclusions, the author indicates the following: "For it is clear that the terrors inflicted on the peasantry have failed to produce the agricultural results promised by theory. At the same time, the crushing of Ukrainian Nationhood was only temporary. Nor is that a local matter merely—if the word local can be used of a nation of nearly fifty million members. Even the true spokesmen of Russia itself, Andrei Sakharov and Alexander Solzhenitsyn, insist that the Ukraine must be free to choose its own future." (p. 347) Reviews: M. Bourdeaux. *The Ukrainian Review* 35:1:92- 93 (Spring 1987). R.H. Johnston. *Canadian Slavonic Papers* 29:2- 3:348-49 (June-September 1987). J. Miller. *Newsweek* (November 17, 1986, p. 95). Bohdan S. Wynar

1336. **Nazi Crimes in Ukraine, 1941-1944: Documents and Materials**, edited by V.N. Denisov and G.I. Changuli. Kiev: Naukova Dumka, 1987. 374 p.

Sponsored by the Institute of State and Law, Academy of Sciences of the Ukrainian SSR, this compilation of documents was edited by V. N. Denisov and G.I. Changuli, who also authored a longer introduction discussing Ukraine's losses during World War II. There are over 100 documents, Soviet and German, published in English translation. Several documents pertain to Nazi war criminals, even those of the most recent period, such as Koziy, Kowalchuk, and others. As one might expect, some documents are reproduced only in excerpts, and the selection of documents reflects Soviet official policy. Bohdan S. Wynar

1337. Edelman, Robert, **Proletarian Peasants: The Revolutions of 1905 in Russia's Southwest**. Ithaca, N.Y.: Cornell University Press, 1987. xv, 1985 p. ISBN: 0801494737 (pbk.), 0801420008. Includes indexes and bibliography (p. 181-183). "This book examines the actions of peasants during the Russian Revolution of 1905. It concentrates on the right-bank Ukraine, an agriculturally advanced region known before 1917 as the southwestern borderland of the Russian Empire.... The work deals at the same time with the larger issues of rural revolution and peasant politics." (p. ix) Reviews: *Russian History* 17:1: 92-93 (Spring 1990). *Russian Review* 49:4:500-01 (October 1990). *Slavic Review* 48:2:302-04 (Summer 1989). *American Historical Review* 94:4:1138 (October 1989).

1338. Ewanchuk, Michael, **Hawaiian Ordeal: Ukrainian Contract Workers 1897-1910**. Winnipeg, Manitoba: Author, 1986. 180 p. Includes bibliography (p. 177-178).
Hawaiian Ordeal describes the events of the last decade of the nineteenth century when the Ukrainian immigrants, many of them displaced farmers, arrived in Hawaii and were induced to sign contracts of indenture to work on the island's vast sugar plantations. As the author comments in the preface, "Their experiences in the 'Paradise Isles of the Pacific' were, however, far from happy: they were maltreated and exploited. Yet after the first group of 1897 arrived, the agents managed to induce more to come, and later they were joined by a much larger group of displaced farmers from the Ukrainian steppes who were sent to Manchuria. In Hawaii both groups were forced by Kackfeld (head of a sugar conglomerate) and other planters to work under 'near slave' conditions." (p. vii) Existing literature on this subject is scant or nonexistent, and Ewanchuk has done an excellent job of bringing to light the sad plight of these early Ukrainian and other European pioneers who, as Ewnachuk puts it, "suffered untold miseries on the sugar cane plantations from the planters and their cow-whip-wielding sadistic lunas." (p. ix) Bohdan S. Wynar

1339. Gross, Jan T., **Revolution from Abroad: The Soviet Conquest of Poland's Western Ukraine and Western Belorussia**. Princeton: Princeton University Press, 1988. 334 p.
In the preface the author indicates that this study was made possible by a discovery in the Hoover Institution of important documents pertaining to Soviet occupation, starting in 1939. The author describes in some detail the social chaos and the terror brought by the Soviet occupation. Many testimonies given by Polish citizens deported to the Soviet Union and later amnestied make a powerful statement of their own. The material is arranged in six chapters: "Conquest," "Elections," "The Paradigm of Social Control," "Socialization," "Prisons," and "Deportations." An extensive bibliography and good index of names, places, and subjects, conclude the volume, which is probably the most comprehensive monographic treatment of Soviet occupation of former Polish territory. The Ukrainian problem is discussed in a more or less objective manner, in spite of the fact that the author used a limited number of Ukrainian sources. Thus, for example, Gross is right in indicating that in general the overwhelming majority of Ukrainians were sincerely glad to see the collapse of the Polish state. "Great excitement circulated among Ukrainians because an intolerable situation of ethnic discrimination had finally come to an end. To be sure, Ukrainians would have preferred German occupation, as is clear from the pattern of immediate population shifts throughout the border area. Whenever the Wehrmacht gave up some territory that belonged in the Soviet zone of occupation, Ukrainians moved out with the Germans." (p.

31) The description of Soviet prisons is quite vivid, but the author obviously had limited resources at his disposal. For example, the description of the Soviet massacre of prisoners in L'viv is not quite accurate or complete, and the use of some Ukrainian sources would benefit the author if this interesting monograph goes into the second edition. All in all, it is a valuable historical study of Soviet occupation of Western Ukraine and Belorussia. Reviews: *Problems of Communism* 39:6:106-11 (November-December 1990). *American Historical Review* 95:1:206-07 (February 1990). *Freedom at Issue* 115:33-35 (June-August 1990). Bohdan S. Wynar

1340.   Harvard University Library, **Famine in the Soviet Ukraine 1932-1933: A Memorial Exhibition, Widener Library, Harvard University**, prepared by Oksana Procyk. Cambridge, Mass: Harvard College Library, 1986. xi, 83 p. ISBN: 0674294262. Includes bibliography (p. 78-83).

This is a catalog of a memorial exhibition held at Harvard University's Widener Library from December 1983 to February 1984 on the occasion of the 50th anniversary of the famine in Ukraine. It contains descriptions of some 250 items, accompanied by 120 illustrations, including title pages or covers of pertinent books and some 30 photographs directly relating to the famine. The material is arranged in ten chapters, the first four offering general background (e.g. "The Ukrainian Revolution 1917-1921" or "The Ukrainian Soviet Socialist Republic and the Policy of Ukrainization"), which are only of marginal interest to the scholar interested in the famine. There is a helpful listing of sources for illustrations and a selected bibliography on famine and related topics in several languages. Review: *Ukrainian Quarterly* 43:1-2:142 (Spring-Summer 1986). Bohdan S. Wynar

1341.   Himka, John-Paul, **Galician Villagers and the Ukrainian National Movement in the Nineteenth Century**. New York: St. Martin's Press, 1988. 358 p. ISBN: 0312016093. Includes index and bibliography (p. 329-343).

According to the author, the present work "may be regarded as another installment in a series of works interpreting the rise of social and national consciousness in Austrian Galicia from the perspective of social history." (p. xv) The author uses firsthand testimony of peasants and rural notables as found in the archives of L'viv in February 1976 in an attempt to establish a connection between class and national consciousness. There are four chapters (with several subdivisions) as well as several appendixes containing information on archival sources. The author discusses serfdom and servitude, the cultural revolution of 1848 in the village in terms of schools, newspapers, and reading clubs, and offers detailed information on village notables, including priests, teachers, and cantors. According to the author, at the turn of the century, Ukrainian peasantry was integrated into the Ukrainian nation in Galicia, furnishing it with a strong backbone. Himka's objective in this monograph is to demonstrate with available evidence the development of this process or, to use his terms, the mechanics of rural nation-building. Reviews: *American Historical Review* 95:2L545-46 (April 1990). *Harvard Ukrainian Studies* 14:1-2:167-70 (June 1990). *Slavic Review* 49:4:655-66 (Winter 1990). Bohdan S. Wynar

1342.   Horak, Stephan M., **The First Treaty of World War I: Ukraine's Treaty with Central Powers of February 9, 1918**. Boulder, CO: East European Monographs, 1988. 202 p. ISBN: 088033133X. Includes bibliography (p. 197-202).

Based on the author's doctoral dissertation at Erlangen University, this volume was published posthumously with an introduction written in October 1986 by the late Professor Horak. Of its 13 brief chapters, the first three provide historical setting, the fourth and fifth chapters discuss negotiations and the nature of the treaty and its implications, followed by chapters on such topics as the demise of the Central Rada, ratification of the treaty, and an interesting chapter devoted to the Brest-Litovsk Treaty in light of the German, Austrian,

Ukrainian, and American literature. Numerous bibliographical notes and a selected bibliography of utilized sources conclude the volume that unfortunately has no index. All in all, it is a welcome addition to the voluminous literature on the subject. Bohdan S. Wynar

1343. Huk, John, **Strangers in the Land: The Ukrainian Presence in Cape Breton**. Sydney, Nova Scotia: City Printers Ltd, 1987. 97 p.

As Reverend John Tataryn indicates in his brief preface, many books have been written about the "men in sheepskin coats" who pioneered the virgin prairies or played a significant role in the industrial development of Ontario and Quebec. This is one such book written about Ukrainian immigrants who came to Nova Scotia, in particular to Cape Breton Island. According to the author, the first immigrants came in early 1898, and the names of these early settlers are mentioned in chapter 1. More than 30 brief chapters are included in this story, describing church activities as well as such things as mushroom pickers, events during World War II, and several social and cultural clubs, This is not a scholarly study, but rather a memoir that may assist the historian in learning about Ukrainian activities in one region.

1344. Kis, Theofil I., **Nationhood, Statehood and the International Status of the Ukrainian SSR—Ukraine**. Ottawa: University of Ottawa Press, 1989. 114 p. *University of Ottawa Ukrainian Studies Occasional Paper*, no. 1. ISBN: 0776601938. Includes indexes and bibliographies (p. 87-101).

In this small monograph the author examines the question of nationhood in Ukraine, using a number of sources published in several languages, including such Ukrainian authors as Bohdan Halaichuk, Vasyl Markus, and Peter Potichnyi. Brief chapters include "The Statehood of the UkSSR: Pretense and Reality," "The Constitutional Deficiency Compromising the Statehood of the UkSSR," and "The International Competence of the UkSSR as Viewed Internationally," among others. The author summarizes well-known views of several scholars usually published in languages other than English, and in this respect this monograph can serve as a good refresher course on the much- debated question of the international status of Ukrainian SSR, the second largest republic of the Soviet Union. Previous works by Kis are listed in his bibliography. Bohdan S. Wynar

1345. Kohut, Zenon E., **Russian Centralism and Ukrainian Autonomy: Imperial Absorption of the Hetmanate 1760's-1830's**. Cambridge, Mass.: Harvard Ukrainian Research Institute, 1988. 363 p. ISBN: 0916458172. Includes index and bibliography (p. 320-351).

Kohut is senior research specialist for Eastern Europe and the Soviet Union at the Library of Congress and for several years was the editor of *American Bibliography of Slavic and East European Studies*. This monograph is based on his doctoral dissertation. The material is arranged under eight chapters: "Russian Centralism and the Borderlands," "The Nature of Ukrainian Autonomy," "Catherine II's Clash with Ukrainian Autonomy: The Removal of Hetman Rozumovs'kyi," "Catherine's Viceroy in the Hetmanate: The Rule of Governor-General Rumiantsev, 1765-1769," "Ukrainian Reactions and Aspirations: The Legislative Commission of 1767-1768," "The Triumph of Russian Centralism: Imperial Reforms and the Integration of the Hetmanate," "Ukrainian Society Adjusts to the Imperial Order," and "Russian Centralism and Ukrainian Autonomy: Conclusions." The study is based primarily on secondary sources (Kohut was denied access to Soviet archives) and focuses on several principal problems. First, in initial chapters, the author shows how a well-ordered police state reinforced Russia's drive toward centralism and uniformity. Second, it shows how Ukrainian society both resisted and accommodated itself to imperial integration. And, finally, Kohut analyzes several dissimilarities in social structure between Russia and Ukraine due to the autonomist outlook that contributed to some difficulties in the integration process, and yet the integration process resulted in the Russification of Ukrainian towns and the reduction of the Ukrainian population to a peasant nation. The author concludes that "although the assimilation of a significant portion of the Ukrainian gentry into Russian imperial society deprived Ukrainians of the leadership of a traditional elite in the initial stages of 'nation-building,' the heritage of the gentry did have an important impact on the development of a modern Ukrainian national consciousness." (p. 304) Reviews: *Russian History* 17:1:110-11 (Spring 1990). *East European Quarterly* 24:3:408 (Fall 1990). *Polish Review* 35:3-4:273 (1990). *Journal of Baltic Studies* 21:2:167-70 (Summer 1990). *American Historical Review* 95:5:1584-85 (December 1990). Bohdan S. Wynar

1346. **A Short History of the Ukraine**, edited by Yuri Kondufor. Kiev: Naukova Dumka, 1986. 314 p.

Sponsored by the Institute of History, Academy of Sciences of the Ukrainian SSR, this brief monograph, first published in Russian, is a collective work by several Soviet historians, among them Y. Kondufor, S. Kulchitsky, A. Likholat, V. Sarbei, and others. The material is arranged in 11 brief chapters covering the primitive communal system, the medieval period, Ukraine's "reunion" with Russia, Ukraine during the crisis of the feudal system, capitalism in Ukraine, World Wars I and II, and the post-war years. Brief mention is made of the early reforms of M. Gorbachev, but no index or bibliography is provided. In spite of the sponsorship of the Institute of History, this is a rather journalistic presentation following Communist party-line directives.

1347. **A Delicate and Difficult Question: Documents in the History of Ukrainians in Canada 1899-1962**, edited by Bohdan S. Kordan and Lubomyr Luciuk. Kingston, Ontario: The Limestone Press, 1986. 174 p. *Builders of Canada Series*, no. 3. ISBN: 091964208X. Includes bibliography (p. 174).

Kordan and Luciuk have organized a volume containing 55 documents dating from 1899 to 1962. The core of the work comprises declassified materials, in addition to which there are a number of significant editorials from the Ukrainian-language press in Canada. The majority of the documents are from public and private archives from North America, and with few exceptions, none of the material has been previously published. The documents illustrate the social and political forces at work within the organized Ukrainian-Canadian community, reflecting the intricacies of the delicate relationship between Ukrainians and the state. It also raises questions on the nature of Ukrainian identity in Canada and how this allegiance has been influenced and shared over the years. After a brief introduction providing the reader with a concise overview of the Ukrainian experience in Canada, the 55 documents are introduced in chronological order. Among the documents included are: "Common Debates, July 1899, Concerning Ukrainian Immigration," "Letter for the National Committee Calling Delegates to a Conference for the Purpose of Forming a National Church, May 27, 1918," "Canadian Ukrainians and War" (editorial), "Secret Memorandum from N. Robertson, the Undersecretary of State for External Affairs, to D. Wilgress, Canadian Minister to the USSR, May 28, 1943, Describing Political Situation Within the Ukrainian-Canadian Community," and others. The volume concludes with a selected bibliography. Review: T.M. Prymak. *Canadian Slavonic Papers* 30:1:169-70 (March 1988). Bohdan S. Wynar

1348. Kozik, Jan, **The Ukrainian National Movement in Galicia: 1815-1849**, edited and with and introduction by Lawrence D. Orton. Edmonton: Canadian Institute of Ukrainian Studies, University of Alberta, 1986. 498 p. ISBN: 0920862403. Includes bibliography.

This monograph is an abridged translation from the Polish of Polish historian Jan Kozik's (1934-1979) two chronologically sequential books, *Ukrainski ruch narodowy w Galiciji w latach 1830-1848 (The Ukrainian National Movement in Galicia, 1830-1848)* (Cracow,

Wydawnitwo Literackie, 1973) and *Miedzy reakcja a rewolucja. Stuia z dziejow Ukrainskiego ruchu narodowego w Galicji w latach 1848-1849 (Between Reaction and Revolution. Studies from the History of the Ukrainian National Movement in Galicia, 1848-1849)* (Cracow, Panstwowe Wydawnictwo Naukowe, 1975). The work is based on Polish archival sources, and the author also had a chance to examine some archival collections in L'viv. Numerous secondary sources were used as well, and in addition to Polish studies the reader will find a number of works published before 1914 (in Polish, Ukrainian, and Russian) as well as Soviet studies, notably by the Ukrainian scholars M. Herasmenko (agrarian relations), F. Steblii (peasantry), etc. In the first part of the study, the author concentrates on the formation of the Ukrainian clerical intelligentsia, emphasizing social and political movements and the conflict between the Poles and Ukrainians. Out of this struggle emerged the national movement that was to establish Eastern Galicia as a "Ukrainian Piedmont" before World War I. As S.F. Jones indicates, discussing the Ukrainian national movement and its problems, "The author explains such 'national' backwardness by the lack of a native noble class, by the division of Ukrainians between Russia and Austria, by the domination of a conservative clergy opposed to Polish and Hungarian ideas of national liberation (and hence loyal to the Austrian throne) and by lack of urbanization (though this is least emphasized by the author)" (p. 470-71) Written from a Marxist point of view, Kozik's study is one of the best in Polish historiography and serves as a comprehensive treatment of the cultural and political life of Western Ukraine during the first half of the nineteenth century. The appended bibliography provides an adequate overview of the most important literature on this subject in several languages, omitting only some Ukrainian "nationalistic" writings, e.g., works by Hrushevs'kyi, Lozyns'kyi, and others, as well as a number of studies done by Western scholars. Reviews: F. Sysyn. *Slavic Review* 47:4:757-59 (Winter 1988). S. Hryniuk. *Canadian Slavonic Papers* 30:1:160-61 (March 1988). S.F. Jones. *Slavic and East European Review* 65:3:470-71 (July 1987). Bohdan S. Wynar

1349. Luciuk, Lubomyr, **A Time for Atonement. Canada's First National Internment Operations and the Ukrainian Canadians 1914-1920**. Kingston, Ontario: Limestone Press, 1988. 32 p.

Luciuk, a member of the faculty at Queen's University, Kingston, is a scholar of the younger generation and the author of several books, including *Anglo-American Perspectives on the Ukrainian Question 1938-1951* and *The Foreign Office and the Famine*. According to the author, before WWI some 170,000 Ukrainians were living in Canada, primarily in the prairie region with significant groups also in Ontario and Quebec, employed in the mining and timber industries. After the entry of Great Britain into World War I the Internment of Canada started to register all aliens of "enemy nationality," including many Ukrainians. Between 1914 and 1920, 8,579 such "enemy aliens" were incarcerated, some 5,000 of Ukrainian origin, were obliged to report regularly to their local police authorities. These tragic events are described in some detail in this short study that cites a number of additional sources pertaining to the topic. Bohdan S. Wynar

1350. **Anglo-American Perspectives on the Ukrainian Question 1938-1951: A Documentary Collection,** with foreword by Hugh A. Macdonald. Kingston, Ontario: The Limestone Press, 1987. 242 p. Includes bibliography (p. 241-242).

This collection of 54 documents pertaining to the relationship between the Ukrainian independence movement and the United States, Great Britain, and Canada, covers the period 1938-1951. The bulk of this collection consists of American and British documents culled from the national archives of both countries, with additional documents from the Canadian government. According to the preface, "these archival materials illustrate how these papers evaluated the impact Ukrainian statehood might have on their international relations, the strengths and weaknesses of the Ukrainian national movement (in particular its role as a political problem for a number of European states), and the question of whether Ukrainians in the emigration posed an internal security risk to their host societies.... The documents reprinted here suggest that, on one level, Western statesmen were well informed about the nature and extent of the Ukrainian national struggle while, on another, they were consistently cynical or indifferent to the idea of Ukrainian self-determination." (p. vii-viii) The 54 documents collected here represent only a small fraction of the available large body of archival materials dealing with the Ukrainian question. Review: J.V. Koshiw. *Canadian Slavonic Papers* 30:2:295-96 (June 1988). Bohdan S. Wynar

1351. **Continuity and Change. The Cultural Life of Alberta's First Ukrainians**, edited by Manoly R. Lupul. Edmonton: Canadian Institute of Ukrainian Studies, 1988. 268 p.

Manoly Lupul, former director of the Canadian Institute of Ukrainian Studies and author or editor of several works dealing with Ukrainian immigrants, edited this useful collection of 19 essays covering several aspects of life and activities of the first Ukrainian settlers in Alberta. Essays written by such authors as John-Paul Himka, Orest Martynovych, R. Bilash, Peter Melnycky, Zenon Pohorecky, Robert Klymash, Bohdan Medwidsky, and others examine the conditions in Western Ukraine that led to immigration, describing in detail early settlements: the nature of rural bloc settlement, material culture, customs and beliefs of early pioneers, and cultural institutions and organizations, including a panel discussion on Ukrainian cultural heritage. The volume resulted from the proceedings of the conference on Continuity and Change: The Cultural Life of Alberta's First Ukrainians, held on May 2-4 1985, at the Ukrainian Cultural Heritage Village. Review: *Studies in Comparative Communism* 23:2:213-222 (Summer 1990). Bohdan S. Wynar

1352. Marples, David R., **Chernobyl and Nuclear Power in the USSR**. Edmonton: Canadian Institute of Ukrainian Studies, University of Alberta, 1986. 228 p. ISBN: 0333441990. Includes index and bibliography (p. 197-201).

This is the first study to analyze the Soviet nuclear power industry in some detail. As Marples points out, "In origin, it predates the Chernobyl accident, but inevitably its format has been determined by that event." (p. ix) Several questions are raised by the author: Why have the Soviet authorities committed themselves so heavily to the development of nuclear energy? Has the speed with which the industry is being developed led to the neglect of safety precautions? Is Chernobyl representative of the nuclear power industry in the Soviet Union? And finally, what will be the long-term effects of the accident at Chernobyl, both on the immediate environment, for agriculture, and for the Soviet energy program? The material is presented in seven chapters using primarily Soviet and some Western sources. The economic and political consequences of this tragedy are discussed in some detail. It is our understanding that the author is preparing another edition taking into consideration the discoveries of new facts during 1987 and 1988. Reviews: W. Huda *Canadian Slavonic Papers* 29:2-3:309-311 (June-September 1987). M.I. Goldman. *Slavic Review* 46:3-4:622-23 (Fall-Winter 1987). T. Chalij. *Ukrainian Review* 35:3:39-56 (Autumn 1987). E.H. Christianson. *Choice* 24:9:1424 (May 1987). Bohdan S. Wynar

1353. ———, **The Social Impact of the Chernobyl Disaster**. New York: St. Martin's Press, 1988. 313 p. ISBN: 0312024320. Includes bibliographical references and index.

In this monograph on Chernobyl, the author concentrates on the environmental impact, economic and political repercussions, restoration and reconstruction of the equipment, and the nuclear power debate in the Soviet Union and abroad. Numerous notes and a brief index conclude the volume. Presenting the aftermath of the world's worst nuclear disaster, the author tries to show what happened to the victims of Chernobyl, how peoples' lives have changed, and, in one chapter, to analyze one of the most controversial topics, namely work in the "special zone." Review: *Contemporary Sociology* 18:5:735-36 (September 1989). Bohdan S. Wynar

1354. **Political Thought and the Ukrainian Underground 1943-1951**, edited by Peter J. Potichnyj and Yevhen Shtendera. Edmonton: Canadian Institute of Ukrainian Studies, University of Alberta, 1986. xxix, 406 p. *Canadian Library in Ukrainian Studies*, ISBN: 0920862454. Includes bibliographies.

This anthology of political writings from the Ukrainian underground (1943-1951) includes essays and articles by leading underground publicists who, according to the editors, "made a significant contribution to the development of Ukrainian political thought. The articles and documents collected here also mark several points at which important ideological shifts took place and changes were made in the organizational structure, strategy, and tactics of the Ukrainian underground." (p. xi) Two periods are covered: 1941-1951, marked by a shift to new forms under Soviet control. The material is arranged in four parts: Part I, "Ukraine in Imperialist Plans;" Part 2, "Ideological Questions;" Part 3, "Strategy and Tactics of the Ukrainian Liberation Movement;" and the fourth section, "Programmatic Documents and Appeals." The book concludes with brief biographical notes on the authors, but there is no index or bibliography pertaining to UPA. Reviews: O.S. Romanyshyn. *Canadian Slavonic Papers* 30:1:163 (March 1988). J.A. Armstrong. *Slavic Review* 46:3-4:628-29 (Fall-Winter 1987). Bohdan S. Wynar

1355. **Ukrainian-Jewish Relations in Historical Perspective**, edited by Peter Potichnyi and Howard Aster. Edmonton: Canadian Institute of Ukrainian Studies, University of Alberta, 1988. 531 p. ISBN: 0920862535. Includes index and bibliographies.

This volume constitutes proceedings of the Conference on Jewish-Ukrainian Relations in Historical Perspective that took place at McMaster University in Hamilton, Ontario, from October 17-20, 1983. All papers were reedited for this publication, and as indicated in the preface, "the perspectives and views expressed by various scholars in their papers reflect their own—and at times highly personal—perspectives on the problems under examination." (p. x) A total of 24 papers are included, plus one roundtable discussion covering some ten centuries of Ukrainian-Jewish relations. Bohdan S. Wynar

1356. Prymak, Thomas M., **Mykhailo Hrushevsky: The Politics of National Culture**. Toronto: University of Toronto Press, 1987. 323 p. ISBN: 0802057373. Includes index and bibliography.

Based on a doctoral dissertation, Prymak's monograph is the only biographical study on Hrushevs'kyi in English that will supplement L. Wynar's *Mykhailo Hrushevs'kyi's Biographical Sources* and other writings about this prominent historian. The material is presented in 11 chapters, e.g., "Youth and Education 1866-1894," "The Young Professor 1894-1897," "Galacian Piedmont 1897-1905," "The Shift Back to Kiev 1904-1914," among others, plus brief sections on conclusions, the fate of the Hrushevs'kyi family and his school, and "The Hrushevsky Legend in the Soviet Union 1934 to the Present." An extensive bibliography and an index conclude this interesting study. In his conclusions, the author indicates, "As in the case of Masaryk, Dubnow, and Iorga, Hrushevs'kyi's role as a national figure is fairly clear. When his career is viewed as a whole, one is struck by the remarkable energy, creativity, and consistency of his endeavor. He never abandoned the ideas of the national awakening that he had first adopted during his youth, and, from his 1894 inaugural lecture on L'viv to this 1920 reflection on the revolution, he reiterated these ideals before many a different audience." (p. 264) Reviews: M. Bohachevsky-Chomiak. *Canadian Slavonic Papers* 30:2:293-94 (June 1988). Bohdan S. Wynar

1357. **Famine in Ukraine 1932-1933**, edited by Roman Serbyn and Bohdan Krawchenko. Edmonton: Canadian Institute of Ukrainian Studies, University of Alberta, 1986. 192 p. *Canadian Library in Ukrainian Studies*, ISBN: 092862438. Includes bibliographical references.

This book, a collective work by a number of scholars, explores several issues connected with the famine: the causes, sources of information about the event, the size of the population lost, and the impact of the famine on Ukrainian society and the Western response. Originally, the papers were presented at a conference held at the University of Quebec in Montreal in 1983 and are re-edited here. A total of ten essays are included. Reviews: *Canadian Slavonic Papers* 29:2-3:349-50 (June-September 1987). *Soviet Union* 14:1:155-56 (1987). Bohdan S. Wynar

1358. Subtelny, Orest, **Domination of Eastern Europe: Native Nobilities and Foreign Absolutism, 1500-1715**. Kingston: McGill-Queen's University Press, 1986. 270 p. ISBN: 0773504389. Includes indexes and bibliographical notes (p. 218-256).

An essential work in comparative history of five East European nations: Poland, Hungary, Livonia, Moldavia, and Ukraine. Subtelny's study shows impressive scholarship, analyzing Eastern Europe as a political region rather than just a number of separate political entities. The volume concludes with a biographical chapter discussing several leaders of the noble opposition such as Johann Reinhold von Patkul, Ivan Mazepa, Stanislaw Leszszynski, Ferenc Rakoczi, and several others. Helpful information is given for each country, as well as a chronological table and a glossary at the end of the volume. Reviews: D. Stone. *Canadian Slavonic Papers* 28:3:314-15 (September 1986). P.F. Sugar. *Slavic Review* 45:3:573 (Fall 1986). Bohdan S. Wynar

1359. ———, **Ukraine: A History**. Toronto: University of Toronto Press in association with the Canadian Institute of Ukrainian Studies, 1988. 666 p. ISBN: 0802058086. Includes bibliographical references and index.

Subtelny is a well-known historian of the younger generation and the author of such books as *Domination of Eastern Europe*, *The Mazepists: Ukrainian Separatism in the 18th Century*, *The Letters of Ivan Mazepa*, *Habsburgs and Zaporozhian Cossacks* (with L. Wynar) as well as a number of essays published in several symposia and many articles dealing with important aspects of Cossack history and periods of the nineteenth and twentieth centuries. The methodology of this significant work is expressed by the author in his introduction: "In dealing with Ukrainian history, I stress two themes. One of them is statelessness. In most national histories the organization and development of the nation-state is a paramount feature, but in the Ukrainian case the opposite is true. The frustration of the Ukrainians' attempts to attain self-government is one of the key aspects of their historical experience. Therefore, the Ukrainian past is largely the history of a nation that has had to survive and evolve without the framework of a full-fledged national state." Modernization is the other major theme of this work, as stated by the author: "Modernization in Ukraine is striking in several ways. Once a quintessentially agrarian society, Ukraine became an industrialized country in an unusually rapid and traumatic fashion. Even more noteworthy is that modernization in Ukraine occurred largely under the aegis of non-Ukrainians" (p. xi) Naturally, the author indicates that there can be subsumed under these two themes, e.g., the period of Kievan Rus', the Cossacks, events during the twentieth century, etc. The material in this volume is arranged in 29 chapters and in 5 parts: "Kievan Rus'," "The Polish-Lithuanian Period," "The Cossack Era," "Ukraine under Imperial Rule," and "Twentieth-Century Ukraine." Several maps, many illustrations, bibliographic notes (unfortunately placed at the end of the book), a glossary, "Selected Readings in English," and an index conclude this large volume. Reviews: *Russian History* 17:1:109-10 (Spring

1990). *Polish Review* 35:3-4:276-80 (1990). *Canadian Historical Review* 71:1: 134-35 (March 1990). *Soviet Union-Union Sovietique* 17:3:314-15 (1990). Bohdan S. Wynar

1360.   Troper, Harold, and Morton Weinfeld, **Old Wounds: Jews, Ukrainians and the Hunt for Nazi War Criminals in Canada**. Toronto: Viking, 1988. 434 p. ISBN: 0670821683. Includes bibliographical references and index.

Written by two Jewish scholars, this monograph examines in some detail the origins of Ukrainian immigration, emphasizing in separate chapters the emergence of war criminals, the Deschenes hearings, and the long and frequently bitter discussion between Jewish and Ukrainian ethnic groups. The authors state: "These historical debates feed into current ethnic sensitivities. Some Ukrainian Canadians are convinced they are under attack as a group while others—equally guilty—are spared, including Jews.... How different, some ask, are eastern Europeans who serve as concentration camp guards from Jewish Kapos who served the same master?" (p. 341) This monograph is not free of Jewish bias but at the same time serves as the only comprehensive treatment of this sensitive issue. It is also very well documented. Review: *American Jewish History* 79:3:415-19 (Spring 1990). Bohdan S. Wynar

1361.   Varvartsev, Nikolai N., **Ukrainian History in the Distorting Mirror of Sovietology**. Kiev: Naukova Dumka, 1987. 173 p. Includes index and bibliography (p. 163-172).

Sponsored by the Institute of History of the Academy of Science of the Ukrainian SSR, this monograph summarizes all the Soviet criticism of Western scholarship (including Ukrainian émigré scholars), which up to this point was available only in articles published in Ukrainian or Russian in such journals as *Ukrains'kyi istorychnyi zhurnal (Ukrainian Historical Journal)* produced by the institute of Kiev. Its three chapters cover "Social Customers for Hostile Stereotypes," "Ukrainian Studies: Centers and Their Purposes," and "Historiography at the Service of Imperialist Policy." Brief conclusions, references, and footnotes, as well as an index of names conclude this publication, which probably has very little to do with scholarship. Nevertheless, the reader will find references to some 100 scholars (Ukrainian and non-Ukrainian) who wrote books and articles dealing with Ukrainian topics as well as typical Soviet propaganda descriptions of such Ukrainian institutions as the Shevchenko Scientific Society and the Ukrainian Academy of Arts and Sciences in New York. According to the author, "falsifying the Leninist ethnic relations policy of the Communist Party of the Soviet Union and its implementation in the Ukraine is part and parcel of politicized historiography in the West." (p. 158) However, "reactionary" nationalism in sovietological centers is only wishful thinking by Mr. Varvarstsev and fortunately or unfortunately has nothing to do with reality. Bohdan S. Wynar

Government and Politics

1362.   **Tragedy of Vinnytsia: Materials on Stalin's Policy of Extermination in Ukraine During the Great Purge, 1936-1938**, edited by Ihor Kamenetsky. Toronto: Ukrainian Historical Association in Cooperation with Bahriany Foundation and Ukrainian Research and Documentation Center, 1989. xviii, 265 p. Includes index and bibliography (p. 253-259).

Nine thousand persons were massacred by the Soviet NKVD in the Ukrainian town of Vinnytsia during 1937-1938. This collection of materials is intended to provide a description and analysis of all the events involving the massacre. The materials are arranged in four parts. Part one is an introduction by Ihor Kamenetsky. Part two consists of testimonies by eyewitnesses and special U.S. congressional hearings devoted to it. Part three contains analytical articles that describe and evaluate the massacre. Finally, part four provides translations of German government reports on the massacre. Review: *Canadian Slavonic Papers* 32:4:516-17 (December 1990).

Religion

1363. Blazejowskyj, Dmytro, **Schematism of the Ukrainian Catholic Church: A Survey of the Church in Diaspora**. Rome: Analecta OSBM, 1988. 1318 p. *Analecta OSBM, Series II, Section I*, vol. 45. Includes index.

Reverend Blazejowskyj is the author of several books published in Latin, Ukrainian, and English, e.g., *Se Potestate Metropolitarum Kioviensium in Clerum Regularem* (1973) and *Ukrainian and Armenian Pontifical Seminaries of Lviv* (1975). The present work, commissioned by the Synod of Ukrainian Catholic Bishops in commemoration of the millennium of Christianity in Ukraine, is a comprehensive encyclopedic work covering in ten chapters such topics as the Catholic church in Rome, the United States, Canada, Western and Central Europe, and other continents including Latin America and Australia. In each chapter Reverend Blazejowskyj provides information on central administration, pastoral districts, parishes, and clergy. Chapters 6 and 7 cover Catholic higher and secondary education and Catholic organizations. Appendixes provide a list of closed parishes, maps and diagrams, as well as an index of names. All in all this is a comprehensive work that will be of substantial assistance to the Ukrainian Catholic church and its followers. Bohdan S. Wynar

1364. **The Millennium of Ukrainian Christianity**, edited by Nicholas Fr.-Chirovsky. New York: Philosophical Library, 1988. 617 p. Includes bibliographical references and index.

The Millennium of Ukrainian Christianity is a collective work by 28 authors covering in four parts several aspects of religious life in Ukraine. Most articles contain footnotes, and this collection concludes with several appendixes and a name index. All in all, it is a useful and adequately edited volume on the millennium of Christianity in Ukraine, bringing to the attention of the English-speaking reader some of the materials published previously in Ukrainian by such authors as Ivan Vlasovksy, Dmytro Dontsov, Vasyl Lypkivsky, Ivan Ohienko, Yaroslav Stetsko, Ivan Keyvan, and Hryhor Luzhnytsky. Bohdan S. Wynar

1365. **The Ukrainian Religious Experience: Tradition and the Canadian Cultural Context**, edited by David J. Goa. Edmonton: Canadian Institute of Ukrainian Studies, University of Alberta, 1989. 243 p. ISBN: 0920862632.

This volume is based on the proceedings of a conference held 13-16 March 1986 at the University of Alberta. It compliments and supplements a number of monographic works such as Paul Yuzyk's *The Ukrainian Greek Orthodox Church of Canada, 1918-1951*. There are two introductory papers—"A Personal Reflection" by Paul Yazyk and "What Really Happened in 988" by O. Pritsak—plus 16 essays by a number of well-known scholars arranged under four headings: "Liturgical Tradition in the Canadian Cultural Context," "Historical Factors in the Maintenance of Religion and Ethnicity," and "Religion, Ethnicity and Jurisdiction: Case Studies." A paper by J. Pekilan, "Eastern Christianity in Modern Culture," concludes this volume, with interesting contributions by Dennis J. Dunn on the relationship between the Vatican and the Kremlin; Bohdan Bociurkiw on Soviet suppression of the Greek Catholic Church in Ukraine; and the role of the patriarchal movement by Vasyl Markus. Bohdan S. Wynar

1366. Hnatenko, Stefania, **Treasures of Early Ukrainian Art: Religious Art of the 16th-18th Centuries**. New York: Ukrainian Museum, 1989. 44 p. Includes bibliographical references.

In this exhibition catalog are icons and iconostases created at the end of the sixteenth and the first half of the seventeenth centuries. The iconostases are those of the Church of St. Paraskeva in L'viv, the Church of the Holy Spirit in Rohatyn, and the Church of the Assumption in the village of Zhovtantsi near L'viv. Well-executed photographs, some in color, and a brief bibliography add to the value of this catalog. This source can be used in conjunction with Hordynskyi's *The Ukrainian Icon*. Bohdan S. Wynar

1367. Hrynioch, Iwan, **Works by Joseph Slipyj: Archbishop Major and Cardinal**. Munich: Suchasnist, 1988. 204 p.

St. Clement's Ukrainian Catholic University has published for a number of years "works" of Cardinal Slipyj, with introductions prepared by Reverend Dr. Hrynioch. This volume contains three introductions, in Ukrainian, Latin, and English. Joseph Slipyj was ordained September 8, 1917, and received his doctoral degree in sacred theology in 1918 from Innsbruck University. For a number of years Reverend Slipyj taught and was a rector of the Greek-Catholic Theological Academy in L'viv. His published works during that first decade have been collected in the first two volumes of the *Opera Omnia*, published in Rome. Later works were published in subsequent volumes of *Opera*, and Hrynioch's introduction provides an appropriate historical setting for those important scholarly contributions by this prominent Ukrainian church leader. Bohdan S. Wynar

1368. Iwanusiw, Oleh Wolodymyr, **Church in Ruins: The Demise of Ukrainian Churches in the Eparchy of Peremyshl**. St. Catharines, Ont.: St. Sofia Religious Association of Ukrainian Catholics in Canada, 1987. 351 p. *Ukrainian Studies*, ISBN: 0969165730. Includes index and bibliography (p. 336).

This book contains excellent illustrations, many in color, of some 690 churches of the Ukrainian Catholic (Byzantine) Rite Eparchy of Peremyshl in present day Poland. While some churches are protected as architectural antiques, most of them were acquired by the Polish Catholic church and a majority of them destroyed. This album in English and Ukrainian illustrates with fine photographs and some drawings Lemko and Boyko wooden architecture. An engineer by profession, the author visited this region four times in order to photograph the remaining churches. He prepared the book in memory of his grandfather's priests in the Lemko region, and this is his contribution to the millennium of Christianity in Ukraine. Indeed, it is a beautiful coffee-table book with excellent illustrations and an intelligent text describing the history of individual churches. Bohdan S. Wynar

1369. **Morality and Reality: The Life and Times of Andrei Sheptytskyi**, edited by Paul Robert Magocsi with the assistance of Andrii Krawchuk and with an introduction by Jaroslav Pelikan. Edmonton: Canadian Institute of Ukrainian Studies, University of Alberta, 1989. xxiv, 485 p. ISBN: 0920862683. Includes bibliographical references.

This volume brings together 21 essays by a number of Western scholars who participated in a conference entitled "Andrei Sheptyts'kyi: His Life and Work," held at the University of Toronto on November 22-24, 1984. As is true of most proceedings, there is some overlap, repetition, and differences in interpretation in several essays; nevertheless, this volume is probably the most significant contribution to the study of Andrei Sheptyts'kyi, an important figure in the history of Christianity and certainly the most prominent leader of the Ukrainian Catholic church during the first half of the twentieth century. Also included are over 50 photographs, 3 genealogical charts, and 2 maps. An introduction by Reverend Jaroslav Pelikan, "The Church Between East and West: The Context of Sheptyts'kyi's Thought," offers a well-rounded analysis of Shertyts'kyi's place in Christianity, specifically the Ukrainian church, indicating that the study of Andrei Sheptyts'kyi's thought is as theologically relevant today as it is fascinating from a historical point of view. Bohdan S. Wynar

1370. Pelikan, Jaroslav Jan, **Confessor Between East and West: A Portrait of Ukrainian Cardinal Josyf Slipyi**. Grand Rapids: Eerdmans, 1989. xiv, 249 p. ISBN: 0802836720. Includes bibliographical references.

Pelikan's book not only explores the life and work of Josyf Slipyi, a Ukrainian cardinal imprisoned by Soviets and subsequently released and exiled to Rome. The book also describes and analyzes the theological and historical context of Slipyj's legacy.

1371. Smotryc'kyj, Meletij, **Collected Works of Meletij Smotryc'kyj**, with an introduction by David A. Frick. Cambridge, Mass.: Harvard University Press, 1987. xxxviii, 805 p. *Harvard Library of Early Ukrainian Literature, Texts*, vol. 1. ISBN: 0916458202. Includes bibliography (p. xxxv-xxxviii).

Meletij Smotryc'kyj was one of the most prominent figures of the cultural revival of the Ukrainian and Belorussian lands of the Polish-Lithuanian Commonwealth in the late sixteenth and early seventeenth centuries. As an advocate of Orthodoxy and, after 1627, an equally ardent defender of the Uniate church, he wrote numerous polemical works and some theological and philological treatises. This volume reproduces in facsimile ten of Smotryc'kyj's most important religious writings beginning with *Threnos* (1610) and concluding with *Exaethesis* (1629). Professor Frick provides a brief introduction to Smotryc'kyj's biography and a selected bibliography of the most important works by this religious leader published in several languages. The facsimile is not adequate and is occasionally unreadable, e.g., p. 517, reproductions of title page on p. 1, etc. Bohdan S. Wynar

1372. **A Thousand Years of Christianity in Ukraine: An Encyclopedic Chronology**, compiled and edited by Osyp Zinkewych and Adrew Sorokowski. New York: Smoloskyp Publishers and the National Committee to Commemorate the Millennium in Ukraine, 1988. 312 p. ISBN: 0914834584. Includes index and bibliography (p. 285-287).

In ten chapters this chronology presents the most important events in the religious life of Ukraine, including some 2,500 entries, over 400 illustrations with some in color, a useful index, and appendixes listing the rulers of Ukraine, and a bibliography. One of the best chapters is chapter 10, which describes Ukrainian churches in the twentieth century (1917-1988) in Ukraine and the diaspora. It is divided into the following sections: general characteristics of the period, chronology (Ukrainian Orthodox Church, Ukrainian Catholic Church, and Ukrainian Protestant churches), principal ecclesiastical activities, destruction of churches and monasteries on Ukrainian territory, and hierarchy of Ukrainian churches. Written by two gifted journalists, one from the older generation and the other from the younger generation, this useful reference source was compiled with the assistance of some 20 individuals representing a good cross section of the Ukrainian diaspora. Bohdan S. Wynar

Architecture and Art

1373. Markovych, Pavlo, **Rusyn Easter Eggs from Eastern Slovakia**. Wien: Wilhelm Braumuller, 1987. 146 p. *Classics of Carpatho-Rusyn Scholarship Series*, ISBN: 3700306954. Includes bibliographical references.

This book was originally published in Ukrainian under the title *Ukrajins'ki pysanky schidnoji Slovachchyny*, and in volume 6, part 2 of the series *Naukovyj Zbirnyk Muzeju Ukrajins'koji Kul'tury v Svydnyku (Scholarly Symposia of the Museum of Ukrainian Culture in Svydnyk)*. It has now been translated using the term "Rusyn." "It is particularly difficult to study the process of the emergence of the pysanka in the pre-Christian era and to determine its original significance, its ancient designs, and its original functions. Only certain remnants have survived in the life of the Rusyn peasants of Eastern Slovakia." (p. 13) Upon making this final introductory comment, the author begins to analyze its history. "The Historic Pysanky" examines the interaction of cultural and ideological influences on the Rusyn pysanky of Eastern Slovakia. In "The Names of Pysanky" we find that pysane jajce, krasanky, maljuvanka, and velykodnje jajce are local names used by the Rusyns for pysanky. "The Origins of Pysanka Ornamentation" examines the purpose of ornamentation, the time and source of its origin, and the methods used to execute it. Also identified are themes, elements and motifs, and the content of agrarian pastoral culture. "The Composition of the Ornament" demonstrates that internal rules of design are used in pysanky and classifies the ornamentation into eight groups (geometric-abstract motifs, phytomorphic motifs, cosmic motifs, etc.). An excellent chart illustrating pysanka motifs used by the Ukrainian population of Eastern Slovakia is included (pp. 91-102) for easy reference. The remaining chapters focus primarily on the processes and techniques used in egg decoration. The book concludes with chapter notes, list of illustrations, and a comprehensive bibliography of some 100 related works in Ukrainian, German, and other languages. Bohdan S. Wynar

1374. Mudrak, Myroslava M., **The New Generation and Artistic Modernism in the Ukraine**. Ann Arbor, Mich: U.M.I. Research Press, 1986. x, 282 p. *Studies in the Fine Arts*, ISBN: 0835716872. Includes index and bibliography (p. 269-274).
Mudrak presents the reader with the only scholarly study of monograph length pertaining to artistic innovations in Ukraine during the period from 1915-1930. The material is presented in three parts: "Panfuturism" (Mykhailo Semenko and the New Generation); "The Painted Image" (beginnings of Formalism and Futurism through Constructivism), and part 3, "The Printed Page," covering typography and the visual arts plus members of the Nova generatsiia. The text ends with a comprehensive bibliography of works connected with a very good section, "Monographic Studies on Ukrainian Artists," with over 20 listings of important works in Ukrainian on such artists as Narbut, F. Krychevs'kyi, Kozhun, Murashko, and others. Reviews: M. Shkandrij. *Canadian Slavonic Papers* 29:2-3:350-52 (June-September 1987). J. Kennedy. *Slavic Review* 46:2:375 (Summer 1987). Bohdan S. Wynar

1375. Tahir, Abe M. Jr, **Jacques Hnizdovsky: Woodcuts and Etchings**. New York: Pelican Publishing, 1987. 261 p. ISBN: 0882894870. Includes index.
This catalog raisonne contains reproductions of 350 wood and linocuts by Jacques Hnizdovsky (1915-1987). As Peter Wick comments in his foreword, "The woodcuts of Jacques Hnizdovsky represent some of the freshest and most original printmaking in American graphic arts of the past thirty years." (p. vii) Hnizdovsky's work was originally influenced by Durer. He experimented with painting, ceramics, sculpture, and other mediums before settling on woodcuts as his preferred medium. It was a long and arduous journey to the top, as Hnizdovsky himself tells in his introductory essay, "Reflection of the Artist." Review: A. Olenska-Petryshyn. *Ukrainian Quarterly* 33:1:70-71 (Spring 1977). Bohdan S. Wynar

Language, Literature, Folklore

1376. **Ukrainian Folk Tales**. 3rd ed. Kiev: Dnipro Publishers, 1986. 388 p.
Translated from Ukrainian by Irena Zhelezova with illustrations by Yuri Kryha, this is
actually the third edition of this anthology published in Kiev. Over 70 folk tales are
included, with such well-known tales as "The Bear and the Bees," "The Goat and the Ram,"
and "Kirilo the Tanner," among others. Bohdan S. Wynar

1377. **Yarmarok: Ukrainian Writing in Canada Since the Second World War**, edited
by Jars Balan and Yuri Klynovy. Edmonton: Canadian Institute of Ukrainian
Studies, 1987. xix, 352 p. ISBN: 0920862527. Includes bibliographies and index.
Literatumyi yamorok was an important Ukrainian literary journal that flourished briefly at
the end of the 1920s. After it was closed in February 1930, literary development was
effectively halted in Eastern Ukraine for a period of thirty years. This anthology, like its
forebear, gathers together a diverse group of writers whose creations express a contemporary Ukrainian identity. It is intended to provide English speaking Canadians "with a
glimpse into a dynamic literary subculture, hitherto accessible only to readers of Ukrainian."
(p. xi).

1378. Gzhytsky, Volodymyr, **Night and Day**. Edmonton: Canadian Institute of Ukrainian
Studies, 1988. 242 p.
Written by one of the most prominent Ukrainian writers, this memoir in novel form is one
of the first attempts to describe Stalin's treatment of writers and the realities of Soviet life
during the 1930s. Originally, "Nich' i den' " was published in the Soviet Ukrainian journal
Zhovten' during the "thaw period following Stalin's death, and 18 years later it has been
translated into English by Ian Press, a senior lecturer at the University of London. In
addition to the translation, a brief introduction to Gzhytsky's writings is provided, including
some discussion of his masterpiece, "The Black Lake," first published in 1919 and
republished in Ukrainian in the West in 1948. Gzhytsky spent several years in Soviet
concentration camps (1933-1948) and was partly rehabilitated in 1956, after the 20th Party
Congress. The author, who was born in Western Ukraine in 1895 and died in L'viv in 1973,
was a member of several literary organizations during the 1920s, and after his rehabilitation
he published a prose collection—"Povernennia" (The Return, 1958), "Opryshky" (Opry-
shoks, 1962), and "Karmeliuk" (1971). Bohdan S. Wynar

1379. Honchar, Oles, **The Cathedral: A Novel,** translated from the Ukrainian by Yuri
Tkach and Leonid Rudnytzky, edited and annotated by Leonid Rudnytzky. Washington: St. Sophia Religious Association of Ukrainian Catholics, 1989. 308 p. *St.
Sophia Religious Association of Ukrainian Catholics*, no. 2.
A translation from Ukrainian of a novel by Soviet Ukraine's leading prose writer. The story
is basically a history of a Ukrainian industrial town called Zachiplianka. The town has
environmental as well as social problems—in most ways a typical industrial center. One
feature that separates it from other industrial towns is the old Cossack cathedral used in
Soviet times as a wildlife museum and storage area. The conflict in the story centers around
the feelings that arise in the population when their cathedral is threatened with destruction.
The storyline thus becomes a metaphor for the struggle between basic human freedoms and
bureaucratic tyranny. The strong ties with religion in Ukraine are also a theme. This is the
author's most controversial work and has had a strong influence on Ukrainian intellectual
life.

1380. Kepley, Vance Jr., **In the Service of the State: The Cinema of Alexander Dovzhenko**. Madison: University of Wisconsin Press, 1986. xi, 190 p. ISBN: 0299106802. Includes index and bibliography (p. 181-185).

In 1973, Marco Carynnyk published *Alexander Dovzhenko: The Poet as Filmmaker*, and the present study is the second monographic volume in English about this outstanding filmmaker. Kepley indicates that Dovzhenko is consistently characterized as the great fold artist of cinema, the cinematic equivalent of a romantic poet, dominated by a pastoral vision of life and embodying historical and timeless themes in his films. Kepley contends that Dovzhenko's projections are not simply of personal and private visions, but that they refer to their historical settings and are highly topical. Kepley's thesis is supported by evidence he collected by examining each film in its original historical and political context. There are nine chapters in this monograph plus several appendixes, including such matters as Dovzhenko's credits, the chronology of his life, etc. The volume concludes with a comprehensive bibliography of works in several languages and an author-subject index. Review: *Film Quarterly* 40:4:36-40 (Summer 1987). Bohdan S. Wynar

1381. Khvylovy, Mykola, **The Cultural Renaissance in Ukraine: Polemical Pamphlets, 1925-1926**, edited and translated by Myroslav Shkandrij. Edmonton: Canadian Institute of Ukrainian Studies, 1986. xi, 266 p. *Canadian Library in Ukrainian Studies*, ISBN: 092086242x. Includes bibliographical references and index.

This volume represents the first English-language collection of Mykola Khvylovy's polemical writings, translated, edited and introduced by Myroslav Shkandrij. Though Khvylovy's outspoken advocacy of and independent literary course for Ukrainian literature led to severe conflict with Stalin's regime, and ultimately to his own suicide in 1933, the issues he raised have survived both him and his antagonists. After his tragic death, Stalin saw to it that Khvylovy's name was expunged from the annals of Ukrainian literature. Thus was the fate of one of the most talented of the post-revolutionary Ukrainian prose writers decided. After a foreword by George S.N. Luckyj and a detailed introduction by Shkandrij, the volume introduces Khylovy's three letters to literary youth: "On Satan in a Barrel or on Graphomaniacs, Speculators, and other Prosvita Types;" "On Copernicus of Frauenburg or the ABC of the Asiatic Renaissance in Art;" and "On the Waters of the Demagogy or the Real Address of Ukrainian Voronskyism, Free Competition, VUAN, etc." These are followed by "Quo Vadis?" and "Thoughts against the Current." But it was Khvylovy's third series, "Apologist of Scribbling," that caused the greatest stir. This essay called for cities to be de-Russified and the Ukrainian Republic to be given rights equal to the Russians. All of the essays are compellingly written, full of striking images and inspired wit. Concluding the text is a previously unpublished pamphlet, "Ukraine or Little Russia," in which Khvylovy accuses the Communist Party in Ukraine of not doing enough to Ukrainize public life because the party was dominated by Russians or culturally Russified elements who represented the worst colonial-settler mentality. Khvylovy spoke as a Ukrainian communist state, and his challenge to the central authority of the party coincided with the dramatic growth of the national movement in Ukraine. His writings reflected a passionate concern for cultural and political questions of the day. This volume presents the essential core of Khvylovy's argument against the communist "establishment" and defines the course of the literary discussion of those years. Review: R. Stites. *Slavic Review* 46:2:337-38 (Summer 1987). Bohdan S. Wynar

1382. **Before the Storm: Soviet Ukrainian Fiction of the 1920s**, edited by George Luckyj. Ann Arbor, Mich.: Ardis, 1986. 266 p. ISBN: 0882335219. Includes bibliographies.

This anthology contains short stories and other works by 17 Ukrainian writers, many of them translated for the first time into English. As Luckyj indicates, "The decade of the

1920's remains the golden decade of modern Ukrainian literature. There is no doubt that the exhilaration of a national awakening on such a grand scale stimulated and nurtured this unprecedented outburst of creativity." (p. 7) Some writers are represented by excerpts, e.g., Mykola Khvylovy, Yurij Yanovsky, Volodymyr Gzhytsky, Victor Domontovych, while others, e.g., Valerian Pidmohylny, Arkadiy Liubchenko, Oleska Slisarenko, have been translated without abridgments. The introduction by Luckyj provides a proper historical background for the major events during the 1920s, and the volume concludes with brief notes on the authors. Reviews: P.M. Austin. *Choice* 24:8:1226-27 (April 1987). Bohdan S. Wynar

1383. Shatulsky, Myron, **The Ukrainian Folk Dance**. Toronto: Kobzar Publishing Company, 1986. 210 p. Includes bibliography.

Folk dances have played a significant role in the lives of the Ukrainian peoples. Together with choral and instrumental music, Ukrainian folk dance has attained a high level of technical and artistic development. As the author states in his foreword, "It is my intention to present the basics of the Ukrainian folk dance in an authentic way. The book deals with dances from the following east-central regions of the Ukraine: Poltava, Kiev, Cherkassy, Dneipropetrovsk, Chernihiv, western part of Kharkiv, Zaporizhia, Kherson, Mykolayiv, north-eastern part of Zhtomyr, and the eastern part of Vinnytsia." (p. x) The book is arranged in four parts: historical development and classification of the folk dance, basic steps and arm positions, national dress, and examples of folk dances. Accompanying the text are clear illustrations and numerous folk song stanzas. This is perhaps the best guide in the English language to the basic steps of the folk dances of Ukraine. Bohdan S. Wynar

1384. Slavutych, Yar, **Standard Ukrainian Grammar**. Edmonton: Slavuta Publishers, 1987. 296 p. ISBN: 0919452191.

Unlike the author's *Conversational Ukrainian*, which follows an oral approach in the treatment of Ukrainian grammar, the present work is exclusively devoted to the process of learning the basic elements of Ukrainian grammar in a more formal way. The material is presented in 20 lectures and may be used in the first year at the university level, for self-education, and probably even in senior high school. In addition to formal lessons, several topics are covered in parts 1 and 3, e.g., systems of transliteration; rules of pronunciation; gender of nouns; hard, soft, and mixed stems; and capital letters. Bohdan S. Wynar

1385. Zaitsev, Pavlo, **Taras Shevchenko: A Life**, edited, abridged, and translated with an introduction by George S. N. Luckyj. Toronto: University of Toronto Press, 1988. xi, 284 p. ISBN: 0802034500. Includes index.

This is the only full biography of Shevchenko in English, translated from the Ukrainian edition that was confiscated in 1939 by Soviet authorities and eventually updated by the author from his proofs for publication in 1955. Zaitsev, one of the best-known authorities on Shevchenko, was the editor of the collected works of Shevchenko in 14 volumes sponsored by the Ukrainian Scientific Institute in Warsaw, and Shevchenko's biography is the first volume in the set. This edition of Shevchenko's works was reprinted by M. Denysiuk in Chicago in 1961-1963. Zaitsev's study is one of the best biographies of this great Ukrainian poet and only Y. Kyryliuk's *T.H. Shevchenko: zhittia i tvorchisti (T.H. Shevchenko: Life and Work)*, published in 1959 and reprinted in 1964, approaches Zaitsev's standards. A glossary and selected bibliography list all important editions of Shevchenko's works as well as works in English containing biographical data. As usual, this translation by Luckyj is very well done, and Zaitsev's study is indispensable for studying not only Shevchenko but also the whole period of Modern Ukrainian literature. Bohdan S. Wynar

Dissident Movement

1386. Bilocerkowycz, Jaroslaw, **Soviet Ukrainian Dissent: A Study of Political Aliena-tion.** Boulder, CO: Westview Press, 1988. xii, 242 p. *Westview Special Studies on the Soviet Union and Eastern Europe*, ISBN: 0813372402. Includes index and bibliography (p. 221-232).

Based on the author's doctoral dissertation, this monograph is probably the most compre-hensive general study in English on Ukrainian dissidents. Dr. Bilocerkowycz provides adequate historical background in eight chapters including "Introduction and Analytical Approach" and "Ukrainian Opposition and Dissent: A Historical and Contemporary Sur-vey," concentrating on types and manifestations of dissent, e.g., religious dissent, with a separate section on *The Chronicle of the Catholic Church in Ukraine*, institutionalized dissent, etc. The author offers a socio-demographic profile of dissidents in a separate chapter plus several case histories on dissidents such as Mykola Rudenko, Lev Lukiianenko, Leonid Pliushch, Viacheslav Chornovil, Leonid Siryi, Nadiis Svitlychna, Father Vasyl' Romaniuk, and Valentyn Moroz. "The Regime's Punitive Response to Dissidents" and general conclusions, including a brief statement on Gorbachev, conclude the volume. Also provided is a very comprehensive, well-documented bibliography of primary and secondary sources in several languages. Among other things, Dr. Bilocerkowycz indicates in his general conclusions that "while Soviet dissidents and exiles debate various facets of Gorbachev's leadership, plans, and policies, most dissidents living in the West have expressed their doubts and criticisms on this issue. If the authorities refuse to restructure dissent and nationality policy of the 1920s, then Ukrainian political alienation will likely fester. The repression of moderate and peaceful dissent may compel a new generation of Ukrainian dissidents to adopt a more militant approach to effecting political change." (p. 199) Review: *American Political Science Review* 84: 1:330-31 (March 1990). Bohdan S. Wynar

1387. Motyl, Alexander J., **Will Non-Russians Rebel? State, Ethnicity, and Stability in the USSR**. Ithaca, N.Y.: Cornell University Press, 1987. xii, 188 p. *Studies in Soviet History and Society*, ISBN: 0801419476. Includes index and bibliography (p. 170-181).

The 10 chapters of this monograph cover ethnic problems in the Soviet Union in terms of concepts of stability of ethnicity, ideology, politics, and language, with a concluding chapter, "Systematic Crisis and the Soviet Russian State." According to the author, the only non-Russian nationality capable of undermining the Russian hegemony and the stability of the Russian position in the Soviet Union is the Ukrainian nationality, and he suggests that its ability to revolt has been and is likely to remain minimal. Continued vitality of the KGB effectively discourages autonomous political action. The book concludes with a selected bibliography of pertinent material in several languages and a detailed index of names and subjects. Reviews: P. Rutland. *Slavic Review* 47:1:144-45 (Spring 1988). P.J.S. Duncan. *Canadian Slavonic Papers* 30:1:144-45 (March 1988). Bohdan S. Wynar

CENTRAL ASIAN REPUBLICS AND PEOPLES

1388. **Tatars of the Crimea: Their Struggle for Survival: Original Studies from North America, Unofficial and Official Documents from Czarist and Soviet Sources,** edited by Edward Allworth. Durham, NC: Duke University Press, 1988. xii, 394 p. *Central Asia Book Series*, ISBN: 0822307588. Includes index and bibliography (p. 357-386).

This volume contains articles, memoirs, and documents relating to the Crimean Tatars. The materials are divided by subject into three sections. Section I, generating group leadership, seeks to come to terms with the ability of the Tatars from Crimea to survive as a group, even in the diaspora. Section II concerns group responses to government and party actions against the Crimean Tatars. Section III deals with the means by which group identity has been sustained. Reviews: *Slavic Review* 49:2:295 (Summer 1990). *Soviet Union* 15:2-3:175-76 (1988).

1389. **Nomads of Eurasia**, edited by Vladimir N. Basilov. Seattle: University of Washington Press, 1989. xiii, 191 p. ISBN: 0295968168. Includes index and bibliography (p. 184-188).

This book was published as a companion to a traveling exhibit on Eurasian nomads. It consists of thirteen essays, each illustrated with photographs of objects or scenes from daily life. Topics covered include Scythians, Sakians, Huns, and Turkic peoples up to the 16th century, folk culture, yurts, rugs and felts, clothing and personal adornment, household furnishings and utensils, harness and weaponry, musical instruments, and religious beliefs. Reviews: *Soviet Union-Union Sovietique* 17:3:301-02 (1990). *American Anthropologist* 92:2:528 (June 1990). *Armenian Review* 43:1:129-30 (Spring 1990).

1390. Dienes, Leslie, **Soviet Asia: Economic Development and National Policy Choices**. Boulder, CO: Westview Press, 1987. xx, 289 p. *Westview Special Studies on the Soviet Union and Eastern Europe*, no. 0163-6057. ISBN: 0813374375. Includes bibliographies and index.

"This work examines the geographic position of Soviet Asia in the overall economy of the USSR and analyzes the impact of major national policy issues on its development and prospects." (p. i) To elaborate these ideas the author has organized the work into three parts. The first serves as the framework for the study describing first the general problem of integration. The author then moves on to the geographic area. Part two focuses on the interaction between economic development in Asian USSR and central economic policy. The third part deals with specific economic issues such as manpower, settlement policy, and regional planning in Siberia, the Far East, and Kazakhstan. The book includes numerous illustrative tables. Reviews: *Geographical Review* 79:2:257-59 (April 1989). *Journal of Comparative Economics* 13:1:141-46 (March 1989). *Canadian-American Slavic Studies* 22:1:83-84 (Spring 1989).

1391. **Domestic Determinants of Soviet Foreign Policy Towards South Asia and the Middle East**, edited by Hafeez Malik. New York: St. Martin's Press, 1990. xiii, 332 p. ISBN: 0312040229. Includes bibliographical references and index.

The sixteen papers presented here are the result of a seminar held at Vilanova University in October 1988. Scholars participating were asked to focus on several key factors affecting Soviet foreign policy in South Asia and the Middle East, such as: 1) Islam, 2) the role of Muslim nationalities in the Soviet Armed forces, 3) decision making processes in Soviet foreign policy, 4) Soviet strategic interest in the area, and 5) Soviet involvement with problems of strategically significant states in the two regions. General agreement on the increasing Soviet interest in the area is apparent in the essays. The essays cover numerous topics: ethnic relations, Soviet-Afghan relations, Soviet Union and the Middle East. The contributors include nineteen scholars from Britain, the U.S., and the Soviet Union, most specialists in political science.

1392. Olcott, Martha Brill, **The Kazakhs**. Stanford, Calif.: Hoover Institution Press, Stanford University, 1987. xxiii, 341 p. *Studies of Nationalities in the USSR, Hoover Press Publication*, no. 338. ISBN: 0817983821 (pbk.), 0817983813. Includes index and bibliography (p. 309-334).
"This book provides an introduction to the history of the Kazakh people: it describes their formation; the rise and fall of the Kazakh Khanate; the annexation, conquest, and colonization; and, finally, the fate of the Kazakhs under Soviet rule." (p. xix) The book has sixteen appendices that provide a wide range of statistical information. Reviews: *Middle East Journal* 42:4:710-11 (Autumn 1988). *Orbis* 32:1:155 (Winter 1988).

1393. Rorlich, Azade-Ayse, **The Volga Tatars: A Profile in National Resilience**. Stanford, Calif.: Hoover Institution Press, 1986. xvi, 288 p. *Hoover Press Publications*, no. 339. ISBN: 0817983910. Includes index and bibliography (p. 253-275).
The first Western language study of the Volga Tatars. The author has sought to be as comprehensive as possible. This chronological study begins with some of the issues relevant to early Tatar history: Islam and the Bulgar Khanate. The author spends some time discussing the Mongol conquests and the rise of the Kazan Khanate, the intrusion of the Russians under Ivan the Terrible and the forced conversion of the Tatars with emphasis given to analyzing the means used to reach the goal of Russification. The revival in Tatar society and the reform movement that arose from 1861 to 1917 are given special attention. The effect of the 1917 revolution and rise of the Tatar republic are carefully examined in the context of Soviet nationality policy. The appendix lists Volga and Bashkir deputies to the Duma and there is a glossary of terms. An extensive and thorough bibliography is helpful for the reader who wishes to pursue the topic.

1394. Rumer, Boris Z., **Soviet Central Asia: "A Tragic Experiment."** Boston: Unwin Hyman, 1989. xix, 204 p. ISBN: 044451466. Includes index.
Rumer concentrates on economic policy in Uzbekistan, Tajikistan, Turkmenistan, and Kirghizistan—Central Asian republics as the Soviets defined it. After two introductory chapters describing regional economic policy and Soviet Central Asia's role in the Soviet economy, he covers problems of industrialization, cotton production, water, labor and employment, standard of living, shadow economy and organizational crime, and the effect of the Gorbachev reforms on Central Asia. Reviews: *Foreign Affairs* 69:2:183 (Spring 1990). *American Political Science Review* 84:3:1047-48 (September 1990). *Russian History* 17:1:105-07 (Spring 1990). *ORBIS* 34:613-14 (Fall 1990).

OTHER REPUBLICS

Armenia

1395. **Armenia at the Crossroads: Democracy and Nationhood in the Post-Soviet Era: Essays, Interviews, and Speeches by the Leaders of the National Democratic Movement in Armenia**, edited by Gerard J. Libaridian. Watertown, Mass.: Blue Crane Books, 1991. ix, 170 p. ISBN: 0962871516. Includes bibliographic references.
A collection of documents most issued by the Armenian National Movement and its leadership. The editor feels that these documents give the reader a picture of the major points of the movement's program. Appendices are included to introduce the views of others many of the contributors to this volume are now leaders of the Armenian Republic. The extensive notes give contextual and biographical information.

1396. **The Armenians**. New York: Rizzoli, 1986. 288 p. ISBN: 0847907312. Includes bibliography (p. 279-288).
Essays sponsored by the Italian Ministry of Foreign Affairs with a contribution by both Armenian and Italian scholars. The main focus of the volume is Armenian architecture. However, the authors seek to place this subject in the larger context of Armenian culture. Thus, essays included cover such topics as the natural environment, historical background, social structure, religion, language, and material culture. The essays also present various viewpoints, no central theory is carried through each. The volume is richly illustrated and includes a historical chronology in an appendix.

Georgia

1397. Garb, Paula, **Where the Old Are Young: Long Life in the Soviet Caucasus**. 2nd rev. ed. Palo Alto, Calif.: Ramparts Press/Common Ground Books, 1987. 175 p. ISBN: 0878671013. Includes bibliography (p. 175).
A study of the centenarians of the Soviet Caucasus, investigating those aspects of their lifestyle that contribute to longevity. The author, raised in America, was studying at Moscow's Institute of Ethnography. The author examines the place the elderly had in Abikhasian society as a factor in their longevity. The book includes information on the history of the area as recounted by the centenarians. The work was originally published in Russian in 1984.

1398. Suny, Ronald Grigor, **The Making of the Georgian Nation**. Bloomington: Indiana University Press in association with Hoover Institution Press, 1988. xviii, 395 p. ISBN: 0253336236. Includes bibliography (p. 381-385).
This history of Georgia focuses on the development of the Georgian national identity. The book is divided into three parts. The first traces the development of the Georgian people into a linguistically and culturally consistent whole. Part two discusses the long relationship between the Georgians and Russians up to the Soviet period. The final section examines the Georgians under the Soviet regime. "Suny comments on these and related questions with special insight and objectivity. He has given us an outstanding work in which he covers the wide range of Georgian history, with a focus on how the Georgians developed into a self-conscious nationality and a nation with its own political institutions." (p. xi) The author includes a glossary to assist the reader. Reviews: *American Historical Review* 95:2:548-49 (April 1990). *Russian Review* 49:4:501-03 (October 1990).

Belorus

1399. Bykau, Vasil, **Sign of Misfortune**, translator, Alan Myers. New York: Allerton Press, 1990. x, 240 p. ISBN: 0898640490.
Bykau, a Belorussian author who writes in Russian and Belorussian, is a popular and widely respected author throughout the Soviet Union. In recent times he has also engaged in political activities as a leader of the Byelorussian Popular Front. This novel, written in 1982, is "a gripping and psychologically truthful story that not only recreates the horror of war through the eyes of small, insignificant peasant characters, but sets the Soviet wartime experience in its proper historical context." (p. vi) The story was also made into a movie.

1400. Urban, Michael E., **An Algebra of Soviet Power: Elite Circulation in the Belorussian Republic, 1966-86**. Cambridge, England: Cambridge University Press, 1989. xvi, 183 p. *Soviet and East European Studies*, no 67. ISBN: 0521372509. Includes bibliographical references (p. 156-175).

A structural analysis of the movement of the political elite within the government from 1966-1986. The author intends to focus on the structure of relations between individuals in various government positions. Therefore there is very little information on personalities of individuals in power or on nationalities. "Rather than a description of the personnel who have held power, the purpose of this study is to describe the personnel system itself as a set of power relations and to inquire into the matter of how it is structured." (p. xii) The book has a thematic arrangement moving from the macro- to the micro- level of analysis. Chapter 1 describes the methodology used in the study and gives an overview of Belorussian history as relevant to the analysis. Chapter 2 discusses elite stratification. The following chapters consider elite structures in Belorussia analyzing the roles of centralization, regionalism, and patronage. Chapter 7 examines specific changes in political succession during the years of the study. Two appendices are included on the stratification of positions in Belorussia and factional groups.

SIBERIAN PEOPLES AND CULTURES

1401. Kennan, George, **Tent Life In Siberia**, with introduction by Larry McMurtry. Salt Lake City, UT: Peregrine Smith Books, 1986. x, 425 p. ISBN: 0879052546.

This is a reprint of Kennan's classic nineteenth-century travel narrative. Kennan's trip was sponsored by Western Union in order to survey Alaska, the Bering Strait and Eastern Siberia for the purposes of linking America and Europe by telegraph line. Enroute to the West after traveling in Siberia for two years, much of it spent in trying to stay alive, they discovered in some old newspapers that the Atlantic cable had been laid and the Russo-American telegraph abandoned. First published in 1870, it went through fourteen printings. The description and observations recorded here of his journey and the people and events encountered have been called sublime.

1402. **The History of Siberia: From Russian Conquest to Revolution**, edited and introduced by Alan Wood. London: Routledge, 1991. xiv, 192 p. *"Third volume of essays on Siberia to result from the activities of the British Universities Siberian Studies Seminar"* (pref.), ISBN: 0415058732. Includes index and bibliographical references.

This series of essays focuses on important topics in the history of Siberia including Siberia's role in Russian history, subjugation and settlement, the Siberian native peoples, vagrancy and crime in Russia's "Wild East," migration settlement and the rural economy, and Siberia in revolution and civil war, 1917-1921. A glossary of specialized terms is included. Review: *Russian History* 18:3:363-65 (Fall 1991).

JEWS

General Studies

1403.   Kahan, Arcadius, **Essays in Jewish Social and Economic History**, edited by Roger Weiss, with an introduction by Jonathan Frankel. Chicago: University of Chicago Press, 1986. xx, 208 p. ISBN: 0226422402. Includes bibliographical references and index.

These essays of Kahan, both published and unpublished, deal "with aspects of Jewish history, particularly with the economic development of East European Jewry, both in the Tsarist Empire and in the new centers established by the great emigrations to the West." (p. xi) Although known primarily as an economic historian, he also explores matters relating to religion and Jewish culture in general. Reviews: *Contemporary Sociology* 16:5:642-43 (September 1987). *Historical Review* 16:1:30-31 (Fall 1987). *Journal of Social History* (Fall 1987) 169-72. *Jewish Spectator* 52:2:146-48 (1987).

1404.   Leskov, Nikolai Semenovich, **The Jews in Russia: Some Notes on the Jewish Question**, with translation, annotation, and introduction by Harold Klassel Schefski. Princeton, NJ: Kingston Press, 1986. xli, 143 p. ISBN: 0940670291. Includes bibliography (p. xxxv-xli).

Leskov was an exception among Russian nineteenth-century writers in that he portrayed Jews with a degree of sympathy and understanding that was not common among his contemporaries. Leskov was commissioned to write this publicist pamphlet by Baron De Gunzburg, a wealthy Jewish merchant in St. Petersburg. De Gunzburg hoped to influence the Pahlen Commission, which had been convened by Alexander III to debate the treatment of Russian Jews. A lengthy introduction by the translator provides the context for the pamphlet and include analyzes of short stories by Leskov that deal with Jews and Jewish topics. Reviews: *Slavic and East European Journal* 31:4:626-27 (Winter 1987). *Slavic Review* 46:2:325 (Summer 1987). *Canadian Slavonic Papers* 29:2-3: 298-99 (June-September 1987).

1405.   Levin, Nora, **Jews in the Soviet Union Since 1917: Paradox of Survival**. New York: New York University Press, 1988. 2 v. ISBN: 0814750184. Includes index and bibliographical references.

This traditional history of the struggle of the Jews during Soviet rule is directed at the nonspecialist and undergraduate. It provides chronological presentation of the complex history of Soviet Jewry. A wide range of topics are covered including antinationalist and antireligious ideology on Marxist-Leninist doctrine, Levin's opposition to the Jewish Labor Bund and it's views on national cultural autonomy, Soviet industrial and agricultural upheaval, the anti-Semitism of key Soviet leaders, especially Stalin, and the victimization of the Jews during political power struggles. The author covers many other issues in this two volume set demonstrating not only the plight of the Jews, but of any national group that struggled to preserve its cultural heritage in the Soviet Union. Review: *Commentary* 88:6:70-72 (December 1989).

1406.   Low, Alfred D., **Soviet Jewry and Soviet Policy**. New York: Distributed by Columbia University Press, 1990. xv, 249 p. *East European Monographs*, no. 281. ISBN: 088033178X. Includes index and bibliographical references (p. 232-241).

This is a study of Soviet policy towards the Jews and of anti-Semitism in the Soviet Union. The history of the policy is presented in eight chapters. After a short introduction that sets the context of Soviet Jewish policy, Low traces the history of the Jews under the tsars and the views of Lenin and Marx regarding Jews. Chapters three through five discuss Stalinism and the rise of nationalism and anti-Semitism, the post WWII years until the death of Stalin, the emergence of Israel, the so-called Black Years of Soviet Jewry, and Soviet policy under Khrushchev. Chapter six examines Soviet policy after the six-day war and the influence of global anti-semitic propaganda. Chapters seven and eight conclude with Gorbachev, glasnost, and the Jews and speculations on the future.

1407. Nudel, Ida, **A Hand in the Darkness: The Autobiography of a Refusenik**, translated and co-written by Stefani Hoffman. New York, N.Y.: Warner Books, 1990. 314 p. ISBN: 0446514454.

In this moving narrative, Soviet "refusenik" Ida Nudel tells of her youth in Moscow and her political involvement that eventually led to her exile, first to Siberia and then to Moldova. In 1986, she was finally permitted an exit visa to Israel.

1408. Pinkus, Benjamin, **The Jews of the Soviet Union: The History of a National Minority**. Cambridge: Cambridge University Press, 1988. xviii, 397 p. *Soviet and East European Studies*, ISBN: 0521340780. Includes index and bibliography (p. 368-379).

Pinkus intends "to present the successive stages in the annals of Soviet Jews since the outbreak of the October Revolution." He does this in four chapters and is highly sensitive in doing so to the previous approaches taken by historians. In chapter one he gives a succinct historical background of the Jews in Russia from the earliest Jewish settlements in the Crimea and the Caucasus to the revolution. Chapter two is confined to the years 1917-1939 when Soviet nationality theory arose. He examines the judicial-political status of the Jews, their autonomy and "statehood," anti-Semitism, and the various religions and socioeconomic processes affecting them. Chapter three analyzes the period of destruction from 1939-1953 and the campaign against Jewish nationalism and cosmopolitanism. The final chapter covers the period 1953 to 1983. Pinkus is always attuned to the ways Jews and other minorities are perceived by the majority and ways in which Jews perceive themselves and the majority within the Soviet state. Reviews: *Russian Review* 49:2:226-27 (April 1990). *Soviet Union* 15:2-3:286-87 (1988). *Orbis* 33:3:461-62 (Summer 1989). *Commentary* 88:6:70-72 (December 1989).

Emigration

1409. Gilbert, Martin, **Shcharansky, Hero of Our Time**. New York: Viking, 1986. xviii, 467 p. *"Elizabeth Sifton Books,"* ISBN: 0670814180. Includes bibliography (p. 431-439).

An account of the life of Anatoly Shcharansky and his battle with the Soviet government to make emigration to Israel possible for Soviet Jews. The author is concerned not only with Shcharansky's personal struggle, but with his more general campaign and the high penalty he suffered for his efforts. Numerous Western sources were consulted and are included in the bibliography. There are several appendices on Soviet Jews imprisoned for their efforts at liberalizing Soviet policies and annual emigration of Soviet Jews 1951-85. The author feels that Shcharansky's story is the story of all Jews who wish to live in their homeland. Review: *Congress Monthly* 53:5:16-18 (July-August 1986).

1410. Roi, Yaacov, **The Struggle for Soviet Jewish Emigration, 1948-1967**. Cambridge: Cambridge University Press, 1991. xvii, 458 p. *Soviet and East European Studies*, vol. 75. ISBN: 0521390842. Includes index and bibliographical references (p. 429-435).

The establishment of the Jewish state in 1948 gave hope and inspiration to Soviet Jews who lived in a country where being Jewish was considered being alien. Roi traces the history of the political and cultural factors surrounding Soviet Jews attempts to emigrate to Israel, beginning in 1948 to the onset of the Six-Day War in 1967. In part one, he explores the euphoria of 1948 occasioned by the establishment of the state of Israel. He then traces Jewish consciousness during the black years, 1948-1953, and the subsequent thaw, 1953-56. In part two he shifts to describing how the outside world became aware of the plight of Soviet Jews and their efforts, prior to 1967 to gain exit visas for Jews wishing to emigrate. In part three he returns to the international side of the story and examines Jewish nationalist activity and the Soviet Jewish national awakening from 1957 to 1967.

1411.   Salitan, Laurie P., **Politics and Nationality in Contemporary Soviet Jewish Emigration, 1968-89**. New York: St. Martin's Press, 1991. x, 180 p. ISBN: 0312061080. Includes bibliographical references and index.

This book analyzes the role of domestic politics in Soviet-Jewish emigration policy. Many previous studies have placed most of their emphasis on the U.S.-Soviet relations as the moving force behind Soviet-Jewish emigration policy. In this study the author uses a comprehensive methodology to discern the nature of emigration policy in general. Thus, a section on Soviet-German emigration is included. "Although there is a considerable degree of differentiation in its application and implementation, I argue that one broad policy governs emigration.... Moreover, emigration policy is strategic and goal-orientated; it is modified when objectives change or when a new approach for achieving goals is adopted." (p. 4) The book is divided into two parts. Part one covers the history of the Jewish emigration movement beginning with the early Soviet period. Part two has one chapter on German emigration and a final chapter covering the details of Soviet emigration policy from 1968-89.

History

1412.   Beizer, Mikhail, **The Jews of St. Petersburg: Excursions Through a Noble Past**, translated by Michael Sherbourne, edited and with an introduction by Martin Gilbert. Philadelphia: The Jewish Publication Society, 1989. xxxv, 328 p. *"An Edward E-Elson Book,"* ISBN: 0827603215. Includes index.

News of Mikhail Beizer reached the West in 1982. A young Jew and "refusenik," Beizer was giving tours of Leningrad sites connected with Jewish activities and famous Jewish inhabitants. This book is a guided tour of those places that Beizer has discovered and researched. His book is much more, however. Part one is the guided tour. Part two contains short biographies of Dubnow, Ravenebbe, and Chagall, information on two special visits to St. Petersburg by Montefiore and Herzl, and a directory of personalities. Part three is a catalog of publications and institutions connected with Jewish life in that city.

1413.   Gitelman, Zvi Y., **A Century of Ambivalence: The Jews of Russia and the Soviet Union, 1881 to the Present**. New York: Pantheon, 1988. xv, 336 p. ISBN: 0805240349. Includes index.

The third largest Jewish community in the world is the subject of this study. The author traces life in Russia for its Jewish population from 1881 to 1987. Always aware of the varying fortunes of this group, the author stresses the ambivalence the Jews themselves felt toward their position in society, Zionism, politics, and many other subjects. The major contributions made in literature, art, philosophy, and many other areas often only made their position vis a vis the larger population more difficult. The volume follows a chrono-logical arrangement covering a wide range of topics including Zionism, the pogroms,

Birobiozhan, the Holocaust, the Six-Day War, Georgian Jews, and Central Asian Jews to name but a few. The book is filled with photographs depicting life for the Jewish population throughout the century. Reviews: *Canadian Review of Studies in Nationalism* 16:1-2:339-41 (1989). *Slavic Review* 48:3:511-12 (Fall 1989).

1414. Klier, John, **Russia Gathers Her Jews: The Origins of the "Jewish Question" in Russia, 1772-1825**. DeKalb, Ill.: Northern Illinois University Press, 1986. xxiv, 236 p. ISBN: 087580117X. Includes index and bibliography (p. 213-223).

Klier aptly summarizes the context of his book by stating that "the purpose of the present study is to provide a survey of Russia's acquisition and administration of her Jewish population which was gradually gathered under Russian control." (p. ii) In it he focuses on three basic questions: 1) "What, for Russians, was the Jewish question? 2) How did they become aware of it? 3) How do they propose to deal with it?" (p. ii) Most of Klier's history concentrates on the period 1772 to 1825. He pays special attention to Judeophobia and its eventual transformation into anti-Semitism in the latter nineteenth century. Review: *Slavic Review* 46:3-4:597-98 (Fall-Winter 1987).

Government and Politics

1415. **The Struggle for Religious Survival in the Soviet Union: Testimony Presented at Hearings of the National Interreligious Task Force on Soviet Jewry, 1985-1986**. New York: American Jewish Committee, Institute of Human Relations, 1986. 76 p. ISBN: 0874950856. Includes bibliographies.

The testimony given at the National Interreligious Task Force on Soviet Jewry, 1985-86 is presented here. The task force seeks to raise consciousness with like-minded groups. Testimony is presented on the situation of various religious groups including Jews, Catholics, Russian Orthodox, Evangelicals, and Muslims.

1416. Lederhendler, Eli, **The Road to Modern Jewish Politics: Political Tradition and Political Reconstruction in the Jewish Community of Tsarist Russia**. New York: Oxford University Press, 1989. ix, 240 p. ISBN: 0195058917. Includes index and bibliography (p. 213-233).

Modern Jewish political development in Eastern Europe is the subject of this study, whose focus is on the period from the 1760s to the late 1870s. It is based on a conceptual analysis of the transition from traditional to modern Jewish politics. Rather than being a definitive history of Russian Jewry in the nineteenth century, Lederhendler deals "chiefly with the internal dynamics of Jewish development and the mutual relationships between the Jewish community and the state." (p. 9) Review: *Russian Review* 49:4:498-99 (October 1990).

1417. Peled, Yoav, **Class and Ethnicity in the Pale: The Political Economy of Jewish Workers' Nationalism in Late Imperial Russia**. New York: St. Martin's Press, 1989. xii, 171 p. ISBN: 031203983. Includes index and bibliography (p. 158-166).

The main theme of Peled's study is the relationship between modernization and ethnic conflict. He uses the development of the General Union of Jewish Workers in Lithuania, Poland, and Russia, known as the Bund, as a case in point for his work. He explores his theme by several means including trying to explain the emergence of ethno-class consciousness among Jewish workers, and the rediscovery of "the debate between the Bund and its main political rivals—the Russian social democrats and the socialist Zionists." (p. 1) Reviews: *International Labor and Working Class History* 38:133-35 (Fall 1990). *American Journal of Sociology* 96:3:766-68 (November 1990).

1418. Rogger, Hans, **Jewish Policies and Right-Wing Politics in Imperial Russia**. Berkeley: University of California Press, 1986. viii, 289 p. ISBN: 0520045963. Includes index and bibliography (p. 271-282).

This is a collection of Rogger's previously published essays on Jews in Russia. Most of them focus on governmental policy from 1880-1917 dealing with the Jewish question. Reviews: *Canadian Slavonic Papers* 29:4:435-36 (December 1987). *Russian Review* 46: 3:331-33 (July 1987). *American Historical Review* 92:4:1006 (October 1987). *Slavic Review* 46:1:157 (Spring 1987).

Special Studies

1419. Dawidowicz, Lucy S., **From that Place and Time: a Memoir, 1938-1947**. 1st ed. New York: W.W. Norton, 1989. xiv, 333 p. ISBN: 0393026744. Includes index.

In 1938-39 Lucy Dawidowicz, in her late 20s, went to Vilna to study the Yiddish press in England. Her memoir touches briefly on her youth and childhood, but focuses primarily on Vilna, a city she says no longer exists. What she means is that although Vilna is still on the map, the prewar Vilna, what Napoleon in 1812 called the Jerusalem of Lithuania, had been destroyed by Nazi extermination policies and years of Soviet occupation. She recounts her time and impressions of Vilna based in part on memory and in part on about 100 letters she had written to her sister and a friend. After leaving Vilna in 1939, she returned to New York. Her memoir follows the fate of Vilna through the war and Dawidowicz's own attempts to salvage remnants from that time and place. Reviews: *Partisan Review* 57:2:306-308 (1990). *American Scholar* 59:1:151-54 (Winter 1990).

1420. Rachlin, Rachel, **Sixteen Years in Siberia: Memoirs of Rachel and Israel Rachlin,** translated from the Danish and with foreword by Birgitte M. de Weille. Tuscaloosa: University of Alabama Press, 1988. ix, 251 p. ISBN: 081730357X. Includes index.

This memoir by Israel and Rachel Rachlin tells the story of their exile from Lithuania in June of 1940 to Siberia. They were part of the 34,260 Lithuanians, many of them Jews, who were sent into exile for being anti-Soviet elements. In 1957 they were allowed to return and to emigrate to Denmark, where they were living at the time this memoir's writing.

1421. Rapoport, Louis, **Stalin's War Against the Jews: The Doctors' Plot and the Soviet Solution**. New York: Free Press, 1990. xvii, 318 p. *The Second Thought Series*, ISBN: 0029258219. Includes bibliographical references (p. 296-300) and index.

On January 13, 1953 the Soviet government announced that nine Kremlin doctors had murdered two of Stalin's closest aides in 1945 and 1948. Six of the nine had ostensibly Jewish names. This was the beginning of the propagandistic and fabricated "doctors' plot." In fact, it was a resurgence of a vile anti-Semitism that was only thwarted by Stalin's death in March. Rapoport traces the roots of Stalin's anti-Semitism, his rivalry with Trotsky, the Great Purge, and the murder of Solomon Mikhoels, the supposed mastermind of the plot. The author, in an epilogue, also recounts his visit to the Solomon Mikhoels Jewish Cultural Center in Moscow in 1989 and it significance in contemporary Russian life.

AUTHOR INDEX

Reference is to entry number.